Charles S. Peirce
Logic of the Future, Volume 2/2

Peirceana

Edited by
Francesco Bellucci and Ahti-Veikko Pietarinen

Volume 2

Charles S. Peirce
Logic of the Future

Writings on Existential Graphs
Part 2: The 1903 Lowell Lectures

Edited by
Ahti-Veikko Pietarinen

DE GRUYTER

ISBN 978-3-11-112499-5
e-ISBN (PDF) 978-3-11-074046-2
e-ISBN (EPUB) 978-3-11-074053-0
ISSN 2698-7155

Library of Congress Control Number: 2021932713

Bibliographic information published by the Deutsche Nationalbibliothek
The Deutsche Nationalbibliothek lists this publication in the Deutsche Nationalbibliografie;
detailed bibliographic data are available on the Internet at http://dnb.dnb.de.

© 2022 Walter de Gruyter GmbH, Berlin/Boston
This volume is text- and page-identical with the hardback published in 2021.
Typesetting: Jukka Nikulainen
Printing and binding: CPI books GmbH, Leck

www.degruyter.com

Acknowledgments

The work on the *Logic of the Future* has taken over fifteen years to complete. A considerable number of people and sources of support have accumulated over the years that are to be acknowledged and deeply thanked for their respective contributions.

An edition on Peirce's graphical logic was conceived during the class I gave at the University of Helsinki on *Peirce's Logic and Philosophy* in autumn 2004. At that time, it became obvious to me that Peirce's logic can never be adequately studied, let alone deeply researched, understood and put into a perspective within the history of ideas, without comprehensive editions.

It was the students of that class of 2004 that ignited the work on the present volumes. Its 20-odd students, including Jukka Nikulainen, Henrik Rydenfelt, Lauri Snellman, Lauri Järvilehto, Michael von Boguslawski, Harry Alanen, Peter Schulman and many others whose names I have forgotten, provided initial assistance in manuscript inspection and transcription.

There is one person without whom this edition would not have been possible to be produced at all. My long-term research assistant, Jukka Nikulainen, who has served as a technical editor of these volumes and has provided the first-ever LaTeX package (EGpeirce) by which one can now typeset any graph, special mark or symbol that ever emanated from Peirce's hand, with ease and uniformity. Jukka also encoded a large majority of the hundreds of complex graphs that appear in the volumes, improving the package along the way and adding new features to it. We believe that by now everything that Peirce ever designed and wanted to design as a special graph, type, character, mark or sign—a plethora of his typographical eccentricities notwithstanding—have been incorporated into the functionality of the Peirce LaTeX package. And much more is available in it than is in fact needed for the purposes of compiling the present editions. Peirce's ethics of notation dictates that pieces of notation are just as important as the prose overall, and that whenever new notation is introduced, reasons for it are not to be taken lightly. Design and typesetting practices have to follow suit, and indeed Jukka has considerably assisted the production of the CRCs of these volumes for the press, honing the notations and checking many of the transcriptions as I slowly progressed with them. He has also searched and compiled information on many of Peirce's references as well as prepared both the index of names and the index of words. Nikulainen, above all, deserves to be acknowledged as having done an amount of work vastly exceeding anything that is to be expected of a technical editor—probably years rather than months since 2004—in order to bring the edition into its present shape.

Claudia Cristalli also went out of her way in helping to bring the edition into its near-completion. Without her many suggestions and concrete advice on organisation and presentation of the material, the progress on these volumes might have slouched altogether. In particular, she gave valuable proposals on organising the editorial, introductory and survey parts.

Francesco Bellucci deserves an equally immeasurable gratitude for pressing on with finalising these volumes. Not only did he check many of the items and transcriptions but also closely researched their content, coming up with important perspectives concerning their interpretation. The volumes and their editorial introductions have benefitted enormously from our scholarly collaboration over the last several years.

Marc Champagne and Liu Xinwen have followed the progress of this project over the years. Both have provided a number of comments and corrections on the introductory parts, and deserve a special thanks for such laborious deeds.

These editions would probably have not seen the light of day had it not been for the enthusiasm and intellectual support of Nathan Houser, with whom I regularly conversed on the prospects of such a work ever since my stay at the Peirce Edition Project in the autumn of 2005 as a post-doctoral Fulbright grantee. It is thanks to Nathan's vocal accentuation on the importance of bringing about a thematic edition on graphs, and above all the unprecedented scholarship that he represents in the Peirce community, that have kept me going with the work. André De Tienne, Director of the Peirce Edition Project, has been equally supportive of the enterprise from the get-go. Conversations with him have supplied vital links and clues by which one could go about navigating the amazing mazes that the literary output of this American mind puts before us.

Over the years, John Sowa, Matthew Moore and Helmut Pape have all provided experienced advice, John on the topical relevance of Peirce's graphical logic, and Matt and Helmut on the challenges of editing Peirce's papers for a thematic collection. Susan Haack has followed the project with interest, and I do not doubt that any new material that might be found in these texts would only support the conclusions she has already arrived at.

My first graduate class on Peirce was given by Risto Hilpinen, who taught logic and philosophy of science at the University of Turku in early 1990s and who was the first to notice that Peirce had arrived at semantic and logical ideas surprisingly similar to those reached much later by others, in particular the game-theoretical semantics independently discovered by Jaakko Hintikka in the 1960s. I am honoured to have an opportunity of including an Introductory Note from Prof. Hilpinen.

Discussions with the late Jaakko Hintikka in 2000–2015 on Peirce's logic have enabled me to put many of the related contributions into a sharper perspective.

"Peirce—miles ahead of Frege in logic and in the philosophy of mathematics", he once told me. The similarities between Hintikka's and Peirce's philosophies are indeed quite striking (Pietarinen 2018), but can be explained by the similarities in the methods of logic and the significance placed on having good logical notations, the relational apparatus of thought, the value placed on proofs, and the semantic (or model-theoretic, semeiotic, notational) outlook on one's philosophical investigations. Both Peirce and Hintikka had put scientific and human inquiry ahead of bare epistemology: both advocated an *action-first* epistemology. That there is reality and truth in such philosophy is reflected in the comment I once received from Jaakko on my presentation that explored connections between the two thinkers. I had suggested that the sheer number of them makes one almost believe in reincarnation, to which he replied: "Yes, but who incarnated whom?"

Discussions with my father, who together with Risto Hilpinen were Hintikka's first doctoral students in philosophy, helped to clarify several conceptions that relate Peirce to philosophical classics, including Spinoza, Kant, Plato and Aristotle. The edition is dedicated to the memory of my parents.

Along the way, Arnold Oostra and Fernando Zalamea provided valuable advice on both the general conception of the edition as well as on the details of Peirce's graphical notation. Zalamea encouraged me to pursue a resolutely comprehensive rather than a critical and limited collation of texts; his answer to my enquiry on what should be included in an edition about Peirce's graphs was, "Everything!" As usual he was right; Peirce's gardening is too precious to be cut off at any branch or ligature, as it may be just another verso of his folios that has the mutation needed for the germinal idea to evolve into a substantially new insight.

I have space left only to enlist a number of colleagues and Peirce scholars who have contributed to the edition either by way of advancing the research on Peirce's graphical logic or explicitly concerning the edition: Christina Barés Gomez, Reetu Bhattarchajee, Angelina Bobrova, Daniele Chiffi, Matthieu Fontaine, Juuso-Ville Gustafsson, Jelena Issajeva, Ma Minghui, Amirouche Moktefi, Marika Proover and Frederik Stjernfelt. They are all to be thanked for having provided important suggestions during our workshops and Peirce Seminars held at the Tallinn University of Technology.

In addition, Jean-Marie Chevalier and Benoit Gaultier have helped with correcting the transcriptions of the letters Peirce wrote in French (LoF 3). Both have provided helpful comments on the edition at various stages of its development.

Over these 15-odd years, several personal research grants have been instrumental in supporting and sustaining the work on the present edition. They are, in reverse chronological order: Higher School of Economics, HSE University Basic Research Program (*Russian Academic Excellence Project '5-100'*, 2018–2020); Nazarbayev University (*Social Policy Grant*, 2018–2019); Estonian Research Council (*Abduction in the Age of Fundamental Uncertainty*, 2013–2018); Academy of Finland (*Logic and Games*, 2003–2005; *Diagrammatic Mind (DiaMind): Logical and Cognitive Aspects of Iconicity*, 2013–2017); Chinese Academy of Social Sciences (*Peirce's Pragmaticism*, 2006; 2016); Joan Nordell Houghton Library Fellowship of Harvard University (*Peirce's Manuscripts on Logic*, 2011–2012); University of Helsinki Excellence in Research Grant (*Pragmaticism and Its Contemporary Applications*, 2006–2009); Kone Foundation (*Peirce's Scientific and Philosophical Correspondence*, 2008); The Jenny and Antti Wihuri Foundation (*Pragmatic Theories of Meaning*, 2007); ASLA–Fulbright Foundation (*Peirce's Manuscripts on Logic*, 2005), and Finnish Cultural Foundation (*Peirce's Scientific and Philosophical Correspondence*, 2005). These sources of support are gratefully acknowledged. In particular, the staff at Harvard's Houghton Library and curator Leslie Morris are to be thanked for their invaluable assistance during my frequent visits to the library over the years to inspect the Peirce collection.

The publisher's team has seen through the final preparation of the edition. It is only appropriate that Peirce's late works on logic appear with the same publisher as Peirce's late works on mathematics (*New Elements of Mathematics*, NEM I–IV) did nearly half a century ago.

The title "Logic of the Future" comes from Peirce's 1909 Christmas Day letter to William James. That letter also explains Peirce's bequest to have his work appear in places that will, first and foremost, advance inquiry and not the sham and fake reasoning that he saw plaguing scholarly minds of his time. Only then, in addition to the advancement of inquiry, one may recognise the value of ideas as those that their author has instigated along the way:

> Now when I die, I want proper justice done to my memory as to these things. Not at all that they are any credit to me, but simply that, by being made to appear considerable, they may invite attention and study, when I think they will do considerable good. For logic and exact reasoning are a good deal more important than you are able to see that they are. So I hope that some account of my work may appear in some publication that people will look into, and not solely in the Biographical memoirs of the National Academy of Sciences. (CSP to WJ, December 25, 1909)

Soon after, Peirce mentions the "pressing questions of our time" (R 678, 1910). He wanted to resolve them by an application of logic and reasoning. Those questions have not gone away. They can be dispelled only by a collective improvement in the art of reasoning. Everyone involved in advancing the present project has done "considerable good" towards that end.

Ahti-Veikko Pietarinen

Abbreviations of Peirce's Works and Archives

Archives:

R *The Charles S. Peirce Papers, 1787–1951*. Manuscripts in the Houghton Library of Harvard University, as identified by Richard Robin, *Annotated Catalogue of the Papers of Charles S. Peirce*, Amherst: University of Massachusetts Press, 1967, and in "The Peirce Papers: A Supplementary Catalogue", *Transactions of the Charles S. Peirce Society* 7, 1971, pp. 37–57. Peirce's manuscripts and letters are available, in part, in *The Charles S. Peirce Papers, Microfilm Edition*, Thirty Reels with Two Supplementary Reels Later Added. Cambridge: Harvard University Library Photographic Service, 1966.[1]

HUA *Harvard University Archives*. Pusey Library, Harvard University.

WJP *The William James Papers*. Houghton Library, Harvard University.

CLF *Christine Ladd Franklin and Fabian Franklin Papers*. Butler Library, Rare Books and Manuscripts Collection, Columbia University.

VW *Lady Victoria Alexandrina Maria Louisa Welby fonds*, York University Archives and Special Collections.

Edited Collections:

SiL *Studies in Logic, by Members of the Johns Hopkins University*. Edited by Charles S. Peirce, Boston: Little, Brown, and Company, 1883. Reissued as a facsimile reprint in *Foundations of Semiotics*, Volume 1, with introductory essays by Achim Eschbach and Max H. Fisch. Amsterdam: John Benjamins, 1983.

DPP *Dictionary of Philosophy and Psychology*. Three volumes. Edited by James Mark Baldwin, 1901–1902. New York & London: The Macmillan Company.

CLL *Chance, Love and Logic: Philosophical Essays*. Edited by Morris Cohen, with a supplementary essay on the pragmatism of Peirce by John Dewey. London: Kegan Paul, 1923.

CP *The Collected Papers of Charles S. Peirce*, 8 volumes. Edited by Charles Hartshorne, Paul Weiss and Arthur W. Burks. Cambridge: Harvard University Press, 1931–1958. Referred to by volume and paragraph number.

---

[1] The microfilm edition is electronically available at https://rs.cms.hu-berlin.de/peircearchive/ Most manuscript and typescript sheets, notebooks and other material from the Harvard Peirce Papers are included in this microfilm edition, but only a minor part of letters and correspondence was included.

PWP   *The Philosophy of Peirce: Selected Writings*. Edited by Justus Buchler. New York: Harcourt, Brace and Company, 1940. Reissued as *Philosophical Writings of Peirce*, Dover, 1955.

CN   *Charles Sanders Peirce: Contributions to The Nation*. Four volumes. Edited by Kenneth Laine Ketner and James Edward Cook. Lubbock, TX: Texas Technological University Press, 1975–1987.

NEM   *The New Elements of Mathematics by Charles S. Peirce*. Four volumes. Edited by Carolyn Eisele. The Hague: Mouton De Gruyter, 1976.

SS   *Semiotic and Significs: The Correspondence between C. S. Peirce and Victoria Lady Welby*. Edited by Charles S. Hardwick with the assistance of James Cook. Bloomington and Indianapolis, IN: Indiana University Press, 1977.

P   *A Comprehensive Bibliography and Index of the Published Works of Charles Sanders Peirce*, with a Bibliography of Secondary Studies. Ketner, Kenneth Laine et al., (eds.). Greenwich: Johnson Associates, 1977. Second edition, *A Comprehensive Bibliography of the Published Works of Charles Sanders Peirce*, Bowling Green, OH: Philosophy Documentation Center, 1986.

W   *Writings of Charles S. Peirce: A Chronological Edition*. Seven volumes. Edited by Max H. Fisch, C. J. W. Kloesel, et al. and the Peirce Edition Project. Bloomington and Indianapolis, IN: Indiana University Press, 1982–2009.

WMS   Manuscripts as cataloged by the Peirce Edition Project, in W.

PLZ   *Charles S. Peirce: Phänomen und Logik der Zeichen*. Helmut Pape (ed.). Frankfurt am Main: Suhrkamp, 1983.

HP   *Historical Perspectives on Peirce's Logic of Science: A History of Science*. Two volumes. Edited by Carolyn Eisele. Berlin, New York and Amsterdam: Mouton De Gruyter, 1985.

RLT   *Reasoning and the Logic of Things: The Cambridge Conference Lectures of 1898*. Edited by Kenneth Laine Ketner. Cambridge, Mass.: Harvard University Press, 1992.

EP 1   *The Essential Peirce: Selected Philosophical Writings*. Volume 1 (1867–1893). Edited by Nathan Houser and Christian J. W. Kloesel. Bloomington and Indianapolis, IN: Indiana University Press, 1992.

PPM   *Pragmatism as a Principle and Method of Right Thinking: The 1903 Harvard "Lectures on Pragmatism"*. Edited by Patricia Ann Turrisi. Albany, NY: State University of New York Press, 1997.

EP 2   *The Essential Peirce: Selected Philosophical Writings*. Volume 2 (1893–1913). Edited by the Peirce Edition Project. Bloomington and Indianapolis, IN: Indiana University Press, 1998.

LoI *Charles S. Peirce: The Logic of Interdisciplinarity. The Monist Series*. Edited by Elize Bisanz. Berlin: Akademie Verlag, 2009.
PoM *Philosophy of Mathematics: Selected Writings*. Edited by Matthew E. Moore. Bloomington and Indianapolis, IN: Indiana University Press, 2010.
ILoS *Illustrations of the Logic of Science, by Charles Sanders Peirce*. Edited by Cornelis de Waal. Chicago: Open Court, 2014.
PSR *Charles S. Peirce: Prolegomena to a Science of Reasoning. Phaneroscopy, Semeiotic, Logic*. Edited by Elize Bisanz. Frankfurt am Main: Peter Lang, 2016.
LoF *Charles S. Peirce: Logic of the Future. Writings on Existential Graphs*. Edited by Ahti-Veikko Pietarinen. Volume 1: *History and Applications*, 2019. Volume 2/1: *The Logical Tracts*, 2021. Volume 2/2: *The 1903 Lowell Lectures*, 2021. Volume 3: *Pragmaticism and Correspondence*, 2021. Berlin and Boston: Mouton De Gruyter.

Introductory Note

Charles S. Peirce was one of the most creative and innovative philosophers of the late 19th and early 20th century. He is known as the founder of American pragmatism, a general philosophical view which he in his later years preferred to call "pragmaticism" to distinguish it from the doctrines propounded by his followers and imitators who, according to Peirce, had "kidnapped" the word 'pragmatism'. He had wide interests, and his pragmaticism permeated his work in many areas of philosophy: logic, semiotics and the philosophy of language, philosophy of science, and metaphysics.

In the 1880s Peirce developed independently of Gottlob Frege a system of quantification theory in which quantifiers were treated as variable binding operators; thus he can be regarded, alongside Frege, as a founder of contemporary formal logic. The standard notation used in contemporary logic is a variant of Peirce's notation rather than that adopted by Frege. As a part of his pragmaticist theory of meaning, Peirce developed a game-theoretical interpretation of logical constants, according to which their meaning is explained by means of a semantical zero-sum game between two parties, an utterer and an interpreter. Peirce also studied modal and many-valued logics, and developed the basic ideas of the possible-worlds semantics for modal logic. In his general theory of reasoning Peirce distinguished three main forms of reasoning, namely abduction, deduction, and induction, and revised the traditional account of non-deductive reasoning. In his work in general semiotics (the theory of signs) and the philosophy of language, he analyzed the sign relation as a triadic relation involving a sign, an interpretant (meaning), and an object, and introduced the distinction between types and tokens into linguistics and the philosophy of language. He made a distinction between iconic, indexical, and symbolic signs, and outlined an account of proper names as "directly referential" indexical signs. Peirce developed a complex classification of signs involving several interpretants and objects, and his rich semiotic system provides a useful framework for the comparison of semiotic theories from the Stoics to the present. He anticipated many significant developments in the later 20th century analytic philosophy and logic.

In the 1890s Peirce reformulated quantification theory by expressing it in a language of diagrams which he called *existential graphs*. The switch from the algebraic notation to the language of graphs seems to have been motivated by his belief that the latter was more suitable for the purposes of logical analysis. According to Peirce, a system of logic can be used as a calculus which helps to draw inferences as economically as possible, or it can be developed for the purpose of representing and analyzing deductive processes. Peirce also thought that a graphical notation was more suitable for logical analysis than an algebraic notation because of its higher degree of *iconicity*. An iconic sign can be said to show what it means in the sense that it resembles its objects in some respect, that is, some features of the sign itself determine its interpretation. Peirce himself regarded the theory of existential graphs as one of his most important contributions to logic and philosophy.

Peirce presented his theory of existential graphs in many papers which also discussed various philosophical topics in semiotics and the philosophy of language. Much of this material remained unpublished during his lifetime, and some scholars became acquainted with it by studying his manuscripts. On the other hand, Peirce was able to get some of these works published, for example, his work *A Syllabus of Certain Topics of Logic* was published by Alfred Mudge & Son, Boston, 1903, and the long paper "Prolegomena to an Apology for Pragmaticism" appeared in the philosophical journal *The Monist* in 1906. However, Peirce's contemporaries ignored these works, perhaps because they were not able to see them as significant contributions to logic and philosophy. It might be said that Peirce was ahead of his times; his work on existential graphs began to receive serious attention only in the 1960s.

The *Logic of the Future* series is the first comprehensive collection of Peirce's writings on existential graphs, especially his previously unpublished writings and unpublished variants of published works. Peirce had the habit of rewriting the same work several times, and the versions often differ from each other in interesting ways. Prof. Ahti-Veikko Pietarinen has performed a valuable service to all students of Peirce's logic and philosophy by making this material easily accessible in book form.

Risto Hilpinen
University of Miami, Coral Gables

Foreword

The *Logic of the Future* edition aims at being both an inclusive and a resourceful set of thematic texts, serving the roles of a diplomatic edition, a handbook, and a multi-volume monograph. Extensive thematic introductions and surveys of selections are included in these books. From editorial points of views, I have attempted to maximise the amount of alternate versions, incomplete drafts and page fragments that one can gather from Peirce's enormous *Nachlass* of over 100 000 surviving pages, while minimising the reader's effort when following his spawning lines of thought and bursts of brilliant insights. The reader will, just as the editor does, despair over the writings that have frequent break-offs, discontinuities and aberrations—explorations left soberly unfinished and rhizoidic—aware as we are that so many of the now-lost pages and forgotten thoughts were once available to fill in the blanks. I hope to share with the reader the view that the numerous alternate versions, even when superficially repetitive, idiosyncratic or seemingly superseded by parallel or later attempts, are all too precious to be left out; too "gravid with young truth" to remain forever undisclosed from the eyes of posterity. If they won't appear in the present edition, chances are that much of that material would never find its way to print.

To wit, let us take to the heart the following passage as an example of such a variant:

> We have only to turn our attention for one moment to a relative term to see that the account given in the logic-books of the composition of concepts is entirely inadequate. The present writer showed the true mode of composition in the seventh volume of *The Monist* by means of graphs. But immediately after that publication he discovered another much better system of graphs, making the whole matter perfectly clear. But he has in vain endeavoured to persuade some journal, academy, or institution to print a sufficient account of it. The time will come when the world will be amazed at this; but then Newton's *Principia* would not have been printed yet if Edmund Halley had not been a very different sort of man from those upon whom publication depends in the United States at this day. (R 280, Alt. pp. 19–20, *The Basis of Pragmatism*, late 1904; LoF 3)[2]

The main purpose of the volumes of the *Logic of the Future* is to facilitate advancement of inquiry on what has remained one of the most neglected topics in the

---

[2] The reference R is to the Charles Sanders Peirce papers deposited at Houghton Library, Harvard University, as listed and catalogued by Richard S. Robin. See "Abbreviations for Peirce's Works and Archives" at the end of the General Introduction for the standard references to the archives, collections and editions of Peirce's work. When the material appears in the present edition of the *Logic of the Future* (LoF for short), a reference to Volumes 1–3 is added.

study of Peirce's thought, the logic of graphs and their role in the eventual completion of his mature logic and philosophy. This oversight shows up in previous editions of his works, which occasionally but quite routinely have left the graphical account out of the picture. Technical limitations are understandable, but the inevitable consequence has been that his favourite method of analysis became unduly suppressed from the perspectives one hopes to gain over the maturation of his later thought, leading to a de-emphasis of the manifold contributions Peirce calculated logical graphs to make towards erecting a fully articulated, architectonic scientific philosophy.

The volumes on Peirce's logic of graphs should be viewed only as the beginnings of a renewed exposition of the kind of inquiry that a comprehensive access to the largely unpublished late works of this poly-pragmatic American philosopher would facilitate. They do little more than identify the relevant minimal corpus that is not to be neglected in the scholarship on Peirce's method of logical analysis, its history, and its applications to the workings of intellectual cognition. Further editions are needed on Peirce's late writings on the algebra of logic, logic of abduction (retroduction), inductive logic and the logic of science, non-Aristotelian (and non-classical) logics, reasoning, definitions, history of logic, semiotics, methodeutic, modality, continuity, vagueness, imagination and perception; the list goes on with anything that was represented in non-graphical notations (such as Peirce's 1909 work on triadic logics), in order to complete the identification of that minimal logical corpus. Any of these areas, when fully available, will open up new insights on, as well as call for some major revisions to, our current understanding of the logical, philosophical and scientific achievements of this agile mind, and what their proper place in the history of logic will end up being. And although electronic repositories of one's literary remains are certainly useful, and although those, too, will appear before long, they are no substitute for organised, systematic and thematic records of one's profound thoughts.

There are also wider issues that have to do with the kinds of historiographies one gets to write on the development of modern logic, including the virtual histories of what the logic of the later centuries would have looked like had the findings that Peirce produced and presented in various occasions been better and more timely disseminated. Misfortunes happened during Peirce's life all too often—yet on balance, we are also fortunate and privileged as much of his literary estate has been preserved for us to continue its future appreciation and critical scrutiny, however fragmentary or prefatory those surviving segments may appear to be. I hope that the present edition will play its part towards achieving these wider goals.

Preface to Volumes 2/1 and 2/2

The second volume in the series of Charles Sanders Peirce's writings on Existential Graphs (EGs) is arranged in two books, Volumes 2/1 and 2/2, and it bears the theme of the 1903 Lowell Lectures, a series of eight popular public talks arranged by the Lowell Institute Peirce delivered in November and December in Boston, Massachusetts. The selection of texts follows the same criteria as for the first volume: the relevant texts chosen for inclusion are those that concern the topic of Existential Graphs (EGs). The first five lectures were largely concerned with logical graphs, and a great majority of his lecture drafts are indeed on that topic. Roughly two thirds of his overall lecture notes, pre-drafts, supplements and worksheets have made it to the selection of the second book of the volume. An ample amount of preparatory material that Peirce produced during the year has also been included as the first book of the second volume, *The Logical Tracts*, a large treatise on logical graphs which Peirce crafted to accompany the planning of his lectures. The introductions are new, including a section on the Gamma part of the theory of EGs, a graphical system of modal logic that Peirce had no time introduce during the allotted eight hours, in Volume 2/1. Editorial survey notes are provided on every selection in the introductory essays.

My special thanks are to André De Tienne, Director of the Peirce Edition Project at the Institute of American Thought, IUPUI, Indianapolis, for permission to consult extensive material at the project's possession about Peirce's 1903 Lowell Lectures during my visits there in 2005, 2012 and 2014. Special thanks also go to Helmut Pape, who has studied and worked on these lectures more than anyone else in the past. As before, this volume could not have been completed without the unfailing assistance of Jukka Nikulainen on technical editing matters, and the loving support of my family on matters of vital importance.

Ahti-Veikko Pietarinen, April 2020

Contents

Ahti-Veikko Pietarinen
General Introduction to *Logic of the Future* —— 1

Ahti-Veikko Pietarinen
Introduction to the Theory of Existential Graphs, Volumes 2/1 and 2/2 —— 15

Ahti-Veikko Pietarinen
Introduction to Volume 2/2: The 1903 Lowell Lectures —— 29

References —— 118

Charles S. Peirce's Writings on Existential Graphs

Part V: *Some Topics of Logic Bearing on Questions Now Vexed* The 1903 Lowell Institute Lectures I–V

32 Lowell Lecture I (R 454) —— 137

33 Lowell Lecture II(a) (R 450) —— 150

34 Lowell Lecture II(b) (R 455, R 456) —— 177

35 Lowell Lecture III(a,b) (R 462, R 457) —— 219

36 Lowell Lecture III(c) (R 464, R 465, R 460) —— 237

37 Lowell Lecture IV (R 467, R 468) —— 256

38 Lowell Lecture V(a,b,c) (R 459, R 466, R 458) —— 280

39 Lowell Lecture V(d) (R 469–R 471) —— 310

40 On the Simplest Branch of Mathematics, Dyadics (R 2–R 3, R 511–R 512) —— 336

| 41 | A Syllabus of certain Topics of Logic (R 478) —— 347

| 42 | Fragments —— 386

Bibliography of Peirce's References —— 419

Catalogue of Peirce's Writings —— 432

Name Index —— 437

Keyword Index —— 439

Ahti-Veikko Pietarinen
General Introduction to *Logic of the Future*

Peirce's Logic

Charles Sanders (Santiago) Peirce (1839–1914) was an accomplished scientist, philosopher, and mathematician, who considered himself primarily a logician. His contributions to the development of modern logic at the turn of the 20th century have been colossal, original, and perpetually influential, albeit his overall influence upon the development of modern logic remained ill-understood for a long time (Fisch 1982, Dipert 1995, Hintikka 1996, Putnam 1982).

Formal, or deductive, logic was just one of the branches in which Peirce exercised his logical and analytical talent. His work developed upon George Boole's algebra of logic and Augustus De Morgan's logic of relations. Peirce worked on the algebra of relatives (1870–1885), the theory of quantification (1880–1885), graphical and diagrammatic logic (1896–1913), trivalent logic (1909), as well as higher-order and modal logics (1898–1911).[1] He also contributed significantly to the theory and methodology of induction, and discovered a third kind of reasoning, different from both deduction and induction, which he called abduction or retroduction, and which he identified with the logic of scientific discovery.

Philosophically, logic became for Peirce a broad and open-ended discipline with internal divisions and external architectonic relations to other parts of scientific inquiry. Logic depends upon, or draws its principles from, mathematics, phaneroscopy (phenomenology), esthetics and ethics (phenomenology), while metaphysics and psychology depend upon logic. One of the most important characters of Peirce's late logical thought was that logic becomes coextensive with semeiotic (his preferred spelling), namely the theory of signs. Peirce divided logic, conceived as semeiotic, into (i) *speculative grammar*, the preliminary analysis, definition, and classification of signs; (ii) *critical logic*, the study of the validity

---

[1] Year ranges are indicative only. The continuous nature of Peirce's explorations and his pluralistic approach to logic routinely challenge pinpointing any definite moment in time when one idea had led to another. For example, higher-order logic was algebraically investigated in his 1885 "On the Algebra of Logic: A Contribution to the Philosophy of Notation" paper but presented in its graphical outfit in 1898. The entire concept of graphical notation for logic is an equally continuous notion and was present in various guises since 1880 (see "Introduction to Volume 1" of Volume 1 of the *Logic of the Future*).

https://doi.org/10.1515/9783110740462-001

and justification of each kind of reasoning; and (iii) *methodeutic*, or *speculative rhetoric*, the theory of methods and an application of the methods of logical analysis to other fields of science, especially mathematics. Peirce's logical investigations cover all these three areas.

In the early 1880s—roughly at the same time as Gottlob Frege (1848–1925) but entirely independently of him—Peirce discovered a notation of quantifiers and variables for the expression of quantificational logic. Unlike Frege, however, Peirce did not stick to any one formalism. He spent the rest of his logical life experimenting with alternative notations to serve the theory of logic and to advance scientific inquiry. The outcome of his notational researches was a system of logical graphs discovered in 1896, which he termed the system of Existential Graphs (EGs).

Sketchy presentations of EGs appeared in print in 1902 in the *Dictionary of Philosophy and Psychology* (DPP) edited by James Mark Baldwin (entry "Symbolic Logic" in Vol. 2, pp. 640–651; LoF 3), in *A Syllabus of Certain Topics of Logic*, a 23-page printed pamphlet that Peirce wrote to accompany his Lowell Lectures of 1903 and circulated in 100 copies, and in the 1906 *Monist* article "Prolegomena to an Apology for Pragmaticism". Apart from these, his prolific writings on EGs remained unpublished in his lifetime.[2]

Peirce continued working on the theory of logical graphs for the rest of his life. On Christmas Day of 1909 he wrote to William James (1942–1910) that this graphical method "ought to be the Logic of the Future". The next sections explain the rationale behind this phrase.

Structure of the Edition

Logic of the Future: Writings on Existential Graphs is a multi-volume edition providing a comprehensive package of Peirce's late writings on the topic of Existential Graphs (EGs). The first volume, subtitled **History and Applications,** consists of three parts, *Reasoning and Diagrams* (Part I), *Development of Existential Graphs* (Part II), and *Theory and Application of Existential Graphs* (Part III). The aim of Part I is to provide a non-technical introduction, in Peirce's own words, to his

---

[2] There are only a few references and hints to them in his other published papers from the early 20th century, such as the "Some Amazing Mazes" series (Peirce 1908a,b; Peirce 1909a). The second *Monist* paper "Issues of Pragmaticism" (Peirce 1905b) makes one reference; the first, "What Pragmatism Is", does not (Peirce 1905a). Nor does the published version of the "Neglected Argument for the Reality of God" (Peirce 1908c) refer to EGs.

method and philosophy of diagrammatic reasoning, especially as conducted and understood in terms of his theory of logical graphs. Part II tells the story of the discovery of EGs and their relation to what Peirce generally calls the "graphical method of logic"; the discovery that largely happens during his immensely productive year of 1896, followed by two years of significant improvements to that original discovery. Part III, which in many ways comprises the most substantial, detailed and technical set of writings of the entire *Logic of the Future* series, portrays the breath and the depth of the theory of EGs, as well as the impact Peirce took the graphical method to have on the advancement of our understanding of the fundamental nature of reasoning, mathematics, science, mind, and philosophy. This third part covers the period from 1899 until some of his last writings on the topic in 1911.

The second volume, **The 1903 Lowell Lectures**, consists of two parts in two books, *The Logical Tracts* (Part IV) and *The 1903 Lowell Lectures* (Part VI), a selection of the first five lectures from the Lowell Institute Lectures series *Some Topics of Logic Bearing on Questions Now Vexed*. *The Logical Tracts* is Peirce's nearly book-length compendium on EGs written while preparing for his upcoming eight lectures in November and December 1903 organised by the Lowell Institute in Boston. The first five of the Lowell Lectures, in turn, contain the most massive body of texts on EGs that Peirce ever undertook to write. Those lectures, their numerous drafts and the accompanying material in *A Syllabus of Certain Topics of Logic* constitute the centerpieces of Peirce's work on EGs. Chronologically, they mark the half-way point in that dozen or so years during which he produced nearly all of the relevant writings. Content-wise, these lectures portray EGs in their matured form, with the system of conventions fully in place and the sound and complete set of rules of transformation ready to be exposed to the audience.

The most philosophical set of writings is found in the third volume, **Pragmaticism and Correspondence**. In its chapters arranged under Part VI on pragmaticism, Peirce is using EGs to elucidate, and even to prove, his philosophical theory of meaning. Thoughts, signs and minds are extensively discussed, and Peirce sends the graphical method to the service of addressing those difficult and penetrating philosophical questions. Selections from 1904 to 1908 make up this sixth part of the trilogy. The third volume also includes, in Part VII, Peirce's extensive exchange of letters with a number of colleagues, collaborators and friends. Among them is a long letter to William James written on December 25, 1909, in which the allusion to the "Logic of the Future" is made. That final part also presents the dictionary entries and their drafts on EGs that were authored or co-authored by Peirce and which—just as most of the other material in the volumes—have remained largely unpublished to date.

Each selection begins with a headnote, and introductory essays to each of the volumes and their individual parts provide further insight into the textual, substantial and editorial encounters that the production of the present collection has involved over the years. In particular, the introductory essays outline the wider context of Peirce's intellectual life and explain the growth and impact of his ideas within that wider context. They also highlight the major novelties and contributions that Peirce is observed to be making in the texts collected in these chapters.

When discussing Peirce's excursions into the theory of EGs and the numerous ventures he had in trying to get his papers published and acknowledged by his peers, I am following the order of the textual selections in their respective chapters. For most if not for all of the texts included in the volumes, philosophical and technical comments are provided on the content. Those comments aim at being a source of information as much as of inspiration, and have no pretension of exhaustiveness.

Editorial Essay

Text Selection Rationale

The selection of copy-texts and their editorial processing follows a number of general and specific guidelines. As to the general ones, first, the edition aims at being *comprehensive* in its coverage of the material Peirce ever wrote on EGs. The number of such manuscript and letter sheets, notebook pages, worksheets, galley proofs, typescripts and published leaves (inclusive of all variant and incomplete draft pages), is nearly 5 000. Virtually all of them have been used as the material for copy-texts of the volumes of the *Logic of the Future* series. This means that important alternative drafts, variants and fragments have also been included as far as possible. Far from making the text redundant, substantive alternatives often contain information not found anywhere else. Peirce worked incessantly, and routinely did not aim at publishing his findings.[3] Even when he did, his submissions, galleys and offprints can be seen to be superseded by the textual and cognitive context within which they were produced. Variants, alternatives, emen-

---

[3] A pertinent example is the destiny of Peirce's 1885 paper "On the Algebra of Logic: A Contribution to the Philosophy of Notation", which was so ahead of its time that is was understood neither by his peers nor the generations that followed (see Ma & Pietarinen 2018a for a recent study). Two decades later Peirce would still feel that it was the aftermath of that paper that led him to give up publishing efforts on the topic of logic altogether; what he would subsequently produce were "written for my eyes solely, like all my logical papers of the last twenty years" (R 253, 1905; LoF 1).

dations, parallel and emerging projects, and even substantial rejections, lacunæ and lost pages supply that important context. Although much editorial effort has been expended on identifying, studying, selecting, organising, transcribing and producing the material in its final format, the present series is a *critical edition* only in the sense of having attempted to identify, select and study the thematically relevant material, with much less contemplation whether that material may have accorded with Peirce's intentions and thoughts about the production of final or ultimate versions of any given piece than what is to be expected of critical editions.

Second, the volumes are *chronological* with respect to their internal thematic organisation. Again, Peirce typically worked simultaneously on many projects, writing assignments, letters, proofs and calculations, producing text and delivering results virtually daily on multiple fronts. (Curiously but understandably, nearly all of the pages included in the first volume were written in the warmth of the months between April and August, 1895–1907; his residence was often too cold during winter to support sustained literary engagements.) *Logic of the Future* aims at preserving thematic unities as far as practicable. This is reflected in the organisation of the material in seven distinct parts. The ordering of writings within those parts is chronological, with a few unavoidable concessions. Peirce's letters are organised in sets of exchanges according to the people involved, and the selections in the first part, *Reasoning and Diagrams*, are presented in a roughly reverse chronological order from 1910 to 1895. The reason for the latter is solely didactic: Peirce's wider perspectives and explanations on the value of the method of EGs find their best formulation in his most mature work deriving from not much earlier than 1910. It is hoped that this retrospective glance helps soften the reader's landing on the more demanding pieces that begin to get off the ground during 1896. Retrospection also aids in placing the superabundant ideas of their inventor into wider philosophical and systematic perspectives.

The methods that have guided the selection of present texts also need an explanation. The leading principle for inclusion is that Peirce writes on, or makes substantial references to, his EGs. The present volumes thus do not cover all of his logic: his pioneering work on the algebra of logic, for example, though in many important ways aiding and abetting the development of EGs and being intimately related to their underlying logical ideas, does not belong to the scope of the present collection. His important other logical, philosophical and semiotic writings that were obviously motivated by the discovery and advancement of the graphical method but do not directly engage with it, have likewise largely been left out.

Often the transitions between algebraic and graphical points of view are without much difference. Sometimes Peirce employs terminology in the logic of the algebra of the copula that may be more familiar from his theory of logical graphs (such as "scriptibility", "sheet of assertion"). For example, in the context of the *Minute Logic* (R 430, ms p. 70, 1902), the writing down of a proposition "on some duly validated *sheet of assertions*" makes the proposition so uttered an assertion that "becomes a binding act". This "we will pretend" to be so "[f]or the sake of fixing our ideas" (*ibid.*). The supposition that one takes there to be the "sheet" upon which an utterance or writing down of a proposition makes it an act of assertion is common in Peirce's algebra of logic just as it is in his graphical method. Likewise is the application of the term "to scribe" or "scriptibility": any algebraic or graphical constituent that has a signification by virtue of the fact that it has been asserted as having that signification, is said to be *scriptible* whenever "it is applicable to V, the *veritas*, in some understood sense" (*ibid.*).

As another example, among Peirce's important writings on logic that are omitted from the present collection is R 501 (c.1901, plus adjacent pages in R 9 and R 11), as these worksheets do not directly employ the notation of logical graphs (and as they are to appear elsewhere).[4] In this treatise, Peirce is seen to present both a general theory of deduction and of the consequence relation, the two cornerstones in the development of modern logic. Its importance thus cannot be overestimated. Peirce is led to these theories by three important generalisations: those of (i) propositions to all signs, (ii) truth to *scriptibility*, i.e. "capable of being written conformably to the purpose" (R 501, late 1901), and (iii) derivation to *transformability*, i.e. "capable of being transformed without changing anything scriptible into anything non-scriptible" (R 430, early 1902). One can also find in R 516 (LoF 1), "On the Basic Rules of Logical Transformation", similar definitions of 'scriptible' and 'transformable' in the context of the graphical method of the logic of existential graphs.

A different set of important texts that regrettably does not have space for inclusion in the present edition consists of Peirce's extensive writings, commentaries and criticism on Alfred Bray Kempe's 1886 publication on mathematical graphical forms (R 708–R 715). Although clearly preceding and influencing Peirce's subsequent studies on logical graphs, these and several other writings of his that antedate the year 1896 have to appear elsewhere.[5] It is ultimately only in connection

---

[4] Ma & Pietarinen (2019) provide a complete transcription of Peirce's "Dragon Logic" of R 501, with an introduction that relate it to later discoveries in modern logic. In brief, Peirce introduces a new Dragon-Head and Dragon-Tail notation: The Dragon Head, Ω, is the implicational sign, and is used in a dual form which Peirce terms the Dragon-Tail, $\hat{C}$, which is an inverse of the head. (Peirce added the circumflex to $\hat{C}$ because C is a singular sign.)

[5] See Grattan-Guinness (2002, 2007) on the account of Peirce's writings on Kempe's theory and their subsequent influence.

to everything that Peirce wrote, throughout his life, on mathematics and algebra, both multiple and logical, that we can assess the place of the graphical method and its genesis in the overall development of these interconnected logical, philosophical, notational and mathematical contributions.

The second criterion for inclusion is that the texts *have not been previously published*. Like the first, this principle has its exceptions, but it is a useful one given how long-lasting the lack of access has been to some of the most important writings dating from Peirce's later years. Duplication of EG-related papers that have long been easily available has been avoided, most prominently that of his 1906 "Prolegomena to an Apology for Pragmaticism" paper. There are, however, copious draft versions and leaves pertaining to "Prolegomena" (the galleys have not been recovered) that have not been published before and those are included in LoF 3. Whenever Peirce's writings that have appeared in print before are published in LoF 1–3, the versions that appear are presumed to be more complete versions of their previous publications. The present edition provides not only the alternative and discrete versions and drafts. It also aims to improve upon previous editions by filling in some gaps and omissions. Details are provided in the volume-specific introductions, individual headnotes and annotations.

Editorial Apparatus

The edition has aimed at narrating the fairly complex technical and graphical notation in a uniform format. The unique 'language' of graphs and other signs and designs peculiar to Peirce's logic and semiotics obviously presents a number of editorial and interpretative challenges. These challenges have been faced by creating a special LaTeX package that produces any graph of whatever kind in a uniform format which is as close to the authorial hand, intentions and explanations as possible. The package includes commands and designs for all logical signs and symbols that have been encountered in Peirce's *Nachlass*. The design of those signs takes into account both (i) how we find them drawn in the relevant autographic sources, and (ii) what Peirce's detailed—and often unfulfilled—instructions to the typesetters were.[6] Fitting several thousand graphs in the volumes, both inline and as display items, would have been impossible in any other

---

[6] For example, in Peirce's algebra of logic the signs similar to sums and products are not the signs of sums Σ and products Π, but those for which "*upright*" type should be used without those little finishing-lines the names of which I forget [Sans Serif]. That is *not* $\Sigma\Pi$ but $\Sigma\Pi$ like inscriptions. You will find many examples in the *Mathematische Annalen*. As a general rule of printing formulae, I like all capitals Roman, all l.c. letters Italics. I only use the small alphabet as sub-

way than by programming a Peirce-specific LaTeX code, commands and environments that can uniformly produce them all. The next section has more details on editing and typesetting these graphs.

Instead of aiming at a clear-text version, *Logic of the Future* edition follows a quasi-diplomatic protocol. Important changes and alterations have been incorporated into the text, displaying inline Peirce's crossed-out texts, deletions and rejections. The default reading is that any portion of text that is stricken-through or crossed out represents an altered portion of text which Peirce replaced with what immediately follows it in the text. Again, this protocol is fallible as editorial discretion must be exercised on what the most meaningful and significant deletions and alterations are taken to be. The gain is an added insight into the evolution of Peirce's thinking and prose at one glance. Double struck-outs are used when an above-text alteration was itself deleted.

Insignificant changes have been emended silently to improve readability. Accordingly, textual apparatus has been kept to a minimum. The downside is that many of the additions of words, lexical units, phrases and sentences that are found in the manuscripts and papers are non-visibly blended into the flow of the text. Marginalia and corrections from Peirce's galleys, books and offprints have been included whenever available, and collateral and external sources have been resorted to in order to verify details and timings of various episodes as well as to confirm the identity of literary sources.

In short, this is an inclusive, thematic, thematically chronological and quasi-diplomatic edition, which aims at maximising novelty and contribution to the advancement of logic and Peirce's logical philosophy. There is a certain urgency in getting the material to appear in print and to reach audiences beyond the communities of scholars who can work directly with Peirce's manuscripts. The impact of his writings on the development of modern logic and on the improvement of human reason becomes understood only through a widespread access to these complex sources.

The abundance of discrete variant texts that derives from Peirce's later period of life—and especially from his profuse works on logical graphs—has necessitated an inclusive editorial approach that makes room for variant texts and versions that diverge from each other in multiple ways yet pertain to the same authorial project or the line of thought. Often Peirce worked without any expressed authorial purpose of aiming at bringing his thoughts, results and diagrams before the public eye. The present edition aims at maximising the amount of alternative but diver-

---

script letters" (CSP to the Open Court, R S-64, draft, 1896; cf. September 2, 1896 CSP to TJMcC [T. J. McCormack, Assistant Editor at the Open Court]; LoF 3).

gent texts while minimising the amount of effort that the reader needs in order to locate the points in which the variant texts show the beginnings of a divergence. Often this has to be carried out at the expense of sacrificing certain critical editing principles that aim at distilling final authorial intentions from textual masses. But what is gained is the lowering of the risk that significant ideas, terms, definitions or results, which notoriously appear in variants, be left out.

Presenting constantly diverging and evolving sets of texts is hardly possible in a strictly linear format. In the present edition, variant pages and alternative segments have been included in the footnotes or, when they are several pages long, appended to the respective chapters. In both cases it is the vicinity of discrete variants that counts in the final output. The reader can observe where the forking has occurred by following the footnoting and boldfaced references **[Alt.** n**]** prefixed to alternative continuations, where n is an index of discrete texts that share the same branching point. Since in many cases there are several substantive alternatives and since at least in some of these cases it is not feasible to venture into guessing whether they represent superseded authorial intentions or whether one or several of them could constitute the final or the maximally authoritative version of the text (or present evidence of the absence of such textual hierarchies), the reader is in such cases presented with options, in hope of furthering the scholarship along the way. It may be that in some cases the alternatives provided in footnotes or appendices in fact represent Peirce's more mature thought, perhaps even those that pertain to some fair copy-text project of his without specific indications. Likewise, substantial deletions and rejections have been retained, either inline or in the footnotes, preceded by editorial tags (**[Del.:]**, **[Rej.:]**). When in rare cases editorial attempts have been frustrated in deciphering a lexical item or a part of an item that occurs in the original source, [*illeg.*] is used in its stead.

When there is an apparent discontinuity in the text either because of physical reasons such as missing, disordered and torn-out pages, or corrupted sheets due to soiling, fire or ink spills, or because of mental reasons such as interruptions of thought, lapses of focus or concentration, but the two texts otherwise can be judged to be parts of the same writing episode, a non-boldfaced flag '[discont.]' is placed in between the conjecturally discontinuous parts. Short editorial omissions and missing text (words or at most a few sentences) as well as incomplete beginnings of alternative texts are indicated by [...]; longer omissions (typically several paragraphs or pages rather than sentences) by [– – –]. Ellipses are used either in order to avoid or curtail excess and irrelevant material or to indicate missing material and lacunæ of any kind, with explanations added. Frequent abrupt endings of the text are indicated by [end].

All editorial annotations are interspersed within the text or given in footnotes and enclosed in upright brackets. Selection titles supplied by the editor are likewise bracketed. Peirce's inconsistent use of brackets has been emended to parentheses to avoid confusion. Identifiers for textual sources are likewise editorial annotations and are included in the text at the beginning of the respective selections, such as **[R 1601]** or [From R S-30] etc. Page references to manuscript sources are to Peirce's own pagination, and when available, are abbreviated by 'ms p.' or 'ms pp.'. ISP pagination numbers are not used.

The editorial approach is thus conservative both as concerns the selection of texts as well as their collation, annotation and textual apparatus. Authorial revisions are visible in the final output with respect to the most significant alterations. Most of the annotations, clarifications and interpretational issues concerning copy-texts and their compositional stages are incorporated in the introductory surveys or in the chapter-wise headnotes. Textual apparatus itself, including detailed information about copy-texts, alternations, variants and editorial emendations, is largely implicit and retained in the source files but not reproduced in the compiled output. Meta-data such as original pagination, running headers and other information about manuscript pages and their organisation are likewise not included in the final output though preserved in the source file layer. Standard and silent normalisations and alterations apply to minor elements of punctuation, such as adding or toggling between single and double quotation marks, typesetting headings and heading punctuation, italization of book titles, and the like. Peirce's original capitalisation of words is preserved. His Latin, Greek, Hieroglyphic, Hebrew, Arabic and other non-English words, phrases, sentences and quotations are given in full but not translated. The sometimes inappropriate vocabulary has been reproduced as is (e.g., "redskin", "negro", "negress", "Flathead Indians", "lover only of a virgin", "lover of every Pope"). In several cases these appear in Peirce's examples (e.g., "Every Hottentot kills a Hottentot") and as such are made up sentences that are entertained, not asserted.

Editing Graphs

In the present edition, graphs are just as important as the text overall. Special note must therefore be made on the methods, techniques and decisions involved in the editorial process of bringing graphs and similar visually pronounced elements into the appearance they have in these volumes. This is not only because of the sheer number of diagrammatic elements involved, but because the totality of instances of graphs also constitutes an actual corpus of a language. As far as the typesetting of the diagrammatic syntax of such graphical languages is concerned, Peirce would typically scribe graphs inline, and only when they grew relatively large in two dimensions, or when there was need to refer to them with running numbers or figure captions, would he display them as individual items or floated or wrapped figures separated from the body of the text. In all cases it is important to keep in mind that graphs are more than mere pictures. They are formulæ of logic and expressions of a language, just as mathematical, logical and natural languages are composed out of designated constituents and lexical units to express relevant and intended meanings. To scribe a graph on the sheet is to assert it. Graphs that appear on the sheet of paper or on the screen of a computer are to be treated as an integral part of the scholarly prose. This needs to be properly acknowledged and accommodated in one's editorial and textual practices, too.

The way the diagrammatic syntax of the language of EGs has been technically handled in the present edition is in terms of developing a special LaTeX package (EGpeirce.sty) that produces uniform, inline-sized graphs that prevent increase in baseline spacing as much as possible. This implies that their "spots" (the predicate terms) that may appear either in natural language, letters (typically upright capital) or some other special marks or mathematical symbols that Peirce used for that purpose, are regularly typeset in small font. For example, A is a graph scribed on a sheet of assertion, and drawing an oval ("the cut") around it produces ⓐ. With two ovals the result looks like ⸨ⓐ⸩, with three ⸨⸨ⓐ⸩⸩, and so on. When some added spacing becomes unavoidable, the preference is to typeset graphs within the text in that case, too. In this manner, the meaningful units of Peirce's diagrammatic syntax—its graph-instances—can be adequately treated as lexical units and utterances in their own right and without discriminating them against the prose of natural language. In those places in which Peirce did write the graphs as display items and when incorporation of them into the text would have cluttered the result and made the text jarring to read, the copy-text layout has been followed as far as practicable. Often Peirce used figure captions to index displayed graphs; those are always preserved and graphs produced in the location nearest to their original appearance in copy-text, always with the caption and reference number given by the authorial hand. To accord with publisher's house style, graphs and figures that appear wrapped in the manuscripts are unwrapped, however.

As mentioned, examples of logical graphs amount to several thousand in Peirce's vast corpus on EGs, often drawn with tinctures of red, blue, brown and green. While all of them have been inspected and studied in their original form at relevant repositories, there are also pages after pages of doodles, seriously incomplete and repetitive examples, sketches too faint or smudged to read; and countless obscure or meaningless ornaments that obviously need not or cannot be included even in the most comprehensive edition, at least perhaps for no other reason than aesthetics. This said, thousands of graphs have been produced in the edition, in uniform and, whenever possible, compressed and space-saving formats, that reduced excess blank space while sacrificing nothing of the readability of graphical texture. (It was a major challenge in Peirce's time to print the graphs, especially the curved lines, at all.) When there are several nests of cuts with only blanks between them, the resulting and sometimes disturbing Moiré effect has been reduced by applying non-symmetric spacing between the cuts. Caption numbers and their in-text references have been made uniform, standardised and corrected when the occasional slip of the pen has happened. These are all silent emendations and standardisations that pertain to the appearance of graphical forms and change nothing in their meaning.

In all cases, graphs are as close to Peirce's original hand as practicable, and they take into account all meaningful features and information visible in original graphs and their respective explanations. The thickness of the lines as well as the shapes of their loose ends are significant features and need to be accurately reproduced. Likewise, Peirce's occasional use of coloured ink in drawing the graphs is preserved in the electronic edition. Typically, he would draw the thick lines of identity in red and the thin cuts in blue ink, especially in 1903 and later when he had better access to ink palettes. Brown and green ink was also availed of in addition to red and blue by the authorial hand to denote specific logical and notational features, especially in reference to second-order graphs (LoF 2). Peirce also resorted to colours for improved didactic effect when educating his students, audiences and correspondents on the fundamentals of EGs. All colours are preserved in the electronic version of the edition, and its grey-scale rendition is expected to reproduce the contrast between light and dark colours as far as possible.

Several images from Peirce's manuscripts are included, either together with their uniform LaTeX rendition or occasionally as stand-alone illustrations. These are marked with **[P.H.]** (standing for "Peirce's Hand"). A couple of facsimiles of entire holograph pages from Peirce's collections have also been included to perfect the material.

While nearly every meaningful piece that Peirce ever wrote or scribed on the topic of EGs is presumed to have been included in the volumes of *Logic of the Future*, this effort is by no means intended to nullify the value of Peirce's original pages, the beauty of which the reader is invited to experience first-hand in the relevant physical and electronic archival locations.

Justification of the Title

It remains to give an explanation of the title chosen to represent the entire edition. On Christmas Day 1909 Peirce wrote to William James that what he had discovered "ought to be the Logic of the Future". What was it that he had discovered? Peirce writes that,

> My triumph in that [algebraic] line, my Existential Graphs, by which all deduction is reduced to insertions and erasures, and in which there are no connecting signs except the writing of terms on the same area enclosed in an oval and heavy lines to express the identity of the individual objects whose signs are connected by such lines. This ought to be *the Logic of the Future*. (R L 224, LoF 3, added emphasis, capitalisation in the original)

This passage epitomises the most important aspects of that new logic. First, historically, EGs represent a natural continuation, application and expansion of algebraic methods that Peirce had worked on for nearly half a century. We now know that everything that can be graphicalised can also be made to work according to algebraic principles. Second, the method Peirce refers to in this passage shows what deduction consists of: a series of insertions and erasures according to certain specified rules of illative transformations. Third, juxtaposition and enclosure completely characterise propositional logic (termed the "Alpha part" of EGs since 1903). These two signs suffice for a system that agrees with a two-element Boolean algebra. An addition of heavy lines moreover extends an Alpha system to (fragments of) first-order predicate logic with identity (termed the "Beta part" of EGs since 1903). Whatever the graphical systems are—and not necessarily only *existential* graphs—they can now incorporate and exploit these three characteristics in full. It is the realisation of the full generality of the graphical method that Peirce predicts is awaiting us in the future.

It may have been only through the advent of modern-day computers, proof theory, mathematics of continuity, cognitive sciences, and a plethora of diagrammatic and heterogeneous notations invented to aid discovery and development of scientific theories, that have put Peirce's prediction into an interesting albeit perhaps somewhat uneasy perspective. How did a single mind not only manage to predict but also contribute to fields that in reality were far ahead in the future? As is the case with a rare number of brains at any epoch of time, Peirce's mind was an anomaly. Largely devoid of academic context and intellectual stimulation of students, in his later years piles of papers accumulated in the attic of his house "Arisbe" in Milford, Pennsylvania, for apparently nothing else than for the sake of advancing the reasoning of posterity. This incremental and exploratory, often painstakingly slow but persistent effort made him realise that an evolution of altogether new logical theories was taking place. This realisation motivated and guided the investigations of this American brain—not the outside influences or recognition expected of them.

"The time will come when the world will be amazed at this" (R 280).

Ahti-Veikko Pietarinen
Introduction to the Theory of Existential Graphs, Volumes 2/1 and 2/2

Introduction

Martin Gardner, in his pioneering book on diagrammatic reasoning, *Logic Machines and Diagrams* (1958), summarised Charles Sanders Peirce's work on the graphical method of logic in the following words:

> We must remember, however, that Peirce undertook his Gargantuan project at a time when symbolic logic was in its infancy. In many aspects of his method he was a pioneer groping in unfamiliar realms. His logic graphs are still the most ambitious yet attempted, and they are filled with suggestive hints of what can be done along such lines. Peirce himself expected successors to take up where he left off and bring his system to perfection. It would be rash to say that no one in the future will be able to build upon it something closer to what Peirce was striving for. In the meantime, it stands as a characteristic monument to one man's extraordinary industry, brilliance, and eccentricity. (Gardner 1958, p. 59)

Peirce self-estimation from mid-1907 was somewhat more modest in kind:

> The author of this book might as well leave his name unmentioned since he has accomplished nothing else but to ~~write this~~ work out the theory sketched in this book and to be more fully set forth and defended in another that he hopes to complete since the day when a diffident boy at this time he picked up from his brother's table a copy of Whatley's *Logic* and asked what logic was and having received an answer stretched himself upon the carpet to devour that book. Now after debating all the points many and many a time within himself a timid old man; he asks himself for the last time whether all this is true. Who can tell? The world will certainly not accept it in a hurry; nor ought it. But the truth will shine clearly out and that in the main the truth is, that which is upheld in these pages is then the belief held with all the strength of head and heart by the author. (R 1608, May 1907)[1]

---

[1] This appears on an unidentified single leaf. It can be dated by the paper type, handwriting status, medical records, and the content that is proximal to Charles's May 1907 letter to his wife Juliette, in which he reveals that "only two things prevent my committing suicide to which I am greatly tempted. One is that I may be useful to you. The other is that I want to write those two little books both of which will do good to many people and bring us money. I am fully resolved to turn over a complete new leaf, give up all my habits of self-indulgence and try to make the rest of my poor life useful" (CSP to JP, May 7, 1907; R L 340).

These words relate to Peirce's planned opening passages for a book (or two) on logic, which he still in his deathbed was convinced is something gravely needed in order to 'make philosophy scientific again'. In his later years, Peirce wanted to save philosophy from the clutches of humanistic studies that scorn scientific practice and pretend to be able to make advances without having to learn and apply the arduous details of methods of logical reasoning.

In that summer, around the time of planning those important books on logic, Peirce receives William James's 1907 book, *Pragmatism*, that contained his popular Lowell Institute Lectures from the previous year, the same series that Peirce had concluded over three years earlier but without success in publishing the lectures. While James's book has often been hailed as no less than the most important contribution to American philosophy, Peirce's 1903 Lowell Lectures were quickly falling into oblivion.[2]

With an allusion to Ferdinand Canning Scott Schiller (1864–1937) among such scholars that had come to deform Peirce's original meaning of pragmatism (Pietarinen 2011b), Peirce had in the meantime drafted a dictionary entry on "Humanism" to drive the point home, with some characteristic satire:

> **Humanism.** Like everybody else I admire humanists and their professed aims. But my admiration of them is by no means unbounded. When they talk of science, as they often do, as abstruse, afflicting, arduous, arid, arenulous, asperous, abstract, abject, apeptic, appallary, abnormal, atrabiliary, abominable, asafetidal, anaclastic, abhorrent, arsenical, abysmal, arithrid, aphagous, and anathema, that simply shows that they ~~like~~ enjoy eating the kindly fruits of the earth better than they do tilling the soil and spreading the manure.
>
> Why should they not abuse the drudges? It is their way of expressing their superior souls.

---

[2] A poignant self-recognition of the implications of his practice of conducting slow science are the autobiographical remarks from the same year, which Peirce recorded on the questionnaire form solicited for the publication of *Men of Science in the United States*, a biographical directory edited by his former student James McKeen Cattell published in 1906:

> **Department of Study:** Logic. [...]
> **Honors Conferred:** Never any, nor any encouragement or aid of any kind or description in my life work, excepting a splendid series of magnificent promises.
> **Books with publishers:** *Photometric Researches* (Leibzig: Wilhelm Engelmann, 1878); Edited *Studies in Logic by Members of the Johns Hopkins University* (Little, Brown & Co, 1883) and B[enjamin] Peirce's *Linear Associative Algebra*, 1882.
> **Chief Subject of Research:** Logic.
> **Where Chiefly Published:** Not published except in slight fragments. See Schröeder's *Logik*.
> **Researches in Progress:** In logic will continue as long as I retain my faculties and can afford pen and ink. (R 1611, 1903)

> But ~~personall~~ for my part, not being able to do everything, I limit my endeavors to make philosophy scientific like the sciences that I was bred in, [end]
> Many of the recent papers upon Pragmatism, Instrumentalism, Humanism, etc. have been attempts to [end] (R S-82, c.1905)

"[H]ave been attempts to apply those doctrines to notions falling outside the domain of their original conception", Peirce might have continued this abandoned passage. Logic, in contrast, and the analytic method of logical graphs in particular, would show what the real definitions consist of, and how such real definitions would follow from applications of the principle or maxim of pragmati(ci)sm. Without the agility and an unceasing desire to rightly follow up on that chief method of the venerable trivium of the liberal arts, logic or dialectics, humanists' aims would remain forever unfulfilled.[3]

Peirce's idea of logic shows, at the same time, to be equally remote from those emerging conceptions of the early 20th century that took logic to be an exercise in how to promulgate formal systems of inference and proof; systems that may be uninterpreted in their languages, non-anthropological in their epistemologies, and in constant danger of ascribing to an empiricist dogma that implies a strict separation of logical and extra-logical affairs (Pietarinen 2011a). Peirce would see dark clouds gathering over both humanists' noble aims and the logicists' narrowly-conceived impressions. The remedy, as he saw it, was to offer a positive solution to both. This was to be carried out by a massive improvement in the theory of logic,

---

3 There is a direct and important connection from these remarks to Peirce's 1903 Lowell Lectures: in a letter to F. C. S. Schiller on May 12, 1905, Peirce recollects his course of lectures in Boston in which he "explained at length how reasoning was analogous—and in fact, a particular case of,—moral self-control, how Logic ought to be founded on Ethics and Ethics on a transfigured Esthetics which would be the science of values, although now wrongly treated as a part of Ethics. After the lectures were over on December 17th, I first laid eyes on the outside of *Humanism* [Schiller 1903], and when, long after, I was able to look at the inside, I was sorry I had not seen it when I wrote those lectures" (CSP to FCSS, May 12, 1905, R L 390). Since Peirce was in a hurry to return to his home in Arisbe, Milford, already on the 18th, it might have been that James had just barely managed to show Peirce the cover of the copy of Schiller's new book that James had recently received. Having suffered from influenza (tonsillitis) since December 10, James was indisposed much of that last week of Peirce's course, and apparently did not attend the last two or three lectures (December 10, 14 and 17), having been "cooped up for three weeks" (WJ to CSP, December 31, 1903, R L 224). It is more likely, then, that Peirce had made a brief visit to see James during the day of the final lecture: "I can see you to morrow if you should be able to call" (WJ to CSP, December 16, 1903; James 2002, p. 345, postmarked "Boston Dec 17, 4am", R L 224). Schiller's book contains a footnote in which Schiller tells to have been corrected—probably by James—that the term 'pragmatism' in fact originates from Peirce, adding, quite misleadingly, that according to the doctrine of pragmatism, Peirce does not have a good claim to the ownership of that designation, since the term did not catch on from the writings and communications of its inventor.

unforeseen since Aristotle, that would offer systems of representation applicable, in the best possible fashion, to the analysis of the meanings of our intellectual conceptions, mental states and rational thoughts as well as to our units of language. This was the ultimate aim of the theory of Existential Graphs (EGs), which reached its most extensive expression in 1903, the *annus mirabilis* of Peirce's scientific life.

Basic Notions

Existential Graphs (EGs) are a graphical method of logic which Peirce gravitated to in 1896 and for which he in the 1903 Lowell Lectures coined the now-customary terminology that divided the method into the Alpha, Beta, and Gamma parts. The logic of the Alpha part is a propositional (sentential) logic and agrees with the two-element Boolean algebra. Peirce often began his presentation of EGs with the second, Beta part of the method that corresponds to a fragment of first-order predicate logic with identity. This introduction follows suit and first provides an informal presentation of the Beta part, followed by a slightly more detailed introduction to the Alpha part. The main ideas of the Gamma part had to do with modal logics, and are presented in the introductory essay to Volume 2/1 of the *Logic of the Future* series.

Peirce defined the central terms "graph", "graph-replica", "existential graph" and "to scribe" in his 1903 Lowell Lectures as follows:

> Every expression of a proposition in conformity with the conventions of this system is called an *existential graph*, or for brevity, a *graph* (although there are other kinds of graphs). Since it is sometimes awkward to say that a graph is *written* and it is sometimes awkward to say it is *drawn*, I will always say it is *scribed*. A graph scribed on the sheet of assent [the sheet of assertion] is said to be *accepted*. We must distinguish carefully between the *graph* and its different *replicas* [instances]. It is the *graph* which is accepted; and the graph is scribed when a *replica* of it is scribed". (R 450, LoF 2/2)

The distinction between the graphs as *types* and graphs as *replicas* (later renamed *instances*) is one of the central distinctions (see also R S-28), and its articulation in this first version of the second Lowell Lecture (R 450, R S-27, R S-28) from September 1903 triggered Peirce to undertake a complete overhaul of this doctrine of speculative grammar during the last quarter of 1903. What is scribed on the sheet of assertion (or on the "sheet or assent") is the replica (instance) of a graph. What the graphs are in general, correspond to their types. What is asserted (or "assented" to) are the graphs as types. The same graph could be scribed on different parts of the sheet as different replicas or instances without thus producing different graphs.

The invention of EGs was in part motivated by Peirce's need to respond to the expressive insufficiency and lack of analytic power of the two systems described, first in the "Note B: The Logic of Relatives" of the *Studies in Logic, by Members of the Johns Hopkins University* (SiL, pp. 187–203), which Peirce later termed the algebra of dyadic (dual) relatives, and soon after in the 1885 paper "On the Algebra of Logic: A Contribution to the Philosophy of Notation", which he termed his general (or universal) algebra of logic. The analytic power derives from subsuming algebraic operations under one mode of composition. This composition of concepts is effected in the quantificational, Beta part of the theory of EGs by the device of *ligatures*. A ligature is a complex line, composed of what Peirce terms the *lines of identities*, which connects various parts and areas of the graphs (see e.g. Dipert 2006; Pietarinen 2005a, 2006a, 2011a, 2015b; Roberts 1973; Shin 2002; Zeman 1964). Here are three examples:

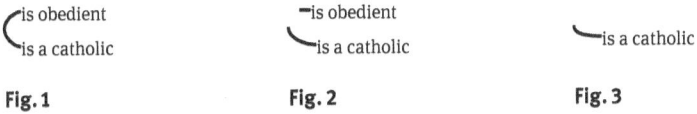

Fig. 1   Fig. 2   Fig. 3

The meaning of these lines is that two or more descriptions apply to the same thing. For example, in Fig. 2 there is a line attached to the predicate term "is obedient". It means that "something exists which is obedient". There is also another line which connects to the predicate term "is a catholic", and that composition means that "something exists which is a catholic", which is equivalent to the graph-instance given in Fig. 3. Since in Fig. 1 these two lines are in fact connected by one continuous line, the graph-instance in Fig. 1 means that "there exists a catholic who is obedient", that is, "there exists an obedient catholic". Ligatures, representing continuous connections composed of two or more lines of identity, stand for quantification, identity and predication, all in one go.

EGs are drawn on the *sheet of assertion*. It represents what the modeller knows or what mutually has been agreed upon to be the case by those who undertake the investigation of logic. The sheet thus represents the universe of discourse. Any graph that is drawn on the sheet puts forth an assertion, true or false, that there is something in the universe to which it applies. This is the reason why Peirce terms these graphs *existential*. Drawing a circle around the graph, or alternatively, shading the area on which the graph-instance rests, means that nothing exists of the sort of description intended. In Fig. 4, the assertion "something is a catholic" is denied by drawing an oval around it and thus severing that assertion from the sheet of assertion:

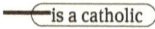

Fig. 4

The graph-instance depicted in Fig. 4 thus means that "something exists that is not catholic".

Peirce aimed at a diagrammatic syntax that would use a minimal number of logical signs, at the same time be maximally expressive while facilitating as analytic a system of reasoning as possible. His ovals, for instance, serve several notational functions: "The first office which the ovals fulfill is that of negation. [...] The second office of the ovals is that of associating the conjunctions of terms. [...] This is the office of parentheses in algebra" (R 430, ms pp. 54–56, 1902; LoF 1). The ovals are thus not only the diagrammatic counterpart to negation but also serve to represent the compositional structure of a graph-formula. Peirce held (see e.g. R 430; R 670, 1911; LoF 1) that a notation that does not separate the sign of truth-function from the representation of its scope is more analytic than a notation, such as that of an ordinary 'symbolic' language, where such a separation is required by the one-dimensional notation. The role of ovals as denials is in fact a derived function from the more primitive considerations of inclusion and implication (Bellucci & Pietarinen 2016; R 300, 1908; LoF 3).

As far as the expressivity of logical languages is concerned, Peirce had already recognised that the notion of *dependent* quantification was essential to the advancement of the theory of logic and that it needed to be captured in any system expressive enough to fully serve the purpose of logical analysis. The nested system of ovals do this in a natural way, much in contrast to algebras that resort to an explicit use of parentheses and other punctuation marks. For example, the graph in Fig. 5 means that "Every Catholic adores some woman". The graph in Fig. 6 means that "Some woman is adored by every Catholic". Peirce notes that the latter asserts more than the former since it states that all Catholics adore the same woman, whereas the former allows different Catholics to adore different women:

Fig. 5   **Fig. 6**

The graph in Fig. 7 means, moreover, that "anything whatever is unloved by something that benefits it", that is, "everything is benefitted by something or other that does not love it":

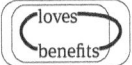

Fig. 7

Graphs can get quite complex, but perhaps still less complex than their natural-language correlates. Peirce occasionally gave examples of some very complicated sentences with intricate quantificational structures, and proposed to model and analyse them with the aid of the graphical method. An example is Fig. 8, which is to be interpreted "in a universe of sentient beings" (R 504, 1898; LoF 1):

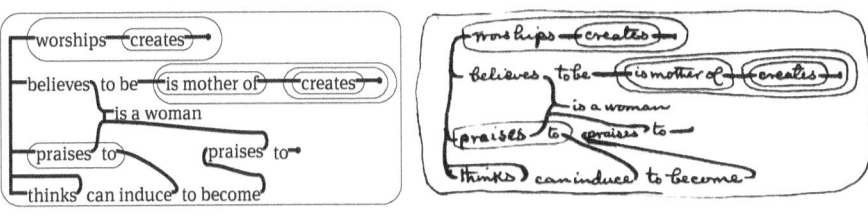

Fig. 8   [P.H.]

The graphical form, Peirce assumes, brings about the meaning of the sentence in a clearer way than what the sentences given in natural language could possibly reveal. For example, the previous graph expresses the following sentence:

> Every being unless he worships some being who does not create all beings either does not believe any being (unless it be not a woman) to be any mother of a creator of all beings or else he praises that woman to every being unless to a person whom he does not think he can induce to become anything unless it be a non-praiser of that woman to every being.

Peirce's example is complicated; the quantificational structure and the dependencies exhibited in the constituents of this sentence are certainly not easily discerned from the linguistic material.

It is on the level of semantics that the power of dependent quantification comes to the fore. Peirce carried his semantics out in terms of defining what today is recognised as two-player zero-sum semantic games that take place between the Graphist/Utterer and the Grapheus/Interpreter.[4] This is explained in a variant of "New Elements (Kaina stoicheia)" (R 517, 1901)[5] as follows. The copulative is *general* and *definite*, as to assert A and B "is to assert a proposition which the interpreter is at liberty to take as meaning A or as meaning B". The disjunctive, on the other hand, is *vague* and thus *individual* in nature, as to assert A or B "is to assert a proposition which gives the utterer the option between defending it by proving A and defending it by proving B" (R 517, ms p. 50). And not only this, Peirce continues that there are strategic advantages according to the order of the choices of selection:

> The asserter of a proposition may be said to [be] *ex officio* a defender of it, or, in the old logical phrase, a respondent for it. The interpreter is, on the other hand, naturally a critic of it and quasi-opponent. Now if a proposition is in one respect vague, so that in that respect the respondent has the choice of an instance, while in another respect it is general, so that in that respect the opponent has the choice of an instance, whichever party makes his choice last has the advantage of being able to adapt his instance to the choice already made by the other. For that reason,
>
> Some woman is loved by all catholics,
>
> where the respondent is obliged to name the woman before the opponent has chosen his catholic, is harder to defend, and less apt to be true, than
>
> Every catholic loves some woman,
>
> where the opponent must instance his catholic, whereupon the respondent can choose his woman accordingly.
>
> It is a curious fact that when there are a number of ~~obvious~~ signified choosings of instances, it is not the later one which has the logical character of an operator upon the one already made, but the reverse. Thus, in the last example [end] (R 517, ms pp. 50–51)[6]

Peircean semantic games were not limited to interpreting natural-language sentences or graph-instances of the theory of EGs.[7] He often applied the same idea

---

[4] Sometimes, and especially in relation to Peirce's *model-building games*, these roles are split so that the Grapheus and the Interpreter are playing separate roles. On this, see Pietarinen (2013). Hilpinen (1982) is the first to notice Peirce's logic as having been importantly erected upon the principles of semantic games. On games in logic, see e.g. Pietarinen (2003b); Majer, Pietarinen & Tulenheimo (2011).

[5] Internal and external evidence suggests that Peirce wrote "Kaina stoicheia" in late 1901 and not in 1904 as has been suggested in the Robin Catalogue and in the publication of that essay in EP 2.

[6] Similar textual evidence for the game-theoretic interpretation occurs in numerous places, see e.g. R 238, R S-64 and the references in Pietarinen (2003a).

[7] How close Peircean semantic games are to contemporary ones has been explored in Pietarinen (2001, 2003a, 2007, 2013).

also to the interpretation of complex quantificational patterns and connectives in his general algebra of logic. In some cases both were considered in unison, as revealed in the following fragment located in R S-64 and probably written sometime in 1893–1894:

> It will be found that the algebraic method is the more convenient; but some persons have such a difficulty with algebra that I add the graphical method.
>   Given a proposition about two things a and b, if you are to select the thing to be represented by a with a view to making the proposition false, and I am to select b with a view to making the proposition true, it may be an advantage to me, and can be no disadvantage to know what your selection is to be, before I ~~determine~~ fix upon mine. Hence, if the proposition be such that it is true even if I make my selection first, much more will it be true if you make the first selection. Accordingly, if a proposition be written either in the algebraic or the graphical system, and that proposition be true, much more will it be true when any letter in a square or affixed to a Π is moved to the left. For a similar reason, of two letters both in circles or in squares, or both attached to Σs or to Πs, it is indifferent which comes first. Thus, to say that every man loves every woman is the same as to say that every woman is loved by every man; and to say that some man loves some woman is the same as to say that some woman is loved by some man; but to say that some man loves every woman is to say much more than that every woman is loved by some man.
>
> [Alt.] There are other interesting systems of representing propositions; but it is not necessary to consider them here. The above algebraic system is the most convenient; but I add the graphical for the sake of the many readers who do not take kindly to algebra.
>   Given a proposition about two subjects, A and B, if *you* are to select the subject A with a view to making the proposition false, if you can,—in which case, plainly, A is universal, for the proposition asserts itself to be true, and hence that you cannot succeed in this,—while *I* am to select B with a view to making the proposition true,—so that B is particular,—then it may be of advantage to me, and can at any rate be no disadvantage, to know what your selection for A is to be, before I fix upon mine for B. That is, if the proposition be true though the particular subject be selected first, much more will it be true if the universal subject be selected first.

The "circles" and "squares" Peirce talks about pertain to the notation of protographs that preceded the discovery of the logical method of EGs (see Introduction to Part II, LoF 1). Importantly, he also emphasises the 'strategic' advantage to those who know what the earlier selections have been, which indeed is a standard property of semantic games (of perfect information) for classical logics.

In another, proof-theoretic sense, it nevertheless speaks to the superiority of EGs over algebraic systems that in it deduction, as follows from Peirce's Johns Hopkins graduate student Oscar Howard Mitchell's (1851–1889) work (Mitchell 1883), is reduced to a minimum number of permissive operations. Peirce termed these operations *illative rules of transformation*, and in effect they consist only of two: *insertions* (that is, permissions to draw a graph-instance on the sheet of assertion) and *erasures* (that is, permissions to erase a graph-instance from the sheet). More precisely, the *oddly-enclosed* areas of graphs (areas within a non-even number of enclosures) permit inserting any graph in that area, while *evenly-enclosed* areas permit erasing any graph from that area. Furthermore, a copy of a graph-instance is permitted to be pasted on that same area or any area deeper within the same nest of enclosures. This is the rule of *iteration*. A copy thus iterated is permitted to be erased by the converse rule termed *deiteration*. An interpretational corollary is that a *double enclosure* with no intervening graphs (other than the blank graph) in the middle area can be inserted and erased at will.

A more detailed exposition of these illative rules of transformation would need to show their application to quantificational expressions, namely applying insertions and erasures to ligatures. Some flavor of such transformations can be gotten from examples. Regarding the graphs in Figs. 1, 2 and 3, an application of a permissible erasure on the line of identity in Fig. 1 results in the graph-instance in Fig. 2, and that another application of a permissible erasure on the upper part of the graph-instance in Fig. 2 results in the graph-instance as depicted in Fig. 3. Thus what is represented in Fig. 2 is a logical consequence of the graph-instance in Fig. 1, and what is represented in Fig. 3 is a logical consequence of the graph-instance given in Fig. 2.

Roberts (1973) has shown that the transformation rules Peirce had reached by 1903 form a semantically complete system of deduction. Roberts did not mention, however, that Peirce had demonstrated their soundness in 1898 and again in 1903 and that he had argued for their completeness in a couple of places, including in unpublished parts of *A Syllabus of Certain Topics of Logic* (R 478) that he wrote to accompany his Lowell Lectures.

Facts like these demonstrate that Peirce was a key innovator in the development of modern logic. And there is more. As observed, it is the polarity of the outermost ends or portions of ligatures that determines whether the quantification is *existential* (namely that the outermost end or a portion of the ligature rests on a positive area) or *universal* (if it rests on an odd area). Unlike in the Tarski-type semantics, but much in the fashion of what happens in game-theoretical semantics, the preferred rule of interpretation of the graphs is what Peirce termed "endoporeutic": one looks for the outermost portions of ligatures on the sheet of assertions first, assigns semantic values to that part, and then proceeds inwards into the areas enclosed within ovals. (In non-modal contexts, ligatures are not well-formed graphs because they may cross the enclosures.)

The diagrammatic nature of EGs consists in the relationship between forms of relations exhibited in the diagrams and the real relations in the universe of discourse. Peirce was convinced that, since these graphical systems exploit a *diagrammatic syntax*, they—together with extensions and modifications that would cover modalities, non-declarative expressions, speech acts, and so forth—can express any assertion, however intricate. Guided by the precepts laid out by the diagrammatic forms of expression, and together with the simple illative permissions by which deductive inference proceeds, the conclusions from premises can be "read before one's eyes"; these graphs present what Peirce believed is a "moving picture of the action of the mind in thought" (R 298, 1906; LoF 3):

> If upon one lantern-slide there be shown the premisses of a theorem as expressed in these graphs and then upon other slides the successive results of the different transformations of those graphs; and if these slides in their proper order be successively exhibited, we should have in them a veritable moving picture of the mind in reasoning. (R 905, 1907; LoF 3)

The theory of EGs that uses only the notation of ovals and the spatial notion of juxtaposition of graphs is termed by Peirce the Alpha part of the EGs, and as noted corresponds to propositional logic. The extension of the Alpha part with ligatures and *spots*[8] gives rise to the Beta part, and it corresponds to fragments of first-order predicate calculus. What Peirce in 1903 termed the *Gamma* part consists of a number of developments, including various modalities such as metaphysical, epistemic and temporal modalities, as well as extensions of modal graphs with ligatures. In Peirce's repositories one can in addition find many proposals developing graphical systems for *second-order logic* and *abstraction* in the logic of *potentials*, logics of *collections*, and meta-logical theories using the language of graphs to talk about notions and properties of the graphs in that language. The latter include encoding of permissive rules of transformation in such languages of "graphs of graphs". He even proposed this idea also to serve as the method of logical analysis of assertions and meta-assertions. In connection to one of his last remarks on EGs in a letter to the chemist, geologist and astronomer Allan Douglas Risteen (1866–1932; R L 376/R 500, December 6–9, 1911) Peirce mentions that one would also need to add a "*Delta* part in order to deal with *Modals*":[9]

> The better exposition of 1903 divided the system into three parts, distinguished as the Alpha, the Beta, and the Gamma, parts; a division I shall here adhere to, although I shall now have to add a *Delta* part in order to deal with modals. A cross division of the description which

---

8 The spots are the graphical counterparts to the predicate terms, similar to simple rhemas that do not contain any logical constants (see Bellucci 2019; Pietarinen 2015c).

9 A. D. Risteen was "assistant to Professor Charles S. Peirce of Stevens Institute of Technology upon pendulum observations summer of 1886; computer with U.S. Coast and Geodetic Survey 1886–87; editor of Power 1887–88; and also an associate editor of the Century Dictionary; assistant to Professor Peirce in U.S. Coast Survey work at Milford, Pa., May-August, 1888", according to the obituary note in *Yale Obituary Record of Graduates, 1932–1933*, New Haven: Bulletin of Yale University, 15 October 1933, p. 191.

here, as in that of 1903, is given precedence over the other is into the *Conventions*, the *Rules*, and the *working* of the System.

While no evidence remains of the details of what the projected Delta could have been, most likely Peirce thought a new compartment was needed to accommodate the ever-expanding amount of graphical systems that had been mushrooming in the Gamma part. Perhaps he planned the Delta part to capture quantificational multi-modal logics in ways similar to those that can be discerned in how he desired his theory of *tinctured graphs* to look like as it was fledgling since 1905 (LoF 3).

As will be observed from Peirce's writings collected in Volume 3, his graphical systems of modal logic included suggestions for defining several types of multi-modal logics in terms of tinctures of areas of graphs. Tinctures enable one to assert, among other things, necessities and metaphysical possibilities, and so call for changes in the nature of how the corresponding logics behave, including the identification of individuals in the presence of multiple universes of discourses. Peirce defined epistemic operators in terms of subjective possibilities which, as in contemporary epistemic logic, are epistemic possibilities defined as the duals of knowledge operators.

Peirce analysed the meaning of identities between actual and possible objects in quantified multi-modal logics. As an example, the two graphs given in Figs. 9 and 10 that he presented in a 1906 draft of the "Prolegomena" paper (R 292a, 1906; LoF 3) illustrate the nature of the interplay between epistemic modalities and quantification:

Fig. 9   **Fig. 10**

The graph in Fig. 9 is read "There is a man who is loved by one woman and loves a woman known by the Graphist to be another". The reason is that in the equivalent graph depicted in Fig. 10, the woman who loves is denoted by the name 'A', and the woman who is loved is denoted by the name 'B'.[10] The shaded area is a

---

10 Fig. 10 is how Peirce presented the graph, apparently forgetting to draw the line of teridentity between the two instances of "loves" and one occurrence of "man", in the same way as in the graph of Fig. 9.

tincture (argent, if given in colours) that refers to the modality of subjective possibility. Thus the graph in Fig. 10 means that it is subjectively impossible, by which Peirce means "is contrary to what is known by the Graphist" (i.e., the modeller of the graph), that A should be B. In other words, the woman who loves and the woman who is loved (whom the graph does not assert to be otherwise known to the Graphist) are known by the Graphist not to be the same person.

Peirce's work on such topics and questions highlights the importance of underlying ideas that were rediscovered significantly later, and often in different guises. In Peirce's largely unpublished works one finds topics that later became known as, for example, multi-modal logics and possible-worlds semantics, quantification into modal contexts, cross-world identities (in R 490 he termed these special relations connecting objects in different possible worlds "references", see Pietarinen 2006b), and what is termed 'Peirce's Puzzle' (Dekker 2001; Hintikka 2011; Pietarinen 2015a), namely the question of the meaning of indefinites in conditional sentences. Peirce himself proposed to analyse the latter in quantified modal extensions of EGs of his own devising.

Far from only anticipating later findings, Peirce's logical innovations have been applied in a number of areas, including philosophical logic, formal semantics and pragmatics, mathematics, mind and language, AI, cognitive and computing sciences, biology, medical diagnosis and prognosis, astrobiology, physics, cosmology and geology, as much as in economics, game and decision theory, history and philosophy of science, archaeology, anthropology, musicology and art studies.[11]

---

[11] For some further work and applications along the lines Peirce had set out to do see, for example, Bellucci & Pietarinen (2020); Bellucci, Pietarinen & Stjernfelt (2014); Brady & Trimble (2000); Lupher & Adajian (2015); Pietarinen (2005b, 2010a,b, 2012a, 2019a,b); Pietarinen, Shafiei & Stjernfelt (2019); Sowa (1984, 2006); Zalamea (2012a,b). For details on Peirce's deductive logic, see the collection of Houser et al. (1997). Hilpinen (2004) is a helpful overview on Peirce's logic.

Ahti-Veikko Pietarinen
Introduction to Volume 2/2: The 1903 Lowell Lectures

In this multi-volume series of the *Logic of the Future*, the development of EGs continues along two trajectories. Volume 2 comprises the bulk of Peirce's 1903 Lowell Institute Lectures and is arranged in two stand-alone books, Volumes 2/1 and 2/2. Together they tell the story of how Peirce wanted the world to receive that theory, and what his sustained efforts were to communicate the fullest possible account of it to his peers, colleagues and public audience.

In Volume 3, *Pragmaticism and Correspondence*, we see Peirce applying EGs to his ultimate philosophical thoughts, and how he took graphs to deliver the proof of his philosophical theory of meaning, among other late innovations buried in the piles of letters, largely unsent, to his friends, colleagues, collaborators and editors.

The second volume has its textual material organised in fourteen selections, arranged in two parts across two books: three selections belong to *The Logical Tracts* (Part IV, LoF 2/1) and eleven in *The 1903 Lowell Lectures* (Part V, LoF 2/2). An account of Part V, its theoretical background and a description of the texts selected in its individual chapters is provided next.

Part V: The 1903 Lowell Lectures

The fifth part of the *Logic of the Future* edition collates the first five of Peirce's eight 1903 Lowell Institute lectures, their lecture drafts and accompanying studies, arranged in eleven individual selections. Over 1 000 manuscript and notebook pages have been chosen for inclusion as the copy-text of the fourteen selections included in the present edition, amounting to 400 printed pages in total.[1]

This section contains two subsections: an introduction to the Lowell Lectures and a survey of the eleven selections that constitute the first five lectures and their supplementary material.

---

[1] The remaining Lectures VI–VIII that have not been included in the present edition have significantly less material associated with them in the archives and would amount roughly to 100 additional printed pages.

Introduction to Part V

The 1903 Lowell Lectures may well be the strongest pillar in Peirce's cathedral of graphs. Unsurpassed not only in the sheer amount of texts that Peirce produced during the year, the philosophical and logical reach of these lecture drafts leaves little doubt that his course lends not only the best possible support to motivate his sustained work on the graphical method, but that it is this very method itself that is now able to reach farther and deeper than virtually anything else that his logical philosophy had so far meant to accomplish—even farther and deeper than what it was going to do during the decade still lying ahead in Peirce's life.

Purpose of the Lowell Lectures

What were the main goals and points of these public lectures? In R 447 (continuing with the first page from R 475 and then in R 447(s)), Peirce sets out to engage his audience with the following plan:

> Ladies and Gentlemen:
> For eight abbreviated hours I am to endeavor to occupy your attention with the subject of reasoning. But can one person inform another what is good reasoning and what is bad?[2]
> About seventy generations have passed since Aristotle gave to logic a scientific form. There has not been one of three generations in Europe which has not been occupied with this study; and it is natural and proper to ask what the harvest has been. At the end of sixty of these seventy generations, Europeans reasoned no better than the personages of Plato's Dialogues are represented as reasoning. They were considerably more adroit,—they reached their conclusions with greater facility; but the conclusions were neither more sure nor further-reaching; and as to the character of the reasoning, it was of a decidedly less vigorous and fecund kind than that of Plato himself. As for the science of logic, it remained substantially the very doctrine that Aristotle had taught.
> Galileo inaugurated the science of dynamics about 1590, and his work was well-known and had its effect, although his book was not published for near half a century later; and it was the study of dynamics, more than anything else, which gradually taught men to reason better on all subjects. I do not say that it was to sole cause; for Tycho Brahe established his observatory half a dozen years before Galileo was appointed professor in Pisa; and the *principle* of our system of numerical notation, the influence of which has been powerful and

---

2 **[Alt.]** [R 447(s):] "For eight abbreviated hours I am to endeavor to occupy your attention with what is now known about right and wrong reasoning, the most of which has been discovered ~~during~~ by the last two of the seventy generations that have held the stage since Aristotle first gave to logic a scientific form. ~~It is a terribly difficult task to present any useful outline of such~~ subject in so very short a course. With a special science, it would not be so difficult. To prompt you in this short course to any useful reflexions upon this subject I will draw upon my abilities to the utmost".

salutary, seems to have been a secret known to a few of the Greeks even in classical times. All these studies, but especially dynamics, forced men to reason with great exactitude; and the spirit of exact think[ing] spread far and wide into all the sciences. [end]

The overarching subject was that of reasoning, and modern scientific reasoning in particular. What makes one piece of reasoning better than some other? What is the true nature of the logic of science? How to distinguish between deduction, induction and abduction, and how do they hang together to reveal something new about reality, in the widest sense of the term?[3]

The Lecture Titles

Peirce was invited to have the lectures early in 1903, and by the end of February he would know they are to take place sometime during the next winter. In mid-March, James Mills Peirce writes to his brother to confirm that A. Lawrence Lowell is offering him "eight lectures at $150 each". Peirce's lecture series, which was the third of the four courses of the autumn arranged by the Lowell Institute, were announced both in the Institute's autumn programme and in the *Monthly Bulletin of Books Added to the Public Library of the City of Boston* (Series 2, Vol. VIII, November 1903, Boston: Published by the Trustees, p. 418) as follows: "**The Third Course** will be eight lectures by Charles S. Peirce, Esq., Member of the National Academy of Sciences, on *Some Topics of Logic bearing on Questions now Vexed*. Mondays and Thursdays at 8p.m., beginning Nov. 23". Boston's local newspaper *Evening Transcript* advertised them on Monday, November 16, also with this full title (p. 5; P 01005). Sometimes called "Topics of Logic" or "Some Topics of Logic", the term that is adopted in the present edition is "The 1903 Lowell Lectures", or just "Lowell Lectures" for short, invariably referring to Peirce's third Lowell Institute Lectures.[4]

The Lowell Institute's office recorded the lectures to have been the following:

---

[3] That Peirce planned his Lowell Lectures of 1903 (same year as the Harvard Lectures on pragmatism) to concern his current views on the logic of science and on the modern theory of the three modes of reasoning is attested in his last (the seventh) Harvard Lecture on pragmatism from early May, in which he told the audience that his views "have naturally developed and matured very much indeed during the twenty-three years that have elapsed since I printed the last of the papers I have mentioned, and I am happy to say that I shall have an opportunity of presenting the matter [or deduction, induction and abduction] afresh next winter in some lectures I am going to give at the Lowell Institute" (R 315).

[4] The previous two installments were the 1892 Lowell Institute Lectures on "The History of Science" that was held from November 28, 1892 until January 5, 1893, and the first, the 1866 lectures on "The Logic of Science; or Induction and Hypothesis", that Peirce delivered from October 24 until December 1.

> From President Lowell's Office: Charles Saunders [sic.] Peirce gave eight lectures at the Lowell Institute in the year 1903–1904. The subjects of the various lectures and the dates on which they were given follows: *Some Topics of Logic Bearing on Questions Now Vexed*. Nov. 23, What Makes a Reasoning Sound? Nov. 27, A System of Diagrams for Studying Logical Relations. Exposition of it Begun. Nov. 30, The Three Universal Categories and their Utility. Dec. 3 Exposition of the System of Diagrams Completed. Dec. 7, The Doctrine of Multitude, Infinity and Continuity. Dec. 10, What is Chance? Dec. 14, Induction as Doing, not mere Cogitation Dec. 17, How to Theorize. (R L 257)

These titles are the ones that Peirce originally proposed, which he would modify during the progress of the course. Taking into account the revised titles penned in the notebook R 470 after the fifth lecture, it is possible to summarise the titles and dates as follows (Peirce's revised titles from R 470 are given in parenthesis):

(1) **Monday, November 23:**
   What Makes a Reasoning Sound?

(2) **Friday, November 27:**
   A System of Diagrams for Studying Logical Relations. Exposition of it begun. (Existential Graphs—Alpha & Beta)

(3) **Monday, November 30:**
   The Three Universal Categories and their Utility. (General Explanations. Phenomenology and Speculative Grammar)

(4) **Thursday, December 3:**
   Exposition of the System of Diagrams Completed. (Existential Graphs: Gamma Part)

(5) **Monday, December 7:**
   The Doctrine of Multitude, Infinity and Continuity. (Multitude)

(6) **Thursday, December 10:**
   What is Chance? (Chance)

(7) **Monday December 14:**
   Induction as Doing, not mere Cogitation. (Induction)

(8) **Thursday, December 17:**
   How to Theorize. (Abduction)

In the beginning of his lecture notes for the seventh lecture (R 473) written between December 10 and 14, Peirce recounts the current progress of the course as follows:

> So far, these lectures have been entirely confined to Deduction. The first lecture contained some essential initial considerations, and the third hurriedly gave what is absolutely indispensable concerning Phenomenology and Speculative Grammar. The second and fourth contained a sufficient introduction to logical graphs which affords the best means of analyzing deductive reasonings. The fifth lecture took up a subject all-important logically and which

serves to illustrate mathematical reasoning in the simplest branch of it, excepting the mathematics of graphs themselves. I had no time, I very much regret to say, to speak of continuity, which is the principal mathematical conception and the most ~~difficult~~ in need of explanation while its logical importance is far greater than is everything else put together that I could bring into the first six lectures. But there was no possibility of crowding it into this course. In the sixth lecture I was only able to make a few detached remarks concerning statistical deductions. This leaves us but two hours in which to treat of the most important kinds of reasoning, Induction and Abduction. Deduction is of small account beside these but unfortunately these can only be understood in the least in the light of deduction. Without that one could not even comprehend what inductive and abductive reasoning are. All that I have said, therefore, is merely a very inadequate preparation for these last two lectures; and the latter of these two will have to be curtailed in a most injurious fashion. Logic, let me tell you, while it is a subject requiring continual stress of mind, is by no means a dry and uninteresting topic. But it becomes so, as any science would, when it has to be compressed to a very injurious and almost fatal degree.

This passage reveals how little Peirce actually managed to present in the handful of hours that he had at his disposal. The actual lectures appear only as a prelude to what he wanted to accomplish, or what he might have accomplished had he been given an opportunity to lecture a full academic course devoted to an examination of all the needed details concerning the theory of modern scientific reasoning. Any such course, as can be inferred from the passage, would have to be multiply times longer than what the popular lecture format, fatally injurious to the substance matter, permitted him to do.

Editing the Lowell Lectures

Most of Peirce's material is in the form of lecture notes, written in thick Harvard Cooperative Notebooks. All the material included in the present volume is located at Houghton Library among the Peirce Papers and constitutes a quite well preserved and relatively complete archival collection, although some specific texts and pages have definitely been lost. 28 thick notebooks survive in the archives, and together with hundreds of related worksheets, rejects and cut-out pages that Peirce amassed in the course of preparing the lectures, the relevant overall corpus provides enough material for a lifetime of excavation, organisation and analysis.

The most important manuscripts for the Lowell Lectures are identified in the Robin Catalogue as follows. Lecture I, R 447–R 454; Lecture II, R 455–R 456; Lecture III, R 457–R 466; Lecture IV, R 467; Lecture V, R 468–R 471; Lecture VI, R 472; Lecture VII, R 473–R 474; Lecture VIII, R 475–R 476. The primary source for the *Syllabus* text is R 478; a number of additional pages is derived from several other folders. This list does not differentiate between delivered and undelivered lectures. Aside from these core texts, relevant pages can be identified and extracted from numerous other supplements, manuscripts, worksheets, typescripts, printed brochures, pamphlets and uncatalogued fragments. The information is given in the surveys of individual selections and in the chapter headnotes. Partial publications of the lectures have appeared in CP 1.15–1.26, 1.324, 1.343–1.349, 1.521–1.544, 1.591-1.615, 4.510–4.529, 5.590–5.604, 6.88–6.97, 7.110–7.130, 7.182n7, 8.176, that of Lecture I in EP 2, pp. 242–257, and in a few other places, most importantly in the third volume of *New Elements of Mathematics* (NEM III, pp. 331–448). Any relevant previous publication has been included in the present collection in its most comprehensive form, with variant texts, extra and discarded leaves and sketches as found in the originals deposited at Harvard's Houghton Library.

The present edition makes no pretension to be an absolutely complete and perfected, let alone critical, reproduction of Peirce's 1903 Lowell Lectures. First, in the present volume they are limited to the first five lectures and their various plans, drafts and supplementary material. This includes those parts and sections of the *Syllabus* manuscript that only pertain to the topic of EGs. The first five lectures directly concern the theory of the graphical logic; Lectures VI–VIII, on the other hand, hardly mention them at all. The total number of notebook pages and manuscript and other sheets is at least 1 300, not counting 500 or so closely related pages of *The Logical Tracts* project presented separately in Part IV of LoF 2/1. The current selections are thus restricted to those lectures, both delivered and non-delivered, that directly bear on EGs and their application to the analysis of the nature of scientific and mathematical reasoning. Quantitatively, the copy-texts that have been selected as the basis for the selections in Part V occupy well over half of the total number of relevant surviving pages. Among the notes and manuscripts not included in the present collection are R 447–R 449 and R 451–R 453 (pre-drafts and drafts of the first delivered lecture), R 458 (though included in part, with alternative versions and rejects from R 458(s)), R 463 (containing a 4-page, early and abandoned draft on multitude), R 469 (but included in part), R 470 (but included in part), and R 472–R 476 (on Lectures VI–VIII). There is also an intermittent item R 477 in the Robin catalogue sequence that lists the items pertaining to the 1903 Lowell Lectures, and although it is a notebook containing "Notes for a Syllabus of Logic", the text cannot be confirmed to be related to the Lowell Lectures.[5] Large portions of the *Syllabus* (R 478), together with many of its subjacent pages located in other folders (e.g., R 538–R 542) have also been left out. Many

---

[5] The reason for not including R 477, "Notes for a Syllabus of Logic", partially published in PSR, pp. 33–34, is that this plan of a syllabus is not connected to the 1903 Lowell Lectures or its syllabus. It may have been produced in June ("...the ~~lonely~~ delightful cool warmth of the June afternoon, the charming sunshine half shaded up by the green bushes outside his windows, the absolute quiet of his study, gave him feelings of joy and of gratitude")—the month when Peirce is back to

other draft, cut-out and assorted pages, rejects and fragments found in miscellaneous folders have been included in the present collection. Yet many more exist that could be contemplated for further inclusion into any comprehensive critical edition of these lectures.[6]

Second, the selections presented here do not attempt to strictly delineate the material that Peirce is presumed actually to have delivered from the abundance of plans and lecture note drafts that did not find their way to Huntington Hall. Some indications of the important material that was quite certainly presented during these evening hours are provided in the introductory essay. In many other cases, it would not be possibly to do so with a reasonable degree of certainty, and one might even question the utility of splitting his lectures in two categories: the actual/oral lectures and the planned/written ones, not least because of the accumulation of surmises that one inevitably would have to entertain in any such attempt to distinguish between what he might have managed and did not quite manage to communicate. His lectures are a moving target. Peirce's organic drafting and cultivation of his ideas is gaining momentum as the lectures progressed. In some cases decisions what to lecture were made perhaps just hours or minutes before the start of the sessions. Characteristically, he would desire certain degrees of freedom, perhaps ad libbing part of the content at will, even discovering and testing ideas on the fly on stage. Whatever happened during any one the evenings influenced both the planning and the delivery of what was happening next. The trajectory that his lectures were taking was unpredictable. Attempts to demarcate between planned and actual lectures are mostly frustrated given the abundance of drafts and the lack of clear reading indications. Eight hours of gross delivery time would only

---

Arisbe from having stayed in Cambridge since late March—but as the text proceeds with remarks on the ingredients of the phaneron and the three states of awareness, the year 1903 is too early. Peirce had not introduced the term "Phaneron" and had not embarked on studies on the indecomposable elements of the Phaneron, before 1906. Such matters pertain to the planned sixth section of the R 477 syllabus plan among the suggested total of its 22 sections, each of which was to be about ten manuscript pages in length. That this "Notes for a Syllabus of Logic" is from 1906 is corroborated both by an inspection of Peirce's handwriting and the type of the notebook used, both consistent with his productions from 1906. The "Notes" plan follows the structure of Peirce's architectonics: it was to exhibit the division of science (sections 1–11), the divisions of logic (sections 12–22), divisions of signs (sections 12–14), and the divisions of scientific reasoning (sections 17–20). Practical reasoning and methodeutic, also somewhat later themes than those that Peirce would have conducted in 1903, were then to conclude this rather extensive plan of whatever this later installment of his as the "syllabus of logic" was projected to contain (sections 21 and 22).

6 An early plan of the Peirce Edition Project has been to have the 1903 Lowell Institute Lectures appear as a stand-alone, out-of-sequence Volume 22 of the critical chronological edition of the *Writings of Charles S. Peirce* (W), of which seven volumes have so far appeared.

be a shallow dive into the depth of ideas recorded in the notes. Quantitatively, well below half of the non-redundant text that has been preserved in notebooks would have been possible to be delivered within the time allotted.[7] Peirce cared much less about what the actual lectures were to be than on the unique opportunity that the preparation of these lectures gave for him once more to concentrate all of his energies on the advancement of the future of the science of logic.

Summary of Lectures

The hour-long lectures were given in Huntington Hall of Rogers Building, 491 Boylston Street, Boston, a lecture theatre seating 938 people. Lectures ran on Mondays and Thursdays at 8pm, with the exception of the second lecture that was held on Friday. A brief sketch of the plan and the content of the lectures is provided next.

Lecture I, delivered on Monday 23, was entitled "What Makes a Reasoning Sound?" (hereafter, WMRS). Versions most likely to have resembled the delivered parts of that first lecture have been published in their main in the *Essential Peirce*, Volume 2, pp. 242–257 and for that reason are not included in the present selection.

The first draft of the first lecture (R 454), which Peirce composed in early summer soon after his Harvard Lectures on pragmatism had ended, was quite different from the one delivered as WMRS. Sometime later in summer and during autumn, Peirce changed his mind about how the material should be presented in the opening lecture. Hearing the echoes of James's advice to avoid alienating his audience in this important first lecture, Peirce would change his plan about the organisation and presentation of his ideas. Reasons are revealed in Peirce's reply to a written question from an anonymous listener given in the beginning of the third lecture (R 465, A1–A8; EP 2, p. 534):[8] "[I]n this short course it seems better to skip such purely theoretical questions". The central theoretical question was the soundness of logic, conceived both in philosophical, mathematical as well as semantic senses of the term. That it indeed was the property of "soundness", and Peirce using that very term to denote the intended key property of reasoning, is

---

[7] Roughly, c. 50–70 notebook pages per sessions of 60 minutes of reading time each. In the best case that would amount to some half a thousand communicable pages, not taking into account the time consumed by other activities, such as projections, blackboard drawings, explanations, questions, distractions or other interruptions.

[8] Peirce's pagination of A1–A8 in the beginning of the notebook R 465 includes other preparatory and introductory remarks besides the answer to the listener's question as well.

attested by Peirce's summary of topics on the cover of the notebook R 465.[9] For one of those topics that he would address in the third lecture was: "Soundness of arguments lies in...".[10] The answer to what sound reasoning is, and which Peirce in his reply admits not to have actually presented in WMRS explicitly, was in that first lecture only informally expounded as "such reasoning that in every conceivable state of the universe in which the facts stated in the premises are true, the fact stated in the conclusion will thereby and therein be true" (EP 2, p. 250). Although WMRS superseded the earlier draft (R 454), it is the latter that is selected here as the opening chapter. This early draft focusses precisely on the theoretical and technical side of the question of the soundness of reasoning.

The notebook cover of that planned first lecture states "Early D. Lowell Lecture I (used for II)". The lecture begins at once with the basic principles and transformation rules for the Alpha and Beta parts of EGs. One finds a technical exposition of properties of EGs, which Peirce wisely avoided in his opening lecture. Yet R 454 is striking precisely because it provides an answer to the initial question: what makes a reasoning sound is the proof of the soundness of the system of EGs and its transformation rules. In R 454 Peirce indeed begins proving the soundness of his four "basic rights". It is this proof that came to be replaced by an informal and what he believed a more listener-friendly exposition. In the delivered lecture Peirce was hoping to reach a point at which the audience could come to realise how the previous accounts of reasoning given in the literature actually compromise the soundness of it. He would nevertheless not proceed to progress beyond the informal exposition of the negative version of the question—namely that concerning what *does not* make a reasoning sound—with a positive answer, as he disliked to "put forth opinions before I am ready to prove them" (EP 2, p. 534). It is only in the planned first lecture, which assumes the addressee to possess some familiarity of Peirce's own system of logic, in which he presents the positive answer, namely by a proof of the soundness of the system of the basic rules of that graphical method.

Lecture II, held on Friday, November 27, was announced with the title "A System of Diagrams for Studying Logical Relations. Exposition of it begun". Relevant drafts of the initial version of second lecture include at least R 450 and the sup-

---

9 R 465 lecture draft is among those that Peirce wanted to have typeset, and probably also published among those in his post-lecture publication plans, as it is both a fairly polished, fair copy of the text ("To be used", Peirce writes on the cover), containing instructions to the typesetter.

10 The other items on the cover of the notebook's table of contents are: "Seven characteristics of great philosophers", "Categories—Hegel 124", "Future not factual 88", "Kinds of laws", "Thirdness—Signs". These are added before the item "Soundness of arguments lies in...". None of these items are visible in the microfilmed copy of R 465.

plementary manuscripts R S-27 ("Graphs, Little Account") and R S-28 ("The Conventions"). The first page of the notebook catalogued R 470, a draft of the fifth lecture, provides an updated list of titles for the all the eight lectures. According to these revised titles, the second lecture was on "Existential Graphs—Alpha & Beta". Clearly Peirce would not manage to lecture on the Beta part during the second lecture. When drafting the several versions of his second lectures, it is also clear that Peirce kept *The Logical Tracts* at his disposal, ready to be used as a comprehensive source-book from which to draw material for the first couple of lectures. "The Conventions" notebook was written on September 15, 1903. Peirce remarks there that "the ten conventions were drawn up about Sep. 1, 1903". *Logical Tracts No. 2* (R 492) presents altogether fourteen elaborate conventions, and was most likely completed after R S-28 and thus sometime between early September and before the beginning of the drafting of the initial versions of the second lecture (R 450). The topic of the second lecture, as the announced subtitle "Exposition of it begun" suggests, was planned to concern the fundamental conventions of setting up the systems of logical diagrams.

The second set of drafts, here denoted by Lowell Lecture II(b), comprises texts from R 455, R 455(s) and R 456, plus the material from the supplements R S-29, R S-32, R S-33 and R S-34. These represent a slightly later and apparently the final plan for the lecture that Peirce actually delivered. Although the updated title announces it as "Existential Graphs—Alpha & Beta", it is evident that during that second lecture Peirce would manage to cover only the rudiments of the Alpha part.

When delivering these lectures, Peirce had at his disposal a device, called stereopticon, to project the diagrams on the stage wall of the large amphitheatre. Lowell Institute had a long tradition of using the stereopticon, and according to the Institute's bylaws the lecturers "were required to furnish the requisite slides". Diagrams for the second lecture were certainly projected by using the device (Peirce notes include instructions and marginal notes on what to project where), and maybe many others from subsequent lectures were projected in this fashion, too. In a draft letter intended for Sedgwick, the curator of the Lowell Institute, Peirce writes in an unsent draft that he had promised to "pay the young gentleman who made my diagrams last night [November 27]" (CSP to WTS, November 28, R L 257). Sedgwick identifies him as Mr. W. C. Lounsbury, working in Sedgwick's Lowell Institute office (WTS to CSP, December 1, 1903). Lounsbury seems to have successfully operated both the blackboard and the stereopticon to help illustrating and projecting Peirce's many diagrams to the audience. This obviously saved some precious time for the speaker to press ahead without many interruptions.

Yet the amount of material that Peirce wanted to communicate especially in the early part of the course was overwhelming, and the incessant lack of time made it necessary, in order to deliver the third lecture on the following Monday, to revisit material from the previous lecture (Lecture II(b)). The third lecture was announced as "The Three Universal Categories and their Utility", with a revised title "General Explanations. Phenomenology & Speculative Grammar" (R 470). Yet the treatment of categories is altogether postponed, as indeed is the important "third chapter" to his theory, namely the Gamma part of EGs. The second lecture ends with a remark ("To fill my hour tonight...", R S-32) on logical properties of possibility, impossibility, necessity and contingency of Alpha and Beta graphs. Peirce then proceeds to present the rule for Beta-possibility, which in modern terms would translate to showing the existence of a model by an application of the construction rules of the semantic tree method, first by reducing the question of the Beta-possibility to that of the question concerning Alpha-possibility, through a procedure somewhat like quantifier elimination (rewriting certain Beta graphs "without junctures"). The five operations that followed these remarks then demonstrate the satisfiability of the problem thus reduced in the "universe of alpha possibility".

From these prescient observations, on which we have every reason to believe that they were actually communicated to what must have been a fairly baffled group of listeners—remembering that the Lowell Lectures were meant to target a popular audience—Peirce's notes move on the composition of the third lecture, the version of which he began drafting on October 5 in R 462 and R S-31. The plan opens with an investigation of Beta-impossible statements. Peirce invents a couple of examples that involve modalities, and concludes that such an impossibility consists of an impossibility of whatever it is that *exists*, that is, whatever it is that is supposed to partake of an individual existence. But there are, Peirce notes, relations between things and their qualities, and between things and laws, and it is those new kinds of relations, which he terms "references" (see also R 490), that do not possess individuality in anything like the sense in which relations in the Beta graphs are expected to possess. This perspective opens up a new, third chapter to the logic of graphs, namely the investigation of those assertions that "deal with what can logically be asserted of *meanings*". Although the doctrine of categories is now mentioned in this third lecture, and although its presence is already much assumed, in this third lecture Peirce seems to have failed to devote any time to the promised exposition of the three universal categories.

The delivered part of the third lecture appears to begin in the middle of Lecture III ("I was advertized to speak tonight [November 30]...", R 464). At this point, it becomes clear that Peirce has not said much about the Beta system at all, at least "nothing more than a few scraps" (R 460), yet he is now compelled to utter things of importance even on the Gamma part. During this fever-pitch evening, categories were skipped altogether, as Peirce fights his way to reach to the Gamma compartment. (Categories are only rampaged in the written notes, though not without some philosophical and phenomenological insight, with a keen eye on their relevance and connection to the ongoing development of the logical method.) The prospected third chapter of the method opens up with a segment on the Gamma possibility, named "substantive possibility", and is represented in the outfit of his newly-developed logic of potentials. In reality, however, the topic of Gamma graphs seems to have been communicated to the audience only during Lecture V (R 469–R 471), and even there in a quite different and condensed form.

Thursday's lecture, held on December 3, was announced to be "Exposition of the System of Diagrams Completed", the revised post-lecture title of it having been "Existential Graphs. Gamma Part" (R 470). It is easy to determine that the exposition was certainly not completed, and although the drafts in notebooks suggest that the Gamma part was to be explained here in the first instance, and by taking into account its multiple compartments, during this fourth lecture Peirce was still desperately behind the schedule. Probably he never said anything about those parts of Gamma graphs that we find him exploring in depth in R 467 that concern graphical modal logic with the broken-cut notation. The logic of potentials that he needed to present the much-needed second-order graphical approach and to argue for the logical character of what otherwise would be a vaguely metaphysical notion of substantive possibility, ties the lecture in with one more of those questions "now vexed". However, also that topic was likewise largely if not entirely suppressed from the actual communication.

To compensate for the loss, the printed part of *A Syllabus of Certain Topics of Logic* (hereafter, the *Syllabus*), first handed out in the beginning of the fourth lecture, contained a few remarks on the system of potentials. That second-order graphical system, indispensable for the understanding of the upcoming fifth lecture to be held on next Monday, "The Doctrine of Multitude, Infinity and Continuity" (in R 470 simply and rightly "Multitude"), would at least be available in a printed form. Peirce might now have attempted to present that part of the Gamma that concerns another remarkable idea of the "graphs of graphs" and which we find scattered over his notes (Lecture IV, R S-31; R 468, "Introduction to Lecture 5, December 4"), likewise indispensable in appreciating the originality of the method by which Peirce is determined to address the upcoming topics in philosophy of mathematics, especially that of the concept of multitude. However, the presentation of even such central topics of the fifth lecture was seriously jeopardised by the lack of time, and eventually Peirce ends up in a predicament in which he is not able to lecture on continuity beyond "the few minutes that remain". He had enlisted continuity among those vexed questions upon which his logic of graphs was calculated to throw much new light.

The delivered lectures were only a pale reflection of masses of topics of logic that Peirce marshalled to bear on "questions now vexed". What is also clear is that the remaining lectures no longer make references to the method of EGs. His lecture plan follows the trajectory of the logic of science, conceived as a three-stage process, and Lecture VI, "What is Chance?" (R 470: "Chance"), delivered on December 10, moves on to discuss the nature of probability and chance, another side of what Peirce argued to belong to the field of deductive logic, in this case statistical rather than non-probabilistic, necessary deduction.[11] The last two Lowell Lectures were on non-deductive and ampliative forms of logic, Lecture VII on the following Monday on "Induction as Doing, not mere Cogitation", retitled simply as "Induction" (R 470), while Lecture VIII, "How to Theorize" ("Abduction", R 470), completed the series on December 17. These last lectures may have somewhat trailed off as Peirce was quite dismayed having only two hours left to spend on what he considered to be the two most important forms of reasoning in science, more important than deduction. Indeed his last appearance on stage seems to have run badly overtime: "Here let those go who had to go", he writes in a margin when the full 50 notebook pages had readily been consumed during this final evening (R 476)—and 36 more pages were still to be read. At any event, the Lowell Lectures deviated from the original plan so much so as to became largely a sustained study of deductive reasoning focussed on its performance as an instrument of logical analysis, implemented with a plurality of new kinds of graphical logics injected into that analysis.

---

11 Since 1907, Peirce appears to have discontinued subsuming deduction under necessary reasoning altogether: in the last lecture of his life—the little that is known of it—which he gave at Harvard University's Emerson Hall B on *Logical Methodeutic* in April 1907 (R 754) Peirce had adopted a surprisingly different view on deduction. In contradistinction to its earlier characterisations as necessary reasoning, deduction is now considered to be "compulsive reasoning":

> I have hitherto defined [deduction] as necessary reasoning; and no doubt much, perhaps most, possibly all deduction is necessary. But on reviewing the subject for this talk, it seems to me more correct to define Deduction as compulsive reasoning. Retroduction seduces you. Induction appeals to you as a reasonable being. But Deduction first points to the premises and their relation, and then shakes its fist in your face and tells you "Now by God, you've got to admit the conclusion". I beg your pardon, with all my heart, I meant to say, "Now by the eternal world forces spiritual and personal [*illeg.*]". Necessary reasoning is reasoning from the truth of whose premises it not only follows that the conclusion is true, but that it would be so under all circumstances.

One could question whether Peirce is making a hasty and unwarranted appeal to the kinds of psychologistic notions of reasoning that he earlier would have denounced. To Peirce's defence, these 1907 remarks are very rambling, exploratory and not written in full mental and physical capacity; it would be worthwhile to attempt giving them a non-psychologistic gloss.

Although not included in the present edition, a few words on the last three lectures are in order. They concern probabilities, induction and abductive reasoning. Lecture VI on chance emphasises the difference between risk-based analyses on the one hand and ignorance and uncertainty on the other. Only the latter, ignorance and uncertainty, and not the probabilistic doctrine of chances, characterise scientific discoveries; any comprehensive logic of science has to be prepared to encompass modes of reasoning that can handle uncertainty, cultivate doubt, and raise new questions to be asked.[12] Peirce then makes pertinent remarks in Lecture VII on the importance of scientists getting the details of statistical reasoning right, and criticises earlier, fallacious proposals that had appealed to regularities or uniformities of nature in order to justify inductive inferences. Finally, Peirce's remarks in Lecture VIII on abduction, economy of research, and the power of reason to guess at scientific hypotheses have stood the test of time well (R 475–R 476), and there is now an abundant contemporary literature of these topics.[13] His last lecture is largely occupied with the logic of the history of science, and one witnesses Peirce describing a prolonged case of appealing to his own abductive powers to guess right at a surprising phenomena. He then offers his experiences as an illustration of abduction not only as a viable method of historical research but a necessary one to be performed in order to explain well whether testimonies are true or false. As the lectures neared their end, one gets the feeling that Peirce had lost some sight of James's advice six months earlier to "avoid collateral matter".

Based on the surviving notes, Peirce did not quite close the circle and revisit these issues from the point of view of the *logic* of the science of abduction. Nor did he attempt anything like a summary or recapitulation of the central points of the entire course. Instead, the last lecture ends with a personal attempt to test the validity of his account of abduction about historical facts and figures, and is largely occupied with the question of making guesses on the life and origins of thought of ancient authors, and Pythagoras in particular, of which "the evidence is extremely slight and where the testimonies are open to grave suspicion" (R 476, p. 96). The course of lectures ends with a specimen of how the suspected procedure of abduction goes about in the author's own mind when applied to some questions concerning the history of intellectual thought: Peirce claims that a certain passage of Boethius (namely the assertion that the Pythagoreans' use of Arabic fig-

---

[12] This approach to the logic and theory of science inspires the work on the logic and epistemology of uncertainty in Chiffi, Carrara, De Florio & Pietarinen (2019); Chiffi & Pietarinen (2017, 2019), and the sub-belief level theory of the logic of abduction and its justification (Chiffi & Pietarinen 2018a; Ma & Pietarinen 2018d; Bellucci & Pietarinen 2020).

[13] See e.g. Chiffi, Pietarinen & Proover (2020), with pointers to the pertinent literature.

ures for numbers is authentic) is indeed authentic, and states that this contrasts with claims by many other authors that the passage is spurious.

Compared to the first five lectures and their drafts, the last three were less systematic and less theoretical. Probably Peirce had much less time to be spent on their preparation. Yet Peirce puts much weight on non-deductive forms of reasoning, which as far as science is concerned were for him the two stages of reasoning that are much more important than deduction; deductive reasoning rather serves as the relay between abduction and induction: it is the brainstem that communicates hypotheses suggested by abduction through such transformations that induction could be applied to them (R 473, pp. 14–15). Yet one must admit that the lecture notes do not reflect his preference: about 90% of the total corpus has deductive reasoning as the focus.

Some Topics of Logic...

What were the Lowell Lectures at bottom about? One should keep in mind that as important as the development of logic was to Peirce, he did not develop EGs merely for the sake of formal interest in them or in order to provide new and useful calculi. Formalism was neither his goal nor his forte. The nature of mathematical reasoning is not revealed in formal expressions and axioms. It ought to be, as he writes in a letter to his friend and Open Court confidant Judge Francis C. Russell in 1910, "obvious to anybody of sufficient grasp of logical analysis to see that logic reposes upon certain positive facts and is not mere formalism" (R 1573; typescript fragment of a letter to FCR quoted by Paul Carus, *The Monist*, 1910). Logic defines what the reality of things could consist of. Talking logic is to tackle questions that would otherwise remain metaphysics unsusceptible of criticism. Logical graphs arise as the method for the analysis of intellectual concepts, thoughts and generalities. The theory of signs co-evolves with the theory of logic.

Equally important in addressing the interpretational questions of Peirce's lectures is the successful identification of the relevant textual corpus and the circumstances that affected its creation, in order to cater for the wider interpretational context to what after all was a very abrupt public appearance. We must keep in mind that the sum total of his lecture plans and drafts, their supplementary material, the reference literature, the companion works of *The Logical Tracts* and the *Syllabus*, together with the communications that took place before, after and during the lectures, vastly outnumber anything one could possibly succeed to communicate, learn or infer from any actual deliveries. The present selections would need to be continued with the reading of the last three lectures, the complete version of the *Syllabus*, and much else besides.[14] Lectures VI–VIII, for example, are nearly without variants and much more straightforward in prose than the first five that made it into the present edition. A separate publication of the *Syllabus* corpus, with its related and expansive documents, is certainly much to be desired just as well.

When assessing, over a century later, the main points of these lectures in that wider context, the question of what was actually delivered, printed or handed out loses some of its importance. James wished Peirce to "gain a bigger audience when living" (WJ to CSP, June 5, 1903, R L 224), but Peirce is after an audience that persists long after he is gone. He converses with an audience that he finds inside his own mind, caring less what any actual ones may happen to be. This attitude is attested in the very design of these lectures. The delivered lectures are only a glimpse, highly uneven and unfocussed, at how logical theories have co-evolved with the development of scientific mind, first throughout the history of civilisation, then throughout his own life, then during the year of 1903, and finally, during the very lectures themselves.

Inspection of the first five lectures reveals three general issues that stand out as those Peirce wished to accentuate.

First, Peirce is struggling to articulate a semantic and model-theoretic treatment of logic and reasoning. This includes what we recognise as a definition of the semantic consequence relation, the method of game-theoretic semantics, a theory of quantification, the notion of truth-in-a-model, the semantic tree method, the properties of soundness and completeness, the idea of various systems of modal logic, and many others. The year 1903 is not the first time he is presenting such ideas, but it is here when preparing for the lectures that the theory of EGs, in the sense of its division into the Alpha, Beta and Gamma parts, and the presentation of the theory in the manner that begins with the now matured system of conventions upon which the whole of that logic is to be erected, reaches its adulthood. Of note is that the conventions are presented first, followed by the systems of permissive rules and rights. It is these conventions that we nowadays recognise as

---

[14] Especially important would be a comprehensive access to those texts that constitute, among others, the third section of the *Syllabus*, "Sundry Logical Conceptions", and whose main segment is 81 manuscript pages in length, with important variants and rejects of at least another 46 sheets. Also, in the privately printed booklet from R 539 ("The Nomenclature and Division of Dyadic Relations", hereon NDDR, deposited in Boxes 4 and 13 of R 1600, Peirce 1903), much of what constitutes the overhaul of Peirce's doctrine of the speculative grammar is seen to be taking place. See Bellucci 2017 on a detailed account of those revisions. To date, the most comprehensive publication of the *Syllabus* and the related documents is available only in German translation, *Phänomen und Logik der Zeichen* (PLZ), edited, introduced and translated by Helmut Pape (1983).

the seeds of the real semantic and model-theoretic approach. Peirce sees the conventions as the most fertile theoretical flora in which his graphical method can blossom. Moreover, most of what he had to say on such semantic conceptions that underlie the development of modern logic was never said or published before, and so the Lowell series and its accompanying material were the first and nearly the only attempt to communicate these pioneering ideas in public.

Second, there is a recurrent theme in the first five lectures that accentuates the service the theory of graphs has to questions that are philosophical in nature. In contrast to the pasigraphies proposed by Peirce's contemporaries, EGs were not developed for the purposes of speedy, efficient or mechanical procedures to calculate logical conclusions. Questions of decidability and algorithmic proof were of secondary concern—such considerations may arise when graphs are subjected to a purely mathematical treatment—the really important qualitative leap happens on (i) the nature of graphs considered as representations, (ii) the significations of logical constants that constitute the graphs and the permissible operations on them, and (iii) the use of those representations and the ensuing sound and complete systems for the purposes of logical analysis, especially for the question of what can be logically said of meanings.

Third, the development of various systems of graphs invariably oriented Peirce's investigations towards the "third chapter", namely how the diagrammatic syntax can elucidate that last question and how, in particular, logical diagrams put before us the true nature of mathematical and scientific reasoning. Peirce's focus in the planned lectures—not in what he struggled and managed to finally deliver but in his draft notes—was on understanding the nature of reasoning that is bound to involve intensional notions. To tackle those questions he develops the Gamma part to deal, among others, with what he in 1906 would call "references", namely the question of identification in modal contexts, and the question of how logical representations can be linked with qualities and laws. Peirce clarifies the importance of references in his 1906 National Academy of Sciences presentation (R 490, LoF 3), a notion that he had carried along for a long time. It is the nature of important mathematical concepts, such as multitudes, as well as the nature of mathematical reasoning in general, that Peirce is largely occupied with when planning his fourth and fifth lectures. The analysis of these mathematical notions was, according to what we find in his many plans, best performed when guided by new logics in the Gamma compartment, which unlike Beta can represent higher-order logical notions (in terms of the logic of potentials), and meta-logical notions (the theory of graphs of graphs), which can self-apply the graphical method to talk about graphs, their notation, properties and proofs.

...bearing on Questions now Vexed

In brief, what were the "vexed questions" that the new logics of graphs were calculated to throw light upon and what Peirce wanted his lectures to resolve? In the *Syllabus*, he would explain that *the* "most vexed question of logic" is to understand the essential nature of propositions:

> Another trichotomy of representamens is into ~~primi~~ single signs, substitutes, or *sumisigns*; double signs, ~~or quasi propositions~~ informational signs, or *dicisigns*, and triple signs, ~~monstrasigns~~ *suadisigns*, or *arguments*. Of these three classes the one whose nature is most easily understood is, by all odds, the second, that is, the quasi-proposition, notwithstanding the fact that the essential nature of propositions is today the most vexed question of logic. (R 478, p. 43, October 1903)

From the context set up by the 1903 Lowell Lectures, the kinds of questions of logic that he at that time regarded as the most vexed ones, the following three can be identified:
(1) What makes a reasoning sound?
(2) What is the best method for logical analysis and what is it an analysis for?
(3) Under what forms of thought should we regard qualities and laws? How can we discover regulative truths in logical theorising about those modes of being that concern qualities and laws?

All these are parts of the principal question concerning the essential nature of propositions. The texts in the present selection are sufficient in finding out what constitutes that essence by identifying some altogether satisfactory answers to the first and the second question. Towards the end, the lectures begin proposing possible answers to the third question, too. Indeed these lectures do have a bearing on metaphysical questions. But the question of finding out the theories that Peirce undertakes to develop, for any future investigation of such questions that are to be of a metaphysical nature, is a strictly logical one. For instance, the question of the relation of representations to laws, where laws are generals, involves solving the issue of how such generalities could become subjects of propositions. And in order to tackle that question Peirce is led to erect a new doctrine of propositions, the theory of dicisigns, which at the same time will be an extension of his older one. The most elaborate accounts of the new doctrine of propositions are found only in the unpublished parts of the *Syllabus* text. In sum, however, it is clear that the lectures, as a textual whole, did succeed in staying on the course Peirce had set in the very first lecture draft (R 454): to exhibit to the public audience the process of modern scientific reasoning.

Common to all eight lectures was the question of the nature of reasoning, in any of its three appearances. The series opened with the question of how to differentiate good reasoning from what is bad, and it ends with the question of the nature of creative scientific reasoning and its history. The topic of reasoning is addressed in the lectures in the customary order: deductive and mathematical reasoning is to be introduced first, as the other two draw their justification from deduction, followed by inductive and abductive kinds as soon as the nature of deductive and mathematical reasoning has become absolutely free from mist. But the introduction and clarification of the first kind consumed the better part of the lectures, and what was left for Peirce to say about the other two modes, especially that of abduction and the logic of discovery of scientific laws, remained sketchy.

Reception and Impact

What was the educational value of these lectures? How were they received? What can we say about Peirce's pedagogical and didactic approach? Did he manage to make the lectures, as he had promised to James, to be as "close to *lessons* as lectures can be"?

On the face of it, events that unfolded surely suggest Peirce was facing an outright didactic disaster. Imagine, for example, getting the printed leaflet of the *Syllabus* at hand right at the beginning of the demanding fourth lecture, while having no time to familiarise with it prior to the deluge on logical analysis of mathematical reasoning. Second, in order to have made the fifth lecture comprehensible, the printed material should have contained an explanation of the notation for metagraphs. Beyond the fifth lecture, the printed syllabus contained nothing on the last three lectures, chance, induction and abduction. The matters of induction and abduction are treated in the third section of the surviving draft of the *Syllabus*, on "Sundry Logical Conceptions", completed after R 462 and thus between October 5 and October 30. That Peirce did plan to write separate sections on these issues is attested in the early table of contents draft, that contained "VI. Principles of Probability. VII. The Two Rules of Induction. VIII. The Principle [of] Abduction" (R 478), but he never really got to writing these planned last chapters of the *Syllabus* to synchronise with the lectures.[15] Possibly Peirce rested content with having man-

---

[15] The draft table of contents also contains a plan for a fifth section, "Sketch of Geometry", of which no draft exists and which at first sight may represent a relative anomaly given the themes of the actual syllabus and the lectures, as none of the material directly appears to have addresses the topic of geometry. However, in a draft of Lecture III (R 464) from October 8 Peirce mentions his "reduction thesis", which would be an appropriate place to have some further accompanying material at hand which he would be unable to cover in that lecture, such as an explanation of the

aged to integrate at least the last two topics into the third section of the syllabus, although none of that made its way to the printed version. Very little was included in the syllabus manuscript on probabilities. The upshot nevertheless was that as soon as the printed booklet was available, it was no longer of much help for the audience members to be able to follow whatever flashes of insights they may have heard emanating in the auditorium. Events like these certainly do not seem to be conducive to good pedagogy.

Some other events and pieces of information that can be garnered from collateral sources suggest that the lectures were in fact a sort of a success, even enjoyable and entertaining to follow. First of all, in defence of the lecturer, we need to appreciate that the request to delay the distribution of the printed syllabus to the audience came from Sedgwick and not from Peirce: "Since you agree with me that it will be unwise to cast your pearls before swine and to waste syllabi upon mere curiosity seekers who may attend the first few lectures there will be time enough to print after you arrive in Boston" (WTS to CSP, November 17, R L 257). A few weeks earlier, Sedgwick also had requested Peirce to prepare an extensive bibliography to accompany the lectures and to arrive his office by November 14: "By an arrangement with the Public Library authorities we are in the habit of printing lists of books of reference for students who desire to read in connection with the lectures. About twenty titles are usually given in by our lecturers ... for your own sake and the sake of any students who might wish to follow your lectures closely, I think you might find it worth while to prepare a list of this kind (WTS to CSP, October 23, 1903, R L 257). Peirce prepares the reading list which Sedgwick acknowledges to have been forwarded to the printer on November 17. The list was printed in *Monthly Bulletin of Books Added to the Public Library of the City of Boston*,[16] and it was promised to be ready from the printer on December 1 and to be available at once for Peirce's lectures, probably since his third lecture. (Only the printed list in the *Monthly Bulletin* has been preserved; there is no surviving letter or manuscript that would evidence what Peirce's autographed list looked like.) The list, for which Peirce included 38 titles, among them Russell's *Principles*

---

basics of topical geometry. Then he could better back up the claim in R 464 that teridentity is a primitive relation: it represents how three representations of facts are united in one representation, the teridentity, which cannot be composed from one and two-place relations. The early plan of the contents of the syllabus could thus derive from the vicinity of his composing of those parts of R 464 that address the reduction thesis. Also, the earlier version of what became the third and long section of "Sundry Logical Conceptions" was planned to be on "Some ~~Logical~~ Definitions and Explanations", replacing here the cancelled and originally the second section heading "Phenomenology. The Three Categories".

16 Vol. VIII, No. 1, January–December 1903, pp. 448–449.

of Mathematics which he had just dismissively reviewed for the October issue of *The Nation*, testifies Peirce's genuine attempt to make the lectures lesson-like, as he had promised James to do in the previous summer.

After the second lecture, Sedgwick wrote Peirce to congratulate him on the "marked success" of the lectures. Sedgwick's account of the early lectures (he attended at most the first two of them) reveals that Peirce had a "very pleasant style and a good voice". Sedgwick compliments his former teacher on "knowing, as you do, how to express your ideas", and that "your lectures are naturally clear and acceptable". "Considering the nature of the subject", he added, "I think this has been quite remarkable and that you have every reason to feel satisfied with the size and quality of the audience" (WTS to CSP, December 1, 1903, R L 257).

William James, who apparently sat through several of the lectures was perhaps the only other person (one member of the audience submitted a question, in writing, concerning the first lecture, which Peirce responds on November 30, see the account of this in EP 2 and R 465, A1–A8) to actually raise some points or questions. James famously epitomised the character of these lectures in his 1907 book *Pragmatism: A New Name for Some Old Ways of Thinking* while he, exactly three years after Peirce, was himself addressing the Bostonite audience on that same platform:

> Whatever universe a professor believes in must at any rate be a universe that lends itself to lengthy discourse. A universe definable in two sentences is something for which the professorial intellect has no use. No faith in anything of that cheap kind! I have heard friends and colleagues try to popularize philosophy in this very hall, but they soon grew technical, and then dry, and the results were only partially encouraging. So my enterprise is a bold one. The founder of pragmatism himself recently gave a course of lectures at the Lowell Institute with that very word in its title—flashes of brilliant light relieved against Cimmerian darkness! None of us, I fancy, understand *all* that he said—yet here I stand, making a very similar venture.[17]

---

[17] Coincidentally, Peirce was in Cambridge on November 23, 1906, attending the meeting of the National Academy of Sciences. He rants James about his experiences of that day:

> The unspeakable 'scientists' kept on reading papers yesterday afternoon until 5:30 and I was forced to sit with strained attention all that time. Meantime Crafts came in and handed me a card asking me, to meet a few 'academicians' at his house in the evening. I nodded assent, not noticing that it was an invitation to dinner. Mrs. Peirce naturally had to receive some attention, however slight she tried to make it; and the result was I got there fatigued, and it was an effort to keep up conversation until near eleven. Now I have got to write my reports, and I fear if I went out to your house in my present state of fatigue combined with a sense of an unfulfilled task, I should only fatigue you and very likely talk heavy things. (CSP to WJ, November 23, 1906).

It is frequently asserted in the secondary literature (including EP 2) that James's description is to be attributed to Peirce's spring Harvard lectures on pragmatism, "Pragmatism as a Principle and Method of Right Thinking" (PPM). But already Josiah Royce remarked that "It was these latter [the Lowell Lectures on Logic of 1903–4] which James described as 'flashes of brilliant light relieved against Cimmerian darkness'—'darkness' indeed to James as to many others must have seemed those portions on 'Existential Graphs' or 'Abduction'. Yet it seems strange that the very striking lectures on 'Induction', 'Probability', 'Chance', and 'Multitude' should have attracted nothing more than a passing notice" (Royce & Kernan 1916, p. 208). Only the Lowell Lectures supplied adequate portions of EGs and abduction and, of course, multitude was the topic of the fifth lecture, chance and probability of the sixth, and induction of the seventh lecture, abduction being the last.

Royce, who was likely to have attended many of Peirce's lectures, could in principle have been mistaken on James's attribution of "cimmerian darkness" to Peirce's second series of lectures. Privately to his wife Alice Howe Gibbens James, William had written, "To think of you with the whole Peirce problem on your back! Alas! alas!—You see that the trouble is that Charlie is impossible. His Lowell lectures were a pure caprice; and Universities wont appoint a man on grounds of pure charity. Nevertheless, when I go to Chicago I will try to talk him up" (WJ to AHGJ, April 14, 1905, in James 2003, p. 8). This might suggest that flashes of light may have been seen inside Sever Hall's room 11 and not at all in Huntington Hall, and that consequently, James did not think very highly of Peirce's performance in the latter.

Peirce would continue to lodge at Prescott Hall for several months more but there is no information of him attending any of the eight Lowell Lectures that now James, in turn, was delivering in November and December. Peirce, still in Cambridge, receives James's book on June 13, 1907:

> I have just this minute received your book *Pragmatism*. I just turned to the index and looked out Peirce, C. Santiago S.—I found a statement of my own thoughts which I can appreciate, having been laboring and crowding my way for months and months,—crowding through throngs of technicalities, objections, and stupidities to try to express. There you have put it on your page with the utmost lucidity and apparent facility. Nothing could be more satisfactory. (CSP to WJ, June 13, 1907)

There is some irony in the last two sentences, and in the last word, that emanated from Peirce's pen. Satisfactory *to what end*? James's book is frequently hailed as the most important book in the history of American philosophy. In Hilary Putnam's estimate, James's opening lecture "The Present Dilemma in Philosophy", in which the allusion to Peirce's 1903 lectures is made, is "one of the finest examples of philosophical prose written in this country" (Putnam 2011). Peirce's story of pragmaticism was, or course, to be told much differently (LoF 3).

Such, however, was unlikely to have been the case. Royce testified that James precisely meant the Lowell Lectures. While James might have missed out on, say, the details of the decision method for the Beta-reduct system of Alpha graphs that suddenly would burst from the podium, he surely would have recognised the intrinsic value of what human fancy and flight, sometimes dull but deep, often protracted and enlightening, is destined to bear when exploring the abysses of the unknown. Peirce's lectures may have been capricious in style,[18] but that would not mean that insights in their content, such as the defence of the new and emerging science of logic, would have gone unnoticed by James.

To conclude this assessment of pedagogical and educational values of his lectures, then, in the light of remarks such as these one might be led to view the intention of the lectures to have been to promote learning, despite whatever defects there may have been in actual performance. One could enlist as many as ten points that attest this. (i) Peirce's lectures were obviously curated with time and care. (ii) Plenty of supporting material was prepared and some printed and handed out. (iii) Extensive reading lists were provided. (iv) Multiple methods of delivery were availed of—including both modern technology and traditional blackboard. (v) Questions were carefully attended to and answered, either orally or in writing: for one, Peirce produced a long rejoinder to James's topics, and he would write down and answer at least another question from the audience member in length. (vi) Teaching was based on the author's original research, and (vii) new and recent findings and results made their appearance into the lectures. Moreover, (viii) the outline of the topics delivered beforehand did not prevent the lecturer from adding new and topical material (witness e.g. Peirce's breaking-news style Herbert Spencer obituary, read in the beginning of the sixth lecture on December 10).[19] (ix) Manners of delivery were testified as pleasant, clear and appropriate for the occasion. (x) Last, Peirce announced during the third lecture his office hours to be had on the next three Sundays, from 3 to 6pm in his dwelling at 6 Prescott Hall, 474 Broadway, Cambridge, Mass (R 464) (he would be back in Milford before the last of those Sundays, though). Maybe only the delay in getting the

---

18 The credence of James's colourful testimony of the lectures to have been "pure caprice" is somewhat doubtful, however, as James was indisposed from attending the last two or three of Peirce's lectures, and as he may have excused some others as well.
19 William James published Spencer's obituary on December 8, the day of Spencer's death, in *New York Evening Post*. Peirce takes his audience to be familiar with James's obituary, and refers to it in his opening remarks on December 10, the day when James would fall ill and may for that reason have been unable to attend this sixth or later terms of the course. Peirce's 10-page obituary, though never published, is more penetrating of the two and adds personal reminiscences of his encounters with Spencer.

Syllabus distributed to the audience in advance should subtract from the final assessment, but that was a decision from the curator's part to not let costly printed material go to the hands of those not seriously interested in studying it.

On the other hand, in another sense Peirce's lectures were likely to have been a failure, at least in the conventional sense of success. Whatever Peirce managed to deliver in one evening, he would also be unlikely to succeed in covering a follow-up material in another, and as a result, whatever attempts there may have been at disseminating the continuity of his original ideas were repeatedly frustrated, and not only by strict time constraints. His important novelties and results came to be buried under the avalanche of definitions, technical nomenclature, classifications and historical passages. Together with the audience's unfamiliarity with his architectonics, the inscrutability of Peirce's terminology made the learning of anything of essence from these lectures an excruciating, if not an impossible, effort, even for the most knowledgeable of the audience members. On the other hand, almost nothing was communicated on the Beta part, which after all is the most important vantage point to motivate EGs, and next to nothing was said on the Gamma graphs, which was the most important novelty of the lectures. Very little was said on non-deductive forms of reasoning, the most important as they were in terms of the overall goal of the lectures, namely to aid audience in understanding the processes of modern scientific reasoning. Peirce appears to be using audience as a vessel; the orator is reciting ideas for one's own avail, occasionally experimenting and improving upon them, untimately hoping that such gesturing will suffice to submit ideas for the perpetual maturation within the future communities of inquirers, but never really able to get in sync with the outside interpreters. Only the totality of the lecture notes, drafts and preparatory material would fulfil the announced goal of the lectures. Was this self-sabotage of an individual, as one is tempted to conclude, Peirce's acknowledged way for science to make progress: here to use the lecture format as an opportunity to immerse oneself ever-deeper into the world of discovery, when no actual constellation of an audience can serve as the real receptable for thoughts whose meaning would lie in the future?

As regards attendance, the little that is know of it one should not expect that Peirce's popular lectures had anything like the full house that James pulled three years later. Only the fact that 100 copies of the *Syllabus* were printed (the upper right corner of the cover of Peirce's copy-text of the syllabus, R 478, bears a lead pencil mark "100 copies" in Sedgwick's hand),[20] and that after Peirce having secured some dozen of them to himself after the fifth lecture—with some half a dozen

---

[20] Sedgwick's enquiry to Peirce on the amount of copies to be printed was sent on November 3, five days after Sedgwick's acknowledgment of Peirce's submission of the *Syllabus* copy-text.

copies left for Peirce to take home to Milford on December 18—stands as the evidence that a good number of people did turn up for the lectures. Sedgwick's estimate before the beginning of the course was that 50–75 people would really "need the syllabus" (R L 257), so it is also likely that this large lecture hall that seated nearly a thousand people was rather reverberant by the time the course was nearing its end. This, again, is an insignificant detail in the light of the meaning of 'real audience' being conceived, as under Peirce's conception it may rather have been the listener as a conceivable, real possibility, that counts.[21]

The *Syllabus*

Something more should be said on the aims and purposes of *A Syllabus of Certain Topics of Logic*, a long text which is preserved as some 250 manuscript leaves and which Peirce eagerly produced to accompany the lectures. Large portions of the preserved draft version are devoted to topics that lectures did not expose, such as the classification of the sciences (Chapter I), the ethics of terminology (Chapter II) and the speculative grammar (Chapter III).

Surely Peirce realised that his classificatory systems and the theory of signs cannot adequately be explained to the audience during these curtate evening hours. But the preserved draft was quickly growing into a full-blown volume—according to Sedgwick, it was a sizable "book" already by October 30—and it was equally clear to Peirce that any printed brochure that was to be offered could only materialise as a much-abridged extract of some of the first four sections that he had produced in the long copy-text. The circular of 23 printed pages that the printer produced included only the first few pages from Chapters I and II, nothing from Chapter III, and only a truncated selection of matters related to EGs, from its Chapter IV.

Peirce's preceding work on *The Logical Tracts*, which he was busy expanding during the fall, served him as something like a proto-syllabus. The *Tracts* is in fact a much more detailed exposition of the basic systems of graphs that what is presented in the *Syllabus*. The purpose of the draft syllabus has to be considered within this wider textual context. Peirce was compelled to change, on relatively

---

Peirce's letter to Simon Newcomb confirms that "[Though] I limited the copies to 100, the money gave out when the printer got so far" (CSP to SN, January 15, 1904, quoted in Eisele 1979, p. 84).
21 James Mills Peirce had written to his brother to be "looking forward to your lecture. The subject is a promising one, and I hope the lectures will not be too abstruse for your public, and at the same time not too trivial for them. The true line in such a field is hard to strike. I don't quite like the word 'vexed' in your title. Would not 'current questions' express your meaning? However, the matter is not very important" (JMP to CSP, October 25, 1903; R L 339).

short notice, those elaborate logical notes into much less technical and more accessible prose, with almost no option to include illustrations. The true *Syllabus* would have to fulfill quite a different role from what it was conceived to do earlier in the summer and autumn. Although adamant in his plans to demand of his audience "close attention and a certain effort of thought" (CSP to WJ), it later dawned on him that six popular lectures could not be the right occasion to marshal hundreds of terms, definitions and formulas.

Only 67 manuscript pages from the newly-written text of over 200 manuscript leaves[22] was selected by Peirce to be printed by Alfred Munge & Son. What the listeners had at their disposal thus does not fit well with the intended purposes of the full *Syllabus*. It is noticeable, however, that when in the beginning of the fourth lecture many copies of the printed pamphlet were finally distributed, this last-minute material bought Peirce extra time to explain something about the Gamma graphs. During the fourth lecture he regrets, however, that he "cannot go into the long explanations that would be needed to expand the theory of the gamma part". Printed in the *Syllabus* were Conventions VII, VIII and IX: namely a short passage on "spot-symbols", which are potentials with selectives rather than lines of identity; this was simply a typographical simplification due to the costs associated with printing tilted lines (Convention VII), an incomplete verbal explanation of the idea of the broken-cut in modal Gamma graphs (Convention VIII), and a likewise brief verbal explanation of the "rim", the "wavy-line", and the "rim shown as a saw line", which were Peirce's notations that he introduced in order to deal with the topic of collections in Lecture V (Convention IX).

Two and a half years later, in his National Academy of Sciences address "Recent Developments of Existential Graphs" (R 490, 1906), Peirce refers to "a certain partly printed but unpublished 'Syllabus of Logic', which contains the only formal or full description of Existential Graphs that I have ever undertaken to give". Then again a few years later, he refers to the printed extract as the other of the two accounts of EGs that he has ever succeeded to present in print, estimating it to be the better than the one that had appeared in *The Monist* after he had held his "Recent Developments" presentation:

> I will here mention that in my latest system of Symbolical Logic, Existential Graphs, of which I have given two independent accounts, first, in some printed pages entitled "A Syllabus of certain Topics of Logic", Boston, 1903, 8vo, where it occupies pp. 15–23 (of which there are probably not half a dozen copies in existence, although it is, in some respects, the better

---

[22] That is, from R 478 and R 508, the former reaching pagination up to 168, with the gap between pages 105 and 137 to be filled by R 539 and largely composed perhaps only over a fortnight or so in mid-October, R 508 being a slightly later undertaking.

exposition of the two); and secondly in *The Monist*, for October 1906, Vol. XVI, pp. 492–546, I regard "lover of ___ " or "lover ___ " (where the dashes represent blanks), as necessarily denoting a lover of some individual unspecified, this individual being whatever one the facts require. (R 646, January 13, 1910)

Peirce consistently takes logical graphs to be systems that pertain to "Symbolical Logic". For some reason he does not mention his "Symbolic Logic, or algebra of logic" article that was published in DPP although that entry also contained an exposition of EGs, and although it was included in his Lowell reading list. At any event, what we can learn from this passage is that by this late date, what Peirce took to be his only decent exposition of EGs, the one that made its way into the *Syllabus*, was quickly passing into oblivion.

The Lowell Lectures Reading List

By the custom and recommendation of the Lowell Institute, Peirce assigned a list of references to books and articles to accompany his lectures. This list has not been mentioned in the secondary literature before, but it was published in the *Monthly Bulletin* of the Boston City Library in early December 1903, pp. 448–449. Its December issue had also advertised rather belatedly the remaining five lectures: "Lectures in **the Third Course,** by Charles S. Peirce, Esq., Member of the National Academy of Sciences, on **Some Topics of Logic bearing on Questions now Vexed**, will be given on Mondays and Thursdays, Dec. 3, 7, 10, 14, and 17" (p. 455). Sedgwick had promised the printed list to be ready by December 1st, and it was made available to the audience for the first time perhaps during the third lecture on November 30, and certainly by the beginning of the fourth talk on December 3. The curator had asked Peirce to furnish the titles well in advance, and definitely to arrive by November 14, which Peirce seems to have adhered to:

> Your list of references is being got ready by the Public Library people and will be ready on December 1st. This costs you nothing and you can get a good number of copies for distribution to friends (and enemies, if as I find it hard to believe you have any). I imagine that not more than 50–75 people will *need* syllabi at the Hall, so you will have of these also a good number for future use. I am surprised to learn that the Carnegie would not help you act by a few hundred dollars for publication. I thought that "discovery and assistance of exceptional men" was their great ambition. (WTS to CSP, November 17, 1903, R L 257)

As can be observed from the list, Peirce's selection contains some of the most important items in the development of modern logic from the late 19th century. Some of the same copies of these items are still available at the City Library of Boston (Boston Public Library) collections, with the same call numbers as announced in the list.[23] The first part of the list contains four titles and they were not assigned to any particular lecture. Next are listed the titles that Peirce had suggested for Lectures I, II, III, V, VI and VIII. There were no readings proposed for Lectures IV and VII. The revised titles in parentheses are editorial additions; notes in brackets are as they appear in the original publication of the list.

The printed list is accompanied with the following note:

> A short list of references suggested in connection with the lectures by Charles S. Peirce, Esq., Member of the National Academy of Sciences, before the Lowell Institute.
>
> All titles in the lists illustrative of the Lowell Lectures are furnished in each case by the lecturer himself, who is responsible for their extent and character. (p. 448)

The boldfaced numbers are the Boston City Library call numbers added to the list by the Lowell Institute's assistant.

---

23 Boston Public Library's Special Collections preserve the books of Schröder (1890–1895, 3 vols.), Russell (1903) and Bertrand (1889) with the same call number, as well as some of the referenced journals. Sigwart (1895) is in the Central Delivery Desk.

Books on Logic, without reference to these lectures.

Arnauld, Antoine, and Pierre Nicole.
The Port Royal logic. Translated by T. S. Baynes. 5th edition. Edinburgh, 1861. **5609.18**

Tredelenburg, Friedrich Adolph.
Elementa logices Aristotelicae. Berolini, 1836. **2979.46**

Watts, Isaac
Logic. New edition. London, 1802. **3609.60**

Whately, Richard, Archbishop of Dublin.
Elements of logic. New York, 1875. **7605.73**

Lecture I.
What makes a reasoning sound?

Bosanquet, Bernard.
Knowledge and reality. A criticism of F. H. Bradley's "Principles of Logic". London, 1892. **3607.126**

Bradley, Francis Herbert.
The principles of logic. London, 1883. **3600.60**

Erdmann, Johann Eduard.
Outlines of logic and metaphysics. Translated by B. C. Burt.[24] London, 1896. [Introductory science text-books.] **3608.166**
The title given by Mr. Peirce is: Benno Erdmann's Logik.

Sigwart, Christoph von.
Logic. 2d edition, enlarged. Translated by Helen Dendy. London 1895. 2 v. **3604.119**

Trendelenburg, Friedrich Adolph.
Logische Untersuchungen. Berlin, 1840. **B.6085.2**

Ueberweg, Friedrich.
System of logic, and history of logical doctrine. Translated by T. M. Lindsay. London, 1871. **B.H.Ref.592.10. (3605.51)**

Wundt, Wilhelm Max.
Logik. 2. Auflage. Stuttgart, 1893–95. 2 v. in 3. **3603.148**

Lecture II.
A system of diagrams for studying logical relations. Exposition of it begun. (Existential graphs—Alpha & Beta)

Kempe, Alfred Bray.
A memoir on the theory of mathematical form. (In Philosophical transactions of the Royal Society. Vol. 177. pp. 1–70. London, 1887.) ***3210.1.177**

Schroeder, Ernst.
Vorlesungen über die Algebra der Logik (exakte Logik). Leipzig, 1890–95. 3 v. ****E.5113.9**

Studies in logic. By members of the Johns Hopkins University. Boston, 1883. **5600.58**

Symbolic logic, or algebra of logic (In Baldwin. Dictionary of philosophy and psychology. Vol. 2, pp. 640–651. New York, 1902.) **B.H.Ref.590.1.2. (*3601.132.2)**

Whitehead, A. N.
The logic of relations, logical substitution groups, and cardinal numbers. (In American Journal of Mathematics. Vol. 25, pp. 157–178. Baltimore, 1903.) ****E.5081.10.25**

Lecture III.
The three universal categories and their utility. (General explanations. Phenomenology and speculative grammar)

Hibben, John Grier.
Hegel's logic. An essay in interpretation. New York, 1902. **3607.196**

Peirce, Charles Sanders.
On a new list of categories. (In American Academy of Arts and Sciences. Proceed-

---

[24] [B. C. Burt was Peirce's student at Johns Hopkins, and a participant in the activities of its Metaphysical Club that Peirce chaired (Pietarinen & Chevalier 2015).]

[25] [This fourth lecture was not included in the original list of readings.]

ings. Vol. 7, pp. 287–298. Boston, 1868.)
*3370.6.7

Lecture IV.[25]
Exposition of the system of diagrams completed. (Existential graphs: Gamma part)

Lecture V.
The doctrine of multitude, infinity and continuity. (Multitude)

Cantor, Georg.
Beiträge zur Begründung der transfiniten Mengenlehre. 2. Artikel. (In Mathematische Annalen. Ban 49, pp. 207–246. Leipzig, 1897.) ****E.5145.1.49**
De la puissance des ensembles parfaits de points. (In Acta mathematica. [Vol.] 4, pp. 381–392. Stockholm, 1884.)
**E.5090.50.4

Dedekind, Richard.
Essays on the theory of numbers, 1. Continuity and irrational numbers. 2. The nature and meaning of numbers. Authorized translation by W. W. Beman. Chicago, 1901. ****E.5129.101**

Peirce, Charles Sanders.
The logic of relatives. (In The Monist. Vol. 7, pp. 161–217. Chicago, 1896–97.)
Per.Room *3604.100.7

Russell, Bertrand Arthur William.
The principles of mathematics. Vol. 1. London, 1903. ****E.5128.44**

Lecture VI.
What is chance? (Chance)

Bertrand, Joseph Louis François.
Calcul des probabilités. Paris, 1889.
**E.5112.41

Boole, George.
An investigation of the laws of thought, on which are founded the mathematical theories of logic and probabilities. London, 1854. ****E.5127.14**

Laurent, Hermann.
Traité du calcul des probabilités. Paris, 1873. **5924.51**

Mill, John Stuart.
A system of logic, ratiocinative and inductive. New York, 1846. **3607.20**

Pearson, Karl.
The grammar of science. 2d edition. London, 1900. **3918.118**

Peirce, Charles Sanders.
Pearson's Grammar of science. Annotations on the first three chapters. (In Popular Science Monthly. Vol. 58, pp. 296–306. New York, 1901.) **Per.Room *5916.50.58**
A theory of probable inference. (In Studies in logic. Boston, 1883.) **5600.58**

Venn, John, F.R.S.
The logic of chance. 3d edition. London, 1888. **3937.59**

Lecture VI.
Induction as doing, not mere cogitation. (Induction)

Lecture VIII.
How to theorize. (Abduction)

Jevons, William Stanley.
The principles of science; a treatise on logic and scientific method. 2d edition. London, 1877. **5607.75**

Mach, Ernst.
Popular scientific lectures. Translated by T. J. McCormack. 2d edition. Chicago, 1897. 2d edition. **3918.123**

Mill, John Stuart.
A system of logic, ratiocinative and inductive. New York, 1846. **3607.20**

Pearson, Karl.
The grammar of science. 2d edition. London, 1900. **3918.118**

Venn, John, F.R.S.
The principles of empirical or inductive logic. London, 1889. **3581.58**

Whewell, William.
History of scientific ideas. Being the first part of the Philosophy of the inductive sciences. London, 1858. 2 v. **5938.5**
Novum organon renovatum. Being the second part of the Philosophy of the inductive sciences. London, 1858. **5589.7**

Survey of Part V: Selections 32–42

This section surveys the eleven items included in the present volume.

Selection 32: What Makes a Reasoning Sound? Lowell Lecture I [Early draft]

R 454. Lectures on Logic, to be delivered at the Lowell Institute, Winter of 1903–1904, Lecture I. Notebook cover states: "Early D. Lowell Lecture I (used for II)". Not delivered.[26]

Composed in late spring–early summer before *Logical Tracts No. 2* (R 492), this lecture represents the earliest draft of the course that came to be superseded by "What Makes a Reasoning Sound?" (WMRS). Terminological inspection suggests its composition to have been underway in early June, soon after the Harvard Lectures were over and around the time Peirce corresponded with James on the upshot of the spring course and on what the next winter's lecture series was going to be like. For example, Peirce uses the term 'sep' for the ovals that are termed 'enclosures' first time in June 27 (*Logic Notebook*, LN) and then in *The Logical Tracts*, the writing of which coincides with his article manuscript on telepathy that reached James in early July. As his terms change in this way, the first lecture was likely to have been completed before June 27.

Indeed the second intensive period in LN out of three that is filled with remarks on EGs falls between Peirce's Harvard and Lowell Lectures. Peirce's preliminary studies in LN helped him compose a detailed account of his logical architectonic in the style that is seen to emerge in *The Logical Tracts* and in his Lowell Lecture drafts. The surprising but very incomplete "Studies of the eight systems of existential graphs", which comes from a separate note (R 1483), indeed derives from the time of the initial planning of his 1903 Lowell Lectures (LoF 1).

Mulling over his upcoming Lowell Lectures promised to him some months earlier, in this early summer Peirce was determined that when writing on logic, one need not make the reading of what one writes "agreeable" to the addressees. The maxims of the ethics of terminology and the ethics of notation present themselves with irresistible force, and technical expressions and precise definitions must therefore be labouriously sought for at every occasion (R 516, R 530; LoF 1). Peirce's unforgiving attitude is attested well in *The Logical Tracts*, the tone of which was premised on the view that logical writings need not "be easily understood by those who are addressed" (R 492).

---

[26] Peirce's own vague dating of this to 1903–1904 evidences that the notebook originates from early plans and thoughts for the course, perhaps first conceived sometime in late spring–early summer when the exact timing of the lectures had not yet been confirmed.

In the present notebook (R 454) one finds an alternative beginning in which Peirce tells having received several letters from his very best friends who tell him how agreeably he could lecture if he chose to do so. They tell that it would be in Peirce's interest to decide to do so. Peirce had James, and perhaps also Royce and Cattell in mind; in early June James patronises Peirce to recycle rather than innovate:

> What I wish myself is that you might *revise these lectures* [the Harvard lectures on pragmatism] for your Lowell course, possibly confining yourself to fewer points (such as the uses of the first, second and thirdness distinction, the generality involved in perception, the nature of abduction—this last to me tremendously important) make each of them tremendously emphatic, avoid collateral matter, except what is illustrative and comparative, avoid polemic as such (you have very successfully done so), keep the ignoramus in view as you auditor, and I have no doubt you'll be a great success. As things stand, it is only highly skilled technicians and professionals who will sniff the rare perfume of your thought, and *after you are dead*, trace things back to your genius. You ought to gain a bigger audience *when living*; and if next year you can only score a popular success, it will do much to help your later prospects. I fear that if you make a new course of lectures altogether, they will prove too technical and wonder arousing and not flagrantly illuminating enough. Whereas, by revising these, you will not only give yourself less trouble, but also do the best possible thing for your audience.
>
> You cannot start with too low an idea of their intelligence.
>
> Look at me, as one! (WJ to CSP, June 5, 1903; James 2002, p. 258)

Peirce's quasi-sarcastic reply on June 8 might lead us to believe that he is meeting James's wishes when he promised "to have just as little pure theory in them as possible" and "to have my Lowell Lectures as near to practical lessons in reasoning as *lectures* can" (June 8, CSP to WJ). The concluding paragraph confirms that he would go over deductive, inductive and abductive reasoning "as fully as" he can "in so very short a course, paying the smallest possible attention to pure theory, but dwelling on the precautions necessary to be observed in practice" (R 454). Yet he ends this first lecture draft by erupting not to give in to those recommendations, professing to be one of those who are "incapable of consulting their interests" (R 454). Defiantly, he decided to set the bar for the upcoming lectures high and demand from the audience "close attention and a certain effort of thought" (R 454).

Some weeks later, when in a more merciful mood, Peirce is planning to replace his first, technical plan with the thoroughly informal prose we find in the actually delivered lecture (WMRS, R 447–R 449). "[I]n this short course," Peirce declares, "it seems better to skip such purely theoretical questions" (R 465; EP 2, p. 534). The upshot was that the opening lecture was altogether divested of graphs and definitions. But this was to be a lone exception. Torn between candor and simplicity, Peirce's internal call of a scientist soon took an upper hand. The demand for precision and highest of standards, while promoting novelty and contribution to knowledge, would shape the rest of the seven hours to come.

It is for such reasons perfectly appropriate to open the selection of Peirce's first five lectures with this original version of the first lecture of the series, thus submitting to the plan that he had in mind all along. Despite the fact that this real plan was never delivered, and not forgetting that his readers and listeners would certainly have judged it too abstract, technical and remote from common experience and background, this superseded draft note is a testimony of Peirce's desire to break new ground with his lectures, even at the expense of being accused of deliberate obscurantism. While the peer pressure to have him succumb to the ideals of an agreeable academic performer never become unfelt, the balance in the lectures tipped towards "…but no simpler"—or, as Einstein reportedly had rather stated, "…the supreme goal of all theory is to make the irreducible basic elements as simple and as few as possible, without having to surrender the adequate representation of a single datum of experience".[27]

As explained in the introduction to Part IV, R 454 sets out to prove the soundness of the system of logical graphs in a formal manner. The graphs are conceived as composing the best possible systems for the representation of processes of reasoning. The manuscript breaks off before completing the inductive proof of the soundness of the basic rights for the system of logical diagrams, but even that suffices to reveal Peirce's intention to have that demonstration as the core of the first lecture: it at once will reveal us what the "thorough and formal refutation of the fallacy" consists of (namely the psychologistic fallacy that what makes a reasoning sound is the "feeling of logicality"). Peirce's demonstration in R 454 of the soundness of the system of EGs is the solution he asserted to have in his possession in R 448 (EP 2, p. 234). The editors of EP 2 have claimed that such refutation "has not been found" (p. 553), but here we have every reason to believe that the refutation is the proof of the soundness of the rules of transformation for EGs: that proof positively replaces any earlier attempt to establish what comprises sound reasoning, such as the feeling of logicality or what consciousness is capable of possessing. In the actually delivered lecture this was only informally and negatively argued for (namely addressing what does *not* make a reasoning sound), for fear that any positive, formal solution would lose the course's popular appeal.

Another salient feature of this early lecture is that it at once reveals Peirce's thoughts on the true analytic virtues of the system of graphs. The graphical method is not meant to draw conclusions that some other system, such as algebraic logic or Peano's pasigraphy could not draw. Nor is the graphical system

---

[27] From "On the Method of Theoretical Physics" by Albert Einstein, The Herbert Spencer Lecture, Oxford, June 10, 1933.

meant to draw those conclusions that others also draw in any easier, more facile or secure manner. The system is intended to be the best method to analyse what the very idea of necessary reasoning consists of, in terms of bringing that reasoning into its smallest elements, discovering along the way what those elements are and how they are connected to each other. This is the true philosophy of the system; it is the theory of the philosophy of logic that Peirce is interested in developing, not formal systems that facilitate proof, calculation or computation.

Peirce communicates in the delivered first lecture (WMRS) that soundness consists in the facts of the case. We evaluate assertions, he tells, in relation to the "states of things" in which they are true. The semantic notion of the consequence relation and the idea of being true-in-a-model virtually desire to come out from his considerations. Further, Peirce is after the character of logical *laws*, in the sense of *real laws*, by virtue of which any reasoning, not necessarily conscious reasoning of human minds, tends towards truth. His conviction, resulting from years of painstaking study, is that diagrams provide the best analytical method by which the character of such laws may be brought to view.

A couple of additional features have the first lecture draft differ from the later versions, including Peirce's actual opening lecture. First, what Peirce in *The Logical Tracts* and later would term "conventions" are here called "principles". Second, we see a curiosity which is found almost nowhere else (but see R 492 and R 513) that Peirce connects the words that are written (asserted) on the blackboard, so that no word would be "understood independently of one another". An idiosyncratic calligraphic script is availed of so that all words come to be serially connected, a practice that happens in the early version of the second *Logical Tracts* but is soon dropped from it as well as from the later drafts of the lectures. One also finds some interesting examples of inconsistent assertions, which Peirce takes to be "pseudo-graphs" and not graphs proper, and which due to their contradictory nature do not "represent any conceivable state of things," that is, they have no model. In the course of the lectures, this would develop into the notion of the "blot".

Deductive reasoning is carried out in terms of "four basic rights of transformation". Peirce had developed the rules of transformation for logical graphs since 1896 (and prior to them, in his algebra of logic) and had gravitated into their final form by August 1898. They are standardly known as the (irreversible) rules of erasure and insertion (Right I), the (reversible) rules of deiteration and iteration (Right II), the rule of the double cut (Right III) and the rule for the pseudograph (Right IV). These rules were published in the entry "Symbolic Logic, or algebra of logic" in the *Dictionary of Philosophy and Psychology* that appeared in the previous year (LoF 3; Rules I–IV for the Alpha part), where for typographical reasons Peirce had to use a different, one-dimensional variant of graphs, with parentheses, brackets and braces instead of the cuts. Peirce's entry was given as the reading for the second lecture.

With the possible exception of the extra eighth Harvard lecture delivered in May (R 316(s), LoF 1), Peirce previously had no chances to explain the sound and complete rules of the system to the live audience. He was obviously looking forward to this opportunity and thus eagerly planned to explain the rules already in the beginning of the lecture series. The matter was postponed to Lectures II and III, however.

A remarkable observation follows the description of these basic rights, namely that "by using these rights we can draw from any premises any inferences that they justify". This is much like how semantic completeness of the system of transformations could be stated. Peirce begins by demonstrating the other direction of the statement, namely that everything that is deducible by these rights is a semantic consequence of the premises. His proof of soundness is a semantic proof in which "a right to transform an entire graph" from M to N, that is, the transformability, or the existence of a derivation sequence that leads from a graph M to a graph N, is taken to mean that "every state of things in which M is true is a state of things in which N is true". This statement was carried over to the informal presentation of WMRS.

The reading list for the first lecture, which Peirce provided in late November, consisted of the following rather bulky items:

Bosanquet, Bernard.
    Knowledge and reality. A criticism of F. H. Bradley's
    "Principles of Logic". London, 1892.   3607.126
Bradley, Francis Herbert.
    The principles of logic. London, 1883.   3600.60
Erdmann, Johann Eduard.
    Outlines of logic and metaphysics. Translated by B. C. Burt. [Introductory science textbooks.]   3608.166
    The title given by Mr. Peirce is: Benno Erdmann's Logik.
Sigwart, Christoph von
    Logic. 2d edition, enlarged. Translated by Helen Dendy. London 1895. 2 v.   3604.119
Trendelenburg, Friedrich Adolph.
    Logische Untersuchungen. Berlin, 1840.   B.6085.2
Ueberweg, Friedrich.
    System of logic, and history of logical doctrine.
    Translated by T. M. Lindsay. London, 1871.   B.H.Ref.592.10. (3605.51)
Wundt, Wilhelm Max.
    Logik. 2. Auflage. Stuttgart, 1893–95. 2 v. in 3.   3603.148

Selection 33: A System of Diagrams for Studying Logical Relations. Exposition of it begun. (Existential Graphs—Alpha & Beta). Lowell Lecture II(a)

R 450, plus R S-27, R S-28. "Lectures on Logic, to be delivered at the Lowell Institute, Winter of 1903–1904". On the cover of this Harvard Cooperative notebook (R 450) is written "L.1? Graphs".

R 450 and R S-27 ("Graphs, Little Account") are the first versions of the drafts for the second lecture, which was held on Friday, November 27. R S-27 is a little later, incomplete draft, also in the form of the Harvard notebook, which ends before completing the description of the fourteen conventions. Peirce wrote on its cover: "See opp. page 17 for important note on sep".

R 450 was probably and R S-27 definitely written soon after the first chapter of *Logical Tracts No. 2* was completed. The writings that here comprise the first batch of the second lecture indeed bear the closest relationship to the *Tracts* both textually and substantially. They were probably written in late September, and in early October Peirce may still have been working on them. R S-28 ("The Conventions") has a date of September 15, and although it presents what perhaps is the most elaborate attempt to explain the basic conventions, it appears to be a slightly earlier undertaking.

"The gist of the reasoning", Peirce proclaims at the outset of R 450, "is to state in the most general terms that relation of the state of things expressed in the conclusion of each inferential step to the state of things expressed in the premisses". What constitutes reasoning is its definition in terms of a semantic consequence relation. This idea, already developed in the first lecture (informally in the delivered and formally in the undelivered early draft of R 454), is the definite and positive refutation of the earlier logicians' attempts to describe the gist of reasoning by appealing to the workings of the mind or to the nature of consciousness. Those attempts fail to analyse changes in the forms of expression. The system prepared to take up the task of analysis of reasoning in its fullest term is the system of diagrams.

Peirce distinguishes diagrams from mere visual signs such as pictures: diagrams have to rely on an elaborate system of conventions for their interpretation. What he had termed "Principles" in the previous, early version of the first lecture undergo here a name-change into "Conventions". Now he is prepared to marshal the full array of fourteen conventions, much in the way he had worked them out in *The Logical Tracts*. R 450 then ends with an index of these conventions which indeed refers to the pagination of *Logical Tracts No. 2* (R 492).

The conventions rely on the fundamental idea of reasoning being "nothing but the discourse of the mind to its future self". Through Plato, Peirce came to be inspired by the ancient idea of the dialogic and interrogative nature of intellectual thought (see Introduction to Volume 1; LoF 1). Today we can elaborate the Socratic–Shakespearean "I says to myself, says I" in terms of logical semantics and using the game theory to define strategies for rational, discursive reasoning. Peirce takes diagrams to provide the best form of expression and the requisite precepts according to which these interactive patterns of discourse between various phases of mind operate. Much of what we find in his system of conventions are attempts to spell out the basic rules and principles that would explicate fundamental workings of reasoning in terms of interactive operations. At the same time, his conventions serve to define meanings of basic logical signs and constants. Throughout his writings on these topics, the description of conventions invariably precede the description of the permissible rules of transformation, which is clear evidence that Peirce realised how fundamentally important it is that semantic and pragmatic (methodeutic) considerations take priority over purely mathematical definitions, in the philosophy of logic.

Peirce might have decided to begin his lectures by trying to motivate fundamental conventions with their underlying Socratic method. Maybe the audience would appreciate philosophical conventions better than they would the technical exposition of graphs in terms of definitions, permissive rules and proofs. In the very least, a philosophically motivated exposition would make the logical behaviour of graphs easier to grasp. In preparing for the second lecture, Peirce does seem to be having the audience and the general aim of the lectures in his mind, for now.

The selection of notes collected under the heading of the "Second Lecture" possesses a wealth of insights and advancements in the philosophy of logic. Four issues are worth highlighting.

First, the practice of the first lecture draft of the previous selection, namely that of writing words as connected, is now dropped, perhaps as an inessential pedantry.

Second, the concept of a sub-graph (partial graph), only briefly mentioned in 1897–1898, is now appropriately defined in terms of the distinction between total/entire graphs and partial graphs. A nearly contemporaneous presentation of these terms is seen to be taking place in *The Logical Tracts*.

Third, the convention number nine hatches the soon-to-emerge idea of the broken cut, which entitles one to refer to alternative universes besides the actual universe of discourse. It is the "mode of dotting the line", Peirce here proposes, that identifies what alternative universes are meant. The idea would soon break out as modal Gamma graphs. The paragraph zero of the ninth convention is also worth highlighting: Peirce writes that "no individual belongs to two different universes", although two individuals may well depend on one another, in the sense in which there is a connection (i.e., an interpretation) of one of them within the universe which involves taking into account that of the other. However, if we were to give up the first stricture of the paragraph zero and permit an individual to occur in two or more universes (such as in two different construction branches of the same semantic tree), we might get new kinds of logic—perhaps something that he was struggling to articulate elsewhere such as in the *Minute Logic* draft from the previous year (R 430, LoF 1). A similar thought appears in Peirce's attempt to apply the idea of the tinctures to related problems concerning logical representation of complex linguistic assertions with anaphora (R 490, LoF 3).

Fourth, in "The Conventions" of R S-28 one finds a unique convention, that of Number 10, which proposes a *wavy* line of identity, with an assigned meaning that the wiggle is a graph asserting such an existential relation between its extremities "as the nature of their universes permits". This unique definition is never developed any further. Perhaps the tadpole that follows was connected to one of the eight alternative systems of EGs which have been lost altogether suggested in "Studies of the Eight Systems of Existential Graphs", a sketchy account which we find in R 1483 and in the *Logic Notebook* on June 27, 1903, and which concerned the possibility of talking about alternative universes with some such variations (LoF 1). In the fourth and the last system that has been preserved in those notes, the nature of the universe is characterised such that an unencircled line resting on a sheet of assertion refers not to *something* but to *everything* in the universe. This would produce a dual system, a Beta version of entitative graphs. Maybe one of the missing four systems is a generalisation of this idea, using the line to refer to alternative modes of existences, some of which he had studied elsewhere without explicitly connecting them to logical analysis. There is also a similar kind of a dotted cut in R S-28 as in the proposed third system in R 1483, in the second paragraph of Convention 9, with an interpretation that takes the conditional to be in another than indicative mood *de inesse*. For conditionals need take into account what *might be* the case, therefore bringing out counterfactual connections between "the state of things supposed in the antecedent and that which is conditionally asserted in the consequent".

The notebook (R S-28) contains about 60 sketches of various graphs which for reasons of space are not reproduced in the present selection (see the last item of the edition, "Fragments", for a selection of a couple of related images). Some of them do stand out with their distinctive logical and notational content, such as (i) collections (both diagrammatic and algebraic notations are used to represent collectives); (ii) qualities, properties of relations such as number-theoretic relations, and multitudes represented by the second-order logic of potentials; (iii) a 'possible-worlds semantics' idea for necessities and possibilities (e.g., "If in every possible state of things either A is false or B is false or C is true..."), using the dual of the envelope-notation of the logic of potentials, which instead of sums takes *products* of two graphs; and (iv) an anticipation of the 1906 tinctured graphs by changing "the universe of the sheet" to "that of logical possibility".

The background reading Peirce provided for his second lecture lists seven items:

Kempe, Alfred Bray.
    A memoir on the theory of mathematical form. (In Philosophical transactions of the Royal Society. Vol. 177. pp. 1–70. London, 1887.)   ***3210.1.177**
Schroeder, Ernst.
    Vorlesungen über die Algebra der Logik (exakte Logik). Leipzig, 1890–95. 3 v.   ****E.5113.9**
Studies in logic. By members of the Johns Hopkins University.
    Boston, 1883.   **5600.58**
Symbolic logic, or algebra of logic. (In Baldwin. Dictionary of philosophy and psychology. Vol. 2, pp. 640–651. New York, 1902.)   **B.H.Ref.590.1.2. (*3601.132.2)**
Whitehead, A. N.
    The logic of relations, logical substitution groups, and cardinal numbers. (In American Journal of Mathematics. Vol. 25, pp. 157–178. Baltimore, 1903.)   ****E.5081.10.25**

Selection 34: A System of Diagrams for Studying Logical Relations. Exposition of it begun. (Existential Graphs—Alpha & Beta). Lowell Lecture II(b)

R 455, R 455(s), R 456, plus pages from **R S-29, R S-32, R S-33, R S-34.** These notes are likely to represent the final plans for the second lecture, which was delivered on Friday, November 27 and initially announced as "A System of Diagrams Studying Logical Relations. Exposition of it begun". Retitled with the more accurate "Existential Graphs—Alpha & Beta" (R 470), these drafts also contain germs of the third lecture, which was delivered on following Monday and advertised as "The Three Universal Categories and their Utility". Peirce now plans to say more about the Alpha part of EGs.

In this second set of notes for the second lecture, Peirce is no longer concerned with the conventions. Now he takes up the issue of the principles of reasoning. What is the real relationship between premises and conclusions? How do we ascertain ourselves of the soundness and validity of a piece of reasoning that is altogether new, have never seen and never thought of before? What makes an instance of reasoning not only sound but *evident* to reason? These are central questions in the philosophy of logic still today. Peirce addresses and cleverly refutes the so-called paradox of the justification of deduction, according to which reasoning that rests upon logical principles must not itself be used to justify those principles. Peirce's solution is that the *statement* of the principle of reasoning, which he had termed leading or guiding principle, and *reasoning according to* that principle are not the same thing: the former is an abstract statement of the principle in another form than the form in which the principle according to which we reason is being used.

There is another objection to the admission of the principles of logic, however, which Peirce here uncovers and which does not appeal to the allegedly question-begging nature of deductive reasoning. To analyse it Peirce first presents the system of EGs, as that system is preferable for the purpose of facilitating the *study* of reasoning: in it, every form is precisely defined and the diagrammatic syntax no longer depends on the confusing syntax of language. Moreover, as the first lecture had made it clear, this method has nothing to do with how we happen to feel about the facts we wish to model with logic. Peirce's presentation of the system of the Alpha part of the method of graphs eats up the full hour, however, and precious little time is left for completing the proposed argument.[28]

In this second lecture Peirce introduces the important terminology of the EGs, such as the "spots". The terminology is not altogether new, as he had used spots since 1896 (R 482, R 483), although they were not used in the early draft of the first lecture (R 454). Peirce's emphasis on "scribing" the graphs, that is, on producing graph-instances on the sheet of assertion as a hybrid procedure of writing and drawing, is equally prevalent in the lecture.

The motivation to tackle the question of basic forms of reasoning is evident in the second lecture. Peirce's communication is occupied with the distinction between conditional propositions *de inesse* and those that make reference to "a whole range of possibilities".[29] How the former is to be represented in EGs leads Peirce to the analysis of conditionals as *scrolls*, the form which he had used already in the very first presentations of EGs, such as his National Academy of Sciences paper in November 1896 (LoF 1). Here the form of illation, central to the understanding of the key principles of reasoning, is appealed to in analysing other notions of logic, including how the concept of the falsity emerges from the concepts of the conditional. The term "blot" (the pseudograph), that is, the filling up of an area of the inner loop of the scroll, which Peirce proposes would trigger the extraction of the concept of negation from the concept of the scroll, is new with

---

28 It is possible to reconstruct the essential elements of this rather complicated argument with the aid of more modern notions of logic; the details are given in Pietarinen (2020).

29 Analysis of conditionals cannot thus be adequately carried out in terms of classical logic that treats conditionals in their *de inesse* modes: "But conditional propositions do not usually mean merely that either the antecedent is true or else the consequent is false. Those which *do* mean no more than this are called conditionals de inesse, where *de inesse* means that they relate merely to the actual state of things" (R 839, ms p. 13, [a single leaf possibly connected to Peirce's June 22, 1911 letter to J. H. Kehler]). See also R S-46 in the last selection on how Peirce in 1903 thought that modalities could help in analysing conditional sentences in graphical logic.

this second lecture, and it occurs contemporaneously with his definition of Convention 10 in *Logical Tracts No. 2*.[30]

One way to approach the problem of reasoning is to define permissible transformations that would never change a true graph into a false one. Such permissions "conform to a general type", Peirce says, which is not a relation of thoughts to what we experience, but a relation of thoughts to "what we may imagine". Importantly, "what we may imagine" is the universe of discourse that is well-agreed upon those who undertake the scribing of graphs and accepting the proposed scribings of graphs, namely is the universe of discourse mutually agreed by the Graphist and the Interpreter of graphs. Graphs permitted to be scribed on the sheet are the true graphs, and so the truth of a graph is the result of transforming a blank sheet into an assertion that has a graph in it (minimally, transforming the blank graph into the blank graph). This means that one is constructing a model for the graph, and all consistent graphs will have a model. Contradictory, absurd graphs—in Peirce's terms "the blot" or "the pseudo-graph"—amount to a quasi-assertion that the universe of imagination "has no being" in it, that is, there is no model that could be obtained for an absurdity.

What is the real objection to the proposed principle of reasoning that Peirce promised to expose at the outset of the lecture? First, Peirce makes an allusion to Euclid and claims to be the first to have found a fallacy in one of Euclid's propositions, namely Proposition XVI in the first book of the *Elements*. Peirce talks on the Euclidean fallacy also in R 514, R 693, R 201 and R 905 and begins, but does not complete, its presentation in the *Tracts* right after Convention 14—another proof of it being a coeval writing project to this present lecture note. Manuscript R 905 (LoF 3) reveals that Euclid's fallacy is not what Peirce means by a *logical* fallacy. It is the *wrong theoric idea* "that his figure essentially represents every possible plane triangle". This statement fails under certain finite configurations of space, which Peirce would detail several years later in R 905. Euclid's reasoning involves a non-deductive, namely abductive (retroductive) moment of thought. Logical reasoning is irreducible to purely demonstrative kind of deductive reasoning. Principle of reasoning involve abductive moments, and that makes them to be of altogether different kind from necessary reasoning.

This, in a nutshell, is the reconstruction of Peirce's objection to what the paradox of the justification of principles of reasoning has been taken to be in the literature. Peirce is not accusing those who attempt to justify deduction deductively of circularity, because leading principles of deductive reasoning would be un-eliminable all the same (Bellucci & Pietarinen 2017a). What he now can

---

30 On details of Peirce's notion of the blot, see Pietarinen et al. (2020).

add to that is that any such justification has to involve forms of reasoning that themselves are not matters of formal demonstration.

It is at this juncture that the notion of *observation* of features of logical diagrams enters the scene. Peirce explains to the audience—if, as it in fact seems that this part was actually delivered—the distinction between *corollarial* and *theorematic* consequences. Notice first that this passage takes place, importantly, right in the middle of Peirce working out the basic permissible rules of transformation for his graphical calculi. Theorematic consequences are characterised by their not being evident until after "some experiment has been performed upon the diagram, such as the addition to it of parts not necessarily referred to in the statement of the conclusion". Peirce then observes how theorematic conclusions are indeed ever-present in logical inferences. This very lecture in fact serves as a living demonstration of the presence of such inferences, as it is right that Peirce derives here the basic, sound and complete principles according to which deductive reasoning is to be performed in EGs. For example, he demonstrates how erasing a double cut from around any graph is far from being a primitive rule of the system. It is a rule derived from more fundamental considerations. The derivation, and thus the rule of the double-cut as a whole, is not primitive because an appeal has to be made to the observation that the graph on the outer close of a double cut is blank.

Such observations on diagrams entitle Peirce then to show the immediacy of what we nowadays recognise as the *residuation lemma* (termed Peirce's Rule in Ma & Pietarinen 2018a), namely that implication is a right residual of conjunction. From this lemma, deduction theorem and many other logical rules follow as corollaries. The connection is immediate, because the only action that is needed to residuate between conjunction and implication is the derived rule of adding and removing of the double cut. In this sense the justification of the guiding principle of reasoning is a sheer observational issue.[31] The analytic virtues of EGs are immediate given that other logical principles, such as contraposition, Modus Ponens and the Law of Excluded Middle, follow from residuation and can in this way be dissected into their simplest possible transformations. Such principles should by no means be assumed to be logical truths. Clearly Peirce is making excursions into non-Aristotelian, non-Fregean, and non-classical territories.

Lastly, Peirce derives permissions for the blank, the blot, and the pseudograph. The resulting seven permissions, which now are results of an argument that has taken into account both reasoning, imagination and observation, show that there is much more to them than what purely formal or demonstrative reason-

---

[31] Nothing depends on the classicality of logic, as one can derive intuitionistic implication by the same residuation, and more generally from adjunction (Ma & Pietarinen 2018b,c).

ing suggests there is. These seven permissions are moreover compressed into the "code of three primary rules", which are erasure/insertion, iteration/deiteration and insignificants/pseudograph. This code of three rules, now finally presented in the form familiar from the secondary literature, is nevertheless the result of elaborate philosophical, diagrammatic and topological considerations, creative observation, and flights of imagination that transgress the boundaries of ordinary demonstration and proof.

The second lecture soon proposes to move on to the description of the Beta part. Peirce was unlikely to have managed to present the Beta extension in the same evening, however. The term *lexis*, a particular kind of a spot roughly corresponding to that of a satisfiable predicate, is new with this draft but is dropped from subsequent explorations. Peirce then rightly observes that the basic code needs an extension that would handle the behaviour of the lines of identity and ligatures. The set of complete rules for the Beta part poses no special difficulty, however, despite many subclauses that need to be added to the code.

After all these insightful points that Peirce desired to communicate to the audience during the second lecture, he calculated to still have a few minutes left of the full hour. To fill the evening's hour, he would present his newly-discovered "five operations" that would ascertain whether a graph is a logical consequence of the system (that is, whether it belongs to the theory of those graphs) or not (that is, does not belong to the theory of those graphs). The operations are found in R S-32. They give an effective method (a rule which in Peirce's term is "as simple as may be") that can show the decidability of the theory in question. As far as the Alpha part is concerned, those operations establish the decidability of the Alpha system.

A closer look at Peirce's operations for the Alpha has been provided in Roberts (1997). Interestingly, Peirce also attempts to give "the simplest rule" he knows "for ascertaining with certainty" whether now also Beta-possibility would hold for any given graph. His rule is limited to those Alpha graphs that are assumed to be juncture-free, that is, they are quantifier-free reducts of Beta graphs. To follow the given five rules of operation mechanistically would describe a "state of things" in which the Beta-reduct is possible, that is, would construct a branch in the semantic tree (a model) in which the graph in question is true.[32]

In the beginning of the next, third lecture Peirce revisits what he had previously mentioned on these operations, and admits (in a deleted paragraph) that "any similar routine" for Beta graphs would be "impractical". As first-order logic is

---

[32] Recall that a tableaux-like method dawned upon him already in the 1885 "On the Algebra of Logic: A Contribution to the Philosophy of Notation" paper, which contains an example of such a model construction for a sentence of propositional logic.

only semi-decidable, and as there is no general method for positively ascertaining whether a graph is Beta-possible or not, his cancellation was premature. Peirce's attempt to apply a decision method to a fragment of Beta graphs in R S-34 is nevertheless of considerable further interest. Perhaps some decidable fragments of first-order logic (such as guarded fragments) are those that could be associated with his purported result of the Beta reducts. For one, his notion of "adaptible pair" from the next lecture suggests that dyadic relations play a central part in the argument (R 538, R 539; Peirce 1903). Unfortunately this and the related pieces are fragmentary and incomplete, without much explanations or helpful variants.

The appendix contains material which in its main is taken from R S-29 ("Existential Graphs: The Initial Conventions").[33] This notebook contains Peirce's studies on the rules of the system, and it includes many sketches of Alpha and Beta graphs which cannot be reproduced here. After a brief capitulation of the initial conventions, of which he presents here only five, Peirce returns to the demonstration of what he termed the basic rights in R 450, and derives some theorems from the nine basic rules. The code of three primary rules is found among the derived ones, which testifies to the non-trivial (theorematic) character of the derivation of the kinds of steps that are typically assumed as exhibiting the standard and primitive graph transformations. We leave it as an exercise to the reader which of Peirce's proofs in R S-29 involve examples of observation and experimentation upon diagrams, and are thus in that sense theorematic.

Selection 35: The Three Universal Categories and their Utility. (General Explanations. Phenomenology and Speculative Grammar).
Lowell Lecture III(a,b)

R 462, R 457. Stated on the notebook cover label of R 462, in Peirce's hand: "The Main holt for Lecture 3". "2nd Draught of 3rd Lecture. Begun 1903 Oct 5 10:30AM". Probably not delivered in most part. Also included in the selection are pages from R S-31 that Peirce cut out from the notebook to keep the planned third lecture of manageable length, as well as an incomplete alternative continuation (R 457).

The presentation of the five operations at the end of the previous lecture plan served Peirce as a bridge not only between the two lectures but also as the much needed transition from how to do proofs in Alpha to the consideration of what

---

[33] Peirce's first subtitle was "The Initial Conditions", which seems to be a slip of the pen and was corrected to "Initial Conventions". The notebook may a little earlier than the other notes for the second lecture in the present selection, and is related in both its character and terminology to Peirce's descriptions of fundamental conventions and basic rules of transformation since 1898 (LoF 1).

Beta graphs teach about philosophical issues of logic. Beginning with the proofs, Peirce dissects the primary permissive rules in two ways: first, into those that *complicate* the graph (insertion, iteration, and adding of the double cut) and those that *simplify* it (erasure, deiteration, and cancelling the double cut). The second division is according to the rules that are *non-reversible* (insertion and erasure), and those that are *reversible* (iteration/deiteration and adding/cancelling the double cut). The latter are equivalence rules.

Peirce also proposes, quite far-sightedly, that because of the "endless multitude" of conclusions that can be derived by rules that complicate the graphs (with only a small number of Beta graphs as premisses), the "the simplest rule" "for ascertaining with certainty" whether Beta-possibility holds is not the kind of "comprehensive routine" that a machine could perform.

Where Beta-impossibility (and intractability) enter the scene is in testing the limits of the expressive power of the system when trying to represent complicated statements of natural language. If those statements involve modal expressions, including *esse in futuro*, in which meanings refer to states of things that fail to obtain in the actual world, their representation, Peirce would notice, have to take place in the Gamma part of the system. Gamma is thus to open up a new chapter in the graphical method which Peirce urges is to be presented at the earliest convenience. However, even in the theory of Beta graphs one might represent meanings not obviously absurd or contradictory that nevertheless are peculiar. A question thus arises: How to discover contradictions in complex Beta graphs?

Finding out contradictions in first-order formulas is a non-trivial task. The semantic tree method tells us that a statement is consistent if and only if it has a model. This method is routinely used in attempts to construct such a model, and a frustrated model-construction in which all branches of the tree lead to a contradiction and thus close will show that the statement in question is inconsistent. Some details to be taken into account include application of the rule of existential instantiation, as that involves introducing new constants. Peirce would it take it to mean a theorematic step in the attempted model construction. Another is to find a right way to treat universal quantification, which being non-deterministic also involves theorematic steps on the development of strategies for the proofs that could avoid infinite branch constructions that would never close.

Peirce presents some examples of complex Beta graphs, of which he wants to find out whether they involve contradictions. His comparison of them with the example a few paragraph later (the graph involving Arthur), leads Peirce to propose a new rule that performs a consistency-check for the Beta graphs. Some new terminology is introduced, such as that of an "adaptible pair". The rule involves iterating the entire graph, followed by a conjoining of adaptible pairs. He then suggests how to introduce new individuals, much like in existential instantiation.

The rule strives to expand the graph to the point in which one could literally see that it is impossible, that is, that the expanded graph involves a contradiction. Peirce concludes that the contradiction in his example is of the same general type as what the pseudograph would do in the Arthur example. Though his explanation of the new rule for checking consistencies is far from clear or completed, the idea of the proposal that when trying to discover hidden contradictions in complicated Beta graphs there must be a rule that can be systematically followed is, even by modern standards, quite remarkably on the right track.

But "the main holt" of this lecture, as indeed of its two other versions, is the promised "third chapter" on Gamma graphs. He needs to communicate to the audience the philosophical motivation first. As the lecture progresses, his topics will bear increasingly more on "questions now vexed": qualities, possibilities and laws are no longer absent in the Gamma analysis. But the music and the language of the lecture is logic, and the analysis of relations and references that link representations to qualities and laws is for Peirce to be a strictly logical affair. What kinds of possibilities are qualities? Why are qualities not related to one another? What is the nature of dyadic relations and relations of existence? What are the triadic relations and how can laws be mental affairs?

This second, undelivered draft of the third lecture breaks off in the middle of the section in which Peirce is explaining the three classes of signs. His explanation of universal categories in terms of qualities, dyadic and triadic relations is to continue with explorations on signs; those separate and later drafts that Peirce added or intended to add to the *Syllabus* text, such as R 508, R 539–R 540, are related to fairly technical and, as far as the dyadic relations are concerned, not very well understood expositions concerning properties of different relations—modal as well as existential—and their role in creating new divisions and taxonomies of signs, especially the three fundamental trichotomies of signs are they are now presented anew in R 540. Part of the purpose of his excursus into the nomenclature of dyadic relations was to see which among the many such relations are of particular interest in the study of logic. On these last two questions, thus, Peirce's planned a last-minute re-edit of the *Syllabus* text that would include R 539 on the classification of dyadic relations and, secondarily, also R 540 (and a one-page orphan leaf which is located in R 799) on the classification of triadic relations. Those studies would have been of special importance to the success of the *Syllabus*, but unfortunately were not included in the final *Syllabus* leaflet due to the lack of funds.

Peirce soon mentions pragmatism, and it is possible that it was in connection to such remarks that some questions arose from the audience, perhaps from William James, as suggested by Peirce's comments on James's syllabus appended to Selection 41 of Peirce's *Syllabus*. Evidence that James's interests are here being addressed comes from multiple sources, including the correspondence between the two scholars and similar remarks James had made earlier that year on Berkeley as an introducer of pragmatism (CSP to WJ, January 23, 1903). Most notably, however, Peirce is addressing James's own preceding course from the previous fall, "The Philosophy of Nature", in which James wanted to achieve something "serious, systematic, and syllogistic". James's syllabus lists the topics covered in the course: "23. Syllabus of Philosophy 3: The Philosophy of Nature (1902–1903) by William James. What Philosophy is: an investigation into object-world as well as into subject-world. "Pragmatism" as our method. Berkeley's Idealism as an example thereof. Kant's argument for Idealism" (James 1988, pp. 257–273). These appear nearly verbatim as titles of Peirce's rejoinder, interspersed within the pages of his own syllabus draft (R 478).[34] Apparently Peirce is now, nearly a year later, alerted to undertake a fresh and more detailed response concerning the topics taken up in James's syllabus, in the context of his own lecturing. Maybe Peirce was asked during the lectures by an unidentified audience member how his pragmatism would relate to what James had taught it to be in his "Syllabus of Philosophy, 3", prompting Peirce to hurriedly write up the long rejoinder.

An earlier and very incomplete attempt from October 2 (R 457) is appended and designated as an alternative version of parts of the third lecture. Labelled as "1st Draught of 3rd Lecture" on the notebook cover label, this attempt confirms that Peirce is after something like a strategic rule that is to aid a tableaux-like model-construction: if it is impossible that an application of transformation rules to a proposition ever leads to a contradiction, how to ascertain oneself of that impossibility? Peirce says that a wrong or a bad application of a rule "may lead

---

[34] Peirce had received James's "Syllabus of Philosophy, 3" in January, and had at once commented it to be

> a work demanding long study & will be extremely valuable to me. I will now make such remarks as occur to me on a first perusal of it.
> Berkeley on the whole has more right to be considered the introducer of pragmatism into philosophy than any other man, though I was more explicit in enunciating it.
> To the question 'How to explain this harmony?' you give a number of answers. None of these *are* explanations but they are *proposals* of *how* to try to explain the harmony. They do not conflict with one another. They simply have different purposes in view. The theistic idea is the only one that satisfies practical needs. But a "design" is a thought. A thought by its nature cannot be present. It only exists in the sense that it is destined to work itself out. (CSP to WJ, January 23, 1903; James 2002, pp. 180–182)

Peirce's evaluation continues for several letter pages and addresses James's points on epiphenomenalism, pragmatism, and the problem of evil, among a number of other issues that had arisen from his initial inspection of James's syllabus. Ferdinand Canning Scott Schiller had also commented on James's syllabus in length (FCSS to WJ, February 4, 1903; James 2002, pp. 194–197).

to a result which can obviously never lead to the cancelling of the sheet when the original graph otherwise treated might have done so". A wrong application of the universal rule may indeed lead to an infinite branch that will never close. Peirce's remedy is to modify rules of transformation such that only the reversible ones are admissible, and then have only those to be applied, so that one is always entitled to backtrack in any branch of the tree to a previous node in which one could try out an alternative strategy.

Peirce seems to have thought that such a restriction to reversible rules is also needed in order to preserve the meaning when translating Beta to Alpha graphs by eliminating the junctures. R 457 ends with a sketch of such a procedure of how to get rid of the junctures to then show the decidability of Beta graphs by reducing them to Alpha graphs and then applying the five operations. Peirce states that "it would be easy enough to describe a way of getting rid of all the lines of identity in a graph while preserving its entire meaning". His sketch of the line-elimination procedure which ends with a proposal to substitute selectives for the lines was left far from complete, and he never really returns to the issue let alone would leave any documentation how "easy" he thought the meaning-preserving line-elimination procedure to be. Marginal notes in the notebook suggest that repeated domestic interruptions that morning prevented him from proceeding with what looks like a significant study on topics of quantifier elimination and decidability.

The list of books Peirce provided for "The three universal categories and their utility" consisted of only two items:

Hibben, John Grier.
    Hegel's logic. An essay in interpretation. New York, 1902.   **3607.196**
Peirce, Charles Sanders.
    On a new list of categories. (In American Academy of Arts and Sciences. Proceedings. Vol. 7, pp. 287–298. Boston, 1868.)   ***3370.6.7**

Selection 36: The Three Universal Categories and their Utility. (General Explanations. Phenomenology and Speculative Grammar). Lowell Lecture III(c)

R 464, R 464(s). The notebook cover states: "To be used for Lecture III. Vol. 1". On page 0: "C.S.P.'s Lowell Lectures of 1903. Part 1 of 3rd Draught of 3rd Lecture. Begun Oct 8, 9am".

Much of what is included here as the second installment of Peirce's third lecture pertains to the final planning stages of the third lecture. The middle part of the lecture plan below (manuscript pages 26–56) was delivered on November 30. This is followed by pages (manuscript pages 56–64) that were delivered as part of Lecture IV on December 3. Also included in this second installment of notes for Lecture III are some non-delivered pages from R 464(s) and R 465.

Peirce began the third lecture by answering a listener's question he had received after WMRS (see the account of this in EP 2, p. 534). He then probably skipped the examples on "methodical reasoning" (methodeutic) that are included in this selection first, and after a brief excursus on categories as a preface to the topic of Gamma graphs ("I was able to say very little about these categories", R 460, Lecture IV), was forced to utter a few words concerning meanings and Gamma graphs, as those would be required for him to be entitled to retitle the lecture as "General Explanations. Phenomenology & Speculative Grammar" (R 470). One also realises now that Peirce never managed to say much at all on the topic of Beta graphs (R 460: "nothing more than a few scraps"). Maybe only the terms "ligatures" and "individuals" were mentioned in passing. At the moment when the seven permissions were finally displayed to the audience, Lecture II was nearing its end and was followed perhaps only by a hasty gesture on the five operations of the decision procedure. For it is right here, at the beginning of the final draft of the third lecture, that Peirce restates those seven rules in terms of what in the earlier drafts were the three primary permissions.

The idea of the third lecture nevertheless is more coherent than its communication ever could have been, and needs to be appreciated in its entirety and read together with this final draft that connects the dots. What Peirce had earlier formulated as a rule for checking Alpha-possibility describes "the states of the universe" to which possibility of an Alpha graph is limited. It is a rule for model construction, and its formulation pertains, Peirce here reveals, to "methodical reasoning", that is, to the part of logic which he later would term the *methodeutic* of logic, not to its *critic* (speculative grammar). Methodeutic is at issue also when one is to apply premisses in the Beta part of the system, since they, such as the application of the rule for universal quantifiers, "can be efficient over and over again endlessly" in the course of a proof. An instructive case for methodeutic comes from mathematical discovery and the ground prepared for it by conceptual innovation and concept-change potential much more than what can come from treating mathematical proofs as demonstrations following mechanistic rules of computation.

The lecture also covers some topics of categories and relations. We see both the negative and the positive parts of Peirce's reduction thesis covered in this draft. Perhaps following James's earlier advice, Peirce adds some examples from science and poetry to illustrate the "real power" of natural thought.

The second part of the third draft starts off with the topic of Gamma graphs, the first example being on representing the relation of "being more multitudinous than". This anticipates what he wished to lecture during the next couple of hours, especially on the topics of multitude and continuity in mathematics, though he never actually gets that far. His diagrammatic representation of propositions about characters in the language of the logic of potentials was probably never explained to the audience, either, and is largely found on the pages cut-out from the notebook. Lacking proper explanations of such preliminaries the complex example that contains three coloured spots (red, brown and black) would have been beyond comprehension anyway. Peirce's notes end with a suggestion to extend Gamma graphs to what he would continue to pursue in the theory of graphs of graphs.

Selection 37: Exposition of the System of Diagrams Completed. (Existential Graphs: Gamma Part). Lowell Lecture IV

R 467, R 468, plus R S-31. On the notebook cover reads: "C. S. Peirce's Lowell Lectures 1903. Lecture 4. Vol 1. (Graphs mostly, C[harles] H[artshorne])". Page 0 contains the title: "C. S. Peirce's Lowell Lectures for 1903. Lecture 4. Vol. I. Gamma Part of Existential Graphs". Published (R 467) as CP 4.510–4.529, with several omissions, inaccuracies and typographic alterations. The rest of the material that appears in the present selection has not been published before. R S-31 contains the cut-out pages from this Harvard cooperative notebook of R 467.

Peirce was unlikely to have had much time to explain his new topic of the graphs of graphs that he planned to do at the end of the third lecture. The delivered lecture five was on multitude, and would presuppose that the audience understand what the second and third compartments of Gamma graphs were, which Peirce summarised in the notebook catalogued at R 468. On its cover reads: "L. V. Vol. I. Graphs. C[harles]. H[artshorne]". Page 0 has Peirce's own title: "C.S.P's Lowell Lectures of 1903. Introduction to Lecture 5. 1903 Dec 4". As the date suggests, Peirce began writing this introduction at once on the day following his third lecture. Since the material of R 468 continues the previous lecture (R 464), it is appended to the present selection collating material on the fourth lecture. A large single sheet "Diagrams for Lecture 5" (from R 468)[35] is written thoroughly with red ink and Peirce seems to have prepared it for projection with the stereopticon device. A transcription of this sheet follows as Appendix C of the fourth lecture as Peirce took it to be co-requisite for the full apprehension of the fifth lecture.

---

[35] This page was microfilmed among the abundant and mostly unrelated assorted pages deposited in the thick folder of R 839. The microfilm image has some lead pencil marks at the top of the page, presumably by later editors (including the phrase "gamma spots"), but those were erased from the original sheet which is now located in the folder R 468 of the Harvard's Houghton Peirce Papers. Another discrepancy between the microfilm edition and the Peirce Papers is, among numerous others, the first ten pages of the *Syllabus* of R 478, which appear in the microfilm edition in R 864, in duplicate.

In the meantime, Peirce had prepared another lecture four, R 467, of which he was unlikely to have managed to communicate much about anything during these crammed evening hours. Although the notebook looks like having been prepared virtually ready for a full hour's presentation, he was unlikely to have been able to fit any of its material into the tight schedule. The exposition of the Alpha part, of which Peirce had just three days earlier given "a tolerably full account", with abundant technical details that he wanted to cover, took much longer than calculated. Despite the fact that these lecture notes contain detailed instructions to the assistant on which graphs to prepare and display to the audience, the important topic of modal Gamma graphs had to be left aside. Some aspects of non-modal Gamma graphs will eventually be briefly introduced during the fifth lecture (R 469–R 471), possibly along the lines of what we find in R 468, as Peirce deemed knowledge of them necessary for the sake of understanding the preferred method of how to analyse mathematical concepts of multitude, infinity and continuity and, ultimately, how to appreciate what the logical method of analysis and definition can do as far as the logic of science and scientific reasoning is concerned. But Peirce might have been forced to abandon his current plan, perhaps literally in the last minute, of revealing to the public what is nothing less than the birthplace of modern modal logic.

The drafting of this undated lecture note took place near the actual lectures. This is evidenced by the instructions Peirce gave to "Mr. Warren" [sic., W. C. Lounsbury], who was in charge of handling the scribing of the graphs and other illustrations on the blackboard and who was operating the stereopticon to project the diagrams as they occur in from Peirce's handwritten notes. Peirce gives a colour code (it is retained in the transcription but shows in the black and white rendering as a grey-scale) to indicate which diagrams were to be projected and which written on the blackboard. (Green ink, which was also part of the code, seems not to have been used in these notes.)

Peirce filled a number of extra notebook pages with various studies on modal Gamma graphs (R S-1, R S-31). In his Lowell lecture notes, there are more studies on modal graphs than on any other topic of his graphical method of diagrams. Peirce was clearly determined to bring this study into a completion and to be fully exposed. Some of his important worksheets are included as holograph pages at the end of the last selection containing assorted fragments from his studies and notes. What Peirce has to say about modal graphs is to be read in conjunction with the *Syllabus*, especially its unpublished parts that follow the seventh convention, including the "archegetic rules of transformation" for Gamma graphs.

Peirce's many attempts to give shape to the Gamma part shows that he was very much immersed in the process of thinking about how to deliver this new graphical version of modal logic as the lectures approached. As soon as a new leaf is turned in one of his notebooks, a new contemplation begins on what could be diagrammatically said of intensions and meanings, and new ideas are seen to materialise on the sheets (The section "Introduction to the Gamma graphs" in the introductory essay of LoF 2/1 presents and analyses only some of his many such suggestions). We can witness Peirce's thoughts to move from questions of Alpha and Beta-possibility to the emergence of new diagrammatic languages that are proposed to represent the concepts of possibility, necessity and contingency in fully logical terms.

Yet the topics of logic that Gamma graphs were invented to diagrammatically analyse were not altogether new with Peirce's 1903 Lowell Lectures. His 1896 "On Logical Graphs" (R 482, LoF 1), which Carus had declined to publish considers "characters of second intention" and how the second-order relatives are represented in logical graphs. Such characters are not properties of things: our knowledge of them is brought about by making observations of logical forms. The idea goes back a long way: Peirce notes that already Thomas Aquinas had made the definition of logic to be the science of second intentions applied to first intentions. Second intentions were the topic of Schröder's algebra, Frege's logic, and had been part and parcel of Peirce's algebraic investigations that antedated the logic of graphs ever since the early 1880s. The reason why Peirce suspended working on them in 1896 and 1897, or indeed before he revisits them later in 1903, was that he was at that time fully occupied with "completely systematizing" the Beta part of the theory first. The Beta was largely systematised by the summer of 1898 (LoF 1), but as other matters to do with health and penury intervened Peirce was unable to return to this projected Gamma chapter until late in 1903.

In R 467 we indeed see Peirce's earlier ideas taking their mature shape, many of which had geminated as early as during Peirce's collaboration with his Johns Hopkins students, especially with Oscar Howard Mitchell, on the topics of many-dimensional universes, universes of logical possibility, qualities, time, and other modalities. Another sustained attempt took place when Peirce proposed to diagrammatise rhemas of second intention: the work that is scattered in many places since the 1896 paper on logical graphs (R 482, LoF 1), such as the 'moustache-notation'[36] in the *Logic Notebook* (LoF 1, LoF 3) and in Peirce's correspondence with Christine Ladd-Franklin, the ρ-notation of *The Logical Tracts*, and the logic

---

[36] Or, and perhaps more appropriately, to be termed the 'wing-notation', as the preferred graphical notation for abstraction may in fact had been originally a Homerian idea: in his letters to William James (in 1894 and 1900; see James 2002), Peirce suggests the distinction between *pteroentic* ("winged") and *apteroentic* ("unwinged") meanings of words to account for James's pair of terms "substantive" and "transitive" streams of consciousness. "Winged meanings" are those produced by imaginative abstractions.

of potentials in the *Syllabus* (LoF 2). During his writing of the Lowell Lectures, and probably by early October, Peirce invents another notation, the 'envelope-notation', which he carries over to the *Syllabus* while abandoning the p-letter notation proposed in *The Logical Tracts* just shortly before.[37] Peirce also never revisits the moustache-notation for potentials that emerged in the interim period of 1898–1901. What is nonetheless common in all these notations for graphs of second intentions is that the order of interpretation of lines connected to the hooks of the spots are explicitly accounted for in the conventions of the systems.

Abstraction (hypostatic or subjective abstraction) is a process of inference that turns thought to an object of another thought. Logically, it is the embedding of predicates in the universe of discourse, making them amenable to connection by lines. Abstraction co-evolves with Peirce's development of notation for second-order logic. Since abstraction was mentioned in the earlier lecture three as the distinctive feature of the upcoming Gamma compartment, Peirce is now obliged to explain it somewhat further. The third lecture had set the ground with its exposition of the three universal categories, so that Peirce can now present abstraction as a strictly logical notion. Moreover, the character of reasoning involved in abstraction is the necessary one, and not abductive or inductive, as abstraction results in that mode of being in which what is inferred is different from necessary reasoning when contrasted with what it is at the Beta level. So maybe Gamma graphs can analyse that special character of deduction better than Beta graphs do. Since under the abstraction the inferred mode of being may be a general (say, "redness"), not all those logical laws derivable in Beta (such as the law of excluded middle) are any longer applicable. But this is no objection to analyse abstraction using some more general form of the graphical method.

Thus what Peirce gravely needs is a new logic that can talk about possibilities and laws as subjects of the discourse—possibilities and laws really being those remaining pieces one needs to apprehend the most vexed of questions. With the full arsenal of Gamma graphs at his disposal, Peirce is hoping to fully apply the method of logical analysis to abstraction. It is logical inference, after all, that creates a new object, which is of the nature of *ens rationis* and which did not appear in the original collection of things. This object can be investigated in a different domain, thereby opening up a new path of inquiry. Peirce conceived abstractive

---

[37] The dating of Peirce's innovation of the envelope notation is aided by the appearance of some sketches of them on the versos of a draft of a book review that was published in *The Nation* on October 1, 1903 (R 1333), as an evidence that he would be working on them prior to producing his *Syllabus* draft (R 478), perhaps sometime since late September and shortly after abandoning the continuation of the text of *The Logical Tracts*. See the last Selection 42 for that R 1333 page, a one-page example from R S-28, and R 464(s) from October 8.

inferences as crucial for scientific inquiry, since abstraction produces general objects of thought.

The significance of performing experiments in one's rational and scientific mind with the aid of diagrams is the leading theme of the lectures as indeed in the *Syllabus*. Some examples of abstractions in graphs are found among the cut pages of what in the previous selection were included in the second part of the second lecture (R 455(s)). In the pages added to the draft of the *Syllabus*, Peirce had replied to several questions or topics that emanated from James during the previous lecture three. Among his replies we find Peirce putting a finger on this important aspect of abstractive thought: "Thought, being of the nature of a Representation, cannot be 'present' to consciousness. A thought is something that has to be *enacted*, and until it is enacted, its meaning has not been given, even to itself" (added emphasis). Moreover, thoughts, in order to be enacted, need to be embodied, too. And indeed all thought, being dialogical (R 499, LoF 3), "is embodied in signs" (R 298, LoF 3), as Peirce would soon argue in length in his pragmaticism papers. The representational, enacted and embodies nature of thought means that whatever the thoughts are, they have to occur in the guise of signs.

In the Lowell Lectures and adjacent writings, Peirce offers a novel account of both the logic and the use of abstraction and symbolic thought in the diagrammatic syntax of the logic of graphs. In Figures 5 and 6 of one of the alternative versions of the previous selection (R 455(s)), Peirce uses a special, jagged line that refers to abstractions. Thus they quantify the beings of *entia rationis*, not individual existences referred to by the standard, thick continuous lines of identity connecting the spots. In the first graph, the abstracted line connects to the envelope-shaped spot of "humanity". The spots that make up Peirce's logic of potentials have a definite order of connection with the lines. For instance, the connection with the abstracted line is to be considered first, followed by a consideration of its second-intentional relation to the other lines connected to the right-hand side of the spot. This is also unlike in the spots of the standard Beta graphs, in which the order of the arguments of the relations, if needed, is separately given (either explicitly or implicitly, maybe as a grammatical or a contextual feature of the spots, denoted or explained by some appropriate means). The rhema denoting the abstracted property in Figure 5 is "possesses humanity". The entire graph thus states that "There is something called 'humanity' which every man possesses".

There is some variation in the precise notation by which Peirce proposes to denote abstraction: the line that bestows abstraction is in R 472 described as a dotted line that encloses whatever is taken in the abstractive sense. It can thus surround standard lines of identity as well as other parts of graphs. "Whatever is enclosed by a dotted line [or a dotter oval] is an *ens rationis*", Peirce explains in an alternative version of (R 492). In one of the examples of abstraction referred to by this remark in *The Logical Tracts*, namely the graph of Fig. 57, Peirce carefully scribes it such that the abstraction is effected by the dotted line that fully encloses the continuous line of identity. That is, a Beta line of identity occurs the line of abstraction; abstraction *embraces* existence, expropriating that character of the line and replacing it with the generality of *ens rationis*.

In the second graph, possessing a "filiation" is a spot to which a line referring to abstracted entities connects. The line of such abstractions connects three envelope-shaped spots. In Peirce's logic of potentials as presented in the *Syllabus* these potentials stand for "being in a two-place relation to". One of the arguments of these relations is "is a human being", the other two are "is a man" and "is a woman" or their negations. The graph of Figure 6 thus states, in Peirce's own words, that "There is a relation, filiation, in which every human being stands to a man and to a woman and if it stands in this relation to anything then that thing is either identical with that man or is identical with that woman". Certainly such abstractions are not "mere words". They take a predicate (quality, relation) an subject it to a logical analysis by these graphs by placing it as an element in the universe that the utterers and the interpreters of these graphs discourse about. This process has the character of a necessity, and thus deduction, as noted in a fragment that was cut out from the opening pages of the previous lecture (R 455(s)):

> The fact that the blade and handle of a knife are strongly connected consists in the truth of the conditional proposition that if one were to wrench them, not too strongly, they would not come apart. Such a law is of the nature of a *graph*. But [it] is *real* in the sense of being really true of the real world. Now we study graphs. We find out what essentially different kinds of parts go to compose them; and since there are real graphs in the real world, we conclude there must be real parts of them such [as] *qualities*, *relations*, etc. These are called *abstractions*. There is a widely prevalent disposition to say that abstractions are *mere words*. That they are of the nature of words is true; and it is also true that a man's words have very little power to produce effects. Nevertheless, such ideas as *justice* and *truth* have enormous power in the world; and what is more pertinent to our present business is that the analysis of mathematical reasoning shows that the gist of it lies mainly in handling abstractions. We must provide for them in our system of existential graphs or it will not be adequate to the expression of all possible assertions.

In the upcoming lectures, the logic of abstraction would become an indispensable set of tools for Peirce to analyse the nature of mathematical reasoning and its service to scientific progress. Given that much of what scientific inquiry is about draws from its activities being powered by mathematics, and from the fact that the power of the graphical method itself draws from abstraction, the ability to analyse abstractions as logical inferences is a manifestly importance part of the theory of science.[38]

Diagrams are symbols representing generality of forms of relations by abstraction. Ideal forms that diagrams put before us are what Peirce analyse in the Gamma part of the logic of existential graphs as "substantive possibilities" (R 467, R 459, R 464). They instruct scientists on how things might be. They refer to possibilities that concern the reality of the results of experiments. They are ideals that occupy the realm of potentiality, entertained by scientists as vital parts of their attempts to construct successful scientific theories. What in the contemporary literature often is proposed as 'idealisation' would in Peirce's view be generality of objects of diagrams, not some intentionally modified and indefinite models. Being symbols, models that have potency to interpret results of scientific experimentation are perfectly definite in this regard.

Indeed the currently standard interpretation of idealisation of models means intentionally modified, partial representations of the phenomena; interpretation that is capable of showing only some essential features of the object of the phenomena in question. From the point of view of Peirce's logical theory of science, the process of idealisation in such model-based reasoning approaches can be put into a sharper focus. Idealisation is the level of generality of objects of diagrams. Ideal models need not in any way be indefinite. Diagrams are symbols, and as symbols, those models that interpret the results of scientific experimentation are perfectly definite.

It follows that claims that purport idealisations to be representations that strictly speaking are false (take fictionalists, who go to such extremes) are strictly speaking false. Substantive possibilities are real and can be discoursed about by virtue of them being elements of the domain of the sheet of assertion of diagrams representing abstraction. Such elements of the domain (ideal or not) and their relationships make diagrammatic representations true or false. What is fictional is, as Peirce would explicitly argue, quite opposite notion to that what is real (Peirce 1906). Abstractions that are of any significant use in science are pertain to the reality and are not fictional creations. One can add that contemporary meanings typically attributed to the notion of models as ideal and abstract entities tend to confuse abstraction, as the process of reasoning, for the property of those models. The real property is that the models, besides being idealisations in the sense of icons, are also generalisations, namely have the character of being symbols. Abstraction, on the other hand, concerns the logical process that is involved in the

---

[38] Cristalli & Pietarinen (2020) argue for the importance of hypostatic abstraction in the 19th century scientific practice of the hand and the eye.

formulation of models that representations of those representative characters of icons and symbols.

Gamma graphs evolved from Peirce's earlier and related considerations of how to distinguish—when such a distinction is called for—between two or more modes of being. The broken-cut notation nevertheless appears to be an innovation rather exclusively confined to the present lecture note. The only precedents of that notation are the few scrolls found in *The Logical Tracts*, but they have different meanings and echo entitative graphs and Peirce's earlier urge to distinguish two kinds of boundaries for the ovals. They are not modal operators. Peirce thought that more than two kinds of cuts may be needed in practice, but he also tells having found real use only for two, and these are the continuous and the broken cuts. If new and different modes of modalities are needed, those are better represented not by changes in the qualities of oval boundaries, which really is nothing but the boundary between the areas inside and outside, but by changes in the types of those areas. That suggests tinctures which he in 1903 is not yet quite prepared to present.

Even without the tinctures, which are to emerge in Peirce's writings two years later, it is not the case that the Gamma graphs endowed with the broken-cut notation would pertain only to representations of alethic modalities. The interpretation of the broken cut may be, and in fact predominantly was taken by Peirce to be, an epistemic one: the broken-cut-p means that an ignorant agent "would not know that p". That is, for all that the agent knows, it is the case that not-p. It is the epistemic possibility that underwrites interpretations of his systems of modal logic.

Furthermore, the remark that possibilities and necessities are "relative to the state of information" anticipates possible-worlds semantics. Such anticipations are investigated in Pietarinen (2006b); the subtle nature of the intended notation is revealed by noticing exactly how the broken-cut-p notation is to be drawn: "that in some assumed state of information which must be specified by some attachment to a hook of the cut, I do not know that it rains" (cf. R S-31: "there is a possible state of information in which the knower is not in a condition to know that the graph is true"; the necessity of p "asserts that there is no such possible state of information"). What follows these definitions is a presentation of the rule of necessitation. Here it also becomes clear that Peirce is treating possible worlds, or rather situations or "states of information", as objects of the model. Modal propositions are about facts that an agent is in a "state of information sufficient to know". A new kind of ligature then emerges, and together with it there will be found "some peculiar and interesting little rules". One such example comes close to what much later was discussed under the heading of the KK-thesis and its validity: that knowledge implies having means of knowing that knowledge, though it by no means implies a simple iteration of that knowledge. Peirce also argues, quite rightly, that if a proposition holds in any state of information from which another follows in terms of being specifically related to it, that proposition is necessary in that former state of information.

Another noteworthy revelation made in the present piece is that the study of Gamma, and especially that ultimate department of the Gamma part that deals with the meta-theory of graphs, is the most demanding of all the three compartments of EGs. The reason is, Peirce explains, that one has to first learn to think in the language of diagrams. Diagrams are not an alternative language, such as your L2 logic, into which you could safely translate every statement of another language, hoping to preserve the meanings and understand anything fully with such translations. Only after learning to think in the language of diagrams first can all meaningful notions of that language—which through abstraction would now become objects of thought proper—be put as objects of logical scrutiny using that very language of graphs.

The fledgling theory of graphs of graphs is indeed another novelty of the present lecture note. To be able to "reason in graphs about graphs" is an "indispensable department of the gamma graphs", which Peirce is thus compelled to explain to his audience. He briefly lists (and presents the list if he ever had time) the main Gamma expressions of Alpha and Beta graphs. An alternative draft (R S-31) further presents four examples of what the permissions of Alpha, and five more examples of what their conventions, would look like in this meta-logical system. Notably, some of them involve broken cuts taken from the modal Gamma graphs, in order to express necessities of permissions and possibilities of scribing, for example.

Peirce's notes on graphical meta-theory carry over to the fifth lecture, during which he appears to have presented the basics of his graphs-of-graphs idea to the audience for the first time (R 468). This latter presentation now included some Beta conventions and permissions expressed as meta-graphs. After that, he had to move on to the mathematical side of the story. Two extra sections have been appended to this fourth batch of drafts that concern graphs of graphs, despite the probable case that Peirce actually presented the idea for the first time during the lecture five.

Such, in summary, are the main novelties which Peirce wanted to share with the audience concerning the preferred methods for the logical analysis of meanings. There were no readings proposed for the fourth lecture, which is understandable as this hour was originally supposed to be spent on concluding the topic of logical diagrams.

Selection 38: The Doctrine of Multitude, Infinity and Continuity. (Multitude). Lowell Lecture V(a,b,c)

R 459, R 459(s) (Lecture V(a)). On the notebook cover label: "Lowell Lectures by C. S. Peirce. 1903. Lecture 3". Crossed out with a remark in Peirce's hand: "Wont do". **R 466** (Lecture V(b)). On the notebook cover label, in Peirce's hand: "?Useful for 3rd or 4th?" **R 458, R 458(s)** (Lecture V(c)). On the cover label of R 458, in Peirce's hand, "May be useful for 3rd and 4th".

Although Peirce seems to have initially planned to spend more than one hour to explain the nature of mathematical reasoning and his new doctrine of multitudes, the lack of time forced him to change his plans at least twice. As a consequence, the two extensive notes for the fifth lecture, R 459 and R 459(s), which make the first section of the present selection, and R 466, which makes its second section, did not find a slot in the tight schedule. The topic of multitudes, as indeed that department of Gamma that deals with the emerging theory of the graphs of graphs, is resumed in the next selection (R 469–R 471), which comprises the main material for the fifth lecture that Peirce eventually did deliver. R 458 or several of its digressions preserved in R 458(s) were unlikely to have been delivered in any length, either. The topic of multitudes, as indeed that department of Gamma that deals with the emerging theory of the graphs of graphs, are resumed in the next selection (R 469–R 471), and unlike the current texts they represent the main material for the fifth lecture that Peirce eventually did deliver.

The reading list for Lecture V, "The doctrine of multitude, infinity and continuity", consisted of the following household titles:

Cantor, Georg
   Beiträge zur Begründung der transfiniten Mengenlehre. 2. Artikel. (In Mathematische Annalen. Ban 49, pp. 207–246. Leipzig, 1897.)   ****E.5145.1.49**
   De la puissance des ensembles parfaits de points. (In Acta mathematica. [Vol.] 4, pp. 381–392. Stockholm, 1884.)   ****E.5090.50.4**
Dedekind, Richard
   Essays on the theory of numbers, 1. Continuity and irrational numbers. 2. The nature and meaning of numbers. Authorized translation by W. W. Beman. Chicago, 1901.   ****E.5129.101**
Peirce, Charles Sanders
   The logic of relatives. (In The Monist.
   Vol. 7, pp. 161–217. Chicago, 1896–97.)   Per.Room *3604.100.7
Russell, Bertrand Arthur William
   The principles of mathematics. Vol. 1. London, 1903.   ****E.5128.44**

Selection 39: The Doctrine of Multitude, Infinity and Continuity. (Multitude). Lowell Lecture V(d)

R 469, R 470, R 471. On page 0 of the notebook R 469 Peirce wrote: "Lowell Lectures 1903. Lecture 5. Vol. 1". On the notebook cover (R 470) it reads in Peirce's hand: "1903 Lowell Lectures. Lecture 5. Vol. 2".

In this final version of the fifth lecture, delivered on December 7, it finally becomes apparent how late in the game it is before Peirce manages to state anything at all on the subject of Gamma graphs. Right in the beginning of this fifth lecture, he sets out to brief the audience on what the concept of the graph-of-graphs is, which he was planning to be able to explain already in the second volume for Lecture IV at the very latest (R 467). Apparently, then, Peirce did not explain anything on his other kinds of Gamma graphs whatsoever: neither the modal graphs nor abstraction or potentials ever made it to the stage. Only one paragraph on the logic of potentials was printed in the *Syllabus* (Convention VII), while no information on the broken-cut notation, which is found in the alternative drafts of the *Syllabus* alongside potentials, was ever disseminated, even though the information in these texts suffices to mark an inception of contemporary modal logics.

The presentation of graphs-of-graphs was brief. Peirce laments that he had ran out of funds to print any explanation of it in the *Syllabus*, of which copies were distributed to the audience at the beginning of the previous lecture and apparently some more during the present evening. The draft of R 478 indeed continues right where the printed version ends, on the "eleven spots signifying parts of graphs", and is followed by some complex examples of graphs of graphs. No doubt this would be the point where the rest of the material could not have been printed, with the limited funds, time and technology available.

Yet it is right here at the beginning of the fifth lecture that Peirce desperately needed the audience to have acquired at least some recognition of the idea of these complicated diagrams, as he would now take them to explain the nature of pure mathematics better than the potentials mentioned in the printed *Syllabus* would do. So he announces a promise to send anyone who might be interested in the subject whatever it may be on these meta-graphs that he would be able to get printed in the future. Nothing will be published on this topic later on, however, and only one reference to the graphs of graphs idea is found in Peirce's subsequent writings years later. "The System of Existential Graphs applied to the Examination of Itself" is a two-page examination on a notebook from mid-February 1909 (R S-3). That attempt is too short and sketchy to constitute a proper study to be presented to anyone, but at least two new things stand out: Peirce proposes a graph type that represents the assertion that "something *justifies* some other thing", and he makes an attempt to continue with the idea of the "Logic of Time" that "involves more than one state of things", a topic which he had been working on in early 1909 (LoF 1). The next day, February 16, 1909, Peirce would embark on the development of three-valued (triadic) logics, first under the heading "Studies of Modal, Temporal, and Other Logical Forms which relate to Special Universes" [341r], followed by an additional couple of pages on related issues later in the month.

Apparently Peirce remained optimistic throughout the semester that he could get much more, and even all the remaining pages from his draft syllabus printed, perhaps with the help of donations from his audience, friends and colleagues. This did not happen, and the reasons why Peirce never really returned to the topic of the graphs of graphs are worth a brief contemplation. The decision not to publish Peirce's Lowell Lectures overall surely meant Peirce's ballooning distrust in the present state of the world and its intellectual poverty unready to receive treatises of considerable complexity and originality. But circumstances that led The Knickerbocker Press not to print a book on logic from him were largely accidental. The matter was decided by George H. Putnam himself (GHP to CSP, December 21, 1903, R L 78), at the time when James McKeen Cattell, Peirce's long-time friend and colleague from Johns Hopkins and its Metaphysical Club, who had been a loyal admirer and supporter of Peirce over the years, had just slightly earlier in that month resigned from the services of the editorship of Putnam's journal *Science*. As Putnam was unable to take "counsel with Professor Cattell", and despite having promised Peirce to arrange for "some other scientific advisor", the turmoils in the office following the disputes that largely concerned Cattell's own academic and professional affairs, left Putnam no other choice than to politely turn down Peirce's proposal. "We have, I am sorry to say", writes Putnam, "not been able to convince ourselves that we should be likely to secure for a book on so very special a subject matter a sufficiently extended sale to render the publication remunerative, or to place the publisher in a position to make a satisfactory return to the scholarly author" (GHP to CSP, December 21, 1903, R L 78).[39] The low sales figures that a book on logic was estimates to have as the official reason, no expert advice on the scientific value of Peirce's course was ever sought for, as Cattell had just made himself unavailable as Peirce's assured champion. As the year was nearing its end, Peirce's dream of getting the lectures printed waned, and so did any further endeavour to raise funds to print the large amount of material remaining in his vaults. The emerging idea of meta-graphs and their use to clarify issues in the foundations of mathematics suffered collateral damage.

---

39 There were enquiries on obtaining copies of Peirce's lectures, such as from Joseph Shippen, attorney-at-law, who wrote one such request to Peirce (JS to CSP, November 17, 1903, R L 406).

In this fifth lecture, Peirce mentions the important distinction between, on the one hand, the purely mathematical interpretation of graphs, which he presents at the end of the printed *Syllabus* (pp. 20–23), and on the other hand, the representational interpretation, which he had presented to the audience during the previous lectures. The latter begins with putting forth systems of conventions and then building the logic of graphs on those semantic and pragmatic notions of the significations of the basic ingredients of the graphical notation. The former, in contrast, has no concern on what the meanings of logical constants may be. One of the key points of the present lecture is that the theory of meta-graphs falls to the side of purely mathematical interpretations. Its graphs do not assert anything about graphs as representations. They treat the language as if it consisted merely of formal relations between its elements. In that sense, the theory of meta-graphs, just as the purely mathematical definition of EGs, need no appeal to the methodeutic of logic.

In these writings, Peirce records about 30 (non-modal) hypotheses that are given in the meta-language of graphs of graphs. R 511, included in the next selection, provides a long list of these hypotheses as expressed in natural language and not in the language of graphs. Peirce uses quotation marks in these hypotheses to denote object-language terms. Objects of the graphs are thus not types but tokens, that is, in the language of graphs of graphs, objects of graphs are graph-instances. He states that there are about "half a dozen" hypotheses that involve the broken-cut notation to denote necessities. Three examples of graphs relying on such hypotheses are given in R S-31 (plus two unannotated ones), two are found in R 468, and one more occurs at the end of the draft segment that pertains to the *Syllabus* and which is located in a folder containing some variant sheets ("Gamma Graphs 3.3.", R 509).

It may be right here, at this moment that goes well into Peirce's presentation of the mathematical versus representational interpretation of graphs, that he went on to show, or had arranged Lounsbury to project, the sheet that is entitled "Diagrams for Lecture 5" (R 468, appended to the previous selection). Whether Peirce also succeeded in presenting some examples of Gamma expressions of conventions and permissions of the Alpha and Beta part cannot be confirmed: the material of R S-31 is on cut pages and would be too sketchy for presentation, as indeed are the pages from the draft version of the *Syllabus*. The ones that are found in R 468 seem to be the most developed of such attempts.

Right after having rampaged through some meta-graphs, which might have been the only topic from the whole Gamma compartment that Peirce ever succeeded to cover, he needed to "hasten to the subject of numbers". This section, which comes from Vol. 1 of the lecture found in another notebook, as well as those parts in which he talks about collections, have been omitted from the text of the current selection (on these missing pieces, see Moore 2010, PoM). The lecture is resumed at the point in which Peirce begins to consider multitudes (cardinalities) of numbers and proposes an example of the kind of logical analysis that he will then carry out in the system of graphs.

This analysis, which we do not find in the antedating drafts (R 459, R 466), should be of considerable interest to historians and philosophers of mathematics and logic. Peirce's graphical analysis of definitions of number and cardinality should also be read in conjunction with his letters to mathematician Eliakim Hastings Moore (1862–1932), a pioneer in early model theory and meta-mathematics (R L 299). Peirce wrote his correspondence right after the lectures and many were left as unsent drafts. For one thing, we can find Peirce's refutation of logicism in this analysis. Logicism could hold truth only if all that graphs are about is how relations are to be formally defined. But such purely mathematical definition, which from time to time Peirce entertains for certain purposes of pure mathematics, is here superseded by semantical definitions and by systems of conventions. These latter provide the desired logical interpretation. For showing the definability of logical properties does not require relevant definitions to be impredicative. Contrary to what Dedekind thought, those interpretations that one is compelled to provide prohibit deriving mathematics from logic. A formal manipulation on graphs such as one that axiomatises the system of natural numbers "could reach every theorem of the mathematics of whole numbers". But when the matter is turned to collections and multitudes, such manipulation, or provability that concerns purely formal definitions, does not exhaust what the *conceptions* of collections and multitudes are. It is such conceptions that require logical analysis, including definitions that apply the principles of pragmatism. Peirce then proceeds to give a "practicable" definition of the conception of the multitude. As an example, and as far as integers are concerned, Peirce also suggests a proof, stated in the language of graphs, of the theorem according to which "there is no multitude intermediate between 3 and 2".

Following the definition of multitude, the topic of continuity which was proposed in the original announcement of the lectures is relegated to "the few minutes that remain". R 473 suggests that the attempt was cut short by the running of the clock, however: "I had no time, I very much regret to say, to speak of continuity, which is the principal mathematical conception and the most difficult in need of explanation while its logical importance is far greater than is everything else put together that I could bring into the first six lectures" (R 473, in the beginning of the seventh lecture on induction). The topic of continuity suffered the same destiny as it did in the supplementary Harvard lecture (R 316(a), LoF 1) earlier in the year, likewise omitted from presentation.

Selection 40: On the Simplest Branch of Mathematics, Dyadics

R 2–R 3, R 511–R 512. Not a lecture but partly related to Lecture V(d) and partly to the next selection concerning the *Syllabus*, the title of the present selection is taken from the longest, five-page segment of R 2; its variations are "On the Simplest Branch of Mathematics" (R 2, R 512) and "On Dyadics: the Simplest Possible Mathematics. First Memoir" (R 3, ms pages D1–D2; R 511, ms pages D3–D7).

This selection consists of segments concerning "Dyadics" written on the same Linen Ledger paper as for instance R S-31, R 508–R 512, R 539, R 540 and R 800. They were likely written during November and perhaps still being worked on in early December, near the preparations for the fourth and especially that of fifth lecture and the projected but unfulfilled completion of the *Syllabus*.

"Dyadics" was what Peirce took to comprise the simplest, two-valued logic, which would also be the logic of pure mathematics. His massive project of "Minute Logic", which consisted of some 2 500 pages of manuscripts many of which were published in NEM, extensively sought to explain that simplest system and its uses in investigating the nature of pure mathematics. The text of the present selection is related to Peirce's attempts that began in the fourth lecture and in the extension of the *Syllabus* pages by R 508 (B1–B5), which together with the manuscript page B6 on gamma graphs was (i) to provide a purely formal definition of the key notions of the theory of graphical logic and (ii) to constitute part of the copy-text for the printed version that replaced the copy-text in the pages 150–154 of the syllabus manuscript of R 478 on the "Rules of Transformation of Existential Graphs". The theory of dyadics was heavily relied on in the fifth lecture, which makes a reference to it as a set of "independent hypotheses" that the "theory of graphs of graphs rests upon", which he announces to have divided "into those which relate to physical possibilities and necessities and those which relate to permissions and prohibitions". Hypotheses related to these physical modalities are "about thirty in number", and they "are all expressible in alpha and beta graphs", while the class of hypotheses that relates to permissions and prohibitions "do not much exceed half a dozen". The latter require the broken-cut notation of the gamma graphs to be added to the graphs of graphs language in order for them to be expressed.

Peirce did not quite complete these lists, and his desires or attempts of actually doing so may have happened after the fifth lecture was over on December 7.[40] In the first of such attempts from R 3 and R 511, paginated as D1–D7, there

---

[40] These lists pertain only to the first of what was the planned series of four "Memoirs" on dyadics. The rest three dealt with an application of dyadics to (i) deductive logic and to the development of principles of logic, (ii) cardinal numbers (multitude), and (iii) continuity and topical geometry, were not written in this context. But see e.g. the roughly coeval pieces "Principles of

are 27 "hypotheses respecting physical possibilities and necessities": 14 for the Alpha part (Hypotheses 2–15) and 13 for the Beta part (Hypotheses 22–34). Hypotheses No. 1 is a fundamental hypothesis of the pure dyadics about the "sheet", the "graphist" and "graph-replicas" that is not counted among either these two categories at all. Six "hypotheses respecting permissions and prohibitions" remain in this first list for the Alpha part (Hypotheses 16–21), while those were not separately enlisted for the Beta part at all. In the other and a slightly more mature attempt from R 2 and R 512 (not paginated as Dn but as SM 1–SM 6, standing for "Simplest Mathematics"), "Hypotheses as to Definitions and as to Physical Necessities" are 16 (Hypotheses 1–16) and "Hypotheses respecting Permissions of Transformation" 6 in number for the Alpha part (Hypotheses 17–22), while there are 13 of the former type of hypotheses for the Beta part (Hypotheses 23–35). The list of hypotheses respecting permissions and prohibitions was not given and only the first number of the item in this list, number 36, was written down. As with the previous list, Peirce might have thought those to be generally redundant with what was given with respect to the Alpha part. In sum, in these lists we find 27 and 29 of those hypotheses that Peirce lectured to be "about thirty", and six of those that "do not much exceed half a dozen".

Peirce took the theory of the graphs of graphs, armed with these fundamental hypotheses of pure dyadics, to "illustrate the nature of Pure Mathematics still better than it is illustrated on pages 20 to 22 of the *Syllabus* [B1–B5 from R 508] distributed last Thursday [lecture four]". He might have wanted to include the list of hypotheses into the Syllabus in the last minute, and the pagination of the first of them as D1–D7 is an indication that that indeed could have well been the case, given that there had been the other and actually printed addition from R 508 on the *Syllabus* pages 20–22 which was paginated in the manuscript as B1–B5 (plus an added page of B6), and that between November 27 and 30 he had added an answer to the listener's question into the beginning of the lecture three, paginated

---

Logic" (R 800) on the themes of the second memoir, and "Considerations concerning the Doctrine of Multitude" (R 27), "Note on the Doctrine of Multitude" (R 30), "On the Theory of Collections and Multitude" (R 31), "Multitude" (R 24), "Topical Geometry" (R 137) and "On Synectics, otherwise called Topology or Topic" (R 139), "Topics. Chapter I. Singular Systems" (R 151) on the themes of the third and the fourth memoirs, among those preserved texts that are significantly related to the contents of the fifth Lowell Lecture on e.g. multitude as well as to the later parts of the *Syllabus* and its projected expansions. These studies are thus to be counted among the totality of contributions to the philosophy of logic and foundations of mathematics during Peirce's *annus mirabilis*. Other texts likely to have emanated in the vicinity of the 1903 Lowell Lectures include "An Apology for the Method of Infinitesimals" (R 238), and "On the Foundations of Mathematics" (the "Dragon-Head Logic", R 7–R 11, R 501; see Ma & Pietarinen 2019).

as A1–A8. (Any prospected addition of supplementary pages C*n* has not been detected among the Harvard's Houghton Peirce Papers, however.)

Peirce argues that the theory of logical graphs, when given a purely mathematical definition, is the ideal logical theory of dyadics. The extant beginnings of the first memoir seek to establish this by presenting a substantial glossary of key terms of EGs, here conceived as the logic of such simplest form of pure mathematics. The language of graphs is not the only possible means to work out such definitions, and in some related papers (e.g. R 5, "Dichotomic Mathematics") he writes long lists of similar hypotheses that nevertheless do not involve explicitly graphical but rather avail themselves of general *symbolic* notations, namely meanings of replicas whose general nature lies in their being represented as objects capable of embodiment of their meanings. These notations, despite being symbolic, are nevertheless seen the apply the graphical notions of the "blank", "sheet", "transformations", and so on. Peirce's list of hypotheses is seen to cover the two general fundamental permissive transformations, namely those that erasure from the graphs and those that insert to the graphs, and they begin with the "entitative development" of the idea of such proofs, much like what he had done in his germinal paper on logical graphs from 1896 (R 482; LoF 1).

Three features stand out in these previously unpublished lists of definitions collated from folders R 2, R 3, R 511 and R 512. First, Peirce's study aims at a pure mathematical definition, which is to say that those definitions do not concern interpretations of signs, that is, they do not consider what the significations of those terms, signs and notations are. For if they did, the system would be the one that performs logical analysis, not the one that would serve as the logic of the science of mathematics. These studies in question are thus intimately related to those "pure mathematical definitions" Peirce had presented earlier in *The Logical Tracts* and soon afterwards in the printed *Syllabus*. Peirce observes in the early part of his delivered fifth lecture that,

> *Pure* mathematics differs from mathematics in general in not admitting into its hypotheses any element that does affect their logical possibility or impossibility. Thus, the pure mathematics of graphs, as you see in those pages of the syllabus, says nothing at all about the logical interpretation of graphs but defines them exclusively by their logical relations to one another. So the pure mathematical presentation of graphs of graphs says nothing at all about the graphs considered being representations of graphs but merely defines the graphs representing the sheet of assertion, a cut, its area, or line of identity, and so forth, in terms of their logical relations to one another. (R 469)

Though the pure mathematical presentation of graphs of graphs is not an instrument for analysis of logical reasoning, the analytical power of the theory of graphs is illustrated in that presentation in terms of the complexity of those graphs (involving modalities) that present in logical precision what is involved in the analysis of proofs, here in terms of analytical presentation of permissive transformations in the language of the graphs of graphs:

> In particular the broken cut enters into everyone, and into some of them with curious complications. One is surprised to find how extremely complicated are the graphs that express some of these fundamentals of the nature of graphs; and this complication puts into a strong light two merits of this system of existential graphs. For on the one hand, it shows the extraordinary analytical power of the system that analyzes conditions which seemed on our first acquaintance with them to be very very simple but which the system of graphs forces us to see are in reality very complex. (R 469)

Peirce's explicit reference to the notion of the broken cut during the fifth lecture is interesting, since he presumably did not have time to introduce the modal logic of Gamma graphs in the previous lecture (nor was it included in the *Syllabus*). If Peirce jumped right into the applications of it in this proposed analysis the content of the permissive transformations, as presented in these complex modal formulation of them in the language of the theory of graphs of graphs, it is hard to see how he could have done that without losing even the most attentive of the audience members during what may in any case have been the most difficult of the eight lectures to follow.

Second, each of the terms to be defined is considered in the theory of pure dyadics to be part of the object-language vocabulary. Peirce carefully encloses all the terms in double quotes. The practice of thus keeping use and mention separate, which in the present selection might strike one as overly pedantic, is implicitly assumed in his subsequent writings, too, despite the fact that such explicit appeals to double quotes to denote mention will be much less overt in his subsequent writings.

Altogether 35 hypotheses of pure dyadics can be recovered from the surviving drafts. They pertain to the Gamma part of EGs now in the form in which it was developed for the fifth lecture. Indeed Gamma is mentioned in one footnote, and perhaps these lists were meant to continue with some further such analytic, Gamma-like representations of the Beta-permissible rules of transformation. It is also worthy of further consideration whether some ideas of provability, or hierarchies of truth, and paradoxes that would inevitably ensue, are fledgling in the hypotheses as presented in the surviving material. To the contemporary reader, Peirce's attempts may indeed resonate with some of the central concerns of modern logic, especially in the areas of discrete mathematics, mathematical logic, and proof analysis.

Third, there is a strictly notational consideration that might have further motivated Peirce to be driven to include these presentations of both the language of the graphs of graphs as well as the analysis of the theory of permissive transformation in the form of the pure dyadics in the supplementary parts of the lecture course. Since by early November it had been clear to Peirce that the printed version of the *Syllabus* could not include many graphs as illustrations (it ended up having only two graphs set with figure captions), Peirce might have thought this purely mathematical and linguistic account ending up distributed to the audience in the printed form in full, yet in an uncompromising form and length that would faithfully communicate all the desired fundamental hypotheses of the language of the Alpha, Beta and (what is here omitted) Gamma parts of the theory of graphs, notwithstanding the fact that they were in this context presented in the nomenclature of the "Pure Dyadics".

Evidence for Peirce having thought of this as a being a sensible strategy is found in terms of another proposed workaround of his, found in fragmentary form in the worksheets of R 510. Here Peirce briefly considered an alternative, non-graphical and linear notation—termed a 'line-feed' notation in Bellucci, Liu & Pietarinen (2020)—of Alpha and Beta graphs that could be better printed than the two-dimensional spreads with complex curves. As this notation would altogether dispense with ovals and lines, it would have been possible to be reproduced with the typesets and sorts commonly available at Peirce's time.

However, by the time these studies were performed and sketched on paper, probably well beyond mid-November, or even when the lectures were half-way through given that Peirce refers to them during his lecture five on December 7 that was prepared between December 3–7 (Lecture V(d); R 469–R 471), it was beginning to be all too late for Peirce to have such planned modifications and additions to be incorporated into the projected final and expanded copy of the *Syllabus* to be printed and distributed in time for the respective terms of the course and certainly before the course would be over. Left aside for the prospected post-lecture publication, perhaps those expansions could find home in one of those renewed opportunities to print his lecture notes along with the revised and completed text of his *Syllabus*.

Selection 41: A Syllabus of certain Topics of Logic

R 478, plus R 478(s), R 508, R 509. "Syllabus of a course of Lectures at the Lowell Institute beginning 1903 Nov. 23. On Some Topics of Logics. By Mr. C. S. Peirce".

The penultimate selection is from Peirce's long manuscript which he intended to become the official syllabus of the series. It begins with what is the fourth and last section of the draft on certain additional topics of logical graphs that Peirce would not cover in full in the lectures. The material for this chapter comes mostly from R 478 (manuscript pages 137–168 plus several variant leaves), with significant additions from folders R 508 and R 509.

The appendix, paginated in R 478 as "Syllabus 2–23" (and pages 9–11 with a *lapsus calami* of "Syllogism"), is written untypically in blue ink with headings in brown. It consists of Peirce's written answers to the topics (or questions or comments) that he may have received from an audience member during or after the third lecture. The person making the comments may have been, as discussed earlier in the survey of the third lecture, William James or one of his students or associates, the issues being related to James's own course of lectures from the previous year.

The transcription provided includes those parts of the manuscript that were printed and distributed in the beginning of lecture four and probably were still available during the next lecture. After the fifth session, Peirce collects some dozen remaining copies for his own use. At most one hundred, and perhaps even somewhat less copies were printed by the Lowell Institute overall. Sedgwick had indicated Peirce that 50–75 printed copies would suffice, asking Peirce in the same letter "*How many copies* of the syllabus will you want printed?" (WTS to CSP, October 30, 1903, R L 257). A few days later Sedgwick estimated that "one or two hundred would be sufficient" (November 3, WTS to CSP, R L 257). The cover sheet of the copy-text segment of R 478 that went to the Lowell Institute has an instruction "100 copies" penciled in the corner by Sedgwick when he forwarded this set of over 130 manuscript sheets to the printer. Peirce's incomplete and unsent letter draft intended to Sedgwick on November 28 contains a calculation in the margin: $75 + 13 = 88$ (R L 257). This could represent the actual number of copies that Peirce calculated to be needed, or was informed that is actually being printed; either way, there is no confirmation which: perhaps 75 was the amount to be distributed to the audience and 13 to be mailed to his friends and colleagues. This letter draft was written less than a week before the printing was completed.[41]

Be this as it may, the booklet, with its slim 23-page selection from 50 manuscript leaves that served as the copy-text,[42] reaches nowhere near the total of 228 manuscript sheets (the pagination of which goes up to 168, with a gap occurring between the pages 105 and 137 that can be bridged with the pages that are found in R 539), variants, drafts and worksheets included, that have been preserved in

---

[41] Another proximal Lowell Lecture sheet has another calculation in the margin "$100-12 = 88$".
[42] Early bibliographies of Peirce mention the printed *Syllabus* to be "a four-page brochure" (CLL, p. 312). This may have been confused with the related *The Nomenclature and Division of Dyadic Relations* (NDDR, another printed pamphlet located in the Harvard's Houghton Peirce Papers, R 1600, R 539, pp. 2–13; CP 3.571–608; Peirce 1903), also printed at the same time with the *Syllabus* and with equal typesetting, and is eight printed pages in length.

R 478. Peirce had sent the majority of the text to Sedgwick by the end of October, and although whether it contained everything from the main segment of R 478 (up to page 168) cannot be confirmed, the printed pages and the copy-text of the relevant leaves from R 478 do have an exact match, save for some inessential typos. In addition, there are also at least 123 pages in other manuscript folders strictly related to the *Syllabus* text or to one of its additional pages, variants and planned addenda (R 509–R 511, R 538–R 542, R 800), and at least R 539 was likely to have gone to Sedgwick together with R 478 in late October. As far as Chapter IV, entitled "Conventions and Rules of Existential Graphs" is concerned (the name comes from Peirce's own table of contents in the *Syllabus* draft), about half of the material that Peirce drafted on EGs made it to the printed version, while nearly half of the material in the pamphlet concerns its fourth section on graphs.

Peirce made no attempt to include Chapter III, "Some leading conceptions of logic" ("Sundry Logical Conceptions", reprinted in part in EP 2, pp. 267–288) in the printed version, as the content of that part was now being overridden by the texts R 539 and R 540 that studied dyadic and triadic relations in depth. The first and the second chapters of R 478, "An Outline Classification of the Sciences" and "The Ethics of Terminology" have been included in full (EP 2, pp. 258–266). EP 2 also included "Nomenclature and Division of Triadic Relations, as Far as They Are Determined" (pp. 289–300, R 540), termed as the "fifth section of 1903 Syllabus", but there is no fifth or later sections in the surviving texts for the syllabus. Peirce repaginated NDDR (R 539), an outgrowth of his many related studies and writings on dyadic relations inspired by Alfred B. Kempe's theory of mathematical forms (see e.g., R 538, R 713) by manuscript pages Syll. 106–134, in order to fill the gap of ms pp. 106–136 in the main sequence of the syllabus draft R 478; the pagination of R 540 on triadic relations then follows that of R 539, overlapping with the fourth section of the *Syllabus* on EGs.[43] Perhaps Peirce planned to

---

[43] This obviously resulted in some discrepancies. The surviving main segment of R 540 was paginated by Peirce from ms p. 134 to p. 155, with the pagination of the fourth section of the syllabus R 478 beginning at ms p. 137. If Peirce ultimately needed to exclude the treatment of triadic relations (R 540) from whatever final version of the syllabus he might have entertained (he probably did not want to exclude it, since R 540 contains instructions for the printer in the margins, such as "The lightly printed designations are superfluous", R 540, ms p. 141), but to retain his study on dyadic relations, then the gap of ms pages 134 and 136 remains between the segments of R 539 and R 478: (i) the ms page 134 is missing from R 439 (while 134 is the page number where R 540 on triadic relations begins), (ii) the ms page 133 may not be the last page of what presumably is the last section of R 439 on modal dyadic relations, (iii) the ms page 135 definitely is not the last page of whatever variant it may represent (the full page ends with "All, however, whether"), and (iv) what is preserved as page 135 is a discontinuous and cancelled variant leaf possibly from another and discrete variant on dyadic relations, while there is no evidence on what the preceding

expand the third section of the syllabus on with the treatise on triadic relations, too, as its draft R 540 has an added pagination in lead pencil that continues that of the treatise on dyadic relations, up to page 155. This would mean that text on triadic relations would overwrite most of the section four on EGs. After all, Peirce remarks that "In this Syllabus, only Speculative Grammar will be touched upon" (R 478, ms p. 42). Perhaps Peirce planned, but did not have the time required, to work on yet another expansion, this time concerning the fourth section on EGs, to match the new pagination of the preceding section. If he planned a rewrite on the *Syllabus* EGs, that could have been renumbered from 156 to continue as a new fourth or fifth section, or it could have preceded the two studies on relations, replacing the third section on speculative grammar from its manuscript page 43 onwards. But then Peirce would have to renumber, once again, the two studies that would begin at manuscript page 106. It is also of interest that inscribed at the end of R 540, ms page 155, there is an added note: "begin Syll. 44", likely in Peirce's hand. This means either that the intention was to preserve much of the speculative grammar of "Sundry Logical Conceptions", with its extensive historical and other expansive accounts, in the full final *Syllabus* text, and to have that long text to follow the exposition of signs in NDTR. Or the note could be a reference to Peirce's planned rewrite of EGs that would precede R 539 and R 540. In either case, the reference to page 44 is one page off from R 478: The section on "Speculative Grammar" of the preserved *Syllabus* copy begins at manuscript page 43. On the other hand, that page is crossed out both on its the title, on the page identifier, and on the page's content. Likewise crossed out is the page identifier of Syllabus 44, indicating that Peirce might have wanted to replace these two pages with other

---

page 134 might have contained. The remaining one or two lost pages of R 539 that would glue the treatise of dyadic relations to Section IV of the syllabus on EGs are thus presumed to be lost. The printed eight-page leaflet *The Nomenclature and Division of Dyadic Relations* (NDDR, Peirce 1903) had used as the copy-text the manuscript pages of R 439 which Peirce had repaginated as 106–117. Omitted were the sections "Third Mode System of Divisions", "Fourth Mode System of Divisions", as well as the last section, "Note on the Nomenclature and Divisions of Modal Dyadic Relations". Especially the latter, the study of the nature of modal dyadic relations, comes close to one of the principal aims of the Lowell Lectures, namely to develop logical tools to analyse the character of the relations between characters and laws, such as qualities and relations of individuals, relations of characters and relations of concepts, and those between symbols and concepts (see CP 3.606 for its publication). In the manuscript original, this section on modal dyadic relations is the only one part in R 539 that has been crossed out, indicating that Peirce might have aimed at getting the study printed until that section. Ultimately the funds were sufficient only to rach Figure 2, covering the second mode of divisions in full but leaving 14 large manuscript sheets unprocessed.

material or with a rewrite of speculative grammar, after that being able to resume with whatever was to follow R 540 at manuscript page 44. The addition of the note "begin Syll. 44" and the cancellation of the pages 43–44 in R 478 are certainly not without interest, as the latter is the only otherwise unexplained, non-trivial cancellation in the main segment of ms pp. 2–105. [44] Overriding the opening pages of the subsection on speculative grammar in R 478 with new material would at this point be inevitable, however, as the original and all of its alternative draft leaves and variants have signs divided into two trichotomies, whereas in R 540 and in its draft versions and variant sheets the three trichotomies are firmly in place.[45]

One should also take a close notice of R 800, which is an earlier draft of R 540, as well as R 792 ("On the Logical Nature of the Proposition"), which is, in turn, an earlier draft of R 800. Peirce might have wanted to have at least R 800 published as part of the *Syllabus*, too, as it bears some annotations that make most sense as preparations and editorial instructions for further processing of the text. Moreover, those penciled emendations are apparently not in Peirce's hand, and rather resemble that of Sedgwick's. Maybe Peirce worked on that draft in the Lowell Institute's office immediately after Peirce's arrival in Boston and his first lecture there on November 23, but soon decided to work out a new version that we find preserved in R 540, the latter becoming the best versions for potential publication in printed form in his second edit aiming at getting the final version of the *Syllabus* copy-text properly arranged. Nevertheless, R 540 was slated to become so important in its content, and to supersede much of what Peirce had to say on speculative grammar in the third section of the first version of the *Syllabus* copy, that only the lack of money would dictate its eventual omission from the final printout.

There is also an earlier version of the table of contents in R 478, which shows that Peirce did plan the *Syllabus* to accompany all eight lectures. In addition, the planned section five of the draft table of contents, entitled "The Sketch of Geometry", does not have a corresponding lecture or a lecture plan. No evidence exists that Peirce went on writing the text of the syllabus beyond the material on EGs and the section four; headings from sections 5 to 8 in the earlier draft table of contents were apparently not worked on separately, and what the *Syllabus* had to say on induction and abduction were confined to their exposition at the end of its section 3, "Sundry Logical Conceptions".

---

[44] The alternative variant segment that exists in R 478 replaces more than the two pages of 43 and 44, namely pages 43–48.

[45] Peirce apparently first tried to salvage the original page 44 by cancelling the sentence "Representamens are divided by two trichotomies", and adding some marginal comments and a footnote. Those penciled emendations have effectively been erased from the original paper sheet, however.

Among notable and regrettable omissions from the printed version were (i) the section on "archegetic rules of transformation", (ii) the presentation of such archegetic codes for Alpha and Beta graphs, (iii) modifications of those rules to suit the purposes of Gamma graphs, (iv) a section entitled "Remark on the gamma rims", (v) the list of rules that can be deduced from the archegetic rules, and last but not least, (vi) the presentation of the Gamma part on graphs of graphs.

The present selection seeks to redeem such omissions. The reader's attention is drawn, first, to "archegetic codes", and especially to Peirce's attempts to modify rules so that such a code be applicable to modal and higher-order logics. The archegetic code is a set of rules in which none of the rules is deducible from others, namely that the rules are independent, admissible rules. But there is also the proposal that the set of rules of transformation be "perfect". Peirce had here a property in mind not far removed from that of semantical completeness—after all, his system of rules for Alpha and Beta were complete, and the set of rules build directly upon his suggestions can be shown to be complete for many systems of modal logics as well. Peirce seems to have had a growing awareness that the behaviour of intensional systems involving modalities, possibilities and potentialities is quite unlike what is to be expected from the behaviour of the extensional parts of the theory. But it must be taken as a pertinent observation that "for the broken cut" "perfect rules" may be given. Indeed broken-cut modal logics that dispense with lines of identity can be completely axiomatised.

The question that occupies him is precisely how the basic rules, the irreversible rules of erasure/insertion and the reversible rules of iteration/deiteration, apply at the presence of the broken cuts. In one of the draft sheets on Convention VIII, broken cut is the denial of the logical necessity of its interior, that is, it denotes the "possibly-not", and he takes the irreversible rules to apply to the broken cut just as if such cuts were the ordinary, continuous cuts. He then states that these irreversible rules of erasure and insertion apply "to the broken cut", and explains this so that evenly-enclosed full cuts may become broken while oddly-enclosed broken cuts may be mended into continuous cuts.

Peirce then proceeds to state in the next paragraph that the reversible "Rule of Iteration and Deiteration does not apply to the broken cut", and that "The Rule of Immaterials [the double cut rule] and the Pseudograph practically does not apply to broken cuts". The precise interpretation of these statements is all-important. What does the "does not apply" mean here? It is left ambiguous as Peirce gives no further explanation: it might mean that no iteration/deiteration is permitted to cross broken cuts, but it might also mean that no graph containing broken cuts, that is, no modal assertion, is permitted to be iterated/deiterated across cuts. We get very different systems of modal logic depending on how we interpret the permission to iterate/deiterate in the context of the broken-cut notation. Systematic variations on restrictions such as these may result in different systems of modal logic, as detailed in the introduction.

We then find an incomplete and somewhat frustrated attempt by Peirce to modify the rules so as to state something on the proof-theoretic behaviour of his second-order logic of potentials. He proposes "a remarkable rule that has no parallel in the Beta graphs" and which "has not been fully formulated". Indeed it cannot yield a perfect system of rules, given that second-order logic is semantically incomplete.

The enigmatic paragraph "Remark on the Gamma Rims" (R 478, ms pp. 163–165) is a criticism of Schröder, and an early though somewhat remote recognition of the difference between standard and non-standard interpretations of second-order logic. Only the Convention IX, paragraphs 1 and 2, which appear earlier than the "Remark", were included in the printed *Syllabus* on Gamma rims. The first sentence of the "Remark" ("The writer knows no way of distinctly formulating the whole transformational value of the three rims"), comes with the note in the margin "This sentence", penciled not in Peirce's but in a later editor's hand. In the full paragraph, Peirce takes Schröder to be an advocate of potentials that quantify over the "whole universe of logical possibility". This made Peirce, among other things, to conclude that his dyadic algebra of logic which had been "Schröder's pet", is "faulty from every point of view". The following distinction between expressing something to be "true of the collection of all men" and something being "one of the possible collections of men" was not, Peirce presumes, something that his own algebra would be capable of drawing. Thus new logics and new signs and notations are needed, which is the task for the Gamma graphs and quite rightly observed at the end of this paragraph to be "a labor for generations of analysts, not for one" (R 478, ms p. 165).[46]

The section on rules of transformation demonstrable from the archegetic rules was likewise not included in the printed *Syllabus*. It is a variation on those standard exercises of deriving a number of theorems which Peirce had presented in his papers on EGs since 1897 (LoF 1). Indeed Peirce had revisited, on June 9, 1903, the rules he had listed in the *Logic Notebook* on June 18, 1898 (119v), adding there

---

[46] The last sentences found at the end of the "Remark on Gamma rims" were quoted also in Roberts (1973, p. 98). Roberts (1973, pp. 75–85) is the only exposition to date that goes at some length to explain Peirce's uses of the gamma rims (dotted enclosures) in their relation to abstraction, *entia rationis*, and the formation and identification of collections ("represented by a wavy line"). In alternative versions of the principles of interpretation recapitulated in *Logical Tracts No. 2*, R 492, items 8 and 9 concern the interpretations of dotted curves, while Figs. 57 and 58 illustrate a couple of proposed uses of enclosures resulting from their application.

a note on Theorem XXVI (LoF 1) which is precisely that of Rule XIV as presented in the list of rules of transformation demonstrable from the archegetic rules.

The final section omitted from the printed version concerns that part of EGs which moves from the "special signs" of potentials to other "special signs", which Peirce now towards the end of the *Syllabus* draft recognises as "adjuncts" of the former, namely "signs of graphs" that signify parts of graphs. It is right here that the idea of the graphs of graphs sees the light of the day. This section may be taken to replace the earlier section on Gamma graphs and Conventions VII–IX which made it to the printed version. That there are no lines in these spot-symbols in the printed version (they exist in alternative manuscript pages) was simply because of technical complications with the printer.

Peirce and Sedgwick agreed that the easiest, fastest and cheapest method of printing the abundance of copy sheets that Peirce has produced by the end of October should be found. Only two examples of graphs were included in the printed brochure, and the draft copy R 478 indeed contains no more as it was readily economised for the printing purposes, without much examples of graphs whatsoever. However, both the surviving manuscript as well as the printed version enumerate these graphs as Figs. 10 and 11, but the preceding figures are nowhere to be seen among the manuscript in R 478 that went to Sedgwick. The original figures captioned as 10 and 11 have been cut out and replaced with rectangular-shaped graphs, a standard procedure to prepare them for printing—yet the numbering of these figures was not changed nor were they corrected later on in Peirce's own offprints. There are no reasonable indications in the manuscript to facilitate any guessed on what Figures 1–9 could have been. These missing figures may add to the suspicion that some more pages, or even a new version of the fourth section, or perhaps some fresh attempts at the syllabus altogether, was somehow in progress at some point. However, there is no evidence that Peirce ever wrote, or even needed or planned to write, a new version of the fourth section on graphs. The matter is resolved by the additional material supplied by the interpolated pages from R 539 on the divisions of dyadic relations that was to immediately precede Section 4 of the *Syllabus* on EGs. Indeed the manuscript page 113 of R 539, "Nomenclature and Divisions of Dyadic Relations" (NDDR, on page 6 of the corresponding printed leaflet of Peirce 1903) begin the running caption numbers with Figure 1, which is a table on "perlations" of various kinds in its "first system of divisions". This is followed by Figure 2 on "suilations" and "ambilations" in its "second system of divisions" on the manuscript page 116 (Peirce 1903, p. 8), a table of ordered pairs of individuals in its "third system of divisions" as Figure 3 on the manuscript page 119 (with instructions to the printer added in the margin; not printed). An example of a transitive relation as a matrix of Figure 4 appears on the manuscript page 121, and two further matrices of relations as Figures 5 and 6 on page 122. Last, Figures 7, 8 and 9 are "all regular two-to-two correspondences" (R 539, ms p. 130) on pages 131–132.⁴⁷ None of Figures 3–9 were printed in the leaflets of Peirce (1903). Moreover, the copy-text of the nomenclature and divisions of triadic relations autograph study (R 540, R 542) did not contain any figures with running caption numbers.⁴⁸ Thus Peirce had the plan firmly in place to include the sections with those preceding Figures 1–9 to the printed syllabus, up to the point when it became apparent that current funds would not suffice to have the separate booklet appear in an equal number of 100 copies. Since Peirce

---

47 All of these manuscript paginations on the leaves of R 539 represent Peirce's final page numbering and have been corrected on each page at least twice, in order to fill the gap of manuscript pages 106–136 between Sections 3 and 4 of the draft of R 478.

48 According to Max H. Fisch's files, on July 19, 1904, a week after Peirce had received an invitation from psychologist Hugo Münsterberg (1863–1916) to present one or two short papers at the Universal Exposition, St. Louis (Louisiana Purchase Exposition) in its International Congress of Arts and Science that was held in September, Peirce proposed that he could present two papers in those sessions on "specialistic contributions" in logic and methodology, papers that Münsterberg instructed to be of 10 minutes each (HM to CSP, July 12, 1904; R L 308). The first of Peirce's papers was for the section on logic, "Classification and nomenclature for triadic relations" (and according to Fisch files he would be sending Münsterberg the section on "Nomenclature and Division of Triadic Relations, as far as they are determined"). The second paper was for the section methodology, entitled "Pragmatism as the Methodeutic of Metaphysics (Outline of the proof of it. Definition. General character of its tendencies. Precautions to be observed in its employment)". According to the notes on the copy of R 540 at the Peirce Edition Project archives derived from Fisch's notes, Peirce would here send Münsterberg parts of R 478, namely ISP pp. 00141–00162, that is, the unprinted alternative sequence of ms pages 2–23 appended to Selection 41 (the first page has not been preserved). This preambulatory section was written in blue ink, and it begins with the definition of philosophy and the classification of sciences, proceeding to a long commentary on one of James's lectures entitled "'Pragmatism' as our Method". These pages, as noted, represent Peirce's replies to James's 1902 syllabus themes, which Peirce could well have desired, still after 1903, to share with the Congress audience as a topical and concise 10-minute paper on methodology. Perhaps he thought that occasion to make up of the time lost during the lectures where he could not afford presenting his commentary on James's pragmatism, and of the unsuccessful effort of publishing the full text of his own syllabus material. And perhaps at that point in July 1904 Peirce had already started to think about the first draft of the "Basis of Pragmatism" series that he would begin writing sometime later in 1904 (R 280; LoF 3). Be this as it may, his proposed submissions to the Congress were not accepted, because Peirce had informed the organisers that he could not attend the conference in person ("I cannot afford to go to St. Louis, but I shall be delighted to respond to your kind invitation by sending two papers on the following subjects [...] Please say on which date copy must be in"; Max H. Fisch Files, quoting CSP to HM, July 19, 1904, a letter deposited at Boston Public Library). This led Münsterberg to inform Peirce that "all papers not presented by the authors themselves" would have to be excluded from the programme of the Congress, programme that consisted of nearly 500 presentations altogether (HM to CSP, August 6, 1904; R L 308).

nonetheless managed to solicit some modest number of printouts of the eight-page booklet of which the first two sections and Figures 1 and 2 of R 539 serve as the copy-text, he did not find it necessary to correct the caption numbers of Figures 10 and 11 in the copy-text or in those offprints of the *Syllabus* that were mailed to his colleagues and friends or remained in Peirce's possession. That the captions remained unchanged also indicates that the addition of the new section on triadic relations (R 541) to the printed version of the *Syllabus* was an unrealised afterthought that occurred to Peirce only in November, when the copy-text of R 478 had already been sent to the Lowell Institute and was soon to be forwarded to the printer. At this point the two figures from the copy-text may already have been typeset and numbered, and the manuscript pages 134 to 136 removed from the preceding section on dyadic relations.

Peirce sent a letter to Sedgwick in early November containing instructions on selection, organisation and printing of the *Syllabus*. The letter has not been preserved. It was received by his secretary Miss Esterbrook and was acknowledged to Peirce by Sedgwick on November 17, to whom it was forwarded from Boston as Sedgwick himself was in Chicago on a business trip that time. The curator assured Peirce that Esterbrook "acted according to your instructions in regards to the printing matter" (WTS to CSP, November 17, R L 257). These instructions probably were about the selection of the texts into the printed pamphlet from R 478. At some point these instructions also had to include the inclusion of the text of R 508 (B1–B5) to be printed in it instead of the "Archegetic Rules" of R 478, and so R 508 was sent earlier or had to accompany one of those instructions. This November 17 letter suggests that Peirce reached an agreement with the Lowell Institute on delaying the printing until after Peirce had arrived in Boston, and to have the *Syllabus* ready for distribution after "the first few lectures" were over. This bought Peirce some more time so that he could continue reworking on the final *Syllabus* content and organisation until at least the beginning of the lectures on November 23. Maybe he brought his "Nomenclature and Division" drafts and the allied planned additions and replacements to the *Syllabus* with him (R 539, R 540, R 508), even including that of R 800, which is a pre-draft of R 540,[49] although it is more likely that he had composed and worked on those drafts when the lectures had already begun, perhaps in Sedgwick's office and in cooperation with him, during the last week of November.[50]

---

[49] Some editorial pencil marks and corrections on R 800 are by hand that resembles that of Sedgwick's more than Peirce's. These additional segments to the *Syllabus* draft that Peirce would produce during November are all written on the same grid (regular graphing) paper type (linen ledger of $8 \times 10\,1/2$), which he might have acquired only when he had arrived in Boston and Cambridge.

The typography of the printed additional pamphlet of the "Nomenclature and Divisions of Dyadic Relations" (NDDR, from R 539) is identical to the printed *Syllabus*. Peirce probably had a few bucks left from the reserved $50 to ask Alfred Mudge to print that study as well, apparently in very small copies. As the initial copy-text contains Figures 1–9 to precede Figures 10–11 of the *Syllabus*, which remained not renumbered, Peirce might have hoped that NDDR could be include in the printed *Syllabus* version. But as the printed version reached only Figures 1 and 2 of the manuscript, Peirce's money gave out there too. Indeed he inserted "Here the fund for printing gave out" at the end of the second copy of the pamphlet (Box 13, R 1600). A few more bucks more might have helped also NDTR (R 540) to reach a printed form, and had both NDDR and NDTR made it to the printed *Syllabus*, it would have been a much more adequate and topical version of much improved use in supplementing the lectures.

The same missing letter from mid-November was also likely to have included Peirce's proposed reading list for the lectures—the list that Sedgwick had urged to Peirce is needed by November 14—as it was acknowledged in the same reply that "list of references is being got ready by the Public Library People" (WTS to CSP, November 17, R L 257). Furthermore, that missing letter may have contained the preface of the *Syllabus*, which was dated November 1, although Peirce could have well written the preface earlier, including it post-dated in the original submission in late October.

There is one more surprise to be excavated from the assorted and supplementary pages of the draft *Syllabus*, thus attesting the value of each and every slip of paper preserved in the Harvard's Houghton Peirce Papers, including those seemingly been abandoned or appearing as uninformative duplicates. On one of such pages (R 478, ms p. 101) within the section entitled "Sundry Logical Conceptions" (a section from which Peirce did not select any material for inclusion in the printed pamphlet, and written in October after R 462), Peirce capitalises on the connection that abduction has with likeness. The text breaks off but is immediately followed by these two graphs (here as they appear in Peirce's hand):

Fig. 1: Peirce's 'abductive graphs' appearing in the *Syllabus* draft (R 478).

---

50 Sedgwick is out of office and out of town starting from Wednesday, December 2 (WTS to CSP, telephone conversation, November 30; WTS to CSP, November 30, R L 257).

These graphs are not the standard Beta or Gamma graphs. The spot *a* is attached to one line in the graph above and, as it appears here, to two lines in the graph below. This cannot happen in standard Beta graphs, because each spot has a fixed arity, the number of "hooks" to which lines can be attached. In the second place, the line attached to the right of the spot *a* is not a standard line of identity, as it shows a peculiar "toothbrush" shape near its innermost extremity. These graphs occur nowhere else in Peirce's corpus. However, they may represent Peirce's unique attempt to begin sketching a graphical logic of abduction.

Indeed another, later segment of the same section "Sundry Logical Conceptions" contains a full page (R 478, p. 101) that explains abduction in the followings terms:

> This synthesis suggesting a new conception or hypothesis, [p. 101] is the Abduction. It is recognized that the phenomena are *like*, i.e. constitute an Icon of, a replica of, a general conception, or Symbol. This is not accepted as shown to be *true*, not even *Probable* in the technical sense,—i.e. not probable in such a sense that underwriters could safely make it the basis of business, however multitudinous the cases might be;—but it is shown to be *Likely*, in the sense of being some sort of approach to the truth, in an indefinite sense. The conclusion is drawn in the Interrogative Mood (there is such a mood in Speculative Grammar, whether it occur in any human language or not). This conclusion, which is the Interpretant of the Abduction, represents the Abduction to be a Symbol,—to convey a general conception of the truth,—but not to *assert* it in any measure. The Interpretant represents the Suadisign as a Symbolical Sumisign.
>
> Abduction having performed its work, it is now [end, the manuscript sequence breaks off here]

Peirce is talking about abduction, and the two graphs are likely to relate to what is going on in the passage. There is also an alternative version of this passage in which Peirce mentions two further points. First, he recognises that abduction has typically been identified not as a separate class of reasoning and has commonly been referred to as generalisation. But the two are, he says, "merely varieties of one class of symbols" (R 478, p. 102). Second, the abduced proposition, under the generalised interrogative mood, is "concluded to be a good question to ask" (R 478, p. 101). These points reveal that in the *Syllabus*, which was written in October 1903, Peirce is already moving away from what in the later literature had been thought be the definite or canonical formulation of the general abductive schema, along the lines of Peirce's Harvard Lectures from spring 1903.

Peirce nevertheless does not explain the meaning of his two doodles in any way and he might have simply forgotten them, failing to recognise the potential importance that a graphical method for abduction could have in completing his theory and logic of science. The sketches themselves do not provide any explanations of their meaning, either. They could, however, be interpreted as sole examples of logical graphs that Peirce ever proposed for abductive reasoning. (This interpretation is based on collateral evidence gathered from R 478 and from a number of his coeval writings documented in detail in Bellucci & Pietarinen 2020a and Pietarinen 2019a).

What was the ultimate fate of the *Syllabus*? What happened during its preparation and plans for publication? The pre-lecture plan took shape as follows. Sedgwick, had received the manuscript for the manuscript from Peirce on October 30. At that time and already for a couple of weeks Peirce had possessed *The Logical Tracts* as his trusted companion for the preparation of the lectures. Both treatises run well over 150 manuscript pages and could claim the title of a *magnum opus* prescribed by Sedgwick. As far as EGs are concerned, the *Tracts* is a positively more thorough treatise of them. R 478, on the other hand, is a much condensed version with long promissory sections on speculative grammar and other classificatory schemes. Together with what is found in the lectures, R 478 nevertheless is the definite presentation of the Gamma part, which is the portion conspicuously lacking from the *Tracts*. Did Peirce initially desire to print *The Logical Tracts* as the syllabus of the lectures? Did he even submit it first to the Lowell Institute?

There is no evidence that the *Tracts* was sent for anyone's inspection. Peirce was back at work on the main four sections of R 478, and it was those sections that he at first submitted to serve as the initial copy-text for the printed syllabus. Indeed Sedgwick returns Peirce's "copy returned by Mudge" to his home in Milford (WTS to CSP, January 1, 1904, R L 257). This is the last preserved communication in the exchange between Peirce and his former student. One should assume, rather safely, that it was the main matter of R 478 (ms pages 1–105 and 137–168), perhaps together with R 508 and possibly R 539 as well, that Peirce received back from the Institute. Given that the text of the printed pamphlet exactly matches those copy-text pages that have been preserved in R 478 (save for a could of typos and printer's errors), the material in that folder represents the bulk of the copy version of the syllabus that Peirce managed to produce for the print.

Since the printing of the abundance of graphs in the style of R 492 was clearly not an option, Peirce was led to write the text of R 478, and rather hastily at that during the busy month of October, from which the selection worth of $50 was made after November 1, and perhaps as late as soon after Peirce had arrived in Boston on November 23. The selection itself had to be made after the majority of the intended copy-texts were sent to the Lowell Institute. Soon the lectures would be well underway, and the shortage of time made it impossible for Peirce to receive the proofs from the printer, Alfred Mudge & Son, before distribution to the audience. A couple of corrections of printer's errors and some marginal notes in Peirce's hand in the surviving copies of the booklet derive from later periods.

Peirce was eager to mail copies of the pamphlet that he would soon receive fresh from the printer to his colleagues and friends. On November 5 Peirce tells Welby about his plans to "be able to get something of importance printed about logic",[51] which he promises to send her when ready. Welby is expecting the material in her November 18 reply which Peirce receives on December 1.[52] Peirce tells Welby of his plan to get "a part of what I said at my lecture last night on the subject [on three categories] type-written and send that [to you]".[53] Part of the delivery of this third lecture, originally entitled "The Three Universal Categories and their Utility" and later renamed "General Explanations. Phenomenology and Speculative Grammar" thus concerned the categories, although in large parts it appears to have been a continuation of the exposition of the Alpha part.

On the same day, Peirce receives a postcard from Welby and writes another letter, wishing Welby to receive some suggestions from the *Syllabus* that he is now "printing".[54] Lecture IV is upcoming in two days, and Peirce has not yet received the item from the printer. He will mail one copy of the pamphlet to Welby on December 4, the next day after the lecture: "I enclose you a piece of the Syllabus, of which I wrote to you. There will be a good deal more of it, if I can raise the money to pay the printer. It has been written hurriedly at different times, and the bits sent to the printer without retaining any copy or receiving any proof".[55] Peirce had no money to pay the printer for any more pages, and the total of 23 printed pages is all that this project amounted to. Welby would enquire after them; Peirce's reply on April 10, 1904 explains that "the reason I did not send more of my syllabus was that after a few very dry pages the money suddenly gave out, quite unexpectedly to me, and I did not think the rest worth sending".[56] Nearly five years later, Welby

---

51 CSP to VW, November 5, 1903, Welby Fonds.
52 Welby also acknowledges Peirce's kind words in his review of her book *What is Meaning?* that had just appeared in October issue of *The Monist* alongside with Peirce's disparaging remarks on Russell's *The Principles of Mathematics*. Welby had read Russell's "amazing" book six times, while Peirce's intimation of it in the published note as "pretentious and pedantic" was grounded on his "slight examination" of it. Russell was, as F. C. S. Schiller reports to Welby, "hugely annoyed" after having read Peirce's review from *The Nation*; Schiller himself was "very glad" that Welby had received such an acknowledgment (FCSS to VW, November 26, 1903, Welby Fonds).
53 CSP to VW, December 1, 1903, Welby Fonds. On this same day Peirce reports to Juliette the previous night having been "very bad" for him and that he has "been miserably shaky all day ...working just as hard as you ever saw me" (CSP to JP, December 1, 1903).
54 CSP to VW, December 1, 1903, Welby Fonds.
55 CSP to VW, December 1, 1903, typescript, Welby Fonds. Original of the letter is missing, with Welby's note, "Here there are two letters missing—One of which I have a fragment and the other a copy of my answer".
56 CSP to VW, April 10, 1904, Welby Fonds. By "not sending more" Peirce probably meant the copies of 8-page NDDR leaflet that he had just received in some small number from the printer

will receive another copy of the *Syllabus* with Peirce's January 31, 1909 letter, as her first copy was by then brimming with hand-written notes and marginalia.

After the fifth lecture, which Peirce planned to be on the doctrine of multitude and which he had told Welby on December 1 to be the topic he is currently having all his focus on, Peirce has some dozen copies at hand that were left over from the distribution. He at once begins to mail them to his colleagues, friends and former students. Copies of the *Syllabus* went at least to James Mark Baldwin, Ernest Cushing Richardson, Fabian Franklin and Christine Ladd-Franklin, Edward Vermilye Huntington,[57] John Dewey, William James, Joseph Jastrow, Francis C. Russell, James Mills Peirce, Simon Newcomb and Victoria Welby. In the letters accompanying the prints, Peirce explains to the recipients how in extreme hurry the syllabus was written and how he did not get to see its proof at all or retained a copy himself, in order to correct some of its formal inconsistencies and typos. To the

---

as well, apparently at the same with the main *Syllabus* (Peirce 1903, in R 1600). That short leaflet may well be considered a dry, dense and formal presentation of the classification and definitions of dyadic relations, at least since that print could not reach the last and most relevant sections that remained in the copy provided (R 539). But certainly Peirce also would not have wanted to surrender one of the very few prints that he was able to secure with the $50 at his disposal, and there is no evidence that he had sent any of those few copies to anyone. Had he mailed one to Welby, Peirce's formal work on relations could have reached Charles Kay Ogden, or even Frank Plumpton Ramsey or Bertrand Russell at Cambridge. Indeed at least Ogden and Ramsey were acquainted with Peirce's *Syllabus* through Welby's efforts.

57 Mathematician Edward Vermilye Huntington (1874–1952) may have been among the visitors Peirce received on December 13, during his Sunday afternoon office hours at Prescott Hall. On December 11, Huntington writes to Peirce his desire to consult him on his recent proof of postulates, and the related matters of mathematical notation, hoping to see him while still at Cambridge:

> I have been recently engaged in working out the independence of the postulates which lie at the basis of the *algebra of symbolic logic*,—one set based on the concepts + and ×, and a second based on the concept $\prec$. The postulates themselves are of course not new, but the complete proofs which I am able to give of their mutual independence may perhaps settle some mooted questions.
>
> It would give me great pleasure if you would permit me to call upon you while you are in Cambridge, to show you my results, and ask your advice on one or two questions of notation, before I write out the paper in full for presentation at the Mathematical Society meeting, and eventual publication. Professor J. M. Peirce was kind enough to tell me that you are usually at home on Sunday afternoon; may I ask whether I may call on you at that, or some other, time? (I have engagements in the evening.) vsy, Edward V. Huntington, Instructor in Mathematics (R L 210).

Peirce would write several drafts and letters back to Huntington on Christmas Eve and later, containing Peirce's comments and the missing proof of the distributivity principle (see Ma & Pietarinen 2017c; LoF 3).

Franklins he uses the wording "It is of the nature of a proof-sheet since I had no opportunity to see the proofs and it was written piecemeal and in great haste without keeping any copy or having any definite recollection of what I had written last. Hence, some formal inconsistencies. There is a lot more in MS. much more than there are funds to print" (CSP to CLF, December 8, 1903, R L 237). To Dewey Peirce writes that the first pages of a Syllabus "is to be regarded as a proof-sheet, since I never had sight of a proof, and it was written in extremest hurry and piecemeal and sent off without retaining any copy and without remembering exactly what I had said in what had before been sent. Hence some formal inconsistencies" (CSP to JD, December 8, 1903, R L 123), adding his distant hope that Dewey's supporting words to the Carnegie Executive Committee Peirce had received from Dewey in 1902 could still enable him to "get some part of my vast load of MS. printed". Accounts such as these suggest, not that Peirce would have written another and a now-lost version of the syllabus on top of the one that reached Sedgwick on October 30, but that when later in November Peirce had to draw up the list of texts and pages for what to include in the selection for the printer, he had to derive at least part of those instructions from memory, trying to recall the contents of what he had earlier sent to Sedgwick in vain. Even though Peirce might have attempted to finalise the composition in Boston with most of these texts now back at his disposal, the complexity of the material, asynchronously produced and still constantly evolving, inevitably resulted in some "formal inconsistencies" in the final output. Although those errors may appear rather minor to the reader, knowing how much text Peirce had amassed for potential inclusion and how much revisions would have to be done to most of them, the output was not much more that a rather haphazardly administered brew of texts all of them in more or less incomplete stages of maturity.

Welby's copy of the *Syllabus* came to have a place in the history of logic that is worthy of an additional note. An inspection of the first part of the transcription of Peirce's 1906 "Prolegomena" paper, which is deposited in the Frank Plumpton Ramsey Papers, reveals that Charles Kay Ogden, who did the second part of the transcription (Welby being the first), added Convention Zero from the *Syllabus* to the "Prolegomena" transcription. We also know that Ramsey made a close study of that paper. Welby, who had acquired Ogden as her secretary in 1911, gave Peirce's offprints, including her annotated copy of the *Syllabus*, to Ogden who would became Peirce's remote disciple at Cambridge. Ogden would show the material that he have received further to Bertrand Russell and others at Cambridge (*The Monist* was not available at Cambridge at that time). One can thus establish a concrete, textual connection between the two transatlantic groups of Cambridgean scholars. In the coming years, Peirce and Welby would exchange long letters many of which would excel in Peirce's pedagogical skill of teaching graphs to students of logic who wishes to learn them. Ogden would gladly join such study group (LoF 3).

After his return to Milford right after the last lecture, Peirce sends out some more copies, this time at least to Eliakim Hastings Moore and James McKeen Cattell. In 1910, Peirce reckons that there are some half a dozen copies of the *Syllabus* in existence, presumably meaning those still in his possession. Four of Peirce's own, corrected copies are presently deposited at Houghton library: one in the folder R 478, one in Box 4 of R 1600, and two that are bound in *[Philosophy and minor writings pamphlet]*, Phil 2225.5.05* (Peirce n.d.,b).

In the accompanying letters to his friends and colleagues Peirce explains that the selection that was printed consisted of "the first pages" of a syllabus. By this he must have meant the first pages of each of the Chapters I, II and IV, having skipped Chapter III entirely from the selection of pages from R 478 that he drew from memory. On the other hand, Peirce managed to include pages from R 508 on the pure mathematical definition of EGs, whose first section, "Existential Graphs. Rules of Transformation. Pure Mathematical Definition of Existential Graphs, regardless of their interpretation" (B1–B5, "I. Alpha Part" and "II. Beta part"), was re-paginated by 150–155 to supersede the pages 150–155 of the long draft manuscript of R 478 which began with the nearly identical general title, "Rules of Transformation of Existential Graphs".[58] This indicates that that segment of R 508, written on a graphing paper different from the main copy-text of R 478 (Crane's 1900 Japanese Linen), was a later addition to the syllabus text and may have been sent or brought to Sedgwick's office separately after the submission of the main text of R 478, perhaps together with Peirce's specification on the exact selection of what those "first pages" were to be that the printer should include in the final printout that he drew up in November.[59]

---

[58] The next page of R 508, designated as "Syllabus B6", was entitled with a section heading "Gamma Part of Existential Graphs", but Peirce did not re-paginate it to 156 and did not appear to propose to include it as a potential later supplement or replacement of the gamma section in the printed syllabus (only the Conventions VII–IX on gamma graphs were included in the print). So the five pages of B1–B5 were the only additions from R 508 on Peirce's proposal of providing the 'pure mathematical definition' that was to replace the pages on the rules of transformation that were originally written in R 478.

[59] No document containing Peirce's instructions on what was to be included in the printed version of the *Syllabus* is preserved in the correspondence between Peirce and the Lowell Institute, but as noted, a reception of that letter was acknowledged by Sedgwick on November 17. Presumably on that occasion, Peirce placed a request for Alfred Mudge & Son to type and print his "The Nomenclature and Division of Dyadic Relations" (NDDR)—the pamphlet of eight printed pages on dyadic relations from the copy-text of R 539—in an unknown but very small quantity. Only two

Peirce then pleads Eliakim Hastings Moore of the University of Chicago to assist in printing the "150 pages more in MS", which Peirce tells are ready but the printing of which was not possible with the money he had in November (CSP to EHM, December 26, 1904, p. 3; R L 299).[60] In addition to the 23 pages already printed (from the selection of about 60 manuscript sheets of R 478 and a couple of more from R 508 as the copy), this would amount to the full array of the surviving drafts of the planned syllabus material in the Peirce Papers (namely R 478, R 508, plus the planned addenda to, or replacement of, the third section of R 539 on dyadic and R 540 on triadic relations, among others), and would still leave room for several variant or perhaps even some entirely new and subsequently lost additional pages and studies that Peirce might have produced in the meantime.[61] No response from Moore is retained in the correspondence to Peirce's December 26 letter, but Cattell does express his wish to print Chapter I ("The Classification of the Sciences") in the newly-established *Journal of Philosophy, Psychology and Scientific Methods* (since 1923 renamed *The Journal of Philosophy*), which following his resignation from the editorship of *Science* he had just assumed with Frederick James Eugene Woodbridge, who writes: "I hope that you will give me the support in this enterprise ... be able to contribute to the early numbers. An article of from 2 000 to 3 000 words on some topics of your special interest ... is suggested. If you could send in copy at once it would be a particular accommodation. I should especially appreciate something dealing with any new material you might have in hand, bearing your interesting philosophy of Tychism" (FJEW to CSP, December 12, 1903; R L 78). Cattell promises to go ahead with the printing of the short first chap-

---

copies of this printed leaflet has been located (Boxes 4 and 13 of the item catalogued at R 1600, consisting of 14 boxes in total among the Harvard's Houghton Peirce Collection).

60 Moore could well have helped Peirce, not least since he was since December actively recruiting projects for the Carnegie Funds, which had proper application forms in place only from that point on and thus much after Peirce's early rejected application (Fenster 2003).

61 Peirce's correspondence with Simon Newcomb suggests that "printing 150 pages more" could even have meant the total of 150 *printed* pages that Peirce would estimate to result from the manuscript material that he would have amassed by early 1904: "I enclose some pages of a Syllabus that may possibly interest you. It certainly would had I been able to print the whole. But though I limited the copies to 100, the money gave out when the printer got so far. The whole would have been about a hundred and fifty such pages. [...] I have a great quantity ready for the press which I think, more keenly the more experience I gain, is of really great importance. But there is no hope of its ever being printed. It seems a fearful piece of egotism to study so deeply for myself alone. But it is not my fault" (CSP to SN, January 15, 1904, quoted in Eisele 1979, p. 84). 150 printed syllabus-sized pages would mean something like 400 pages existing in fair copy, vastly exceeding those that have been preserved in the archives. Did Peirce write or projected to write extensive continuations of what have been preserved as the various beginnings, drafts and sketches drafted in late November and December, such as R 792, R 800 and R 510?

ter, but unfortunately Peirce added to his reply an unwise proposal that he be nominated as the Area Editor on Logic of that new journal. Following this, the plans to publish even the first chapter waned, and the proposal to endow Peirce with editorial duties of the journal was passed over in silence. The first articles published in that journal on Peirce's work were written by his Johns Hopkins alumni, published in the journal's 1916 commemorative issue.[62]

Such were the far-reaching implications of the Carnegie Institute Trustees's infamous decision not to aid work in logic and philosophy, by a scholar who without dispute was America's most inventive mind in exact sciences at the turn of the century. That decision meant not only the burial of Peirce's massive 1902 *Minute Logic* (which still remains, in large parts, unpublished), but also the perennial lack of sponsorship to publish his equally notable and extensive studies from the following years, including the Lowell Institute Lectures and its long companions such as *The Logical Tracts* and the *Syllabus*. One can only conjecture what might have happened to the sciences of logic, foundations of mathematics, and the emerging sciences of computing and cognition, had a less supercilious and more farsighted decision been reached at that crucial moment when Peirce's lifelong, and in all measures exactly the kind of 'high-risk-high-reward' research promoted in Carnegie's charter,[63] was showing signs of coming to its real fruition.[64]

---

[62] Peirce wrote an anonymous, one-paragraph notice of his own *Syllabus*, which appeared within his book review of Robert Flint's *Review of Philosophy as Scientia Scientiarum, and a History of the Classification of the Sciences* published in *The Nation*, volume 80, on May 4, 1905, pp. 360–361. Peirce's notice concerns the first chapter of the *Syllabus* on the classification of the sciences:

> The second title at the head of this notice is that of a brochure distributed last winter [December 1903], which gives an outline sketch in four pages of a somewhat elaborate inquiry into the relations of the actual living and advancing studies as they are conceived by the researchers themselves. The outline embraces only theoretical sciences of research; but the study on which it is based allots considerably more space to the practical sciences. (p. 361; see R 1493a(s) for fragments of draft pages of the Flint review)

Apparently the review was written sometime in early 1905 that Peirce took to be the present winter. It is not known whether Peirce received a copy of his own *Syllabus* from *The Nation* in order to review the whole pamphlet or whether it was his own idea to include a short notice only on its first chapter on the classification of sciences after having been solicited to assess Flint's book, but one may guess that the latter is more likely to have been the case.

[63] The statutes stated: " 'To promote original research, paying great attention thereto as one of the most important of all departments', discovering 'the exceptional man in every department of study whenever and wherever found, in side or outside of schools, and enabling him to make the work for which he seems specially designed his life-work' " (quoted in Newcomb 1904, p. 174).

[64] The report on Peirce's application solicited from Simon Newcomb opined it to be, "so far as I have been able to see their purport ...discussions and reviews ...rather than well-reasoned

Selection 42: Fragments

R S-28, R S-1, R 510, R 478, R 1333, R 496, R S-46, R 1070. The last chapter included in the present book is a collection of assorted graphs and holograph pages from Peirce's many sketchbooks and manuscript leaves that pertain to his planning and preparation of the Lowell Lectures. They are largely scattered across the Peirce Papers: relevant notebooks, drafts, worksheets, manuscript sketches, doodles and cut-out pages arise from a number of folders and supplementary material. Some of them are from isolated and uncatalogued leaves lacking clear indications of which lecture topics they would belong to.

Several holograph reproductions of important study pages are included in the selection. A majority of them are sources from supplementary folders indexed in the Robin catalogue as R S, rediscovered over half a century after Peirce's *Nachlass* was deposited in the Harvard library collections (Robin 1971). Many of the graphs contained in this selection are unique and represent Peirce's repeated attempts to take the logical theory of graphs to novel directions, as explained in the introduction to the present volume and in its other selections. Most of them were not pursued after 1903, partly because Peirce had neither time nor patience to develop them and partly because a lot more was to be discovered in the graphical method of logical analysis in the forthcoming years that took precedence. Nonetheless, the scraps preserved in the notebooks are important reminders of the lasting value that inventing new logical notations can have to the theory of logic and scientific reasoning, and as Peirce remarked in R 467 are likely to be material for "genera-

---

scientific development of any one subject ... buried so deeply in the mass of preliminary discussion that it is difficult to exhume them" (SN to the Carnegie Institution, March 13, 1903, quoted in Brent 1993, p. 288). This pseudo-review bears the characteristics and turns of phrases of a politician of science having decided the recommendation before the clichés are penned down, demonstrating little or no effort of having processed the content of the application in the least. The next year, Newcomb praised Carnegie's pioneering efforts in funding science in the United States, seeing nothing but success of its endowment and defending its policies and decisions: "So far as has yet become apparent, the main functions of the Institution have been to carefully collate and study all the applications for assistance which have been made to it by individual investigators, and to comply with such of them as seemed most worthy and important" (Newcomb 1904, p. 175). No admission of error of judgment or bias was forthcoming from the eminent astronomer, once a student of Peirce's father, Benjamin Peirce, and whom Charles Peirce himself described, in a draft review of Newcomb's *Reminiscences*, to be "without doubt, the most distinguished man of science in this country today, and one of the most distinguished in the world" (R 1479, c.1903). Earlier, Newcomb had rejected Peirce's proposal, collaboratively designed with his special assistant Allan Douglas Risteen (see Introduction to W8 by Nathan Houser, p. 25), for an experimental project to determine whether the sum of the angles of triangles at astronomical distances was exactly 180 degrees, among others.

tions of analysts" that could bring the general method of logical graphs—and its Gamma part in particular—to some sort of completion.

Conclusions

The year 1903 was the indisputable *annus mirabilis* of Peirce's professional life. That year—even when taking only its second half into account—saw the discovery of modal logics, a decision method for logic (Alpha and Beta-reduct graphs), the theory of meta-graphs, second-order logic of potentials, logic of abstraction, reformation of speculative grammar, and an application of these concepts and tools to the foundations of mathematics, theory of science, epistemology and constructions of knowledge structures, metaphysical and ontological nature of relatives, philosophy of mind and cognition, as well as to the emerging ideas of computation, automated reasoning and logical and intelligent machines.

During that year, Peirce also achieved the perennial classification of the sciences (Kent 1987; Pietarinen 2006c), the formulation of the ethics of notation and terminology, and some of the best-known characterisations of abductive reasoning and its linkage to the philosophy of pragmatism. All this happened while having produced a number of paper and lecture drafts, paid book reviews, reports and notices that appeared nearly fortnightly throughout the year (25 such items appeared in *The Nation* that year alone). Obituaries and translation works appeared, while the preserved manuscripts papers witness Peirce having recorded a wealth of computations, commentaries, recreational studies and inventions of scientific, mathematical and practical throughout the year. Extensive correspondence was maintained with colleagues, friends and relatives, including the beginning of an intensive exchange with Victoria Welby (SS).

A considerable effort from Peirce's part was made to package his researches into didactically and pedagogically solicitous presentations, both in their oral and literary forms, although the actual deliveries may have left a lot to be desired. No doubt such efforts took their toll as the year neared its end, as attested by a report from one of his popular course participants: "Near the end of Peirce's lecture course [December 13], I went to see him at his lodgings, and introduced myself. He was very untidy as to dress, and covered with tobacco stains, as I judged, but was very simple, kindly and genial" (a personal report from F. Green, as listed in Pfeifer 2014, p. 80).[65]

---

[65] This encounter probably took place on Sunday, December 13. Also one of William James's sons visited Peirce during his 'office hour' on this last Sunday of his stay in Cambridge (WJ to CSP,

Should Peirce have succumbed to William James's advice to "gain a bigger audience when living"? (Exactly three years later, Huntington Hall is filled to the brim as William James enters the stage.) Or rather, did Peirce succeed gaining a larger audience in the future, when not living, as soon as he resolutely decided not to cave in? From the perspective of Peirce's own philosophy of pragmaticism, his demand of "highest of attention" from the audience sounds much less like a prelude to a pedagogical fiasco than a reference to the notion of an audience conceived as a real possibility. Surely his audience was not destined to be some actual, curiosity-seeking "popular audience" that happens to pass by at any given epoch. Rather, the true notion of an audience was an element of Peirce's own discursive mind, or of the mind of those who contemplate the same thoughts.

A lot was thus at stake for Peirce throughout the year. With his Lowell Institute Lectures, Peirce might have hoped to finally have made a permanent difference to the way philosophy is being observed and practiced, if not immediately then reassuringly in the long run, both by improving on its exact methodology and by deepening its relevance to science.

This watershed year being hardly over, Peirce would witness pragmatism and logic becoming increasingly separated, increasingly detached from their historical roots, and increasingly associated with ideas that did not conform well to the original purpose and meaning of the these two terms. As a long-lasting corrective to the emerging narrative, the Lowell Lectures were of little or no avail. Volume 3 of the *Logic of the Future*, entitled *Pragmaticism and Correspondence*, will attend to such final issues in Peirce's enduring project.

December 1903; James 2002), sent by William in order to bring an item (maybe a copy of Schiller's *Humanism*) to Peirce from their household. That item nevertheless was forgotten. Had Peirce had a chance of viewing Schiller's book in that advance occasion, he might have wanted to embark on an exchange with Schiller, and to launch his assessment and critique of humanism earlier than he actually did (Pietarinen 2011b).

References

Only those of Peirce's manuscript writings are included in the reference list below which do not appear in the *Logic of the Future* editions. Titles are those given in the Robin Catalogue, unless otherwise indicated by brackets. The textual sources of Volume 2 are listed in the separate "Catalogue of Peirce's Manuscripts". Peirce's own references are included in the backmatter, listed as "Bibliography of Peirce's References".

Bellucci, Francesco 2017. *Peirce's Speculative Grammar: Logic as Semiotics*. New York: Routledge.
Bellucci, Francesco 2019. Analysis and Decomposition in Peirce. *Synthese*. In press.
Bellucci, Francesco, Moktefi, Amirouche and Pietarinen, Ahti-Veikko 2013. Continuity, Connectivity and Regularity in Spatial Diagrams for *N* Terms. In Burton, Jim and Choudhury, Lopamudra (eds.), *Diagrams, Logic and Cognition: Proceedings of the First International Workshop on Diagrams, Logic and Cognition*. CEUR Workshop Proceedings 1132, pp. 23–30.
Bellucci, Francesco, Pietarinen, Ahti-Veikko and Stjernfelt, Frederik (eds.) 2014. *Peirce: 5 Questions*. Copenhagen: VIP/Automatic Press.
Bellucci, Francesco and Pietarinen, Ahti-Veikko 2015. Charles Sanders Peirce: Logic. *The Internet Encyclopedia of Philosophy*. http://www.iep.utm.edu/
Bellucci, Francesco and Pietarinen, Ahti-Veikko 2016. Existential Graphs as an Instrument for Logical Analysis. Part 1: Alpha. *The Review of Symbolic Logic* 9(2), pp. 209–237.
Bellucci, Francesco, Chiffi, Daniele and Pietarinen, Ahti-Veikko 2017. Assertive Graphs. *Journal of Applied Non-Classical Logics* 28(1), pp. 72–91.
Bellucci, Francesco, Moktefi, Amirouche and Pietarinen, Ahti-Veikko 2017. *Simplex sigillum veri*: Peano, Frege, and Peirce on the Primitives of Logic. *History and Philosophy of Logic* 39(1), pp. 80–95.
Bellucci, Francesco and Pietarinen, Ahti-Veikko 2017a. Two Dogmas of Diagrammatic Reasoning: A View from Existential Graphs. In K. Hull & R. K. Atkins (eds.). *Peirce on Perception and Reasoning: From Icons to Logic*. New York: Routledge, pp. 174–195.
Bellucci, Francesco and Pietarinen, Ahti-Veikko 2017b. From Mitchell to Carus: 14 Years of Logical Graphs in the Making. *Transactions of the Charles S. Peirce Society* 52(4), pp. 539–575.
Bellucci, Francesco and Pietarinen, Ahti-Veikko 2017c. Assertion and Denial: A Contribution from Logical Notation. *Journal of Applied Logics* 24, pp. 1–22.

Bellucci, Francesco and Pietarinen, Ahti-Veikko 2019. Icons, Interrogations, and Graphs: On Peirce's Integrated Notion of Abduction. *Transactions of the Charles S. Peirce Society* 56(1), pp. 43–62.
Bellucci, Francesco and Pietarinen, Ahti-Veikko 2020. Methodeutic of Abduction. In Shook, John and Paavola, Sami (eds.), *Abduction in Cognition and Action*. Springer. In press.
Bellucci, Francesco and Pietarinen, Ahti-Veikko 2020. Notational Differences. *Acta Analytica* 35, 289–314.
Bellucci, Francesco, Liu, Xinwen and Pietarinen, Ahti-Veikko 2020. On Linear Existential Graphs. *Logique & Analyse* 251, pp. 261–296.
Brady, Geraldine and Trimble, Todd H. 2000. A Categorical Interpretation of C. S. Peirce's Propositional Logic Alpha. *Journal of Pure and Applied Algebra* 149, pp. 213–239.
Brent, Joe 1993. *Charles Sanders Peirce: A Life*. Bloomington: Indiana University Press.
Brünnler, Kai 2003. *Deep Inference and Symmetry in Classical Proof*. PhD thesis. Technische Universität Dresden.
Carroll, Lewis 1895. What the Tortoise said to Achilles. *Mind* 4, pp. 278–280.
Carus, Paul 1910. Non-Aristotelian Logic. *The Monist* 20(1), pp. 158–159.
Caterina, Gianluca and Gangle, Rocco 2016. *Iconicity and Abduction*. Dordrecht: Springer.
Champagne, Marc and Pietarinen, Ahti-Veikko 2019. Why Images Cannot be Arguments, But Moving Ones Might. *Argumentation* 34, pp. 207–236.
Chiffi, Daniele and Pietarinen, Ahti-Veikko 2017. Fundamental Uncertainty and Values. *Philosophia* 45, pp. 1027–1037.
Chiffi, Daniele and Pietarinen, Ahti-Veikko 2018a. Abductive Inference within a Pragmatic Framework. *Synthese* 197, pp. 2507–2523.
Chiffi, Daniele and Pietarinen, Ahti-Veikko 2018b. Assertive and Existential Graphs: A Comparison. In: Chapman P., Stapleton G., Moktefi A., Perez-Kriz S., Bellucci F. (eds.). *Diagrammatic Representation and Inference. Diagrams 2018. Lecture Notes in Computer Science* 10871. Springer, pp. 565–581.
Chiffi, Daniele and Pietarinen, Ahti-Veikko 2019a. On the Logical Philosophy of Assertive Graphs. *Journal of Logic, Language and Information.* 29, pp. 375–397.
Chiffi, Daniele and Pietarinen, Ahti-Veikko 2019b. Risk and Values in Science: A Peircean View. *Axiomathes* 29(4), pp. 329–346.
Chiffi, Daniele, Pietarinen, Ahti-Veikko, Proover, Marika 2020. Anticipation, Abduction and the Economy of Research: A Normative Stance. *Futures: The Journal of Policy, Planning and Futures Studies* 115, 102471.

Chiffi, Daniele, Carrara, Massimiliano, De Florio, C. and Pietarinen, Ahti-Veikko 2019. We Don't Know We Don't Know: Asserting Ignorance. *Synthese*. In press.

Clark, Glenn 1997. New Light on Peirce's Iconic Notation for the Sixteen Binary Connectives. In Houser, N., Roberts, D., Van Evra, J. (eds.). *Studies in the Logic of Charles S. Peirce*. Bloomington and Indianapolis, IN: Indiana University Press, pp. 304–333.

Couturat, Louis 1914. *The Algebra of Logic*. Chicago: Open Court.

Cristalli, Claudia and Pietarinen, Ahti-Veikko 2020. Abstraction and generalization in the logic of science: Cases from the 19th-century scientific practice *HOPOS: The Journal of the International Society for the History of Philosophy of Science*. In press.

Dekker, Paul 2001. Dynamics and Pragmatics of 'Peirce's Puzzle'. *Journal of Semantics* 18, pp. 211–241.

Dipert, Randall 1995. Peirce's Underestimated Place in the History of Logic: A Response to Quine. In Ketner, K. L. (ed.), *Peirce and Contemporary Thought*. New York: Fordham University Press, pp. 32–58.

Dipert, Randall 2006. Peirce's Deductive Logic: Its Development, Influence, and Philosophical Significance. In Misak, C. (ed.). *The Cambridge Companion to Peirce*. Cambridge, Mass.: Cambridge University Press, pp. 257–286.

Edwards, A. W. F. 2004. *Cogwheels of the Mind: The Story of Venn Diagrams*. Baltimore: John Hopkins University Press.

Eisele, Carolyn 1979. *Studies in the Scientific and Mathematical Philosophy of Charles S. Peirce*. The Hague: Mouton Publishers.

Fenster, Della D. 2003. Funds for mathematics: Carnegie Institution of Washington support for mathematics from 1902 to 1921. *Historia Mathematica* 30, pp. 195–216.

Fisch, Max H. 1982. Peirce's Place in American Life. *Historica Mathematica* 9, pp. 265–287.

Fisch, Max H. 1986. *Peirce, Semeiotic, and Pragmatism: Essays by Max H. Fisch*. K. L. Ketner and C. J. W. Kloesel (eds.). Bloomington and Indianapolis, IN: Indiana University Press.

Fisch, Max H. and Turquette, Atwell 1966. Peirce's Triadic Logic. *Transactions of the Charles S. Peirce Society* 2(2), pp. 71–85. Reprinted in Fisch, M., *Peirce, Semeiotic, and Pragmatism: Essays by Max H. Fisch*. K. L. Ketner and C. J. W. Kloesel (eds.). Bloomington and Indianapolis, IN: Indiana University Press, pp. 171–183.

Floridi, Luciano 2006. The Logic of Being Informed. *Logique & Analyse* 196, pp. 1–28.

Frege, Gottlob 1879. *Begriffsschrift: eine der arithmetischen nachgebildete Formelsprache des reinen Denkens*. Halle: Louis Nebert.

Gardner, Martin 1958. *Logic Machines and Diagrams*. New York: McGraw-Hill.

Gentzen, Gerhard Karl Erich 1934. Untersuchungen über das logische Schließen. I. *Mathematische Zeitschrift* 39(2), pp. 76–210.

Gil J., Howse J., Kent S. and Taylor J. 2000. Projections in Venn-Euler Diagrams. *IEEE Symposium on Visual Languages*, pp. 119–126.

Grattan-Guinness, Ivor 2002. Re-Interpreting 'Λ': Kempe on Multisets and Peirce on Graphs, 1886–1905. *Transactions of the Charles S. Peirce Society* 38(3), pp. 327–350.

Grattan-Guinness, Ivor 2007. From A. B. Kempe to Josiah Royce via C. S. Peirce: Addenda to a recent paper by Pratt. *History and Philosophy of Logic* 28(3), pp. 265–266.

Hilpinen, Risto 1982. On C. S. Peirce's Theory of the Proposition: Peirce as a Precursor of Game-Theoretical Semantics. *The Monist* 65(2), pp. 182–188.

Hilpinen, Risto 1995. Peirce on Language and Reference. In Kenneth Laine Ketner (ed.) *Peirce and Contemporary Thought: Philosophical Inquiries*. New York: Fordham University Press. pp. 272–303.

Hilpinen, Risto 2004. Peirce's Logic. In Gabbay, Dov M. and John Woods (eds.). *Handbook of the History of Logic. Vol. 3: The Rise of Modern Logic From Leibniz to Frege*. Amsterdam: Elsevier, pp. 611–658.

Hilpinen, Risto 2016. Peirce, Perfect Knowledge, and the Gettier Problem. *Cognitio* 17(2), pp. 303–312.

Hintikka, Jaakko 1962. *Knowledge and Belief. An Introduction to the Logic of the Two Notions*. Ithaca: Cornell University Press.

Hintikka, Jaakko 1996. The Place of C. S. Peirce in the History of Logical Theory. In Brunning, J. and Forster, P. (eds.). *The Rule of Reason: The Philosophy of Charles Sanders Peirce*. Toronto: University of Toronto Press, pp. 13–33.

Hintikka, Jaakko 2011. What the Bald Man Can Tell Us. In Biletzky, A. (ed.). *Hues of Philosophy: Essays in Memory of Ruth Manor*. London: College Publications.

Holm, Jacob and Rotenberg, Eva 2019. Fully-dynamic Planarity Testing in Polylogarithmic Time. arXiv:1911.03449v2 cs.DS.

Hookway, Christopher 2012. *The Pragmatic Maxim: Essays on Peirce and Pragmatism*. Oxford: Oxford University Press.

Houser, Nathan 1985. *Peirce's Algebra of Logic and the Law of Distribution*. Dissertation. University of Waterloo, Ontario.

Houser, Nathan 1991. Peirce and the Law of Distribution. In: Drucker, T. (ed.). *Perspectives on the History of Mathematical Logic*. Boston: Birkhäuser, pp. 10–32.

Houser, Nathan, Roberts, Don D., Van Evra, J. (eds.) 1997. *Studies in the Logic of Charles S. Peirce*. Bloomington and Indianapolis, IN: Indiana University Press.

Huntington, Edward V. 1904. Sets of Independent Postulates for the Algebra of Logic. *Transactions of the American Mathematical Society* 5, pp. 288–309.

James, William 1988. *Manuscript Lectures*. Cambridge, Mass.: Harvard University Press.

James, William 1907. *Pragmatism, A New Name for Some Old Ways of Thinking*. Popular Lectures on Philosophy. New York: Longmans, Green, and Co.

James, William 2002. *The Correspondence of William James*. Vol. 10: 1902–March 1905. Edited by Ignas K. Skrupskelis, Elizabeth M. Berkeley and John J. McDermott. Charlottesville: University Press of Virginia.

James, William 2003. *The Correspondence of William James*. Vol. 11: April 1905–March 1908. Edited by Ignas K. Skrupskelis, Elizabeth M. Berkeley and John J. McDermott. Charlottesville: University Press of Virginia.

Kent, Beverley 1987. *Charles S. Peirce: Logic and the Classification of the Sciences*. Kingston and Montreal: McGill-Queen's University Press.

Kempe, Alfred Bray 1886. A Memoir on the Theory of Mathematical Form. *Philosophical Transactions of the Royal Society of London* 177, pp. 1–70.

Ketner, Kenneth 1987. Identifying Peirce's "Most Lucid and Interesting Paper". *Transactions of the Charles S. Peirce Society* 23(4), pp. 539–555.

Lemanski, Jens 2017. Logic Diagrams in the Weigel and Weise Circles. *History and Philosophy of Logic* 39(1), pp. 3–28.

Liu, Xinwen 2005. An Axiomatic System for Peirce's Alpha Graphs. In F. Dau, M.-L. Mugnier, & G. Stumme (eds.). *Common Semantics for Sharing Knowledge: Contributions to ICCS 2005*, Kassel: Kassel University Press, pp. 122–131.

Lupher, Tracy and Adajian, Thomas (eds.) 2015. *Philosophy of Logic: 5 Questions*. Copenhagen: VIP/Automatic Press.

Ma, Minghui 2018. Peirce's Logical Graphs for Boolean Algebras and Distributive Lattices. *Transactions of the Charles S. Peirce Society* 54(3), pp. 320–340.

Ma, Minghui and Pietarinen, Ahti-Veikko 2016. Proof Analysis of Peirce's Alpha System of Graphs. *Studia Logica* 105(3), pp. 625–647.

Ma, Minghui and Pietarinen, Ahti-Veikko 2017a. Graphical Sequent Calculi for Modal Logics. *Electronic Proceedings in Theoretical Computer Science* 243, pp. 91–103.

Ma, Minghui and Pietarinen, Ahti-Veikko 2017b. Gamma Graph Calculi for Modal Logics. *Synthese* 195(8), pp. 3621–3650.

Ma, Minghui and Pietarinen, Ahti-Veikko 2017c. Peirce's Sequent Proofs of Distributivity. *Logic and Its Applications: 7th Indian Conference, Lecture Notes in Computer Science* 10119, Springer, pp. 168–182.

Ma, Minghui and Pietarinen, Ahti-Veikko 2018a. Peirce's Calculi for Classical Propositional Logic. *Review of Symbolic Logic* 13(3), pp. 509–540.

Ma, Minghui and Pietarinen, Ahti-Veikko 2018b. A Graphical Deep Inference System for Intuitionistic Logic. *Logique & Analyse* 245, pp. 73–114.

Ma, Minghui and Pietarinen, Ahti-Veikko 2018c. A Weakening of Alpha Graphs: Quasi-Boolean Algebras. In Chapman P., Stapleton G., Moktefi A., Perez-Kriz S., Bellucci, F. (eds.). *Diagrammatic Representation and Inference. Diagrams 2018. Lecture Notes in Computer Science* 10871. Springer, Cham, pp. 549–564.

Ma, Minghui and Pietarinen, Ahti-Veikko 2018d. Let Us Investigate! Dynamic Conjecture-Making as the Formal Logic of Abduction. *Journal of Philosophical Logic* 47, pp. 913–945.

Ma, Minghui and Pietarinen, Ahti-Veikko 2019. Peirce's Logic of Dragon Head (R 501). Preprint.

Majer, Ondrej, Pietarinen, Ahti-Veikko and Tulenheimo, Tero 2009. Introduction to Logic and Games. In O. Majer, A.-V. Pietarinen and T. Tulenheimo (eds.). *Games: Unifying Logic, Language, and Philosophy*. Dordrecht: Springer, pp. ix–xxiii.

Menger, Karl 1939. On the Logic of the Doubtful: On Optative and Imperative Logic. *Reports of a Mathematical Colloquium Notre Dame* 2(1), pp. 53–64.

Menger, Karl 1994. *Reminiscences of the Vienna Circle and the Mathematical Colloquium*. Edited by Louise Golland, Brian McGuinness and Abe Sklar. Dordrecht: Kluwer Academic.

Mitchell, Oscar Howard 1883. On a New Algebra of Logic. In: C. S. Peirce (ed.). *Studies in Logic, by Members of the Johns Hopkins University*. Boston: Little, Brown & Company, pp. 72–106.

Moktefi, Amirouche and Pietarinen, Ahti-Veikko 2015. On the Diagrammatic Representation of Existential Statements with Venn Diagrams. *Journal of Logic, Language, and Information* 24(4), pp. 361–374.

Moktefi, Amirouche and Pietarinen, Ahti-Veikko 2016. Negative Terms in Euler Diagrams: Peirce's Solution. In Jamnik, M. et al. (eds.), *Lecture Notes in Artificial Intelligence* 9781, pp. 286–288.

Moore, Matthew (ed.), 2010. *New Essays on Peirce's Mathematical Philosophy*. Chicago: Open Court.

Newcomb, Simon 1904. The Carnegie Institution. *The North American Review* 178, pp. 172–185.

Øhrstrøm, Peter 2000. Graphs for Time and Modality. In Øhrstrøm, P. & Hasle, R. (eds.) *Temporal Logic: From Ancient Ideas to Artificial Intelligence*, pp. 320–343. Dordrecht: Kluwer Academics.

Pape, Helmut (ed.) 1983. *Charles S. Peirce: Phänomen und Logik der Zeichen*. Frankfurt am Main: Suhrkamp.

Peirce, Charles S. 1867a. On an Improvement in Boole's Calculus of Logic. *Proceedings of the American Academy of Arts and Sciences* 7, pp. 250–261. (Presented March 12, 1867. Reprinted in W2, pp. 12–23; CP 3.1–19.)

Peirce, Charles S. 1867b. On the Natural Classification of Arguments. *Proceedings of the American Academy of Arts and Science* 7, pp. 261–287. (Presented April 9, 1867. Reprinted in W2, pp. 23–49; CP 2.461–516.)

Peirce, Charles S. 1867c. Upon the Logic of Mathematics. *Proceedings of the American Academy of Arts and Science* 7, pp. 402–412. (Presented September 10, 1867. Reprinted in W2, pp. 59–69; CP 3.20–44.)

Peirce, Charles S. 1868. On a New List of Categories. *Proceedings of the American Academy of Arts and Sciences* 7, Boston, pp. 287–298. (Reprinted in W2, pp. 49–59; CP 1.545–559; EP1, pp. 1–10.) [Lowell Lecture's reading list, Lecture III.]

Peirce, Charles S. 1870/1873. Description of a Notation for the Logic of Relatives, Resulting from an Amplification of the Conceptions of Boole's Calculus of Logic. *Memoirs of the American Academy of Arts and Sciences* 9, pp. 317–378. (Communicated on January 26, 1870; a separate publication by Welch, Bigelow, and Company for Harvard University, 1870. Reprinted in W2, pp. 359–429; CP 3.45–149.)

Peirce, Charles S. 1878. *Photometric Researches*. Leibzig: Wilhelm Engelmann.

Peirce, Charles S. 1880. On the Algebra of Logic. *American Journal of Mathematics* 3(1), pp. 15–57. (Reprinted in W4, pp. 163–209; CP 3.154–251.)

Peirce, Charles S. 1881. On the Logic of Number. *American Journal of Mathematics* 4, pp. 85–95. (Reprinted in W4, pp. 299–309.)

Peirce, Charles S. c.1882. [Fragments on Logic] (R 747). Houghton Library.

Peirce, Charles S. 1882. Letter (draft) to Oscar Howard Mitchell, December 21, 1882 (R L 294). Houghton Library.

Peirce, Charles S. 1883a. A Communication from Mr. Peirce (P 245). *Johns Hopkins University Circulars* 2(22) (April 1883), pp. 86–88. (Reprinted in W4, p. 470.)

Peirce, Charles S. 1883b. Note B: The Logic of Relatives. In Peirce, C. S. (ed.). *Studies in Logic*, pp. 187–203. (Reprinted in W4, pp. 453–466; CP 3.328–358.)

Peirce, Charles S. (ed.) 1883c. *Studies in Logic by Members of the Johns Hopkins University*. Boston: Little, Brown, and Company. (SiL) [Lowell Lecture's reading list, Lecture III.]

Peirce, Charles S. 1883d. A Theory of Probable Inference. In Peirce, C. S. (ed.). *Studies in Logic*, pp. 126–181. (Reprinted in W4, pp. 408–450; CP 2.694–754.) [Lowell Lecture's reading list, Lecture VI.]

Peirce, Charles S. 1885. On the Algebra of Logic: A Contribution to the Philosophy of Notation. *American Journal of Mathematics* 7(2), pp. 180–196. (Reprinted in W5, pp. 162–190; CP 3.359–403.)

Peirce, Charles S. c.1886. Qualitative Logic (R 736). Houghton Library.
Peirce, Charles S. 1889a. Notes on Kempe's Paper on Mathematical Forms (R 714). Houghton Library.
Peirce, Charles S. 1889b. Kempe Translated into English (R 715). Houghton Library.
Peirce, Charles S. 1891a. Algebra of the Copula [Version 1]. In *Writings of Charles S. Peirce* Vol. 8 (1890–1892), pp. 210–211. Bloomington and Indianapolis, IN: Indiana University Press, 2010.
Peirce, Charles S. 1891b. Algebra of the Copula [Version 2]. In *Writings of Charles S. Peirce* Vol. 8 (1890–1892), pp. 212–216. Bloomington and Indianapolis, IN: Indiana University Press, 2010.
Peirce, Charles S. 1893a. *How to Reason: A Critick of Arguments*. Division I. Stecheology. Part I. Non Relative. Chapter VIII. The Algebra of the Copula. (R 411). Houghton Library.
Peirce, Charles S. 1893b. *How to Reason: A Critick of Arguments*. Chapter XI. The Boolian Calculus. (R 417). Houghton Library.
Peirce, Charles S. 1893c. *How to Reason: A Critick of Arguments*. Book II. Division I. Part 2. Logic of Relatives. Chapter XII. The Algebra of Relatives. (R 418). Houghton Library.
Peirce, Charles S. c.1894a. [On the Algebra of Relatives] (R 553). Houghton Library.
Peirce, Charles S. c.1894b. [The Three Categories and the Reduction of Fourthness] (R 915). Houghton Library.
Peirce, Charles S. c.1894c. [Logic: Fragments] (R S-64). Houghton Library.
Peirce, Charles S. 1894. Letter to Francis C. Russell, September 6, 1894 (R L 387). Houghton Library.
Peirce, Charles S. 1896. The Regenerated Logic. *The Monist* 7(1) (October), pp. 19–40. (Reprinted in CP 3.425–455; LoI, pp. 170–185.)
Peirce, Charles S. c.1897. Memoir § 4. Algebra of Copula (R 737). Houghton Library.
Peirce, Charles S. 1897. The Logic of Relatives. *The Monist* 7(2) (January), pp. 161–217. (Reprinted in CP 3.456–552; LoI, pp. 186–229.) [Lowell Lecture's reading list, Lecture V.]
Peirce, Charles S. 1898. Reply to Mr. Kempe (K) (R 708). Houghton Library.
Peirce, Charles S. 1901a. New Elements (Kaina stoicheia) (R 517). Houghton Library. (Reprinted in NEM IV, pp. 235–263; EP 2, pp. 300–324.)
Peirce, Charles S. 1901b. [The Logic of Dragon Head] (R 501, R 9, R 11). Houghton Library. (Ma & Pietarinen 2019).
Peirce, Charles S. 1901c. Pearson's Grammar of Science. Annotations on the first three chapters. *Popular Science Monthly* 58, pp. 296–306. [Lowell Lecture's reading list, Lecture VI.]

Peirce, Charles S. and Ladd-Franklin, Christine. 1902. Symbolic Logic, or algebra of logic. In James Mark Baldwin (ed.), *Dictionary of Philosophy and Psychology*. Volume 2, pp. 640–651. [Lowell Lecture's reading list, Lecture III.]

Peirce, Charles S. c.1902. A Treatise on the Calculus of Differences (R 91). Houghton Library.

Peirce, Charles S. 1902. Logic, Regarded As Semeiotic (The Carnegie Application of 1902), Version 1: An Integrated Reconstruction. Joseph Ransdell (ed.), *Arisbe*, preprint. (R L 75), Houghton Library.

Peirce, Charles S. 1903a. *A Syllabus of Certain Topics of Logic*. Boston: Alfred Mudge & Son. (Copies annotated by Peirce located in R 478; R 1600, Box 4; plus two bound in *[Philosophy and minor writings pamphlet]* Phil 2225.5.05*; all at Houghton Library.)

Peirce, Charles S. 1903b. *The Nomenclature and Division of Dyadic Relations*, privately printed (Alfred Mudge & Son). (R 539; R 1600, Boxes 3 and 13).

Peirce, Charles S. 1905a. What Pragmatism Is. *The Monist* 15(2) (April), pp. 161–181. (Reprinted in CP 5.411–437; LoI, pp. 230–244.)

Peirce, Charles S. 1905b. Issues of Pragmaticism. *The Monist* 15(4) (October), pp. 481–499. (Reprinted CP 5.438–463; LoI, pp. 245–258.)

Peirce, Charles S. 1905c. Rough Sketch of Suggested Prolegomena to your [James Mills Peirce's] First Course in Quaternions (R 87). Houghton Library.

Peirce, Charles S. 1906. Prolegomena to an Apology for Pragmaticism. *The Monist* 16(4) (October), pp. 492–546. Errata: *The Monist* 17(1) (January), 1907, p. 160. (Reprinted in CP 4.530–572; LoI, pp. 307–342.)

Peirce, Charles S. 1907. Second Talk to the Philosophical Club and Second Talk. On Deduction. April 12, 1907 (R 754). Houghton Library.

Peirce, Charles S. 1908a. Some Amazing Mazes. *The Monist* 28(2), pp. 227–241. (Reprinted in CP 4.585–593; LoI, pp. 394–403.)

Peirce, Charles S. 1908b. Some Amazing Mazes (Conclusion). Explanation of Curiosity the First. *The Monist* 28(3), pp. 416–464. (Reprinted in CP 4.594–642; LoI, pp. 404–445.)

Peirce, Charles S. 1908c. A Neglected Argument for the Reality of God. *Hibbert Journal* 7, pp. 90–112. (Reprinted in CP 6.452–485; EP 2, pp. 434–450.)

Peirce, Charles S. 1909a. Some Amazing Mazes, A Second Curiosity. *The Monist* 29(1), pp. 36–45. (Reprinted CP 4.643–646; LoI, pp. 446–451.)

Peirce, Charles S. 1909b. Studies in Meaning. March 25–28, 1909 (R 619). Houghton Library.

Peirce, Charles S. 1911a. A Letter (draft) to James Howard Kehler, June 22, 1911 (R L 231, R 514, R 515). Houghton Library.

Peirce, Charles S. 1911b. A Letter (draft) to Allan Douglas Risteen, December 6–9, 1911. (R L 376, marked "moved to R L 376" from R 500, though located at

R 500 in the Harvard's Houghton Peirce Papers at least until 2012). Houghton Library.

Peirce, Charles S. n.d.,a. Note on Kempe's Paper in Vol. XXI of the *Proceedings of the London Mathematical Society* (R 709); Notes on Kempe's Paper (R 710); Notes on Kempe's Paper (R 711); (Kempe) (R 712); (Kempe (R 713). Houghton Library.

Peirce, Charles S. n.d.,b. *[Philosophy and minor writings pamphlet]* Phil 2225.5.05*. Houghton Library.

Peirce, Charles S. n.d.,c. *[Peirce's Reprints and Books from his Library; Editor's Materials and Preliminary Catalogues of the Collection].* (R 1600), 14 Boxes. Houghton Library.

Pfeifer, David 2014. Peirce Medical History Excerpts. Complied from the Max H. Fisch Records. Mimeograph. Institute for American Thought, IUPUI, Indianapolis.

Pietarinen, Ahti-Veikko 2001. Most Even Budged Yet: Some Cases for Game-Theoretic Semantics in Natural Language. *Theoretical Linguistics* 27(1), 20–54.

Pietarinen, Ahti-Veikko 2003a. Peirce's Game-Theoretic Ideas in Logic. *Semiotica* 144(14), pp. 33–47.

Pietarinen, Ahti-Veikko 2003b. Games as Formal Tools versus Games as Explanations in Logic and Science. *Foundations of Science* 8(1), pp. 317–364.

Pietarinen, Ahti-Veikko 2004. Peirce's Diagrammatic Logic in IF Perspective. *Lecture Notes in Artificial Intelligence* 2980, Berlin: Springer-Verlag, pp. 97–111.

Pietarinen, Ahti-Veikko 2005a. Compositionality, Relevance and Peirce's Logic of Existential Graphs. *Axiomathes* 15(1), pp. 513–540.

Pietarinen, Ahti-Veikko 2005b. Cultivating Habits of Reason: Peirce and the *Logica Utens* versus *Logica Docens* Distinction. *History of Philosophy Quarterly* 22, pp. 357–372.

Pietarinen, Ahti-Veikko 2006a. *Signs of Logic: Peircean Themes on the Philosophy of Language, Games, and Communication* (Synthese Library 329). Dordrecht: Springer.

Pietarinen, Ahti-Veikko 2006b. Peirce's Contributions to Possible-Worlds Semantics. *Studia Logica* 82(3), pp. 345–369.

Pietarinen, Ahti-Veikko 2006c. Interdisciplinarity and Peirce's Classification of the Sciences: A Centennial Reassessment. *Perspectives on Science* 14(2), pp. 127–152.

Pietarinen, Ahti-Veikko 2007. *Game Theory and Linguistic Meaning.* (Current Research in the Semantics/Pragmatics Interface 18). Oxford: Elsevier Science.

Pietarinen, Ahti-Veikko 2008. Diagrammatic Logic of Existential Graphs: A Case Study of Commands. In G. Stapleton, J. Howse, & J. Lee (eds.). *Diagrammatic*

Representation and Inference, Lecture Notes in Computer Science 5223, Heidelberg: Springer, pp. 404–407.

Pietarinen, Ahti-Veikko 2009a. Significs and the Origins of Analytic Philosophy. *Journal of the History of Ideas* 70(3), pp. 467–490.

Pietarinen, Ahti-Veikko 2009b. Pragmaticism as an Anti-Foundationalist Philosophy of Mathematics. In B. Van Kerkhove, R. Desmet & J. P. Van Bendegem (eds.). *Philosophical Perspectives on Mathematical Practices*. London: College Publications, pp. 305–333.

Pietarinen, Ahti-Veikko 2010a. Is Non-Visual Diagrammatic Logic Possible? In A. Gerner (ed.). *Diagrammatology and Diagram Praxis*. London: College Publications, pp. 73–85.

Pietarinen, Ahti-Veikko 2010b. Peirce's Pragmatic Theory of Proper Names. *Transactions of the Charles S. Peirce Society* 46(3), pp. 341–363.

Pietarinen, Ahti-Veikko 2010c. Which Philosophy of Mathematics is Pragmaticism? In M. Moore (ed.). *New Essays on Peirce's Mathematical Philosophy*. Chicago, IL: Open Court, pp. 59–79.

Pietarinen, Ahti-Veikko 2011a. Existential Graphs: What the Diagrammatic Logic of Cognition Might Look Like. *History and Philosophy of Logic* 32(3), pp. 265–281.

Pietarinen, Ahti-Veikko 2011b. Remarks on the Peirce–Schiller Correspondence. In E. H. Oleksy & W. Oleksy (eds.), *Transatlantic Encounters: Philosophy, Media, Politics*. Frankfurt am Main: Peter Lang, pp. 61–70.

Pietarinen, Ahti-Veikko 2011c. Moving Pictures of Thought II: Graphs, Games, and Pragmaticism's Proof. *Semiotica* 186, pp. 315–331. (Translated in Portuguese as 2013, "Grafos, Jogos e a Prova do Pragmaticismo", in Lafayette de Moraes and João Queiroz, *A lógica de Diagramas de Charles Sanders Peirce: Implicacões en Ciêcia Cognitiva, Lógica e Semiótica*. Editora UFJF, pp. 83–104.

Pietarinen, Ahti-Veikko 2012a. Peirce and the Logic of Image. *Semiotica* 2012(192), pp. 251–261.

Pietarinen, Ahti-Veikko 2012b. Why is the Normativity of Logic Based on Rules? In Cornelis De Waal and Kristof P. Skowronski (eds.), *The Normative Thought of Charles S. Peirce*, Fordham: Fordham University Press, pp. 172–184.

Pietarinen, Ahti-Veikko 2013. Logical and Linguistic Games from Peirce to Grice to Hintikka. *Teorema* 33(2), pp. 121–136.

Pietarinen, Ahti-Veikko 2014a. The Science to Save Us from Philosophy of Science. *Axiomathes* 25, pp. 149–166.

Pietarinen, Ahti-Veikko 2014b. A Scholastic-Realist Modal-Structuralism. *Philosophia Scientiae* 18(3), pp. 127–138.

Pietarinen, Ahti-Veikko 2015a. Two Papers on Existential Graphs by Charles S. Peirce: 1. Recent Developments of Existential Graphs and their Consequences for Logic (R 498, R 499, R 490, S-36; 1906), 2. Assurance through Reasoning (R 669, R 670; 1911). *Synthese* 192, pp. 881–922.

Pietarinen, Ahti-Veikko 2015b. Exploring the Beta Quadrant. *Synthese* 192, pp. 941–970.

Pietarinen, Ahti-Veikko 2015c. Signs Systematically Studied: Invitation to Peirce's Theory. *Sign Systems Studies* 43(4), pp. 372–398; Recent Studies on Signs: Commentary and Perspectives, pp. 616–650; [Division of Signs, by Charles Peirce], pp. 651–662.

Pietarinen, Ahti-Veikko 2016. Four Papers Extensions of Euler Diagrams in Peirce's Four Manuscripts on Logical Graphs. In Jamnik, M. et al. (eds.), *Lecture Notes in Artificial Intelligence* 9781, pp. 139–154.

Pietarinen, Ahti-Veikko 2018. To Peirce Hintikka's Thoughts. *Logica Universalis* 13(2), pp. 241–262.

Pietarinen, Ahti-Veikko 2019a. Abduction and Diagrams. *Logic Journal of the IGPL*. In press.

Pietarinen, Ahti-Veikko 2019b. Semeiotic Completeness in the Theory of Signs. *Semiotica: Journal of the International Association for Semiotic Studies / Revue de l'Association Internationale de Smiotique* 228, pp. 237–257.

Pietarinen, Ahti-Veikko 2020. How to Justify Deductive Reasoning: Peirce's Solution. *British Journal for the History of Philosophy*. In press.

Pietarinen, Ahti-Veikko and Snellman, Lauri 2005. On Peirce's Late Proof of Pragmaticism. In T. Aho and A.-V. Pietarinen (eds.). *Acta Philosophica Fennica* 79. Helsinki: Societas Philosophica Fennica, pp. 275–288.

Pietarinen, Ahti-Veikko and Bellucci, Francesco 2014. New Light on Peirce's Conceptions of Retroduction, Deduction and Scientific Reasoning. *International Studies in the Philosophy of Science* 28(4), pp. 353–373.

Pietarinen, Ahti-Veikko and Chevalier, Jean-Marie 2015. The Second Metaphysical Club and Its Impact to the Development of the Sciences in the US. *Commens Working Papers no. 2*. Commens: Digital Companion to C. S. Peirce.

Pietarinen, Ahti-Veikko, Shafiei, Mohammad and Stjernfelt, Frederik 2019. Mutual Insights on Peirce and Husserl. In Pietarinen, A.-V. and M. Shafiei (eds.). *Peirce and Husserl: Mutual Insights on Logic, Mathematics and Cognition*. Dordrecht: Springer, pp. 3–15.

Pietarinen, Ahti-Veikko and Chiffi, Daniel 2020. From Knowability to Conjecturability. *Contemporary Pragmatism* 17(2-3), pp. 205–227.

Pietarinen, Ahti-Veikko; Bellucci, Francesco; Bobrova, Angelina; Hayden, Nathan and Shafiei, Mohammad 2020. The Blot. In Pietarinen, A.-V. et al. (eds.), *Diagrammatic Representation and Inference—11th International Conference, Diagrams 2020, Tallinn, Estonia, August 24–28, 2020, Proceedings*. Lecture Notes in Computer Science 12169, Springer.

Putnam, Hilary 1982. Peirce the Logician. *Historia Mathematica* 9, pp. 290–301.
Putnam, Hilary 2011. The Story of Pragmatism. *Comprende* 13(1), pp. 37–48.
Prior, Arthur N. 1964. The Algebra of the Copula. In Moore, E. and Robin, R. (eds.), *Studies in the Philosophy of Charles Sanders Peirce*. Amherst: The University of Massachusetts Press, pp. 79–94.
Ramharter, E. and Gottschall, C. 2011. Peirce's Search for a Graphical Modal Logic (Propositional Part). *History and Philosophy of Logic* 32, pp. 153–176.
Robin, Richard 1971. The Peirce Papers: A Supplementary Catalogue. *Transactions of the Charles S. Peirce Society* 7, 1971, pp. 37–57.
Roberts, Don D. 1973. *The Existential Graphs of Charles S. Peirce*. The Hague: Mouton.
Roberts, Don D. 1997. A Decision Method for Existential Graphs. In Houser, Nathan et al. (eds.). *Studies in the Logic of Charles S. Peirce*. Bloomington and Indianapolis, IN: Indiana University Press, pp. 387–401.
Rodgers, Peter, Flower, Jean and Stapleton, Gem 2012. Introducing 3D Venn and Euler Diagrams. In Chapman, Peter and Micallef, Luana (eds.), *Proceedings of the 3rd International Workshop on Euler Diagrams*. CEUR-WS 854, pp. 92–106.
Royce, Josiah with W. Fergus Kernan 1916. Charles Sanders Peirce. *Journal of Philosophy, Psychology, and Scientific Methods* 13, pp. 701–709.
Russell, Bertrand 1901. Sur la logique des relations avec des applications á la théorie des séries. *Revue de mathématiques/Rivista di Matematiche* 7, pp. 115–148.
Russell, Francis C. 1908. Hints for the Elucidation of Mr. Peirce's Logical Work. *The Monist* 28(3) (July 1908), pp. 406–415.
Serene, E. F. 1981. Anselm's Modal Conceptions. In Knuuttila, S. (ed.), *Reinforcing the Great Chain of Being: Studies of the History of Modal Theories*, pp. 117–163. Dordrecht: Springer.
Schiller, Ferdinand Canning Scott 1903. *Humanism. Philosophical Essays*. London: Macmillan and Co.
Schröder, Ernst 1890. *Vorlesungen über die Algebra der Logik*. Volume 1, Leipzig: Teubner.
Schütte, Kurt 1977. *Proof Theory*. Berlin: Springer-Verlag.
Shields, Paul 1981/2012. *Charles S. Peirce on the Logic of Number*. 2nd ed. Boston: Docent Press.
Shin, Sun-Joo 2002. *The Iconic Logic of Peirce's Graphs*. Cambridge, Mass.: MIT Press.
Sowa, John 1984. *Conceptual Structures: Information Processing in Mind and Machine*. Addison-Wesley.

Sowa, John 2006. Peirce's Contributions to the 21St Century. *Proceedings of the 14th International Conference on Conceptual Structures*. Lecture Notes in Computer Science 4068, pp. 54–69.
Stapleton, Gem, Howse, John and Taylor, John 2005. A Decidable Constraint Diagram Reasoning System. *Journal of Logic and Computation* 15, pp. 975–1008.
Stjernfelt, Frederik 2007. *Diagrammatology: An Investigation on the Borderlines of Phenomenology, Ontology, and Semiotics*. Dordrecht: Springer.
Sylvester, James Joseph 1878. On an Application of the New Atomic Theory to the Graphical Representation of the Invariants and Covariants of Binary Quantics. *American Journal of Mathematics* 1, pp. 64–104.
Venn, John 1883. Review of "Studies in Logic", *Mind* 8, pp. 594–603.
Winslow, C.-E. A. 1921. William Thompson Sedgwick (1855–1921). *Journal of Bacteriology* 6(3), pp. 255–262.
Zalamea, Fernando 2012a. *Synthetic Philosophy of Contemporary Mathematics*. Urbanomic.
Zalamea, Fernando 2012b. *Peirce's Logic of Continuity: A Mathematical and Conceptual Approach*. New York: Docent Press.
Zellweger, Shea 1997. Untapped Potential in Peirce's Iconic Notation for the Sixteen Binary Connectives. In Houser, Nathan et al. (eds.). *Studies in the Logic of Charles S. Peirce*. Bloomington and Indianapolis, IN: Indiana University Press, pp. 334–386.
Zeman, Jay J. 1964. *The Graphical Logic of C. S. Peirce*. Ph.D. dissertation, University of Chicago. Online edition 2002: http://users.clas.ufl.edu/jzeman/graphicallogic/
Zeman, Jay J. 1967. A System of Implicit Quantification. *Journal of Symbolic Logic* 32, pp. 480–504.

Charles S. Peirce's Writings on Existential Graphs

An admission ticket for Peirce's 1903 Lowell Institute Lectures (Harvard Peirce Papers, R 1600).

Huntington Hall, Rogers building, c. 1903.

Part V: *Some Topics of Logic Bearing on Questions Now Vexed*
The 1903 Lowell Institute Lectures I–V

32 Lowell Lecture I [early draft]

[Copy-text is the full text of R 454. On the notebook cover label is inscribed: "Early D. Lowell Lecture I (used for II)".] Presumably composed in late spring-early summer roughly contemporaneously with the composition of *Logical Tracts No. 1* (R 491) and the early version of *Logical Tracts No. 2* (R 492), this non-delivered, early pre-draft of the planned first lecture represents Peirce's initial thoughts on the opening of the course of eight lectures. Later superseded by its non-technical version, "What Makes a Reasoning Sound?" (EP 2, pp. 242–257), which was delivered on November 23, this early plan of Peirce's, despite being clearly incomplete and considerably shorter that the allotted 60-minutes of reading, sets the tone for the rest of the course. By proposing, and to some extent actually embarking on sketching out the elements of the proof of the soundness and completeness of the system of logical graphs, Peirce sets out to resolve, once and for all, what constitutes the "thorough and formal refutation of the fallacy" (R 448; EP 2, p. 243) advertised in the actually delivered lecture, the fallacy that Peirce took to have indisposed all earlier attempts to justify logical reasoning. Equally salient feature of this early plan is its emphasis on the analytic virtues of logical graphs. The graphical method is not meant to facilitate conclusion-drawing. Instead, it is intended to offer the best method hitherto developed to analyse what the very idea of necessary reasoning consists of, breaking the process of reasoning down to its smallest elements and discovering how those elements are chained to one other. This is the true philosophy of the system of logic, Peirce avers, proceeding to advance the method of graphs as the backbone of the new theory of the philosophy of logic soon to be articulated during the full term of the course.

The list which Peirce collated in late November presented the following famous titles as the suggested reading for the first lecture:

Lecture I.
What makes a reasoning sound?

Bosanquet, Bernard
    Knowledge and reality. A criticism of F. H. Bradley's
    "Principles of Logic". London, 1892.   **3607.126**
Bradley, Francis Herbert
    The principles of logic. London, 1883.   **3600.60**
Erdmann, Johann Eduard
    Outlines of logic and metaphysics. Translated by B. C. Burt. London, 1896. (Introductory science text-books.)   **3608.166**
    The title given by Mr. Peirce is: Benno Erdmann's Logik.
Sigwart, Christoph von
    Logic. 2d edition, enlarged. Translated by Helen Dendy. London 1895. 2 v.   **3604.119**
Trendelenburg, Friedrich Adolph
    Logische Untersuchungen. Berlin, 1840.   **B.6085.2**
Ueberweg, Friedrich
    System of logic, and history of logical doctrine.
    Translated by T. M. Lindsay. London, 1871.   **B.H.Ref.592.10. 3605.51**
Wundt, Wilhelm Max
    Logik. 2. Auflage. Stuttgart, 1893–95. 2 v. in 3.   **3603.148**

Ladies and Gentlemen:

I intend in these lectures to exhibit to you, as far as possible in so brief a course, the processes of modern scientific reasoning, and to explain what precautions have particularly to be attended to. I shall briefly explain why we ought to proceed as I say, while refraining from entering profoundly into the theory. In cases where views opposed to my own are supported by respectable reasons, I shall briefly examine them without going into any detailed controversy.

This evening I am going to explain to you a method for expressing any assertion with such precision as to enable us to deduce its precise consequences without danger of committing any errors, so long as certain evident rules are adhered to. I wish you to understand what the purpose of this system of expression is. It is *not* its purpose to enable us to draw any conclusions which we could not draw without it, nor to draw any conclusions that we could not just as easily and just as securely draw without it. If that should be the result, in some cases, well and good: but that I wish to say with all emphasis and distinctness is not what I aim at. The only thing I aim at is to obtain machinery by which I can pick necessary reasonings into their smallest parts, to carry the analysis of them to their very elements, and thus to discover what those elements are and how they are put together. If my aim were to facilitate reasoning, instead of endeavoring to separate every inference into as many distinct steps as possible, I should endeavor to construct a system of expression which should enable me to jump over as many inferential steps as possible at one bound, without danger of slipping. But my purpose is just the reverse of that.

Here is the blackboard. It is nothing but a wooden thing with a plane black surface. But with your coöperation, I will ~~effect~~ work a metamorphosis of it. It shall be a representation of the universe,—not necessarily the universe of experience, but a universe of my creation which may coincide with that real universe. So be it.

So now the blackboard is quite another thing than pieces of wood with a plane black surface. It is something wherein you can discover my universe if you look attentively.

But what kind of a representation is it? Not a mere copy or diagram or any kind of icon. I can tell you that the blackboard in no way resembles my universe, although in certain particulars I am going to make it so. Neither is it a mere index or symptom of my universe by virtue of any physical connection with it. To be sure, it is so to some extent, since I intend by my muscular force to make certain marks on the board by which you can learn something of the characters of my universe. But the blackboard is already and is going to be still more so, a more intellectual sort of representation of the universe, representing it by virtue of certain intelligible ~~Rules~~ PRINCIPLES which you and I are going to agree upon.

Let the first of these ~~rules~~ principles be this:

Principle I. Whatever is written on the board shall be asserted to be true of the Universe in question.[1]

This is clear. We all know what it is to *assert* anything. An act of assertion is a contract, the effect of which is that if what is asserted is not true, the assertor forfeits in a measure his reputation for veracity.

The lilacs are in bloom.

Here is an example.[2] It is asserted that in my universe the lilacs are in bloom.

Now I wish to ~~write~~ assert something else. But to enable me to do that, I shall ask you to agree to a second ~~rule~~ principle.

Principle II. Anything written shall have its meaning independently of anything else that may be written on another part of the board and that is, not joined to it by any line of connection. If so joined the meaning shall only undergo such modification as that line imports.

Our **principles** must be perfectly strict; and therefore, in order to conform to this ~~rule~~ one, I must modify

The lilacs are in bloom **[P.H.]**

and make it

The lilacs are in bloom **[P.H.]**

For if the words were separate, they would have to be understood independently of one another. I will exemplify this principle by making some additional assertions about my universe.

The lilacs are in bloom.
Something moves over something.
Something is the ground.
Something is rustling.

No matter how near together they are written, those assertions are nevertheless written on different parts of the board, and are disconnected. They are therefore

---

1 [Principles I–IV are inscribed in blue ink in the original, as are the basic Rights of Transformation I–IV.]
2 [Examples of assertions and graphs, both inline and displayed, are inscribed in red ink in the original copy-text.]

asserted separately. I have therefore asserted that the lilacs are in bloom in my universe, that there is ground in my universe, that something moves over something in my universe, and that something rustles in my universe.

I want to free myself from the necessity of writing so often the long word "something". I therefore propose for adoption ~~the following rule~~ the **provisional principle** that

A heavy ~~dot~~ dash shall stand for an indefinite individual existing object.

I call this principle provisional, not because I do not mean to stick to it but because I mean to extend it.

We can by virtue of this rule write

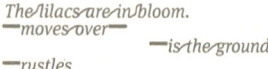

But now I wish to add two more assertions. Namely, I wish to assert that that something which rustles is the very same thing as that something which moves over something; and I further wish to assert that that something,—that existing object,—which is the ground is the very same thing as that something over which the rustling thing moves. In order to enable me to do this and other similar acts of assertion, as an extension of the provisional principle, I propose the following:

Principle III. All the ~~points~~ parts of any one heavy line, called a "line of identity", or "line of connection" shall denote the same existing object.

I now write

But there are other things than facts in my universe. There are *Laws*. For example, I do not say that there will ever be a flash of lightening in my universe. The creator of this universe has not made up his mind whether it ever shall lighten or not. But to one thing he has made up his mind, and it may be set down as true of this universe; namely, that if ever it shall lighten, then it shall thunder. But we have, as yet, provided no means of asserting this analytically. It might be written down as a whole. But it is necessary so to write it as to show the relation between the fact of lightening, should it lighten, to the thunder which the law would then compel. I propose then a fourth principle, in the enunciation of which I use the word "proposition" to mean an expression capable of being asserted, conceivably true.

Principle IV. The writing of ⒜̆ⒷÌ, an enclosure with an enclosure within it, and with a proposition, or possible assertion, singly enclosed in the outer enclosure and ~~an assertion~~ a proposition doubly enclosed in the inner enclosure shall ~~signify~~ assert that in case the singly enclosed proposition is true, then doubly enclosed proposition is also true, the conditional sentence being understood *de inesse*, that is, as meaning that either the antecedent is false or the consequent true.

We can write, then, ⟨*It shall lighten* ⟨*It shall thunder*⟩⟩.

Those four principles are all the fundamental principles of expression of which I shall make use. I shall introduce one or two little simplifications, writing something in one shape rather than another, but no new principles of expression will be used.[3]

---

3 [Alt.] [Two cut-out pages from R 36(s), ms pp. 11, 12] [...] new principles of expression will be used.

Having then established this system of expression, this simple language, the next ~~thing~~ task before us is to ~~make~~ ascertain the rules of ~~permissible~~ logical transformation of expressions of this system.

When anything is written on the blackboard, no matter what, say

ERASE and write
M

I may have a logical right to transform this into

N

This will be the case if the state of things that M asserts to exist involves as a part of the whole of it the state of things that N asserts to exist. But if N asserts anything not involved in the state of things asserted by M, then we have no logical right to transform M into N.

We wish to dissect the transformations as much as possible; because the very purpose of our study is to ascertain and describe the elements of the logical procedure.

Now it will be found that every transformation say of

L M

into

L N

where L represents ~~the part of~~ all in the assertion which remains unchanged, may be separated into two steps, in the first of which L M is changed to

Before going any further, I must show you how the third and fourth principles work when they are taken together. For there are some quite puzzling forms.

But first of all I must make you acquainted with a few words that are convenient in talking about these expressions.

In the figure last drawn, "It shall lighten" is singly enclosed; that is, one line, and one only, completely encircles it. "It shall thunder" is doubly enclosed, since two portions of the line, and only two, completely encircle it.[4] Suppose I make this assertion:

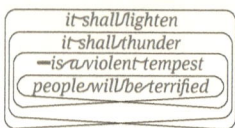

This means that if it shall lighten then two things will be true; first, it shall thunder, and second, if there is a violent tempest, people will be terrified. Again we might write this:

This means that if these two things are both true; first that if a house is struck by lightening property will be destroyed; and second, that [if] it shall lighten, then it will be true that insurance will be high.

Here parts of the expression are three and four times enclosed. Now I say of any part of an expression which is encircled any odd number of times that it is *oddly enclosed* and of any part that is encircled any even number of times, reckoning *zero* as an even number, that it is *evenly enclosed*. Therefore I say of a part that is not enclosed at all that it is evenly enclosed. This will be found convenient.

———

L M N

and in the second of which this is changed to

L N

[end]
4 [Del.:] Let us now examine the combination of the principle of the line of identity with the principle of enclosures.

I call this whole system of expression the **System of Existential Graphs**.⁵ By an *existential graph*, or as I shall commonly call it, a *graph*, I mean anything which ~~written alone~~ taken by itself would, according to the principles of this system, ~~assert~~ represent some conceivable state of things to exist ~~not absurd~~ even if it have no positive meaning. For example, if the board is a perfect blank, I call that a graph, because it represents my universe to exist, although it conveys no positive meaning, because that is among the things of which we had to take cognizance in the fundamental principles of the system upon which you and I agreed at the outset. So likewise I call any blank portion of the board a graph, because it represents the same state of things that the whole board, when blank, represents. So also this is a graph

though it conveys no positive meaning, any more than a blank space. This

―

is a graph that merely asserts that merely asserts that⁶ something exists. It would be a nice question whether that has any positive meaning or not.⁷

On the other hand, here is something that I do not call a graph.

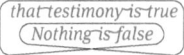

For that does not represent any conceivable state of things.⁸ I therefore call it, not a *graph*, but a *pseudograph*. Of a similar character is this

Nothing is false.

Such a pseudograph may be a part of a graph. Thus

is merely a way of saying that that testimony is not true.

---

5 ["**System of Existential Graphs**" inscribed in blue ink in copy-text.]
6 [Peirce wrote "merely asserts that" twice.]
7 [Its positive meaning is that "Something exists that is identical to itself".]
8 [Namely, does not have any model.]

Let us now examine the various modes of combinations of the principle of the line of identity with the principle of enclosures. The following

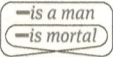

means that if there is a man in my universe then there is, in my universe something that is mortal.⁹ The following

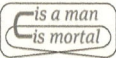

means that if there be anything in my universe that is a man that same thing is mortal. That whatever man there be in my universe is mortal; or either there is no man in that universe or all the men there are are mortal.

Here is something requiring a clear head for its interpretation:

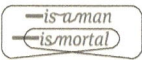

In order to make the meaning of this clear, first consider this

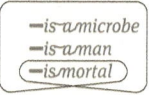

If there is a microbe and also a man then something is mortal. But this may be read: If there is a man coexistent with a microbe something is mortal; and we see that a blank space may be read "Is coëxistent with".

So

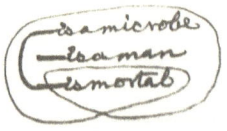 [P.H.]

means if there be a man then whatever is a microbe is mortal; or in other words, if there be a man whatever microbe be coexistent with that man is mortal. Now going back [three steps] to the figure

---

9 [Peirce's inscribing of words as connected strings does not occur in this and the next example in the original.]

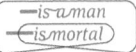

we see it reads: if there be a man then whatever there is, is mortal.[10]

The principal secret of the matter is readily explained, if you will give me your attention. Considering every line of identity to be as much enclosed as its least enclosed part, if this part is evenly enclosed it denotes *something suitably chosen*, but if it is oddly enclosed it denotes *any thing you please*. For example

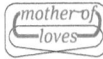

means: take any two things you please and if the first is mother of the second, that first loves the second; that is every mother loves everything of which she is the mother.

But the following,

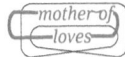

means that there is something A such that, taking anything you please, B, if A is mother of B, A loves B; that is something loves everything of which it is the mother.

Now if any of you care to practice with this form of expression, as I recommend you to do, as excellent training in exact thinking, you will, with care find no particular difficulty as long as you take care to ~~make~~ keep the innermost line of connection between every pair of connected graphs inside all the enclosures that both graphs are inside of. If you do not do that, your difficulties will be apt to surpass your skill in dealing with them. If, for example, you were to write

you would be very apt to interpret that to mean that something loves something and if a lover is a man then the object loved is a woman. For you are puzzled by the fact that the line of connection between "is a man" and "is a woman" runs outside of their common enclosure, through "loves". But what is here written may otherwise be written, thus:

---

10 [More accurately, "If there be a man then whatever *else* there is, is mortal".]

and means simply "If whatever loves anything is a man, then something loves a woman". This of course implies that something loves something.

But all this will be made infinitely clearer by studying how a graph once written may be altered without danger of rendering its assertion false. There are four

Basic Rights of Transformation

Right I. Any evenly enclosed graph may be erased; and under odd enclosures, already written, any graph can be inserted.

Right II. Any graph precisely like another that is written under no other enclosures than its own, and connected with the same graphs, can be erased.

Any graph can be repeated under the same or any already written additional enclosures, with the same connections.

Right III. Two enclosures one within the other with nothing between can anywhere be erased or inserted.

Right IV. Under an enclosure containing a pseudograph, it makes no difference what else is written, and the enclosure with all it encloses may be erased.

By using these ~~rules~~ rights we can draw from any premises any inferences that they justify, and not merely the stupid syllogisms of the Logic-books.

I will now proceed to ~~show~~ prove to you that we have these rights, and you will thereby gain a new light on the interpretation of graphs. The proof is excessively simple; but of course it is necessary to pay attention in order to follow it.

Of course, we have at any moment a right to ~~rub out~~ clean everything off the blackboard by a general erasure; for that is merely to cease insisting on our assertion. It cannot introduce any falsity since it introduces nothing at all.

Next, what is thus true of the entire graph is true of any partial graph which is unenclosed and disconnected from the rest. Thus, if this be true:

$$\begin{array}{c}\text{It snows}\\ \text{It blows}\end{array}$$

That is, if it is true that it snows and it blows, it is true that

$$\text{It snows.}$$

So this establishes Right No. 1 so far as it concerns graphs that are unenclosed and disconnected.

But to say that we have a right to transform an entire graph

$$\text{M} \quad \text{into another graph} \quad \text{N}$$

means that every state of things in which M is true is a state of things in which N is true. That is the sense in which these rights are asserted. Suppose then that we have written the graph

That means that K is true and that if L is true, M is true. If then M, were it written unenclosed, would be transformable into N, so that if M is true N is true, then the truth of the graph just written involves the truth of this:

which means that K is true (as before) and that if L is true, N is true. Now every graph without connections in which M is doubly enclosed can be put in the above form.

Thus we have proved that if a graph M can logically be transformed into a graph N when written unenclosed as an entire graph then M can equally be transformed into N when it forms the entire contents of an enclosure within another and is entirely disconnected with any other graph in a graph containing no lines of connection. Bear that principle well in mind. I shall have to refer to it more than once in this proof and will call it for the time being the

Principle of Barbara.[11]

Now suppose that Right No. 1 had been proved for every partial graph, entirely disconnected with other parts of the graph, and enclosed within any even number of enclosures less than a hundred. Then suppose we had a graph of this form:

where Q is a complicated graph containing M as partial graph, disconnected, and within 98 enclosures. Then were this graph Q written alone, the M in it could be transformed into N. Consequently, by the Principle of Barbara, we have a right to transform M into N in the graph just written, where it occurs under one hundred enclosures.

Therefore if Rule 1 Right No. 1 holds good for disconnected graphs within any even number of enclosures up to any number, it holds good also for the next higher even number of enclosures. But we have already proved it for 0 and for 2 enclo-

---

[11] The Principle of Barbara represents the principle of substitution in logic.

sures, and therefore it holds good for any even number of enclosures that can be reached by successive additions of 2.¹²

Reasoning is self-controlled thought. The majority of men have very little power of reasoning. They think, but they have no strong grip over their thoughts. Many men and women of sweet natures, without bad impulses or stormy passions, never need to acquire any athletic self-control. Others have been taught in childhood to control their actions and their feelings, but have never learned to control their thoughts.

The result is that not only do individuals fall into bad or insufficient reasoning; but whole nations, whole generations do so. Fortunately, the natural tendencies of the human mind are right in the main to just about the same degree that the natural tendencies of the human heart are right, knowledge does advance and methods of inquiry do improve. But the world would advance much more rapidly toward the truth, if men would put forth their energy to control their thoughts, and would train themselves, not in that medieval way of reasoning that the logic books teach but in the best ways of thinking that modern inquiry can make out.

God forbid that I should waste a single breath in trying to induce anybody to control his thoughts who is not inclined to take the trouble to do so. My services belong exclusively to those who do want to reason rightly, and who hunger and thirst after it.

When I was appointed to deliver a course here,¹³ I received several letters from my very best friends telling me, in flattering terms, how very agreeably I could lecture when I chose to make myself agreeable, and pointing out to me how greatly it was for my interest to make these lectures agreeable. I know well enough that it would be for my interest. But the world is full of men who, for one reason or another, are ~~unable to~~ incapable of consulting their interests; and I am one of them. For nearly half a century the best of my energies have been devoted to learning all I could about reasoning; and now it is high time I gave the benefit of what I have learned to those who care to make the necessary effort to comprehend it. I mean

---

12 [The main segment of the early pre-draft of the first lecture in R 454 ends here. Included next as the last five paragraphs of the present selection are written on the first couple of verso pages of the same notebook as the above main segment. They represent an alternative beginning of Peirce's introductory remarks and may be been his very first attempt to write the opening remarks of the course. The closeness of these remarks to his June 8 letter to James suggests that this undated notebook was near the correspondence that took place between the two men soon after Peirce's Harvard Lectures had finished in mid-May.]

13 [Peirce was confirmed of his appointment to deliver the Lowell Lectures in the upcoming academic year in early March.]

to consider them exclusively. Therefore these lectures will require close attention and a certain effort of thought.

I shall ~~examine~~ consider all the main classes of reasoning, Deductive, Inductive, and Abductive, as fully as I can do in so very short a course, paying the smallest possible attention to pure theory, but dwelling on the precautions necessary to be observed in practice. Mathematical reasoning, which is the easiest kind of reasoning, and which is essentially involved in all reasoning, will command our attention first.

33 Lowell Lecture II(a)

[Copy-text is R 450, plus a selection of relevant pages from R S-27 and R S-28. The notebook catalogued R 450 represents the first version of the pre-drafts for the second lecture, which was held, exceptionally, on Friday, November 27. R S-27 ("Graphs, Little Account") is a closely related, incomplete draft, also written on the Harvard Coop notebook. R S-28 contains another related notebook, entitled "The Conventions".] R 450 was probably and R S-27 definitely written soon after the completion of the first mature chapter of *Logical Tracts No. 2*. The writings that comprise the present selection constitute the first batch of the second lecture. They resemble, both textually and substantially, the content of the most mature version of *The Logical Tracts*. The likely dating of these writings is from September until at most early October. Only R S-28 ("The Conventions") has been dated to indicate its composition during the first half of September, and although that text presents the most elaborate attempt to explain the basic conventions of the theory of logical graphs preserved in the Peirce Papers, it appears to be a slightly earlier undertaking.

"The whole gist of the reasoning", Peirce proclaims at the outset of the second lecture, "is to state in the most general terms that relation of the state of things expressed in the conclusion of each inferential step to the state of things expressed in the premisses". In modern terms, what constitutes sound reasoning is the definition of the system of logical representation such that a semantic consequence relation arises from it. This important idea, which Peirce had already started to develop during the first lecture (informally in the delivered and formally in the undelivered early draft of R 454), matures into Peirce's definite and positive statement of the refutation of the earlier logicians' attempts to justify reasoning by appealing to the workings of the mind or to the nature of consciousness, as those attempts fail to analyse systematic and consistent changes in the forms of expression. The instrument best prepared to assume the task of the analysis of reasoning is, as Peirce now seeks to establish, the graphical system of logic.

The readings Peirce provided for his second lecture consisted of the following five items:

Lecture II.
A system of diagrams for studying logical relations. Exposition of it begun. (Existential graphs—Alpha & Beta)

Kempe, Alfred Bray
 A memoir on the theory of mathematical form. (In Philosophical transactions of the Royal Society. Vol. 177. pp. 1–70. London, 1887.)   ***3210.1.177**
Schroeder, Ernst
 Vorlesungen über die Algebra der Logik (exakte Logik). Leipzig, 1890–95. 3 v.   ****E.5113.9**
Studies in logic. By members of the Johns Hopkins University
 Boston, 1883.   **5600.58**
Symbolic logic, or algebra of logic (In Baldwin. Dictionary of philosophy and psychology. Vol. 2, pp. 640–651. New York, 1902.)   **B.H.Ref.590.1.2. *3601.132.2**
Whitehead, A. N.
 The logic of relations, logical substitution groups, and cardinal numbers. (In American Journal of Mathematics. Vol. 25, pp. 157–178. Baltimore, 1903.)   ****E.5081.10.25**

Ladies and Gentlemen:

Reasoning is not an art to be taught in eight lessons; but I can show you how you can improve yourselves in it. The first kind of reasoning to study is deduction, and of deduction, *necessary deduction*.

It has taken two generations to work out the explanation of the reasoning of mathematics.[1] The reasoning itself is everywhere evident; but to state in general terms and with precision how it proceeds, what the relation of the conclusion to the premisses is in each step has been no easy task. Logicians of all degrees of incompetence have imagined they could describe the reasoning. But when their explanations were examined, it was found that they passed over certain steps without explaining them, and that it was precisely in those steps that the whole gist of the reasoning was contained. How could those logicians so deceive themselves[?] Some of them mistook the nature of the problem, which really is to state in the most general terms that relation of the state of things expressed in the conclusion of each inferential step to the state of things expressed in the premisses;— that relation, I say,—wherein lies the impossibility of the premisses being true without the truth conclusion being true. Instead of doing this, those logicians endeavored simply to describe the phenomena of consciousness during the reasoning. But men who were so capable of missing the point of the problem had not the subtlety of thought that was needed even for the solution of the easier problem to which they addressed themselves. Others who saw what the problem really was, including most of the English logicians, failed because they attempted to penetrate beneath the forms of expression language to the very concepts of the mind. The consequence was that when such a logician was challenged to state the precise line of reasoning in any given demonstration of Euclid, for example, and he produced his statement, a sharp critic would ask, 'Well, how are you justified in passing from this statement to this?' and he would reply, 'Oh, that is a mere change in the form of expression'. But it would invariably be found that the entire gist of the demonstration lay in these changes in the form of the expression. After this sort of thing had happened many times, we all became convinced that[2] [t]he attempt to divest thought of expression and to get at the naked thought itself, which some logicians have made, is like trying to remove the peel from an onion and get at the naked onion itself. Reasoning is nothing but the discourse of the mind to its future self. What is required is simply to adopt a system of expressing

---

1 [This long paragraph was crossed out from "The reasoning itself ..." to "...we all became convinced that", continuing uncancelled from "The attempt to divest thought of expression..."]
2 [The preceding was crossed out from the present paragraph, except the first sentence. The continuation was with the capitalised "The attempt to divest thought of expression..."]

ourselves which admits of no ambiguity and is as simple as possible; and in that system of expression to state fully all the different stages of the demonstration to be explained, and to show that the passage from each one to the next takes place according to a rule which can evidently never authorize a passage from the representation of one state of things to a representation of a different state of things.

The first thing to be done, therefore, is to agree upon such an unambiguous and simple system of expression. The present lecture will be devoted to a description in outline of such a system. The present course is too short to enable me to do much toward illustrating the use of it. But if you will only learn this system, which is very easy, and will then ~~practice by~~ train yourselves in expressing facts in this way and in reasoning in this system, I can promise you that it will do wonders for you in helping to unravel tangles of thought.

But let the aim of this system not be mistaken. I wish to say ~~emphatetically~~ with all the emphasis I can command and once for all, that it is *not* intended to afford a speedy or ready passage from premisses to conclusion. It aims in the very opposite direction; namely, to break up reasonings into their smallest fragments, so that their constitution can be fully understood. Were it our aim to effect a speedy and ready passage from premisses to conclusion, we should want, on the contrary, to reduce long series of reasoning to single steps; which is precisely what we shall aim to avoid. In short, this system is not at all intended for an aid in reasoning, but only for an aid in the analysis of reasonings. But the study by means of it of the constitutions of different reasonings, and practice with it, helps immensely to make thought clearer, and thus is indirectly conducive to skill in reasoning.

The system of expression which I am about to describe is a system of *diagrams*. A diagram appeals to the eye like a picture, while it differs from a picture in that it obtrusively involves *conventional signs*. A conventional sign has, since Aristotle and earlier, received the name of *symbol*; but besides conventional symbols there are ~~symbols that are natural~~ signs of the same nature except that instead of being based on express conventions they depend on natural dispositions. They are natural symbols. All thought takes place by means of natural symbols and of conventional symbols that have become naturalized. Every symbol is employed over and over again, and we call all the occurrences of it occurrences of the same *symbol*. That is to say, it is the general type that makes the *symbol*, or its being made according to certain general precepts. A word is, therefore, wanted for the single embodiment of the symbol. I call it a *replica*. For example one word, namely *the*, will generally be repeated in ordinary English about once in from fifteen to twenty five words, according to the author's style. I express this by saying that one replica out of every 15 to 25 is a replica of the single word *the*.

The system of diagrams I am about to describe is called the *Method of Existential Graphs*.³ This system involves 14 *conventions*, or agreements that you and I shall have to come to as to the significations of parts of our graphs. ~~But of these 14 conventions, only 9 are of~~ ~~an arbitrary~~ a very general nature, the other 5 merely conventions called for by in the name of establishing each a special sign for occasional ~~simplification~~ use. To these fourteen I may prefix one which I will call Convention 0, since it does not pertain to this particular system but to every system of conventions of whatever kind.

Convention 0. Whatever feature of the signs is not the subject of an express convention can be freely varied without influence in the meaning.

To begin, every act of expression or of representation supposes two persons, one who makes the signs, and another who interprets them, that is in whose mind an interpreting sign is determined. In this case, we may call the sign-maker the *graphist* and the other the *interpreter*. The interpreter may be the graphist's future self. These two persons in order to have any intercourse must go upon a basis of common past experience, well-understood between them. When one says to the other 'It is cold', the other knows that he does not mean that it was cold in Iceland during the glacial period or that it was cold in the Laputa of Gulliver's travels. The sum total of what they understand one another to be talking about, is what logicians call the *universe of discourse*. De Morgan introduced the term in November 6, 1846. Exact logic dates from that day. There are certain truths which they well-understand one another to hold as indubitable concerning that universe. ~~I shall assume that that universe is the creation of some mind. It certainly is so in some cases, as when men dispute as to the~~ In particular, they always agree that the universe is a collection of *individuals*, by which I mean that of every object in it, every possible predicate is either wholly true or wholly false. If there were in the universe such an object as "Any triangle" that would be an object of which it could neither be said that "Any triangle is equilateral" nor that "Not any triangle is equilateral". They also agree that these individuals are *definite* individuals, so that no ~~assertion~~ predicate concerning any of them is at once both true and false. That is, there is no such object existing in the universe as "Some triangle" of which it would be true at once that "Some triangle is equilateral" and also that "Some triangle is non-equilateral".

In addition to the graphist and the interpreter, if we assume that the universe of discourse is the creation of some mind, as it obviously is when men dispute for

---

3 [Del.:] The system of expression which I am going to describe is a system of diagrams; and these diagrams I call *existential graphs*. Everything we call a diagram appeals to the eye, and yet at the same time involves conventional signs.

example about the sanity of Hamlet, and as we shall find in a future lecture that it must be wherever necessary reasoning is admissible,[4] and as still later in the course we shall find that we virtually assume it to be whenever we reason at all, then we shall have to take account of this author of the universe of discourse who may be called the *grapheus*.[5]

The first convention or agreement which I shall ask you to join me in establishing is this:

Convention No. 1. The surface of this blackboard, excepting such parts as we may find it convenient to sunder from the rest, and with an extension to be indicated in another convention, shall be called our *sheet of ~~assertion~~ assent*, and every proposition the regular expression of which the imaginary graphist, ~~that is, the lecturer~~ with the concurrence of the interpreter shall at anytime ~~express~~ place upon that sheet of ~~assertion~~ assent, shall be understood ~~as asserted~~ to be mutually agreed to by them both, as representing a truth upon my universe of discourse.[6]

Every expression of a proposition in conformity with the conventions of this system is called an *existential graph*, or for brevity, a *graph* (although there are other kinds of graphs). Since it is sometimes awkward to say that a graph is *written* and it is sometimes awkward to say it is *drawn*, I will always say it is *scribed*. A graph scribed on the sheet of assent is said to be *accepted*. We must ~~always~~ distinguish carefully between the *graph* and its different *replicas*. It is the *graph* which is accepted; and the graph is scribed when a *replica* of it is scribed.

Some oranges have red pulp.

The sheet of assent itself is of the nature of a *graph*; for it represents the idea of the universe which graphist and interpreter mutually ~~understand~~ agree to be true

---

4 **[Del.:]** we must avoid being led into any discussion that can be avoided and therefore you may, if you like, regard my assumption that the universe of discourse is in every case the creation of a mind as a fiction which becomes convenient owing to my not having been able to find any way of describing the simplest proposition, without winding myself up inextricably unless I make this assumption.

5 **[Del.:]** The universe of discourse, it is to be understood, is in every respect determinate and definite, so that every possible assertion about it is either true or false, while no assertion about it is both true and false.

6 **[Del.1:]** with the full assent of the interpreter. **[Del.2:]** and such expression shall be called a *graph*. Since I do not know whether it is more proper to say that a graph is written or drawn, I will say that it is *scribed*. I cannot tarry to inquire into the nature of this act of assertion. Suffice it to say that it is similar to writing one's name on the back of a ~~check~~ note. It renders the graphist responsible for the truth of the proposition he writes.

at the outset of their conversation. The sheet together with all that is at any time ~~written on~~ scribed on it is likewise a *graph*.

I now hasten to Convention No. 2 which is of all the conventions the one which is most arbitrary and most characteristic of this ~~peculiarity~~ special system of expression.

Convention No. 2. If different graphs are scribed on entirely different parts of the sheet of assertion, each shall have the same significance as if the other were not there. All that is scribed shall be called the *entire graph*, the entire graph together with the sheet of assent itself shall be called the *total* graph, and *graphs* scribed in presence of others shall be called *partial graphs*.

Some oranges have red pulp.
Natural expression is the last perfection of style.

Of course, in case different diagrams have a common part, they will not be written on different parts of the sheet; and this convention will not apply.

The following is a

Supplement to Convention No. 2. It is best to conceive that *replicas* are movable upon the sheet of assent and that the blackboard is only a part of ~~the sheet of assent~~ that sheet, namely, that part to which attention is directed at the moment. The rest of the sheet of assent is an imaginary extension of the board. Thus, when a graph is erased from the board, assent to it is not necessarily withdrawn. It is only moved ~~off~~ away to a distant part of the sheet.

Convention No. 3 requires a little introductory explanation. The conditional form of sentence "*If* one thing is true, *then* another thing is true", is employed in everyday language in several different senses. In theoretical assertions, it most commonly refers to a universe of possibilities and asserts that throughout that whole range of possibility whenever the antecedent, or protasis, is true, the consequent, or apodosis is true along with it. This form of sentence, however, is sometimes used without any reference to any state of things than the actually existing state. This makes what logicians call a conditional proposition *de inesse*. I will not stop to explain how the word *inesse* comes to have this meaning. But *de inesse* means regardless of what *might be* and considering only what *actually is*. The conditional *de inesse* does not imply that there is any connexion between the state of things supposed in the antecedent and that which is conditionally asserted in the consequent, because any such connexion would be an affair of possibilities. That is to say, there is no further connection than this, that the assertor of the proposition says he knows that the consequent is true unless the antecedent be false. Consider, for example, this conditional proposition: "If some oranges have red pulp, then naturalness is the last perfection of style". If this be understood *de inesse*, then in any universe in which there were no oranges with red pulp, it would be true regardless of what might be the last perfection of style. For the proposition asserts nothing at all about the case of there being no oranges with red pulp, and consequently it asserts nothing false. But every proposition is either true or false. Hence, it is true. So likewise in any universe in which naturalness is the last perfection of style, the proposition would be true regardless of the character of the oranges. The only sort of universe in which it would be false would be one in which there were oranges with red pulp but in which naturalness was not the last perfection of style. It is obvious that in the ordinary use of language there can hardly be any occasion for this form of proposition. But in the logical analysis of meaning, it is very convenient. Thus, consider the ordinary conditional proposition, "If a spark should fall into this barrel of gunpowder, it would go off". The meaning of this may be very conveniently analyzed as being that in each possible state of things either no spark will fall in or else the gunpowder will go off; that is, in each possible state of things the conditional proposition will be true *de inesse*. It thus becomes highly desirable to have a form which shall signify a conditional proposition de inesse without any danger of its being interpreted as any other kind of conditional proposition. Let us fulfill this desideratum by drawing a scroll around antecedent and consequent thus:

$$\boxed{\text{Some oranges have red pulp} \atop \boxed{\text{Natural expression is the last perfection of style}}}$$

Here the scroll with its contents is scribed on the sheet of assertion, and asserts the conditional proposition *de inesse*. But the two members of that proposition, the antecedent and the consequent, are cut off from the sheet of assertion by the line of the scroll. I may mention that no significance is attached to the fact that the line crosses itself. That is a mere convenience in drawing it. The essential feature of the scroll is that it consists of two closed lines one inside the other. Each of these lines is called a *sep* and the space within it its *close*. The word *enclosure* will be used to mean the *sep* together with whatever is in its *close*. An *enclosure*, therefore, is a replica of a *graph*, that is, the expression of a proposition in this system. Namely, it is the sep, considered not as a mere chalk-mark but as a sign which refers to what is in its close. The agreement to understand the *scroll* as the sign of a conditional proposition *de inesse* constitutes Convention No. 3. I beg you particularly to observe that a sep, or enclosing line, that is not itself enclosed lies on the sheet of assertion. But no point of its close is on the sheet of assertion, since the *sep* cuts it off. This constitutes **Convention No. 3**.

You may well be surprised at my rating the Convention No. 3 as less arbitrary than Convention No. 2. But that is simply because I have not time to develop the reasons that almost compel it.

The flight of time forces me to pass over the next ~~five six~~ five conventions in a very summary manner. They all relate to certain heavily drawn lines which I call *lines of identity*. The best way of introducing these conventions to you will be by examples.

I write •has red pulp to mean that there exists in the universe something that has red pulp. I write •teaches• to mean something teaches something, •is greater than• to mean something is greater than something, •gives•to•in exchange for• to mean that something gives something to something in exchange for something. Each heavy dot stands for some undesignated individual object existing in the universe. This is **Convention No. 5**, which reads: Every heavily marked point shall denote a single individual object (undesignated by the dot itself).

If a proper name were inserted in place of each dot the result would be a *proposition*. I must inform you that quite regardless of this particular system of expression which I am expounding, the word *rhema* is used in logic to denote any proposition and any blank form which would become a proposition if every one of its blanks were filled with a proper name. Thus, the following are rhemata

Cain killed Abel
Cain killed———
———killed Abel
———killed———

In this system every expression of a rhema whose meaning the diagram does not analyze is called a *spot*. Around this spot are places where *dots* may be placed so as to produce *graphs*, that is assertions expressed in this system. These places round a spot, where the dots may be placed are called its *hooks*. I have now told you the substance of **Convention No. 4**.

The following graph •is an orange •has red pulp asserts that something is an orange and something has red pulp. Now if I wish to express that the very same thing is an orange and has red pulp, I scribe it thus (is an orange has red pulp That heavy line expresses *individual identity* which logicians call numerical identity. So (teaches) asserts that somebody teaches himself. That is the substance of **Conventions 5** and **6**. The former asserts that a point which belongs at once to two diagrams each of which by itself would be a graph, shall be understood to denote one individual object. **Convention 6** introduces the continuous line.

Let us allow lines of identity to branch. Thus

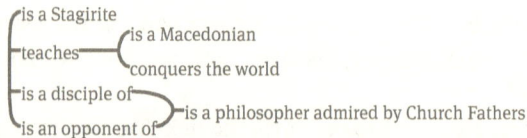

will mean that there is a Stagirite who teaches a Macedonian conqueror of the world and who is at once a disciple and an opponent of a philosopher admired by Fathers of the Church. That is the substance of **Convention No. 7**.

Look at the following

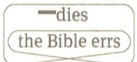

This means that, if it be true that there is something that dies, then the Bible errs;— a manifestly false assertion. Suppose, however, we extend the line of identity to the outer sep thus:

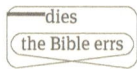

Now this point on the sep denotes an existing individual. I assume that our universe of discourse is the totality of all historical men. We can hardly avoid interpreting the graph as meaning that if that individual man dies (say perhaps Enoch or Elijah), the Bible errs. So take this.

It means that if there be a salamander something lives in fire; and the meaning will not be affected by prolonging the outer line of identity to the inner sep. If however we join the two lines of identity, thus,

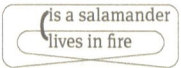

we can hardly resist the interpretation, 'If anything is a salamander that very something lives in fire', that is, 'Whatever salamander there may be lives in fire'. This is the substance of **Convention No. 8**, which reads that the junction by a line of identity of a point on a sep to a point within the close of the sep expresses the identity of the individuals, either hypothetically or conditionally, just as any predicate in the same close is expressed.

I may remark that propositions whose expressions in this system involve lines of identity are called *categorical* propositions; and the ordinary logic books teach that they are simpler than conditional propositions which in this system would be written without such lines. It is a blundering sort of way of looking at the matter.

I have now set forth the nine principal conventions of the system; and I now proceed to the five subsidiary conventions. But I may here remark that I have not thought it proper to count it as a convention of this system that ~~accidental~~ no feature of graphs which is unmentioned in the conventions has any significance; because this is a matter of course in all conventions relating to all subjects. For example, we have said nothing in our conventions about the shape or size of lines of identity or of seps. Consequently, it makes no difference what their shapes and sizes may be.[7]

Convention No. 10 requires a few words of introduction. I have called your attention to the fact that the graphist and interpreter necessarily have some common experience and firm belief and understand one another to have it. That may be regarded as expressed by the blank sheet of assertion before anything is written upon it. Any graph which should merely assert any part of that common basis, as a dot standing alone, for example, • does, has no meaning. That is, it leaves the sheet with the same meaning after it was written that it had before. Nevertheless, I call it a graph. I call the blank sheet of assertion a graph. For it stands to graphist and interpreter for all that they agree to. On the other hand, any expression which contradicts what graphist and interpreter have agreed that they will not deny, such as 'Nothing is true', or

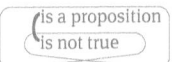

violates the first convention, and is therefore not properly an expression of this system. I do not call that a graph, but *pseudograph*. I say not *a* pseudograph but *the* pseudograph because all such expressions are equivalent in this system, all being alike violations of the conventions. To write the pseudograph on the sheet of assertion would be equivalent to burning up the sheet, since the sheet only exists, as such, in the minds of the graphist and the interpreter, and *that* by virtue of the agreement which the writing of the pseudograph destroys. Notwithstanding this, it is often useful to write the pseudograph in the inner close of a graph. Take this for example

---

7 [This is what Peirce elsewhere lists as Convention 0.]

This says 'If Washington was a commonplace man, then every assertion is false'. That is as much as to say that Washington was not a commonplace man.

Now **Convention No. 10** is that filling up a close so as to leave no room in it shall be understood as inserting the pseudograph in the close. Hence in order to deny that Washington was a commonplace man, we can write

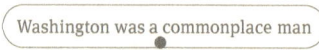

or since the size of a sep is not a significant feature

Washington was a commonplace man

Or making the loop infinitesimal, we shall understand a sep as denying what is written in its close.

There are a number of important corollaries from this convention which I have not time to point out. You will easily make them out for yourselves.

It sometimes happens that lines of identity have to cross one another and produce confusion. Conventions 11 and 12 provide means of remedying this inconvenience. **Convention No. 12** is that in such case the lines of identity may have parallels drawn on either side of them near the intersection. Thus

Convention No. 11 allows to put a capital letter as the proper name of an undesignated individual. These are called *Selectives*. At first sight, this device seems an admirable simplification, and tempts us to abandon the use of lines of identity altogether. It results however in endless complications especially in transforming the graphs. Nevertheless, it is occasionally useful in a very high degree.

Conventions Nos. 13 and **14** are perhaps the most important of all, notwithstanding my reckoning them as merely subsidiary. I do so because they merely introduce special kinds of signs. It is by means of these conventions that I have been enabled, at last, to discover the real gist of mathematical reasoning which lies in the operation of *abstraction*, whereby we reflect or turn round upon thought itself and make it the object of thought. [end][8]

---

8 [40 blank notebook pages follow the end of this first part of the second lecture. The page numbers in the third column of the table below make a cross-reference to the pagination of the

Convention	No. 1	p. 21	Sheet
"	No. 2	25	Two graphs
"	No. 3	31	Scroll
"	No. 8	59	Sep on sheet
"	No. 4	43	attachment to spot
"	No. 5	45	dot
"	No. 6	45	Continuous line
"	No. 7	47	Branching
"	No. 12	75	╬
"	No. 9	60	⊖
"	No. 11	71	Selectives
"	No. 10	64	Pseudograph
"	No. 13	81	$p_1 p_2 p_3$ etc.
"	No. 14	82	[*entia rationis*: line of identity placed between two rows of dots / dotted ovals with dotted lines]

Graphs: Little account

[Copy-text is R S-27, a Harvard Cooperative Society notebook. An alternative and possibly a slightly later draft of the second lecture than R 450, which nevertheless ends before completing the description of the fourteen conventions. Peirce wrote on the cover of the notebook: "See opp. page 17 for important note on sep".]

Ladies and Gentlemen:

The first kind of reasoning to be studied is *Deduction*. Deduction is that kind of inference in which the fact expressed in the conclusion is inferred from the facts expressed in the premisses, regardless of the manner in which these facts have come to the reasoner's notice. Deduction is either necessary or probable. *Necessary deduction* is that sort of inference in which the fact concluded is conceived to be involved in the facts premissed. It is the reasoning of mathematical demonstration.

It has taken two generations to work out the explanation of mathematical reasoning. This delay has been partly due to many writers entirely missing the point and directing their energies to ascertain the sequence of mental phenomena in reasoning instead of the logical sequence of the argument, which need not be closely related to the psychological sequence. The delay has also been due in part to the circumstance that some students attempted to divest thought of its garment of expression and to get at the naked thought itself, an attempt analogous to that to remove the peel from an onion so as to get at the naked onion itself. Reasoning is nothing but the discourse of the mind to itself. Divest thought of signs and it ceases to be thought, and becomes, at best, direct perception.

---

manuscript pages of the main mature segment of the text of R 492, the *Logical Tracts No. 2*. Peirce listed the conventions hitherto expounded in this table that appears in the last page of the notebook.]

What is requisite is to take really typical mathematical demonstrations,—and state each of them in full, with perfect accuracy, so as not to skip any step, and then to state the principle of each step so as perfectly to define it, yet making this principle as general as possible. For routine demonstrations there is no particular difficulty; but for the major theorems there is much. If we attempt to make the statement in ordinary language, the task success is practically impossible. Our syntax was not made with a view to such propositions; and it sometimes defies ingenuity to express them, I do not say clearly, but accurately with whatever intricacies of expression in words. At all times, the burden of language is felt severely, and leaves the mind no energy for its main work. Yet this is the least of the disadvantages of ordinary speech. After we have weeded out its ambiguities, it presents so many forms whose precise difference of meaning we are not prepared to define that we are very apt to pass over important steps of reasoning as mere changes in grammatical transformations; and in many cases we see pretty clearly that an inference holds good but are provided with no sure way of stating its principle in general terms. Mathematicians have found themselves obliged to resort to algebraic arrays of letters in order to express themselves. But their algebras were devised for a purpose quite inconsistent with that of logical analysis, and are of no material help. It is necessary to devise a system of expression for the purpose which shall be competent to express any proposition whatever without being embarrassed by its complexity, which shall be absolutely free from ambiguity, perfectly regular in its syntax, free from all disturbing suggestions, and come as near to a clear skeleton diagram of that element of the fact which is pertinent to the reasoning as possible. I am going to devote this lecture to a brief description of a system of expression which, if it does not quite satisfy my ideal of what such a system ought to be, is at any rate the best I have been able to devise during forty years study of the problem. If you will learn this system and will then train yourselves to the use of it, I can promise that it will help you much to unravel tangles of thought.

Only, let not its aim be mistaken. I wish to declare distinctly and once for all that it is *not* intended to furnish a speedy or ready way by which to pass from premisses to conclusion. It aims in the diametrically opposite direction, namely, to break up reasoning into the greatest possible number of distinct steps, so that the constitution of reasoning may be studied. If we wished to obtain a speedy passage from premisses to conclusion, we should, on the contrary, seek to make the steps as few and as large as we could. In short this system is meant not as an aid in reasoning but as an aid in the minute analysis of reasonings. Practice with it, however, will make thought clearer, and will so conduce indirectly to skill in reaching conclusions.

This system is a system of *diagrams*. A diagram has the advantage of appealing to the eye, and to that adds others due to the prominence it gives to *conventional signs*. Every conventional sign or other symbol is employed over and over again. The word *the* will occur several times on every page of English print; and it is everywhere one and the same word. Thus, it is the general type that constitutes the self-identity of the symbol; that is, it is its being formed in conformity to certain general precepts. But everyone of those single embodiments of the word *the* which we find on a page; what are we to call them? A word is wanted for the purpose. I will call the single embodiments of a symbol, whether conventional or natural, its *replicas*.

The special system of diagrams that I am about to describe is called the *Method of Existential Graphs*. This system will repose upon 14 conventions or agreements into which you and I shall have to engage as to the significations of parts of our graphs. When I say there are 14 conventions, there is one that I do not count for the reason that it does not belong to this particular system any more than it does to any other system of conventions relating to no matter what subject. I will therefore number this Convention Number Zero. It reads as follows:

Convention No. 0. Whatever feature of a sign of this system is not the subject of any express convention can be varied indefinitely, without affecting the meaning of the sign.

For example, nothing being said about the size of certain parts of our diagrams,[9] they can be made excessively small. Nothing being said about the length or shape of certain lines, we are free to give them any length and shape that may suit purposes.

Convention No. 1 depends upon the consideration that an act of expression is a performance in which two persons take part, the one making the signs, the other interpreting them. It is essentially the same when a man deliberates with himself. He impulsively formulates an assertion, not necessarily in words, but in some kind of expression; and the self of a moment later criticizes and accepts or rejects, which requires him first to interpret the ~~sign~~ expression, that is, to reexpress it in his consciousness of a moment later. Vernacular language often embodies sound psychology, and the vulgar phrase "I says to myself" is endorsed by the most scrupulous science. Milton and Shakespeare speak of the "discourse of reason".

But if one person is to convey any information to another, it must be upon the basis of a common experience. They must not only have this common experience, but each must know the other has it; and not only that but each must know the other knows that *he* knows the other has it; so that when one says 'it is cold' the other may know that he does not mean that it is cold in Iceland or in Laputa, but right here. In short it must be thoroughly understood between them that they are talking about objects of a collection with which both have some familiarity. The collection of objects to which it is mutually understood that the proposition refer is called by exact logicians the *universe of discourse*. A certain amount of truth about this universe is taken for granted between the two. So far they have the same idea of the universe; upon that universe the attention of both is fixed; and when one makes any assertion to the other, and the other assents to it, what happens is simply that their common idea of the universe becomes more definite; for their whole discourse is about that and nothing else. Now the first convention or agreement, which I shall ask you to join in establishing is this:

Convention No. 1.[10] The whole surface of this blackboard, excepting such parts as we may agree to sunder from the rest, together with any other surface which we may hereafter adjoin to it, shall be

---

9 [Alt.] [...] about the size of certain parts of our diagrams they can be made excessively small. Nothing being said about the length or shape of certain lines, they can be given any length and shapes we find convenient.

Convention No. 1 depends upon the consideration that an act of *expression* is an operation performed by two persons, of whome one makes the signs, while the other interprets them. That it is essentially the same thing when a man thinks, is attested by the common phrase, "I says to myself". The most scientific examination of the matter only ~~ratifies~~ endorsed this vulgar conception. Milton and Shakespeare call reasoning "discourse of reason". However, for simplicity, we will suppose that there are two different persons, the *graphist* who makes the diagrams, and the *interpreter* who reads them [end]

10 [Alt.] Convention No. 1. The whole surface of a certain paper page or blackboard, together with whatever other surface which we may hereafter see fit to adjoin to it, both excepting such parts as we may sever from the rest, shall, under the name of the *sheet of assertion* be considered as a representation of the universe of discourse; and every proposition of which ~~the imaginary graphist shall, with the assent of the interpreter, render~~ an expression ~~according~~ conforming to the conventions of this system shall be made legible upon the ~~sheet shall thereby be understood to be~~

called our *sheet of assertion*, and every proposition the regular expression of which our imaginary graphist shall, at any time, render legible upon this surface, shall be understood to be thereby asserted of the universe, thus rendering the blackboard a more definite representation of the universe.

For example, the graphist writes

Some orange has red pulp

We are thus informed that the universe is one in which there is an orange with red pulp.

Throughout this course, I shall avoid all questions of theoretical logic as far as I possibly can. I shall, therefore, not stop to inquire what assertion consists in. There will be the less need of doing so inasmuch as it will be quite foreign to our purpose to inquire into the truth of assertions placed on the board. The word *assertion* means etymologically *braiding to*; and in this connection it is used [to] mean that that proposition which might be written elsewhere quite idly or to practice one's handwriting, or for any other purpose when put upon this board is meant to be attached to the universe of discourse. The interpreter is supposed to assent to all that the graphist asserts.

I ask attention to the following definition. Every expression of a proposition according to the conventions of this system is called an *existential graph*. But since we shall have no occasion to refer to other kinds of graphs, we may say *graph* simply when we mean an existential graph. The *graph* is the symbol, it is only a replica of it that can be placed on the sheet of assertion; but we may say that the graph is *scribed* on the sheet when a replica of it is placed there.

The sheet of assertion is itself a *graph*, and what is scribed upon it is a *graph*, and the two taken together form a *graph*.

I now hasten to the second convention which is, of all the conventions, the one that is the most arbitrary and the most characteristic of this special system of expression.

Convention No. 2.[11] Two different graphs legibly scribed on the sheet of assertion in such a way that either might be removed without disturbing the other shall each have the same significance as if the other was not there.

For example, our graphist writes something further on the sheet

Some orange has red pulp
Naturalness is the last perfection of style

Thus our idea of the universe becomes still more determinate.

We shall do well to conceive that the graph-replicas are movable over the sheet of assertion, and that the blackboard is not the whole sheet, but only the part of it to which attention is directed at the moment. Accordingly, when a replica on the board is rubbed out we need not understand

---

~~known to be true~~ asserted of the universe, ~~rendering the representation of it more definite.~~ board or page shall be understood thereby ~~assertorically applied to that universe~~ ~~to receive an assertory application to the universe~~ ~~applied to the universe assertorily~~ ~~with assertory force~~ asserted of the universe.

11 [Alt.] Convention No. 2. A graph-replica no part of which coincides in position with any part of another graph-replica shall (whatever others may be on the sheet) ~~have the same significance~~ ~~have the same assertory value~~ make the same assertion [were it to stand] alone.

that the graphist retracts his assertion, since he may merely have shoved the replica away to a distant part of the sheet.

I must here trouble you with three definitions. *Partial graphs* are graphs ~~scribed in~~ on the sheet of assertion that are not the only ones scribed on the sheet. The *entire graph* is all that is scribed on the sheet. The *total graph* is the entire graph together with the sheet of assertion itself.

Convention No. 3 will require a few introductory words. In ordinary language the conditional form of sentence, 'If one thing, then another thing' is employed for various purposes. Most commonly, in theoretical assertions, at least, it refers to a universe of possibilities—a "range of possibility", as we say,—and means that, throughout this range of possibility, in whatsoever state of things the protasis, or antecedent, would be true, in that same state of things the apodosis, or consequent, would likewise be true. It is only rarely that in ordinary language the conditional form is used in a sense which is of the highest importance in logic, in which no range of possible states of things is considered, but merely the actual state of things. A conditional proposition which has this meaning is called a conditional *de inesse*. To say that there is a *connection* between one fact and another fact is to talk of *possibilities*. Since, therefore, the conditional *de inesse* does not refer to possibilities, but only to the actual state of things, it does not imply any connection between the facts expressed by antecedent and consequent. Take for example the proposition "If any orange has red pulp then naturalness is the last perfection of style", understanding this *de inesse*. Now there are four possible cases, as here shown:

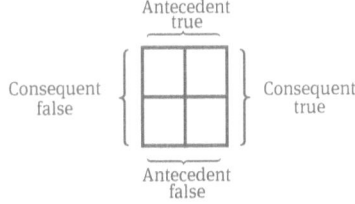

If the Antecedent is false, the proposition asserts nothing at all. It therefore contains no falsity. But every proposition is either true or false. Hence, the Conditional *de inesse* is in this case true, no matter how it may be with the consequents. If the Antecedent and Consequent are both true, then all that the Conditional asserts is true. Hence the Conditional *de inesse* is true if the consequent is true, regardless of the Antecedent. If however the Antecedent is true and the Consequent false, the Conditional *de inesse* is false. This therefore is the only one of the four possibilities which this form of proposition excludes.

It is absolutely indispensable that our system of expression should be provided with a way of expressing a conditional *de inesse*; and if it can express this kind of conditional, other conventions will enable it to express all other kinds of conditional propositions without difficulty. Now let the conditional *de inesse* be expressed in this way:

'If any orange has red pulp, then naturalness is the last perfection of style'.

The line consists of two ovals. The whole of it is called a *scroll*. Each oval is called a *sep* Sep .[12] The inner sep of a scroll is called its *loop*. The space enclosed by a sep is called its *close*. When one sep encloses another the space within the outer sep but not within the inner sep is called the *immediate* close of the outer *sep*, while this immediate sep together with the *close* of all the enclosed seps is the *entire* close of the outer sep. A sep together with all it contains is called an *enclosure*. It will be necessary to bear those terms in mind. A scroll is a curve consisting of one oval within another. A sep is a single oval. The inner sep of a scroll is its *loop*. The surface inside a sep is its *close*. Its *immediate close* is enclosed in no inner sep; its *entire* close embraces the whole space within it. An *enclosure* is a *sep* together with all it contains; or better, the *enclosure* is the sep considered as having its meaning as a sign determined by what it contains.

We now have two conventions, as follows:

Convention No. 3.[13]
1. A self-returning cut in the sheet of assertion or in any area enclosed within that sheet shall be considered to be itself, with every point of it, that sheet or area.
2. It is not a graph and shall not affect the meaning of any graph-replica placed upon its line.
3. It shall cause the entire area within it to denote a world of ideas then and there created by the graphist.
4. The peculiar special quality of the cut shall assert a corresponding peculiar special relation between the world of ideas represented by the area it encloses and the world represented by the area in which the cut is made.

---

12 [The latter "Sep" was inscribed on this notebook leave (pagination 17) in red ink. Probably this was meant to mark a reference to what Peirce intended to provide on the opposite leave (the verso of page 16), as suggested by what he wrote on the cover of the present notebook: "See opp. page 17 for important note on sep". The verso of 16 is left blank, however, and no proximal notebook or loose leaf contains a separate note on the sep either. What he did write concerning seps in the present notebook are located within the definition of Convention 3 and in its several rejected variants, and are provided in the present selection below.]

13 [Del.:] A self-returning cut in the sheet of assertion or in any other area shall be considered to be itself with every point of it on that sheet or in that area; together with every point of it and to be there in its semantic character as referring to its contents shall differ from a mark in that it leaves but it is not itself a graph and does not affect the signification of any point or line of a graph or of another cut entirely which may lie upon it. The cut shall have two effects. First, it shall cause show that the area within it is intended to refer to a world of ideas there and there created by the graphist. Secondly, the cut, being fact that the cut is in the sheet of assertion or other area shall show that what is asserted of its world of ideas is asserted only in so far as it affects the world of the area in which it lies.

[Del.:] **Convention No. 3.** A sep scribed on the sheet of assertion or in any close shall be understood to sunder its entire close from the area in which it is itself scribed. The sep itself and all points upon it shall be considered to be quite outside the sep Points upon that sheet and a sep scribed in the immediate close of another sep shall be understood to sunder its entire close from the immediate close of the outer sep.

Convention No. 4.[14] A sep scribed on the sheet of assertion and containing another sep shall be understood to assert *de inesse* that if all that is expressed in its immediate close expect the inner sep be true when interpreted as it would be if legibly scribed on the sheet of assertion then all that is expressed in the close of that inner sep is true, when interpreted in the same manner.

You will probably be surprised that I should say that these conventions are less arbitrary than Convention No. 2. But that is because I have not time to develop the argument to show that the conditional *de inesse* can only be expressed in a manner essentially the same as that described.

The next seven conventions relate to the expression of individual identity and will call for little comment.

Convention No. 5. The heavy marking of a point on the sheet of assertion causes that point to denote a single individual existing in the universe of discourse, and therefore asserts such existence without distinguishing that individual from others.

Thus • asserts that some individual objects exists. But ⁚ does not assert that two individuals exist; for by Convention No. 2 each dot means just what it would if the other were not there; so that the pair merely asserts twice over that some individual object exists.

I am forced to inflict upon you one or two definitions more. A *rhema* is either a proposition or a blank form that would become a proposition if all its blanks were filled with proper names. Here are examples:

Rhemata
Cain killed Abel
killed Abel
Cain killed
killed

A rhema which is made a part of a graph and is not itself compounded according to the rules of existential graphs is called a *spot* and the places where proper names might be inserted are called the *hooks* of the spot.

Convention No. 6. The placing of heavily marked points at all the hooks of a legible spot on the sheet of assertion shall be understood as asserting that there exist in the universe individuals related to one another as would be the individuals denoted by proposer names filling the blanks of the rhema.

For example •kills• will mean assert something kills something. •gives•to•in exchange for• will assert that something gives something to something in exchange for something.

---

14 [Alt.] **Convention No. 4.** A *conditional cut* is constituted to be such by possessing a peculiar quality (represented on paper by a smooth fine line on the blackboard by a blue line, and in either case, if deemed desirable, with a little minus sign just within it). If on the sheet of assertion there be a conditional cut in whose area there be nothing but a graph A and together with a consequential cut [is] constituted by being in the area of a conditional cut (and by possessing a peculiar quality represented on paper or blackboard like a conditional cut except that a little *plus* sign replaces the little *minus* sign), in whose area is a graph B, then the whole wound of the conditional cut makes the replica of a graph on the sheet of assertion asserting *de inesse* that if A is true, B is true.

Convention No. 7. A heavily marked continuous line on the sheet of assertion shall assert that the individuals denoted by its two extremities are identical.

For example •is a bird asserts that something is a bird and something is blue. But  asserts that something is a bird and that that very same individual is blue. So ⟨kills⟩ asserts that some individual kills itself.

Such a line is called a *line of identity*.

If three or more lines of identity have extremities at one point, then by Convention No. 5, those three lines denote the same individual. For example

will mean that some blue bird kills itself.

Convention No. 8. If two different lines of identity cross one another, they must be interrupted and placed between parallels near the intersection, to show that this is not a point of branching:

Make afflus to unknown graphs.¹⁵

The Conventions

[Copy-text is from R S-28, the first 31 pages of a large notebook largely written during the first half of September, 1903. Houghton Library. The notebook also contains later drafts and worksheets connected to Lectures III and IV. This notebook possesses the most elaborate presentation of the conventions of the method of existential graphs, including Convention 10 and some notions and terminology that do not appear elsewhere.]

Preface. The ten conventions were drawn up about September 1, 1903.¹⁶ They are merely exacter and more systematic formulations of what I have used for the past ~~ten~~ (six?) years, existential graphs having been invented by me within a month of the entitative graphs described by me in Vol. VII of *The Monist*.

The fundamental rules are substantially what I have always used and were added in this book September 15, 1903.

Convention No. 0.

Whatever feature of a sign of this system is the subject of no express convention may be varied indefinitely without altering the meaning or application of the sign.

---

15 [A penciled note on the verso of the last inscribed page (paginated 23) of the notebook. All the rest of the notebook leaves are blank. On the verso of the penultimate page (paginated 22), appears the following graphs: ◯ ◯ . This is of note given that these graphs illustrate shading of negative areas, the convention which Peirce would propose to be the preferred notation of EGs in explicit fashion only since June 1911 (LoF 3).]

16 [This refers to the ten conventions that are found in R 492, *Logical Tracts No. 2*.]

Convention No. 1.

¶0. We agree to adopt the following ~~imaginary~~ fanciful hypothesis as the basis of the system of Existential Graphs:

¶1. We are to imagine a person called the *graphist* and another called the *interpreter*; and we are to imagine that the graphist conveys a variety of information to the interpreter which the latter accepts without question, having no other source of information.

As to the manner in which this information is conveyed, we are to imagine that there is before the mind of the interpreter a certain field of consciousness ~~and speaking of this as if it were a visual field in two dimensions as, plane surface~~ —and for facility of imagination we will call it the *sheet of assertion* and suppose it to have a vague analogy with a sheet of paper without ~~meaning it to be confined~~ definitely supposing it to be confined to two dimensions or to be a visual image, and we are to suppose that the graphist exercises a power of "*scribing*" upon that surface; that is, of causing ~~diagrams~~ a sign to appear there which conforms to ~~a system~~ general rules of expression established in the habits of graphist and interpreter.

[Without such habits, a variety of information could not be conveyed.[17] Without some general habit, no information at all could be conveyed; since there would be nothing to cause the interpreter to regard objects appearing on the sheet of assertion as signs of anything else.

Moreover, in order that the signs should make sense, they must, ~~in the same way, purport to relate,~~ by the graphist be intended to be understood to relate, and must by the interpreter be understood to be intended to relate, to something independent of the appearance of the signs themselves. Otherwise, they would be mere apparitions, and not signs at all. This would be so even were the signs to purport to relate to nothing but a creation of the graphist's fancy. In all cases, indeed, that to which the information relates must be the creation of thought, since it is to be the object of general thought. For thought proper,—general thought,—can only think thought. The ~~general~~ signs, whose meaning is determined exclusively by general rules, cannot themselves inform the interpreter what it is to which they themselves are intended to relate; for any description, however minute, would give room for an infinite variety of possible different things to which it might relate. A description would have to be infinitely detailed, covering every possible question which might be asked of the subject, in order to indicate what was meant; and were such a description (impossible for a finite being to grasp), once conveyed, no room ~~at all~~ would be left for any information on that subject. The subject of that information must, it is true, be the creation of thought; but it can only be the creation of infinite thought. The only way of conveying to a finite mind the notion of what it is, is by that which the French lawyers expressively call *des voies de fait*. That is, by brute force;—that is to say, what appears as such to the finite mind.

Such a force is a force of experience. For no matter how surprising to reason a fact may be, yet once it is actually experienced, that closes all questioning. It is necessary, therefore, to imagine that graphist and interpreter should have, should understand one another to have, a common basis of already existing experience, and that they should agree that the sheet of assertion together with all that is scribed upon it should relate to a definite object of this common experience.[18]

Now blind force only takes place between what we call single objects; since what we mean by a "single object" is merely that which is subject to blind force.]

---

[17] [The bracketing of the next four paragraphs is Peirce's.]
[18] [Del.:] No information (true or false) can ever be conveyed from one mind to another unless it relates to a well-understood object of common previous experience.

We are to imagine that graphist and interpreter mutually understand that the sheet of assertion, together with that which is scribed upon it, is a representation of experimentally well-known collection of single objects having intelligible characters. This collection shall be called the universe of discourse.[19]

The features of the imaginary situation that are now to be stated are less essential, but will render our idea more distinct. First, we may imagine that some truths about the universe of discourse are well-understood between graphist and interpreter to be so familiar to the latter that he will not need to be informed about them. Second, we may imagine that the signs are movable upon the sheet of assertion, and that the interpretant at any time is only attending to a part of the sheet away from which he may shove some or all of what is scribed.[20]

¶ 2. We will actually take a page of paper or a blackboard, and will regard this surface, less such parts as we may ~~sever~~ sunder from the rest, as an accurate ~~picture~~ representation of a part of the sheet of assertion ~~to which the interpreter is attending~~, though only in respect to the meanings of the signs. We will make the sign we place on the page or board exactly correspond to whatever may be on that part of the sheet of assertion,—so exactly that we shall not ordinarily need to distinguish between our page or blackboard and that part of the sheet of assertion.

¶ 3. Any legible expression conforming to the conventions of this system, signifying an intelligible state of things, shall, when the graphist places it upon the sheet of assertion, be understood thereby to go to determine the interpreter's idea of the *universe of discourse*, and so to be asserted of it.

A sign on the sheet of assertion or on any other area, made by a single action or series of acts of scribing and expressive according to the conventions of this system, of an intelligible state of things, shall be called a *graph-replica*. The general type of all possible graph-replicas which would be similar to a given graph-replica in every significant respect, shall be called a *graph*. (So when we say that the word 'the' occurs twenty times on a page, we use the word 'word' in the sense of a general type; but when we say that there are three hundred words on a page, we speak of word-replicas.)

¶ 0. We will make the following addition to our imaginary hypothesis:
(1) The interpretant's [sic, interpreter's] mind shall have a stretch in time.
(2) The graphist shall ~~exercise his power of scribing~~ scribe one sign on the sheet of assertion at ~~different times~~ one time and others at other times.
(3) Whatever the graphist has scribed shall continue indefinitely to remain on the sheet of assertion.
(4) There shall be a part of the sheet of assertion which is, as it were, ~~illuminated~~ bright; and another part which is dark.[21]
(5) The interpreter shall have the power of moving any signs scribed upon the sheet of assertion from the bright to the dark part and back again. (In this way there may be on the bright part of the sheet at two different times two different signs which at a third time may both be there.)

---

19 [Opposite page:] This hypothesis may be supplemented in subsequent conventions.
20 [Marginal note:] Transfer to Convention No. 2.
21 [Peirce would soon in the drafts of the next version of this second lecture (II(b), see the next selection) introduce "the blot" in order to delineate white and black, or bright and dark, areas of the sheet.]

¶1. That part of the sheet of assertion which our page or board (excepting sundered parts) shall be understood to represent at any time shall be the bright part of that sheet as it is at some one time.

Convention No. 2.

¶2. Two graph-replicas on entirely different parts of the bright sheet of assertion shall each have the same signification as if it stood alone.

Convention No 3.[22]

¶ 0. ~~We will supplement of our fanciful hypothesis as follows:~~[23]

[Although it is impossible that one person should convey any assertion to another that does not relate to an object of common previous experience, well-understood between them to be such, ~~yet nothing prevents the assertion from relating to other things, as well. Thus, the assertor may say, "There is something called Orion". At first,~~ this is only known as being something in some way connected with the common object of experience, the universe.

~~For the universe is the creation of thought. Let its creator, from whom, by some way, the graphist derives his information, be called the *grapheus*. The graphist may learn something concerning the habits of the grapheus as far as the universe of discourse is concerned; and this information~~ yet ~~because by means of relation~~ by asserting the relations of the previously known objects to other objects, he may convey information concerning these others. Such relations are ~~either~~ in some cases real, ~~or~~ in some cases rational. By means of the assertion of ~~former~~ real relations, the collection of individual objects constituting the universe of discourse is enlarged. By ~~means of the latter~~ asserting rational relations, the discourse is led to objects which are never joined to that collection called the universe of discourse; namely, to characters, to relations, and to abstractions of other kinds. These are *entia rationis*, that is, are subjects created by the interpreter, which would appear mere fictions if the graphist did not disclose their reality ~~by showing that the objects of the~~ by enunciating truths relating to the universe of discourse of a higher

---

22 [Del.:] Convention No. 3. ¶ 0. We will supplement our fanciful hypothesis as follows:

First, the interpreter, as shall be imagined as to have no other source of information than the scribings of the graphist.

Second, nevertheless he shall be able to ~~think~~ have signs of objects not in the universe of discourse. For the universe of discourse cannot directly embrace among its individuals any of the ~~replicas~~ graphs scribed on the sheet of assertion; otherwise the entire graph would be a ~~conventional sign~~ symbol indicating its own object. But the interpreter is to be imagined capable of ~~making~~ having signs of ~~these replicas~~ graphs.

Third, since these signs cannot be directly on the field of assertion, he is to be imagined to have the power of setting up what we may describe as a special area of consciousness for them, altogether similar to the sheet of consciousness, except that it is understood not to represent the universe of discourse but a universe of signs. ~~We will describe such a setting~~

Fourth, that which is described in such a specially set up area may have some intelligible ~~applicability~~ relation to the universe of discourse; and the graphist may inform the interpreter of this by an act equivalent to indirectly scribing the special area with its entire graph on the sheet of assertion. For this reason, we shall describe the setting up of such an area as consisting in ~~making a cut~~ separating by a cut a part of the sheet of assertion as described, in ¶1. The following ¶5.

23 [The next four paragraphs were bracketed by Peirce.]

degree of practical importance than any others, which truths essentially involve reference to such abstractions, cannot be even expressed or thought otherwise, and indeed do not expressly practically refer to the universe of discourse if at all only in an accidental manner. Thus, when we say I am told that all bodies gravitate toward one another, it is true that I should get this would mean nothing to me if I did not know that he meant my informant referred to the bodies I have known by *past* experience, among others. But the whole value of the information to me is due to its leading one to expect, in *future* experience, events that otherwise would surprise me. It is a general rule; and as such its signification transcends every collection of individuals. This signification has its most literally accurate expression, not in the concrete statement about "all bodies", as if it were an accidental coincidence confined to the particular bodies that happen to exist, but in the abstract statement, "A component acceleration of part to part is a universal property of mass".

In order to adapt our fanciful hypothesis to these facts and considerations, All *entia rationis* have their birth in the consideration of general signs,—indeed, we may say in the consideration of general conventional signs, meaning not the replicas but the types. It is true that these types are not singulars; that is, are destitute exert no brute force, and can therefore not be objects of the universe of discourse nor be objects of direct perception. But they govern replicas which can be perceived; and by a process of thought of which logic can give no other account than that, measured by the steps of which it is able to take account, it is an infinite process,—by such a process of thought, the mind is led to a perceptual judgment that the type, or rule, governs the replicas. The mind then proceeds goes on to create a new universe,—a universe which may be, in the first instance, fictitious, until the fiction turns out to be fact,—a collection of singulars each of which is an abstraction, like "beauty" "truth", "right", "inclusion", this or that collection, an orbit, a solid, "matter", and the like. These are properly enough, although in a secondary way, singulars; for though the force they exert is, in one sense, not blind, yet it is always mysterious; and the blindness of force in all cases really consists in our inability to fathom its reasonableness. Guided by these abstract ideas, the mind hazards a conjecture as to a law, experimental as defining the hidden mode of intelligibility of certain phenomena. If, then, experimental induction verifies that conjecture, the abstractions involved in the strict expression of the law as such ceases to appear foolish need no longer any indulgent sufferance: they have proved their reality.

Such considerations show that in order to render our system of expression existential graphs adequate to the expression of all kinds of truth we must make an addition to it for which the following supplement to our fanciful hypothesis will supply the background.]

The graphist shall be imagined to make assertions each of which brings the universe of discourse into relation to another universe represented by an area on which graphs are scribed by the interpreter, this area being altogether analogous to the sheet of assertion, except that it represents a different universe, except that it fills a hole cut out in the sheet of assertion, and except that the manner of the cutting shall be significant of the relation in which the graphist asserts that it stands to the universe of discourse.[24]

¶ 1. The term *cut* shall be applied to a linear separation of a surface, which line of separation returns into itself, so as to enclose a space within which the material of the surface in which the

---

24 [Del.:] The interpreter shall be imagined to be able to create imaginary universes make holes in the sheet of assertion do something which we will describe as making holes in the sheet of assertion, filling each with a sheet of its own, referring to a universe of his own imaginary creation, related in a definite manner to graphs

cut is made is replaced by a different material, either by stripping off the original material and disclosing a new surface below, or by putting on a patch fitting into the cut. The new surface of the interior shall be called the *area* of the cut, the outer surface the *place* of the cut, while the cut and its area, as a single whole, shall be called the *hole* ~~wound~~ of the cut. Upon the page or blackboard the cut shall be represented by a line; but it shall not be said to be scribed, nor conceived to affect the meaning of any sign scribed in the line-locus of the cut, which locus shall be conceived to be in the place of the cut, and not in its area.

¶ 2. The area of a cut, together with all signs placed upon it shall have the same signification as the place of the cut, except that it shall refer to a different universe, peculiar to that area.

¶ 3. The character of the relation of the total graph of the area of the cut to the universe of the place of the cut shall be imagined to be signified by a peculiarity of the cut, called its *quality*, which shall be represented on the page or board in any convenient way.

¶ 4. The relation whose character is signified by the quality of the cut between the universe of the area and that of the place of the cut shall be conceived to be asserted of the latter universe by the ~~wound~~ hole of the cut.

Convention No. 4.

¶ 0. The graphist may assert that a certain graph is so related to the universe of discourse that the scription of it upon the sheet of assertion would allow the interpreter to scribe a certain other graph on the sheet of assertion.

This assertion may be conveyed by a hole whose cut has a certain quality and on whose area shall be the first graph together with a hole in that area made by a cut of a certain quality and containing on its area the second graph.[25]

¶ 1. A cut having an area sufficiently large to contain legible signs and having a quality represented on the page by a fine line, on the board by a blue line, in either situation, further distinguished, if desired, by its bending inward to a node, shall be called a *sep*. A cut in the area of a sep, having a quality represented on the page or board like a sep, except that it may extend outward to the node of the line representing the sep, shall be called an *antisep*.

¶ 2. A ~~wound~~ hole consisting of a *sep* on whose area there is, besides the replica of a graph A, only an antisep containing a replica of a graph B, being placed on the sheet of assertion shall be understood to assert *de inesse* that if A is true, B is true, and nothing more.

Convention No. 5.

~~The expression according to the conventions of this system, of an unintelligible (i.e. absurd) state of things, is not a graph, but may be called the pseudograph.~~[26]

¶ 0. [Hitherto our fanciful hypothesis has provided no way in which the possibility of anything being false should ever present itself to the mind of the interpreter. It is evident that the idea must

---

25 [Del.:] The interpreter having ~~formed the idea of a universe into which one graph would be applicable and in another independently~~ in one area one graph and in a second area a second graph may be informed by a scription of the graphist that the ~~relation of the second graph to the universe to which the first applies is the same as the relation of the first to the universe of discourse~~ universe of discourse is related to the first graph as the universe of the area in which this graph is scribed is related to the second graph.

26 [The following two paragraphs were bracketed by Peirce.]

first come from a surprise. But how can the interpreter ever be surprised? It can only be by some rule leading him to expect something which is not borne out. But how can he know or suspect that it is not borne out[?] Let us suppose the rule leads him to expect to find that something appears blue, and that when it comes it appears red. Still, why should it not appear blue, also?

It seems to be tolerably plain that we must supplement our fanciful hypothesis as follows:]

The interpreter is to be imagined as having a direct power of pronouncing that a quality is *not* a quality which in fact it is not, or that there are two graphs that are unintelligible in combination.

[As soon as he can do this, he can suppose an unintelligible assertion to be expressed according to the

¶ 1. The assertion of that which is unintelligible (i.e. absurd) not being a graph shall be called *the pseudograph*, and may be represented by filling the entire area in which it is, so as to leave room for nothing else.

["The" pseudograph, because all such assertions are equivalent in representing no intelligible state of things. No further assertion added to the pseudograph can modify it. It must remain the sign of nothing. Hence, it is suitable that it should leave no room for any apparent addition.][27]

Convention No. 6.

¶ 0. [When a person hears a *pure* proper name, that is one having no classifying implication, for the first time (in which occurrence of its embodiment may be called its *prime replica*) it is precisely equivalent to "something". He learns that it The mere mention of it teaches the hearer that the object exists, by the very fact that it has a proper name,—and one learns whatever is said. But at all subsequent occasions of hearing the name, it identifies an object already known; so that then the mere mention of it means nothing conveys no information. Still, the mention calls the existence of the object to mind.][28]

¶ 1. The name of an individual written scribed on the sheet of assertion shall be considered asserting the existence of the object of the name.

¶ 2. A capital letter shall be called a *selective*, and shall be considered as a new proper name. Its prime replica shall not be in within any cut outside of which there is a replica of it; and the prime replica may be heavily lined (**N** but later N). [It will be wise to confine the use of selectives only to cases in which they can obviously lead to no difficulty. For the rules governing them are complicated; and they are never indispensable.][29]

¶ 3. A heavily marked point called a *dot* on the sheet of assertion shall be a graph asserting the existence of an undesignated individual object. It is to be understood that the dot is not the mark but a movable place carrying the mark. No point shall denote more than one individual, although different points may denote the same individual.

¶ 4. A graph heavily scribed shall be understood to have further undesignated determinations rendering it individual.

---

27 [Peirce's bracketing of the paragraph.]
28 [Peirce's bracketing of the paragraph.]
29 [Peirce's bracketing of the sentence.]

Convention No. 7.

¶1. Either a proposition or a blank form of proposition that will become a proposition if every blank of it is filled with a proper name is called a *rhema* and a proper name or other designation of an individual is called an individual subject, or for brevity, a subject.

    A rhema, when not represented as complete, shall be represented in this system by a kind of sign called a *spot* having a special place upon its periphery called a *hook* for each blank of the rhema.

¶2. A dot or selective at or abutting upon a hook of a rhema shall become the corresponding subject of the proposition which will result from so filling every hook.

Convention No. 8.

¶1. A heavily marked uninterrupted line on the sheet of assertion, having two extremities and no branching shall be called a *line of identity* and shall be a graph asserting the identity of all the individuals denoted by its points (all which being heavily marked denote individuals).

    A line of identity ~~must be continuous as~~ cannot cross a cut, where it would be interrupted. ~~nor can it have a point of branching~~ A line of identity together with all that are connected with it by common points either directly or through other such lines, a cut being no interruption shall be called a *ligature*.

Convention No. 9.

¶0. It is to be understood that no individual belongs to two different universes although two individuals may be such that the "existence", or factual connection with the universe of discourse, of either involves that of the other.

¶1. A hole whose cut is represented by a dotted line shall denote an individual, usually indesignate, and usually belonging to a universe other than the universe of discourse, which universe shall be identified by the mode of dotting of the line.

¶2. In case the area of the cut contains the graph of a proposition, the individual denoted shall be such that its "existence", that is, its factual connection with the universe of discourse, is *constituted* by the truth of the proposition of the universe of discourse. [For example, if the proposition is that something is other than something, as in the figure

the individual denoted is some *pair* of individuals of the universe of discourse.][30]

¶ 3.

- The sign ρ_0 shall denote an indesignate *medad*, or proposition;
- The sign $\cdot\rho_1$ (where the single hook is marked by a little dot) shall denote an indesignated *monad*, or rhema of one blank;
- The sign $\cdot\rho_2\cdot$ (where the two hooks is marked by little dots) shall denote an indesignate *dyad*, or rhema of two blanks;
- The signs $\cdot\dot{\rho}_3\cdot$, $\cdot\dot{\rho}_4\cdot$, $\cdot\dot{\rho}_5\cdot$, etc. shall have analogous values.

---

30 [Peirce's bracketing of the sentence.]

These signs ought strictly to be surrounded by dotted cuts.[31] But these may be omitted.

Convention No. 10.

¶1. A wavy line on the sheet of assertion shall be a graph asserting that its extremities are in such ~~positive~~ existential relation (that is, in such positive connection in reference to the universe of discourse) as the nature of their universes permits.[32]

[Thus, the figure, were it upon the sheet of assertion,

$$\sim\!\sim\!\sim \sigma_1$$

would assert that of some individuals of the universe of discourse some proposition was true.][33]

Fundamental Rules of Illative Transformation of Existential Graphs[34]

(1) *Rule of Erasure and Insertion.* Within an even number of cuts (or none), any partial or total graph can be erased, and in an odd number of cuts any graph can be inserted.

This rule is to be understood as permitting the cutting of any line of identity within an even number of cuts and the junction of any two lines of identity within an odd number of cuts.

(2) *Rule of Iteration and Deiteration.* Any partial or total graph may be iterated within the same or additional cuts, the new replica having *junctures* connecting each hook with the corresponding hook of the original graph.

And if any graph is so iterated, it may be deiterated by erasing any replica provided it does not lie outside any cut which no other replica of the same graph joined to the same junctures is outside of.

(3) *Rule of Two Cuts.* Two cuts within the other with nothing between except junctures passing from outside the outer to inside the inner may be together erased or inserted anywhere.

(4) *Rule of the Point on a Cut.* A marked point on a cut is, so far as outside lines of identity are concerned, subject to the same rules as if it were entirely outside of and away from the cut; but so far as inside junctures are concerned is to be treated as lying inside the cut; so that the cut being evenly enclosed a marked point on it can be joined to any marked point within it but cannot be disjoined except by deiteration, while if the cut is oddly enclosed the rule is reversed.

(5) The innermost effective juncture between two graphs lies wholly within every cut that both graphs are within; so that if the innermost juncture does not so lie, it is ineffective and can be disjoined or created.

Thus ⊏loves‒benefits⊐ is the same as ⊏loves‒benefits⊐. But ⟦loves‒benefits⟧ asserts more than ⟦loves‒benefits⟧.

---

31 [This is the qualification of the convention inherited from Convention 14 of *Logical Tracts No. 2*.]

32 [Convention 10 is almost unique, but see "Studies of the Eight Systems of Existential Graphs", written in summer 1903 (R 1483, LN [237r]; LoF 1, pp. 611–613).]

33 [Peirce's bracketing of the sentence.]

34 [According to Peirce's declaration in the preface, it is these rules that were added to this notebook on September 15.]

34 Lowell Lecture II(b)

[Copy-text is R 455, R 455(s) and R 456, plus pages from R 461, R S-29, R S-32, R S-33, R S-34 and R 1574. These lectures notes represent Peirce's final plans for the second lecture, delivered on the evening of Friday, November 27, having largely been composed already by early October. Initially announced with the title "A System of Diagrams Studying Logical Relations. Exposition of it begun", Peirce retitled the actually delivered lecture it in R 470 more accurately as "Existential Graphs—Alpha & Beta".] No longer occupied with the intricacies of the conventions of graphical logic, in this second lecture Peirce planned to advance the nature of reasoning as it is being excavated by the Alpha part. The issue at hand concerns the principles of reasoning: What is the real relationship between premisses and conclusions? How do we ascertain ourselves of the soundness and validity of a piece of reasoning that is altogether new, never seen and thought of before? What makes a reasoning not only sound but *evident* to reason? Peirce addresses and refutes the so-called paradox of the justification of deduction, according to which reasoning that rests upon logical principles must not itself be used to justify those principles. The statement of the principle of reasoning and reasoning according to that principle are, Peirce argues, not the same thing: the former is an abstract statement of the principle in another form than one in which the principle according to which we reason is used. He also uncovers another objection to the admission of the principles of logic, objection that does not appeal to the allegedly question-begging nature of deductive reasoning. To analyse it, he first has to present the system of EGs in the light of facilitating the study of reasoning, for in EGs, every form is precisely defined, and its diagrammatic syntax no longer depends on the confusing and arbitrary syntax of language. His presentation of the Alpha system eats up the full hour, however, and precious little time is left for completing the proposed argument. The draft then proposes a description of the Beta part which is was unlikely to have reached that evening. Peirce observes that the basic code needs a new fourth rule that applies to the lines of identity and ligatures; other than that the set of complete rules for the Beta part poses no particular difficulty.

Following the surge of these insightful lessons, Peirce calculated to have a few minutes left to present his newly-discovered "five operations". Their application is meant to ascertain with certainty whether a graph is a logical consequence of the system (that is, whether it belongs to the theory of those graphs) or not (that is, does not belong to the theory of those graphs). These operations, found in R S-32, provide an effective method (a rule "as simple as may be") that shows the *decidability* of the theory of Alpha graphs. Notably, Peirce attempts to give "the simplest rule" that he can find "for ascertaining with certainty" whether also *Beta-possibility* would hold for any given graph. The rule of operations is limited to graphs that are juncture-free, that is, are quantifier-free reducts of Beta graphs. To mechanistically follow the given five rules of operation would describe a "state of things" in which the Beta-reduct is possible. In the beginning of the lecture three Peirce then revisits what he had previously mentioned on these operations, and admits (in a deleted paragraph) that "any similar routine" for Beta graphs would be "impractical". His proposal to apply a decision method to Beta-reducts appear among the assorted loose leaves and fragments of R S-34, while the application of "adaptible pairs" described in the follow-up selection suggests that dyadic relations that Peirce was busy drafting in connection to the *Syllabus* text play a central part in this version of the decidability argument. The appendix is from R S-29 ("Existential Graphs: The Initial Conventions"), another notebook filled with studies on the rules, theorems and corollaries of the system, including dozens of esquisses of Alpha and Beta graphs.

To prompt you, in this short course, to any thoughts that ~~will~~ may hereafter prove of much value to you will draw upon such abilities as mine for all that they can render. Were I dealing with a special science the case would be different. The lecturer upon electricity, for example, if he lays down a general principle, at once shows you an experiment to illustrate it. If the experiment does not fully prove the principle,[1] it is because an experiment to be exhibited to an audience cannot be subjected to all the ~~necessary~~ precautions that are required in research, and also because it has to be completed in a few minutes, instead of being repeated with all sorts of variations in the course of months. But it affords you a clear idea of how the principle is proved; and it manifestly comes as near to a proof as could reasonably be expected under the circumstances. If is does not prove that the precise principle enunciated is true, it shows, at least, that something like it is true.

But in regard to a principle of reasoning, suppose I assert that a certain conclusion follows from certain premisses in case a certain condition is fulfilled, but that if that condition is not fulfilled the conclusion does not necessarily follow. Then, if the case is altogether analogous to cases you are quite familiar with, you know all about it already, and my enunciation of it, unless I have some ulterior purpose in view, is superfluous. But suppose it is ~~something~~ a sort of reasoning you never thought of before. Then you will certainly not be satisfied that I should simply inform you that the reasoning is sound under such and such circumstances but otherwise is not so. You will demand that it be made evident to your own reason.

Take, for example, these premisses:

1. It the old days of southern slavery every woman *born* a slave (for I do not speak of importations from Africa) became the mother of at least one yellow girl. At any rate, statistics show that it was so on the average.
2. Still during these years myriads and myriads of full-blooded negro girls were born.

Now, then, I will inform you that assuming those two premisses to be true,—which of course I do not assert to be the ~~case~~ actual fact,—but assuming them to be true, it necessarily follows that,

3. During the days of southern slavery myriads and myriads of daughters of slave women were themselves born free.

---

[1] [The preceding was cancelled by Peirce as the opening of the dozen pages cut out from the notebook currently located in R 455(s). The content of those cut-out pages is transcribed here first, and is followed by another, and the most mature, version of the second lecture from R 455–R 456.]

Are you satisfied to accept upon my say-so the ~~statement~~ assertion that that would be a necessary consequence from these premises? Of course you are not, and ought not to be so easily satisfied in a matter of such possibly vast concern as the correctness of a mode of reasoning. Then how am I to proceed with you[?] Shall I illustrate the principle by examples? That is just the way in which bad reasoning comes to be admitted. To persuade you to believe in any form of reasoning on the strength of examples would be to hold up to you a model of bad reasoning.

Shall I give you, then, a strict demonstration of each principle? There is a logical objection to that, too. I do not mean the objection which has sometimes been urged, that since reasoning is to rest upon logical principles, therefore logical principles must not be made to rest upon reasoning. For this objection arises from a pedantic confusion of thought. I call it pedantic because it is not the outcome of any unsophisticated natural reasoning. It is essentially a logician's fallacy. That is, it comes about, as many other fallacies of professional logicians come about, from the mistaken application of a logical rule. The person who ~~made it~~ first raised the objection was thinking of the form of fallacy which logicians call "begging the question". That fallacy really consists in assuming as a premiss ~~the very~~ some thing ~~you wish to prove. It is quite true that you must not do this; for a premiss is assumed to be true and therefore you want to prove the truth of~~ not admitted to be true,[2] a statement of a principle of reasoning,—which supposes, of course that that statement is not already evident,—you must not assume that statement as a premiss. But there may be no objection to your reasoning according to that principle, if it really does render your reasoning evident. Your proof of it will only consist in showing that the statement in question merely states a principle that in another form is already admitted. What objection is there to using a principle which is evident as it [is] applied in order to prove the truth of a statement which seemed at first doubtful but which this reasoning shows to be nothing more than that very principle that is so evident in another form? The truth is that the people who raise this ridiculous objection that you must not ~~appl~~ reason according to a logical principle to prove the truth of an abstract statement of that principle

---

2 [Del.:] a principle of reasoning, which of course cannot be done if it is ~~self~~ evident already [that] you must not assume that principle as a premiss. But there ~~is no~~ may be no objection to your reasoning according to that principle, which is quite a different thing from assuming it as a premiss. ~~No act of necessary reasoning rests on an~~ If from a premiss, P, we draw a conclusion, C, as evidently necessary, the only premiss of that reasoning is P. The conclusion evidently follows; and since this is perfectly evident it cannot be rendered more evident. For instance, let the premiss be 'This is a large hall', and let the conclusion drawn from that premiss be, 'This is a hall'. That evidently follows. What is meant by the *logical principle* of this reasoning is simply a proposition which would necessarily [end]

imagine that the fallacy of begging the question consists in assuming as a premiss anything which would be false if the conclusion were false. But to declare that to be a fallacy is simply to declare that all necessary reasoning is fallacious and is fallacious for the very reason that the conclusion necessarily follows from the premiss.

So then that is not my objection to asking you to ~~resting my principles~~ admit the ~~logical~~ principles of logic ~~on the~~ because of formal demonstrations which I may present. In order to explain what my objection is, let me ~~state you tell~~ recount to you a bit of history. Euclid, the author of that celebrated ~~book~~ mathematical treatise called the *Elements*, for that is the complete title of it, was an extremely acute and accurate reasoner. He polished and elaborated the reasoning of the first book of his treatise with that inexhaustible patience which the ancients used to bestow upon their finest writings. The result of his pains was that the work was universally adopted as the introductory text-book of geometry by all mathematicians of all ages down to the publication of Legendre's recension of it in 1794, and has been very widely used ever since that time. The reasoning of no book has ever been half so critically scrutinized as that of the first book of Euclid's *Elements*. Nevertheless, at least one fundamentally important fallacy in it certainly escaped detection for more than two thousand years; and indeed I do not know that I am not the first to remark it. There is no possible doubt that it is a fallacy; for it is much easier to make quite sure that reasoning is fallacious than to make quite sure it is sound.

Now if this could happen for a small book so carefully criticized by hundreds of acute minds in each of the sixty or seventy generations since Euclid, what warrant would there be that a demonstration given orally in a public lecture only once, would be flawless. Would you do wisely to make sure that any demonstration I might give was really sound, because during my delivery of it you had not detected any fallacy of it? I think not. I think it will be much better for me to ~~describe the~~ give a sufficient description of the demonstration and for you to take notes of it and go over it with great care by yourselves when you get home.[3]

~~Ladies and Gentlemen:~~[4]

Let us take up the subject of necessary reasoning, mathematical reasoning, with a view to making out what its elementary steps are and how they are put together.

---

[3] [End of R 455(s). What follows as Peirce's most definite version of the pre-draft of the second lecture is taken from R 455 and R 456.]

[4] [The salutation was cancelled by lead pencil and may suggest that some of the preceding (despite being cut-out pages), or perhaps some other unidentified material was to precede as the opening remarks of the present version of the planned second lecture (II(b)).]

In order to do this it is necessary to replace the confused syntax of ordinary language by a system in which the meaning of every form is exactly defined, which is free from forms that cast a tinge of passion or of any kind of subjective feeling on the facts, and which has no more forms than are requisite in order to express every kind of fact or truth ~~so analytically as to~~ in such a way as to enable us to carry the dissection of reasoning to its smallest steps.

~~I shall~~ Let us devote this evening's hour to forming such a system of expression.

~~To begin with,~~ Before beginning, let us distinctly recognize the purpose which this system of expression is designed to fulfil. It is intended to enable us to separate reasoning into its smallest step so that each one may be examined by itself. Observe, then, that it is *not* the purpose of this system of expression to facilitate reasoning and to enable one to reach his conclusions in the speediest manner. Were that our object, we should seek a system of expression which should reduce many steps to one; while our object is to subdivide one step into as many as possible. Our system is intended to facilitate the *study*[5] of reasoning but not to facilitate reasoning itself. Its character is quite contrary to that purpose.

Let the blackboard represent the universe. As thus significant we will call it the sheet of assertion.

Let whatever I write upon the blackboard or sheet of assertion go toward making the representation of the universe more determinate. Thus, I write[6]

A pear is ripe.

blackboard

That represents that there is a pear and a ripe pear in the universe.

Necessary reasoning can never ~~ascertain~~ answer questions of fact. It has to assume its premises to be true. Therefore, in order to avoid the possibility of questioning what is written on the board, let us say that it is not the real universe that is represented by the board,[7] but a universe existing in my imagination, concerning which you have no source of information except my testimony. By the *universe* I mean the entire collection of things, or subjects of force, to which ~~I imagine there are in the universe~~ all that is going to be written on the board will relate. Logi-

---

5 [The word "study" is underlined with lead pencil, probably during the preparation of the document for presentation.]

6 [In what follows, Peirce inscribed in the margins presentation instructions next to the examples, such as "blackboard" for preparing the example on the blackboard prior to the lecture, or "diagram" to prepare its projection with the stereopticon.]

7 [The phrase "by the board" as well as "on the board" in the preceding bracketed by lead pencil, with accompanying marginal noted, but those have been erased beyond legibility. A conjecture: Peirce altered these phrases to "on the board or on the page" and "by the board or by the page".]

cians call such a collection of things, or subjects of force, to which the whole of a discussion relates, the *universe of discourse*.[8]

This universe consists in the first place of certain mutually well-understood centres, or subjects of force, well-understood to be different from one another; secondly, of certain subjects of force well-understood to exist, but not thoroughly understood to be known to be different from any of those of the first class; and thirdly of an indefinite supplement of subjects of force presumed to exist but of which there has been no definite recognition. Summing up the matter, we may say that the universe of discourse is the aggregate of subjects of the complexus of ~~well-known~~ experience-forces well-understood between the graphist, or he who scribes the graph, and the interpreter of it.

The system of expression which I have thus begun to describe will be found to be a system of diagrams. The mathematicians call a diagram that is composed mainly of *spots* of different kinds and of *lines*, a *graph*. This system is called a system of *existential graphs*. In this system, the spots may be conveniently differentiated from one another by words written in them. The consequence is that a sign of this system is partly drawn and partly written. For brevity, I always say it is *scribed*. Any sign conforming to the rules of this system which, if it were ~~written~~ placed on the board, or sheet of assertion, would ~~represent~~ assert some intelligible state of things to be true of the universe of discourse, is called a *graph*. Strictly, I ought to say an *existential graph*; but for brevity since existential graphs will be the only ones dealt with, I shall call it a *graph*, simply. For example, what I have just ~~written~~ scribed is a *graph*. The board itself is a *graph*, since it represents the universe as consisting of single imaginary things. The board and what is written on it together make up another *graph*.

~~We want~~ It is quite important, however, to distinguish between a *graph* and a *graph-replica*. Suppose an editor writes to me and asks for an article of 4 000 words. You know what he means by *words* in that case. In what I write the single word "the" may occur twenty times on every page. Every time it will count as a separate word. Yet in another sense, it is the same word. In this latter sense, the word *the* consists in the sum total of general conditions to which ink-marks or voice-sounds must conform in order to be understood in a certain way. In this sense the word *the* is, strictly speaking, never written; but what is written conforms to it, or, as we say, embodies it. In the other sense ~~every~~ a written word is written once and only once, since every act of writing makes a new word. Now when I speak of a *graph*, I mean the general type of whatever means the same thing and expresses

---

[8] [Reading instruction penciled: "go opposite". The next paragraph appears on the opposite page.]

that meaning in the same way, so far as the ~~rules~~ conventions of this system ~~are concerned~~ take cognizance of the ways; while that which is scribed once and only once and embodies the graph, I call a *graph-replica*. For brevity, however, I speak of "scribing a graph" just as we speak of writing the word *the*. The phrase may be defended as employing the word "scribe" in a special sense.

I will now put an additional replica upon the board, or sheet of assertion.

It rains

A pear is ripe

Let us agree to understand that each of those ~~graphs~~ replicas has the same meaning as if it stood alone; and that it shall be the same with any other two replicas on the sheet. So that I now assert not only that there is a ripe pear, but also that it rains.

By calling this system a system of *existential graphs*, my meaning is that two graphs at different parts of the board, *whether far or near*, are both asserted, each, *just as much as if the other were not there*.

The most immediately useful information is that which is conveyed in conditional propositions, "*If* you find that this is true, *then* you may know that that is true". Now in ordinary language the conditional form is employed to express a variety of relations between one possibility and another. Very frequently when we say "If A is true (antecedent), then B is true (consequent)",[9] we have in mind a whole range of possibilities, and we assert that among all possible cases, every one of those in which A is true will turn out to be a case in which B is true also. But in order to obtain a way of expressing that sort of conditional proposition, we must begin by getting a way of expressing a simpler kind, which does not often occur in ordinary speech but which has great importance in logic. The sort of conditional proposition ~~to which I allude refer is a~~ I mean is one in which no range of possibilities is contemplated, which speaks only of the actual state of things. "If A is true then B is true", in this sense is called a conditional proposition *de inesse*. In case A is not true, it makes no assertion at all and therefore involves no falsity. And since every proposition is either true or false, if the *antecedent*, A, is not true, the conditional *de inesse* is true no matter how it may be with B. In case the *consequent*, B, is true, all that the conditional *de inesse* asserts is true, and therefore it is true, no matter how it may be with A. If however the antecedent, A, is true, while the consequent, B, is false, then, and then *only* is the conditional

---

9 [An inline addition occurs here in red ink, as an instruction to the assistant to prepare an illustration of it as a projection or blackboard item: "If A is true (Antecedent), then B is true (Consequent)", and a larger table on the opposite page: If A is true, then B is true.]
Antecedent   Consequent
(Consequence above "is true, then B is true")

proposition *de inesse* false. This sort of conditional says nothing at all about any real connection between antecedent and consequent; but limits itself to saying "If you should find that A is true, then you may know that B is true", never mind the why or wherefore.

The question of the proper way of expressing a conditional proposition *de inesse* in a system of existential graphs has formed the subject of an elaborate investigation with the reasonings of which I will not trouble you. Suffice it to say that it is found that there is essentially but one proper mode of representing it. Namely, in order to assert of the universe of discourse that if it rains then a pear is ripe I must put ~~on the blackboard~~ down[10] this:

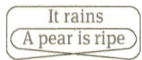

I draw the two ovals which taken together I call a *scroll* in blue because I do not want you to regard them as ordinary lines. I want you to join me in making believe that they[11] are cuts through the surface, and that inside the outer one the ~~surface~~ skin of the board has been stripped off disclosing another surface below. This I call the ~~area~~ *bottom* or *area*. Therefore "It rains" is not scribed on the blackboard or, as I say, is not scribed on the sheet of assertion. For what is scribed on that sheet is asserted to be true of the universe of discourse; while the statement "It rains" is a mere supposition. Let us say that that ~~area~~ *bottom* inside the outer cut represents another universe, a universe of supposition, and that it is only in that universe that it is said to rain. Besides this graph, "It rains" the ~~area~~ *bottom* of the outer cut contains the inner cut which interrupts its surface; and inside the inner we will make believe that a *patch* is put on with a surface like that of the blackboard, although cut off from it. I use the word 'area' for any part of the surface unbounded or bounded by cuts, never extending through a cut.

The outer cut is itself on the sheet of assertion although the whole of its interior is severed from that sheet. Now this outer cut, by being on the sheet of assertion, represents the conditional proposition *de inesse* to be true of the universe of discourse. A fixed terminology is a great comfort. Let us term the area on which a cut stands the *place* of the *cut*, while the *area* or *bottom* of the cut is the area within the cut. The cut itself is not a graph nor the replica of a graph. No more is the *scroll*. But the scroll with the two graphs scribed in its two *closes* or *areas*

---

10 ["on the blackboard" struck out and "down" added inline by lead pencil.]
11 [The word "they" struck out by lead pencil, replaced by a note in the margin that has been erased beyond legibility.]

makes up a graph, or graph-replica; and this I call an *enclosure*. The term may be used indifferently to mean the graph or the replica.

In order to get an insight into *how* the scroll represents the conditional proposition *de inesse*, we must make a little experimental research.

~~At present~~ Thus far, we have no means of expressing an absurdity. Let us invent a sign which shall assert that *everything is true*. Nothing could be more ~~absurd~~ illogical than that statement inasmuch as it would ~~annihilate~~ render logic false as well as needless. Were every graph asserted to be true, there would be nothing that could be added to that assertion. Accordingly, our expression for it may very appropriately consist in completely filling up the ~~space on~~ area on which it is asserted. Such filling up of an area may be termed a *blot*.

Take the conditional proposition *de inesse*, "If it rains then everything is true":

That amounts to denying that it rains. But there is no need of making the inner cut so large. Let us write 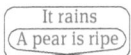 or even 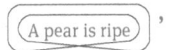.

This suggests that the relation which the cut asserts between the universe of discourse and what is scribed within it is simply that what is scribed within is false of the universe of discourse.

Then we may interpret

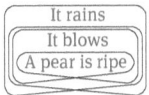

as meaning "It is false that it rains and that a pear is not ripe". But we have already seen that this is precisely the whole meaning of the conditional *de inesse*; namely that it is false that the antecedent is true while the consequent is false. Thus, that which the cut asserts is precisely that that which is on its bottom is not, as a whole, true.

This agrees with the fact that if there is nothing on the bottom except the inner cut, its patch, and what is on that patch, the latter may be asserted. Thus

(A pear is ripe) ,

since a blank merely asserts known truth, means, "if the truth is true then a pear is ripe", or it is not false that a pear is ripe. So in the following

It rains
It blows
A pear is ripe

or "if it rains, then if it blows, a pear is ripe" the two cuts with nothing between can be taken away without altering the fact expressed.

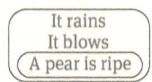

If it both rains and blows, a pear is ripe.

So much of the system of existential graphs as I have thus far described I term the *alpha* part of the system.[12]

[[Del:]][13] There are certain ways in which graphs scribed on the sheet of assertion can be modified *without any possibility of changing a true graph into a false one*. Such modification, I call *permissible transformations*. In particular those which can be proved ~~by the principles of the alpha part of the system~~ to be permissible, that is, never to be capable of changing a true graph into a false one are called *alpha-permissible transformations*. The alpha part of the system establishes three ~~kinds of~~ signs besides the graphs themselves. The first sign consists in ~~writing~~ scribing two graphs together on the sheet. As long as we recognize a blank as a graph, the ~~writing~~ scribing of a single graph is a case of scribing two graphs together, of which a blank is one. The second sign is the scroll. These two are the only indispensable signs; but we recognize as a third sign the filling up of an area with a *blot*.

I just defined a *permissible transformation* as one which can never change a true graph to ~~a false one~~ one not true. Very good. But why should we regard this ~~as a definition of~~ statement as constituting a definition of a permissible transformation rather than as constituting a definition of truth? Why might not truth be defined as that which we can assert with impunity? If the idea of penalties for breaking rules is more familiar to us than the idea of truth it might not be a bad definition.

In like manner we might define the three signs of the alpha part of existential graphs by means of ~~permissible~~ what is permitted. Since every act of definition involves two propositions,—they may be variously stated, but these will always be two,—one for example stating that if a word is used a certain interpretation is justi-

---

12 [R 456(s):] So much of the system of existential graphs as I have thus far described I term the *alpha* part of the system.

There are certain ~~ways in which~~ general methods by which graphs scribed on the sheet of assertion can be modified without any possibility of a true graph being changed into a false one. Transformations according to su[ch methods] I call *permissible*.

13 [This bracketed material was crossed out by Peirce with a light brown ink. The lecture might have continued several pages later from "I now pass to ...", thus skipping the presentation of the technical material on the permissions altogether.]

fied, the other stating that in given cases the use of the word will be legitimate,—if, I say we remember this double character of definition, we shall see that the definitions of the three signs will give six propositions. These six are as follows:

First, if two graphs are together on the sheet of assertions either may be cancelled or erased.

Second, if either of two graphs might be ~~written~~ scribed, both may be scribed together.

The ~~second~~ third rule is that a cut with nothing within is a *replica* of the pseudograph and may be scribed ~~on the sheet of assertion with~~ enclosed in a cut on the sheet of assertion, while two coincident cuts may be removed.

Third, if it would be permissible to transform one graph, *a*, into another, *b*, it is permissible to scribe

Fourth, whenever it is permissible to scribe it would be permissible, were *a* scribed, to scribe *b*.

Fifth, a vacant enclosure ~~may be called a *blot*, and is not permissively scriptible~~ is not permissively scriptible, and as such is called a *blot*.

Sixth, any enclosure having a blot in its area may be cancelled or erased.

Here we have the three signs defined purely in terms of what logical transformations from them and to them without one word being said about what the signs really mean. They are left to be applied to whatever there may be that corresponds to them. This is the Pure Mathematical point of view, a point of view far from easy to a person as imbued with logical notations as I am.

These six rules are not quite so convenient as are three rules, each double, which can without difficulty be proved to follow from these six. These three double rules are what I call the three *fundamental alpha rules of existential graphs*.

~~They are as follows:~~ I proceed to state them
(1)   Rule of Erasure and Insertion
(2)   Rule of Iteration and Deiteration
(3)   Rule of ~~Double Enclosure~~ the Double Cut.]

~~We now have three rules of necessary inference.~~ First, from any premiss A, we can necessarily include B, if and only if we know that it is not the case that A is true while B is false.

We may, therefore, rub out everything on the board, because we know that the blank sheet of assertion asserts nothing false. Hence if two graphs are written we may erase either of them, because each has the same signification as if it stood alone, and either standing alone might be erased.

But now if any graph, G could if it were scribed on the sheet of assertion be transformed into another graph H without fear of introducing falsity then if H were scribed on the bottom of a cut it could be transformed into G without ~~fear~~ danger of introducing falsity.[14] For if G is transformable into H it is that we know that it cannot be that G is true while H is false. If then ⊙H is on the sheet of assertion, that is, if H is on the bottom of a cut, G cannot be true and therefore we may scribe ⊙G That is H on the bottom of a cut can be transformed into G. This is called the *principle of contraposition*. From all this it follows that [a]ny graph on the sheet of assertion or within an even number of cuts can be erased. While within an odd number of cuts *already* made, any graph can be inserted. This does not justify us in *making any new cut* within an even number of cuts. That, then, is the first rule, called the rule of *erasure and insertion*.

~~The second is that a cut with nothing in it is a *replica* of the pseudograph and that which we may always scribe in a cut on the sheet and consequently a pair [of] cuts one within the other with~~ nothing ~~no graph between them can anywhere be made or anywhere be destroyed. This is called the *rule of two cuts*.~~

☞ The ~~third~~ second rule is that any graph scribed on any area can be *iterated*, that is, scribed in a new replica, ~~either~~ on the same area or within any additional cuts; and if a graph is already so iterated, it can be *deiterated* by erasing the inner replica. This is called the *rule of iteration and deiteration*.

It follows by means of the principle of contraposition from the fact that if we have on the sheet of assertion

It rains

we can write

It rains

It rains

The ordinary logics give a form of inference called the *modus ponens*. The premisses are: If A is true, B is true and A is true. The conclusion is that B is true. Our system analyzes this into three inferential steps.

We have

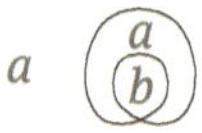

$$a \quad \overline{\left(a \atop \overline{(b)}\right)}$$

---

14 [The rest of this segment was cancelled by Peirce with a light brown cross until "I now pass to the beta part of the system of existential graphs".]

The rule of iteration and deiteration gives us a right to

$$a \;\; \overline{\textstyle\underline{b}}$$

The rule of two cuts gives

$$a \;\; b$$

Finally, the rule of erasure and insertion gives

$$b$$

I shall presently describe a *beta* part; and in another lecture the system will be completed by a *gamma* part.

There are certain ways in which graphs that are scribed on the sheet of assertion can be modified without any danger of changing a true graph into a false one. Transformations according to any general method that can never change a true graph into a false one I term *permissible transformations*. In particular, those which the principles of the alpha part of the system render permissible shall be termed *alpha-permissible transformations*, and in general I shall use "alpha" freely as a prefix to signify a reference to these principles. Thus, I shall say that the *alpha-signs*, that is to say the signs of this system heretofore described apart from the *graphs* themselves are two, and there are besides two peculiar graphs. Namely, the two peculiar graphs are the blank place which asserts only what is already well-understood between us to be true, and the *blot* which asserts something well understood to be false. The two signs which are not graphs are the ~~writing scribing~~ putting of two graph-replicas upon the same area, which if we remember that a blank is a graph, is seen to include the scribing of a single graph as a special case. This idea that scribing a graph is a transformation of a graph already accepted is a very useful one. The other sign is the scroll.

I have just defined a *permissible transformation* as one which conforms to a general type which in no case can transform a true graph into a false one. But what do we mean by a *true* graph and *false* one? I will not stop at present to analyze fully the meaning, because this system of existential graphs is not intended to inquire into the conformity of ~~ideas~~ thoughts to experiences. The universe of our discourse is to be a universe of my imagination, and therefore any graph which I permit to be *scribed* will be true, unless it is absurd and so amounts to telling you that my universe has no being even in my imagination. Therefore, for our purposes, a true graph is nothing but a graph which will result from a special permission to transform the blank sheet of assertion into the sheet with that graph scribed upon it.

As for the general alpha-permissions, they are nothing but the ~~descriptions~~ definitions of the four general alpha signs in terms of permissibility.

Let us draw up statements of them. You know that every definition consists of two propositions. Thus, if man is defined as a featherless biped, the one proposition, Every *man* is a featherless biped ~~asserts~~ predicates the *definition* 'featherless biped' of the *definitum*, 'man'; while the other proposition 'Every featherless biped is a man' predicates the *definitum* of the *definition*.

Consequently, each sign of the system should furnish us with two ~~rules~~ permissions of transformation.

Beginning then with the sign which consists in ~~writing~~ scribing together, or as we may term it, *compounding* two graphs, the definition of it in terms of permission will be:

First, predicating the definition of the definitum, if it is permitted to scribe on the sheet of assertion a replica of a compound graph, then it is permitted to scribe on the sheet of assertion a replica of either component. Or, stating this in terms of transformations: Any replica of a compound graph may on the sheet of assertion be transformed into a replica of either component. That is to say, under a more practical aspect, any partial graph on the sheet of assertion may be erased or cancelled. This shall head our list of alpha permissions.

diag **Permission No. 1.** Any graph on the sheet of assertion can be erased.[15]

Second, predicating the definitum of the definition; if it be permitted to scribe on the sheet of assertion a replica of which we please of two graphs then it is permitted to scribe the replica of the compound graph of which those two are the sole components. Or in terms of transformation, if it be permitted to transform the blank sheet into either we please of two graphs, it is permissible to transform it into the compound of the two. That is to say, under a more practical aspect, whatever might be scribed on the ~~blank~~ sheet of assertion were this blank, can be scribed regardless of what is already scribed. This shall be our second alpha permission.

diag **Permission No. 2.** Whatever is permissibly scribable on the sheet of assertion is so regardless of what is already scribed.

Let us now treat the scroll in the same way.[16]

---

15 [Permissions 1–7 inscribed in red ink on the opposite (verso) pages of the notebook text. They are also accompanied by an instruction "diag" penciled in the margin, to prompt preparation of these permissions for projection to the audience by the stereopticon device.]
16 [The following variant begins on the manuscript page 47, written on a dozen notebook pages that Peirce cut out from the notebook, now located in R 456(s). Their reconstruction is a follows:]

Now let us treat the scroll in the same way: First, predicating the definition of the definitum, $\left(\genfrac{}{}{0pt}{}{x}{y}\right)$ if it be permitted to scribe a scroll with any two graph-replicas, *x* and *y*, within its outer and its inner close, or upon its bottom and upon its patch, respectively, then whenever it may be permitted to put a replica of *x* on the sheet of assertion, it will be permissible to scribe a replica of *y* or the sheet of assertion. Or stating this in terms of transformation, whenever an enclosure has been permissibly scribed on the sheet of assertion, this enclosure containing another enclosure on its area, then [the] graph consisting of all the rest of the contents of the enclosure may whenever it is scribed on the sheet of insertion [sic,] be transformed by the insertion into as a component of it of what graph which is contained in the inner enclosure while the entire graph upon its area, with the exception of one enclosure upon that area, is also **[Alt.1]** scribed upon the sheet of assertion, it is always permissible to transform a blank on the sheet of assertion into any the graph that is scribed on the area patch of that enclosed enclosure. In order to state this in a more practical shape, **[Alt.2]** I will draw your attention to a *corollary* from it. By a corollary from a proposition is meant a necessary consequence of it that is easily drawn. Now I will tell you a great secret about necessary consequences which it is exceedingly useful to know, but which the logicians are generally quite ignorant of. It is that the drawing of such a consequence always depends upon the *observation* of some fact about some diagram or something of the nature of a diagram, whether on paper or in the imagination. The fact here to be observed is that one kind of graph always does lie on the sheet of assertion outside of a scroll. That graph is the blank. Consequently since when $\left(\genfrac{}{}{0pt}{}{x}{y}\right)$ *x* is on the sheet of assertion, the present predication of the definition of the definitum makes it permissible to scribe *y* on the sheet of assertion whatever graph *x* may be, it follows that if the graph *x* is a blank so that what is on the sheet of assertion is $\left(\genfrac{}{}{0pt}{}{}{y}\right)$ we are permitted to scribe *y* on the sheet of assertion. In other words, two *coincident* cuts or a *double cut* as I call it, that is a scroll with its outer close vacant; permits us to write scribe what is in the inner close directly on the sheet of assertion. Let us take this for our third permission:

Permission No. 3. The graph within a double enclosure on the sheet of assertion may be scribed unenclosed.

Now then the remainder of the substance of the predication of the definition of the scroll of its definitum amounts only to this, that if all that is in the outer close of a scroll on the sheet of assertion is also scribed on that sheet it may be erased from the outer close. That is, if $\left(\genfrac{}{}{0pt}{}{x}{y}\right)$ *x* is scribed, we may transform it into $\left(\genfrac{}{}{0pt}{}{}{y}\right)$ *x*. For this by Permission No. 3 will give us all that the present predication of the definition of the definitum authorizes. But I am not quite yet ready to put this upon our list of permissions. Now going onto the predication of the definitum of the definition, this predication is that if it is permitted to scribe any certain graph, *y*, on condition that it shall be permitted to scribe a certain graph, *x*, then it is permitted to make a scroll with *x* scribed alone in its inner outer close, or on its bottom, and with *y* scribed in its inner close, or on its patch. Stating this in terms of transformation, if it would be permitted to transform a graph *x*, should it occur on the sheet of assertion, into a graph *y*, that permission is permissively transformable into gives the permission to transform a blank of the sheet of assertion into a *scroll*, having *x* alone on its bottom and *y* on its patch.

    We can now formulate that permission which I just now postponed formulating. Suppose we have on the sheet of assertion $\left(\genfrac{}{}{0pt}{}{x\,z}{y}\right)$ *x* Then as soon as we are permitted to scribe *x z* on the sheet of assertion we shall be permitted to scribe *y* But we are already permitted to scribe *x*; and therefore as soon as we are permitted to scribe *z* we can scribe *y*. Hence by our present predication we are already permitted to scribe $\left(\!\!\begin{array}{c}\boxed{z}\\ y\end{array}\!\!\right)$ That is to say, we find that if we have on the sheet of assertion a scroll and also a partial graph of the entire graph in the outer close of that scroll, then we are permitted to ~~write~~ scribe the scroll without that partial graph in its outer close. That is we get

Permission No. 4. Any graph in the outer close of a scroll on the sheet of assertion which graph is also scribed on the sheet of assertion may be permissively erased from the ~~bottom inner~~ outer close of the scroll.

From [the] predication of the definitum of the definition we can draw a corollary. For suppose y is scribed on the sheet of assertion. We ~~accept whatever is written as true~~ assume what has been scribed has been permitted to be scribed. It is therefore permissible to scribe y on the sheet of assertion. But by Permission No. 2, whatever it is permissible to scribe on the sheet of assertion it is permissible to scribe whatever else may be scribed there, say z. Therefore, by the present predication, it is permissible to scribe $\left(\!\!\begin{array}{c}\boxed{z}\\ y\end{array}\!\!\right)$ whatever z may be. We thus have

Permission No. 5. It is permitted to put upon the sheet of assertion a scroll having in its inner close a replica of any graph already on the sheet of assertion, and in its outer close whatever graph we please.

Now let us see what further transformation the predication of the definitum of the definition of a scroll authorizes. This practically amounts to two rules, first that in all cases it is either permissible to scribe any graph x on the sheet of assertion or to scribe a scroll with x alone on its bottom and with whatever we please on its patch; and second, that it is always permissible to transform y on the sheet of assertion into a scroll with y on its patch and whatever we please on its bottom.

It now remains to treat the blank and the blot in the same way. Taking first the blank, we find that when we attempt to predicate the definition of the definitum there is nothing to predicate. The presence of a blank does not involve any permission at all. To say this, that is to say that there is no express permission to ~~write~~ scribe anything in place of a blank except what is expressly permitted to be scribed there would be a needless and meaningless form of assertion with no ~~substance~~ matter. We therefore pass to ~~fifth~~, the predication of the definitum of the definition, which consists in saying that the presence of a blank on the sheet of assertion is always permitted. It is fortunate that it is permitted, because it is physically impossible that a blank should not accompany whatever graph-replica is scribed on the sheet of assertion or any other area. Practically, therefore, this permission amounts to nothing.

In short, the system of existential graphs has been so contrived that the blank takes care of itself by physical necessity.

Omitting this, then, we come to the blot. Since, the meaning of the blot is that everything is true, the predication of the definition of the definitum is that where the blot is scribed anything whatever is permitted to be scribed. The blot, however, fills its whole area so that it is physically impossible to scribe anything else. But we have already ~~shown~~ seen that any enclosure having a blot on its area can be erased, provided we interpret a cut as precisely denying the truth of the entire graph which it encloses. [End of sequence, R 456(s)]

[Alt.1] [...] scribed upon the sheet of assertion, it is always permissible to transform a blank on the sheet of assertion into any graph that is ~~enclosed~~ scribed on the area of that enclosed enclosure. But when we ~~take this in connection with another permission that is soon to follow, it will be seen~~

First, the predication of the definition with the definitum as subject is that when it is permitted to scribe upon the sheet of assertion a scroll with two graph-replicas, x and y, in its ~~inner~~ outer and in its inner close, or on its bottom and on its patch, respectively, $\left(\dfrac{x}{y}\right)$ then whenever it is permitted to put the graph x upon the sheet of assertion, it will likewise be permitted to put the graph x upon the sheet of assertion. Or in terms of transformation it will be permissible on the sheet of assertion to transform x by the insertion into it of y as a component of a compound graph $x\,y$.

In order to put this into a more explicit shape, I will first call your attention to a corollary from it. A *corollary* to a proposition of Euclid is a necessary consequence drawn from it by some editor of Euclid's *Elements* and inserted by him, originally, I suppose, marked with a little crown in the margin. These additions are, for the most part, ~~trifles~~ propositions that Euclid thought ~~not worth~~ too obvious for special notice. Hence, any easily drawn necessary consequence of a proposition is termed a corollary. Here I will tell you a secret about necessary consequences.[17] It is a very useful thing to know, although most logicians are entirely ignorant of it. It is that not even the simplest necessary consequence can be drawn except by the aid of *Observation*, namely, the observation of some feature of something of the nature of a diagram, whether on paper or in the imagination. I draw a distinction between *Corollarial* consequences and *Theorematic* consequences. A corollarial consequence is one the truth of which will become evident simply upon attentive observation of a diagram constructed so as to represent the conditions stated in the conclusion. A *theorematic* ~~diagram~~ consequence is one which only becomes evident ~~when the diagra~~ after some experiment has been performed upon the diagram, such as the addition to it of parts not ~~mentioned~~ necessarily referred to in the statement of the conclusion. In the present case, I am going to draw a conclusion about a *double enclosure*, that is, two cuts one within the other and with the annular space between them blank like this $(\!(y)\!)$. The observation which I ask

---

~~to amount to this, that any graph replica on the area *bottom* of a cut whose *place* is the sheet of assertion remembering that~~ remembering that by the *bottom* of a cut we mean the area it encloses, while by the *place* of it we mean the area in which the cut stands, [sheet abandoned]

[Alt.2] [...] it ~~will be well to anticipate a permission shortly to be reached, that of transforming $(\!(y)\!)$ into y. With that in~~view, ~~the present permission amounts to this that~~ view, and remembering that by the *bottom* of a cut we mean the area it encloses while by its *place* we mean the area upon which it had been made, this ~~rule~~ permission ~~is seen to amount to this, that any graph replica that is scribed on the bottom of a cut whose place is the sheet of assertion can be erased provided another replica of the same graph is scribed on the sheet of assertion. But this statement is not precisely the present permission.~~

17 [See the variant exposition of this "secret" that precedes the emergence of Permission No. 3 that Peirce wrote on the cut-out draft pages located in R 456(s).]

you to make is that in every such case there will be a graph of which one replica is in the outer close ~~which is also~~ while another is on the sheet of assertion outside. Namely, that graph is the *blank*. And since the present principle permits us to transform $\binom{x}{y}x$ [into] $\binom{x}{y}xy$ *whatever x may be*, it allows this transformation when *x* is the blank; so that we can transform (y) into $(y)y$. We may count this as our third permission, so that we have

board

Permission No. 3. A graph within a double enclosure on the sheet of assertion may be scribed on the sheet of assertion, unenclosed.

diag

The consideration of what further explicit permission is involved in the predication of the definition, the definitum being the subject, had better be postponed until we have considered the predication of the definitum the definition being the subject. This predication is that in case the permission to scribe on the sheet of assertion a replica of a graph, *x*, would carry with it in every case a permission to scribe on the sheet of assertion a replica of a graph, *y*, then it is permissible to scribe on the sheet of assertion a scroll containing in its outer close only a replica of *x* and in its inner close a replica of *y*. Or in terms of transformation, if it would be permissible to transform a graph, *x*, should it occur on the sheet of assertion, into a graph, *y*, then it is permissible to transform a blank on the sheet of assertion into a scroll having only *x* in its outer close, and having *y* in its inner close.

We may here draw a corollary analogous to, but much more obvious. Namely, to say that it is permissible to scribe any graph, *y*, on the sheet of assertion is to say that, it is permissible to transform a replica of the blank into a replica of *y*. But this, according to this part of the definition of the scroll, permits us to place on the sheet of assertion the scroll (y). Hence we have

diag

diag

Permission No. 4. If a graph could be permissively scribed on the sheet of assertion a double enclosure containing that graph may be placed on the sheet of assertion.

By combining the two parts of the definition of the scroll we get the highly useful graphical form of the *principle of contraposition*. Namely, suppose that a replica of the graph $\genfrac{}{}{0pt}{}{x}{x}$,[18] were it scribed on the sheet of assertion, would be permissively transformable into a replica of the graph, $\genfrac{}{}{0pt}{}{y}{y}$, and suppose that the scroll $\binom{y}{z}$ were permissively placed on the sheet of assertion. Then, by the predication of the definition concerning the definitum, *y*, if scribed on the sheet of assertion, would be transformable into *z*. So *x* being transformable into *y* and *y* in its turn into *z*, it follows that *x* would on the sheet of assertion be transformable into *z*.

Board

---

18 [Peirce added the graphs, in red, on top of the expressions of them that appear inline in black. The presentation instruction "Board" is added in the margin.]

Hence by the predication of the definitum concerning the definition, it would be permitted to place on the sheet of assertion the scroll $\left(\overline{x \atop \overline{z}}\right)$. That is to say, the permissibility of the transformation on the sheet of assertion of x into y, carries with it the permissibility of the transformation on the bottom of a cut placed on the sheet of assertion, of the reverse transformation of y into x. Here is a principle which involves many permissions.

Permission No. 5. *The Principle of Contraposition.* Of whatever transformation is permissible on the sheet of assertion, the reverse transformation is permissible within a single cut.

Thus if

and so on indefinitely. In short, whatever transformation is permissible on the sheet of assertion is permissible on the sheet of assertion within any even number of cuts while the reverse transformation is permissible within any odd number of cuts. For example, since any graph can be erased on the sheet of assertion any graph can be erased within any even number of cuts while any graph can be inserted within any odd number of cuts. Since any graph already scribed on the sheet of assertion can by Permission No. 2 be iterated on the sheet of assertion, that is can have another replica of it placed on the sheet, it follows that if one replica of a graph is on the sheet of assertion and another replica of the same graph is oddly enclosed, the latter can be erased. Thus, $x \left(\overline{x \atop \overline{y}}\right)$ can be transformed into $x \,\overline{(y)}$ and thence by Permission No. 3 into $x\, y$, and thence by Permission No. 1 into y . This [is] what the logic books call the *modus ponens*.

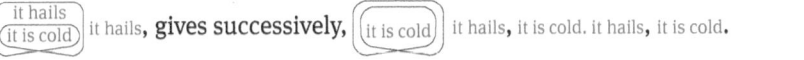 it hails, **gives successively,** it is cold it hails, it is cold. it hails, it is cold.

The fact that our system breaks this up into three steps goes to show that our main purpose, that of dissecting reasoning into its simplest elements, has been, in some measure at least, attained.

It still remains to treat the blank and the blot in the same manner.

But when we undertake to predicate of the blank as definitum any definition we find that no specific permission follows from the existence of a blank, although the whole possibility of writing graphs depends upon it. That has therefore to be passed over. As to the predication of the definitum concerning the definition this renders it permissible for a blank to accompany any and every graph scribed on the sheet of assertion. It is truly fortunate that this is permitted, inasmuch as it would be physically impossible that a blank should not accompany every graph. The truth is that the system of existential graphs was intentionally contrived so that this matter should take care of itself. Here, again, therefore, no permission is called for.

Passing to the *blot*, or *pseudograph*, of which, you remember the meaning is that everything is true, the predication of the definition concerning the definitum is that within any even number of cuts where the blot is ~~scribed~~ any graph we please may be ~~pointed and~~ inserted and within any odd number of cuts where the blot is any graph may be erased.[19] The blot, it is true, fills its whole area, so as to leave no room for any other graph. But there is an equivalent of it of which this is not true. For since by Permission No. 1 every graph on the sheet of assertion ~~evenly~~ enclosed can be transformed into the blank, it follows, by the principle of contraposition that an enclosure containing nothing but a blank can when evenly enclosed be transformed into anything we please, and consequently into the pseudograph. The vacant enclosure is, therefore, a form of the pseudograph. For evenly enclosed it can be transformed into the blot, as the blot can be transformed into it. And since these two transformations are the reverse of one another, it follows, by the principle of contraposition that the same is true within any odd number of cuts. When the vacant enclosure is oddly enclosed as in this figure y ,the enclosure on whose area it stands is evenly enclosed and can be erased by Permission No. 1. But when the vacant enclosure is evenly enclosed as in the next figure z all other graphs, in the same enclosure (here represented by x), being evenly enclosed can be erased by Permission No. 1, and then Permission No. 4 which allows a double enclosure round any graph under even enclosures, permits the double enclosure to be removed under odd enclosures. I mean the double enclosure formed of the cut of the vacant enclosure together with the cut enclosing it. This done nothing but a blank remains; and so, within odd and even numbers of cuts alike, the whole enclosure containing the pseudograph may be suppressed. We thus get

Permission No. 6. Any enclosure containing a blot or other pseudograph may [be] suppressed whether evenly or oddly enclosed.

---

19 [R 1574] [A loose, abandoned sheet] [...] graph may be erased. ~~The blot, however, it is true, fills the whole area in which it is, so as physically to leave no room for anything else. But there is an equivalent pseudo-graph of which this is~~ Now since it is destructive of logic to suppose that everything is true [end]

The predication of the definitum concerning the definition may be regarded as giving the last Alpha Fundamental Permission.

Permission No. 7. A vacant cut may be treated as a pseudograph.

diag

These seven permissions being, however, somewhat confusing, I replace them by a compact little code which I call the **Three Primary Rules**. It runs as follows:[20]

diag

Rule of Erasure and Insertion. Within even cuts (or none) any graph can be erased; and within odd cuts any graph can be inserted.

Rule of Iteration and Deiteration. Any graph of which a replica is already scribed may be iterated on the same area as the primitive replica or within any additional cuts already existing; and of two replicas of the same graph, one of which is enclosed by every cut that encloses the other, the former may be erased, this process being termed deiteration.

Rule of Insignificants and the Pseudograph. A double enclosure can be circumposed about any graph or be removed from any graph; and any enclosure containing a vacant cut or other form of pseudograph can be suppressed or inserted.

I now pass to ~~another part of the~~ the beta part of the system of existential graphs. It is far more interesting and important than the alpha part, but incomparably less so than the gamma part.

When one hears a proper name mentioned for the first time, one generally learns, of the individual person or thing denoted by that name that it exists. It may, of course, be identified with a subject of force already well-known; but that will be exceptional. It will frequently be ~~obvious~~ apparent that it is a thing quite different from any hitherto mutually recognized. In this case, it will make an addition to the universe of discourse, brought about by means of the assertion [of] a real relation of it to an object previously recognized. Sometimes, it will be doubtful whether it is one of the recognized subjects of force or not. But what I want to ~~call~~ focus your attention upon is, that at the first mention of a proper name, apart from any special information about its subject that may then be conveyed, the name merely tells us that *something exists*, that is, is a factor of the entire complexus of forces that we partly have known by experience. But at any *subsequent* mention of the proper name, though this assertion of existence is reiterated, yet that being known already is of no importance. The importance of the name at all occurrences after

---

20 [Presentation instruction "diag" penciled in the margin next to the definitions of all three rules inscribed in red ink.]

the first is that it *identifies* what is mentioned with something we had heard of before.

If you bear in mind these characteristics of proper names, you will perceive that when lawyers and others use the letters A, B, C as a sort of improved relative pronouns, saying for example that if A owes B money and C owes A money, then B may "trustee" C for the debt (as you say in Massachusetts), these letters differ from new proper names only in the accidental circumstance that they are first introduced in the antecedent of a conditional proposition while proper names are first introduced in positive assertions. I call such improvised proper names *selectives*.

There is nothing to prevent our using the capital letters as such individual names, provided we distinguish the *first replica*, by scribing it heavily or otherwise. I cannot say that this is a bad way; it serves the purpose of putting out of view confusing trifles. But I do say that it is inferior requires rather complicated rules, and from every other point of view except that of putting unimportant circumstances out of view and the convenience in printing, is usually inferior to another way of accomplishing fulfilling the same purpose, which I proceed to describe.

Since the blackboard, or the *sheet of assertion*, represents the universe of discourse, and since this universe is a collection of individuals, it seems reasonable that any decidedly marked point of the sheet, should stand for a single individual; so that • should mean "something exists". We cannot make this ⁚ to mean that two things exist, since this would conflict with our convention that graphs on different parts of the sheet shall have each the same meaning as if each stood alone, so that consequently the second point merely *reiterates* that something exists.

You will ask me what use I propose to make of this sign that *something exists*, a fact that graphist and interpreter took for granted at the outset. I will show you that the sign will be useful as long as we agree that *although different points on the sheet may denote the same individual, yet different individuals cannot be denoted by the same point on the sheet*.

If we take any proposition, say

diagram
A sinner kills a saint

and if we erase portions of it, so as to leave it a *blank form* of proposition, the *blanks* being such that if everyone of them is filled with a proper name, a proposition will result such as

diagram
―――kills a saint
A sinner kills―――
―――kills―――

where *Cain* and *Abel* might for example fill the blanks, then such a blank form, as well as the complete proposition, is called a *rheme*, provided it be neither by logical necessity true of everything nor true of nothing. But this limitation may be disregarded. If it has one blank it is called a *monad* rheme, if two a *dyad*, if three a *triad*, if none a *medad* (from μηδεν).

Now such a *rheme* being neither logically necessary nor logically impossible, and represented as a part of a graph without being represented as ~~as compunded~~ a combination by any of the signs of the system is called a *lexis* and each replica of the *lexis* is called a *spot*. (*Lexis* is the Greek for a single word and a lexis in this system corresponds to a single verb in speech. A *lexis* is therefore an incomplex *contingent* graph. The plural of *lexis* is preferably *lexeis* rather than *lexises*.) Such a spot has a particular point on its periphery appropriated to each and every one of its blanks. Those points, which, you will observe, are mere places, and are not marked, are called the *hooks* of the spot. But if a *marked point*, which you remember we have agreed shall assert the existence of an individual, be put in that place which is a hook of a graph, it must assert that something is the corresponding individual whose name might fill the blank of the rheme. Thus

• gives • to • in exchange for •   diagram

will mean "something gives something to something in exchange for something".

Now let us further agree that a heavily marked line —, all whose points are *ipso facto* heavily marked and therefore denote individuals, shall be a *graph* asserting the identity of all the individuals denoted by its points. Then (is a pear / is ripe) will mean that there is a ripe pear, that is, something is a pear and that very same thing is ripe.

Blackboard

We call such a heavy line a *line of identity*. A point from which three lines of identity proceed has the force of the conjunction 'and'.

⎧is a bird
⎨is black
⎩is mischievous   diagram

There is no need of a point from which four lines of identity proceed; for two triple points answer the same purpose ✕. Therefore a figure like this ✛ is to be understood as two distinct lines of identity crossing one another. Nevertheless, in order to avoid possible mistake a *bridge* may be represented thus: ⊥⊤ One line passes under the bridge, the other upon it.

diag
diag
diag

The more you scribe on the bottom of a cut, the less you assert. Thus

⟨—returns to earth⟩   ⟨—is translated⟩   diag

means: It is not true that somebody returns to earth nor is it true that somebody is translated. But

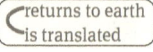

merely says that *both* are not true. That is one or other is false. Either nobody returns to earth or else nobody is translated.

Add to this a line of identity joining the two

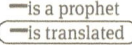

and still less is asserted. Either nobody is translated or if anybody is translated, that person does not return to earth.

Now take this

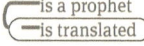

That means somebody is a prophet but nobody is translated. If we continue the outer line to the cut, it will make no difference:

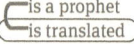

For no significance attaches to the shape of the line. If, however, the inner line be extended to join the point on the cut, much less is asserted:

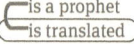

This means: Somebody is a prophet and this person is not translated; that is, Some prophet is not translated.

Lines of identity bring only one new rule of illative transformation. (*Illative* transformation, by the way, is transformation of the nature of necessary inference.) But lines of identity require some slight changes to be made in the three primary rules already given.

Under the rule of omission and insertion, it is to be noted that a line of identity may be broken within an even number of cuts or on the sheet of assertion, while two lines may be joined within an odd number of cuts. We also have the curious fact that as far as this rule is concerned a point on a *cut* is to be treated as being within the cut, although in other respects it is to be treated as being outside the cut. The cause of this is that we take it for granted that something exists. How this cause produces this effect I shall leave it for you to make out.

The rule about the double enclosure receives an extension since not only are two cuts of no effect when ~~nothing~~ no graph is between them, but they are equally so when nothing is between them except lines of identity that traverse the space between the two cuts.

The rule of iteration and deiteration takes a form which cannot easily be expressed without defining a new term, *ligature*. Namely, a line of identity is, as I have said, a graph and as such it cannot be part on one side of a cut and part on the other side. In the graph

there are two lines of identity. But their having a common point on the cut identifies the individuals they denote. By a ligature is meant a line of identity together with all other series of identity that have points in common with it. For example

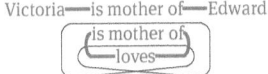

means any man loves himself. It has four lines of identity, one attached to the monad spot "is a man", two attached to the dyad spot "loves" and one joining the triple point to the inner cut. But all those make a single "ligature". Now the reformed rule of iteration and deiteration is, that any partial graph, detached or attached, may be iterated within the same or additional cuts provided every line or hook of the iterated ~~spot~~ graph be attached in the new replica to identically the same *ligatures* as in the ~~old~~ primitive replica; and if a partial graph be already so iterated it can be deiterated by the erasure of one of the replicas which must be within every cut that the replica left standing is within. For example, suppose we have these premises:

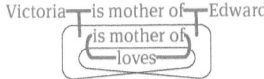

We can iterate the two outside lines of identity with in the outer cut, thus:

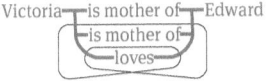

Within one enclosure we can join the two lines on each side, thus:

We can now deiterate "mother of", thus:

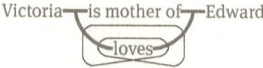

We can now erase the two cuts which have nothing between them but lines of identity, thus:

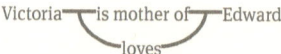

We can now erase "mother of", thus:

I now proceed to the new fourth rule. It runs as follows:

The New Fourth Rule. The innermost effective ligature between two spots lies within every cut that encloses both those spots.

In order to illustrate the meaning of this I take these graphs:[21]

diag

The first three of these mean, respectively, "Nobody loves anybody whom he does not respect", "Somebody loves nobody whom he does not respect", "Somebody is loved by nobody who does not respect him".[22] Those three propositions cannot be expressed, with the same degree of analysis without the ligatures, the innermost of which is within the cut that encloses both spots. But the fourth, which means "There is somebody whom somebody does not love unless he respects him" will not have its meaning changed by breaking both ligatures, as in the fifth

---

21 [Cf. Fundamental Rule 5 at the end of Lecture II(a), R S-28 of the previous selection.]

22 **[Alt.]** [R 455(s), notebook page 29] The first three mean "nobody loves anybody whom he does not respect", "somebody loves nobody whom he does not respect", "somebody is loved by nobody who does not respect him". Those three cannot be expressed without the ligatures, the innermost of which is within the cut that encloses both spots. But the fourth which means, "There is somebody whom somebody does not love unless he respects him", will not have its meaning changed by breaking both ligatures and making it read "Either somebody does not love somebody or else somebody respects somebody", or "If everybody loves everybody then somebody respects somebody". [This cut-out segment continues with "I have now left very little time for the third chapter of this exposition…" in the footnote below.]

graph, so as to make it read "Either there is somebody who non-loves somebody or else somebody respects somebody" or "If everybody loves everybody somebody respects somebody". The junctures protruding through two cuts could be cut without altering the meaning.

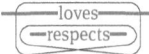

By putting two cuts round the "loves" and retracting the junctures through two cuts we get the equivalent graph[23]

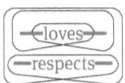

diag

The third chapter of the exposition of existential graphs is by far the most important and interesting or the three. The whole gist of mathematical reasoning depends upon it. I shall have to remit it to another [R S-32] lecture.[24] To fill my hour tonight, I will give a rule for solving a problem which often arises in connection

---

23 [Presentation instruction "diag" penciled in the margin of the previous and the following example.]

24 [Peirce's draft of the lecture that was delivered on November 27 continues in R S-32 to be written, for the first time, not on the Harvard notebook pages but on a linen ledger grid paper of 8 × 10½ that he apparently acquired only after having arrived in Cambridge, Massachusetts on November 23. This last part of the lecture, as transcribed in the main segment of the text, was apparently to replace the last two cut-out pages from the notebook of the draft of Lecture II(b), located at R 455(s), produced below and in the subsequent footnote. The intended final version of the ending of the second lecture, in which we find Peirce having largely completed the elaboration of the rules (the "Five Operations") of the suggested decision procedure for the Alpha and the Beta-reduct graphs, was probably composed near the end of the month, perhaps only during the days between the first and the second lecture, that is, November 24–26. Time permitting, the five operations it may well have been communicated to the audience instead of the following earlier plan, which was to concern abstraction, also because the topic of abstraction would find its more natural place within the later lectures of four and five.] **[R 455(s)]** [Four notebook leaves paginated 31–34 and inscribed on the rectos of last two pages that have been cut out from the notebook of R 455 (on the versos of the same notebook leaves appears another rejected segment paginated 29, 31, 33 and 35, "…lecture and will fill up…a vacant enclosure", transcribed in the next footnote):] I have now left very little time for the third chapter of this exposition which [is] by far the most important and ~~if I had time to develop it would be infinitely the most interesting.~~ most interesting of the three. I will say what I can of it tonight and remit the rest to another lecture. Among existing things which attract our attention there are some whose existence consists in facts concerning other things. Thus, a knife consists in the fact that its blade and its handle have been joined together so as not easily to come apart. The existence of anything extended in space ~~exists by~~ consists in the coherence of its parts. Yet we must conceive that there are ultimate subjects of force which do not consist in facts about anything else. When we examine any one

of such constitutive facts, we find that it has reference to a *law*, to a conditional proposition. The fact that the blade and handle of a knife are strongly connected consists in the truth of the conditional proposition that if one were to wrench them, ~~pretty~~ not too strongly, they would not come apart. Such a law is of the nature of a *graph*. But [it] is *real* in the sense of being really true of the ~~external~~ real world. Now we study graphs. We find out what essentially different kinds of parts go to compose them; and since there are real graphs in the real world, we conclude there must be real parts of them such [as] *qualities*, *relations*, etc. These are called *abstractions*. There is a ~~common~~ widely prevalent disposition to say that abstractions are *mere words*. That they are of the nature of words is true; and it is also true that a man's words have very little power to produce effects. Nevertheless, such ideas as *justice* and *truth* have enormous power in the world; and what is more pertinent to our present business is that the analysis of mathematical reasoning shows that the gist of it lies mainly in handling abstractions. We must provide for them in our system of existential graphs or it will not be adequate to the expression of all possible assertions.

Let me introduce you to a certain series of spots. I write them and mark their hooks

•/0\ •/1\• •/2\: •/3\• •/4\: etc.

I will ~~explain~~ illustrate the meanings of two of them.

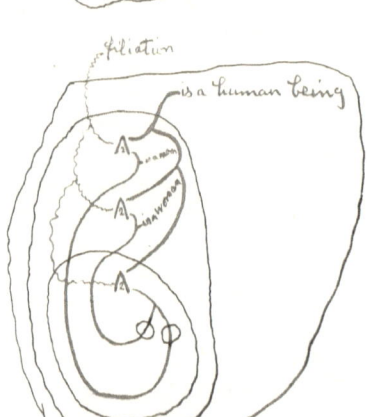

There is something called humanity which every man possesses.

There is a relation, filiation, in which every human being stands to a man and to a woman and if it stands in this relation to anything then that thing is either identical with that man or is identical with that woman.

[The segment from R 455(s), ms pp. 31–34 ends at the end of the page 34, and was either abandoned here or had a continuation that has been lost. What follows is a nine-page segment, shortly abandoned, which refers to the above examples and is written in the notebook R 461 that bears the title of "Lowell Lectures of 1903 by C. S. Peirce ~~Lecture IV, Begun Sep. 30. 2pm. Second Draught of continued. Lecture 3. After page 9. beginning p. 90"~~.]

Ladies & Gentlemen: I continue the subject of my last lecture. From what I was saying it evidently amounts to the same thing to say that an object possesses the quality of humanity and to say that it belongs to the collection of men. Nevertheless, there is considerable difference between a quality and a collection; for though the essence of the collection is the essence of the quality, yet its existence is the existence of all its members. A quality has no individual identity; it has no existence. But a collection is a single ~~object~~ individual object; it exists. Not only is a heap of sand a single individual object; but

Gaius Julius Caesar

the collection composed of Julius Caesar, of this piece of chalk, and the replica of Caesar's name that I have put on the board is a single object. Thus a collection has a mixed nature. It shares in part the nature of a substantive possibility, like a quality; while in part it shares the nature of what we call in philosophy a *first substance* that is an individual object existing in an act of brute reaction. Some of the qualities of a collection are like the qualities of first substances and consist in what is true of its members. Thus, when we say the United States has free government, we mean, that all those states are largely inhabited by voters whose majority determines who is to fill the offices, together with other such facts. When we say that a people is turbulent we mean that ~~some of the a considerable part of the people~~ many men who are members of it forcibly oppose other members who are a part of it. On the other hand a collection also has qualities which are similar to those general respects in which qualities agree and differ. Chief among ~~these potential~~ these respects is *multitude*, or *maniness*. Let me repeat that I never use the word multitude to mean a large collection. I invariably use it to mean ~~a respect~~ a character of a collection ~~by virtue of~~ consisting in that collection being greater than every collection than which it is greater and being at least as small as every collection that it is [at] least as small as. The multitude of a collection may be compared to the luminosity of a color. Like luminosity, it is a *serial* respect or *quantity*. But even in the qualities of this respect, multitude, we find marked traces of the existential nature of collections. For all the quantities or serial respects in which substantial qualities differ are ~~infinitely~~ *continuous*; that is, between any two grades, say of luminosity of a color, or of pitch of a note there is room for any multitude, however great, of others; while multitude on the contrary varies by *discrete steps*. This difference is dues to the fact that a collection consists of existing objects while a quality is a mere general possibility.

The doctrine of multitude ~~was first~~ dates from the year 1851 when an accurate definition was published of what it means to say that one collection is greater than another, in the posthumous work of the catholic theologian and logician, Bernhard Bolzano. You will search in vain for Bolzano's name in the histories of philosophy, unless in some encycloædic work like the revised Überweg; because historians of philosophy confine their attention to works that have created more or less sensation, and works that can be appreciated only by readers who are capable of accurate and solid reasoning never can create a sensation, since there is not one reader of philosophy in a thousand who is so capable. But you may be sure that so clear-headed a thinker, venturing into the field of theology, did not escape persecution; and that is why this work was posthumous.

The negative of *being greater than* is being *as small as*. Let me seize this opportunity to ~~explain two more~~ repeat explanations of two peculiarities of my use of language. When I say that

with the third chapter.[25] Namely, the rules of transformation of graphs enable us to perform necessary inferences. If a graph *a* can be transformed into a graph *b*,

---

one thing is *as small as* another, I invariably [mean] that *at most* it is *[at] least as small as* that other, that it is equal to or smaller than that other. ~~I never mea~~ For the relation of "being at least as small as" is demonstrably the simplest of the relations of comparison of two magnitudes. The other peculiarity of my language is similar to that, in that I ~~choose~~ adopt that one of two possible meanings which asserts the less. Namely, when I say that anything is either *a* or *b*, either a bird or blue, either a lover or a son of, I do not mean to exclude the possibility of it being both *a* and *b*, both a bird and blue, both a lover of and a son of.

Now, then, to say that a collection, say that of the *a*s, is as small as a collection, say that of the *b*s, is true, if, and only if, there is some relation in which every *a* stands to a *b* to which no other *a* stands in this same relation.

What we may call, after a phrase of the mathematicians, a one-to-one ~~correspondence~~ relation is a relation in which ~~every member of one class stands to one nothing~~ no one individual stands to two different ~~things~~ individuals, nor any two individuals to the same individual. Such for example is the relation of ~~husband of~~ in a monogamous country. Now according to a certain very simple ~~proposition~~ theorem of the doctrine of substantive possibility, ~~to say that~~ the fact that there is a relation, *r*, in which every *a* stands to some *b* to which no other *a* stands in the same relation, implies and is implied by the fact that there is a one-to-one relation in which every *a* stands to some *b*. In point of fact, this one-to-one relation is easily defined, provided the Bs are capable of being arranged in serial order, which we shall see is always the case. Namely, letting ρ denote the one-to-one relation; and adopting the locutions "U is ρ to V" or "U is ρ'd by U" in place of the longer phrase "U stands in the relation ρ to V", then to say that "U is ρ to V" shall mean the same as to say that "V is ρ'd by U which is an *a* and is the first of the *b*s in serial order that is ρ'd only by U". [end]

25 [The following alternative continuation of the main segment of the text appears on the versos of four cut-out pages of the notebook R 455 preserved in R 455(s), paginated 29, 31, 33 and 35, and have been merged with the main folder at the Harvard Peirce Papers. This rejected segment represents Peirce's early and rejected attempt at the decision rule, appealing to the operation of the newly introduced sign termed the "blot" in the course of that attempt.]

[R 455(s):] [...] lecture and will fill up the hour this evening by considering a problem which often occurs in that third part of the subject but which does not properly belong to it.

In the logical analysis of mathematical reasoning,—even of reasoning so simple that everybody employs it,—we often find that a reasoning is sound unless a certain state of things would be logically impossible. Now the question is, how are we to ascertain for certain, in a complicated case, whether the state of things represented by a graph is logically possible or not. What is wanted is as simple a rule as may be for making positively sure of this.

We have seen that a logical impossibility ~~evenly enclosed~~ acts by the rules of graphs to destroy the entire enclosure within which it is. Thus the graph "If *a* is true then *b* and *c* are true" ⓐ(ⓑc), become in case *b* is logically impossible **[P.H.]**[26]

then if *a* is true, *b* is *necessarily* true; or if *b* is false, *a* is *impossible*. It will be convenient to speak of *alpha-possibility, beta-possibility*, and *gamma-possibility* to distinguish what the principles of three chapters of our exposition permits. Namely, if those rules of graphs which refer only to *cuts* but not to ~~junctures~~ ligatures would destroy the entire area in which a given graph is scribed, I shall call that graph, *alpha-impossible*. If the same effect would be produced by all the rules thus far considered, I call the same graph *beta-impossible*; so that a graph may be alpha-possible but beta-impossible. If the rules of the third chapter would have the same effect, I call the graph *gamma-impossible*. The rules hitherto given, then, enable us to say that certain graphs are *beta-necessary* and that certain graphs are *beta-*

The impossibility destroys the cut and all it contains. In like manner if in the same graph *a* is logically impossible, so that it means "if the logically impossible were true *b* and *c* would be true" is saying nothing whatever. The whole enclosure disappears.

What is wanted, therefore, is a simple rule for determining whether if a given graph were scribed on the sheet of assertion, it would act, by the rules of graph-transposition, to destroy the entire sheet. This is a kind of problem which I am accustomed to leave my pupils to work out. I have [...] [The rest of this sentence written horizontally in the margin of this loose page of the cut-out sheet has disappeared with the cutting.] However, I will say something about it. This graph ◯ consisting of a blank ~~oval~~ enclosure or cut with nothing in its area is logically impossible, since it asserts that nothing is true, which would destroy logic. Therefore our purpose would be attained if we had a simple rule which would show when the rules of graphs would authorize our putting a vacant enclosure on the sheet of assertion. The precise denial of the logically impossible is the logically necessary. And the logically necessary is that which the rules of graphs would authorize us to write on a blank sheet. Therefore a simple rule which should determine what the rules of graphs authorize our scribing on a blank sheet will answer our purpose. For if they authorize our making a cut with a given graph in it, that graph is impossible; and if not, it is not. Consequently what we want is a simple summary of the rules of graphs. [[**Del:**]] The only thing that we can ~~at once~~ immediately scribe on a blank sheet is a scroll ⌽ or any number of them anyhow placed. Having thus obtained cuts we can ~~write~~ scribe anything we like in them and that done we can iterate. Thus we can successively scribe ⌽ ⌽ ⌽ . We are never authorized to scribe a spot unless that spot be itself logically necessary. Therefore if a graph contains under one cut any spot not logically necessary and not scribed unenclosed we know at once that the graph is logically possible.]

Since I may not be able to give the whole rule to-night, I will divide it into two parts; and will begin by giving that part of it which shows how to proceed when the junctures have been completely disposed of. [[**Del:**]] This part of the rule depends on this principle:

Suppose an entire graph ~~involves~~ contains, no matter how enclosed, a graph *x* which is logically *contingent*, that is, is neither logically impossible nor logically necessary. Then the entire graph is logically impossible if, and only if, it would be impossible if *x* were everywhere erased, and would also be logically impossible if *x* were everywhere changed into a vacant enclosure] [end, page full, continuation missing]

impossible. If a graph is neither *beta-impossible* not *beta-necessary* it is said to be *beta-contingent*. Now we may have a complicated graph and after transforming it according to the rules, may fail to find it either beta-impossible or beta-necessary; and yet we may be unable to make quite sure that there is not some mode of transforming it that we have not thought of which would prove one or the other. We thus stand in need of a rule, as simple as may be, which shall determine whether or not the rules of transformation of graphs would in any way result in the cancelling of ~~any~~ every area on which that graph ~~was~~ should be scribed. If this effect would be produced the graph is *beta-impossible*; if not it is *beta-possible*. In the latter case, we examine its negative, and if that be *beta-impossible* the graph itself is *beta-necessary*. But if ~~neither~~ both the graph and its negative are *beta-possible*, they are both *beta-contingent*.

I will give you the simplest rule I know for ascertaining with certainty whether any graph is *beta-possible* or not. I do not believe it is the simplest rule that could be devised for the purpose; but it is the business of my scholars to find out such ~~things~~ simplifications. I am fully occupied with other problems. The rule has two parts; of which the first reduces the question of *beta-possibility* to a question of *alpha-possibility*, while the second part solves the problem of alpha-possibility. Since I may not have time this evening to give the whole rule, I will begin by giving the second part. This second part, then, dealing with the possibility of *a graph without junctures* is as follows:

> Representing the graph under investigation by the letter x, scribe on the sheet of assertions an enclosure containing the letter x and also an enclosure containing on its area the graph under examination. Separate this inner area into ~~half~~ two parts by a dotted line, leaving one part, to be called the *upper region*, vacant, the entire graph being in the *lower region*.

This being done, the rule presents a numbered list of five operations, and recommends that now and ~~on the compl~~ after each operation, you perform the first of these operations that is practicable, as long as any is practicable. These five operations are as follows:[27]

---

[27] [R S-34:] Establish a separate sheet of assertion whose universe is that of unexcluded possibility.

At the beginning and after ~~each of the~~ performing any one of the following operations (unless ~~it results in there being~~ there be a vacant cut on the sheet of ~~assertion~~ the graph under examination), perform on that graph ~~whose possibility is in question~~ the first of these operations that can be performed.

Operation 1. Cancel ~~every~~ an enclosure containing a vacant cut.

Operation 2. Cancel a pair of cuts one of which contains nothing but the enclosure of the other, leaving the contents of the latter to stand in the area in which the outer cut stood.

Operation 3. Transfer one *lexis*, or incomplex alpha-contingent graph that stands otherwise unenclosed in the ~~inner~~ lower region of an enclosure on the area of the outermost cut (where x is scribed) to the upper region, and cancel it wherever it occurs, however enclosed, in the lower region.

Operation 4. For every replica, however enclosed, one incomplex alpha-contingent graph which occurs as the sole contents of an unenclosed cut in the lower region of an enclosure on the area of the outermost cut (where x is scribed), substitute a vacant enclosure throughout that region, ~~in every occurren~~ at the same time inserting in the upper region an enclosure containing that graph and nothing else.

Operation 5. Select, to be next dealt with, one, incomplex alpha-contingent graph which remains, anyhow enclosed, in the lower region. Iterate on the same area every enclosure on the area of the outermost cut (where x is scribed). In the upper region of each of the original replicas of the iterated enclosures scribe the graph selected, ~~treating the lower region~~ cancelling that graph throughout the lower region, as in Operation 3. In the upper region of

---

Operation 1. Cancel ~~every~~ an area containing a vacant cut.

Operation 2. Cancel a pair of cuts one of which contains nothing but the enclosure of the other, leaving uncancelled what is on the area of the latter.

Operation 3. Cancel wherever it occurs ~~any simple~~ an incomplex contingent graph which occurs unenclosed, ~~writing it, unenclosed on a separate slip as an unexcluded poss~~ at the same time scribing it unenclosed on the sheet of unexcluded possibility.

Operation 4. Substitute a vacant cut for an incomplex contingent graph which is the sole contents of an unenclosed cut, at the same time scribing on the sheet of unexcluded possibility a cut containing only this graph.

Operation 5. ~~Copy the~~ Iterate entire graph under examination (omitting cancelled parts) enclosing each replica in a cut, and enclosing both cuts in an outer cut, and do the same with the entire graph of unexcluded possibility etc.

A juncture is enclosed by a cut if, and only if, every part of it is enclosed by that cut.

If any juncture is unenclosed by any cut, select one of the unenclosed junctures, and in the area of its unenclosed part ~~write~~ scribe "A exists" (but this need not be done if it joins a hook of a contingent spot in the same area) and scribe A against every hook which this ~~graph~~ juncture joins erasing the juncture itself.

If now there is another unenclosed juncture, enclose the whole, excepting the "A exists", in two cuts with nothing between, and proceed to the following operations. Otherwise proceed to them, at once.

each of the new replicas of the iterated enclosures scribe an enclosure containing only the graph selected, and throughout the lower region substitute a vacant enclosure for that graph, as in Operation 4.

When all these operations practicable have been performed, no ~~contingent~~ alpha-contingent graph will remain in the lower regions. The graph remaining is ~~then~~ to be understood as referring to the universe of alpha possibility, and to be accepted as true.

Example.

diag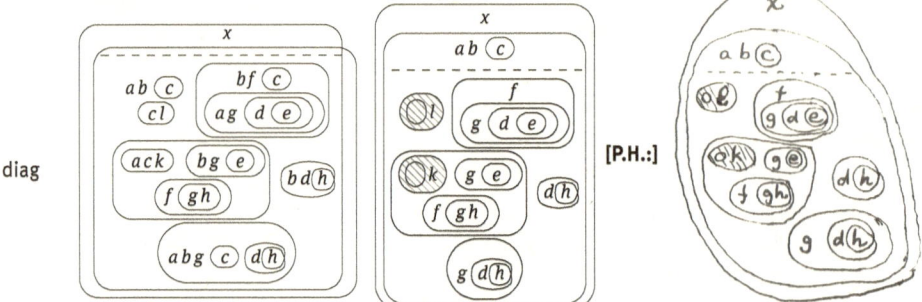

I first deal with *a*, *b*, *c* together.

Practically I should next deal with ⓓⓗ although this would violate the rule. But when one has a mastery of the subject, one can see whether or not it would make any difference. But I will pursue the rule and will next deal with *g*.

diag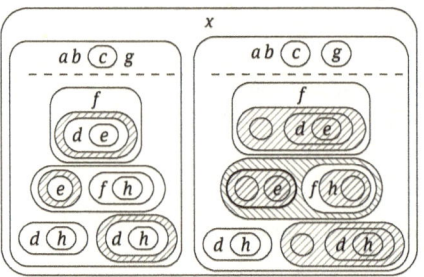

On the *g* side, we can now deal with *d* by Operation 3. On the right we can deal with *f* by Operation 4. We thus get

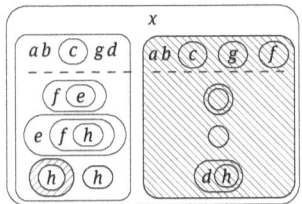 [P.H.:] 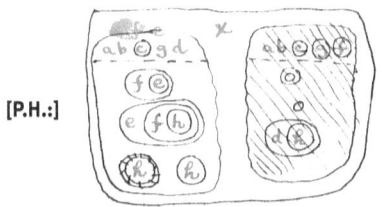 diag

The ~~blank~~ vacant enclosure on the right destroys the entire enclosure in which it is and it is easy to see that the h will destroy the other showing that the graph is impossible. But if the h had not occurred at the bottom of the original graph, we should have had the graph[28]

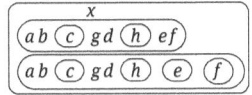 diag

showing that if the original graph were true a, b, g, d would be true c and h false and e and f both true or both false. [End of R S-32]

Existential Graphs: The Initial Conventions

[R S-29, R S-33. This appendix contains a study from the notebook catalogued R S-29, entitled "Existential Graphs: The Initial Conventions" (initially corrected from "The Initial Conditions"), plus variants. This study might be earlier than 1903, as it is related both in character, handwriting and internal terminology to Peirce's descriptions of the fundamental conventions and the basic rules of transformation of EGs that we find in his studies since 1897 (LoF 1; see esp. Selection 10, R 497, on nine basic rules). However, the study is not unrelated to the second Lowell Lecture and to *The Logical Tracts*, either, and serves as a reminder of what Peirce had earlier accomplished in relation to the topics of the second lecture draft. In this notebook we find Peirce's study of the rules of the system. After the capitulation of the initial conventions, of which only five are presented in the study, Peirce returns to the demonstration of what he in the pre-draft of the second lecture (R 450) had termed the basic rights, and derives some theorems from the nine basic rules. The Code of Three Primary Rules is found among the derived ones, and hence the proofs illustrate well their non-trivial (theorematic) character, showing that those primary rules are not primitive rules of inference. Many other of Peirce's proofs in R S-29 likewise involve the kinds of observation and experimentation upon diagrams take make the present study a good example of the extend in which theorematic reasoning is involved deduction, and how philosophy of logic penetrates the analysis mathematical reasoning.]

---

28 [An arrow pointing from the word "graph" to the example below. Presentation instruction "diag" occurs inscribed in lead pencil in the margin.]

Existential Graphs: The Initial ~~Conditions~~ Conventions

1. It is agreed that whatever is written on a certain sheet shall represent objects ~~existing~~ reacting in pairs in a certain universe. Thus, Hamlet ~~can~~ may be written if Hamlet ~~belongs to that~~ reacts with the objects of that universe; otherwise Hamlet must not be written. "Man" can be written if there is a man in the universe. A proposition can be written if there is ~~an object~~ a set of objects ~~whose existence in the universe~~ being one of a class the existence of any member of which in the universe renders the proposition true while the non-existence of any ~~object~~ member of the class renders the proposition false. Thus writing a proposition on the sheet ~~of assertion~~ asserts it of the recognized universe.[29]

---

29 [Alt.1]

1. Each and Every ~~state of things represented~~ conceived fact written unenclosed on the sheet of the graph is ~~asserted, no matter what else may be written~~ thereby asserted to be realized in the universe of actuality.
2. Enclosing ~~a proposition represented state of things~~ the expression of a conceived fact within a lightly drawn o[val] excludes it from the ~~book of truth or the realm of existence~~ universe of actuality.
3. ~~Every part of a continuous heavy line asserts the identity of the parts it connects and so ultimately of its extremities.~~ Contact of individuals signifies identity, and every part of a heavy line asserts the identity of its extremities.

[Alt.2] [R S-33]

Existential Graphs: The Initial Conventions

1. The writer of the graph and the interpreter agree that a certain sheet of paper shall have nothing written upon it except the writer's settled ideas about a certain universe, or collection of objects, with which both parties are acquainted; so that what is written on that sheet is asserted of that known universe. (To write ~~anything~~ any proposition implies there exists something which exists only in the universes for which the proposition is true. To write something implies it exists. A written proposition denotes an object whose existence makes the proposition true.)
2. Two propositions are both asserted; and a blank space asserts nothing.
3. If an individual subject is not indicated, the meaning shall be that an individual of the recognized universe can be found of which the proposition is true.
4. A heavy line (branching or not) shall assert the identity of all its extremities.
5. A lightly drawn oval wholly enclosing a verb shall be understood to remove that verb from the sheet of assertion; and such an oval is to be conceived as drawn tightly round the enclosed assertion so as to leave no blank space within it; but one oval enclosing another and nothing more restores the enclosed proposition to the sheet of assertion. The whole enclosure, consisting of the oval and its contents is to be understood as a verb meaning that its subject is something ~~whose existence in any universe involves the truth for that universe of the enclosed proposition~~ which belongs to a universe for which the enclosed proposition is true.

[Alt.3] [R S-33] **Existential Graphs: The Initial Conventions**

1. To write a proposition in the area devoted to the graphs is to assert it of the universe recognized.

2. If two propositions are written both are asserted. (*Corollary.* A blank place ~~asserts no~~ has no meaning, and is always true.)
3. If an object is not precisely indicated, but only partially described the meaning is that the precise description being completed to suit ~~the interest~~ the writer it becomes true.
4. A heavy line (whether it furcates or not) shall assert the identity of its extremities.
5. A lightly drawn oval wholly enclosing an object removes the object from the sheet of assertion, and if it is left indefinite the interpreter can complete the description to suit himself.

The Nine Basic Rules

I. We have a right to a blank sheet.
II. Two graphs that can be written separately can be written side by side.
III. All basic rules for transformation of graphs apply to unenclosed parts of graphs.
IV. If an unenclosed part, A, of a graph is transformable into an enclosure consisting of an oval containing ~~only~~ a graph B then B in the same situation in which A was is transformable into an enclosure consisting of an oval of like contents except that B is replaced by A.
V. If an unenclosed part of a graph being an enclosure consisting ~~only~~ of an oval containing only A is transformable into a graph B, then a similarly placed enclosure consisting of an oval containing only B is transformable into A.
VI. Two designate individuals transformable the one into the other may be joined by a heavy line, or being joined may be separated.
VII. Designate individuals joined by a ~~connecting~~ heavy line uncrossed by any oval line are mutually transformable.
VIII. Every unenclosed heavy line might be joined to a designate individual, did we know what one to choose. And all medads should be considered as designations of the same individual.
IX. It makes no difference whether a designate individual is enclosed or not, though it does make a difference[30] whether ~~a portion of~~ the heavy line attached to it ~~passes through~~ is ~~so enclosed~~.

---

2. To write two propositions is to assert both.
3. If a subject is left undesignated, the meaning is that of some individual of recognized universe the proposition is asserted.
4. A heavy line asserts the identity of all its extremities.
5. A ~~light~~ proposition wholly enclosed in a lightly drawn oval is not asserted; but the whole is a verb asserting that its subject is the substance (or meaning) of the enclosed proposition. But, for the sake of convenience, if the oval is not so connected with any subject, it is considered to be connected by a heavy line to the verb "is false". And it is to be remarked that a proposition within an oval may have its subjects connected by heavy lines to subjects not in the oval. These lines not being wholly enclosed are assertions of identity. It is an imperfection of this system that two ovals one enclosing only the other do not obliterate one another.

30 [Peirce peppered "though it does make a difference" with four question-marks.]

Theorems. X. Any graph, A, which, being unenclosed, is transformable into another, B, is transformable into that other wherever it is evenly enclosed, while that other, B, is transformable into A wherever it is oddly enclosed.[31]

Demonstration.

1. Whatever graph A may be, (A) is transformable into itself; for this is no transformation, at all.
2. Hence, by basic rule IV, A is transformable into (A).
3. If A unenclosed is transformable into B, then (BC_0) C is transformable into (AC_0) C_1. For by basic rule III, AC_0 is transformable into BC_0 and, by 2, BC_0 is transformable

---

[R S-33:] **X.** A transformation within any certain number of ovals is illative within every number congruent to the first to the modulus two, while the reverse transformation is illative under all other numbers of ovals.

Demonstration.

1. Whatever graph A may be, (A) is transformable into (A); for this is no transformation at all.
2. Hence, by basic rule IV, A is transformable into (A).
3. And by basic rule V, ((A)) is transformable into A.
4. If A is transformable into B, then (B) is transformable into (A). For, by 2, B is transformable ((B)), so that A is transformable into ((B)), whence, by basic rule IV, (B) is transformable into (A).
5. If (A) is transformable into (B), then B is transformable into A. For, by basic rule IV, B is transformable into ((A)) and by 3 ((A)) is transformable into A.
6. If A is transformable into B, then A enclosed in any even number of ovals is transformable into B enclosed in the same number of ovals and B enclosed in any odd number of ovals is transformable into A. For suppose this is true for all numbers up to $2N$ then it is true for $2N+1$ $2(N+1)$. For let α be A enclosed in $2N$ ovals and β be B enclosed in $2N$ ovals. Then α is transformable into β, and by 4, (β) is transformable into (α) and ((α)) into ((β)). Now for $N = 0$ the proposition is evident. Hence, it is true for all values of N.
7. If A is transformable into B within any certain even number of ovals or B into A within any certain odd number, then A unenclosed is transformable into B. For suppose this true for all numbers up to $2N$. Then it is also true for $2N + 1$ and for $2(N + 1)$. For let α be A enclosed in $2N$ ovals and β be B enclosed in $2N$ ovals. Thus by 5, α is transformable into β, (β) is transformable into (α) and this is true if ((α)) is transformable into ((β)). Consequently, if (β) be transformable into (α) or ((α)) be transformable into ((β)), α is transformable into β. Now when $N = 0$, the proposition is manifestly true. Hence, it holds for all numbers.
8. If A be transformable into B under any certain even number of ovals, or B be transformable into A any certain odd number, then the same is true for all even and odd numbers. For by 7 A unenclosed is transformable into B and by 6 A with every even number of ovals is transformable into A.
9. Since this is true when A and B are entire graphs it is, by basic rule III, true when they are parts of graphs.

into ⓑ(B₀), whence, by basic rule IV, ⓑ(BC₀) is transformable into ⓑ(AC₀). Whence, by basic rule III, ⓑ(BC₀) C₁ is transformable into ⓑ(AC₀) C₁.

4. If A unenclosed is transformable into B, then ⓑ(ⓑ(AC₀) C₁) C₂ is transformable into ⓑ(ⓑ(BC₀) C₁) C₂. For, by 3, ⓑ(BC₀) is transformable into ⓑ(AC₀); whence by 3, ⓑ(ⓑ(AC₀) C₁) C₂ is transformable into ⓑ(ⓑ(BC₀) C₁) C₂.

5. Suppose it to be proved for a particular whole number, N, that if any graph, A, is transformable into another, B, then wherever A is enclosed in an even number of ovals not exceeding $2N$, it is transformable into B, while wherever B is enclosed in an odd number of ovals not exceeding $2N$, it is transformable into A. Then, the same proposition is true for the number $N + 1$, next greater than N. For, by 3, when B is within $2N + 1$ ovals, it can be transformed into A; and, by 4, when A is within $2(N + 1)$ ovals, it can be transformed into B.

6. But, by 3 and 4, the proposition is true for $N = 0$. Hence, it is true for every integral value of N. Q.E.D.

Corollary from X.[32] If one graph M is transformable into another N, then an enclosure consisting of an oval containing only N is transformable into an enclosure consisting of an oval containing M.

Demonstration. For by basic rule IV, if A ⌐ Ⓑ then B ⌐ Ⓐ. Let A be M and let B be Ⓝ. Then if A ⌐ Ⓝ, Ⓝ ⌐ Ⓐ but by V N ⌐ Ⓝ. Hence if A ⌐ N, Ⓝ ⌐ Ⓐ. Q.E.D.

XI. Two ovals, the one enclosing the other but enclosing nothing outside that other, neutralize each other's effect and are equivalent to none.

Demonstration.

1. Whatever graph A may be, Ⓐ is transformable into Ⓐ.
2. Hence, by basic rule V, ⓑ(Ⓐ) is transformable into A.
3. But, by basic rule IV, A is transformable into ⓑ(Ⓐ).
4. Thus, A and ⓑ(Ⓐ), being mutually transformable, are for purposes of transformation equivalent.

Corollary. Any blank space may be enclosed by an oval provided another be drawn within it. Q.E.D.

XII. If an enclosure consisting of an oval enclosing a graph, A, is transformable into a graph containing an unenclosed enclosure consisting of an oval enclosing only a graph, B, then B is transformable into A within any even number of ovals, and A is transformable into B within any odd number of ovals.

Demonstration. If Ⓐ C is transformable into Ⓑ D then, since by basic rules I and III, Ⓑ D is transformable into Ⓑ, it follows from basic rule IV that B is transformable into A C. But, by basic rules I and III, A C is transformable into A. Hence, by X, B is transformable into A wherever it is evenly enclosed, and A is transformable into B whenever it is oddly enclosed. Q.E.D.

Corollary from XII.[33] If an enclosure containing only one graph, P is transformable into an enclosure containing only another graph Q, then Q is transformable into P.

---

32 [Initially numbered as theorem **XIV**, with the cancelled roman numeral and a marginal note: "This is a mere corollary from **X**".]

33 [Initially numbered theorem **XV**, with the cancelled roman numeral and a marginal note: "This is a mere corollary from **XII**".]

Demonstration. For by IV if (P) ≺ (Q) then Q ≺ (P). But by XI (Q) ≺ P so that Q ≺ P. Q.E.D.

XIII. *Rule of deletion and insertion.* Any evenly enclosed part of a graph may be deleted and within any odd number of ovals any insertion may be made.[34]

Demonstration. For since the graph A standing alone may by basic rule I be erased, it follows, by basic rule III, that A B can be transformed into B. Whence, by X, the same transformation may be made within any even number of ovals, while within any odd number B may be transformed into A B. Q.E.D.

XIV. If a heavy line is partly inside and partly outside an oval, it makes no difference whether a branching point in it is outside or inside.

Proved by the basic rules about heavy lines. Q.E.D.

XV. *Rule of iteration and deiteration.* Whether within an even or odd number of ovals, any part of a graph standing outside of any number of ovals, or of none, may be iterated inside inside those ovals, its attachments to heavy lines being preserved; and any part of the graph precisely like, and with the same connections as, a part of the graph reached from the former by passing out through any number of ovals, or none, may be erased.

Demonstration.

1. By the rule of deletion and insertion A (B) C ≺ A (BA) C
2. By XIV and III, if A M ≺ A N then A (N) ≺ A (M). But by II A B ≺ A B A B and by the rule of deletion and insertion A B A B ≺ A B A so that A B ≺ A B A. For M put B and for N put B A. Then A (BA) ≺ A (B) and by III A (BA) C ≺ A (B) C.
3. By the rule of deletion and insertion D (A BA / C) ≺ D (A B / C)
4. By 2 and XIV (A (B) C) ≺ (A (BA) C) and by III (A (B) C) D ≺ (A (BA) C) D
5. It is thus proved that a medad may, whether it be enclosed or not, be iterated under one oval and that the reverse deiteration may be performed. Whence by X it follows that this may be done when the outer medad is anyway enclosed.
6. Suppose it proved that medad may, however placed, be iterated within N ovals that it stands outside of, and that the reverse deiteration may be performed. Then by 5 the same is true of $N + 1$ ovals. But by 5 it is true of one oval. Hence, it is true of any number. Thus the proposition is proved for a medad.
7. Such a graph as A⟩─B / C is transformable into A⟩─B / C⟨A by the rule of deletion and insertion.

---

[34] [R S-33:] *Rule of iteration and deiteration.* XIV. Whether within an even or an odd number of ovals, any part of a graph standing outside any number (including zero) of ovals may be iterated inside those ovals, its attachments to heavy lines being preserved; and any part of the graph precisely like and with the same connections as a part of the graph reached from its place by passing out through any number (including zero) of ovals, may be erased.

8. Such a graph as ⟮A—B, C—A⟯ is by VIII transformable into Y—⟮A—B, C—A⟯ and by IX this is transformable into $^{Y-A-X}_{Y-C}$ ⟮X—B, Y—A, X⟯ and by 2 this is transformable into $^{Y-A-X}_{Y-C}$ X—B and by VI this is transformable into $^{Y-A-X\, X-B}_{Y-C}$ and by deletion this into ⟮A—B, C⟯.

9. & 10. These by contraposition can be performed under single ovals.
etc etc.

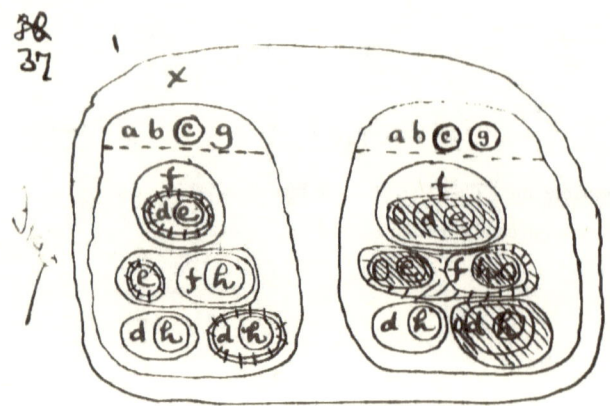

On the g side, we can now deal with d by Operation 3. On the right we can deal with f by Operation 4. We thus get

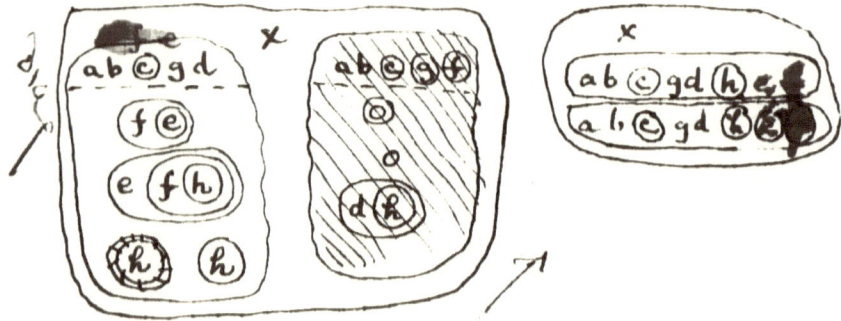

The vacant enclosure on the right des[t]roys the entire enclosure in which it is and it is easy to see that the h will destroy the other showing that the graph is impossible. But if the h had not occurred at the bottom of the original graph we should have had the graph showing that if the original graph were true $ab\bar g d$ would be true c and h false and e and f both true or both false.

[One holograph page illustrating Peirce's decision procedure. With presentation marks "diag" and letters in red ink, with some smudging (Harvard Peirce Papers, R S-32).]

35 Lowell Lecture III(a,b)

[Copy-texts are R 462 (III(a)) and R 457 (III(b)). On the notebook cover label of R 462 is written, in Peirce's hand, "The Main holt for Lecture 3. 2nd Draught of 3rd Lecture. Begun 1903 Oct 5 10:30am". Also included in the selection of this non-delivered pre-draft of the third lecture are cut pages located in R S-31 that Peirce had removed from the notebook in order to keep the planned third lecture within the 60 minute reading time. Included in the appendix is an earlier and incomplete attempt from October 2, R 457, designated on the notebook cover label as "1st Draught of 3rd Lecture".] The presentation of the five operations at the end of Peirce's foregoing lecture plan served as a bridge between the two lectures in articulating the much needed transition from how to do proofs in Alpha to the consideration of what Beta graphs can teach us about philosophical issues of logic. Beginning with the matter of proofs, Peirce bisects the primary permissive rules in two ways: first, there are those that *complicate* the graph (insertion, iteration, and adding of the double cut) and those that *simplify* it (erasure, deiteration, and cancelling the double cut). The second division is according to the *non-reversible* (insertion and erasure) and *reversible*, equivalence rules (iteration/deiteration and adding/cancelling the double cut). Peirce also proposes, quite far-sightedly, that because of the "endless multitude" of conclusions that can be derived by rules that complicate the graphs (with only a small number of Beta graphs as premisses), "the simplest rule" "for ascertaining with certainty" whether Beta-possibility holds is not the kind of "comprehensive routine" that a machine could perform.

The "main holt" of this lecture as indeed of its two other extant versions nonetheless is the promised "third chapter" on the Gamma part of existential graphs. Peirce first needs to communicate its philosophical motivation. As the lecture progresses, the topics touch increasingly more on "questions now vexed": qualities, possibilities and laws will no longer be absent in the analysis provided by the method of Gamma graphs. What kinds of possibilities are qualities? Why are qualities not related to one another? What is the nature of dyadic relations and relations of existence? What are the triadic relations and how can laws be mental affairs? The analysis of relations and references that link representations to qualities and laws is for Peirce to be a strictly logical affair.

The third lecture was originally announced as "The three universal categories and their utility". The main pre-drafts of the lecture notes actually dealing with Peirce's theory of universal categories are located in R 464, composed beginning in October 8 and portraying the second, and a slightly more mature version of the present draft of R 462, and ultimately, in R 465, the writing of which began on October 12 and which was designated as the second part of the third draft of the third lecture, anticipated by both R 462 and R 464. The list of references that Peirce provided under the original heading consisted of two titles only:

Lecture III.
The three universal categories and their utility. (General explanations. Phenomenology and speculative grammar)

Hibben, John Grier
    Hegel's logic. An essay in interpretation. New York, 1902.   **3607.196**
Peirce, Charles Sanders
    On a new list of categories. (In American Academy of Arts and Sciences. Proceedings. Vol. 7, pp. 287–298. Boston, 1868.)   ***3370.6.7**

At the end of the last lecture [Lecture II(b); R S-32, R S-34, R 457] I gave a rule for positively ascertaining whether a graph is alpha-possible or not.¹ It also ~~determines~~ furnishes a description of the state of things in which it is possible. I said I supposed it was not the best possible rule; but it is reasonably speedy. Considering that the system of existential graphs is not intended to be used as a calculus, it satisfies all requirements.²

The idea of that rule was double corresponding to two different distinctions among the six fundamental alpha-permissible operations. Namely, of these six, there are three that complicate the graph and three that simplify it. The three that complicate it are insertion, iteration, and ~~placing~~ making of a double cut. The three that simplify it are erasure, deiteration, and the cancelling of a double cut. Furthermore, there are of the six operations, two only that are not reversible, that is which ~~cannot~~ may not be *undone* as well as done. These are erasure and insertion. Now my idea in drawing up the rule was, in the first place, to define to myself precisely on what occasions the complicating operations might be indispensable in ascertaining whether a graph was possible or not, and to restrict their virtual employment to those cases, and in the second place, so to modify the non-reversible operations as to render them reversible.

The ~~rule~~ method given is such a comprehensive routine that it would be easy to devise a machine that would perform it. But when ~~junctures~~ ligatures have to be taken into account, the immense diversity and complexity of the case renders any such procedure quite impracticable.

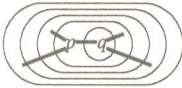 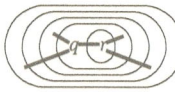 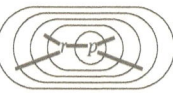

Thus, from these three premisses, which are certainly not of more than ordinary complexity, yield no less than ninety entirely independent conclusions without iterating the premises.³ With iteration there would be strictly an endless multitude, of which several hundred would have some interest. I say this without very careful examination, but I believe it is correct.

---

1 [At the top of the page: "Use *ligature* in place of *junctive* throughout".]

2 **[Del.:]** When we come to beta-possibility, it is impracticable to work ~~by any similar~~ in the same comprehensive routine. It might be done; but the waste of time would be enormous in any but the simplest cases.

3 [Aligned with the three premisses, Peirce wrote in the margin: "These should be twisted to make right and left hand spots alike".]

The beta-part of the system of existential graphs is distinguished by its taking cognizance of individual identity and individuality. Perhaps, therefore, we ought to consider the following statement as *beta-impossible*:

> A certain institution will pay every dollar it has borrowed or shall borrow with a borrowed dollar; and the payment of a dollar cannot balance debts of more than one dollar. Nevertheless, there will be some dollars borrowed that never will be repaid.

I have, however, introduced no rule into this part of the exposition which would stamp that statement as impossible. If the institution in question had an eternal existence it might, ~~conceivably~~ as far as my rules take cognizance of impossibilities, go on forever borrowing more and more dollars each year and after paying up all its ~~old~~ last year's debts have an ever-increasing surplus of borrowed money in hand. But this possibility does not consist in any state of things that ever will be an accomplished fact. It consists in a predicted endless future that never can ~~come to pass~~ become positive fact.

However, rightly or wrongly, I postpone all consideration of the distinction between *esse in futuro* and positive individual existence to the gamma part of the subject; and as long as I do this, there is no impossibility in the beta part of the development which[4] is not essentially of the same nature as the absurdity of the following ~~statement~~ proposition and graph:

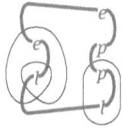
Arthur likes everything exhibited by a certain dealer who exhibits a picture painted by an artist who paints nothing that Arthur likes.

An impossibility like that of this second graph appears to have a different character.

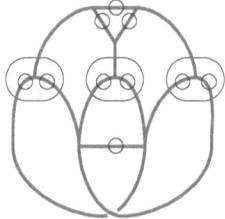

---

4 **[Del.:]** [does] not appear to consist in a violation of the principle of contradiction, like an alpha-impossibility. There is, however, a difference as will appear. As a simple example of the kind of impossibility which my rules do condemn, we may take this graph, which may be read as follows: [end]

You should have no difficulty in reading it. The heavy lines assert each the *identity* of an individual. The oval cuts with lines running through them assert the otherness of the individuals on the two sides. An oval cut with two lines running into it and there joining any graph assert that the individuals denoted by those lines are not in the relation signified by that graph. All these things were explained in the last lecture. They are perfectly simple. Yet if any of you is able without difficulty to see the meaning of that graph, if his mind is not rendered dizzy by the multiplicity of signs exactly alike, let me tell him that he has the making of an excellent mathematician in him.

The absurdity which this graph asserts is that there is a certain triplet of ~~different~~ individuals and there is a pair of individuals; and each member of the triplet is a member of the pair. That is manifestly absurd. But it strikes the mind as a different kind of absurdity from a ~~simple~~ self-contradiction,—say like that about ~~Alfred~~ Arthur and the picture. This impression deserves careful examination.

We remark that if the member of the triplet and of the pair were mere *predicates* or general subdivisions, there would be no absurdity. It is not absurd to say that every special science is either *nomological, classificatory,* or *descriptive,* and is at the same time either *physical* or *psychical*; although to Aristotle this seemed impossible when the predications were essential.

Let us see how it will be if from that graph we remove the junctures and simply leave a triplet of graphs and a pair of graphs. The graph will then become, let us say, this:

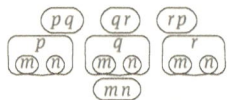

On testing this by the rule given in the last lecture, we find that the graph is perfectly possible, as it stands, but that it will cease to be possible if more than *one* of the triplet *p, q, r,* are true or if more than one of the pair *m, n* are true, as is obvious on inspection. This suggests that the absurdity of the first graph is due, not to the relation of identity, but to the fact of *positive existence* of the members of the triplet and of the pair. In order to test this let us substitute in that graph some other relation for that of identity. Let us assert first that there are *three* individuals, each of which, instead of being non-identical with each of the others, does not stand in an undefined reciprocal relation to each of the others which we will represent by $\overset{B}{\underset{A}{\frown}}$, that is, A is *r* to B and B is *r* to A. And instead of adding that each of these is a member of a certain triplet [we] will simply say that they agree in ~~some~~ having a certain graph *t* true of them. We shall have then this graph,

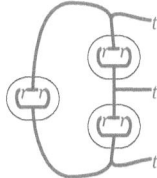

Next, instead of talking of a pair, let us talk of individuals of whom a certain graph —p is true, and say that it is not true that there are three of these related to one another like the three of which t is true. This will give us

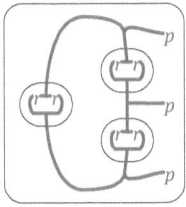

Now we have to assert ~~something~~ or question able absurdity concerning the relation between t and p.

Our absurdity has hitherto consisted in saying that every member of a triplet ~~could not be~~ is identical with a member of a pair. But there was not need of introducing the relation of identity here. It is equally absurd to say that every member of a triplet *is checked off* against a member of a pair, provided it be essential to the idea of "checking off" that if two objects not identical are checked off, then the objects ~~with~~ against which they are checked off are not identical. Let us use this relation of checking off. Only in the definition of it, we must replace the relation of non-identity by that same reciprocal relation which we have hitherto used. We shall thus have this graph ~~perfectly~~ sufficiently defining checking off, which we will express by the letter c:

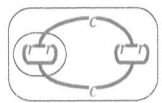

Now the question is whether it is absurd to say that everything of which t is true is checked off against something of which p is true; that is

The answer is that it is absurd, and that the impossibility is of the same general type as that about Arthur and the picture. But it is evidently the same as the impossibility of and consequently this is like the Arthur impossibility.

In short the difference between alpha-impossibility and beta-impossibility is that alpha-impossibility is implicit self-contradiction violating the principle of contradiction and therefore being an impossibility for anything that has any kind of *being*. A *beta-impossibility* is an impossibility for whatever *exists*, so that the principle of excluded middle holds of it, whether this existence be accomplished or be *in futuro*.

A rule for finding whether a graph is β-impossible, or if not ~~how near it comes to that condition~~ what graph would have to be scribed along with it to render it so, is as follows:

First, find in the graph some lexis (regarding ──⊖── as a lexis) of which one replica is oddly enclosed and another is evenly enclosed, the latter not being within every cut enclosing the former. Call every such pair of spots an *adaptable pair*.[5] And having found such a lexis, iterate the entire graph.[6] Now in the new replica of the graph *conjoin* as far as possible the adaptable pairs (*conjoining* them consisting in joining all the junctures of corresponding hooks) ~~Second, now of the graph, join by junctures such junctures as can be joined by~~ using the following permissive operations:

1. Any graph may be iterated (with identical junctures) within any even number of additional enclosures.
2. Regarding a juncture as enclosed by a cut only if every part of it is so enclosed, every oddly enclosed juncture may be extended outwardly so as to be enclosed by two cuts fewer, and every evenly enclosed cut may be retracted inwardly so as to be enclosed by two cuts fewer.
3. Every juncture may be extended or retracted inwardly, but since two lines of identity can only be joined when oddly enclosed, the permission substantially is to join any two junctures of which one is oddly enclosed and is enclosed in every cut that encloses the other.

Secondly, repeat this operation until all adaptable pairs have been ~~completely~~ conjoined, as far as possible, in the same replica in which other pairs are conjoined (or until you clearly see that the graph is impossible).

---

5 [This sentence added in the margin.]
6 **[Alt.]** [from R S-31, ms p. 20] [...] iterate the entire graph, and in the new replica *conjoin*, as far as possible the adaptible pairs, the operation of conjoining them consisting in permissively joining all the ligatures of their corresponding hooks, ~~employing~~ availing yourself, for this purpose, of the following permissions: A. ~~Any two lines of identity oddly enclosed~~ A ligature being regarded as enclosed within a cut only if every part of it is enclosed by a cut, and the phrases "oddly enclosed" and "evenly enclosed" being understood to mean enclosed by an odd or an even number of cuts and [end]

I now pass to the third chapter of the exposition treating of the gamma-part of the system of existential graphs. The alpha part considers only the general relations of ~~truths~~ simultaneous assertions and of the members of a conditional proposition *de inesse*. The beta part considers individual existence, though without discriminating between past or future; and thereby treats of the logic of all those relations which suppose the individual existence of their correlates. When I speak of a *relation*, it is that kind of relation that I usually mean. I endeavor so to restrict the use of that word. I distinguish other relations by calling them *references*. Thus I speak of the *reference* of a thing to its qualities, if I do not consider them as having individuality. The gamma part of the System deals with what can logically be asserted of *meanings*.

An *ens rationis* is something whose being consists in the possibility of something being true about something else. An ordinary adjective when applied to an object does not assert any accomplished fact. It ~~says~~ tells how an experiment will in future experience turn out. To say that a body is soft means that the experiment of trying to scratch it by the moderate pressure of a knife will always succeed. To say that a body is *hard* will mean that the same experiment will always fail. We so rarely meet with a body on which such experiments will give *variable* results without any ~~obvious~~ assignable reason that the need of an adjective to express *this* quality has not been felt. To possess a quality *now* usually means that experiments of a certain kind that may be made in the future will turn out uniformly in a certain way or ways. Of course, there are qualities which we immediately feel, such as colors; these are what they are without reference to anything else. We may suppose and ordinarily do suppose that external things have qualities in themselves independently of anything else. We suppose that a hard or soft body is rendered such by something that is true of that body in itself whether anybody ever tries to scratch it or not. But of such qualities we can have no further knowledge; and when we apply an adjective the *meaning* of it refers to a conditional prediction as to the results of possible future experience. That, then, is what it is to be hard and to be soft. But now what is this thing *hardness* or *softness* in itself? ~~It is something whose being consists in the possibility how the experiment of trying to scratch a thing should have one or the other uniform result.~~ It is something which has no other being than [what] *consists* in possibility that the experiment of trying to scratch a thing should have certain uniform result. I am talking *logic* and nothing else. These lectures have no doubt a *bearing* upon metaphysics and upon other vexed questions; but upon those questions themselves I have no time to touch. I am not, then, talking Metaphysics. Still less am I talking Epistemology.

Kant has a famous distinction between *constitutive* principles and *regulative* principles. A constitutive principle expresses what *is* so, whatever that may mean. A *regulative* principle expresses how you must think about a matter in order to attain your purposes, whether it *be* so, or not. For example, in a hand of whist, when only three rounds remain to be played and you have the lead, you must *think* of the cards as lying so that it will be possible for you to win the odd trick, although you have no evidence that it is so. You must think so, because if it is not so, your thinking it is ~~cannot~~ can make matters no worse for you, while if they do lie that way, your going on that assumption may save you the trick. Now when I say I am only talking logic and not metaphysics, I mean that for the time being I do not care one straw what the occult truth may be about the real natures of qualities, but all I care for is under what aspect or form of thought you ought to regard them if you do no want to fall into grievous practical errors and to miss important practical truth. There is a logical doctrine called *Pragmatism*. It is the doctrine that what any word or thought means *consists in* what it can contribute to an expectation about future experience, and nothing more. This doctrine has been supposed to have sceptical tendencies; and as the author of it, I have been set down in one History of Philosophy as a sceptic, and in another criticism of my opinions I have been called a second Hume. It is strange to me that it should not have occurred to those writers that a person who thinks that as soon as it is fully proved ~~that holding~~ that the going upon any given proposition will be salutary, it is proved that all that proposition can possibly mean is true, will rather be led by this opinion to believe *more* things than *fewer*. At the same time it is obvious enough that it is a doctrine that may very easily be carried to extremes, if one does not ~~tread with~~ mind one's logic very closely. It is like walking among eggs. I do not intend in this ~~part of my~~ course to ~~touch~~ allude further to *pragmatism*. I content myself with saying that logic is the science of regulating your thoughts so as not to be surprised when it can be avoided; and therefore whatever is said in logic about the modes of being of qualities, of laws, etc. must be understood as *regulative* truth in Kant's sense.

There is an old chestnut,—a now *very* old and never very meaty chestnut, about some physician of the days when medicine and logic were ~~supposed to be kindred studies, closely allied, if not related by blood,~~ allied studies, who on being asked *why* opium should put people to sleep, replied that it was because it had a *dormitive virtue*. When the joke was first popped, doubtless about A.D. 1600, medical men lived who were almost capable of such nonsense; and the jeer had some point. But the hundreds of writers who have, since that time, made merry over it have evidently supposed that such abstractions are absolutely of no account at all in thinking or only serve to confuse our ideas. Now in this they are entirely mistaken; for the microscopic dissection of mathematical reasoning shows that the gist of it lies very largely in thus turning what one may call adjective elements of thought into substantive objects of thought. An obvious example is where mathematicians treat *operations* as themselves things to be added, multiplied, and raised to powers. But the practice penetrates all parts and kinds of mathematics to a degree little suspected.

If I define redness as that whose being CONSISTS in the logical possibility of something being red, you cannot deny that redness really has the being that its definition implies without denying that it is logically possible for anything to be red, unless you mean to say that redness in general would have contradictory properties. Locke does say something like this. He says that a *triangle in general* is neither equilateral, isosceles, nor scalene, but all and neither of these at once. ~~But he is wrong.~~ But when he wrote that, his pen ran away with him. A triangle, in general, is indeed, as he says, *neither* equilateral, isosceles, nor scalene, and this shows that it does not *exist*,—that is, is not a subject of brute force,—but it does not prove that it has no *being* at all. ~~He is quite wrong when he says that~~ If a *triangle in general* were, as he says it is, *both* equilateral, isosceles, and scalene, then he would be quite right in calling it nothing at all, not even an idea. But his assertion that it is so, ~~is a piece of bad logic, not in the least true.~~ simply has no foundation whatsoever. It arose from his inadvertently begging the question by assuming that there is no other kind of being than existence. I should like to ask him whether there is no such thing as a law of nature. I know very well what his answer would be; namely that a law of nature is a *mere word*. But to this I should reply, it is undoubtedly of the general nature of symbol. But what I asked was whether it has no being in nature because we can base predictions on it which come true. He will reply they come true because nature is uniform. I reply events may be uniform by mere *chance* without any special cause. Successive throws of a die may be alike to any number. But nobody bases any sound prediction on that, and that proves that mere uniformity is not sufficient to support a prediction and consequently that the laws of nature are not mere uniformities among events.

But whatever your metaphysical opinion may be, you must in logic look upon *mere possibilities* as having a certain mode of being, or you will entangle yourself in difficulties. They do not *exist*, it is true. But they *are* possible, and are distinctly *not* at the same time impossible; nor do they reunite *any* contrary characters. As long as they do not you can never disprove their being. It is an absurdity, a logical impossibility. Now that whose being omniscience itself could not disprove has being enough for logic.

Qualities are a certain kind of possibilities. They have themselves qualities. It is a *fact*,—and a not unimportant one,—that colors, themselves qualities in respects in which individual things may agree or differ, have in their turn the three independent qualities,—or respects in which *they* can agree and differ,—namely, their *luminosity*, their *chroma*, or chromatic intensity, and their *hue*. A *sound*, which is just as much a quality as is a color, is usually thought of as a thing, being confused with the *occurrence* of it at a definite time and place. It is that occurrence of it that is the individual thing. The sound of a *note* which is its quality, itself has many qualities such as duration, intensity, pitch, timbre, mode of stress, expression, purity, etc. These qualities of qualities *themselves* again have qualities, or ~~modes~~ respects in which they may agree and differ. Thus duration, intensity, and pitch have the character of varying ~~along one line~~ serially only in two directions, that is in another direction, while timbre, mode of stress, expression, purity have the quality of varying in many different directions. These qualities of qualities of qualities themselves have qualities, or respects in which they might agree or differ. For serial variation may be continuous or discrete with other distinctions of which the definition would be too long. In short, without saying that this succession of one order of qualities upon another could go on forever, I am not prepared to say where it would stop.

Qualities are mere possibilities. As such, they have no existence and no individuality. Two qualities are more or less alike; but individual identity of qualities is impossible. Of two qualities one may admit the other or exclude the other. The negative of a quality is itself a quality. Existence cannot transcend possibility. Whatever exists is possible. But it is impossible that all ~~qualities~~ possibilities should exist. It is possible that everything that exists should be ~~crimson~~ scarlet. It is possible that everything that exists should be ~~chrome yellow~~ ultramarine blue. But it is impossible that both these possibilities should be realized.

In thus speaking of qualities, I am leaving time out of consideration and am not drawing any distinction between those things which remain true and those which happen on a certain occasion. I shall continue to neglect time in what follows, except where it is quite necessary to consider it.

Relations are qualities of sets of subjects. They are dyadic if the sets are pairs, triadic if the sets are triads. Some relations may subsist between sets of indefinite multitude, such as the relation of *similarity*; but these should be regarded as *dyadic*, since they may subsist between pairs. Existence being an act of brute force, has its origin in a dyadic relation, although we are apt [to] forget this. ~~Thought An intellectual relation, on the other hand,~~ All purely brute relations like physical forces are dyadic, that is subsist between two subjects.

All dyadic relations are of two kinds; first, relations between ~~two~~ pairs of existing objects, which I usually mean when I speak of relations, and which I might distinctively call *re-relations* by reduplication of the first syllable, since doubleness is so essential to them; and secondly, those relations which I prefer to call *references*, each subsisting between a subject having relatively, at least, an independent position and a *possibility* embodied or actualized in that subject.

You may ask why there should not be a class of relations between qualities. I answer that qualities *per se* apart from the possibility of their being possessed have no relations of any kind, not even references. Each is what it is irrespective of anything else. If one cannot coexist with another, that means that one subject cannot possess both. If one ~~implies~~ involves another, that means that every possible subject which should possess the former would possess the latter.

If a ~~dyadic relation, or any~~ relation be considered in the abstract, it is nothing but a quality, the quality of a set of things; and of course whatever is true of all quality is true of it. In order to appreciate the distinctive character of dyadic relations, they must be considered in the concrete, as facts. Every accomplished fact is a dyadic relation; and every dyadic relation is an accomplished fact. Positive existence is *dual* in its very essence. The idea of it comes to us from the experience of effort. Now ~~a sense of~~ an experience of effort and ~~a sense of~~ an experience of resistance are nothing but the same two-faced experience. It is from that experience that we draw our conception of existence,—if it can be called a conception. Properly it is not a conception; because a conception is general idea,—a sort of picture or diagram which we think of as variously applicable. But to think existence is to have a slight inward repetition of the experience of effort and resistance ~~essentially something that happens~~, that is to say, of that very experience;—an experience of its nature capable of repetition but incapable of the sort of generalization ~~of being pictured or diagrammatized~~ that is performed by picturing or diagrammatizing its object. It is right here and now, or else you have no other cognition of it than a purely symbolical one based on an index. Of course you might use the *word* by habit with tolerable correctness without having the thing itself before your consciousness, were it not that we are never during waking hours for more than a few seconds without the experience. And to that double-sided experience present to you, you tack on pictures and diagrams as you might pin them up upon a wall. I must apologize for this wandering out of logic. It was merely ~~for the sake of memor~~ to fetch a vehicle for the logical idea.

We now come to triadic relations. I think I may affirm that all triadic relations are without exception more or less of the nature of *thought* in a very general sense. Take a few examples for yourselves and you will see that it is so. Only let your first examples be genuine triadic relations and not mere combinations, or else you may find a difficulty in apprehending their true nature.

Take the relation of *giving*. The *donor* gives a *donation* to the ~~givee~~ donatee. Giving is not a mere physical fact. It does not consist in the giver's throwing away the object and that object's striking the other. Even if the thrower had aimed his shot at the other, that aiming would have been an act of thought. Even if he had thrown it without any reference to the other and it had merely hit that other by chance, the regarding these two events which would be thus merely casually connected as one act, would be a creation of thought. But genuine *giving* is not necessarily accompanied by any physical act except that of the expression of an idea. "I give it". Its essence lies in the transfer of the right of property. Now *right of property* is a matter of *law*; and *law* is a mental affair.

Take the relation between two parts making up a whole and that whole. That is a ~~triple~~ triadic relation. Now either these parts make the whole by being brought together or otherwise modified or else their mere being constitutes the whole. In the former case the whole is an *ens rationis*,—a thing of thought. For an *ens rationis* is, by definition, that whose being *consists* in some fact about other things. Now the whole consists in the fact of the necessary modification of the parts in order to constitute it, these parts not being, *in* their *mere* being, identical with that whole. If, on the other hand, the parts are *not* brought together and there is nothing at all true of them to make them into the whole; as when we consider the precession of equinoxes and the American eagle as constituting a whole, the purely mental, not to say fanciful, character of the whole comes out all the more plainly.

You can multiply examples for yourselves. ~~Conversely, every thought involves a triadic relation.~~

Conversely, every thought proper involves the idea of a triadic relation. For every thought proper involves the idea of a sign. Now a sign is a thing related to an object and determining in the interpreter an interpreting sign of the same object. It involves the relation between sign, interpreting sign, and object. There is a three-fold distinction between signs, which is *not in the least psychological in its nature*, but is purely logical, and is of the utmost importance in logic.

Three kinds of elements can be discerned in ~~every object which~~ whatever comes before the mind. The first is the element of Quality, such for example, as Red; and including all the positive suchness of the idea in itself, as mere ideal suchness. It is that which is such as it is, positively and ~~utterly~~ quite irrespective of anything else. I call this element the element of Firstness. ~~The second element~~ Besides its direct presence we attribute to things out of us natures of their own irrespective of ~~other things~~ actual reactions. The second element is directly experienced in our sense of being here, in our sense of present fact, which is the experience of actual reaction with a non-ego. It consists in anything's being that which another makes it to be here and now. I give to this element of doubleness the name of Secondness. Besides, directly experiencing it, we regard outward objects as compelling one another, as exerting force upon one another. The third element is the moulding of brute reactions into conformity to ~~the pure~~ ideas. It is the growth into expression of ~~an idea~~ a thought which can only be thought in the expression, this expression consisting of a bending of reactions to the form of the idea. But, dear me, what a fearfully abstruse matter I am making of that which is the easiest thing in the world to understand, the *nature of a general sign*. Yes, strictly speaking the very easiest of all things to understand; for what we call understanding anything else merely consists in seeing that it is of the nature of a sign. Every little child understands it perfectly. But as he grows up and loses his ~~faculty~~ gift of language, it becomes more difficult; and the more he studies and cultivates his mind the more inscrutable this simple business of a sign, which is the only comprehensible thing in the universe, appears to him to be. Ah, what says Wordsworth to the child?[7]

> Thou, whose exterior semblance doth belie
>   Thy Soul's immensity;
> Thou best philosopher, who yet dost keep
> Thy heritage, thou eye among the blind,
> That, deaf and silent, read'st the eternal deep,
> Haunted for ever by the eternal Mind,—
>   Mighty prophet! Seer blest!
>   On whom those truths do rest
> Which we are toiling all our lives to find.

Oh, it is difficult to have patience with people who imagine that the action of blind force can explain all the phenomena of this world, or even a single one of them. What happens? I observe nature. I think I detect a regularity, and I hazard a prediction. Well, I am often wrong. But not infrequently the event turns out according to the prediction; and not the first time only, nor the second, nor the tenth, nor the hundredth, nor the thousandth, but right straight along. And yet there are people that will tell you that Laws are not real! The prediction gets verified. That is the whole story, provided you realize all that that means. Provided, for example, you perceive that the making of a prediction is an action; and that *every* action consists in making a prediction. The air in my study is stuffy. I say to myself, The window should be opened. Well, then I shall have to open it. Then I shall have to cross the room. Then I shall have to rise. And presently I find myself crossing the room, and the window gets opened. This case in its most general features is just like the other. It is a prediction. Of course the presence of my body and its self-control was a large factor of it. If people would only dismiss from their minds the stupid notion that this universe is ruled by brute force, considering that predictions are verified and actions shaped to purposes solely by the *regularity* of the reactions and that regularity, relating as it does to *what is about to happen*, is necessarily an affair of *thought*, and certainly not the predictor's thought but the thought of God, they would then see what signs really amount to. This element of our daily and hourly experience, the element of the conformity of fact to thought,—this element whose being such as it is consists in this that it has such reference to an object in-

---

7 [From William Wordsworth (1770–1850), "Ode on Intimations of Immortality from Recollections of Early Childhood".]

dependent of it as to bring a third thing (the interpretation) into the same triadic relation to that same object,—this character of a *sign*, the being [of] an exponent of thought, is what I call the element of Thirdness in the phenomenon.

Now, as I was saying, there are three kinds of signs. The first consists of *Icons*, which like all signs are such only by virtue of being interpreted as such, but whose significant character which causes them to be so interpreted is their possessing a quality, in consequence of which they may be taken as representative of anything that may happen to exist that has that quality. Of course there are no signs that are exclusively iconic. But a geometrical diagram, for example, represents, say, a triangle, simply because it is like it.

The second class of signs consists of *Indices*, whose significant character which causes them to be used as signs lies in a matter of *positive fact*, the fact that they are really ~~connected~~ related, re-related, to the objects they denote. This ~~class~~ genus of signs has two species, of which the first consists of those that are merely connected with their objects and call attention to them, of which an example would be Bunker Hill Monument which its designer, Horatio Greenough, declared he meant should say "Here!" merely that, and nothing more. The other species ~~are compounded of~~ consists of Indices of the first species which carry attached to them and thus calling attention to them Icons of these same objects. Such is the weather-cock which is not only connected with the wind but points in the same direction.

The third class of signs are *Symbols*, which not only, like all sings, function as such only in being interpreted as such, but further have for their special significant character merely the certainty, based on some habit, natural disposition, or convention, that they will be understood in certain ways. Thus the word "man" bears not the smallest resemblance to a man, nor is it physically connected with a man, nor otherwise sufficiently connected to make that much reason for ~~interpreting~~ using it as a sign of a man; but which is certain to be understood to mean a man and therefore an excellent sign of one. This genus of signs[8] has three species. The first consists of those [end]

---

8 [The "Main holt" (pp. 0–88, pagination by even numbers except also including page 87) of the present notebook is completed as the notebook becomes full at this point of reaching its last page of 88. The first leaf of another notebook, R 461, bears a heading "Lecture IV, Begun Sep. 30. 2pm. Second Draught of Lecture 3, continued. After page 9. beginning p. 90". The continuation that occurs after ms page 9 is indeed paginated as 90, but consists only of one line "[…] has three species. The first consists of those". The sentence breaks off right when Peirce begins to inscribe the first letter of the next word to be written after "those". Apparently he never continued this particular draft of the planned and abruptly interrupted third lecture, and indeed 90 pages or more would have been too much to be covered in a single lecture. But as Peirce was now occupied with explaining both his newly discovered extension and revision of the doctrine of speculative gram-

Lowell Lecture III(b)

[R 457. "~~Lectures on Pragm.~~ Lowell Lectures III, 1903. 1ˢᵗ Draught of 3ʳᵈ Lecture. Begun 1903 October 2. 10:30am".]⁹

Ladies and Gentlemen:

I explained at the end of the last lecture [Lecture II(b); R S-32, R S-34] how to ascertain speedily and certainly whether a graph is absurd or not after the junctures are got rid of. I now give the rule for getting rid of the junctures. Let me repeat that I think there are probably better rules than that which I give; but it is the duty of any students to find these out. ~~My rule, until I learn of a better one is as follows:~~ Perhaps I shall do well to ~~expound~~ set forth to you the ~~cause of reasoning~~ line of thought by which my rule, such as it is, has been derived; because it is comparatively simple, and will give you some rough idea of the kind of reasoning required in establishing a system of logic.

I begin by asking myself, How is it that I need any such rule? The first answer is that I want some means of determining with certainty whether a graph is possible or not. Oh, but that answer won't do. The means I seek is a ~~means by mode of~~ method of transformation of graphs. What, then, does the word *possible* mean, when translated into terms of transformation of graphs? The answer is that a graph is alpha-possible if the alpha rules of graph-transformation being performed on a sheet on which this graph is scribed can never result in the cancelling of the entire sheet. Very well; then what is wanted is a method by which to ascertain whether, to begin with, the alpha rules of graph-transformation could ever lead to the cancelling of the entire sheet on which the graph in question is scribed. But I ask, Why not simply apply those rules and see whether they lead to that result or not? The answer is, that such operations performed upon a graph may lead to a result which can obviously never lead to the cancelling of the sheet when the original graph otherwise treated might have done so. But this would not be so, if you only made such

---

mar and the related theory of graphs of graphs emerging as a novel department of Gamma graphs, he would be exceedingly busy during much of October in order to produce the *Syllabus* text and its accompanying documents, including the draft of Lecture IV (R 467), in which the division of symbols into three species (qualisign, legisign, sinsign) comes out as the desired new extension of his late 1903 theory of signs. Likewise, the inclusion of the theory of the graphs of graphs into the Gamma part as the desired new extension of his current theory of logic is continued to be presented in the *Syllabus* draft. Soon, however, in the morning of October 2, Peirce begins drafting another continuation of his previous attempt at completing the notes for his third lecture (R 457). In this document, he planned to revisit another disrupted topic of his, namely the decision procedure for the fragment of the logic of Beta graphs in which the lines (junctures, quantifiers) have been eliminated. These sparse notes written on the first ten pages of the otherwise empty notebook of R 457 are included here next.]

9 [Page 0:] Begun 1903 Oct 2. 10:30 A.M. Time Lost by Interruptions
  First interruption by Juliette at   10: 31   15ᵐ
    Work resumed   10: 36
  2ⁿᵈ interruption (Adolphine with message)   10: 50   10ᵐ
    Work resumed   10: 58
  3ʳᵈ interruption   11: 12   25ᵐ
    Work resumed   11: 26

transformations as could be reversed; for in that case any result could be reconverted into the original graph. Let us see then what are the unreversible transformations. They are none other than the operations of erasure within even numbers of cuts and of insertion within odd numbers of cuts. Now, as to the erasure that may, without inconvenience, be restricted to unenclosed partial graphs, and instead of erasing them entirely, they may be simply moved away into another region. This you will observe is just what our rule does. As to insertions, they may be restricted, without losing any result which they could bring about, to the insertion unenclosed of a scroll with the same graph in its two areas. Suppose, for example, you have the graph g and you wish to introduce a spot a. You have only to write $g\,\begin{pmatrix}a\\\overline{a}\end{pmatrix}$. Then putting a double cut about the outer a, you get $g\,\begin{pmatrix}\overline{a}\\a\end{pmatrix}$. Then by twice iterating g you get $\begin{pmatrix}g\ a\\\overline{ga}\end{pmatrix}$. This is precisely the 5th Operation of our rule. Now, then, is there any further difficulty? Yes there is. What is it? It is that half the operations, those of insertion, iteration, and adding a double cut, complicate the graph, and thus lead to a result who[se] possibility or impossibility is ~~less evident~~ even harder to make out than was that of the original graph. The cure for this is carefully to study these complicating operations, ~~and to limit their employment to cases in which~~ to ascertain precisely what are the cases in which they are indispensable in proving graph to be impossible, and to restrict their employment to those cases. This I have done. The operations of insertion and iteration receive their due recognition in Operation 5, while the useful effect of the operation of putting a double cut is fully attained in Operation 4. Namely, in case one has $(a)\,(a\,b)$, one would insert a double cut round the right hand a thus, $(a)\,(\overline{(a)}\,b)$ and then, by deiteration, one would get $(a)\,(\bigcirc b)$. Arrived at this stage we put a double cut about b giving $(a)\,(\bigcirc \overline{(b)})$ and by erasure $(a)\,(\bigcirc\bigcirc)$ by deiteration $(a)\,(\bigcirc)$ and removing the double cut (a). But Operations 4 and 1 accomplish this and thus obviate the necessity of any direct employment of the complicating operations.

I have thus sketched this line of thought in order to give you a rough notion of the kind of reasoning needed in this business. The reasoning which determined the first part of the rule is altogether too complicated to be explained orally. It would be easy enough to describe a way of getting rid of all the lines of identity in a graph while preserving its entire meaning. But the difficulty would be that in the case of a not excessively complicated graph, the different spots would run up into the thousands. But an overwhelming majority of them would be entirely useless. What is wanted is to ~~connect~~ join the junctures of corresponding hooks of all the different replicas of the same spot which ~~sometimes~~ occurs both within an odd number and within an even number of cuts. The first thing, therefore, that is to be done is to note all the hooks which it is desirable to join. Then the first thing to be done is to make such iterations, ~~as may be necessar~~ each within an even number of additional cuts as may be necessary to bring ~~the~~ like spots either within exactly the same enclosures or else so that one is within only one more enclosure than another. Suppose, for example, we have this graph, which is an excessively simple case. $\begin{pmatrix}^c\\_w\end{pmatrix}\begin{pmatrix}^c\\\overleftrightarrow{l}{-}w\end{pmatrix}\begin{pmatrix}^{l-w}\\_w\end{pmatrix}$

The w's and the c's already conform to the desired condition of being all either within the same ~~enclosure~~ cut or the same except that one replica is in one more cut than another. But an iteration is necessary in order to make this true of the l's. It must be an iteration within an even number of additional enclosures.

We perform the iteration of $w\!-\!l\!-\!w$ and then of $\begin{pmatrix}^c\\_w\end{pmatrix}$ and of $-w$ and we prolong the junctures

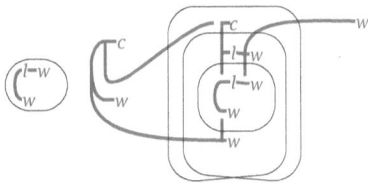

so as to bring them within the same cuts *odd in number*. So far we have performed no operation that is not reversible. We have a right to join the lines within the odd enclosures.[10] But we must be careful to do nothing that cannot be undone. We need not disturb ourselves about the three joinings in the enclosure , because this whole enclosure could afterward be erased leaving us free by a new iteration to restore the present state of things should we desire to do so. But with the joining of the two *c*'s it is different. One way would be to iterate the whole of the large enclosure and scribe

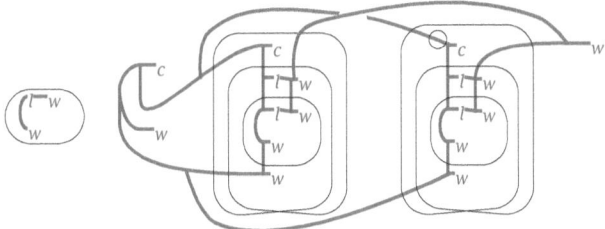

This is an ideally excellent way, suited to some difficult cases. It is ~~never~~ hardly necessary, ~~and in the present case it is preferable simply to iterate the *c* within the cut.~~ in so simple a case as this. But we may let it go. We now simply follow the second part of the rule taking care not to consider two spots as alike unless their corresponding hooks have identically the same junctures. Cancelling the *c* and the two *w*'s and putting capital letters in place of the different junctures we get

$$x$$
$$A c\ A w\ B w\ Z c$$

$$A / B$$
$$A / B$$

$$X w\ X / Y\ Y w$$

---

10 ~~Should we do so we could not break them again. But then, what we could do would be to erase the evenly enclosed , and could then iterate it again if we liked. Nothing will, therefore, be endangered by joining the lines, and we proceed to do so.~~

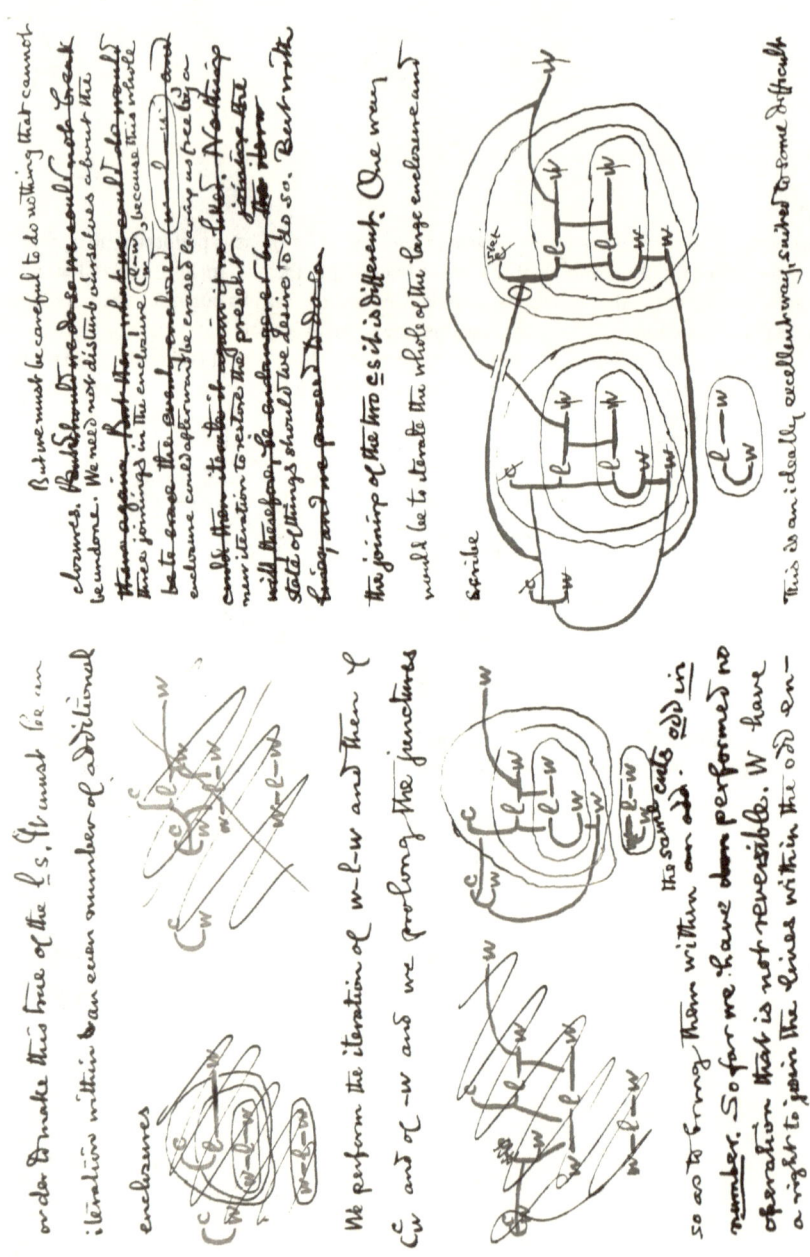

[One holograph page (Harvard Peirce Papers, R 457, notebook pages 8 and 9), red and black ink. Some spots in the last graph are cancelled by Peirce in order to demonstrate the procedure of juncture elimination.]

36 Lowell Lecture III(c)

[Copy-text is R 464, R 465, R 460, with additional pages from R 464(s). On the notebook cover of R 464 is written: "To be used for Lecture III. Vol. 1", and on page 0, "C.S.P.'s Lowell Lectures of 1903. Part 1 of 3rd Draught of 3rd Lecture. Begun Oct 8, 9am". Much of what is included here as the second installment of Peirce's third lecture pertains to its final planning stages. The middle part of the plan below (manuscript pages 26–56) was delivered on November 30, followed by the text segment (manuscript pages 56–64) that Peirce read as part of Lecture IV on December 3. Also included in this second set of notes are some non-delivered pages from R 464(s) and R 465, and last, text from R 460, which comprises part of the actually delivered fourth lecture.] The design of Peirce's third lecture is more coherent than many of its extant variants might suggest, this final draft now connecting the dots. What Peirce had earlier formulated as the rule for checking the Alpha-possibility describes "the states of the universe" to which the possibility of an Alpha graph is limited. It is a model-construction rule, the characteristics of which Peirce explains to pertain to "methodical reasoning" (methodeutic), that is, to the third compartment of logic and semiotics, and not to the second compartment (critic) or to the first (speculative grammar). As in the course of a proof the premisses in the Beta part of the system "can be efficient over and over again endlessly" (such as when applying the rule for universal quantifiers), any prudent application of those rules is governed by methodeutical considerations. A case in point is mathematical discovery and the underlying conceptual innovation and concept-change potential that leads to novel discoveries: methodical reasoning takes into account certain other factors of living intelligence besides demonstrative proofs, as the latter are patterns mechanical applications of permissive rules of transformation.

~~Ladies and Gentlemen:~~

At the end of the last lecture [Lecture II(b); R S-32, R S-34] I gave a rule for positively ascertaining whether or not a graph is alpha-possible.[1] In case it be so, the rule further furnishes a description of the states of the universe to which its possibility is limited. If I had time to set ~~forth~~ before you the ~~process of reasoning~~ train

---

[1] [R 464(s), the two cut-out opening pages] Ladies and Gentlemen: At the end of the last lecture, I gave a rule for positively ascertaining whether a graph is alpha-possible or not, the rule further serving, in case the graph is possible, to furnish a description of the cases in which it is so. I am sure you would be interested in an account of the process of reasoning. I very deeply regret that this course is so miserably short that I can not only not touch upon one third part of logic,— methodeutic, which shows how to use reasoning, but I have not even time to give you a single illustration of the process of methodical reasoning. I bitterly regret that I ever consented to give such a course.

Instead of setting before you the interesting and instructive course of thought which led to the formulation of this rule, I am limited to stating briefly the principles of that reasoning, which is a very different thing. [end]

of thought which ~~led to the~~ determined the formulation of that rule, it would afford an instructive simple example of methodical reasoning. Unfortunately, there is not time for any such illustration in this course; far less can the science of methodeutic be touched upon that great third of logic that teaches the principles upon which reasonings are to be arranged into systematic developments of theory. I will only say that in formulating that rule, I considered that of the six fundamental permissible operations, two are non-reversible, namely, erasure and insertion. That is where either of these can be performed the reverse operation cannot be performed. I further considered that three of the six fundamental permissible operations complicate the graph, while the other three simplify it. Namely, insertion, iteration, and the ~~placing of making~~ introduction of a double cut, complicate the graph, while erasure, deiteration, and the removal of a double cut simplify it. It is necessary for the purpose to modify the non-reversible operations so as to render them reversible; and it fortunately happens that this can be done without erasure, the only one of them that is simplicative, being rendered complicative. In the next place, since the result aimed at must be of extreme simplicity, it is necessary to place restrictions upon the employment of the complicative operations. To this end, each of these was studied and the precise ways in which it could further the general purpose of the rule were ascertained; and thus in place of the complicative operations were substituted a set of operations conducive to the purpose.

The process of the rule is, as I said, probably not the most facile. But since the system of existential graphs is not intended as a calculus or general ~~instrument~~ tool of reasoning, but is only meant for use in the study of logic, where it ~~only occasionally~~ quite infrequently happens that it is necessary to ascertain whether or not any very complicated graph is alpha-possible, the waste of time due to this rule not being the simplest possible, is not of much importance.

The rule prescribes a routine calling for the exercise of so little intelligence that a machine might be devised to perform it. When we pass to the problem of beta possibility, that is, of formulating a rule for positively ascertaining whether a graph with ligatures is logically possible or not, it would be quite easy to formulate a similar routine. But the performance of it would be utterly impracticable owing to the stupendous complications that it would lead to. For example, here is a graph, not particularly intricate:

Yet from this graph as a premiss no less than ninety entirely independent conclusions can be drawn, showing the misconception involved in the popular expression, "the conclusion" from given premisses. Moreover, none of these 90 conclusions uses any part of the assertion of the graph more than once. By repeated making use of the same assertion, any number of conclusions could be drawn. In the alpha-part of logic to which the ordinary textbooks of logic are virtually confined, because although if the problem they consider were stated in graphical form, there would be ligatures, yet they are only such as can all be joined throughout the graph, so that the rules of operation become the same as if there were no ligature at all,—this is not a minutely accurate statement because the books are so unsystematic that no brief statement of what they contain could be quite accurate, but it is substantially so—in this alpha-part of logic a premiss can only be efficient *once*. But in the beta part of logic premisses can be ~~applied~~ efficient over and over and over again endlessly. A moment's reflexion on any simple branch of mathematics will show that it must be so. For instance, the whole theory of numbers depends upon five premisses represented in this graph

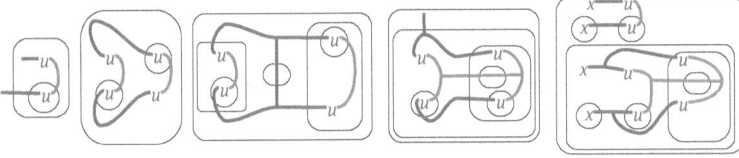

The red ligatures refer to numbers, the brown ligatures to any universe such that there is a relation that *u* may be understood to express, that will make the entire graph true.[2]

x is to be understood to be replaceable by any monad graph whatever without altering the truth of the entire graph.

We shall see, in due time, what those five premisses are. Suffice it for the present to say that there are only five. Now if each of them could be efficient and that in only one way, as one would have a right to infer from the account of reasoning given in the text-books, it would necessarily follow that there could not be but 32 theorems of the theory of numbers in all; whereas of highly interesting theorems already known there are hundreds. Euclid's *Elements*, which was never designed to be more than an introduction to geometry and algebra (or that theory which with the Greeks served the purpose of our algebra) has only 5 postulates, which are the main premisses, together with 9 axioms and 132 definitions. From these Euclid deduces 369 theorems, 96 problems, 17 lemmas, and 27 corollaries. There are also 2 scholia. At the same time, I ought to remark that, while the possible conclusions are innumerable, yet after all premisses have been iterated so as to exhaust all the different ways of using them together with all simpler ways,

---

[2] [In the black & white rendering, red is represented by dark and brown by light grey.]

there will be no more theorems of any particular interest, and the branch of mathematics in question may be said to be substantially exhausted. The theory of conics is an instance. The great geometer Charles after he attained to a great age continued to grind out, by the bushel-basket full, such theorems as that in a plane the number of conics that touch five given conics is 3264. I think that when a mathematical theory has nothing new to discover but such propositions as that it may be said to be exhausted. Every given mathematical theory must, in that sense, eventually become exhausted. Whether or not new theories of interest will continue to offer new problems or not, I am not prepared to say.

But to come back to the matter in hand, I give you without further preface, the following rule for positively ascertaining whether or not a given graph is beta possible.

In the first place, find in the graph every lexis (regarding —⊖— as a lexis), of which one replica is oddly enclosed (that is, is within an odd number of cuts) and another evenly enclosed (i.e., is within an even number of cuts), the latter not being enclosed by every cut that encloses the former; and call every such pair of spots an *adaptible pair*. An adaptible pair is said to be *conjoined* when, and only when, every hook of one of its spots is joined by a ligature to the corresponding hook of the other spot. Your object will be as far as possible to leave no adaptible pair unconjoined, and if this be impossible, at any rate, to produce every possible combination of conjunctions in some replica of an evenly enclosed part of the graph, unless you see clearly that ~~nothing would be gained by~~ a given combination would not serve your purpose in any degree. In order to do this you are permitted to perform any of the following operations upon ligatures, provided that before performing a non-reversible operation you iterate an evenly enclosed part of the graph including every part that will be affected by the operation and only operate upon the new replica so produced.

Operation A. Two oddly enclosed lines of identity in the same area may be joined; and an evenly enclosed line of identity may be severed. These operations are irreversible.

Operation B. From any line of identity lying just outside a cut a branch may be made extending into the cut; and this operation is reversible.

Operation C. A disconnected ~~line of identity~~ ligature can anywhere be scribed or erased.

But what is generally useful is to iterate an evenly enclosed partial graph within an even number of additional cuts, or an oddly enclosed partial graph within an odd number of additional cuts, to extend a branch from an evenly enclosed line of identity into an odd number of cuts and there join it to another, ~~to deiterate an~~

~~oddly get rid of an oddly enclosed replica, and to erase an evenly enclosed replica~~ of the same graph. Of course, this operation is irreversible.

Secondly, when all possible combinations of conjunctions of applicable pairs have been made, the second part of the rule is to be applied, all spots not conjoined by all their corresponding hooks being treated as replicas of different lexeis and all spots that are so conjoined being treated as replicas of the same lexis, and no further attention being paid to the ligatures during the process.

The process will be found to be simpler in practice than it sounds in an abstract statement. I regret that the brevity of the course forbids my illustrating it.

I desire now to say that, in order to be of as much help as I can to those who may be interested in the subject, it is my intention for the next three Sunday afternoons from 3 to 6 o'clock to be at my room at No 6 Prescott Hall, 474 Broadway, Cambridge, where I shall be extremely happy to see any of you who may wish for any explanations from me.

I was advertized to speak tonight [Monday, November 30] of the three Universal Categories. I will try to say something about them; but my last lecture was not half-finished owing to untoward circumstances, and tonight I must begin with the brat part of existential graphs.

I did succeed, last time, in explaining alpha graphs. The blackboard except such portions as may be separated from the rest by "cuts", so-called, is the *sheet of assertion*. Even *graph*, or proposition, scribed upon it is asserted. If two *graphs*, or propositions, are scribed upon it, each is asserted independently of the other; and it makes no difference on what part of the sheet a graph is scribed, so long as they are on separate parts of the sheet. The sheet is itself a graph-replica, or the expression of a proposition; namely it is to be interpreted as expressing whatever is well-known to be true concerning the universe of discourse. Every blank of the sheet is to be understood as forever asserting that.

A *cut* is a self-returning line which I draw on the board with green chalk, but on paper merely as a fine line. A *cut* is not a graph-replica: It does not itself assert anything. But the cut together with all that is within it is called an *enclosure*; and an enclosure is a graph. The surface outside the cut is called its *place*. The surface inside the cut is called its *area*.

I gave you 7 Permissions;[3] but I can state these more neatly as follows:

Rule of Erasure and Insertion. Within even cuts (or none) any graph can be erased; and within odd cuts any graph can be inserted.

---

3 [See Lecture II(b).]

Rule of Iteration and Deiteration. Any graph of which a replica is already scribed may be iterated on the same area as the primitive replica or within any additional cuts already existing; and of two replicas of the same graph, one of which is enclosed by every cut that encloses the other, the former may be erased, this process being termed deiteration.

Rule of Insignificants and the Pseudograph. A double enclosure can be circumposed about any graph or be removed from any graph; and any enclosure containing a vacant cut or other form of pseudograph can be suppressed or inserted.

The beta part of the system of existential graphs is distinguished from the alpha-part by the presence of ligatures in its graphs; and it is therefore natural to think that the distinction between alpha-possibility and beta-possibility lies in the latter's taking account of the relation of identity. But it could easily be demonstrated that this is not the truth of the matter. The true distinction lies in the fact that beta-possibility takes account of individuals, so that whereas in the alpha part all the spots are regarded simply as propositions and may be general, in the beta part, besides these, individuals which form an entirely different category, enter into the graphs. I now go on to a preface to the gamma part of the subject, which is by far the most important of the three, and which is distinguished by its taking account of *abstractions*.

I begin by a remark drawn from Phenomenology.[4] Phenomenology is the science which describes the different kinds of elements that are always present in the Phenomenon, meaning by the Phenomenon whatever is before the mind in any kind of thought, fancy, or cognition of any kind. Everything that you can possibly think involves three kinds of elements. Whence it follows that you cannot possibly think of any one of those elements in its purity. The most strenuous endeavors of thinking will leave your ideas somewhat confused. But I think I can help you to see that there *are* three kinds of elements, and to discern what they are like. I begin with that one which the rough and tumble of life renders most familiarly prominent. We are continually bumping up against hard fact. We expected one thing or passively took it for granted, and had the image of it in our minds, but experience forces that idea into the background, and compels us to think quite differently. You get this kind of consciousness in some approach to purity when you put your shoulder against a door and try to force it open. You have a sense of resistance and at the same time a sense of effort. There can be no resistance without effort: there

---

4 [Cf. R 470, the lecture retitled as "General Explanations. Phenomenology and Speculative Grammar". In the margin, Peirce wrote an instruction to the typist in brown ink: "Type Writer begin here and give me two copies to the middle of page 74".]

can be no effort without resistance. They are only two ways of describing the same experience. It is a double consciousness. We become aware of ourself in becoming aware of the not-self. The waking state is a consciousness of reaction; and as the consciousness *itself* is two-sided, so it has also two *varieties*; namely, ~~willing~~ action, where our modification of other things is more prominent than their reaction on us, and perception where their effect on us is overwhelmingly greater than our effect on them. And this notion, of being such as other things make us, is such a prominent part of our life that we conceive other things also to exist by virtue of their reactions against each other. The idea of other, of *not*, becomes a very pivot of thought. To this element I give the name of Secondness. But now there are elements of what is before the mind which do not depend upon others, each of them being such as it is positively, in itself, regardless of anything else. Such, for example, is the quality of purple. Contrast may cause it to strike us more; but however little it strikes us, the quality of the purple remains the same, peculiar and positive; and we can only say of it that it is such as it is. We attribute to outward things something analogous to our Qualities of feeling. We conceive that a hard body, that is to say a body not readily scratched with a knife, is hard just the same when nothing sharp presses upon it, or even if nothing sharp ever presses upon it. Its hardness, in that case, is nothing but an unrealized possibility. Now what is that? It is certainly no subject of reaction. It does not belong, then, to the category of Secondness. I call this element of thought the conceived being such as it is positively, regardless of aught else, the element of Firstness. Everything you can possibly think of has its Firstness. It is just what it is thought to be or otherwise is regardless of other things. It must be conceived to be something in itself in order to be in relation to other things.

But it is impossible to resolve everything in our thoughts into those two elements. We may say that the bulk of what is actually done consists of Secondness,— or better, Secondness is the predominant character of what *has been* done. The immediate present, could we seize it, would have no character but its Firstness. Not that I mean to say that immediate consciousness (a pure fiction, by the way), would be Firstness, but that the *Quality* of what we are immediately conscious of, which is no fiction, is Firstness. But we constantly predict what is to be. Now what is to be, according to our conception of it, can never become wholly past. In general, we may say that *meanings* are inexhaustible. We are too apt to think that what one *means* to do and the *meaning* of a word are quite unrelated meanings of the word 'meaning', or that they are only connected by both referring to some actual operation of the mind. Professor Royce especially in his great work *The World and the Individual* has done much to break up this mistake. In truth the only difference is that when a person *means* to do anything he is in some state in consequence of which the brute reactions between things will be moulded in conformity to the form to which the man's mind is itself moulded, while the meaning of a word really lies in the way in which it might, in a proper position in a proposition believed, tend to mould the conduct of a person into conformity to that to which it is itself moulded. Not only will meaning always, more or less, in the long run, mould reactions to itself, but it is only in doing so that its own being consists. For this reason I call this element of the phenomenon or object of thought the element of Thirdness. It is that which is what it is by virtue of imparting a quality to reactions in the future.

There is a strong tendency in us all to be sceptical about there being any real meaning or law in things. This scepticism is strongest in the most masculine thinkers. I applaud scepticism with all my heart, provided it have four qualities: first, that it be sincere and real doubt; second, that it be aggressive; third, that it push inquiry; and fourth, that it stand ready to acknowledge what it now doubts, as soon as the doubted element comes clearly to light. To be angry with sceptics, who, whether they are aware of it or not, are the best friends of Spiritual Truth, is a manifest sign that the angry person is himself infected with scepticism,—not, however, of the innocent and wholesome kind that tries to bring truth to light, but of the mendacious, clandestine, disguised, and conservative variety that is afraid of truth, although truth merely means the way to attain one's purposes. If the sceptics think that any account can be given of the phenomena of the universe while they leave Meaning out of account, by all means let them go ahead and try to do it. It is a most laudable and wholesome enterprise. But when they go so far as to say that there is no such idea in our minds, irreducible to anything else, I say to them, "Gentlemen, your strongest sentiment, to which I subscribe with all my heart, is that a man worthy of that name will not allow petty intellectual predilections to blind him to truth, which consists in the ~~harmony~~ conformity of his thoughts to his purposes. But you know there is such a thing as a defect of candor of which one is not oneself aware. You perceive, no doubt, that if there be an element of thought irreducible to any other, it would be hard, on your principles, to account for man's having it, unless he derived it from environing nature. But if, because of that, you were to turn your gaze away from an idea that shines out clearly in your mind, you would be violating your principles in a very much more radical way".

I will sketch a proof that the idea of meaning is irreducible to those of Quality and Reaction. It depends on two main premisses. The first is that every genuine triadic relation involves meaning, as meaning is obviously a triadic relation. The second is that a triadic relation is inexpressible by means of dyadic relations alone. Considerable reflexion may be required to convince yourself of the first of these premisses, that every triadic relation involves meaning. There will be two lines of inquiry. First, all physical forces appear to subsist between pairs of particles. This was assumed by Helmholtz in his original paper, *On the Conservation of*

Forces [1885]. Take any fact in physics of the triadic kind, by which I mean a fact which can only be defined by simultaneous reference to three things, and you will find there is ample evidence that it never was produced by the action of forces on mere dyadic conditions. Thus, your right hand is that hand which is toward the *east*, when you face the *north* with your head toward the *zenith*. Three things, east, west, and up, are required to define the difference between right and left. Consequently chemists find that those substances which rotate the plane of polarization to the right or left can only be produced from such active substances. They are all of such complex constitution that they cannot have existed when the earth was very hot, and how the first one was produced is a puzzle. It cannot have been by the action of brute forces. For the second branch of the inquiry, you must train yourself to the *analysis* of relations, beginning with such as are very markedly triadic, gradually going on to others. In that way, you will convince yourself thoroughly that every genuine triadic relation involves thought, or *meaning*. Take, for example, the relation of *giving*. A *gives* B to C. This does not consist in A's throwing B away and its accidentally hitting C, like the date-stone, which hit the Jinnee in the eye. If that were all, it would not be a genuine triadic relation, but merely one dyadic relation followed by another. There need be no motion of the thing given. Giving is a transfer of the right of property. Now right is a matter of law, and law is a matter of thought and meaning. I there leave the matter to your own reflection, merely adding that, though I have inserted the word 'genuine', yet I do not really think that necessary. I think even degenerate triadic relations involve something like thought.

The other premiss of the argument that genuine triadic relations can never be built of dyadic relations and of Qualities is easily shown. In Existential Graphs, a spot with one tail —x represents a quality, a spot with two tails —r— a dyadic relation. Joining the ends of two tails is also a dyadic relation. But you can never by such joining make a graph with three tails. You may think that a node connecting three lines of identity ⋏ is not a triadic idea. But analysis will show that it is so. I see a man on Monday. On Tuesday I see a man, and I exclaim, "Why, that is the *very* man I saw on Monday". We may say, with sufficient accuracy, that I directly experienced the identity. On Wednesday I see a man and I say, "That is the same man I saw on Tuesday, and consequently is the same I saw on Monday". There is a recognition of triadic identity; but it is only brought about as a conclusion from two premisses, which is itself a triadic relation. If I see two men at once, I cannot by any such direct experience identify both of them with a man I saw before. I can only identify them if I regard them, not as the *very* same, but as two different manifestations of the same man. But the idea of *manifestation* is the idea of a sign. Now a sign is something, A, which denotes some fact or object, B, to some interpretant thought, C.

It is interesting to remark that while a graph with three tails cannot be made out of graphs each with two or one tail; yet ~~every graph with four tails~~ combinations of graphs of three tails each will suffice to build graphs with every higher number of tails:

And analysis will show that every relation which is *tetradic, pentadic,* or of any greater number of correlates is nothing but a compound of triadic relations. It is therefore not surprising to find that beyond the three elements of Firstness, Secondness, and Thirdness, there is nothing else to be found in the phenomenon.

As to the common aversion to recognizing *thought* as an active factor in the real world, some of its causes are easily traced. In the first place, people are persuaded that everything that happens in the material universe is a motion completely determined by inviolable laws of dynamics; and that, they think, leaves no room for any other influence. But the laws of dynamics stand on quite a different footing from the laws of gravitation, elasticity, electricity, and the like. The laws of dynamics are very much like logical principles, if they are not precisely that. They only say how bodies will move after you have said what the forces are. They permit any forces, and therefore any motions. Only, the principle of the conservation of ~~forces~~ energy requires us to explain certain kinds of motions by special hypotheses about molecules and the like. Thus, in order that ~~friction and viscosity~~ the viscosity of gases should not disobey that law we have to suppose that gases have a certain molecular constitution. Setting dynamical laws to one side, then, as hardly being positive laws, but rather mere formal principles, we have only the laws of gravitation, elasticity, electricity and chemistry. Now who will deliberately say that our knowledge of these laws is sufficient to make us reasonably confident that they are absolutely eternal and immutable, and that they escape the great law of Evolution? Each hereditary character is a law, but it is subject to development and to decay. Each habit of an individual is a law; but these laws are modified so easily by the operation of self-control, that it is one of the most patent of facts that ideals and thought generally have a very great influence on human conduct. That truth and justice are great powers in the world is no figure of speech, but a plain fact to which theories must accommodate themselves.

The child, with his wonderful genius for *language*, naturally looks upon the world as chiefly governed by thought; for thought and expression are really one. As Wordsworth truly says, the child is quite right in this;—he is an

"eye among the blind",

"On whom those truths do rest
That we are toiling all our lives to find."[5]

But as he grows up, he loses this faculty; and all through his childhood he has been stuffed with such a pack of lies, which parents are accustomed to think are the most wholesome food for the child—because they do not think of his future,— that he begins real life with the utmost contempt for all the ideas of his childhood; and the great truth of the immanent power of thought in the universe is flung away along with the lies. I offer this hypothetical explanation because, if the common aversion to regarding[6] thought as a real power, or as anything but a fantastic figment, were really natural, it would make a powerful an argument of no little strength against its being acknowledged as a real power.[7]

But we must settle down to the gamma part of existential graphs. Suppose I wish to express in that system that the population of Boston is greater than that of Baltimore, but so as to speak, not of the cities, but of their persons inhabitants. The Bostonians are more multitudinous than the Baltimoreans. What does it mean, precisely to say *more multitudinous*? I avoid the phrase "more numerous" because that is applicable only to collections not exceeding every number. Now infinite collections can be compared as to their multitudes. The correct analysis of the idea was first given in 1851 in a posthumous work by the logician and catholic theologician, Bernard Bolzano, a theologian far too-clear-headed for his own comfort. You won't find his name in any ordinary history of philosophy; for exact logic requires too much from the reader to make any noise in the world. His definition was substantially this: One collection is more multitudinous than another if, and only if, these can be no relation in which every member of the former collection

---

5 [From William Wordsworth (1770–1850), "Ode on Intimations of Immortality from Recollections of Early Childhood".]
6 [The lecture draft forks here. A long continuation is preserved in R 465, labelled as "2nd Part of 3rd Draught of Lecture III. Begun Oct 12. 9:30AM".] [...] thought as a real power, or as anything but a fantastic figment, were really natural, it would make an argument of no little strength against its being acknowledged as a real power.
  Those of you, ladies and gentlemen, who are interested in philosophy, as most of us are, more or less, would do well to get as clear notions of the three elements of Firstness, Secondness, and Thirdness as you can. Very wretched must be the notion of them that can be conveyed in one lecture. [- - -] [The rest of the text of this long variant of the draft is omitted. It spans the notebook pages 68–126 (evenly numbered) and contains an extensive exposition of universal categories, phenomenology, and the definition of representamen, among others.]
7 [The rest is from R 464(s), comprising the text of the cut-out pages from R 464, beginning at ms page 66, "-ing thought as a real power".]

can stand to a member of the latter collection to which no other member of the former stands in the same relation.

In order to scribe a graph expressing this statement I must have a sign for a relation. So far, we have no sign which will answer the purpose. In the alpha-part, we have besides the sheet and the cuts only graphs, which are propositions. A relation is not a proposition. In the beta-part, we have in addition only the lines of identity which represent individuals. But a relation does not possess individuality; and we should be in danger of error if we assumed that it had.

ABC
ACB
CAB
CBA
BCA
BAC

Fig. 1

What is a relation? It is the character of a set of things. By a *set*, I mean an ordered collection, so that [Fig. 1] represents six different sets, although they represent the same collection. A *quality* is a character of an individual. A *relation* is a character of a set of individuals. This is a mere explanation of the word, not an attempt to analyze the idea. And I should say that the word is often so used that we speak of the relation of a thing to its qualities, though qualities are not individuals. I endeavor to avoid that use of the word and to speak of the *reference* of a thing to its qualities. But to guard against mistake I sometimes reduplicate the first syllable and speak of *re-relations* to emphasize the fact that I limit what I am saying to relations between sets of existing individuals.

~~Characters~~ Qualities and Relations, then, are characters. What is a character? A character is an *ens rationis*, or ~~thing creation of thought~~ creature of thought. It is not a figment or fictitious thing; but it is something whose being CONSISTS in something being true of something else. This is the *definition* of it; and it is a perfectly legitimate definition and cannot be denied. If, then, that which it consists in is not true, so that it consists in the truth of what is not true, it is not a real *ens rationis*. But if what it consists in is true, you cannot deny the real being of the *ens rationis*, as an *ens rationis*, since that would be to deny that which is all that its real being consists in. Of course, an *ens rationis* has no existence, since existence means being a subject of brute force; and the fact that anything is true does not exercise or suffer brute force. The particular kind of truth in which the being of a character consists is a truth of β-possibility. There is such a character as ~~having green hair~~ breathing flames, because it is logically possible that ~~an animal~~ a dragon should breathe flames. There is such a relation as that of being at once wife and a grandmother of; because it is logically possible for a man to marry his grandmother.

Characters themselves have characters. Thus "being of an ultramarine blue" has the characters of being ~~visual~~ a color, of being of a warm kind of blue, of being intensely chromatic, of having low luminosity, etc. 'Being ultramarine blue' and 'being yellow' stand in the *relation* to one another of being nearly complementary. Being ultramarine blue stands in the relation to being blue of being a more determinate species of it.

Characters of characters themselves have characters. Thus 'having a low luminosity' has the character of being a degree of a series.

The doctrine of gamma-possibility, or, as I have also called it, of *substantive possibility*, is absolutely indispensable to the understanding of the logic of the fundamental ~~doctrines~~ branches of mathematics. Its questions are decidedly puzzling. As an example, take the question whether or not it is logically possible that all logically possible varieties of individuals should exist, at once.

I will first explain how I represent in existential graphs propositions about characters; and then I will touch some of the questions to which answers will be required when we come to study the logic of mathematics.

Although characters are not individuals, yet they have a sort of relation of identity. To signify this I use a heavy line of identity which in these lecture diagrams I scribe in a different color from that of the lines of individual identity. But for ordinary work that would involve too much delay and trouble. In my own work I frequently assign to each character its own selective capital letter. I naturally scribe those spots which relate entirely to characters in the same color as the lines of identity. I use these [five] abbreviations:

—I —is an individual   —r —is a relation
—p —is a possible state of things   —s —is a sign
—q —is a quality

I also use these characters

⌐q
⋏—I   = An individual possesses a quality

⌐r
⋏⊂I
 ⋏I   = An individual is in a dyadic relation to an individual

⌐s
⋏⊂I
 ⋏I   = An individual is in a triadic relation to an individual for an individual.

I use these same ~~signs~~ symbols for characters of characters and for characters of characters of characters, but in the diagrams in different colors.[8] Thus

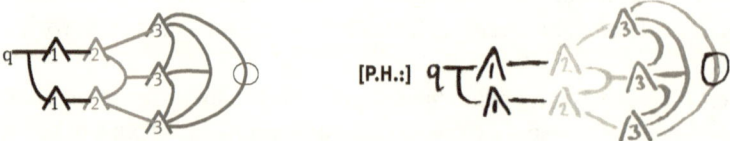

will mean that there are five objects between which there are three triadic relations, one of the objects being the second correlate of all three relations, two the third correlate of the first and first correlate of the second and third correlate of the second and first of the third while the first correlate of the first and third of the third are different individuals; and the first triadic relation has one relation to the second and the second a relation to the third these two dyadic relations having a common quality.

The notation is now nearly complete. I use a dotted enclosure to denote the single character which consists in the logical possibility of the rhema written within it.[9] It is the *name* of a single character, analogous to a proper name.

Here are illustrations [P.H.]:[10]

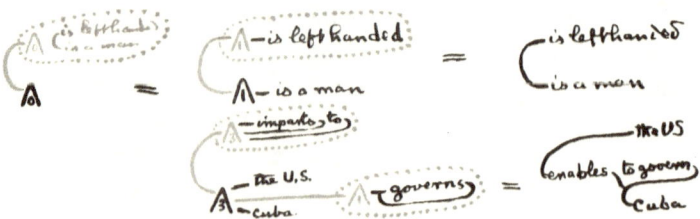

We now only need the following signs:

G_1, G_2, G_3 etc. are single graphs

—g   =   —is a graph, i.e. a possible apparent graph

—/—   =   —is an unenclosed heavy line of—

---

8 [The graphs and definitions above and below use black, red and brown ink, represented in the version of the edition devoid of colours from dark to light grey, respectively.]

9 [Peirce added a sentence in the margin, but it is illegible as it was partly cut out from this sheet that itself was cut out from the notebook.]

10 [In draft sketches of similar graphs found in R 461, the broken-cut oval notation of R 467, and not the dotted ovals, is seen to appear, anticipating the undelivered fourth lecture of R 467. Thus R 464(s) was most likely written in late November.]

—⌒—	=	—is permissively transformable into—
—n—	=	—precisely denies—

You will please remember that, as I use the words, an apparent graph is not really a graph unless it is possible.

This scheme shows many uses of the terms

An *apparent graph* is either { a *necessary graph* into which any graph is permissively transformable or else a *contingent graph* or else a *pseudograph* transformable into any graph. } in these two cases only, it is a graph.

Now let us trace out the permissions of transforming these gamma-graphs. Given any beta-graph, the possibility of this constitutes, in the first place, the being of a possible state of things; in the second place, the being of a quality for each of its unenclosed ligatures, since a quality is nothing but a logical possibility; in the third place; the being of a dyadic relation for each ordered pair or dyad of its unenclosed ligatures; in the fourth place; the being of a triadic relation for each triad of its unenclosed ligatures. These statements are so many gamma-necessary propositions represented by the graphs

Lecture III or IV

[R 460. Lecture III or IV. On the cover label of this Harvard Cooperative notebook is marked, in red crayon (by CP editors), "Lect. III a b d".]

Ladies and Gentlemen:

I have not yet succeeded in making up for the time lost by my not having overlooked the state of my diagrams at my Second Lecture. My last lecture, according to the programme, should have been about Firstness, Secondness, and Thirdness, and tonight's about the gamma graphs. But I was able to say very little about these categories, which it is indispensable to consider a little further in order to render the gamma graphs intelligible; and without the gamma graphs I should not be able to make myself understood about Multitude, Infinity, and Continuity, one of the subjects concerning which the thought of our generation has made decidedly the most extraordinary and indisputable advances that it has made in any direction. Besides, the doctrine of three categories is a matter of supreme interest.

Very early in my studies of logic, before I had really been devoting myself to it more than four or five years, it became quite manifest to me that this science was in a bad condition, entirely unworthy of the general state of intellectual development of our age; and in consequence of this, every other branch of philosophy except ethics,—for it was already clear that psychology was a special science and no part of philosophy,—was in a similar disgraceful state. About that time,—say the date of Mansell's *Prolegomena Logica*,—Logic touched bottom. There was no room for it to become more degraded. It had been sinking steadily, and relatively to the advance of physical science by no means slowly from the time of the revival of learning,—say from the date of the last fall of Constantinople. One important addition to the subject had been made early in the eighteenth century, the Doctrine of Chances. But this had not come from the professed logicians, who knew nothing about it. Whewell, it is true, had been doing some fine work; but it was not of a fundamental character. De Morgan and Boole had laid the foundations for modern exact logic, but they can hardly be said to have begun the erection of the edifice itself. Under these circumstances, I naturally opened the dusty folios of the scholastic doctors. Thought generally was, of course, in a somewhat low condition under the Plantagenets. You can appraise it very well by the impression that Dante, Chaucer, Marco Polo, Froissart, and the great cathedrals make upon us. But logic, relatively to the general condition of thought, was marvellously exact and critical. They can tell us nothing concerning methods of reasoning since their own reasoning was puerile; but their analyses of thought and their discussions of all those questions of logic that almost trench upon metaphysics are very instructive as well as very good discipline in that subtle kind of thinking that is required in logic.

In the days of which I am speaking, the age of Robert of Lincoln, Roger Bacon, St. Thomas Aquinas, and Duns Scotus, the question of nominalism and realism was regarded as definitively and conclusively settled in favor of realism. You know what the question was. It was whether *laws* and general *types* are figments of the mind or are real. If this be understood to mean whether there really are any laws and types, it is strictly speaking a question of metaphysics and not of logic. But as a first step toward its solution, it is proper to ask whether, granting that our common-sense beliefs are true, the analysis of the meaning of those beliefs shows that, according to those beliefs, laws and types are objective or subjective. This is ~~more properly~~ a question of logic rather than of metaphysics,—and as soon as this is answered the reply to the other question immediately follows after.

Notwithstanding a great outburst of nominalism in the fourteenth century which was connected with politics, the nominalists being generally opposed to the excessive powers of the pope and in favor of civil government, a connection that lent to the philosophical doctrine a factitious following, the Scotists, who were realists, were in most places the predominant party, and retained possession of the universities. At the revival of learning they stubbornly opposed the new studies; and thus the word *Duns*, the proper name of their master, came to mean an adversary of learning. The word originally further implied that the person so called was a master of subtle thought with which the humanists were unable to cope. But in another generation the disputations by which that power of thought was kept in training had lost their liveliness; and the consequence was that Scotism died out when the strong Scotists died. It was a mere change of fashion. The humanists were weak thinkers. Some of them no doubt might have been trained to be strong thinkers; but they had no severe training in thought. All their energies went to writing a classical language and an artistic style of expression. They went to the ancients for their philosophy; and mostly took up the three easiest of the ancient sects of philosophy, Epicureanism, stoicism, and scepticism. Epicureanism was a doctrine extremely like that of John Stuart Mill. The Epicureans alone of the later ancient schools believed in inductive reasoning, which they grounded upon the uniformity of nature, although they made the uniformity of nature to consist in somewhat different characters from those Stuart Mill emphasizes. Like Mill the Epicureans were extreme nominalists. The Stoics advocated the flattest materialism, which nobody any longer has any need of doing since the ~~doctrine~~ new invention of Monism enables a man to be perfectly materialist in substance, and as idealistic as he likes in words. Of course the Stoics could not but be nominalists. They took no stock in inductive reasoning. They ~~considered~~ held it to be a transparent fallacy. The Sceptics of the *renaissance* were something like the agnostics of the generation now passing away, except that they went much further. Our agnostics contented themselves with declaring everything beyond ordinary generalizations of experience to be unknowable, while the sceptics did not think any scientific knowledge of any description to be possible. If you turn over the pages, for example, of Cornelius Agrippa's book *De incertitudine et vanitate scientiarum et artium* (1531), you will find he takes up every science in succession, arithmetic, geometry, mechanics, optics, and after examination pronounces each to be altogether beyond the power of the human mind. Of course, therefore, as far as they believed in anything at all, the sceptics were nominalists. In short, there was a tidal wave of nominalism. Descartes was a nominalist. Locke and all his following, Berkeley, Hartley, Hume, and even Reid, were nominalists. Leibniz was an extreme nominalist, and Rémusat who has lately made an attempt to repair the edifice of Leibnizian monadology, does so by cutting away every part which leans at all toward realism. Kant was a nominalist; although his philosophy would have been rendered compacter, more consistent, and stronger if its author had taken up realism, as he certainly would have done if he had read Scotus. Hegel was a nominalist of realistic yearnings. I might continue the list much further. Thus, in one word, all modern philosophy of every sect has been nominalistic. In a long notice of Frazer's Berkeley, in the *North American Review* for October, 1871, I declared for realism. I have since very carefully and thoroughly revised my philosophical opinions more than half a dozen times, and have modified them more or less on most topics; but I have never been able to think differently on that question of nominalism and realism. In that paper I acknowledged that the tendency of science has been toward nominalism; but the late Dr. Francis Ellingwood Abbot in the very remarkable introduction to his book entitled *Scientific Theism* (1885), showed on the contrary, quite conclusively, that science has always been at heart Realistic, and always must be so; and upon comparing his writings with mine, it is easily seen that these features of nominalism which I pointed out in science are merely superficial and transient.

The heart of the dispute lies in this. ~~All~~ The modern philosophers,—one and all, unless Schelling be an exception,—recognize but one mode of being, the being of an individual thing or fact, the being which consists in the object's crowding ~~its way into~~ out a place for itself in the universe, so to speak, and reacting by brute force of fact, against all other things. I call that existence. Aristotle, on the other hand, whose system, like all the greatest systems, was evolutionary, recognized besides an embryonic kind of being, like the being of a tree in its seed, or like the being of a future contingent event, depending on how a man shall decide to act. In a few passages Aristotle seems to have a dim *aperçue* of a third mode of being in the *entelechy*. The embryonic being for Aristotle was the being he called matter, which is alike in all things, and which in the course of its development took on Form. Form is an element having a different mode of being. The whole philosophy of the scholastic doctors is an attempt to mould this doctrine of Aristotle into harmony with christian ~~ideas~~ truth. This harmony the different doctors attempted to bring about in different ways. But all the realists agree in reversing the order of Aristotle's evolution by making the Form come first, and the Individuation of that form come later. Thus, they too recognized two modes of being; but they were not the two modes of being of Aristotle.

My view is that there are three modes of being. I ~~maintain~~ hold that we can directly observe them in elements of whatever is at any time before the mind in any way. They are the being of positive qualitative possibility, the being of actual fact, and the being of law that will govern facts in the future.

Let us begin with considering actuality, and try to make out just what it consists in. If I ask you what the actuality of an event consists in, you will tell me that it consists in its happening *then* and *there*. The specifications *then* and *there* involve all its relations to other existents. The actuality of the event seems to lie in ~~relationship~~ its relations to the universe of existents. A court may issue *injunctions* and *judgments* against me and I not care a snap of my finger for them. I may think them idle vapor. But when I feel the sheriff's hand on my shoulder, I shall begin to have a sense of actuality. Actuality is something *brute*. There is no reason in it. I instance putting your shoulder against a door and trying to force it open against an unseen, silent, and unknown resistance. We have a ~~double~~ two-sided consciousness of effort and resistance, which seems to me to come tolerably near to a pure sense of actuality. On the whole, I think we have here a mode of being of one thing which consists in how a second object is. I call that Secondness.

Besides this, there are two modes of being that I call Firstness and Thirdness. Firstness is the mode of being which consists in its subject's being positively such as it is regardless of aught else. That can only be a possibility. For as long as things do not act upon one another there is no sense or meaning in saying that they have any being, unless it be that they are such in themselves that they may perhaps come into relation with others. The mode of being a *redness*, before anything in the universe was yet red, was nevertheless a positive qualitative possibility. And redness in itself even if it be embodied is something positive and *sui generis*. That I call Firstness. We naturally attribute Firstness to outward objects, that is we suppose they have capacities in themselves which may or may not be already actualized, which may or may not ever be actualized, although we can know nothing of such possibilities so far as they are actualized.

Now for Thirdness. Five minutes of our waking life will hardly pass without our making some kind of prediction; and in the majority of cases these predictions are fulfilled in the event. Yet a prediction is essentially of a general nature, and cannot ever be completely fulfilled. To say that a prediction has a decided tendency to be fulfilled, is to say that the future events are in a measure really governed by a law. If a pair of dice turns up sixes five times running, that is a mere uniformity. The dice might happen fortuitously to turn up sixes a thousand times running. But that would not afford the slightest security for a prediction that they would turn up sixes the next time. If the prediction has a tendency to be fulfilled, it must be that future events have a tendency to conform to a general rule. "Oh", but say the Nominalists, "this general rule is nothing but a mere word or couple of words!" I reply, "Nobody ever dreamed of denying that what is general is of the nature of a ~~symbol~~ general sign; but the question is whether future events will conform to it or not. If they will, your adjective 'mere' seems to be ill-placed". A rule to which future events have a tendency to conform is *ipso facto* an important thing, an important element in the happening of those events. This mode of being which *consists*, mind my word if you please, the mode of being which *consists* in the fact that future facts of Secondness will take on a determinate general character, I call a Thirdness.

Next define the sign and the three trichotomies.

The peculiarity of gamma graphs is that they make abstractions, or mere possibilities as well as laws the subjects of discourse. I have been in the habit of defining an abstraction or *ens rationis* as something whose being consists in the truth of a proposition concerning something else. The definition is not exact; but it will answer tolerably our question. If the proposition is that some description of thing is possible, this is a roundabout way of describing a Firstness. If the proposition is that something always will be, it describes a Thirdness. Now the subject of a proposition is necessarily an individual or in relative propositions a set of individuals, in this sense, that when I say 'All crows are black', I may be understood to mean 'Select any crow you like and that crow is black'.

But how can a law which is essentially general, which must relate to more than experience ever can cover ~~of~~ or it is not a general rule at all, how can this be the subject of a proposition?

The difficulty lies in the nature of a dicisign. [end][11]

---

[11] [See R 478, segments on the "Sundry Logical Conceptions" section, on Peirce's ongoing revision of speculative grammar and the evolving expansion of the notion of the proposition and the dicisign. The evolution will continue in Peirce's 1904–1908 series of papers and correspondence on pragmaticism and related matters, arranged in LoF, Volume 3.]

37 Lowell Lecture IV

[Copy-text is R 467, R 468, with additions from S-31. On the notebook cover of R 467 reads "C. S. Peirce's Lowell Lectures 1903. Lecture 4. Vol. 1. (Graphs mostly, C[harles] H[artshorne])". Page 0 bears a decorative title "C. S. Peirce's Lowell Lectures for 1903. Lecture 4. Vol. I. Gamma Part of Existential Graphs". R 467 has been published in CP 4.510–529, with several omissions, inaccuracies and typographic alterations. The rest of the material in the present selection has not been previously published. Folder R S-31 contains the cut-out pages from this Harvard cooperative notebook of R 467. On the cover of R 468 reads "L. V. Vol. I. Graphs. C[harles] H[artshorne]". Page 0 has Peirce's own title, "C.S.P's Lowell Lectures of 1903. Introduction to Lecture 5. 1903 Dec 4".] Halfway through the term of the course, Peirce was unlikely to have had enough time to explain many of the planned developments on the method of logical graphs, such as the emerging idea of the graphs of graphs, something that he initially planned to do already at the end of the third lecture and which had profound implications to the reformation of his theory of speculative grammar as well as to how the logical analysis of mathematical reasoning is to be exposed. The delivered lecture five, on the other hand, was to be on multitude and would presuppose the audience the understanding of the second and the third compartments of Gamma graphs as summarised in the notebook catalogued as R 468. As its date reveals, Peirce began writing the introduction to the lecture five the day after the third lecture was delivered on December 3. The material from R 468, appended to the present selection, is a revision of the topics of the previous lecture (R 464). Also appended is "Diagrams for Lecture 5" (from R 468), a large sheet inscribed in red ink and prepared to be projected to the audience with the stereopticon device, which illustrates the method of graphs of graphs that was co-requisite for understanding the main point of the fifth lecture.

The body of the present selection concerns, however, Peirce's undelivered material on modal Gamma graphs (R 467). Perhaps just days before having composed R 468, Peirce had completed another plan of his to make the fourth lecture, found in an undated Harvard notebook catalogued as R 467. The purpose of this alternative lecture note was to introduce the Gamma part, in its three compartments of the broken-cut notation for modal Gamma graphs, the second-order graphical logic of potentials, as well as the theory of meta-graphs (the graphs of graphs), the last which was also the main topic of R 468. Despite virtually ready for a full hour's presentation, Peirce was unlikely to have managed to fit any of that material into the tight schedule of the term. The exposition of the Alpha part, which he just three days earlier had given "a tolerably full account" took much longer than calculated, and while the Beta part was still to be covered, new topics for the fifth lecture were awaiting around the corner. Despite its manifest novelty, the theory of the broken-cut graphs had to be left aside altogether. Some aspects of non-modal Gamma graphs were eventually briefly introduced during the fifth lecture (R 469–R 470), without which the audience would be unable to follow the exposition of the method of how to logically analyse the mathematical concepts of multitude, infinity and continuity—concepts that Peirce planned to become the pinnacles of the entire course. However, he was forced to abandon, perhaps literally in the last minute, this most detailed and pioneering scheme of systems of modal logic that has been preserved in R 467 and in the accompanying studies (R S-1, see "Fragments") and drafts of the *Syllabus* (R 478, R 478(s)). Consequently, what amounts to nothing less that the birthplace of the theory of modal logic was withheld from public presentation.

There were no additional readings proposed for Lecture IV, originally announced with the title "Exposition of the system of diagrams completed" and afterwards renamed "Existential graphs: Gamma part".

Ladies and Gentlemen:

The alpha part of graphs, of which I gave you a tolerably full account, although without illustrating the use of it, since there was no time for that, is able to ~~deal with~~ represent no reasonings except those which turn upon the logical relations of general terms.[1]

The beta part of which I was able to give you nothing more than a few scraps has been thoroughly elaborated. It is able to handle with facility and dispatch reasonings of a very intricate kind, and propositions which ordinary language can only express by means of long and confusing circumlocutions. A ~~man~~ person who has learned to think in beta graphs has ideas of the utmost clearness and precision which it is practically impossible to communicate to the mind of a person who has not that advantage. Its reasonings generally turn upon the properties of the relations of individual objects to one another.

But it is able to do nothing at all with many ideas which we are all perfectly familiar with. Generally speaking it is unable to reason about abstractions. It cannot reason for example about qualities nor about relations as subjects to be reasoned about. It cannot reason about ideas. It is to supply that defect that the gamma part of the subject has been invented. But this gamma part is still in its infancy. It will be many years before my successors will be able to ~~give~~ bring it to the perfection to which the alpha and beta parts have been brought. For logical investigation is very slow, involving as it does the taking up of a confused mass of ordinary ideas, embracing we know not what and going through with a great quantity of analyses and generalizations and experiments before one can so much as get a new branch fairly inaugurated.

Exact logic was started by Augustus De Morgan in 1846, who produced a great variety of necessary reasonings entirely beyond the scope of the traditional logic, and in particular made a considerable investigation of the logic of relations, of syllogisms of transposed quantity, and of numerically definite syllogisms.

In 1847, George Boole, a great genius, produced an algebra of logic which was equivalent to the alpha part of existential graphs; but he subsequently used it to take important steps toward ~~setting~~ correcting the doctrine of probabilities ~~right~~.

De Morgan had many pupils, and among them Jevons who did some good work. I took up the subject about 1860, and lectured at this Institution upon it in 1866. I published various papers relating to the beta part of the subject, always employing some modification of the Algebra of Boole which I brought to

---

1 [A couple of preceding pages were cut out from the notebook but have been preserved in R S-31; see Appendix A.]

perfection in Note B appended in 1882 to the Johns Hopkins *Studies in Logic* ~~and in another pub~~.

Meantime Schröder, beginning in 1877, had been working up the details of the matter. Schröder's work was almost entirely in details. In the fundamentals he was less strong.

The Johns Hopkins *Studies*, however, contained an essay of extraordinary power, fairly rivalling that of De Morgan, if not Boole's, by Dr. Oscar Howard Mitchell. In consequence of the study of that paper, in 1885, I ~~took the fur~~ first broke ground in the gamma part of the subject.

In 1895 Schröder published the third huge volume of his logic, which consisted mainly of a vast elaboration in detail of the logical algebra of my Note B. That I never ~~thought~~ considered that algebra to be a great masterpiece is sufficiently shown by my giving my exposition of it no other title than "Note B". The perusal of Schröder's book convinced me that the algebra was not what was wanted; and in *The Monist* for *January 1897* I produced a system of graphs which I now term Entitative Graphs. I shortly after abandoned that and took up Existential Graphs. The beta part and portions of the gamma part were in running order in a few months; but the work of completely systematizing the beta part was not a job to be hurried up,—or, at any rate, was not so as I conceive such work ought to be done. It was a process like the ripening of corn, requiring the heat of hard work, indeed, but above all the ripening effect of time. Meantime, I have been making many and many an attack upon the gamma fortress, and have captured sundry redouts ~~but I have no~~. Of course, I can work with it. But that only supposes such a degree of mastery as one has of a language when one can think in that language. How many people fancy that they know a language very well when they can think in it[?] If they pursue the study, they will afterward turn back and see that that was merely the time at which their real knowledge of the language was making its first beginning! It is precisely so in graphs. When you have learned to think in them easily without translation then you are ready to begin the real study of them.

The gamma part of graphs, in its present condition, is characterized by a great wealth of new signs; but it has no sign of an essentially different kind from those of the alpha and beta part. The alpha part has three distinct kinds of signs, the *graphs*, the *sheet of assertion*, and the *cuts*. The beta part adds two quite different kinds of signs, *spots*, or *lexeis* and *ligatures* with *selectives*. It is true that a line of identity is a graph; but the terminal of such a line, especially a terminal on a cut where two lines of identity have a common point, is radically different. So far, all the gamma signs that have presented themselves, are of those same kinds. If anybody in my lifetime shall discover any radically disparate kind of sign, peculiar to the gamma part of the system, I shall hail him as a new Columbus. He must be a mind of vast power. But in the gamma part of the subject all the old kinds of signs take new forms.

If I were ~~to treat the possibli~~ to expound to you fully the theoretically needed new forms of spots, cuts, and ligatures that are required in the gamma part, you would find the complexity of it,—presented in the hurried way that would be necessary,—to be not only tedious but also confusing.

It will be better to give you examples of what I have found most useful, and leave it to you to study out the rest if you care to do so. I shall have a printed *Syllabus* ready for distribution at the next lecture which will be a great help; but even in that I cannot go into the long explanations that would be needed to expand the theory of the gamma part.[2]

Thus in place of a sheet of assertion, we have a book of separate sheets, tacked together at points, if not otherwise connected. For our alpha sheet, as a whole, represents simply a universe of existent individuals, and the different ~~points~~ parts of the sheet represent facts or true assertions made concerning that universe. At the cuts we pass into other areas, areas of conceived propositions which are not realized. In these areas there may be cuts where we pass into worlds which, in the imaginary worlds of the ~~first~~ outer cuts, are themselves represented to be imaginary and false, but which may, for all that, be true, and therefore continuous with the sheet of assertion itself, although this is uncertain. You may regard the ordinary blank sheet of assertion as a film upon which there is, as it were, an undeveloped photograph of the facts in the universe. I do not mean a literal picture, because its elements are propositions, and the meaning of a proposition is abstract and altogether of a different nature from a picture. But I ask you to imagine all the true propositions to have been formulated; and since facts blend into one another, it can only be in a continuum that we can conceive this to be done. This continuum must clearly have more dimensions than a surface or even than a solid; and we will suppose it to be plastic, so that it can be deformed in all sorts of ways without the continuity and connection of parts being ever ruptured. Of this continuum the blank sheet of assertion may be imagined to be a photograph. When we find out that a proposition is true, we can place it wherever we please on the sheet, because we can imagine the original continuum, which is plastic, to be so deformed as to bring any number of propositions to any places on the

---

2 [Added in the top margin:] Insert p. 21 and Skip to p. 42. [Page 21 consists of the previous two paragraphs; page 42 begins at "I will begin with one of the *gamma cuts*", preceded by one cut-out page given as an alternative version beginning "[...] the general purpose of using different sorts of cuts as practice should prove them to be desirable; but up to this time I have only found occasion for two". Peirce seems to have added such instructions in order to shorten the draft for a better fit into the schedule of the course.]

sheet we may choose. So far I have called the sheet a photograph, so as not to overwhelm you with all the difficulties of the conception at once. But let us rather call it a map,—a map of such a photograph if you like. A map of the simplest kind represents all the points of one surface by corresponding points of another surface in such a manner as to preserve the continuity unbroken, however great may be the distortion. A Mercator's chart, however, ~~presents~~ represents all the surface of the earth by a strip, infinitely long, both north and south poles being at infinite distances, ~~but comparatively~~ so that places near the poles are magnified so as to be ~~much~~ many times larger than the real surfaces of the earth that they represent, while in longitude the whole equator measures only two or three feet; and you might continue the chart so as to represent the earth over and over again in as many such strips as you pleased. Other kinds of map, such as my Quincuncial Projection which is drawn in the fourth volume of the *American Journal of Mathematics*, show the whole earth over and over again in checkers, and there is no arrangement you can think of in which the different representations of the same place might not appear on a perfectly correct map. This accounts for our being able to scribe the same graph as many times as we please on any vacant places we like. Now each of the areas of any cut corresponds exactly to some locus ~~point or plae~~ of the sheet of assertion where there is mapped, though undeveloped, the real state of things which the graph of that area denies. In fact it is represented by that line of the sheet of assertion which the cut itself ~~follows~~ marks. By taking time enough I could develop this idea much further, and render it clearer; but it would not be worth while, for I only mention it to prepare you for the idea of quite different kinds of sheets in the gamma part of the system. These sheets represent altogether different universes with which our discourse has to do. In the Johns Hopkins *Studies in Logic* I printed a note of several pages on the universe of qualities,—*marks*, as I then called them. But I failed to see that ~~this was trespassing upon~~ I was then wandering quite beyond the bounds of the logic of relations proper. For the relations of which the so-called "logic of relatives" treats are *existential* relations, which the non-existence of either relate or correlate reduces to nullity. Now, *qualities* are not properly speaking individuals. All the qualities you actually have ever thought of might, no doubt, be counted; since you have only been alive for a certain number of hundredths of seconds; and it requires more than a hundredth of a second actually to have any thought. But all the qualities, any one of which you readily can think of are certainly innumerable; and all that might be thought of exceed, I am convinced, all multitude whatsoever. For they are mere logical possibilities, and possibilities are general, and no multitude can exhaust the narrowest kind of a general. Nevertheless, within limitations, which include ~~all~~ most ordinary purposes, qualities may be treated as individuals. At any rate, however, they form an entirely different universe of existence. It is a universe of logical possibility. As we have seen, although the universe of existential fact can only be conceived as mapped upon a surface by each point of the surface representing a vast expanse of fact, yet we can conceive the facts are sufficiently separated upon the ~~surface~~ map for all our purposes; and in ~~like manner~~ the same sense the entire universe of logical possibilities might be conceived to be mapped upon a surface. Nevertheless, in order to represent to our minds the relation between the universe of possibilities and the universe of actual existent facts, if we are going to think of the latter as a surface, we must think of the former as three-dimensional space in which any surface would represent all the facts that might exist ~~at once~~ in one existential universe. In endeavoring to begin the construction of the gamma part of the system of existential graphs, what I had to do was to select from the enormous mass of ideas thus suggested a small number convenient to work with. It did not seem to be convenient to use more than one actual sheet at one time; but it seemed that various different kinds of cuts would be wanted. ~~I adopted~~[3]

I will begin with one of the *gamma cuts*. I call it the *broken cut*. I scribe it thus

This does not assert that it does not rain. It only asserts that the alpha and beta rules do not compel me to admit that it rains, or what comes to the same thing, a person altogether ignorant, except that he was well versed in logic so far as it ~~brought~~ embodied in the alpha and beta parts of existential graphs, would not know that it rained.

The rules of this cut are very similar to those of the alpha cut.

---

3 [Alt.] [From R S-31, a notebook page 42 cut from the notebook R 467] [I adopted] the general purpose of using different sorts of cuts as practice should prove them to be desirable; but up to this time I have only found occasion for two.

One of them is the interrupted cut which I draw with little lines about equal to the spaces. Thus, this graph

does not positively deny that it rains, but merely asserts that in some assumed state of information which must be ~~indicated~~ specified by some attachment to a hook of the cut, I do not know that it rains.

Rules of the Broken Cut.[4]

Rule 1. In a broken cut already ~~scribed~~ on the sheet of assertion any graph may be inserted.

Rule 2. An evenly enclosed alpha cut may be half-erased so as to convert it into a broken cut, and an oddly enclosed broken cut may be filled up to make an alpha cut.

Whether the enclosures are by alpha or broken cuts is indifferent.

Consequently,

will mean that the graph g is beta-necessarily true. By Rule 2, this is converted into

which is equivalent to

g

the simple assertion of g. By the same rule is transformable into

which means that the beta rules do not make g false.[5] That is g is beta-possible.
So if we start from

which denies the last figure and thus asserts that it is beta-impossible that g should be true, Rule 2 gives

 equivalent to

the simple denial of g.
And from this we get again

---

4 [Inscribed in red ink in copy-text.]
5 [See "Fragments" (R S-1) and "Introduction to Existential Graphs, Volume 2", for related studies of such 'provability' of the system of graphs.]

It must be remembered that possibility and necessity ~~relate to some~~ are relative to the state of information.

Of a certain graph g let us suppose that I am in such a state of information that it *may be true* and *may be false*; that is I can scribe on the sheet of assertion[6]   Board

Now I learn that it is true. This gives me a right to ~~assert~~ scribe on the sheet

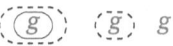

But now relative to this new state of information, (g̅) ceases to be true; and therefore relatively to the new state of information we can scribe ((g̅))

You thus perceive that we should fall into inextricable confusion in dealing with the broken cut if we did not attach to it a[7] sign to distinguish the particular state of information to which it refers. And a similar sign has then to be attached to the simple g, which refers to the state of information at the time of learning that graph to be true. I use for this purpose cross marks below. Thus

These selectives are very peculiar in that they refer to states of information as if they were individual objects. They have, besides, the additional peculiarity of having a definite order of succession, and we have the rule that from ₁⁹ [P.H.] we can infer ⁹ [P.H.]. These signs are of great use in clearing up the confused doctrine of *modal propositions* as well as the subject of logical breadth and depth.[8]

There is not much utility in a *double broken cut*. Yet it may be worth notice that

---

[6] [A presentation instruction written on the opposite page:] Mr. Warren: From this point on, I will scribe everything in *brown* that goes on the board with the "cuts" in *blue* and everything in *red* and *green* is to [be] made into a diagram.

[7] [Del.:] ... ~~an indexical symbol~~ sign, ~~that is,~~ not strictly an index, but a symbol ~~representing itself~~ whose interpretant represents it to be an index, that is to say, a *selective*, which shall indicate what state of information it refers to.

[8] [A loose, abandoned sheet from R S-34 reads:] [...] or depth which refers to a state of information in which the meanings of terms is known but there is no other real knowledge, is called the *essential* breadth and depth. That informed breadth or depth which refers to omniscience is called substantial breadth and depth. The difference of informed breadth and depth between the

 and g

can neither of them be inferred from the other. The outer of the two broken cuts is not only relative to a state of information but to a state of reflection. The graph  asserts that it is possible that the truth of the graph *g* is necessary. It is only because I have not sufficiently reflected upon the subject that I can have any doubt of whether it is so or not.

It becomes evident, in this way, that a modal proposition is a simple assertion not about the universe of things but about the universe of ~~things propositions~~ facts that one is in a ~~conditi~~ state of information sufficient to know. The graph ⟨*g*⟩ without any selective, merely asserts that there is a possible state of information in which the knower is not in a condition to know that the graph *g* is true, while ⟨*g*⟩ asserts that there is no such possible state of information. Suppose however we wish to assert that there is a conceivable state of information of which it ~~is not~~ would not be true that in that state the knower ~~is not~~ would not be in condition to know that *g* is true. We shall naturally ~~scribe~~ express this by  [P.H.].[9] But this is to say that there is a conceivable state of information in which the knower ~~does~~ would know that *g* is true. That is ⟨*g*⟩ [P.H.]

Now suppose we wish to assert that there is a conceivable state of information in which the knower would know *g* to be true and yet would not know another graph *h* to be true. We shall naturally express this by

 [P.H.:]

Here we have a new kind of ligature, which will follow all the rules of ligatures. We have here a most important addition to the system of graphs. There will be some peculiar and interesting little rules, owing to the fact that what one knows one has the means of knowing that one knows,—which is ~~often~~ sometimes incorrectly stated in the form that whatever one knows one knows that one knows, which is manifestly false. For if it were the same to say "A whale is not a fish" and "I know

---

terms is *certain* and *doubtful*, according as it is certain or doubtful whether [end] [The sheet is Crane's 1900 Japanes Linen, the same paper type on which the text of R 430 ("The Simplest Mathematics", *Minute Logic*, 1902, see LoF 1) was written, and the examples of graphs and algebraic formulas on this and the verso of the page are specifically those of R 430.]

9 [Peirce draws this graph so that the little selective sign protrudes the cut directly south continuously from the dash of the broken cut, and through the lower part of the letter *g*. This is intentional, and should be carefully reproduced when scribing the modal gamma graphs with selectives: their attachments are to be made "to a hook of the cut" (R S-31).]

that a whale is not a fish", the precise denials of the two would be the same. Yet one is "A whale is ~~not~~ a fish" and the other is "I do not know that a whale is not a fish".

The truth is that it is necessary to have a graph to signify that one state of information follows after another. If we scribe

$$A \longrightarrow B$$ [P.H.]

to express that the state of information B follows after the state of information A, we shall have  [P.H.]

It is clear, however, that the matter must not be allowed to rest here. For it would be a strangely, and almost an ironically, imperfect kind of logic which should recognize only *ignorance* and should ignore *error*.

Yet in order to recognize *error* in our system of graphs, we shall be obliged still further to introduce the idea of time, which will bring still greater difficulties. *Time* has usually been considered by logicians to be what is called "extra-logical" matter. I have never shared this opinion. But I have thought that logic had not reached that state of development at which the introduction of temporal modifications of its forms would not result in great confusion; and I am much of that way of thinking yet. The idea of time really is involved in the very idea of an argument. But the gravest complications of logic would be involved, in so far as taking account of time to distinguish between what ~~I~~ one *knows* and what ~~I am perfectly confident of~~ one *has sufficient reason to be entirely confident of*. The only difference that there seems to be room for between these two is that what one *knows*, one always will have *reason to ~~know~~ be confident of* while what one now ~~entirely~~ has ample reason to be entirely confident of one may conceivably in the future, in consequence of a new light, find reason to doubt and ultimately to deny. Whether it is really possible for this to occur, whether we can be said truly to have sufficient reason for entire confidence unless it is manifestly impossible that we should have any such new light in the future, is not the question. Be that as it may, it still remains *conceivable* that there should be that difference, and therefore there is a difference in the *meanings* of the two phrases. I confess that my studies heretofore have not progressed so far that I am able to say precisely what modification of our logical forms will be required when we come to take account, as some day we must, of all the effects of the possibilities of error, as we can now take account, in the doctrine of modals of the possibilities of ignorance. Nor do I believe that the time has yet come when it would be profitable to introduce such complications. But I can see that when that time does come, our logical forms will become very much more metamorphosed by introducing that consideration than they are in modal logic, where we take account of the possibility of ignorance as compared with the simple logic of propositions *de inesse*, as non-modal propositions in which the ideas of possibility and necessity are not introduced are called.

I will here take leave of this department of the gamma graphs in order to consider another. Instead of saying that opium puts people to sleep we may say that opium has a dormitive virtue. In that particular case little or nothing is gained by the more complicated expression. But in some cases there is a great gain. When, for example, instead of saying that a *particle moves* we say that the *particle describes a line* we introduce an abstraction in the same manner as when we talk of a dormitive virtue. But the advantages here are manifest, since we may imagine a *filament* to occupy the whole line at once, and we may further imagine that that filament moves in such a manner that at each moment it altogether quits the line which it is momentarily occupying. Here again we may introduce an abstraction and say that the filament *generates a surface*. Then we may imagine a material *film* to occupy the whole surface at once, and may imagine that the *film* moves in such a way that at each moment it is quitting the surface at which it is just arriving; and if it is not restricted to the space of our ordinary intuition we may say that the character of its motion ~~describes defines~~ determines a particular ~~solid~~ space, tridimensional at each point of it. This space, probably much more peculiar than the simple space we know, might, for aught we can see, be occupied all at once by a *body*. And we cannot see why this body should not move so that at every instant ~~every part of it with possible exceptions should~~ it should altogether quit the space that it at that instant occupies; and so on.

Here we see that the introduction of abstractions has led us to conceptions some of which, at any rate, are of the highest value. The others teach us still more if it can in any way be shown that they are impossible, and how they are so.

Hegel, I suppose, would regard a point as far more abstract than three dimensional space. This is, ~~in my opinion~~ according to my principles of terminology, an abusive, or at any rate, an unadvisable use of the word abstraction. But what Hegel means is that it is nearest to experience in its totality. In the case of space we pass backward in this way. Here is a glass object. ~~But~~ Everything is not glass. There is besides air. No air is glass. There is however something ~~that is neither~~ no part of which is altogether glass and no part altogether air. It is glass-air. This is the surface between the glass and the air.

Now we place a little water against a part of that surface. There are now three surfaces, one of glass-air, a second of glass-water, a third of air-water. There is some thing that is, in the same sense, between the glass-air surface and the glass-water surface; and this must necessarily also be between either of those and the water-air surface. It is the line where glass air and water meet. Now let us put a piece of putty over a portion of that line. There are now three additional surfaces, the putty-glass surface, the putty-air surface, and the putty-water surface, and there are three additional lines, the putty-glass-air line above the putty-glass-water line below, the putty-air-water line on the level surface. These four lines all come together at some even number of different points.

I will not stop to explain the metaphysical explanation of our coming out with an even number of points except in peculiar cases when two of them coincide, but will merely say that it is owing to pure space being of the nature of a law, while a body in space has individual existence; ~~in consequence~~ now existence is an affair of Secondness, and thence it would be found, upon ~~close~~ minute analysis, to be necessary that if anything exists there should exist something else, upon which it may react, and in order that the law of space should not unite the two things a twofold condition has to be satisfied from which it results, I will not stop to explain how, that the points reached should be two.

Here is a logical proposition[10]

A particle moves	A pear is ripe
A particle passes over a path	A pear possesses ripeness

I mean that in the two columns the forms of statement on the upper line have the same relation to the forms of statement under them. Here is another proposition of the same kind.

A filament moves from its place	Ripeness is more or less
A filament ~~generates~~ passes over a surface	Ripeness possesses degree

In order to ~~represent~~ make such forms of statement in graphs, I introduce ~~the following~~ certain spots which I term Potentials. They are shown on this diagram:

The Potentials.[11]

A—p	means	A is a primary individual
A—q	means	A is a monadic character, or "quality"
A—r	means	A is a dyadic relation
A—s	means	A is a legisign
A—⋏	means	A is a ~~monad~~ graph
A—⋏—B	means	B possesses the quality A

---

10 [The two tables below inscribed in red ink in the original.]
11 [The diagram below inscribed in red ink in the original.]

268 — 37 Lowell Lecture IV (R 467, R 468)

A—/2⥸ᴮ_C   means   B is in the relation A to C

A—/3⥸ᴮ_C⤸_D   means   B is in the triadic relation A to C for D.

It is obvious that the lines of identity on the left-hand side of the potentials are quite peculiar,[12] since the characters they denote are not, properly speaking, individuals. For that reason and others, to the left of the potentials I use selectives not ligatures.

As an example of the use of the potentials, we may take this graph, which expresses a theorem of great importance:[13]

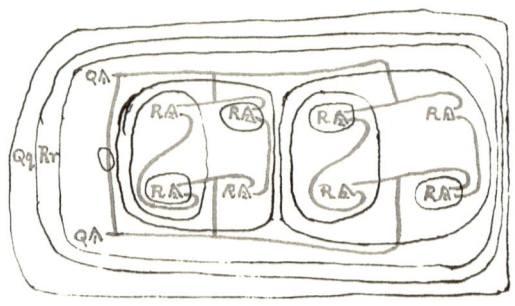

---

12 **[Alt.]** [A cut-out page from R S-31] [...] since the characters which they denote are not properly speaking individuals. For that reason and others, I use selectives instead of lines of identity on the left of the potentials.

As an example of the use of the potentials, we may take this graph.

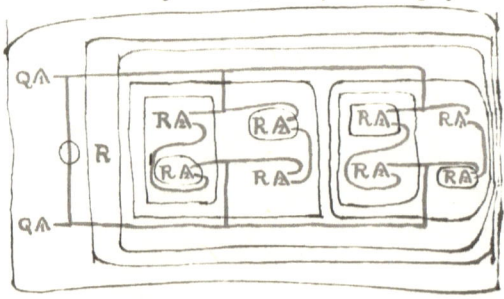

This states a theorem of immense importance which I will prove to you in another lecture, if there is time. It states that [end of fragment; see Peirce's letter to Josiah Royce on November 13, 1903 (LoF 3).]

13 [Marginal note, crossed out:] This diagram would be less confusing if the angles weren't so sharp and the lines so straight and parallel and right-angled. [This refers to the diagram of the cut-out graph given in the previous note. The diagram below is purported to be its emended version.]

The proposition is that

> for every quality, Q, whatsoever, there is a dyadic relation, R, such that, taking any two different individuals both possessing this quality, Q, either the first stands in the relation R to some thing to which the second does not stand in that relation while there is nothing to which the second stands in that relation without the first standing in the same relation to it, or else it is just the other way, namely that the second stands in the relation, R, to which the first does not stand in that relation while there is nothing to which the first stands in that relation, R, without the second also standing in the same relation to it.

The proof of this, which is a little too intricate to be followed in an oral statement (although in another lecture I shall substantially prove it) depends upon the fact that a relation is in itself a mere logical possibility.

I will now pass to another ~~most~~ quite indispensable department of the gamma graphs. Namely, it is necessary that we should be able to reason in graphs about graphs.[14]

The reason is that a reasoning about graphs will necessarily consist in showing that something is true of every possible graph of a certain general description. But we cannot scribe every possible graph of any general description, and therefore if we are to reason in graphs we must have a graph which is a general description of the kind of graph to which the reasoning is to relate.

For the alpha graphs, it is easy to see what is wanted.

Gamma Expressions of Alpha Graphs[15]

A	the sheet of assertion	W—κ—Z	A is the area of the cut W
—y	is a graph	U—(V)	U precisely expresses V
Y→X	A is placed on Y		

Let A, the old Greek form of the letter A, denote the sheet of assertion. Let —y [mean] is a graph. Let Y→X mean that X is scribed or placed on Y. Let W—κ—Z mean that Z is the area of the cut W. Let U—(V) ( [P.H.]) mean that U is a graph precisely expressing V.[16] It is necessary to place V in the *saw-rim*, as I

---

14 [The lecture draft continues in another notebook of R 467, with the heading on the first leaf:] "C. S. Peirce's Lowell Lectures of 1903. Lecture IV. 2nd Volume".
15 [The diagram in the table below are inscribed in red ink in copy-text. The follow-up examples in the next two paragraphs use both black, blue, red and brown ink, in the order of the decreasing intensity of the grey-scale.]
16 [In the first, crossed-out attempt on this, Peirce placed a spot (in brown ink) λ between U and V outside of the saw-rim. See Roberts (1973, pp. 73) for a study of these saw-cut graphs and a proposed correction to what Peirce had here presented.]

call the line about it, because in thus speaking of a sign *materialiter*, as they said in the middle ages, we require that it should have a hook that it has not got. For example, 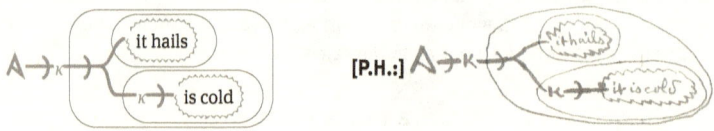 asserts, of course, that if it hails, it is cold *de inesse*.

Now a graph asserting that this graph is scribed on the sheet of assertion, will be

[P.H.:]

This graph only asserts what the other does assert. It does not say what the other does not assert. But there would be no difficulty in expressing that. We have only to place instead of  wherever it occurs

We come now to the graphical expressions of beta graphs. Here we require the following symbols:

Gamma Expressions of Beta Graphs[17]

X→Y — means Y is a ligature whose outermost part is on X.

X→(g)→Y — means g is expressed by a monad spot on X whose hook is joined to the ligature Y on X.

X→(g)⇉Y,Z — means g is expressed by a dyad graph on X whose first and second hooks respectively are joined on X to the ligatures Y and Z.

X→(g)⇉Y,Z,W — means g is expressed by a triad graph on X whose first, second, and third hooks are joined on X to the ligatures Y, Z, W, respectively.

[P.H.] means g is expressed by a tetradic spot on X whose first to fourth hooks are joined on X to Y, Z, U, V, respectively.

Appendix A. Lecture IV [Variant A]

[Copy-text is the cut-out pages from the notebook of Lecture IV (R 467) located in R S-31. Peirce was unlikely to have had time to explain the new and "quite indispensable department of the gamma

---

17 [This section inscribed in red ink in the original.]

graphs", namely the graphs of graphs, in his fourth lecture. The delivered lecture five was on multitude, presupposing from the audience an understanding of what the graphs of graphs are, the gist of which he attempted to summarise, in addition to what he wrote as the last segment of the main lecture draft above, in the next three segments appended to the present selection of Lecture IV as Appendices A, B and C.]

Ladies and Gentlemen:

The time has come for introducing you to the Gamma Part of Existential Graphs. This part of the subject has only recently been opened up. The part I have already sketched is about six years old; but I have but a limited amount of time that I can give to logical studies, and of this limited time the subject of graphs is not entitled ~~to a very large~~ by any means to the largest share; for like every investigator, I must chiefly devote myself to branches in which I have some facilities that others have not.

We now have permission to scribe the following graphs:

[Gamma Expressions of Alpha Graphs]

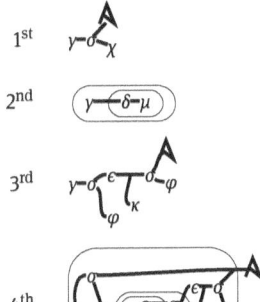

1st — There is a graph-replica on the sheet.
For if there be no other, the blank is a graph replica.

2nd — Every graph-replica contains a blank as a part of it.

3rd — It is permitted to place on the sheet as the entire graph-replica an enclosure on whose area it is permitted to place some graph-replica as the entire graph-replica of that area.

4th — If it is permitted that the sheet should carry an enclosure which carries nothing but an enclosure [end]

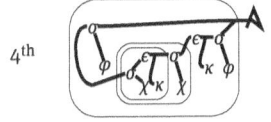

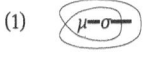

(1) A blank is on every area.

(2) Every blank is a graph-replica.

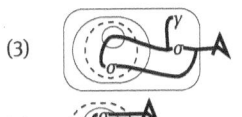

(3) If any graph-replica is on the sheet it is not necessary that anything else should be on the sheet.

(4) It is permissible that there should be an enclosure on the sheet of assertion.

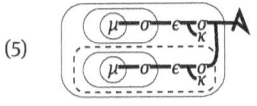

(5) If the sheet carries an enclosure whose area carries nothing but blanks then the sheet must carry an enclosure whose area carries nothing but blanks. [Written next to the graph:] Doubt the necessity of this.

[One holograph page of Lecture IV (Variant A), showing the sketches and the layout of the Gamma Expressions (1)–(5) (Harvard Peirce Papers, R S-31).]

Appendix B. Lecture IV [Variant B, for Lecture V]

[R 468. Cover: "L. V. Vol. I. Graphs. C[harles].H[artshorne]". Page 0: "C.S.P's Lowell Lectures of 1903. Introduction to Lecture 5. 1903 Dec 4". Fifteen notebook pages of sketches of the theory of graphs of graphs.]

There are some features of gamma graphs about which it is necessary that I should add a few words. In the first place, I must say of the graphs which make assertions about graphs, that since a graph or any other proposition must essentially be represented by its interpretant to be true, that is to say to be which implies that it is really affected by its object, it follows that the object of a proposition must be represented as a subject of force, and therefore as an individual. A graph, however, is not an individual but is a general type. Accordingly a proposition can only have a graph for its subject indirectly and I do not know that there is any other way than that the proposition should relate immediately to a replica of the graph, considered as such. Accordingly, all the graphs of graphs are strictly graphs of graph-replicas and parts of graph-replicas. I here introduce you to the following list of those that I shall have early occasion to use. Others will be mentioned soon. Here is the list:

⊣	is the sheet	θ	is a point of
⊣α	is an area		is a point
⊣ε⊢	is area of	τ	is a line whose ends are at — and —
⊣φ	is a permission	⊣∝	is coreplica with or is equivalent to
⊣χ	is a fact	⊣ζ⊢	is a graph-replica
⊣μ	is a blank	⊣γ	is a dot
⊣κ	is an enclosure	⊣ω	is a point of teridentity[a]
		⊣ψ	the rules of logic and graphs do not require g to be true
		(g̃)	

***

a [See R 2–R 3, R 511–512, LoF 2, and R L 231, LoF 3.]

Facts not involving permission:

[Gamma Expressions of Alpha Graphs]

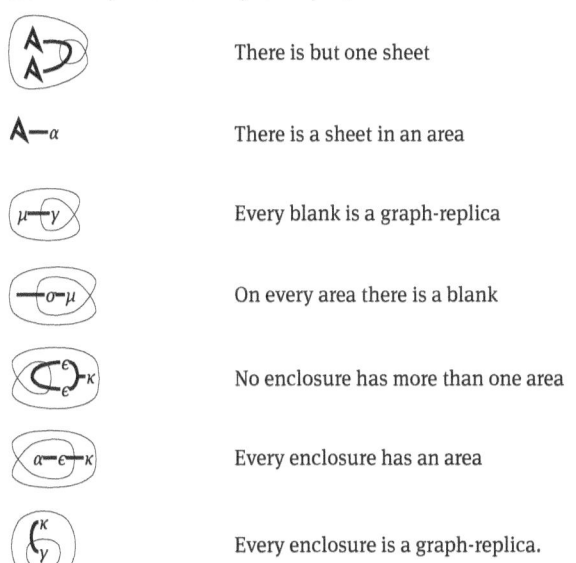

There is but one sheet

There is a sheet in an area

Every blank is a graph-replica

On every area there is a blank

No enclosure has more than one area

Every enclosure has an area

Every enclosure is a graph-replica.

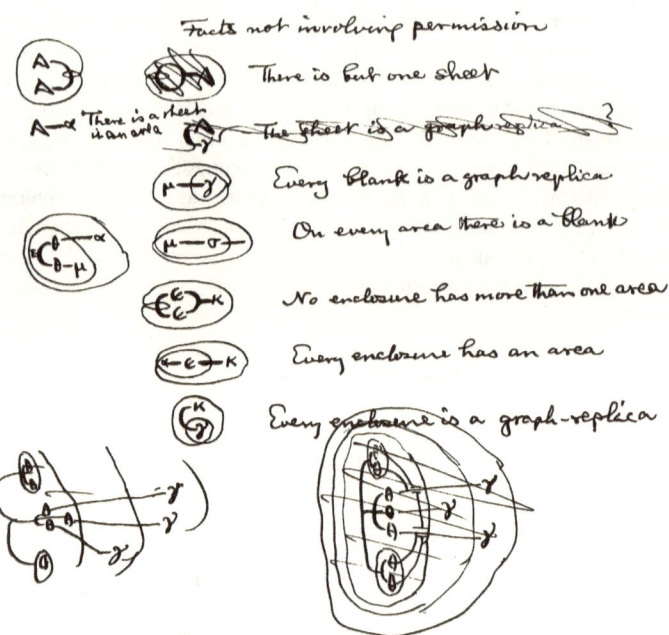

[A holograph page of the preceding list of the Gamma Expressions of Alpha Graphs (Harvard Peirce Papers, R 468, notebook page 3).]

[Facts involving] Permissions:

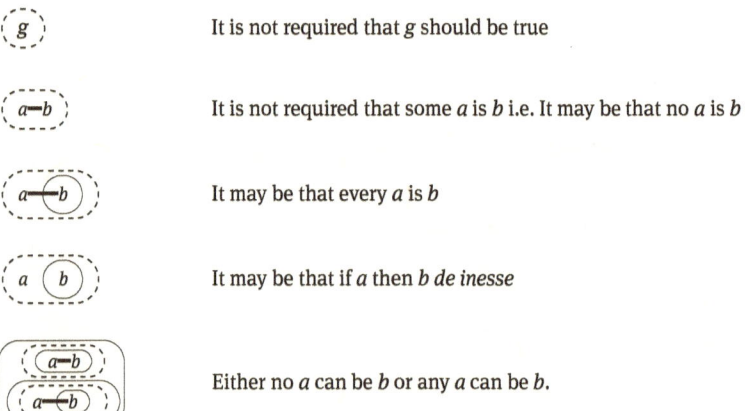

It is not required that g should be true

It is not required that some a is b i.e. It may be that no a is b

It may be that every a is b

It may be that if a then b de inesse

Either no a can be b or any a can be b.

[Gamma Expressions of] Beta Part.

 There is a point in a dot.

 If in any dot there is a point A or a point B, these are identical.

 No point is in two dots.

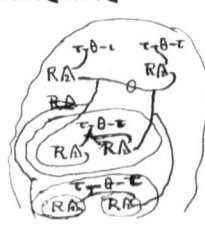 [P.H.] Taking any two individuals A and B and any relation R either there is a point of the line that is not R to A and is not R to B or there is a point of the line that is R to A and R to B. (If there is a point of the line that is R to A and a point of the line that is R to B [sic.]).

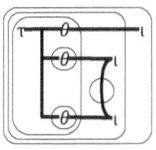 If there is a line of identity there are two individual lines of identity such that every point of the line is either in the one or in the other.

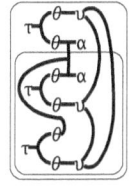 The question is whether this is not deducible from the last.

 Every line of identity is a graph.

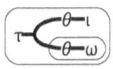 At whatever point on a line of identity there is a dot.

[Facts involving Permissions]

 It is always permitted to scribe a line of identity on the sheet of assertion with its extremities attached to blanks.

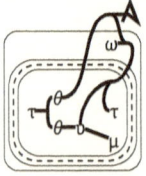
If a dot is on the sheet of assertion it is permissible to attach to it a line of identity with the other extremity at a blank.

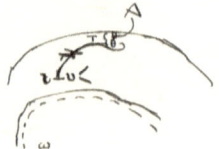
[P.H.] If a line of identity is scribable on the sheet of assertion, it is permitted to ~~add~~ insert a point of ter-identity upon any point of it.

A continuous line is such that if there is any dyadic relation, r, and any class of objects, the p's, such that the existence of a p does not consist in the existence of anything else such that no point of the line can be in the relation r to two different p's and if A is an individual p and B is an individual p every point of the line is either r to A or r to B any point of the line, is r to A and a point is r to B, it follows *ipso facto* that A and B are identical.

A continuous line is a place such that if there are two different individuals, A and B, whose existence does not consist in any proposition expressing a more direct Secondness, and if there is a dyadic relation r such that every point of the line is in this relation, r, to one or other of the individuals A and B, then there is *ipso facto* a point which is in that relation r, to both A and B.[18]

---

18 [These two paragraphs appear on the opposite page of the notebook page on "[Gamma Expressions of] Beta Part".]

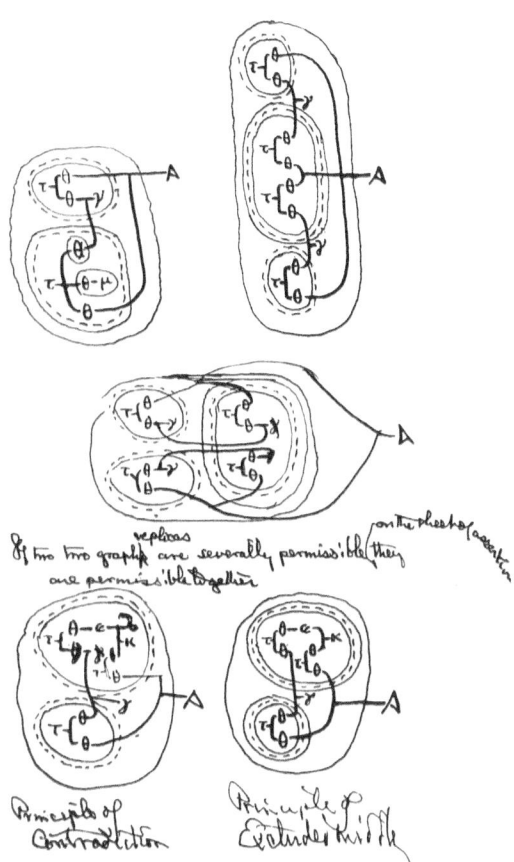

[Three holograph notebook pages showing further examples of graphs of graphs concerning permissions, the first two without captions (Harvard Peirce Papers, R 468).]

Appendix C. "Diagrams for Lecture 5"

[A one-page Linen Ledger sheet inscribed in red ink and deposited in R 468. Previously published in CP 4.529n. Probably what Peirce refers to as "If I could present it" in the Lowell Lecture V(c) (R 469; see the next selection): "This matter of the graphs of graphs if I could present it would also illustrate the nature of Pure Mathematics, still better than it is illustrated on pages 20 to 22 of the *Syllabus* distributed last Thursday [December 3]".]

X—A means "X is the sheet of assertion."

X—ϵ—Y means "X is the area of the enclosure Y."

X—φ means "X is a permission."

X—χ means "X is a fact."

X—μ means "X is a blank."

X—κ means "X is an enclosure."

X—$\alpha\genfrac{}{}{0pt}{}{Y}{Z}$ means "Y is on X by virtue of Y" "X carries Y as its entire graph in so far as it is of the nature of Z to make it do so". That is to say, for example,

$\alpha\genfrac{}{}{0pt}{}{\kappa}{\chi}$ means "An enclosure is the entire graph on the sheet of assertion as a fact".

means "It is permitted to place on the sheet of assertion as the entire graph an enclosure on whose area an enclosure is placed as a fact".

X—δ—Y means "The graph-replica denoted by X contains as a part of it the replica Y".

X—$\iota\genfrac{}{}{0pt}{}{Y}{Z}$ means "X is a line of identity having its terminals at Y and Z".

X—ζ—Y means "X is a replica of the same graph of which Y is a replica, or is equivalent to Y".

X—γ means "X is a graph-replica".

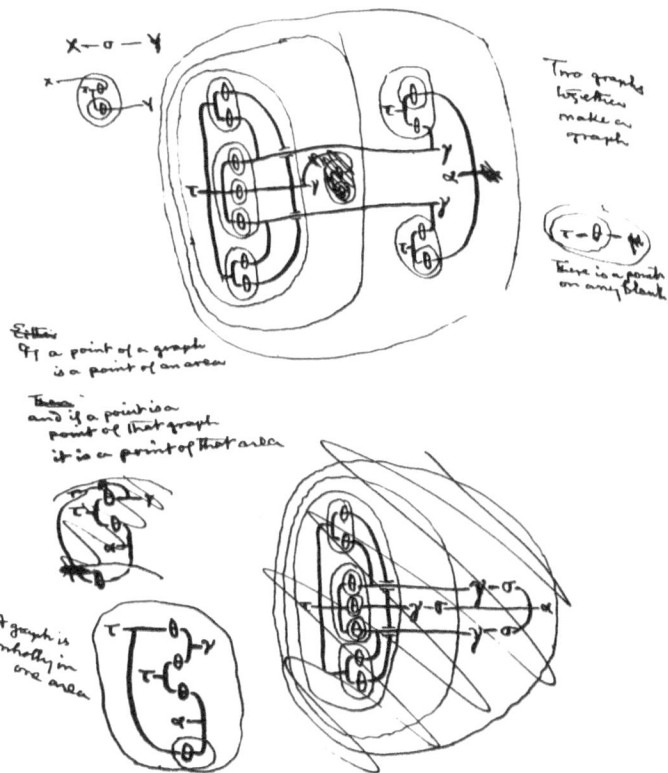

[A holograph page (Harvard Peirce Papers, R 468). Alternative formulations of some examples of Gamma expressions of the Beta part, appearing on the opposite page of "Facts not involving permission", verso of the notebook, page 2.]

38 Lowell Lecture V(a,b,c)

[Copy-text of the first selection (Lecture V(a)) is R 459 and R 459(s), the second (Lecture V(b)) R 466 plus pages from R S-31, and the third (Lecture V(c)), R 458 and R 458(s). On the notebook's cover label (R 459) reads, in Peirce's hand: "Lowell Lectures by C. S. Peirce. 1903. Lecture 3", crossed out with a remark inscribed in Peirce's hand: "Wont do". On the notebook cover of R 466 is written in Peirce's hand: "?Useful for 3rd or 4th?". On the cover label of R 458 is written, also in Peirce's hand, "May be useful for 3rd and 4th". On the cover of R 458 also appears a list of some of the content as: "Pure mathematics. Collection (Bolzano). All understanding refers to future, to possibility. Achilles & Tortoise".] Initially, Peirce planned to spend more than one full hour's lecture to explain the nature of mathematical reasoning and his doctrine of multitudes. The lack of time forced him to change his plans at least twice. As a consequence, the two extensive and rather early sets of notes for the fifth lecture of the course (R 459 and R 459(s), which comprise the first section of the present selection, and R 466, likewise a pre-draft which comprises the second section), did not find a slot among the eight curtate hours. R 458 or several of its digressions preserved in R 458(s), which are the earliest of these pre-drafts, were unlikely to have been delivered in any length, either. All these efforts were superseded by R 469–R 471 written closer to the lectures (Lecture V(d), provided in the next selection). The topic of multitudes, as indeed that department of Gamma that deals with the emerging theory of the graphs of graphs, are resumed in the next selection, and unlike the current texts represent the main material for the fifth lecture that Peirce eventually did deliver. The dating of the early versions is unclear, but most likely they were written before October, sometime during early autumn between the discontinuation of *The Logical Tracts* and the initiation of the composition of the *Syllabus*, while also in proximity to the drafting of R 455.

The reading list for Lecture V consisted of the following titles:

Lecture V.
The doctrine of multitude, infinity and continuity. (Multitude)

Cantor, Georg
  Beiträge zur Begründung der transfiniten Mengenlehre. 2. Artikel. (In Mathematische Annalen. Ban 49, pp. 207–246. Leipzig, 1897.)   ****E.5145.1.49**
  De la puissance des ensembles parfaits de points. (In Acta mathematica. [Vol.] 4, pp. 381–392. Stockholm, 1884.)   ****E.5090.50.4**
Dedekind, Richard
  Essays on the theory of numbers, 1. Continuity and irrational numbers. 2. The nature and meaning of numbers. Authorized translation by W. W. Beman. Chicago, 1901.   ****E.5129.101**
Peirce, Charles Sanders
  The logic of relatives. (In The Monist. Vol. 7, pp. 161–217. Chicago, 1896–97.)   **Per.Room *3604.100.7**
Russell, Bertrand Arthur William
  The principles of mathematics. Vol. 1. London, 1903.   ****E.5128.44**

Mathematics is the science which draws necessary conclusions.[1] Such was the definition first given by my father, Benjamin Peirce, in 1870. At that day the new mathematics was in its early infancy and the novelty of this definition was disconcerting even to the most advanced mathematicians; but today no competent man would adopt a definition decidedly opposed to that. The only fault I should find with it is that if we conceive a science, not as a body of ascertained truth, but as the living business which a group of investigators are engaged upon, which I think is the only sense which gives a natural classification of sciences, then we must include under mathematics everything that is an indispensable part of the mathematician's business; and therefore we must include the *formulation* of his hypotheses as well as the tracing out of their consequences. Certainly, into that work of formulation the mathematicians put an immense deal of intellectual power and energy.

Moreover, the hypotheses of the mathematician are of a peculiar nature. The mathematician does not in the least concern himself about their truth. They are often designed to represent *approximately* some state of things which he has some reason to believe is realized; but he does not regard it as his business to find out whether this be true or not; and he generally knows very well that his hypothesis only approximates to a representation of that state of things. The substance of the mathematician's hypothesis is therefore a creature of his imagination. Yet nothing can be more unlike a poet's creation. The reason is that the poet is interested in his images solely on account of their own beauty or interest as images, while the mathematician is interested in his hypotheses solely on account of the ways in which necessary inferences can be drawn from them. He consequently makes them perfectly definite in all those respects which could affect the ways in which parts of them could or not be taken together so as to lead to necessary consequences. If he leaves the hypotheses determinate in any other respects, they are hypotheses of *applied* mathematics. The pure mathematician generalizes his hypotheses so as to make them applicable to all conceivable states of things in which precisely analogous conclusions could be drawn. In view of this I would define Pure Mathematics as the science of pure hypotheses perfectly ~~determinate~~ definite in respects

---

[1] [R 459(s):] Mathematics is the Science which draws necessary conclusions. Such was the definition first given by my father, Benjamin Peirce, in 1870. At that day, its novelty was disconcerting even to the profoundest mathematicians; but today no definition would be given which did not come substantially to that. The only respect in which I should hesitate to accept it would consist in the recognition that it is a part of the business of the mathematician to form that distinct and definite assumption from which he reasons. Some of the mathematicians who have most deeply studied the fundame [end]

which can ~~affect the~~ create or destroy forms of necessary consequences from them and entirely indeterminate in other respects.

I am confident that this definition will be accepted by mathematicians as, at least, substantially accurate. As for the old definition that mathematics is the science of quantity first appears, I believe, in Boëthius, about A.D. 500 when mathematics at its lowest ebb; and at that time three words that occur in it had entirely different meanings from those they now carry. Those three words are *Mathematics*, *Science*, and *Quantity*. First, under mathematics were then included only four sciences called Arithmetic, Astronomy, Geometry, and Music. But by arithmetic was not meant anything now called by that name; for our arithmetic was called *logistic* and was not included in mathematics. Secondly, by *science* was then meant *comprehension* through principles, which we now call *philosophy*, a thing which a modern mathematician would not touch with a nine foot pole. Thirdly, by *quantity* was meant simply things *measurable*. Therefore, the true meaning of that phrase 'Mathematics is the science of quantity' was that four branches of learning, of which all but geometry are now utterly forgotten, constituted the philosophy of measurement. You see it is one of the many cases in which a phrase has quite survived its meaning. The relation of Quantity to Mathematics is, in fact this, that it is found that in one way or another the conception of quantity has an important bearing upon almost every branch of mathematics, as it has upon logic itself. But it is by no means the principal subject of all branches of mathematics. Thus the theory of Linear Perspective is a branch of Mathematics. Yet it is properly and primarily not concerned with quantity; and if it is made to appear so, it is badly taught.

Some very eminent and profound mathematicians go so far as to say that Mathematics is a branch of Logic. Dedekind is one of these whose little book published by the Open Court Company under the title of *Essays on Number* I beg leave to recommend to your study. But Mathematics is not Logic for the reason that the mathematician deals exclusively with assumptions for whose truth he in no wise makes himself responsible, while logic deals with positive truth. The mathematician's interest in reasoning is to get at the conclusion in the speediest way consistent with certainty. The logician, on the contrary, does not care particularly what the conclusion is. His interest lies in picking the reasoning to pieces and discovering the principles upon which its leading to truth depends. As far as necessary inference is concerned, the mathematician and the logician meet upon a common highway. But they face in contrary directions.

Still, the mere fact that mathematicians of high rank consider mathematics as a branch of logic may serve as sufficient justification for my denoting a part of this course to the examination of mathematics.

A *mathematical reasoning* may be defined as a reasoning in which the following of the conclusion does not depend on whether the premisses represent experience, or represent the state of the real universe, or upon what universe it may be that they apply to. This erects, as we shall see, a definite ~~boundary~~ party-wall between the reasoning of mathematics and much of the reasoning of all the positive sciences including philosophy. But, of course, all the other sciences have recourse to the mathematician very frequently, and none so constantly as logic. There is no science more infested with a vermin of ignorant pretenders than logic; and there is one simple question by which they can commonly be detected. Ask your pretended logician whether there are any necessary reasonings of an essentially different character from mathematical reasonings. If he says no, you may hope he knows something about logic; but if he says "yes", he is contradicting a well-established truth universally admitted by sound logicians. If you ask for a sample, it will be found to be a very simple mathematical reasoning *blurred* by being confusedly apprehended. For a necessary reasoning is one which *would* follow under all circumstances, whether you are talking of the real world or the world of the Arabian Nights' or what. And that precisely defines mathematical reasoning. It is true that a *distinctively* mathematical reasoning is one that is so intricate that we need some kind of a diagram to follow it out. But something of the nature of a diagram, be it only an imaginary skeleton proposition, or even a mere noun with the ideas of its application and signification is needed in all necessary reasoning. Indeed one may say that something of this kind is needed in all reasoning whatsoever, although in induction it is the real experiences that serve as diagrams.

One of the most striking characters of pure mathematics,—of course you will understand that I speak only of mathematics in its present condition, and only occasionally and with much diffidence speculate as to what the mathematics of the future may be,—but one of the characters of latter day pure mathematics is that all its departments are so intimately related that one cannot treat of anyone as it should be treated without considering all the others. We see the same thing in several other advanced sciences. But so far as it is possible to break mathematics into departments, we observe that in each department there is a certain set of alternatives to which every question relates. Thus, in projective geometry, which is the whole geometry that is allied to perspective *without measurement*, namely, the geometry of planes, their intersections and envelopes, and the intersections and envelopes of intersections and envelopes, the question always is whether a figure lies in another figure or not: whether a point one way described lies on a point another way described, whether a point lies on a line or nor, whether three lines coincide or not. Here there are two alternatives. On other departments, the alternatives are all the integer numbers; in still others, the alternatives are all the analytical numbers, etc. The set of alternatives to which a branch of mathematics constantly refers may be considered as a system of values; and in that sense, mathematics seems always to deal with quantity. It would seem that if any lines of demarcation are to be drawn between different mathematical theories they must be according to the number of alternatives in the set of alternatives to which it refers; but I am bound to say that this is ~~an idea of my own and that I have not complete confidence in its truth. Accepting it, however, for the moment, it at least shows~~ a notion personal to myself—and that I have my doubts as to its worth as the basis of a complete classification of mathematics. We may, however, accept it in so far as it shows that the simplest possible kind of mathematics will be that all whose questions relate to which one of a single set of two alternatives is to be admitted. Now in Existential Graphs, all questions relate to whether a graph is true or false; and we may conceive that every proposition has one or other of two values, the *infinite* value of being true, and the *zero* value of being false. We have, therefore, in Existential Graphs an exposition of this simplest possible form of mathematics. It is Applied Mathematics, because we have given definite logical significations to the graphs. But if we were to define the graphs solely by means of the five fundamental rules of their transformation, allowing them to mean whatever they might mean while preserving those rules, we should then see in them the Pure Mathematics of two values, the simplest of all possible mathematics.

Were we to follow out the same principle, we should divide all mathematics according to the number of alternatives in the set of alternatives to which it constantly refers and also to the number of different sets of alternatives to which it refers. Perhaps that would give as natural a classification of pure mathematical inquiries as any that could at this time be proposed. At any rate, we may so far safely trust to it, to conclude that the very first thing to be inquired into in order to comprehend the nature of mathematics, is the matter of *number*.

Certainly, of all mathematical ideas, next after the idea of two alternatives, the most ubiquitous is the idea of whole numbers. Dr. Georg Cantor is justly recognized as the author of two important doctrines, that of *Cardinal Numbers* and that of *Ordinal Numbers*. But I protest against his use of the term *Cardinal Number*. What he calls cardinal number is not number at all. A cardinal number is one of the vocables used primarily in the experiment called counting a collection, and used secondarily as an appellative of that collection. But what Cantor means by a cardinal number is the *zeroness, oneness, twoness, threeness*, etc.,—short the *multitude* of the collection. I shall always use the word multitude to mean the *degree of maniness* of a collection. By *ordinal numbers* Cantor means certain symbols invented by him to denote the place of an object in a series in which each object has another next after it. The character of being in a definite place in such a series may be called the *posteriority* of the object.

Since I have alluded to Cantor, for whose work I have a profound admiration, I had better say that what I have to tell you about Multitude is not in any degree borrowed from him. My studies of the subject began before his, and were nearly completed before I was aware of his work, and it is my independent development substantially agreeing in its results with his, of which I intend to give a rough sketch. And since I have ~~praised~~ recommended Dedekind's work, I will say that it amounts to a very able and original development of ideas which I had published six years previously. Schröder in the third volume of his logic shows how Dedekind's development might be made to conform more closely to my conceptions. That is interesting; but Dedekind's development[2] has its own independent value. I even incline to think that it follows a comparatively better way. For I am not so much in love with my own system as the late Professor Schröder was. I may add that quite recently Mr. Whitehead and the Hon. Bertrand Russell have treated of the subject; but ~~I have not, as yet, had time to examine their work.~~ they seem merely to have put truths already known into a uselessly technical and pedantic form.

The two doctrines of Cardinal and Ordinal Numbers, or of Multitude and Posteriority, though necessarily running parallel are curiously unlike one another. The doctrine of Ordinal Numbers is a theory of Pure Mathematics. For the relation of coming after is defined by this graph **[P.H.]**:

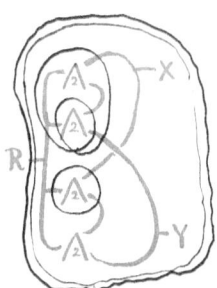

That is to say, to say that X is posterior to Y is to say neither more nor less than that there is a relation R in which Y stands to whatever X stands in that relation to as well as to something to which X does not stand in that relation.

---

2 **[Alt.]** [R S-31] [...] development has its own independent value, and follows, I incline to think, the better way. The definite form of the doctrine still remains to be made out. I may add that recently Mr. Whitehead as well as the Hon. Bertrand Russell have taken up the subject. But I have not yet studied their work.

The two doctrines are curiously unlike one another, although precisely parallel. The doctrine of Ordinal Numbers is a theory of Pure Mathematics. For the relation of being after is defined by this graph ⟨graph⟩ = A is posterior to B and the relation of being next after is defined by [end]

The relation R may be any relation whatever. The letter is attached to it and the two cuts simply to show that it must be a relation fixed in advance. To change from one relation, R, to another would generally be to change the order of sequence.

The relation of posteriority is composed of two parts which are the negatives of one another. It is that x is at least as late as y while y is not as late as x. The relation of being at least as late as is represented by this graph. I usually call it the relation of *inclusion of correlates*, for it implies that everything that u stands in any fixed relation to is included among the things to which v stands in that same relation.

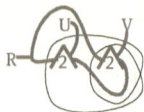

This form of relation is of immense importance in mathematics. I will tell you presently what renders it so.

The relation of posteriority as defined by the graph is such sequence as there is among events in time but not such as there is among the milestones of a road. The difference is that two events in time may be contemporaneous, while two milestones cannot ~~come together~~ be reached simultaneously. We may express that in a given case the succession is ~~linear~~ serial by the graph [P.H.:][3]

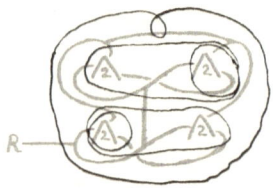

that is, if u is as late as v and v is as late as u, then u and v are identical. We can express this more neatly by taking for the correlates certain qualities; namely, the quality of being the first in the assumed order in the series, the quality of being one of the first two, the quality of being one of the first three, and in general the quality of being as early in the series as some given one. Then taking *p* as an abbreviation *p* = possesses one of the "as early" qualities, namely_____ , we may write the graph thus:

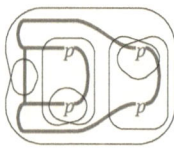

---

3 [The lines of identity and the spots are drawn in red ink in the copy-text of this graph.]

I ~~promised to~~ will now show you *why* the relation of ~~begin as late as~~ inclusion is so important in mathematics. The system of existential graphs was invented for the purpose of representing the reasoning of mathematics in as analytical form as possible. It is not perfect. It is open to objections which I know well. For instance, the fact that a and $(\!(a)\!)$ represent the same state of things, without either being more analytical than the other, is a grave fault which I shall have to leave future logicians to cure. The system is merely the best I could do. But it does express, in highly analytical form, all ~~mathematical~~ necessary reasoning. Now in constructing it, I was forced to introduce into its very forms four distinct kinds of signs of relation. Namely first, the relation expressed by writing anything on the sheet of assertion; second, the relation expressed by writing two graphs together on the sheet; third, the relation expressed by the heavy line; and fourth, the relation expressed by the scroll. Now since these four relations are the relations that thus enter into the very form and essence of necessary reasoning, it follows that every relation whose law has the same form as the laws of these must be of the highest importance for pure mathematics, since pure mathematics is precisely what results from abstracting from all the special meaning of necessary reasoning and considering only its forms. Of these four relations there is one which enters into the very ~~idea~~ definition of necessary reasoning. For necessary reasoning is that whose conclusion is true of whatever state of things there may be in which the premiss is true. Now this is expressed in a graph thus:

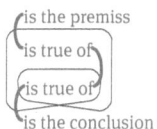

The pure mathematician substitutes for these logical terms defined symbols *x, y, z*, which are to mean whatever they may mean; and he thus gets this graph, which is precisely the graph of inclusion.

I cannot stop to consider the other three relations but must hurry back to the subject of numbers. The doctrine of ordinal numbers, then, is a theory of pure mathematics and, as matters stand today, is the most fundamental of all branches of pure mathematics after the mathematics of the pair of values which existential graphs illustrate. The doctrine of multitude is not pure mathematics. Pure mathematics can see nothing in multitudes but a linear series of objects, having a first member, each one being followed by a next, with a few other such formal characters. A multitude, as such, Pure Mathematics knows nothing of. Multitudes are characters of collections; and the idea of a collection is essentially a logical conception. How would you define a collection, in general, without using the idea itself in your definition? It is not easy. In order to explain the matter, it is necessary to begin with the conception of a quality. There is an essential part of the doctrine of Existential Graphs,—essential to it, I mean, as a logical, not as a mathematical doctrine,—and of such importance as quite to overshadow all the rest which I have been forced to pass over for lack of time. It treats of the general properties of qualities and relations. Without it there are most important inferences that cannot be drawn. I call it the doctrine of *substantive possibility*, because qualities and relations are possibilities of a peculiar kind. In a secondary sense a quality may be said to exist when it has, as it were, a replica in an existing thing. But strictly speaking, a quality does not exist. For to *exist* is to be a subject of blind ~~force~~ compulsion. A quality not only neither exerts nor suffers such force, but it cannot even be called an *idea* of the mind. For things possess their qualities just the same, whether anybody thinks so or not. The being of a quality consists in the fact that a thing *might be* such or such like. In saying this, I am not talking metaphysics nor epistemology. I am confining myself to logic. You can entertain whatever opinion seems good to you as to the real nature of qualities and as to the genesis of ideas in the mind. I have in this course quite nothing at all to say to all that. I simply say that you must use this form of thought, whether you regard it as corresponding to facts literally, metaphorically, symbolically, or however you may prefer. But you must use the form of thought or your threads will be inextricably entangled. For my part, when I think about logic I dismiss irrelevant questions of metaphysics and psychology entirely from my mind. But that requires some training. Qualities, then, and Relations are pure possibilities; and as such they have no individual identity. Two qualities are more or less unlike. Identity belongs only to subjects of blind compulsion or force. There is no sense for example in asking how many shades of red there are,—unless you mean how many a man can distinguish,—which is a question of psychophysics, not logic. These substantive possibilities,—that is, qualities, relations, and the like,—are *prior* to existence, in the sense that non-existence is not a necessary proof of non-possibility, but non-possibility is a necessary proof of non-existence. For it is logically impossible that existence should exhaust pure possibilities of any kind. These truths are strictly deducible from the facts of phenomenology, or the analysis of the phenomenon; meaning by the *phenomenon* whatever is present to the mind in any kind of thought.

From these truths there follows a most important rule of existential graphs, having two clauses. The first clause is that any graph which does not relate to what exists but only to pure substantive possibilities of the same order is true if the outermost part of its innermost ligature is enclosed in an even number of cuts, but is false if that number be odd. The second clause is that in case existence is in question along with the substantive possibilities of one order, and if the truth or falsity of the proposition is contrary to what the first clause would be if it were not limited to cases in which no existence is spoken of, then ~~it can be made to agree with that rule by a sufficient substitution from~~ the discrepancy may be regarded as due to insufficiency of the things that it says exist or to the excess of the things that it says do not exist. For example, although propositions about every quality are normally false yet it is true every quality ~~presents~~ is susceptible of varieties greater than existing things can embody. But this is because of the insufficiency of existing things.

What is meant by the order of substantive possibilities will be explained in the next lecture.

The doctrine of substantive possibility is an extensive one. You will understand that I only mention bits of it.

The variety of qualities, as is easily proved, literally exceeds not only all number, but all multitude finite or infinite; and anybody who should assume the contrary would be liable to great errors of reasoning. But the Qualities with which we are familiar are a small number. Certainly a figure *one* with only twenty or thirty zeros after it would denote a greater number; and these are naturally regarded by us as composed of a *very* small number of qualities which we do not analyze. Therefore for all those purposes for which we regard the qualities themselves, they may be considered as comparatively few.

Qualities are general respects in which existing things *might* agree or differ. They are as I have said, mere possibilities. But qualities have themselves *general* respects in which they agree or differ. Thus, musical notes differ in respect to duration, intensity, pitch, timbre, stress, expression, and some other respects. These qualities of qualities differ very much from qualities of existing things. Considering the qualities of any one class of qualities, we find them to be innumerable indeed but not in excess of all multitude; and a set three or four of some such small number of them that are independent of one another will fully suffice to describe the rest. These respects, or qualities of qualities, themselves again have general respects in which they agree and differ. Thus duration, pitch, and intensity are serial, that is each can only vary along one line of variation, while timbre, stress, and expression are multiform. These modes of variation of respects correspond to the possible whole numbers.

After these explanations, you will be able to understand this definition of a *quality*:

> A *quality* is anything whose being consists in such logical possibility as there may be that a definite predicate should be true of a single subject.

It is said to be actually *embodied in* or *possessed by* whatever there is of which that predicate is true.

But somebody may ask, Has a quality any being? I reply, Why of course it must have being because by the terms of its definition to say that it has being is at the very most, no more than to say that something is logically possible. Remember, we are not talking metaphysics; we are talking logic. A quality is an *ens rationis* of course. That is, it consists in a certain proposition having a meaning. The term *Essence* means being such as the subject of the essence necessarily is. Quality then has *essence*. But it has no *existence*, because it neither exercises nor suffers brute compulsion.

I am now prepared to give you the definition of a collection; and remember that by a collection I do not mean that whose members are in any sense actually brought together, nor even that whose members are actually thought together; but I mean that whose members *might*, in logical possibility, be thought together. But to think things together is to think that something might be true of them all that was true of nothing else. But to do this amounts to thinking that they have a common quality. Therefore the definition is plain:

> A *collection* is anything whose being consists in the existence of whatever there may exist that has anyone quality; and if such thing or things exist, the collection is a single thing whose existence consists in the existence or all those very things.

According to this definition a *collection* is an *ens rationis*. If its members are ~~physically~~ actually brought together like the atoms which compose my body, it is more than a mere *collection*. As collection it is an *ens rationis*, but that reason or *ratio* that creates it may be among the realities of the universe. A *collection* has *essence* and may have *existence*. It has *essence* from all eternity, in the logical possibility that it should be described. It has *existence* from the moment that all its members exist. Thus, all men constitute a collection; and not a very small one. But in the carboniferous period in a certain sense that collection had no existence. By saying it was so 'in a certain sense' I mean if by *men* be meant the men that live at the moment. In this same sense, the existence of this collection is constantly changing; the same collection in essence is becoming a different collection in existence. There is a collection or men with ~~bright~~ grass green hair; but having only essence and not existence, it has no individual identity. It is the collection that we call *Nothing*. It must be counted among collections; but it differs from all the rest in having no existence. Of course, for ordinary purposes, this is the emptiest nonsense. Nevertheless, it is a matter that has to be put straight for logical purposes. I may remark that nonsense often repays logical study and by that study enables us to avoid fallacious reasoning about serious questions. Another such little point is the following. According to the definition, there must be a collection of luminaries of the day. But there happens to be only one luminary of the day; namely, the Sun. Here then is a collection having but one member. Is not that collection the sun itself? I reply, Certainly not. For a collection is an *ens rationis*. Its being consists in the truth of something. But the Sun is not an *ens rationis* and its being does not consist in the truth of any proposition. It consists in the act of brute force in which it reacts with everything in its neighborhood. So then the Sun is one thing and exists, and this collection containing only the sun is something different and exists, and there would be a collection embracing as its sole member this collection, and this too exists and so on *ad infinitum*. This is true. Yet there is only one *existence*; for the existence of the collection is the existence of its sole member. Thus, that collection embracing the sun alone is different from the Sun but its existence is the same as the existence of the sun. In that sense, it is the same as the Sun.

In the next lecture I will show you what *multitude* is and what different grades of multitude there are; and then you will see how some of the hair-splitting of this lecture is, after all, very useful.

Lowell Lecture V(b)

[Copy-text is R 466, with pages from R S-31. On the notebook cover it reads: "?Useful for 3rd or 4th?" The text in this version of the pre-draft represents Peirce's second attempt at giving shape to a lecture on continuity and multitude.]

Mathematics is the science which draws necessary conclusions. Such was the definition given first by my father as early as 1870. At that day, when the new mathematics was in its infancy, the novelty of this definition was disconcerting even to the profoundest mathematicians; but today nobody would propose a definition differing much from that. The only doubt that should entertain is whether we ought not to recognize as a part of mathematics, what is certainly a most important part of the mathematician's business, the formation of the assumptions on which his reasoning is to be based.

Some of the mathematicians who have most deeply studied the fundamentals of their science have even gone so far as to pronounce mathematics to be a branch of logic. Dedekind is one of these whose two little books published in one volume in translation by the Open Court Company [Dedekind 1901], which is doing so much for American culture, I should strongly recommend to your attention. The fact that so profound a mathematician can hold this opinion is a sufficient justification of my devoting several lectures of this short course to a study of ~~the reasoning of~~ the nature of mathematics.

I do not quite agree with Dedekind, myself; and I will tell you why presently. The question of whether mathematics was a branch of logic was the subject of careful discussion between my father and me at the time he had his definition under consideration. But first I had better notice ~~a more superficial objection~~ an objection which will seem weighty to superficial minds. Namely, it will be said that much necessary reasoning is not at all mathematical. On that I take direct issue. Eminent jurists, moralists, and philosophers can be found whose powers of reasoning are famous, and who yet declare that they have no head for mathematics. This is, in part, a delusion owing to bad instruction which has given rise to such an aversion to everything that seems mathematical that as soon as one talks to them of x, y, z, they stop thinking. But what is also true of those persons is that they cannot hold clearly before their minds intricate relations between objects that are almost exactly alike except in respect to abstract relations. But when I ask one of those gentlemen to give me an example: of a necessary reasoning that he considers not to be mathematical, it turns out to be one of those that are most readily amenable to mathematical representation, differing only from the reasoning he cannot grasp in its extreme simplicity. But that which conclusively stamps all necessary reasoning as mathematical is that in such reasoning, it makes not the slightest difference whether the premises ~~relate to~~ express observed facts (as strictly speaking they seldom do) or whether they describe wholly imaginary states of things. The conclusion follows as necessarily concerning the imaginary state of things as it would if that state of things had been observed. This, indeed, is precisely what the *necessity* of such reasoning consists in. For the purposes of the reasoning, therefore, the premises are mere assumptions. If they happen to be more, it has nothing to do with the reasoning. Now the only science which deals with pure assumptions regardless of their real truth is mathematics. That is, on the whole, the best definition of mathematics. All necessary reasonings, therefore, are pieces of mathematics.

The only reason I do not agree with Dedekind in making mathematics a branch of logic is that logic is *not* a science of pure assumptions but is a study of positive truth. The mathematician seeks only to trace out the consequences of his assumptions in the readiest and speediest way. The logician does not care much what the conclusions from this or that system of assumptions may be. What he is interested in is in dissecting ~~the mathematicians'~~ reasonings, in finding out what their elementary steps are, and in showing what positive facts about the real universe of things and of thoughts it is from which the necessity of the mathematician's reasonings and the validity of other kinds of reasonings depend, and exactly what the nature of that dependence is. I have already pointed out that the characters that make a system of symbols good for mathematical purposes are quite contrary to those which would make it good for logical purposes. The truth is that the mathematician and the logician meet in one department on a common highway. They *meet*; but one is facing one way while the other is facing just the other way. Each of them, it is true, finds it interesting to turn round occasionally and take a glance in the opposite direction.

The mathematician, however, has little or nothing to learn of the logician. Mathematics differs from all the special sciences whether of physics or of psychics in never encountering ~~serious~~ logical difficulties, which it does not lie entirely within his own competence to resolve. The logician on the other hand has everything to learn from the mathematician. Mathematics is, with the exception of Phenomenology and Ethics, the only science from which he can draw any ~~fundamental~~ real guidance. There is therefore every reason in the world why we should not delay examining the fundamental nature of mathematics.

The simplest possible kind of mathematics would be the mathematics of ~~two values~~ a system of only two values. Do we in experience meet with any case in which such mathematics could have any application? I reply that we do. There are just two values that any assertion can have. It is either true when it has all the ~~truth~~ value it can have, or it is false, and has no value at all. It follows that our system of Existential Graphs is precisely an application of the mathematics of two values. It will give you an idea of what Pure Mathematics is to imagine the Existential Graphs to be described without any allusion whatever to their interpretation, but to be defined as symbols subject to the fundamental rules of transformation. Namely,

1. Graphs are figures drawn on a surface and composed of any finite number including zero of each of these three kinds of elements, first, oval cuts of which no two intersect, second, heavy lines, and third, spots each with definite places each of which is at an extremity of a heavy line.[4]
2. Any graph within an even number of cuts can be erased and any within an odd number of existing cuts can be inserted.
3. Any graph can be iterated or deiterated provided the iterated or deiterated replica is not outside of any cut that the other is inside of.

---

4 [Del.:] A graph is composed of spots with definite hooks from each of which one heavy line extends. [NEM III(1), p. 357, in which the main segment of R 466 appears, erroneously transcribes this deleted sentence instead of its dominant alteration.]

4. Two cuts one inside the other with nothing between except heavy lines passing from within the inner to outside the outer, can either be made or destroyed anywhere.
5. A heavy line ~~passing in~~ of which both ends connect with lines inside a cut which lines do not connect spots connected inside the cut can anywhere be erased or inserted.

From those assumptions everything universally true of existential graphs could be deduced, and that would be the Pure Mathematical Treatment. I have defined Mathematics in general as the science which draws necessary conclusions and which formulates the assumptions from which such conclusions can be drawn. I now define *Pure* Mathematics as that Mathematics which leaves its assumptions entirely indeterminate in respects which have no bearing upon ~~the forms of inference which can be drawn from them~~ the manner in which they can be combined to produce conclusions.

The Pure Mathematics of the System of Two Values would leave us free to regard the Graphs as representing anything for which their fundamental transformations would hold good.

In like manner there would be a Mathematics of a System of Three Values[5] which would not be without utility and which has been in some measure developed. The theory of numbers furnishes partial developments of the mathematics of every system having a finite ~~number~~ multitude of values.

I particularly call your attention to my use of the word *Multitude*. I never use this word to mean a *Collection* or *Plural*, I always use it as an abstract noun denoting that character of a Collection which makes it greater than some collections and less than others. Thus, two-ness, ten-ness, three-hundred-and-sixty-five-ness, are individual Multitudes, as I use the word.

At the very outset of the study of the logic of mathematics our attention is forced to the subject of Multitude. Everybody knows that there is a Mathematics of Multitude; and I am going this evening to tell you some elementary things about it that you probably do not know.

It is desirable to remark at the outset that the Mathematics of Multitude is not pure mathematics. The reason is that the whole application of Numbers to Multitude is based on the four propositions. I will state these propositions although it is not necessary you should follow them exactly. It will be sufficient to apprehend their general character. The first is, that if you take any two numbers say 3 and 7 and there is a collection that 3 is used in counting: one, two, *three*, four,

---

5 [See the segment from R S-31 in a footnote below. Here Peirce makes an early allusion to a 'triadic logic' of which records are preserved in his *Logic Notebook* from February 1909.]

five,—and there is a collection that seven is used in counting ⦂⦂ then either 7 is used in counting the first or else 5 is used in counting the second. That is the first proposition represented by the graph

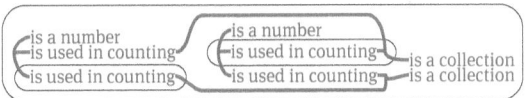

and the other proposition is that there are not two different numbers that are used in counting precisely the same collections, that is, if two numbers A and B are not identical there is either some collection that A is used in counting and B is not, or there is some collection that B is used in counting and A not.[6]

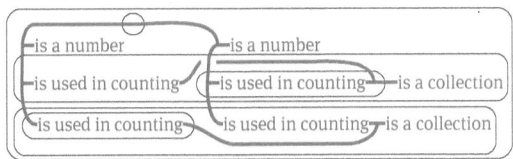

The third proposition is that there is a number next greater than any given number or taking any number whatever, there is a number (namely, the next greater one) such that taking any number you please either this third number (being no greater than the first) is used in counting every collection that the first is used in counting or else (being as great as the next greater number) is not used in counting any collection unless that that next greater is used in counting it.[7]

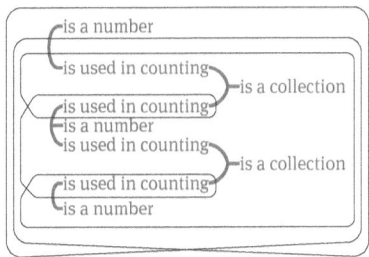

---

6 [Del.:] But the manner in which these two premises can be combined to form the mathematical conclusions of arithmetic has nothing to do with the particular words that are written in these two graphs.

7 [On an alternative, cut-out page (R S-32, ms p. 15) this is phrased as follows:] The third proposition is that taking any number whatever there is a next greater number such that whatever third number you may take either this third number is not greater than the first so that whatever collection it is used in counting, the first number is used in counting M's and if the third number is used in counting the N's then either the first number is used in counting the N's or the third number is used in counting the M's.

The fourth proposition is that the count of any finite collection stops at some largest number used in counting it, what we call the number of the collection, that is, for any collection that some number is used in counting and that some number is not used in counting there is a number (namely the number of its count) used in counting it that is such that whatever number is used in counting this collection is used in counting every collection that this number is used in counting.

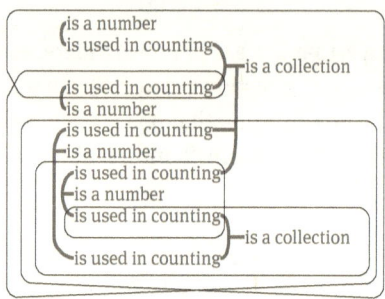

I might add a fifth proposition to express that there is an absolutely smallest number; but I do not think that of much importance.

By manipulating those four graphs according to the rules of graphs we could reach every theorem of the mathematics of whole numbers. But the rules of the transformation of graphs do not depend upon what is written in the different spots. So long as they are preserved the same or different, as the case may be, letters or any other meaningless expressions might be substituted. In particular, in place of "collections" any other universe might be adopted, and in place of "is used in counting" a general symbol for any one dyadic relation. If this change were made in the four graphs, the result would be that they would define the relations of *ordinal* numbers to one another, except of course that they omit to say that there is a smallest number; and in fact there is not, if negative numbers are included.

Thus, the Arithmetic of Ordinal Numbers is Pure Mathematics; but the Arithmetic of Cardinal Numbers is Applied Mathematics. The conception of a Collection is, therefore, not a mathematical conception and the conception of Multitude is not a purely mathematical conception. But the conception of a collection is a highly important logical conception and for that reason, we will turn our attention to *Multitude*.

But why should the conception of Multitude be an important conception in logic? I will tell you. We have seen that there are three relations which subsist between the parts of graphs. The first is the relation expressed by the scroll ⓐ/ⓑ . This is the most important of all, since this is the relation of premiss and conclusion; that is, if it be true that if A is true B is true, then should A occur as a premiss we have a right to conclude B. The second relation is that expressed by writing two graphs side by side A B, that is to say, the relation of coexistence, and the third is the relation of individual identity expressed by the heavy line. Now whatever relation is analogous to one of these three relations will be expressed by graphs into which the corresponding element of graphs enters and will therefore affect reasoning and hence will be of logical importance. Now the relation expressed by saying that one collection is at least as great as another is precisely analogous to the relation expressed by the scroll in graphs; and that is why *multitude* which is the character of a collection which constitutes it as great as what it is as great as, is so very important for logic.

Everything depends, in logic, upon formulating precise definitions. Now what precisely do we mean by saying that one collection is at least as small as another? The best definitions are those which express how the ~~assertion or denial~~ truth or falsity of the term defined ~~can affect our future experience~~ will affect what we can do in the future. To say that a thing *is soft* is to say that it can easily be scratched. To say that it is hard is to say that it never will easily be scratched, unless it turns soft. The relation of greater and less was first defined in this fashion by the Catholic logician Bolzano in his posthumous work which appeared in 1851. He said a collection, say that of the A's is at least as small as another collection say that of the B's, if, and only if, every single A can be placed in a relation to B to which no other A stands in the same relation. But just as to say that a body *can* easily be scratched is the same as to say that it *is* soft, so to say that one thing *can be* placed in relation to another thing is to say that it already *is* in relation to that thing; and it is simpler to say that the collection of the A's is at least as small as the collection of the B's, if and only if there is a relation in which every A stands to a B to which no other A stands in the same relation **[P.H.:]**[8]

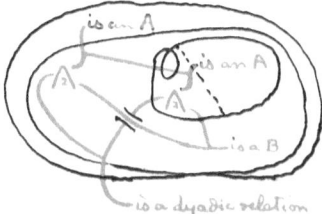

[Fig. 1:] There is a certain dyadic relation such that if there is an A it stands in that relation to a B and if there is any A and it stands in that same relation to that same B then it is identical with that first A.[9]

---

8 [The lines of identity and the spots are drawn in red ink in the copy-text of this graph.]
9 [Peirce wrote next to the graph:] The inner scroll might have left the A outside. No: not so.

To deny this is to say that there is no such relation, which we express by enclosing the whole in a cut. But every fact whatever consists in the existence of a relation. To say that there is no relation of one kind is to say that there is a relation of another kind. All things are related to one another in every combination. The brevity of this course ~~does not permit~~ forbids my going into the general theory. But if a relation not in itself absurd and therefore having all the ~~existence~~ being that belongs to a relation in itself fails to exist in any case, it is simply because *existence* by its very nature must fall short of possibility. It must be because the things fail to exist that would ~~make the relation exist~~ bring the relation into existence in the particular case. If there is no one-to-one relation of ~~every~~ whatever A there is to a separate existent B, it is simply because[10] the B's which this would require do not exist. Add other things, say C's to the B's and every A would be provided with its own separate B or C. Take no more C's than are required, and conversely every B or C would have its own separate A and therefore every B has its own ~~particular~~ separate A.

Hence we get the proposition if the collection of A's is not as small as the collection of B's then the collection of B's must be as small as the collection of A's.

This proposition has been a great puzzle to the mathematicians. They have endeavored in vain to prove it. The truth is that it never can be mathematically proved because it depends upon the peculiar nature of relations which is a question of logic, not of mathematics. Hence, every ~~attempt~~ proposed mathematical demonstration of it, of which there have been more than one, will necessarily be found upon examination to be fallacious.

Whatever things we may take it into our heads to regard as forming a collection,—say the milky way, this bit of chalk, and King Peter of Servia,—have some character in common not possessed by anything else in the universe. For it is a fact that they might be regarded as forming a collection which should exclude everything else; and just as the fact that a piece of chalk *could* easily be scratched ~~makes~~ constitutes it eternally true that it *is* soft now so the fact that any thing could be regarded as forming a collection containing nothing else constitutes a character which they all possess and they alone. *Qualities* or characters, like *relations* are in themselves mere possibilities. Many possible things do not *exist* but

---

10 [The following fragment appears on four loose notebook leaves (ms pp. 22–25, from R S-31) that were removed from the notebook's centrefold (R 466) without having to cut the pages. The fragment is an alternative but abandoned continuation of the present topic of the fifth Lowell Lecture. It is also an interesting anticipation of Peirce's work on three-valued, or triadic logic preserved on a couple of pages of the *Logic Notebook* from February 16–23, 1909.] **[R S-31:]** […] correlatives. But nobody has discovered any such relation. I can show you a *fictitious* way of accomplishing the purpose. To say that a thing is *hard* is not the logically precise denial of saying that it is *soft*.

whatever at any time exists or is even imagined to exist is *possible*. You must try to understand, what I know is difficult to understand without long explanations for which I have no time, that I do not at any time in this course touch upon metaphysics and that here at least I have nothing to do with epistemology. I must be understood in a purely logical sense, when I say that *qualities* and *relations* are not creatures of the mind, but are in themselves eternal possibilities, whether the mind thinks them to be so or not. They acquire existence only in the sense that they determine existent individual subjects. One of you may say to another "For all the lecturer says, I think qualities are creations of the mind". In saying that, you mean one or other of two things. You are either speaking as a metaphysician or as an epistemologist. I neither affirm nor deny what you say. I am simply talking logic. You are thinking either of the nature of the being of qualities or of the processes of human cognition. I have nothing to do with either. I simply say that

---

Because to say that it is hard is to say that the experiment of trying to scratch it with the moderate pressure of a knife will always result in failure while to say that it is soft is to say that the same experiment will always result in success. Now it is conceivable that the experiment would sometimes fail and sometimes succeed. We may, therefore, conceive that all the qualities of individual objects are of two kinds, *affirmative* qualities, each of which consists in the fact that a certain conceivable experiment would always result in a given way, and *negative qualities*, which consist in the fact that the experiment aforesaid will *not* always result in that way, as shown in this scheme

$$\text{not soft} \begin{cases} \text{hard} \\ \text{variable} \\ \text{soft} \end{cases} \Big\} \text{soft}$$

in the case of hard and soft. Now if we confine ourselves to almost any class of qualities, it is easy to imagine that one object should have all the affirmative qualities of another and more beside. Imagine for example two barrels of sugar. The one, A, is pure or has but a single impurity in spots. The other, B, has some impurity [in] some places [and] various other impurities in various different parts of the barrel. Then alchemist testing the two will find that every experiment that gives an invariable result will give the same result for both barrels; but many experiments that result invariably for A will not result invariably for B. Now if two individuals had precisely the same affirmative and negative qualities of all descriptions there would absolutely be no meaning in saying that they were different. But not to have any given ~~positive~~ affirmative quality is to have the corresponding negative quality. If therefore we write *p* as the abbreviation for 'possesses the positive quality' we have by logical necessity the

graph and it won't be necessary to write it. But I call this a fictitious way of getting over the difficulty because if you take *all* qualities into account [end] [This fragment is abandoned at ms p. 25.]

in order to avoid getting wound up in your reasoning, you are to regard qualities in a certain *aspect*. You need not say what they really are nor what the genesis of the ideas is, but leaving that quite aside you are to ~~look upon~~ regard *qualities* as eternal and immutable possibilities *prior* to existence in the sense that no fact of existence can affect in the least the qualities themselves. A *collection* is also a possibility, a mere possibility. But it differs from a quality in that it is a possibility *posterior* to existence. ⁙ Here are five dots and the existence of those five dots constitutes the *existence* of the collection. I might put in a sixth dot, and the possibility of that sixth constitutes the *possibility* of a collection of six dots. The existence of those five dots not only constitutes the existence of the one collection of five dots but also the existence of five collections of 4 dots each as well as 10 collections of 3 dots each, 10 collections of 2 dots each; collections of 1 dot each, and 1 collection *nothing*; and these 32 collections constitute one collection of collections. Or we may say there is a collection of six collections each of which latter collections is a collection of equal collections of dots.

The members of every collection possess some quality common to them and possessed by nothing else in the universe; and for that reason it is for some purposes much the same thing to say that an object belongs to a collection and to say that it possesses a quality. But for other purposes the distinction is important. Qualities possess no individual identity but only similarity while a collection is a single individual collection, though possessing it is true only a *derived* individuality.

A quality possesses, in itself, few positive qualities, which few are mostly of the particular kind called quantities. Thus, any particular kind of red, has its degree of light, its degree of fullness of color, and its peculiar quality of hue. This third is something more than a mere quantity. But it varies only in two opposite ways like a quantity. A collection, on the other hand, has all sorts of qualities discoverable by experience. Thus, a man's body is a collection of molecules; and its qualities are what is true of some of these molecules in relation to each other and to other things.[11] *Multitude* is a quality of a collection or something like that; and accordingly it possesses only one quality which is its quantity. It consists in the collection's being more than some and less than others. But I do not know [end][12]

---

11 [Peirce was well versed in his long-time colleague and assistant, chemist, geologist and astronomer Allan Douglas Risteen's (1866–1932) relevant research on molecules and human body (Risteen 1895).]

12 [The text on the notebook of R 466 ends in the middle of the notebook page 28, and may have been here abandoned altogether.]

Lowell Lecture V(c)

[Material in the notebook R 458 and in its cut-out leaves located in R 458(s) consists of sketchy accounts on multiple topics, including logical graphs and mathematical reasoning, with more unfinished sentences and uncorrected prose than is characteristic of other drafts written for the lectures. This early draft was initially planned to become the third lecture of the course, but when revising the plans for the lectures the topic of mathematical reasoning Peirce decided to postpone it to the fifth lecture. The main material of R 458 was published in NEM III, pp. 331–342. Produced below is the beginning of that main segment, with its three alternative and previously unpublished digressions preserved in R 458(s).]

I am going to devote this evening's curtate hour in endeavoring to convey to you some notion of the conceptions of mathematics.

What is mathematics? Traditionally it is defined as the science of quantity; but at the time when that definition was first adopted, three words bore entirely different acceptations from those they bear today. Those three words are *mathematics*, *science*, and *quantity*. Under mathematics were included the four sciences of Geometry, Arithmetic, Astronomy, and Music. But by Arithmetic was not meant what is now so called, but was then called *Logistic*. The arithmetic of those days was a wordy system of naming *ratios* mainly. It is now deservedly forgotten. That was not considered as any part of mathematics. The word *science* in those days did not mean what it now means, devoted single-minded research. Neither did it mean what Coleridge called science, i.e. *systematized knowledge*. It meant *comprehension*, understanding the metaphysical principles of things; nearly what we call philosophy. Finally the four branches of philosophy meant were said to relate to quantity because they all at that time were confined to the study of *measures*. Thus the definition of Mathematics as the Science of Quantity is simply a case of the frequent phenomenon of a phrase or formula being stoutly adhered to long after its original meaning has been forgotten. The truth is that *quantity* plays a very considerable part in mathematics; but there is much mathematics that has nothing al all to do with it.

If you take a paper ribbon, give it a half twist, paste the ends together to make a ring, and slit it along the middle till you come round, the result will be a single ring. That is a proposition in mathematics. But it has nothing to do with quantity.

The truth is that it is only within the last generation that mathematicians have come to understand the nature of their own science. My father was the first, in 1870, to define Mathematics as the science which draws necessary conclusions. This is now universally acknowledged by competent men to be substantially correct. Some self-conceited fool may assert that there are necessary conclusions not mathematical; but that is simply due to superficial study or no study at all. There is no room for a difference of intelligent opinion. Dedekind, one of the leaders of modern mathematics, whose little book published by the Open Court Company I strongly recommend to you,[13] goes so far as to call mathematics a branch of logic. But that overlooks the circumstance that the mathematician and the logician though standing on the same ground face in diametrically opposite directions. The mathematician is trying to draw the necessary conclusions, the logician is trying to find out how inferences necessary and probable are composed. One study is synthetic, the other analytic.

Mathematics is the science of hypotheses,—the science of what is supposable. Supposable does not mean directly imaginable; it means what makes sense. For instance, we cannot *imagine* an endless succession of instants. We can, however, imagine a *graph* which asserts that between midnight and any instant before midnight, there is an instance; and we can suppose that that graph is true. If so, there is an endless succession of instants before midnight. It makes sense, although we cannot actually call up the idea of so many distinct instants. It would obviously require an endless series of exertions for which an endless life would be requisite.

Mathematics may be divided according to the complexity of its hypotheses. The simplest kind of mathematics would be the mathematics of existential graphs. Let us look at this subject mathematically. Any graph has one or other of two grades of value. The lower grade is that of a *false* graph, which must not be **[Alts. 1–3]** scribed on the sheet of assertion. The higher grade is that of a true graph, which may be scribed on the sheet of assertion.

Now the pure mathematical way of looking at this matter would be something like this. The mathematician always thinks in diagrams. He would put two spots

f v

for truth and falsity marking them with letters to distinguish them in writing about them. Below these he would ~~mark~~ imagine a whole collection of spots, to represent the graphs, and would actually draw some of them. Each graph spot would be joined either to the f spot or to the v spot,—none to both.[14]

---

[13] [Richard Dedekind's 1901 *Essays on the Theory of Numbers* was included in Peirce's list of references for Lecture V.]

[14] **[Del.:]** [This deleted and abandoned fragment appears on the opposite of the cut-out pages of Alternatives 1–3, thus originally preceding those pages that Peirce crossed out when the pages were removed from the notebook. See R 496 in "Fragments", Selection 42.] Let us write this

He might now draw arrowhead lines from one to another of the graph-points, attaching a new graph-point to each. These would denote conditionals[15] *de inesse*. Then if it were possible to pass from the v points to the f point along the line of such a graph-point in the direction of its arrow, he would connect that point with f. Otherwise with v.

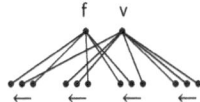

By some such means as that he would study out the laws of these things. I have not time to go further. What I have said will give you an inkling into the pure mathematics of logic.

[– – –][16]

[Alt.1] [...] scribed on the sheet of assertion. The higher grade is that of a true graph which may be ~~in~~scribed on the sheet of assertion.

Although ordinary algebra is contrived for dealing with a much more complicated hypothesis than this and to employ it for this purpose is like using a vast triphammer to crack a nut, yet it might be so applied. *Boole* did substantially just that. Let v (*verum*) be any numerical value you please, which we may arbitrarily assign as the value of every true proposition and let f (*falsum*) be any different numerical value you please which we arbitrarily assume as the value of every false proposition.[17] Then, in order to express that the value of any proposition is either v or f, that is, that proposition is either true or false, we may write

$$(v - x)(x - f) = 0$$

---

to assert that the graph A is permissibly scribable on the within *m* cuts at the time B, within *m* cuts being either any whole number including 0, There one rule will be and within any *n* other cuts [end, cf. R 456(s)]

15 [NEM III, p. 332, misspells ~~pro~~conditionals as "preconditionals".]

16 [Omitted is the rest of the notebook text of R 458, notebook pages 6–33, which is available in most parts in NEM III(1), pp. 331–342. Produced below are the pages cut out from the notebook after its page 4, representing three alternative rejects located in R 458(s) that continue the text from its bifurcation point above ([**Alts. 1–3**]).]

17 [The tall characters v and f, as well as all the display equations, are inscribed in red ink in the original copy sheets.]

For if the product of these two factors is zero one or other must be zero. If $(v-x) = 0$, $x = v$ and the proposition is true. But if $x \neq v$, $v-x$ is not zero and $x-f$ must be zero and x must be equal to f, or the proposition is true. Let us write l_{ab} for the value of the proposition that a loves b. This value varying according to what individuals a and b denote. Let m_{ab} be the value of the proposition that a is the mother of b and let k_{ab} be the value of the proposition that a kills b.

If then we write

$$\Sigma_a \Sigma_b (m_{ab} - f)^2 (v - l_{ab})^2 = 0$$

where I square each factor to ~~make it positive~~ prevent it from having a *minus* value and there the $\Sigma_a \Sigma_b$ means that you must take the sum of all the results obtained by ~~putting~~ making a and b successively all the individuals in the world, then this equation will signify that every mother loves that of which she is the mother. In like manner,

$$\Sigma_a \Sigma_b (k_{ab} - f)^2 (l_{ab} - f)^2 = 0$$

will mean that nobody loves a person whom he is killed.

The algebraic solution is got by considering that for each pair of a and b

$$(m_{ab} - f)(v - l_{ab}) = 0$$
$$(k_{ba} - f)(l_{ab} - f) = 0$$

Multiplying the first by $(k_{ba} - f)$ and the second by $(m_{ab} - f)$ we get

$$(m_{ab} - f)(v - l_{ab})(k_{ba} - f) = 0$$
$$(m_{ab} - f)(l_{ab} - f)(k_{ba} - f) = 0$$

Adding

$$(m_{ab} - f)(v - f)(k_{ba} - f) = 0$$

Striking out the factor $v - f$ which cannot be *zero*

$$(m_{ab} - f)(k_{ba} - f) = 0$$

which means that no mother is killed by her child.

[Alt.2] [...] scribed on the sheet of assertion. The higher grade is that of a true graph which may be scribed on the sheet of assertion.

Let us write this[18]

$$\text{co}\overset{A}{\underset{B}{\text{v}}}\text{ers}\text{---}C$$

to mean that a graph A permissibly covers a part of the sheet of assertion B at the time C.

Now I want to call your attention to a general rule applicable to all relations. As examples of relations in general I usually select one which begins with one of the seven tall letters b d f h k l ſ

b ~~benefits betrays~~ blames
d defends
f fools
h hates
k knows
l loves
ſ serves

Taking any of these, say the monosyllabic "blames" my proposition is that if A blames everybody that is blamed by B and B blames everybody that is blamed by C, then A blames everybody that is blamed by C, then A blames everybody that is blamed by C. It is obviously so. But I will prove it by existential graphs. In order to express that A blames everybody blamed by B, we note this simply denies that there is anybody blamed by B and not blamed by A. Therefore we ~~write~~ scribe

So to say that B blames everybody that is blamed by C we scribe

Or dropping the capital letters

---

18 [The graphs in this fragment are inscribed in red (the lines and letters for spots), and in black or blue ink (the continuous and broken cuts and the scrolls).]

Now I call your attention to the fact that if any graph g is on the sheet of assertion together with a cut $g \bigcirc$ enclosing another graph p

$$g \;(p)$$

we may first iterate g by the rule of iteration and deiteration

$$g \;(g\,p)$$

and may then erase the outside replica by the rule of ~~omission~~ erasure and insertion

$$(g\,p)$$

So that ~~we have the rule~~ it comes to this that any graph not in an odd number of cuts can be shoved into any additional cuts that may be *already made*.

Acting on this rule, let us shove the whole of the upper graph into the inner cut of the lower one; thus:

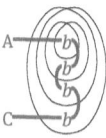

Now whatever rule holds good for every graph is true of every line of identity, since a line of identity is a graph. We therefore have a right to iterate the lower right hand line in one more cut thus

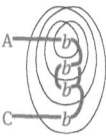

Now by the rule of omission and insertion within three cuts, three being an odd number we can make any insertion we like. We can therefore join the two lines there thus

38 Lowell Lecture V(a,b,c) (R 459, R 466, R 458) — 307

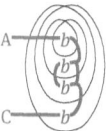

Now the two ~~inner~~ middle *b*'s having the same ~~connections~~ ligatures, we can ~~deiterate~~ erase the inner one by the rule of iteration and deiteration thus

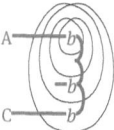

And now, the middle *b* being in an even number of cuts can be erased, making

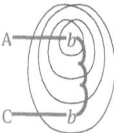

Finally, the two cuts with nothing between except traversing cuts destroy one another and we have

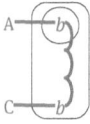

That is A blames everybody blamed by C which is what I undertook to prove.

[Alt.3] [...] ~~written~~ scribed on the sheet of assertion. The higher grade is that of a true graph which may be ~~written~~ scribed on the sheet of assertion. If a graph cannot be ~~written~~ scribed on the sheet of assertion then another graph consisting of a cut enclosing that graph can be scribed on the sheet of assertion.
    ~~In any case we may scribe this~~[19]

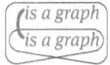

If we write

---

[19] [The graph below was crossed out by Peirce.]

to mean something can be ~~scribed~~ scribable[20] on the sheet of assertion, then we may write

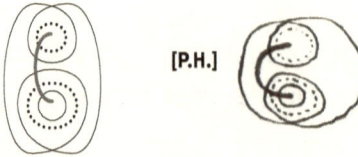

to mean that if a graph cannot be scribed on the sheet of assertion then a cut enclosing it can be so scribed [end][21]

---

20 [Peirce replaced 'scribed' by the modalised word 'scribable', not by his more usual spelling of 'scriptible'.]

21 [Fragment abandoned.]

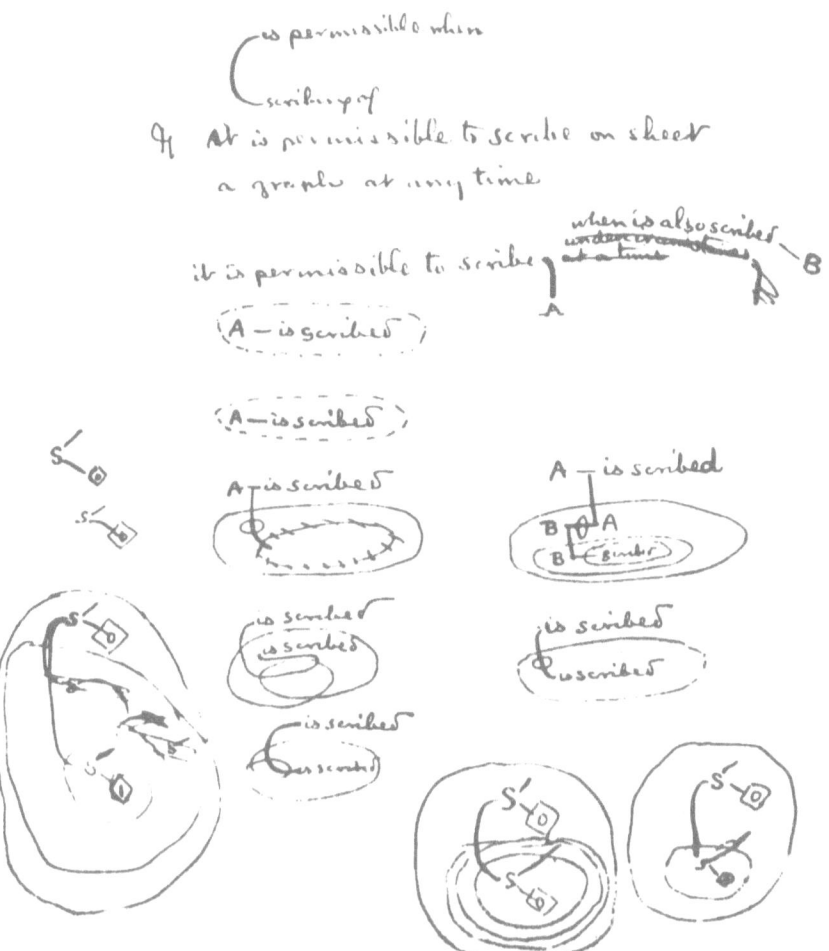

[A holograph page from R 458(s) (Harvard Peirce Papers). All inscriptions on the page originally in red ink.]

39 Lowell Lecture V(d)

[Copy-text is from R 469, R 470 and R 471, plus two pages from R S-55. On page 0 of the Harvard coop notebook R 469 Peirce wrote: "Lowell Lectures 1903. Lecture 5. Vol. 1". On the notebook cover (R 470) it reads, in Peirce's hand: "1903 Lowell Lectures. Lecture 5. Vol. 2".] In this final version of the fifth lecture, delivered on December 7, it finally becomes apparent how late in the game it is before Peirce manages to state anything at all on the subject of Gamma graphs. Right in the beginning of this fifth lecture, he sets out to brief the audience on what the concept of the graphs of graphs is, the theme which he was hoping to be able to explain no later than in the second volume for Lecture IV (R 467). The presentation of the graphs of graphs was at all events very brief, and apparently Peirce did not manage explaining anything on other kinds of Gamma graphs: neither the broken-cut modal graphs nor abstraction or potentials ever made it to the stage. Only one paragraph on the logic of potentials was printed in the *Syllabus* (Convention VII), while no information on the broken-cut notation, which is found in the alternative drafts of the syllabus draft alongside potentials (R 478), was ever disseminated.

In the fifth lecture of the course, Peirce's leading idea is the important distinction between, on the one hand, the *purely mathematical interpretation* of graphs, which he had disseminated at the end of the printed *Syllabus* (pp. 20–23), and on the other hand, the *representational interpretation*, which is the approach to EGs that Peirce had presented to the audience during the second lecture in terms of the elaborate system of conventions. In coeval writings, Peirce had recorded about 30 (non-modal) hypotheses that are given in the meta-language of graphs of graphs. The text of the next selection provides lists of such hypotheses as expressed in natural language instead of the language of graphs, with double quotation marks in these hypotheses to denote object-language terms. Objects of the graphs are thus not types but tokens. In the language of graphs of graphs, thus, objects of graphs are graph-instances. Peirce states that there are about "half a dozen" hypotheses that involve the broken-cut notation to denote necessities. Three examples relying on those hypotheses appear in the language of graphs on loose sheets within the folder R S-31 (plus two not annotated), two more are found in R 468 (see the last selection on "Fragments"), while another one occurs at the end of the draft segment that pertains to the *Syllabus*, and is located in a folder containing several variant sheets ("Gamma Graphs 3.3.", R 509).

Peirce's graphical analysis of definitions of number and cardinality provided in this fifth lecture is of considerable interest to historians and philosophers of mathematics and logic. Following the definition of multitude, the topic of continuity proposed in the original announcement of the lectures is relegated to "the few minutes that remain". What he recorded in R 473 suggests that even the attempt to do so was cut short by the running of the clock.

[R S-55] Ladies and Gentlemen

I have been all along saying that I was not talking Metaphysics but Logic.[1] I did not mean by that that what I had to say would have no effect upon metaphysics. Far from that, metaphysics, to be sound, must draw all its principles from logic and apply these principles to its own analyses of familiar observations. No, I did not mean that; but what I did mean is that logic is the prior science. That it is bad logic when you are studying logic to be squinting at what in effect will be upon metaphysics. That is something that no devoted logician will tolerate; and the metaphysician who is guilty of such practices will simply prevent the establishment of any truth at all. It will be something like a repetition of what we have seen in religion, the religionists always insisting on this or that color being taken by sciences prior to their own, and the result has been almost to destroy religion for the thinking part of mankind and to prevent men from seeing the simple truths that they would soon have some to if the roadway of science had not been blocked by the religionists with their very deficient faith in religion and their want of any desire to learn the real truth whatever it may turn out to be. Something like this will happen if metaphysicians insist on shaping their logic so as to accord with this or that favorite dogma of metaphysics.

[R 470] I am going to speak to you tonight about *multitude* or *maniness* and shall, I hope, be able to give you a glimpse of its logical importance. Some kinds of *infinity* will come under our notice, but I fear I shall not have time to speak of other kinds. I shall say a few words only concerning *continuity*. All of these subjects become intensely interesting and of great importance if one can go into them in some detail. But the difficulty with a course of this kind is that it is not possible to go deeply enough into the subjects to reach the really valuable parts of them.

I must begin by ~~referring to so~~ a few words concerning gamma graphs; because it is by means of gamma graphs that I have been enabled to understand these subjects, and I do not believe it is possible really to understand them except by some method equivalent to that of gamma graphs.

In particular, it is absolutely necessary to representing the reasoning about these subjects that one should be able to reason with graphs about graphs and thus that we should have graphs of graphs.

It is essential to a graph or any other expression of a proposition that it should be represented by its interpretant sign to be *true*. But to say that it is true implies

---

1 [Alt.] Logic is a study of great utility not merely as a training in thought, but also for the information that it brings. But it is of very little use or none at all, if not worse than useless, unless it be exact; and in order to render it exact it is necessary to go through a long course of study of matters in themselves calculated to try one's patience.

that it really is affected by its object; and in order that this object should have a real effect upon it, this object must be a subject of force, which is an individual. Consequently, an adequate interpretant of a graph must represent it as a sign of an *individual*. How, then, can there be a *graph* of a *graph*, considering that a graph is a *legisign*, or sign which has the mode of being of a *general type*, just as any word is a general type, and not a single individual object in a single definite place at a single instant. The answer is that a graph can only have a graph for its object indirectly. Directly, it can only refer to a graph-replica. But it can assert what it asserts of *any graph-replica* you please so long as it be *equivalent* to a given graph replica.

The matter is unsuitable to presentation in a course like this, although it is indispensable that something should be said about it. If I can ever get the funds to print it, I shall be very happy to send copies to ~~anybody who cares fo~~ all who may care for them.

This matter of the graphs of graphs if I could present it would also illustrate the nature of Pure Mathematics, still better than it is illustrated on pages 20 to 22 of the *Syllabus* distributed last Thursday [December 3].[2] Mathematics, in general, is the science of the logical possibility and impossibility of hypotheses. Upon that definition first put forth by my father Benjamin Peirce in 1870, mathematicians are now pretty unanimously agreed. *Pure* mathematics differs from mathematics in general in not admitting into its hypotheses any element that does affect their logical possibility or impossibility. Thus, the pure mathematics of graphs, as you see in those pages of the syllabus, says nothing at all about the logical interpretation of graphs but defines them exclusively by their logical relations to one another. So the pure mathematical presentation of graphs of graphs says nothing at all about the graphs considered being representations of graphs but merely defines the graphs representing the sheet of assertion, a cut, its area, or line of identity, and so forth, in terms of their logical relations to one another.

The theory of graphs of graphs rests upon a larger number of independent hypotheses than do most branches of pure mathematics. I divide these hypotheses into those which relate to physical possibilities and necessities and those which relate to permissions and prohibitions. The former class, thirty in number, are all expressible in alpha and beta graphs.[3] The latter class which ~~there are less than~~ do not much exceed half a dozen require, one and all of them, gamma graphs to

---

[2] [See R 508, B1–B6, Selection 41 of the *Syllabus*.]
[3] [See Selection 40, especially R 2 and R 511 on "Dyadics", in which one can find 23 such hypotheses defined in natural language (*Hypotheses* 1–30).]

express them. In particular the broken cut enters into everyone, and into some of them with curious complications.⁴

One is surprised to find how extremely complicated are the graphs that express some of these fundamentals of the nature of graphs; and this complication ~~illustrates two almost an~~ puts into a strong light two merits of this system of existential graphs. For on the one hand, it shows the extraordinary analytical power of the system that analyzes conditions which seemed on our first acquaintance with them to be very very simple but which the system of graphs forces us to see are in reality very complex; while on the other hand, this same complication shows ~~the quite extraordinary diagramm~~ that the system of existential graphs possesses to an extraordinary degree the ~~peculiar~~ virtue that belongs more or less to all diagrams that of the putting a matter a really extremely complicated into a light under which it is fully and adequately represented and yet seems as easy and natural as ~~rolling~~ slipping off a floating log.⁵

But I must hasten to the subject of numbers.⁶

Whole numbers can on the one hand be studied in two ways which are surprisingly different from one another throughout. They can be studied as qualities of collections, making the members of one collection many and those of another few, which is called by the Germans with their usual incapacity for language the doctrine of *Cardinal Numbers*; but ~~I call it~~ which ought to be called the doctrine of *Multitude*. Or, on the other hand, numbers may be considered simply as objects in a sequence, as *ordinal numbers*. The latter study is a branch of pure mathematics, because it makes no difference what kind of objects they are that are in series, nor whether it is a series in time, in space, or in logic. The doctrine of multitude, on the other band, is not pure mathematics. For the objects it studies, the multitudes are in a linear series exactly as the doctrine of ordinal numbers supposes; and since the doctrine of ordinal numbers permits the members of the series to be objects of any kind, it follows that it permits them to be multitudes. Thus the doctrine of multitude is nothing but a special application of the doctrine of ordi-

---

4 [See Lecture IV, R 467; R 511, *Hypotheses* 17–22, *Hypotheses* 31–36; and the *Syllabus*, "Gamma Graphs 1–5".]

5 [In Peirce's own pagination, here followed Herbert Spencer obituary (notebook pp. 140–158, evenly paginated), followed by an instruction to continue on page 36 of Vol. 1 ("What has been said of qualities…" of the notebook, or "What I have said of qualities…" of its cut-out fragment in R S-31). The obituary is preceded by an instruction to skip to "Vol. 1, p. 2", which continues the present lecture on the subject of numbers and multitude, and which is the instruction that is here followed.]

6 [The sentence preceded by a deleted passage:] As a specimen of mathematical logic in action, I am going to tell you this evening something about the new doctrine of *maniness*, or *multitude*.

nal numbers. But the special objects of its series have a special character which permits them to be studied from a special point of view; and that point of view is a logical point of view. It is not the pure mathematical forms that we study in the doctrine of multitude. It is on the contrary a branch of logic which, like all logic, is directly dependent upon mathematics. The first question we come upon in the study of multitude is very obviously a purely logical question; and there is nothing at all corresponding to it in the doctrine of ordinal numbers: it is the question what is multitude. Multitude is obviously a relative quality of *collections*, or plurals. Therefore the question becomes, What is a *collection*? That is obviously a most important question for logic; and it is about as difficult a one as could be found. In speaking of a collection, we do not mean that its members are physically or in any way existentially brought together. We mean by a collection merely a plural, whose objects are collected together by thought. The collection exists just as much as its members. Their existence is its existence. Yet in another point of view, it is a creation of thought. It is an *ens rationis*. An *ens rationis* may be defined as a subject whose being consists in a Secondness, or fact, concerning something else. Its being is thus of the nature of Thirdness, or thought. Any abstraction, such as Truth and Justice, is an *ens rationis*. That does not prevent Truth and Justice from being real powers in the world without any figure of speech. They are powers, just as much, and in the same way, as I am a power if I can open my window should the air seem to me stuffy. A collection is an abstraction, or is like an abstraction in being an *ens rationis*. But it is unlike an abstraction in that it *exists*. Truth and justice do not *exist*, although they are powers. I myself, properly speaking, do not exist. It is only a replica of me that exists, and I exist in that replica as the effect of my being as a law. A collection, however, exists, and this existence is derived from the existence of its members which may be pure Secondness. Our bodies are of course much more than so many collections of molecules; but as far as its *existence* is concerned, the existence of our bodies consists in the existence of the molecules. But the word *collection* and other words of the same general meaning have two different meanings with a very fine distinction between them. This makes a large part of the difficulty of defining a collection, and the non-recognition of this distinction makes a serious stumbling block in the doctrine of cardinal numbers. In accordance with my views of the Ethics of Terminology, I am going to make two new words to distinguish these two meanings. The one I shall call a *gath* which is simply the word 'gather' with the last syllable dropped. The other I call a *sam* which is the word 'same' with the last letter dropped. I also like this word because it is so much like the word sum, in the phrase *sum total*. It also recalls the German word *Samlung*. A collection, in the sense of a *gath* is a subject which is a pure Secondness without Firstness, and whose only mode of being is whatever existence it may have; and this consists in the existence of certain other existents, or pure Seconds, called its *members*. Thus, the ~~collection~~ gath of human beings at this moment in Boston, consists in the existence of this man and that man. No matter how those men might be transformed, ~~say into corpses, or into pieces of butcher's meat~~ no matter if some of them were to leave Boston, that same gath exists, although it would cease to be the gath of the inhabitants of Boston. But were a single member of the collection to cease to exist, that ~~collection~~ particular gath would no longer exist. There would still be a ~~collection~~ gath of inhabitants of Boston but it would be a different ~~collection~~ gath. The description, 'All the inhabitants of Boston' describes a ~~collection~~ gath. But as time goes on it will describe a different ~~collection~~ gath.

The description 'the inhabitants of Boston' is a proper name. It applies to but a single individual object, the ~~total~~ whole of all the inhabitants of Boston. This ~~total~~ whole, what I call a *sam* is not exactly a ~~collection~~ gath; and it is important to get a distinct idea of the difference. Just as the molecules that compose a man's body are continually changing by the loss of some and the gain of others, while there remains the same man, so the population of Boston is ever changing, yet remains the same individual whole. I propose to say it is the same sam. But it does not remain the same ~~collection~~ gath. At ~~every~~ each instant it is identical with a ~~collection~~ gath. Always there is a ~~collection~~ gath in the existence of which consists the existence of the ~~whole~~ sam of the inhabitants of Boston. Were the city to be devastated and not one inhabitant left, still, as long as it remained Boston, ~~there would be a 'whole'~~ the 'sam, or sum total, of the inhabitants of Boston' would have a *being*, although it would under those circumstances have ceased to *exist*. It would continue to *be*, since the description would retain its meaning. The *essence* of the ~~whole~~ sam would remain, although its existence had departed. But as for the ~~collection~~ gath, since it has no other being than existence, and its existence consists in the existence of its members; and since under those circumstances no members would exist, the ~~collection~~ gath would altogether cease to be. It is important to have this distinction clearly in mind. I do not mean to say that it is usually important to ~~make~~ hold this distinction clear in regard to any collection that we may happen to speak of; but I mean that for certain purposes it is indispensably necessary. Whatever ~~collection gath~~ sam there may be to whose members, and to them alone, any sign applies is called the *breadth* of the sign. This word *breadth*, originating with the Greek commentators of Aristotle, has passed into our vernacular. We speak of a man of *broad* culture. That means *culture* in many fields. *Breadth* of mind is the character of a mind that takes many things into account. If a man has *broad* and *deep* learning, the breadth consists in how many different subjects he is acquainted with, and the depth in how much he knows about whatever subject he is acquainted with. Now the *breadth* of a descriptive appellation has an *essence*, or Imputed Firstness; which is the signification, or *Depth*, of the appellation. Take the word *phenix*. No such thing exists. One naturally says that the name has *no breadth*. That, however, is not strictly correct. We should say *its breadth is nothing*. That breadth is precisely what I mean by a *sam*. Therefore I define a *sam* as an *ens rationis* ~~which has a First Firstness (or essence, which is any quality) and an existence, or Second Firstness, or Firstness of Secondness, whose identity~~ having two grades of being, its *essence*, which is the being of a definite quality ~~attributed~~ imputed to the sam, and its existence which is the existence of whatever subject may exist that possesses that quality. A *gath*, on the other hand, is a ~~an ens rationis~~ subject having only one mode of being which is the compound of the existence of subjects called the *members* of the *gath*.

You ~~should~~ may remark that a *sam* is thus defined without any reference at all to a gath. I repeat the definition, so that you may observe this:

> A *sam* is an *ens rationis* whose essence is the being of a definite quality (imputed to the *sam*) and whose existence is the existence of whatever subject there may be possessing that quality.

On the other hand, it is impossible to define a gath without reference to a sam. For when I say that a gath is ~~an ens rationis~~ a subject whose only mode of being is the compound existence of definite individuals called its members, what is the meaning of this *compounded* existence[?] It is plain that the idea of a compound is a triadic idea. It implies that there is some sign, or something like a sign, which picks out and unites those members. Now the fact that they are all united in that compound is a quality belonging to them all and to nothing else. There is thus here a reference to a possible *sam* which does this. Thus, we might as well at once define a *gath* as ~~an ens rationis~~ a subject which has but one mode of being which is the existence of a *sam*. From this fact, that a *gath* cannot be defined except in terms of a *sam*, it follows that if by a *collection* be meant, as ordinarily is meant, a *gath*; while a *gath* is not distinguished from a *sam*, it becomes utterly impossible to define what is meant by a collection.

This would not be true if the two clauses of the definition of the *sam* were two distinct ideas which have to be put together; but it is not so. Secondness involves Firstness, although it can be discriminated from it; and consequently the idea of the existence of that which has an essence, which is simple Secondness, is decidedly a simpler notion than that of existence without essence, or a Secondness discriminated from Firstness. For it is only by a rectification applied to the former notion that the latter can be attained.

No doubt the ~~simplest~~ easiest way to conceive of the *sam* is to imagine that you have a ~~general~~ common noun, without specifying what noun it is, and to think that that noun signifies some quality which is possessed by anything to which it applies, but is not possessed by anything to which is does not apply. Now you are to imagine a single thing which is composed of parts. Nothing is done to these parts to put them into their places in the whole: their mere existence locates them in the whole. Now, think of this rule as describing the whole. If any individual object can properly have that common noun predicated of it, it is a part of the single object called a *sam*; if not, it is not. That gives you the idea of the *sam*. Now to get the idea of a *gath*, you are to consider that those individual objects might change their qualities without losing their individual identity; so that limiting ourselves to any instant, any individual object which at that instant forms a part of the *sam* forever forms a part of an object of which no object not at that instant a part of the *sam* is a part, and this individual composite whole which has nothing to do with the qualities of its members is a *gath*.

For every *gath* there must be a corresponding *sam*. This is what we should ordinarily express by saying that whatever exists is possible. Or, as De Morgan put it, the individuals of whatsoever collection have some quality common to them all that is peculiar to them, i.e. possessed by nothing else. Kant, I dare say, would remark that this is a Regulative principle but that it cannot be proved to be a Constitutive principle. That is, it is proper to assume it, but you cannot prove it is so. But I reply that every principle of logic is a Regulative Principle and nothing more. Logic has nothing to do with Existence. And I should add: Herr Professor Dr. Hofrath Kant, permit me to say that in saying this is not a Constitutive principle you speak of *qualities* as if they were existent individuals. A quality has no other being in itself than possibility and to say that a quality is possible is to say that it has all the being that in the nature of things a quality could have. If as you say there *may* be a quality common and peculiar to all the members of a *gath*, then there certainly is such a quality; and you yourself have in this very same breath described one such quality, in saying that they are all members of the *gath* in question. So for every *gath* there is a corresponding *sam*. But it is not true that for every *sam* there is a corresponding *gath*. Since there is the *sam* of the phenix, although it happens not to exist up to date. But there is no such *gath* since there is no phenix. Another point which I observe puzzles the Hon. Bertrand Russell in his *Principles of Mathematics* is whether a collection which has but a single individual member is identical with that individual or not. The proper answer is that if by a collection you mean a *sam*, the *sam* of the sun is not the sun, since it is an *ens rationis* having an essence, while the individual has no essence and is not an *ens rationis*. But if you mean the *gath*, the gath of the sun has no being at all except the existence of the sun which is all the being the individual existent sun has. Therefore, having precisely the same being they are identical and no distinction except a grammatical or linguistic one can be drawn between them. Mr. Russell's being puzzled by this is a good illustration of how impossible it is to treat of philosophy without making a special vocabulary such as all other sciences make. It is, however, far more needed in philosophy than in any other science, for the reason that the words of ordinary speech are needed by philosophy for its raw material.[7]

What has been said of qualities is equally true of relations, which may be regarded as the qualities of sets of individuals. That is to say, if any form of relation is logically possible between the members of two given *gaths*, a relation of that form actually exists between them.

In order to illustrate this principle, I will consider a proposition which the ablest mathematicians have been endeavoring for half a century to demonstrate to be either true or false. The proposition assumes that there are two *gaths*, which we may call the A's and the B's. And now if we use the phrase a "one to one relation" to denote such a relation that no ~~individual~~ relate stands in that relation to two different correlates nor any two relates to the same correlate; like the relation of husband to wife in a monogamous country, or better of father to eldest child, then it is assumed that there is no one-to-one relation in which every B stands to an A. Then the question is whether there is necessarily any one-to-one relation in which every A stands to a B.

---

[7] [Alt.] [Seven cut-out pages from R 469 located in R S-31] [...] than in any other science for the reason that the words of ordinary speech are needed by philosophy as its raw material.

What I have said of qualities is equally true of relations which may be regarded as qualities of sets. If any form of relation is logically possible between members of two *gaths*, a relation of that form actually exists between them.

For example, take the relation which consists at once in being in a given relation to and in not being in that relation to anything other than. Two gaths say the A's and the B's may be such that it is logically impossible that there should be a relation of that form in which there is [The rest of the paragraph is from the last, unnumbered loose sheet of R S-31, which is presumed to fit here between ms pages 36 and 40. This page which Peirce may forgotten to paginate as 38 has a crossed-out graph which is replaced below by a graph found on the verso of loose ms page 36.] an A to every B. That is to say, either this graph is true or else it is logically impossible. But that form of relation is not in itself absurd. For there is a relation such as the next graph shows. More than that there is a *gath* which substituted for A would make the graph true of B, and there is gath that substituted for B would make the graph true for A. For the relation of identity satisfies the condition. If therefore the first graph is logically impossible there must be a peculiar relation between the two gaths that renders it so. What is that relation? In order to answer that question we observe that there is a relation of the form shown in the third graph. For identity is such a relation.

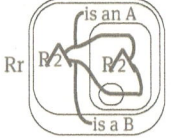 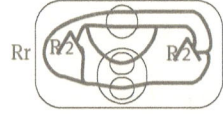

Since there is no one-to-one relation in which whatever B that may be stands to an A, it must be logically impossible that there should be any such relation. But since the form relation in itself is not absurd, and since in point of fact every B does stand in such a relation to some member of a *gath*; for every B stands in

---

That is, this is a relation in which no two relates stand to the same correlate and no relate to two correlates. Now the B's are all in such a one-to-one ~~relation~~ correspondence to some gath. But it is supposed to be logically impossible, that is to involve a contradiction, for every member of this gath to be an A. Unless this contradiction be due to some special fact about the A's, a supposition which I will put aside for the moment, it can only be that it would involve the connection of an A with two or more B's. That is, we may suppose every B to be connected with only one thing and that one thing an A but we may suppose that in every such case it is inevitable that ~~two A's are~~ the same A is connected with two present B's. [The last sentence is partly cut out and is reconstructed from matching parts of the words and characters preserved in the notebook's page stems (R 469).]

But now I say that it manifestly cannot be necessary that the same A's should be connected with two B's in any distribution in which there are any A's uncollected. This is a point over which mathematicians have made vast difficulty. They say this is not manifestly necessary. But this, I am confident, is because they misapprehended the argument. They understand, as I suppose, that the argument is that after we have joined as many B's as possible to separate A's, there can be no need of joining another B to an A already joined to a B as long as there remain A's unjoined to B's. If this were the argument, it would unquestionably be unsound, because it would assume that there was a state of things in which as many B's as possible had been joined to separate A's, which there might not be any such ultimate condition if the A's were innumerable. But that is not the argument. I am not speaking of any ultimate stage. I simply say this. It is ~~supposed~~ assumed to be necessary that if every B is joined to an A some A should be joined to two B's. This it is assumed is a necessity. But a necessity cannot come about at random. There has got to be something in the state of things that makes it necessary; and I say that there is nothing to make this necessary there being an A not joined to any B. I am not contemplating a gradual process of making the connections. I simply say if there was such a *necessity*, that necessity must have been due to a definite state of things; and the only definite state of things producing that necessity supposes every A to be joined to a B. This seems to me to be evident.

As to the supposition of anything peculiar about the A's rendering a relationship impossible which would otherwise be possible, it is absurd, since it would forbid each relationship; and the prohibition of each such relation would itself be a relation of the very kind that it undertook to prohibit.

I am particularly desirous of making this reasoning clear to you; and it is the process of reasoning that is more important than the conclusion. Let me restate it.

We begin with the assumption that it is impossible that there should be a one-to-one relation, that is, a relation in which no one individual stands to two and no two to any one, that it is impossible there should be such a relation in which every B stands to an A.

Now every B does stand in such a relation to something. So that what is logically impossible is that the correlates should be, all of them, A's. Now a logical impossibility is a contradiction and therefore there must be some definite state of circumstances making the supposition that all the correlates as A's to be directly contradictory of the relation being a one-to-one relation [end] [The segment is abandoned in the middle of ms p. 48, R S-31.]

the relation of identity to ~~every~~ some B, it follows that the logical impossibility lies in some existential limitation of the A's. However, dropping at the outset the assumption about the one-to-one relation and considering any two *gaths*, the A's and the B's, there is a relation in which no relate stands to two different correlates (though two relates may stand in it to the same correlate) in which every B stands to an A; for the B's may so stand to any one A.

Relates
⫯ ⫯ V V
Correlates

Now setting out with such a relation, let us ask whether by a change of it so as to change each correlate into some other individual of the universe, it is possible so to change it as to make every A a correlate of it. Let us trace out the consequences of supposing this not to be possible. Let us under this hypothesis change our relation by a change of correlates so as to render it a one-to-one relation, and let us suppose this to be done in every possible way so as to give a vast multitude of different one to one relations. Among these different relations there must be some all of whose correlates are A's because every possible variation of our relation occurs, and they could not all agree in any respect unless it were logically compelled. But since we are going on the hypothesis that every one of these relations leaves some A that is not a correlate, it follows that there is nothing to compel any correlate to be non-A; for the only logical requirement is that no two correlates shall be identical and since even when we do not care whether they are so or not there are A's that are non-correlates, it follows that there is nothing to compel any correlate to be a non-A, since there are A's that it may be. But there cannot be any compulsion that does not affect any individual, and therefore there is nothing to compel correlates to be non-A's and consequently in some cases none will be non-A's. But now if we bring in the assumption that there is no one-to-one relation in which every B stands to an A, this result is rendered impossible, and with it disappears the hypothesis of which it is a necessary consequence; namely, that there is no relation in which no relate has two correlates and in which some B stands to every A. This hypothesis being overthrown appears then that there is such a relation in which no B stands to two A's yet of which every A is correlate to some B. But we have only to exclude from this all but one of the relations of different B's to the same A for every A to reduce its converse to a one-to-one relation of every A to a B. Thus we have proved that if there is no one-to-one relation of every B to some A there is a one-to-one relation of every A to some B.[8]

---

8 [Penciled in the margin "Skip to p. 60", indicating omission of the explanation of Cantor's ordinal numbers from the delivered lecture, until "But I might give several lectures elucidating this

Let us now look into another problem. Dr. Georg Cantor has a wonderful system of Ordinal Numbers which I must explain to you. It begins with the ordinary ordinal numbers

1, 2, 3, 4, 5, 6, 7, 8, 9, 10, 11,...

That series is endless. That is to say, it has no last. But neither in logic nor in fact does that interfere with its being gone completely through provided the objects numbered are not in the nature of existences. When for instance Achilles runs after the Tortoise and we choose to divide his course into a first stage in which he goes to the place where the tortoise was at first, a second stage in which he goes to the place where the tortoise was at the end of the first stage, a third stage in which be goes to the place where the tortoise was at the end of the second stage, and so on, the series of stages is endless. But nothing in logic, or in fact, prevents Achilles from accomplishing them all, since they are only possibilities. So then there will be other ordinal numbers, after the first endless series is gone through. And the first of these Cantor denotes by ω then every ordinal number having one next after it, the series runs

$\omega + 1, \omega + 2, \omega + 3, \omega + 4, \omega + 5, \ldots$

and after this endless series is accomplished there will come $\omega + \omega$ which he calls $w \cdot 2$. Then according to the rule must come

$\omega \cdot 2, \omega \cdot 2 + 1, \omega \cdot 2 + 2, \omega \cdot 2 + 3$
$\omega \cdot 3, \omega \cdot 3 + 1$
$\omega \cdot 4$
$\omega \cdot 5$ etc.

This series $\omega, \omega \cdot 2, \omega \cdot 3, \omega \cdot 4, \omega \cdot 5$ is endless and after it is accomplished we shall have $\omega \cdot \omega$ or ω^2. Then

$\omega^2, \omega^2 + 1, \omega^2 + 2$
$\omega^2 + \omega$
$\omega^2 + 2\omega$ and so on
$\omega^2 + \omega^2 = \omega^2 \cdot 2$ and so at length $\omega^3, \omega^4, \omega^5$

And endless series, after which ω^ω. Then there will be

---

matter. I must hurry on to other things". Likewise marked as omitted is the material on Bolzano, until about "For example there is no possible one-to-one relation in which every one of five things stands to one of three things". On that page 60 there is another note in the margin, "Skip to 68", indicating a further omission of the material up to the beginning of "Let us see then what all the different grades of *multitude* are". Display maths is inscribed in red ink in copy-text.]

$\omega, \omega^\omega, \omega^{\omega^\omega}, \omega^{\omega^{\omega^\omega}}$

Cantor gives no other way of writing these. But[9] suppose that instead of ω^ω we write $\omega(1, 2)$. For ω^3, ω^4 we write $\omega(1, 3), \omega(l, 4)$. For $\omega^\omega, \omega^{\omega^\omega}$, etc. we write $\omega(l, 1, 2), \omega(1, 1, 3)$. So that $(\omega^{\omega^{\omega^\omega}})^5 \cdot 6$ will be written $\omega(6, 5, 4)$. Then we shall at length get $\omega(1, 1, \omega)$ which [we] may write $\omega(1, 1, 1, 2)$. So we shall get $\omega(1, 1, 1, 1, 2), \omega(1, 1, 1, 1, 1, 2), \omega(1, 1, 1, 1, 1, 1, 2)$ and after all these we may put $\omega((1), 2)$.

Then we shall have at length $\omega((1), (1), 2)$ and so forth and then $\omega(((1))2)$ and so $\omega((((1)))2), \omega(((((1))))2)$ and after that we may put $\omega[2]$. In short, there will be no end to the need of new symbols. It all follows from two principles, first, every number has another number next after it. Second, every endless series of numbers accurately describable in any manner whatever has a number next after it.

Cantor calls such a series a *wohlgeordnet* series. But I propose, in admiration of the genius that has discovered it, to call it a *Cantorian succession*.

Cantor has conjectured that, given any collection whatever, any universe you please of independent quasi-individuals, there is a relation (and if one of course innumerable such) that in passing from relate to correlate and from correlate to correlates correlate, this relation arranges the whole universe in a Cantorian collection.

Indeed, Cantor puts forward this as more than a conjecture,—as a consequence of an unacknowledged law of thought. But the proposition has been received by mathematicians with the gravest doubt.

If I have time, I will say more about this very important question later; but at present I will only say this. The relation is *per se* possible. It only supposes that certain individuals shall have special one-sided connections. Now every ~~dyad of~~ two individuals have special one-sided connections.

Neither can any limitation of existence render this form of relation self-contradictory. Therefore, Cantor is right. This cannot be clear to you. It is the merest hint. But I might give several lectures elucidating this matter. I must hurry on to other things.

Having made it clear what a collection is, the next thing I have to do is to define *Multitude*. If we regard plural nouns, such as *men, horses, trolley-cars*, as names describing *sams men* meaning a sam of which any member is a man, etc. then the adjectives *two, ten, myriad, innumerable*, express qualities of collections of a certain class, and any quality of this class is a *multitude*. Of course, this is not a definition. It is only the framework for a definition. In order to define multitude,

---

9 [Del.:] [...] if we write the $\omega_1 \omega_2 \omega_3 \omega_4$ etc. we shall at length come to ω_ω and then there will be $\omega_{\omega_\omega} \omega_{\omega_{\omega_\omega}}$ and so on without end.

it is necessary to begin by analyzing our meaning when we say that one collection is greater than another. This analysis was first published in a posthumous work of Bernard Bolzano, which appeared in 1851 and has since been reprinted *Paradoxeien des Unendlichen*. Bolzano was a catholic theologian of Hungary and the author of a logic in four volumes. He was far too clear-headed to escape persecution in his position, you may be sure. Bolzano's definition amounts to this. If one *gath*, say that of the B's, is so related to another gath, say the A's, that there can be no one-to-one relation in which every B stands to an A, then, and only then, the gath of the B's is *greater* than that of the A's, and the latter is less than the former.

For example there is no possible one-to-one relation in which every one of five things stands to one of three things.

Then it follows from the proposition I proved a little while ago that one collection cannot be at once greater and less than another. It may however be neither greater no less.

On Bolzano's definition of greater and less can be based a definition of Multitude. That is the *multitude* of a collection will be defined as consisting in its being greater than those collections that is greater than and being less than those it is less than. This definition is at least a practicable one. It can be put to use in demonstrations. In that respect it is infinitely better than what Cantor puts forth as a definition in the style of Kant, who was a superb logical genius but who never studied logic and therefore sometimes commits grievous faults of logic. Namely Cantor tells us that if we think of a collection and then put out of view this and that element of our idea, what remains is multitude. But that is no definition at all. It is an experiment telling us, granting for the sake of argument that it obtains its aim, how to find and identify multitude. A definition ought to be an analysis of a conception useful in demonstration. The purely relative definition based on Bolzano's definition of greater and less does that. But it takes too narrow and formal a view of the matter. It fails to show the immense logical significance of *multitude*. It also makes it to be purely relative between one collection and others. That is not true.[10]

---

10 [Del.:] Bolzano's definition has the merit of accurately distinguishing the different multitudes; but it looks upon the matter in a purely formal way. It fails to bring out the great logical significance that there is in multitude. Let me give you my definition. A *multitude* is a quality of a *gath* consisting of the degree of indeterminacy with respect to forms of relationship of the members of the gath insofar as they are merely defined as such.

The multitude of a collection would be just what it is if there were no other collection in the world. Let me offer a definition. The multitude of a *gath*,—remember, it is a pure gath and the special Firstnesses or *flavors* of the characters of its units and sets of units is put out of the question,—consists in the complexity of the relations existing between its units in virtue of its peculiar character purely as a gath. But what is meant by the complexity of relations? What does it consist in? In order to bring this home to you I compare a greater collection with a smaller. Among the units of any gath of multitude five or more there is the relation shown in this graph [the same in **P.H.** on the right]:

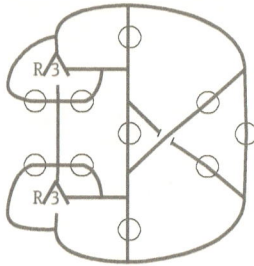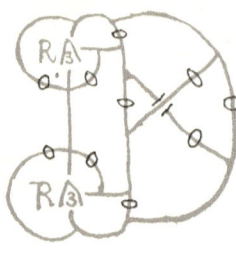

In no smaller gath is such a scheme possible. It is in the possession of such schemes that multitude consists. But every such scheme holds for every gath, except for the cuts that ligatures traverse. That is to say every form of relationship exists between the members of all gaths alike, except in respect to the identity and diversity of the correlates. We may go further. Every scheme holds for every gath if there are no cuts. Therefore multitude consists in the complexity of indefinite relationships between the units of a gath as such. But this complexity consists solely in the diversities of correlates. Hence the multitude of a gath consists in the othernesses among its units that the multitude permits. This is so obvious that it is truly wonderful that nobody has ever said it before this minute, when I say it to you. On the other hand, the smallness of a collection expressed by enclosing such a scheme in a cut, consists in the necessitation of identities.

Now some logicians look upon every proposition as expressing a description of identity. That may be a contorted conception of a proposition, but it is not false. Adopting it for the moment, we see that the smallness of a collection compels descriptions of identities that in a larger collection are not compelled. But this is as much as to say that propositions follow as necessary consequences from premisses relating to members of smaller collections when in a larger collection no such conclusion would follow. If one collection is larger than another this will in-

---

This means that if you compare a greater [end of deletion]

variably be true. From this point of view you see the immense logical significance of multitude.

For instance, suppose you want to find out who committed certain murders, who some Jack the Ripper is. Plainly if you can ~~ascertain~~ make sure that he belongs to a certain small collection of persons your investigation may be greatly helped. You have ways of reasoning open to you that you had not before. Indeed if you can reduce the multitude of that collection to *unity*, your problem is solved.

Let us see then what all the different grades of *multitude* are. The lowest is *unity* for *Nullity* is not a multitude. *Unity* is that quality of a collection which consists in the absence of all diversity of its members. Add a single diverse individual to a collection of one, and you get a larger collection. Let me prove this by graphs. In each graph which I write, the universe of discourse will be the members of the *gath* I am dealing with. Then nullity will be expressed by ⊖ which is of course the pseudograph. For a universe with nothing in it is absurd. I add one to this. That is I express that there is something such that if anything is different from this the graph of nullity holds for it. That is ⊖⊖ or ⊖ . It is the graph of *Unity*. I add a unit to this. That is I express that there is something other than what the graph of unity asserts, for all that is not this that graph holds. This gives 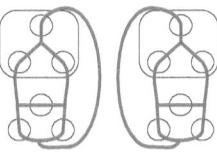 .

It is the graph of Twoness. I again add a unit, asserting that there is something else but that apart from this new unit the graph of Twoness holds. This gives

which is the graph of Threeness. In order to express that the gath taken as the universe is greater than a given number you must assert all the diversity that the graph of that number asserts and also the diversity it denies. That is, we must remove the large cut. Then in order to assert that our gath is not more than the number we must enclose the last graph in a cut. Thus to express that that *gath* in question is more than three we have the graph

To assert that it is not more than three we scribe

To assert that it is neither three nor more than three, that is that it is less than three, we scribe

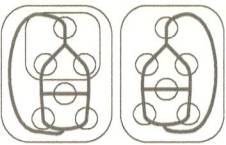

We now iterate the right-hand graph in the second cut of the left-hand one thus

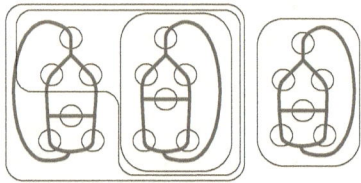

We extend the ligature by the rule of Iteration and join them inside three cuts by the Rule of Insertion. We thus get, after erasing the left-hand part,

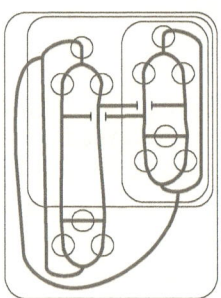

We now deiterate so as to get

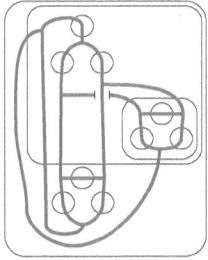

We erase within two enclosures giving

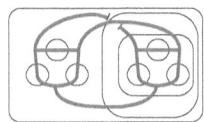

We remove the double cut getting

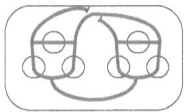

and finally we deiterate getting . This signifies that the gath is not more than two. That is we have proved by graphs that there is no multitude intermediate between 3 and 2.

I am sorry there is no time to go further into the graphical treatment, because it becomes more and more interesting as we go on, and the results are very important. For instance, in order to prove by graphs that the Syllogism of Transposed Quantity holds good for all finite multitudes, since it is evidently impossible to scribe the graphs of all ~~finite~~ enumerable multitudes it is necessary to scribe a graph which shall describe what a graph of any ~~finite~~ enumerable multitude is like. The idea of a graph of a graph is in itself interesting. But it becomes far more so when we see what the character of that graph must be. In that way it can be proved what is, I confess, pretty plain, without the graphs that the smallest multitude that is greater than all finite multitudes is the multitude of a ~~collection gath~~ sam for which there is *some* relation, and some individual unit of the *sam*, such that whatever quality there may be that is possessed by that particular *unit*, that quality being of such a nature that if it be possessed by any *unit*, say M, it is necessarily possessed by a *unit* in that particular relation to the unit M,—any quality I say of which these two propositions hold is necessarily possessed by every member of the collection. This is the property of the denumeral multitude which is made use of in Fermatian reasoning, a mode of reasoning that was invented by Pierre de Fermat, who was born in 1601 and died in 1666, and who was probably the greatest mathematical genius that ever lived. He also invented the mode of reasoning of the differential calculus. Fermatian reasoning has to be used in order to prove, rigidly *prove*, almost any proposition about whole numbers.

We call a collection of the members of which the Syllogism of Transposed Quantity necessarily holds an *enumerable* collection and one of which this is not true, or where there is a *Fermatian* relation, a denumeral collection—in German *abzählbar*. It follows that it is true of every *enumerable* collection.

All the whole numbers, properly so called, that is, all numbers of which our system of so called Arabic notation affords a definite symbol,—all the numbers up lo any one form an enumerable collection. But the entire collection of whole numbers capable of representation in that system is a collection not enumerable, but innumerable. And the particular single multitude of all the whole numbers, or of any such endless series of which all the members up to any member form an enumerable collection is called the *denumeral* collection, "abzählbar" in German. The denumeral multitude is a single multitude of the class of innumerable multitudes.

I was saying that all collections less than a given collection can be reasoned about in ways that greater collections cannot.[11] The mode of reasoning which is applicable to all enumerable collections, but to no others was first discovered, or first put into a logical treatise by Augustus De Morgan. He called it the syllogism of transposed quantity. Here is an example:

Every dollar borrowed requires a borrowed dollar to be paid out
No borrowed dollar paid out covers more than one dollar borrowed
∴ Every dollar borrowed has to be paid out.

Now I need not tell you that sundry business schemes are based on the idea of evading this conclusion. The notion is that dollars borrowed can partly be spent and can all be paid out by means of new dollars borrowed. It was at the great fire of 1835 in New York, if I remember rightly that this scheme first emerged. All the insurance companies declared themselves bankrupt except only the Etna of Hartford which advertised that it would pay all losses. It had not the money to do so; but its advertisement brought so many new policies that it did pay, and laid the foundations of a great future. Paying out of the increase of one's business is, of

---

11 [Here begins Lecture V, Vol. 2 (R 470, ms p. 78).]

course, fatal in the long run. And yet after all that is what we are all doing. A young man marries without having the money in the bank to support a dozen children. It is not in accordance with sound business; but the human race would progress little if they did not bank upon the future. But restricting myself to teaching logic, I limit myself to saying that the syllogism of transposed quantity is valid for every *enumerable* universe and for such alone. Here is a specimen of this reasoning applied to a question of philosophy:

No second of past time was immediately followed by two different seconds of past time.

But the last second of past time has no second of past time immediately following it.

Hence there must have been some second of past time that did not follow any second, that is time must have had an absolute beginning.

Whatever *definitely exists or has existed forms an enumerable collection, and the reasoning about time must be accepted* so long as you suppose the passage of seconds to be so many events that actually did take place. The past and the future stand upon an altogether different footing in this respect.

The entire collection of all whole numbers is not enumerable, since if we prefix *zero* to them, the resulting series has zero for its first, one for its second, two for its third member and so on, and has no capacity for diversity greater than that of the collection of whole numbers without the zero.

From a denumeral collection, such as that of the whole numbers, you may take away, not merely an enumerable part, but a denumeral part, equal to the whole, without thereby making the whole less.

Thus from all numbers, take away all the odd numbers, and the remaining collection of even numbers is equal to the whole, since corresponding to every number N there is a distinct and separate even number, its *double*. So likewise the multitude of powers of ten, or numbers written by a single figure 1, followed by zeros 1, 10, 100, 1000, 10 000, etc. is just as great as that of all whole numbers.

[– – –][12]

This series of multitudes is endless. That is there is no *largest*. But that does not in the least prevent there being a multitude greater than them all, just as the multitude of all whole numbers is greater than each whole number though there is no largest whole number. What then would come next? Collections of each of these multitudes is possible, notwithstanding that the least of the ultranumerables far exceeds the multitude of all the atoms in the universe. Still a collection

---

12 [Text of the notebook pages 86–114 (evenly paginated) is omitted; see NEM III, pp. 383–387 for the transcription.]

of any ultranumerable multitude not only is possible but once it ~~actually~~ *really* IS, in the sense in which any plural is apart from its having ever been thought of as such. Now, then, let collections of all these multitudes be aggregated. What sort of a collection will that be? It is easy to answer that question infallibly, though not so easy to comprehend the answer. The aggregate of those collections would falsify my proposition that the collection of collections of the M's is greater than the M's. It would not be so for such an aggregate. But that bas been proved to be necessarily true for all collections. Then such an aggregate would not be a collection. It would be *too many* to be a collection. How so? I haven't time to show you; but I will tell you. It is because you have then so crowded the field of possibility, that the units of that aggregate lose their individual identity. It ceases to be a collection because it is now a continuum.

I regret exceedingly that I cannot give you a lecture on continuity because my discoveries in that field are of quite a different order of importance than those about multitude. I foresee that I shall die without getting my say said, although I strain every nerve in my work. The world will have to wait, I fear, a good while for the explanation of continuity if my work is not made public.

In the few minutes that remain I give you one or two scraps; but they are perfectly useless without the whole. One might as well, when a battle-ship is wanted, bring a quarter of a pound of boiler-iron.

I have in these lectures no concern with metaphysics. That is not saying that what I say has no importance for metaphysics. But for present purposes I care not what the real nature of time and space may be. But what I mean by a truly continuous line is a line upon which there is room for any multitude of points whatsoever. Then the multitude or what corresponds to multitude of possible points,—exceeds all multitude. These points are pure possibilities. There is no such gath. On a continuous line there are not really any points at all. Two lines which intersect, intersect in a point. That is true for the intersection breaks the continuity and makes a point where there was none before the intersection.

[R 471][13] I have now said all I need say about rationals. It is plain that in order to consider analytic continuity I must take up irrationals. I shall not need to consider any other ordinal. In order to consider true continuity I must consider the doctrine of multitude; and it will be more convenient to consider multitude first and irrationals afterward.

But at the very threshold of multitude, I am met by a great logical difficulty. For the whole doctrine of Multitude is founded upon a conception of the relation

---

13 [The lecture draft loosely continues in R 471 (unpaginated, published in NEM III(1), pp. 389–391).]

of ~~being~~ one collection's being greater than another which is by no means the common-sense idea of that relation and which was first given to the world by Bernard Bolzano, who was at once a logician and a catholic theologian, a combination of specialties pretty sure to lead to grave personal inconvenience, as it did in his case and has done in most cases where the logician has attempted to advance his science. The common-sense idea of being greater than is that if one collection contains a member representative of every member of another collection and more beside it is greater than that other; and consequently an infinite collection is greater than itself. But Bolzano's definition does not allow any collection to be greater than itself, if ~~every member~~ there are two collections the A's and the B's and if there is any possible relation, r, in which every A stands to a B to which no other A is r, then, says Bolzano, we will say that the collection of A's is *not greater* than that of the B's. If there be no possible relation of that sort the collection of A's is greater than that of the B's. But, thereupon, there at once arises the question, why may not two collections each be greater than the other?[14] Now if that be possible, the idea of magnitude breaks down. There are logico-mathematicians who think it is possible.[15]

But there are others, Cantor among them, who think not. To me the notion that ~~there should be no possible relation in which every A's are left over~~ every one-to-one relation between A's and B's should leave over some A's unrelated to any B's ~~and at the sa~~ although there are B's to which no A's are related, and that there should be no relation whatever in which these unoccupied A's could stand to those unoccupied B's is contrary to the nature of *relation* and of *possibility*.

~~No doubt,~~ If by the *possible* you mean no more than that ~~whose contrary~~ which you do not know to be ~~true~~ false, then everything in mathematics not already demonstrated to be false is possible. No doubt, that logical situation is the basis of the conception of possibility. But so defining the possible a relation of the kind in question ~~exists unless~~ is possible until you ~~can demonstrate~~ have demonstrated that the collections of A's and of the B's have definite characters which ~~render demonstrate that there is~~ conflict with the supposition that there is such a relation.

But I think it would be more convenient to say not that everything in mathematics about which you happen to be ignorant is possible but that only that is possible of whose falsity no ~~definite~~ demonstration ever will be given. The question then would be whether ~~the A's can ever be prevented~~ anything can render it

---

14 [Del.:] To this an obvious reply is that if nothing *at all* be considered as a collection, as a mathematician would naturally consider it, that collection is greater than itself.
15 [See e.g. Peirce–Josiah Royce correspondence, and Peirce's letter to Royce on November 13, 1903 (LoF 3).]

demonstrable that the A's cannot be put into a one-to-one relation to B's except by showing that there are no B's for them to be in one to one relation to. Now it is plain there cannot be such a demonstration.

It cannot be said that this definition of possibility is satisfactory.

Not to trouble you with logical subtleties ~~any more than~~ where I can avoid it, let us say that an ~~statement~~ assertion is *general* if no amount of actual fact could certainly fulfill the truth of it. It says you *never will* find this falsified, ~~and nothing that has happened can exhaust the fut~~ the future never will have been exhausted. A general assertion leaves it to the hearer to take any instance he can. To say "all men are mortal" is as much to say, You can take any man you please, and experience will prove he is a liar.

Of an opposite kind are indefinite assertions, where the speaker does not fully commit himself as to what is the instance he is speaking of. As the ~~general~~ is that which no amount of fact can constitute true, so the *indefinite* is that which no amount of fact can constitute false; for its asserter only says ~~some time~~ the future will produce a case of such and such a kind.

Those two definitions will be found helpful in discussing the question whether or not two collections can be each greater than the other. But first we must answer the question, What is meant by a *collection*? I answer, It is a whole of ultimate parts which are *discrete* objects. What, then, is meant by discrete objects? I answer, objects which, whether it be in human power to distinguish them, are supposed to be in themselves of such a nature as to be susceptible of being so described that everyone is distinguished from every other. In other words by *discrete* objects are meant individuals of a system of *definite* individuals—Definite each in its own nature although we may not be able to define them singly.

That being the case, I assert that given any definite collection whatsoever, there is some general character which belongs to all its members and belongs to nothing else, a character common and peculiar to the members of that collection. For if it were not so, the collection would not be a definite collection. If it were not so, you could instance such a collection. "Very well" you would say, look there! Look where, I should naturally ask; and you would have either to describe the collection unmistakably when your description would involve a ~~general~~ common and peculiar character of its members, or you would have to *do* something bringing that collection and no other to my attention when you would *create* such a character. If you object that that character would not have existed before you had created it, I should reply that all general characters refer to what will take place in the future.

Now relations are characters of sets of objects; and therefore the proposition just enunciated includes the proposition that there is dyadic relation common and peculiar to all the pairs of objects of a collection.[16]

Then proof that $2^m > m$. p. 17

No maximum multitude.

We now go to irrationals. These are the limits of converging series of rationals. It is easily proved that every positive ~~real~~ irrational is expressible to any desired degree of approximation though never exactly by a secundal ~~decimal~~ fraction.

- The whole shows that all number rational or irrational can express nothing but order in a series
- Now take up Multitude and go through the whole doctrine
- Beginning with the doctrine of possibility
- Then return to irrationals
    - Show their multitude
    - Show how gaps can be made in the series
    - Show that it is pure assumption that there are no other points on a line.
- Now to the true nature [of] continuity
- Next take up Time
- Then ~~To[pical]~~ Singularities

Expressions of π and G in secundals.[17]

More zeros than ~~ones~~ units. (p. 16, 17)

The multitude of irrationals nothing but the first abnumerable multitude.

Analytic continuity thus differs from true continuity most markedly.

---

16 [A remark occurs here:] Now p. 23. The proof that two collections cannot be each greater than the other. [See R S-1, "Notes on the Theory of Multitude", notebook pages 1–57, on Peirce's extensive notes on these matters, written in July 1903.]

17 [The latter character is Charles Peirce's preferred design to notate the Napier–Euler constant e. Earlier he had introduced a slight modification to his father Benjamin Peirce's original proposal, which was used by James Mills Peirce in his works, to create two mirror-symmetric signs for π and for e, the "Neperian base" ("Note on Two New Symbols", *Mathematical Monthly* 1(5), 1859, p. 167–168). The first of the signs is to represent a modification of c (from "circumference") and the second a modification of b (from "base"). Charles Peirce introduced his further emendations, ∂ for "the ratio of the circumference to the diameter", and G for the "Napierian base", in his *Century Dictionary* entry on "Notation" (CD V:4022).]

more than the number we must enclose the last graph in a cut. Thus to express that that in question is ~~~~ ~~If we assert at once that~~ putts it all in a

more than three we have the graphs [graph] To assert that it is not more than three we scribe [graph] →

To assert that it is neither three nor more than three, that is that it is less than three, we scribe [graphs]. We now iterate the right hand graph in the second cut of the left hand one thus

[graphs]

We extend the ligature by the rule of Iteration & join them inside 3 cuts by the Rule of Insertion. We thus get after erasing the left hand parts

[A holograph page, crossed out (Harvard Peirce Papers, R 469).]

40 On the Simplest Branch of Mathematics, Dyadics

[Copy-text of the first version is R 2 and R 511, and of the second version R 3 and R 512. The title is from the longest, five-page segment of R 2; its variations are "On the Simplest Branch of Mathematics" (R 2, R 512, ms pages SM 1–6) and "On Dyadics: the Simplest Possible Mathematics" (R 3, ms pages D1–D2 and R 511 ms pages D3–D7).] These 2 + 2 interlocking segments included in the present selection are on the topic of "Dyadics", likely to have been written shortly prior to the preparations of the final draft of the fifth lecture (R 469–R 470), possibly as late as in early December but before December 6. The topics are substantially those characterising the fifth lecture, which makes a direct reference to the set of "independent hypotheses" that the "theory of graphs of graphs rests upon": "those which relate to physical possibilities and necessities and those which relate to permissions and prohibitions". In the fifth lecture, Peirce tells hypotheses related to these physical modalities to be "about thirty in number", "all expressible in alpha and beta graphs", while the class of hypotheses that relates to permissions and prohibitions "do not much exceed half a dozen". The "Dyadics" is thus also connected both to (i) the printed *Syllabus* that included the first part of R 508 (B1–B5) on the purely formal definition of the key notions of the theory of existential graphs, and (ii) that part of the copy-text for the printed version of the *Syllabus* that replaced the copy-text found in manuscript pages 150–154 of R 478 by the section "Rules of Transformation of Existential Graphs". This makes "Dyadics" closely related to Peirce's efforts to collate and compose the final set of copy-texts for the printing of the *Syllabus*, and could have been produced during November as well.

    Two features stand out in these previously unpublished lists of definitions. First, they aim at a purely mathematical definition, which is to say that these definition do not concern the interpretations of signs, that is, what the significations of the terms and notations of the theory of logic are. For if they did, the system would be the one that performs logical analysis, not the one that would best serve as the logic of the science of mathematics. The resulting piece is thus related to those "pure mathematical definitions" that Peirce presents not only in the additions to his *Syllabus* text (R 508) but also are present in *The Logical Tracts* (LoF 2/1). Second, each of the terms to be defined is considered to be part of the object-language vocabulary. Peirce carefully encloses them in double quotes, the practice which is implicitly assumed in his subsequent writings although not explicitly notated in the way here portrayed. From the surviving drafts we can recovered the first 35 hypotheses that Peirce proposed (the total of 34 hypotheses are proposed in the first, and apparently a little later version from R 2 and R 511). All these lists remain incomplete, ending where the "second section" of the Beta part on "hypotheses respecting permissions and prohibitions" was projected to continue. Several additional hypotheses, as well as three additional chapters (Peirce calls them "Memoirs") were in the pipeline, although Peirce did not appear to have written them down. Those follow-up hypotheses may also have pertained to the Gamma part of existential graphs, including the broken-cut notation, in the form in which it was planned to be exhibited by the time the fourth lecture would be over. Indeed Gamma is mentioned in a footnote, and one might well assume that these incomplete lists were meant to continue, during the fifth lecture (and time permitting), with an orated description or projection by stereopticon of the Gamma representations of Beta-permissible rules of transformation. That would involve presenting rather complex formulations of those definitions and hypotheses, involving logical modalities of necessity and possibility in the meta-language similar to the graphs-of-graphs theory that exists in many of his coeval drafts and pre-drafts of the lectures and their purported companions.

Written on the same regular linen ledger grid paper of 8 × 10½ as for instance R 31, R 508–R 512, R 539, R 540 and R 800, Peirce's study on the simplest, dyadic logic of mathematics is presented in plain language, closely related in content to the series of planned later additions and completions to the *Syllabus* text (see the next selection). The most likely date of completion of the "Dyadics" is November 1903, thus representing one of the follow-up segments to the initial submission of the first copy-text of the main segment of the *Syllabus* (R 478), which reached the Lowell Institute by the end of October. Since already by early November it became clear to Peirce that the printed version of the *Syllabus* could not include many of the graphs at all (it ended up having only two graphs as figures), Peirce might have thought this purely mathematical and linguistic account as an opportune workaround that could in fact be distributed to the audience in the printed form in full, and in an uncompromising form and length that would faithfully communicate all the desired fundamental hypotheses of the diagrammatic language of the Alpha, Beta and (what is missing here) the Gamma parts of the theory of graphs. Such account was needed in order to perform the analysis of the fundamental nature of mathematical truths, here given in the nomenclature of the "Pure Dyadics". By the time these studies were nearing their completion, perhaps well beyond mid-November, it was getting too late for Peirce to incorporate these planned additions into the copy-text of the printed material that was to accompany the lectures.

On Dyadics: the Simplest Possible Mathematics. First Memoir

First Division. Pure Dyadics and Existential Graphs. The Fundamental Hypotheses

The purpose of this series of memoirs are as follows:[1]

In the First of them, to lay the foundations of the simplest possible of all theories in Pure Mathematics, to furnish a system of diagrams for the study of it, and to deduce its main propositions and a method of working with it;

In the Second Memoir, to apply this pure mathematical theory to deductive logic, and to develop, by the aid of it, certain principles of logic that are required in the following studies;

In the Third Memoir, to use the results of the Second in order to clear up certain doubts hanging over the doctrine of Multitude, or "Cardinal Numbers";

In the Fourth Memoir, to consider the proper working definition of continuity and in what way problems in Topical Geometry can be solved.

Mathematics will here be understood to be the science which sets up hypotheses with a view to doing what it proceeds to do, namely, to deduce their con-

---

1 [Copy-text of this first item is R 3, pages D1–D2, and R 511, pages D3–D7, entitled "On Dyadics: the Simplest Possible Mathematics. First Memoir".]

sequences, and to study the methods of doing so. Pure Mathematics will be understood to be a kind of mathematics which, as far as possible, eliminates from its hypotheses all that does not concern the forms of deduction of consequences from them.

The technical terms used in the pure mathematical part of this memoir will be chosen with a view to their convenience in the principal application of the theory, namely, in its application to logic.

Chapter I. The Fundamental Hypotheses of Pure Dyadics

It will be convenient to divide Dyadics into three parts, to be called the Alpha Part, the Beta Part, and the Gamma Part. The Alpha part is confined to what is absolutely requisite to making any dyadics. The Beta part adds a conception necessary for the fuller development of dyads, even as a pure mathematical theory. The Gamma part introduces certain conceptions which become necessary for the full development of the subject, when it is applied to logic. This Gamma part will, therefore, not appear in the present chapter.

Hypothesis No. 1. Let it be supposed that there is an object called a *sheet* and that there is an intelligent agent called a *graphist* who can cause determinations of a sheet, called ~~graphs~~ "graph-replicas", if, and only if, these accord with two sets of general principles, namely, a certain set of general hypotheses concerning what is supposed to be actually true of a sheet and its determinations, and another set of general hypotheses describing what general sorts of modifications of the "graph-replicas" would be permissively possible under different general conditions.

Alpha Part: Section 1. Hypothesis respecting Physical Possibilities and Necessities.

Hypothesis No. 2. There is but one "sheet". Any determination of the "sheet" which has actually been made by the Graphist is an individual object, called a "graph-replica". (It will presently appear that certain other objects are likewise so called.) The act of *determination* production of a "graph-replica" may involve the production of one or more objects not considered to be determinations of the sheet, but to be individual objects of like nature with the " sheet", called "areas". (No. 3.) The sheet itself is called an "area"; but (No. 4) every "area" other than the "sheet" belongs to a "graph-replica", and (No. 5) to one only. Every "area" considered in the alpha part is called a "true area" and belongs to a "graph-replica" of a particular kind called as such an "enclosure". (No. 6) Every "enclosure" has an "area", and has (No. 7) only one. The "area" of which the "enclosure" is a determination is called its "place". Every "true area" is of the same nature as the "sheet" and it is physically possible that a determination can be produced upon it, precisely like any determination possible upon the sheet.

Hypothesis No. 8. For the more convenient statement of the relations of different "areas" and "graph-replicas" to one another, let it be supposed that there are certain abstractions termed "points" which have no other being than that which consists in the existence of those relations- Every "point" is in a relation to an area called being "upon" it, and most points (including all considered in the alpha part) are in this relation to only one "area"; and (No. 9) every "point" is in a relation to a "graph-replica" also called being "upon" it, provided we regard a non-determination of an "area" to any other "graph-replica" as a determination to a formal "graph-replica" termed a "blank". Although a "point" is a mere abstraction, yet it is to be conceived as of its essence that it is "upon" the "area" "upon" which it is; while it is only by a further determination that it comes to be "upon" this or that "graph-replica" (No. 10). Every "graph-replica" has at least one "point" "upon" it, and every alpha "graph-replica" has innumerable "points". (No. 11) Every "area" has at least one "point' upon it; and (No. 12) every "true area" has a "point" "upon" it that is "upon" a "blank". (No. 13) All "points" that are "upon" the same "graph-replica" are "upon" the same "area", and the "graph-replica" itself may be said to be "upon" that "area", which is termed the "place" of the "graph-replica". Every "graph-replica" every "point" "upon" of which is "upon" another "graph-replica" may be termed a "part" of the latter. (No. 14) There is no limit to the multitude of "graph-replicas" having no common "part" which may be "upon" any "true area".

Hypothesis No. 15. Let it be supposed that any two "graph-replicas" "upon" the same "area" constitute one "graph-replica" "upon" that "area"; and let the first two be called "components" of the last, and the last the "compound of the first two. Consequently, any alpha "graph-replica" may be regarded as having a "blank" as a "component" of it.

Alpha Part. Section 2. Hypotheses respecting permissions and prohibitions

Hypothesis No. 16. A "graph-replica" is an individual object actually "upon" some "area". A permission, as merely rendering something possible, in some sense, cannot refer immediately to an individual; since an individual is an actual subject of force. A permission, therefore, or a prohibition refers to a general class of possible "graph-replicas"; and any one of the class is permitted to be upon an "area" when any one is so permitted. Let two "graph-replicas" of possible "graph-replicas" such that "upon" whatever "area" either is permitted to be, the other is permitted to be, be said to be "equivalent" to one another. Let two "graph-replicas" which are such that, disregarding the "points" that are "upon" them (and consequently the "areas" that the "graph-replicas" are "upon"), are in themselves alike in every respect which under any circumstances affects a permission (and are thus necessarily "equivalent" to one another), be said to be "replicas" of the same "graph"; while two "graph-replicas" which, though they be "equivalent", nevertheless, even though the difference of the "points" that are "upon" them be disregarded, differ in a respect which under some circumstances affects a permission, be said to be "replicas" of different "graphs". (So that every "graph-replica" is a "replica" of one "graph" and of one only.)

Hypothesis No. 17. Let it be supposed that every "graph-replica" actually having any "point" "upon" it is permitted to exist and to have that "point' upon it, whether by virtue of some of the general hypotheses, or owing to some special fact or truth, or by a tentative permission recognized as having that character.

Hypothesis No. 18. Let it be supposed that all "points" "upon" any one "area" in the same relation to all permissions, except so far as they may be "upon" "graph-replicas" other than "blanks"; so that, while a permission for two "points" to be "upon" "replicas" of two "graphs" will not necessarily be a permission for the same "point" to be "upon" "replicas" of those "graphs", nor *vice versa*, yet a permission in regard to any set of "points" is *ipso facto* a permission with regard to any other set of "points" "upon" the same "areas" and "upon" "replicas" of exactly the same "graphs".

Hypothesis No. 19. Let it be supposed that if, in the existing state of permissions, it is permitted that a "point" "upon" the "sheet" should be "upon" an "enclosure" "upon" whose "area", besides "blanks" and possible "enclosures", there is only a "graph-replica", G, which may be "compound", then if, in this state of permissions, it is permitted that a "replica" "equivalent" to G should be "upon" the "sheet", it is likewise permitted that there should be "upon" the "sheet" some "equivalent" of a "graph-replica" which is alone (except for "blanks") "upon" the "area" of some "enclosure" that is "upon" the same "area" as G.

Hypothesis No. 20. Let it be supposed that in case it is not permitted that any "point" upon the "sheet" should be "upon" a ' 'replica" of a given "graph", G, then it is permitted that a "point" on the "sheet" should be "upon" an "enclosure" upon whose "area" there is no "point" that is not either "upon" a "blank" or "upon" a "replica" of G.

Hypothesis No. 21. Let it be supposed that there is a "graph" of which a "replica" would conform to all the Hypotheses Nos. 2 to 15, yet which is not permitted to have a "replica" "upon" the "sheet".

Beta Part: Section 1. Hypotheses respecting Physical Possibilities and Necessities

Hypothesis No. 22. Let it be supposed that there are certain objects called "lexis-replicas",[2] each of which is a "graph-replica", but the determination of each of which creates certain objects of the general nature of "areas", in that they are not "graph-replicas" but are capable of being determined to "graph-replicas, these objects being called the "hooks" of the "lexis-replica", (No. 23) each "hook" belonging to a single "lexis-replica", (No. 24) only one "point" being "upon" one "hook", and (No. 25) different "hooks" having, in all cases, different "points" upon them. Indeed, the "hooks", as having a being consisting in a possibility of determination, may very well [be] regarded as identical with the "points" "upon" them, since these "points" are of the nature of possibilities capable of determination to existence. But let it be supposed (No. 26) that a "hook" differs from the "area" of an "enclosure" in that a "hook" is "upon" the "place" of the "lexis-replica" to which it belongs. Let an object of the general nature of an "area", as being a subject of determination and not a result of determination, but which differs from a "true area" in that there is but a single "point" "upon" it, and also in that it is "upon" a "true area" of which that object which creates it is or involves it is itself a determination, be called a "quasi-area".

Hypothesis No. 27. Let it be supposed that there is a class of objects called "lines", each of which is a "lexis-replica" of two "hooks" but having two remarkable properties, as follows. First, in whatever dyadic relation every "point" that is "upon" a "line" stands to the one or the other of two individual objects, if one "point" "upon" the "line" stands in that relation to one of those two individuals, while another "point" "upon" the line stands in the same relation to the other of the two, then there must be a third "point" "upon" the "line" which stands in the same relation to them both. Secondly, (No. 28), every "line" has two "points", A and Z, upon it, called its "ends", that are (or are "upon") its "hooks"; and these "hooks" have the property that any third "point", M, that is "upon" the "line", there is a "line" whose "hooks" (or the "points" "upon" them) are M and A (whence there is also a line whose "ends", or "hooks", and M and Z), these lines being such (No. 29) that no other "point" is at once upon them both. Let the "end" of a "line" which "end" is either not the sole "point" that is "upon" both of two "lines" or else is "upon" these lines at once, and is the sole "point" that is "upon" any two of them, be termed a "terminal" of every "line" that it is "upon"; and let a line both whose "ends" or "hooks" are "terminals" be termed an "entire line". Then, (No. 30) let it be supposed that every "line" is such that all the "points"

---

[2] ["Lexis-replica" is here a new term, called the "dot" in the earlier draft below. Copy-text of the present section from R 511 apparently represents the final surviving draft of the relevant texts.]

"upon" it are "upon" one "entire line". Let any "graph-replica" which has "upon" it all the "point" of every "entire line" of which two are "upon" it be termed an "entire graph-replica". Then, (No. 31) let it be supposed that if it be true of any "point" "upon" an "entire line" that it is "upon" any other "entire graph", this is true of a "terminal" of that "entire line"; and (No. 32) let it be supposed that every "entire line" is an "entire graph-replica".

Hypothesis No. 33. Let it be supposed that "upon" the "area" of any enclosure there may be any multitude of "entire-lines" of each of which a "terminal" shall not only be "upon" that "area" of that "enclosure" but also "upon" its "place", so that these "terminals" shall be "hooks" of the "enclosure" giving it the properties of a "lexis-replica", except that the "hooks" of a "lexis-replica" are fixed in number and nature.

Hypothesis No. 34. Let it be supposed that one "point" can be "upon" two "graph-replicas" only by being at once the "terminal" of an "entire-line" and a "hook" of a "lexis-replica" or of an "enclosure". [end]

On the Simplest Branch of Mathematics, Dyadics [Variant]

The purposes of this memoir are, first, to ~~develope~~ lay the foundations of the simplest possible theory of pure mathematics, to furnish a system of diagrams for the study of it, and to deduce some of its main propositions; second, to apply this theory to deductive logic, and to draw certain corollaries, not strictly mathematical but logically necessary; third, to use these principles to clear up certain doubts in the theory of Multitude, or "Cardinal Numbers"; fourth, to present some reflections resulting from these studies concerning the proper method of investigating topical geometry.[3]

The Alpha Part. First Section. Hypotheses as to Definitions and as to Physical Necessities

1. Let us suppose that there is something called a "sheet".
2. Let us suppose that there is but one "sheet".
3. Let us suppose that the sheet is an individual of a class of objects, called "areas".

---

[3] [Copy-text of this section is R 2 and R 511, which Peirce paginated as SM 1–6.]

4. Let us suppose that there is a class of possible objects called "points" and of relation, called "being upon"; and let us suppose that, given any "area" whatever, it is always physically possible that there should be a "point" "upon" it other than any "point" already "upon" it.
5. Let us suppose it physically impossible that a "point" should be "upon" two different "areas", except in the case of Hypothesis No. 34.
6. Let us suppose that there is a class of objects called "graph-replicas", and that "upon" any "graph-replica" it is physically possible that there should be a "point".
7. Let us suppose that it is physically impossible that any "point" should be "upon" a "graph-replica" without being "upon" some "area".
8. Let us suppose that if two "points" are "upon" the same "graph-replica", then "upon" whatever "area" one of these "points" is, the other is likewise, by physical necessity, except in the case of hypothesis No. 34.
9. Let us suppose that there is a certain class of objects called "blanks", that every "blank" is a "graph-replica", and that "upon" every "area" it is physically possible that there should be a "point" which is upon a "blank".
10. Let us suppose that if "upon" a "graph-replica", A, any "point" that there might be would by physical necessity be "upon" a given "area", and if "upon" a second "graph-replica", B, any "point" that there might be would by physical necessity be "upon" the same "area", then by definitional necessity, there would be a "graph-replica", C, such that any "point" whatever would either be neither "upon" A, nor B, nor C, or else it would be "upon" A and ' "upon" C. (But were there not "points" upon A and B that were "upon" the same "area", this should not be true, by Hypothesis 7.)
11. Let us suppose that there is a certain class of objects called "enclosures" and that every "enclosure" is a "graph", that there is a certain relation called "has belonging to it", that every "enclosure" has an "area" "belonging" to it, that (12) every area except the sheet "belongs to" some "enclosure", that (13) no two different "enclosures" have the same "area" belonging to them, and (14) that no two different "areas" "belong to" the same "enclosure". ~~Let it further be supposed (15) that if any "point" is at once "upon" an "enclosure" and "upon" another "graph-replica", then~~
15. Let us further suppose that there is a relation called being "within", that if a "point" could be at once "upon" an "enclosure" and "upon" an area, then that enclosure would be "within" any "enclosure" to which that "area" might belong, and that whatever "enclosure" is "within" any "enclosure" is "within" every "enclosure" that the latter "enclosure" is "within", and that no "enclosure" is "within" another unless necessitated to be so by this requirement; and that (16) no "enclosure" is "within" itself.

Second section. Hypotheses respecting Permissions of Transformation

17. Let us suppose that whenever it is permitted that a "graph-replica" should be so circumstanced that a "point" "upon" it would by physical necessity be "upon" the sheet, then it is permitted that the state of things should be such that it would be physically impossible for a "point" to be "upon" the "sheet" without being either "upon" a "blank" or "upon" that "graph-replica".
18. Let us suppose that whenever it would be permitted that a "graph-replica", A, should be so circumstanced that a "point" "upon" it could be "upon" the "sheet", while the same thing is permitted concerning a "graph-replica", B, then it is permitted that both A and B should be so circumstanced that a "point" "upon" A could be "upon" the "sheet", and at the same time a "point" "upon" B could be "upon" the "sheet".
19. Let us suppose that there is a reciprocal relation of being "equivalent" between certain pairs of "graph-replicas", such that a permission ~~to place one in certain~~ in reference to either is *ipso facto* a like permission in reference to the other, or would be so, were that which is permitted physically possible.
20. Let us suppose that it is never at once permitted that a "graph-replica" should be so circumstanced that a "point" could at once be "upon" it and "upon" the "sheet" and that an "equivalent" "graph-replica" should be so circumstanced that a "point" could at once be upon it and "upon" an "area" "belonging" to an "enclosure" so circumstanced that a "point" could at once be "upon" it and be "upon" the "sheet".
21. Let us suppose that in every case one or other of two things is permitted (could we know which), namely, either that a "graph-replica" ~~similar to any~~ "equivalent" to any definite possible "graph-replica" should be so circumstanced that a "point" could at once be "upon" it and "upon" the "sheet", or else that an "equivalent" "graph-replica" should be so circumstanced that a "point" could be at once "upon" it and "upon" an "area" "belonging" to an "enclosure" so circumstanced that a "point" could at once be "upon" it and "upon" the "sheet".
22. Let us suppose that it would be absurd to suppose it permitted to put any "graph-replica" we pleased in such circumstances that a "point" could be at once "upon" it and "upon" the "sheet".

The Beta Part. First Section. Hypotheses respecting definitions and physical necessities

23. Let us suppose that there is a class of objects called "dots", such that any "dot" is a "graph", while (24) it is physically impossible that two different "points" should be "upon" the same "dot".
25. Let it be supposed that there is a class of objects called "lines", each of which is a "graph", and that each "line" has these two physical properties. First, (26) if there be any dyadic relation in which every "point" that is "upon" a "line" stands to one or other of two individual objects, and if some "point" that is "upon" the "line" stands in this relation to one of these and some "point" "upon" the "line" stands in the same relation to the other, then there is some "point" "upon" the line that stands in this relation to both individuals. Secondly, (27), "upon" every "line" there are two different "points", A and Z, called its "ends", whose property is that, taking any "point", M that is "upon" the "line", there is a "line" whose "ends" are M and A, whence also there is a line whose "ends" are M and Z, and every "point" that is "upon" the first "line" is either "upon" the "line" whose "ends" are M and A or is "upon" the "line" whose "ends" are M and Z. (Whence, by (26), the "point" M is "upon" both the last two "lines".)
28. Let it be supposed that if there is a "graph-replica", X, such that every "point" that is "upon" it is "upon" a certain "enclosure", then the "graph-replica" X can neither be a "line" nor any other kind of "graph-replica" than a "dot".
29. Let us suppose that there is a class of objects called "spots", each of which is a "graph-replica" and is such that if there be any "graph-replica", X, other than the "spot" itself, such that any "point" that is "upon" X is "upon" a "spot", then the "graph-replica", X, can only be a "dot". In this respect, a "spot" agrees with an "enclosure"; but let it be further supposed (30) that a "point" which is at once "upon" a "dot" and "upon" a "spot" is one or another of at most three "points" "upon" the "spot" called its "hooks"; and let it be further supposed (31) that a "spot" has no "area" "belonging to it".
32. Let it be supposed that every "end" of a "line", ~~besides being~~[4] which is an "end" of every "line" that it is "upon" (such an "end" that is only an "end" being called a "terminal" of a "line" both of whose "ends" are of this character) is also either a "hook" of a "spot", or is "upon" an "enclosure", or is "upon" a "blank", or is "upon" a "dot".

---

[4] [The text of R 2 ends here. The continuation is from R 512, ms p. SM 6.]

33. Let it be supposed that no "point" "upon" a "line" except a "terminal" can be a "hook" of a "spot", or can be "upon" an "enclosure", or can be "upon" three "lines" "upon" all three of which there is no other "point".
34. Let it be supposed that a "point" "upon" an "enclosure" may be a "terminal" of a "line" such that every other "point" "upon" it is "upon" the "area" of that "enclosure". The best way of reconciling this hypothesis with Hypotheses Nos 5, 8, and ___ , is to regard such a "terminal" as not being, strictly speaking, "upon" the "enclosure", but to be trimmed with an "equivalent" "dot" that is "upon" the "enclosure".
35. Let it be supposed that "terminals" of three different "lines" may be one "point" provided that that "point" is "upon" a peculiar kind of "dot" called a "dot of teridentity".

Second Section. Hypotheses respecting Permissions and Prohibitions

36. [end][5]

---

5 [The writing of this fragment from R 512 is abandoned here at the beginning of the item numbered 36.]

41 A Syllabus of certain Topics of Logic

[Copy-text is R 478, plus pages from R 478(s), R 508 and R 509. On the manuscript cover "Syllabus of a course of Lectures at the Lowell Institute beginning 1903 Nov. 23. On Some Topics of Logics. By Mr. C. S. Peirce".] The bulk of the current selection comes from Peirce's long manuscript of R 478, the text that Peirce intended as the official syllabus for the course of lectures submitted to the printer with several later intended revisions, additions and replacements (R 508–510, R 539, R 540, R 792, R 800). The selection begins with the fourth and the last section of the final draft, on existential graphs, and it includes material that Peirce was unable either to cover in his lectures or select for inclusion in the printed, 23-page version. The transcription is mostly drawn from R 478 (the continuous segment of manuscript pages 137–168 plus several variant leaves), with significant inclusions from the sheets located in folders R 508 and R 509. The text in the appendix, which is paginated in R 478 as "Syllabus 2–23" (the first ms page is missing) and which Peirce inscribed in blue ink, consists of Peirce's written rejoinders to the topics that are found in William James's syllabus of "Problems of Philosophy 3".

The shortage of funds forced Peirce to select only severely truncated excerpts from the long manuscript to be typed and printed. Important material had to be omitted at the printing stage, or was planned to be superseded by new material that nevertheless remained not completed, including (i) the section on "archegetic rules of transformation", (ii) the presentation of such archegetic codes for Alpha and Beta graphs, (iii) modifications of those rules to suit the purposes of Gamma graphs, (iv) the section "Remark on the Gamma Rims" in full, (v) the list of rules that can be deduced from the archegetic rules, and (vi) the presentation of the Gamma part on the graphs of graphs. These omissions, all of which have remained previously unpublished, are included in the present selection, with complete sets of alternative variants and drafts.

The material that made it into the printed extract of the text is indicated in the textual annotations.

Preface.[1]

This syllabus has for its object to supplement a course of eight lectures to be delivered at the Lowell Institute, and by some others not easily carried away from one hearing. It is intended to be a help to those who wish seriously to study the subject, and to show others what the style of thought is that is required in such study. Like the lectures themselves, this syllabus is intended chiefly to convey results that have never appeared in print; and much is omitted because it can be found elsewhere.

Milford, Pa., 1903 Nov. I.

Preface[2]

This syllabus has for its object to supplement a course of eight lectures to be delivered in 1903 at the Lowell Institute. Everything is excluded which can easily be carried away from a hearing of the lectures, as well as everything which has been satisfactorily treated in print. For, like the lectures themselves, the matter of this syllabus is entirely new, except so far as restatements of old matter are necessary in setting forth the new matter. Milford, Pa. 1903 Nov. 1.

Contents.

I. Classification of the Sciences of Discovery.
II. The ethics of Terminology.
III. Some leading conceptions of logic.
IV. Conventions and Rules of Existential Graphs.

---

1 [This is the preface from the printed version of the *Syllabus*. The draft preface and the draft Table of Contents reads as follows:] **Preface.** The purpose of this syllabus is to furnish printed statements of some points not easily carried away from an oral delivery. It includes some matters which there will not be time to state in the lectures, and omits much that will be given in the lectures. **Contents.** I. A ~~Natural~~ Classification of the Sciences. II. The Ethics of Scientific Terminology. III. ~~Phenomenology. The Three Categories.~~ Some ~~Logical~~ Definitions and Explanations. IV. Existential Graphs: the Conventions of the System and its Fundamental Rules; with a few deduced rules. V. Sketch of Geometry. VI. Principles of Probability. VII. The Two Rules of Induction. VIII. The Principle [of] Abduction.

2 [This is the preface of the pre-draft copy of R 478.]

Syllabus
137

Existential Graphs Vol 4
The Conventions.
Alpha Part

Convention № I. ¶1. These Conventions are *supposed to be* mutual understandings between two persons; a *Graphist*, who expresses propositions according to the system of expression called that of *Existential Graphs*, and an *Interpreter*, who interprets those propositions and accepts them without dispute.

A *graph* is the propositional expression in the System of Existential Graphs of any *possible* state of the universe. It is a Symbol and, as such, general, and is accordingly to be distinguished from a graph-replica. A graph remains such though not actually asserted. An expression, *according to* the conventions of this system, of an impossible state of things (anything with what is taken for granted at the outset or has been asserted by the graphist) is not a graph, but is

[margin notes:]
Convention № Zero. Negative of these diagrams that may be varied at will. This convention is numbered zero, because it is an unfulfilled expression of the conventions to have a given character, or by previous conventions of language

is not in all agreements.

[A holograph page of the beginning of page 15 of the printed *Syllabus* (Harvard Peirce Papers, R 478, ms p. 137).]

EXISTENTIAL GRAPHS.

THE CONVENTIONS.

Alpha Part.

Convention No. Zero. Any feature of these diagrams that is not expressly or by previous conventions of languages required by the conventions to have a given character may be varied at will. This "convention" is numbered zero, because it is understood in all agreements.

Convention No. I. ¶ 1. These Conventions are supposed to be mutual understandings between two persons: a *Graphist*, who expresses propositions according to the system of expression called that of *Existential Graphs*, and an *Interpreter*, who interprets those propositions and accepts them without dispute.

A *graph* is the propositional expression in the System of Existential Graphs of any possible state of the universe. It is a Symbol, and, as such, general, and is accordingly to be distinguished from a *graph-replica*. A graph remains such though not actually asserted. An expression, according to the conventions of this system, of an impossible state of things (conflicting with what is taken for granted at the outset or has been asserted by the graphist) is not a graph, but is termed *The pseudograph*, all such expressions being equivalent in their absurdity.

¶ 2. It is agreed that a certain sheet, or blackboard, shall, under the name of *The Sheet of Assertion*, be considered as representing the universe of discourse, and as asserting whatever is taken for granted between the graphist and the interpreter to be true of that universe. The sheet of assertion is, therefore, a graph. Certain parts of the sheet, which may be severed from the rest, will not be regarded as any part of it.

¶ 3. The graphist may place replicas of graphs upon the sheet of assertion; but this act, called *scribing* a graph on the sheet of assertion, shall be understood to constitute the assertion of the truth of the graph scribed. [Since by ¶ 1 the conventions are only "supposed to be" agreed to, the assertions are mere pretence in studying logic. Still they may be regarded as actual assertions con-

Existential Graphs

The Conventions

Alpha Part.

Convention No. Zero.[3] Any feature of these diagrams that is not expressly or by previous conventions of languages required by the conventions to have a given character may be varied at will. This "convention" is numbered zero, because it is understood in all agreements.

Convention No. I. ¶ 1. These Conventions are supposed to be mutual understandings between two persons; a *Graphist*, who expresses propositions according to the system of expression called that of *Existential Graphs*, and an *Interpreter*, who interprets those propositions and accepts them without dispute.

A *graph* is the propositional expression in the System of Existential Graphs of any possible state of the universe. It is a Symbol and, as such, general, and is accordingly to be distinguished from a *graph-replica*. A graph remains such though not actually asserted. An expression, according to the conventions of this system, of an impossible state of things (violating conflicting with what is taken for granted at the outset or has been asserted by the graphist) is not a graph, but is termed *the pseudograph*, all such expressions being equivalent in their absurdity.

¶ 2. It is agreed that a certain sheet, or blackboard, shall, under the name of *the Sheet of Assertion*, be considered as representing the universe of discourse, and as asserting whatever is taken for granted between the graphist and the interpreter to be true of that universe. The sheet of assertion is, therefore, a graph. Certain parts of the sheet, which may be severed from the rest, will not be regarded as any part of it.

¶ 3. The graphist may place replicas of graphs upon the sheet of assertion; but this act, called *scribing* a graph on the sheet of assertion, shall be understood to constitute the assertion of the truth of the graph scribed. (Since by ¶ 1 the conventions are only "supposed to be" agreed to, the assertions are mere pretence in studying logic. Still they may be regarded as actual assertions concerning a fictitious universe.) 'Assertion' is not defined; but it is supposed to be permitted to scribe some graphs and not others.

Corollary. Not only is the sheet itself a graph, but so likewise is the sheet together with the graph scribed upon it. But if the sheet be blank, this *blank*, whose existence consists in the absence of any scribed graph, is itself a graph.

---

3 [Printed in the *Syllabus* was the section on conventions, until "Rules of Transformation of Existential Graphs".]

Convention No. II. ¶ 1. A graph-replica on the sheet of assertion having no scribed connection with any other graph-replica that may be scribed on the sheet shall, as long as it is ~~scribed, no~~ on the sheet of assertion in any way, make the same assertion, regardless of what other replicas may be upon the sheet.

The graph which consists of all the graphs on the sheet of assertion, or which consists of all that are on any one area severed from the sheet, shall be termed the *entire* graph of the sheet of assertion or of that area, as the case may be. Any part of the entire graph which is itself a graph shall be termed a *partial* graph of the sheet or of the area on which it is.

Corollaries. Two graphs scribed on the sheet are, both of them, asserted, and any entire graph implies the truth of all its partial graphs. Every blank part of the sheet is a partial graph.

Convention No. III. ¶ 1. By a *Cut* shall be understood to mean a self-returning linear separation (naturally represented by a fine-drawn or peculiarly colored line) which severs all that it encloses from the sheet of assertion on which it stands itself, or from any other area on which it stands itself. The whole space within the cut (but not comprising the cut itself) shall be termed the *area* of the cut. Though the area of the cut is no part of the sheet of assertion, yet the cut together with its area and all that is on it, conceived as so severed from the sheet, shall, under the name of the *enclosure* of the cut, be considered as on the sheet of assertion or as on such other area as the cut may stand upon. Two cuts cannot intersect one another, but a cut may exist on any area whatever. Any graph which is unenclosed or is enclosed within an even number of cuts shall be said to be *evenly enclosed*; and any graph which is within an odd number of cuts shall be said to be *oddly enclosed*. A cut is not a graph; but an enclosure is a graph. The sheet or other area on which a cut stands shall be called the *place* of the cut.

A pair of cuts, one within the other but not within any other cut that that other is not within, shall be called a *scroll*. The outer cut of the pair shall be called the *outloop*, the inner cut the *inloop*, of the scroll. The area of the inloop shall be termed the *inner close* of the scroll; the area of the outloop, *excluding the enclosure of the inloop* (and not merely its area), shall be termed the *outer close* of the scroll.

The enclosure of a scroll (that is, the enclosure of the outer cut of the pair) shall be understood to be a graph having such a meaning that if it were to stand on the sheet of assertion, it would assert *de inesse* that if the entire graph in its outer close is true, then the entire graph in its inner close is true. No graph can be scribed across a cut, in any way; although an enclosure ~~may be part of graph~~ is a graph.

(A conditional proposition *de inesse* considers only the existing state of things, and is, therefore, false only in case the consequent is false while the antecedent is true. If the antecedent is false, or if the consequent is true, the conditional *de inesse* is true.)

¶ 2. The filling[4] up of any entire area with whatever writing material (ink, chalk, etc.) may be used shall be termed *obliterating* that area, and shall be understood to be an expression of the pseudograph on that area.

Corollary. Since an obliterated area may be made indefinitely small, a single cut will have the effect of denying the entire graph in its area. For to say that if a given proposition is true, everything is true, is equivalent to denying that proposition.

Beta Part

Convention No. IV. ¶ 1. The expression of a rheme in the system of existential graphs, as simple, that is without any expression, according to these conventions, of the analysis of its signification, and ~~so that the expression occupies~~ such as to occupy a superficial portion of the sheet or of any area shall be termed a *spot*. The word 'spot' is to be used in the sense of a *replica*; and when it is desired to speak of the symbol of which it is the replica, this shall be termed a *spot-graph*. On the periphery of every spot, a certain place shall be appropriated to each blank of the rheme; and such a place shall be called a *hook* of the spot. No spot can be scribed except wholly in some ~~one~~ inner areas.[5]

¶ 2. A heavy *dot* ~~placed~~ scribed at the hook of a spot shall be understood as filling the corresponding blank of the rheme of the spot with an indefinite sign of an individual, so that when there is a ~~spot~~ dot attached to every hook, the result shall be a proposition which is particular in respect to every subject.

Convention No. V. ¶ 1. Every heavily marked point, whether isolated, the extremity of a heavy line, or at a furcation of a heavy line, shall denote a single individual, without in itself indicating what individual it is.

¶ 2. A heavily marked line without any sort of interruption (though its extremity may coincide with a point otherwise marked) shall, under the name of *a line of identity*, be a graph, subject to all the conventions relating to graphs, and asserting precisely the identity of the individuals denoted by its extremities.

Corollaries. It follows that no line of identity can cross a cut.

Also, a point upon which three lines of identity abut is a graph expressing the relation of ~~tri-iden~~ *teridentity*.

---

4 [Corrected from "fitting" by Peirce in the copies of R 478 and of R 1600 (Nos. 1 and 2).]
5 [The printed version reads "…wholly in some area", which is printer's error uncorrected by Peirce in the offprints.]

¶ 3. A heavily marked point may be on a cut; and such a point shall be interpreted as lying in the place of the cut and at the same time as denoting an individual identical with the individual denoted by the extremity of a line of identity on the area of the cut and abutting upon the marked point on the cut. Thus, in

Fig. 10   [P.H.]

~~the figure~~ Fig. 10, if we refer to the individual denoted by the point where the two lines meet on the cut, as X, the ~~meanin~~ assertion is, "Some individual, X, of the universe is a man, and nothing is at once mortal and identical with X"; i.e., some man is not mortal.⁶ So in ~~the second figure~~ Fig. 11, if X and Y are the individuals denoted by the points on the [inner]⁷ cut, the interpretation is,

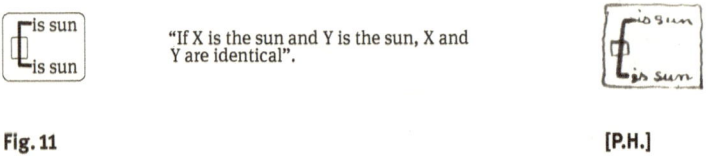

Fig. 11   [P.H.]

A collection composed of any line of identity together with all others that are connected with it directly or through still others is termed a *ligature*. Thus ligatures often cross cuts, and in that case, are not graphs.

Convention No. VI. ¶ 1. A ~~sign~~ symbol for a single individual, which individual is more than once referred to, but is not identified as the object of a proper name, shall be termed a *Selective*. The capital letters may be used as selectives, and may be made to abut upon the hooks of spots. Any ~~line junct~~ ligature may be replaced by replicas of one selective placed at every hook and also in the outermost area that it enters. In the interpretation, it is necessary to refer to the outermost replica of each selective first, and generally to proceed in the interpretation from the outside to the inside of all cuts.

---

6 [The original figures were cut out in the copy and replaced by these two printer-friendly renderings with captions renumbered as Fig. 10 and Fig. 11. The renumbering took place during or after Peirce's composition of the prospected additional syllabus material on dyadic relations (R 539).]
7 [Peirce's insertion to the copies located in R 478, R 1600 and Peirce (n.d.,b).]

Gamma Part

Convention No. VII. ¶ 1.[8]

The following spot-symbols shall be used, as if they were ordinary spot-symbols, except for special rules applicable to them (selectives are placed against the hooks in order to render the meanings of the new spot-symbols clearer):

Aq,	A is a monadic character;	x⌒,	X is a proposition or fact;
Ar,	A is a dyadic relation;	x⌒Y,	Y possesses the character X;
As,	A is a triadic relation;	x⌒^Y_Z,	Y stands in the dyadic relation X to Z;
		x⌒Z (Y, W),	Y stands in the triadic relation X to Z for W.

[A holograph page (Harvard Peirce Papers, R 478, ms page 147).]

---

8 [Alt.] The following special spot-graphs may be used, much as if they were ordinary spots (selectives are placed at the hooks in order to render them more readily intelligible):

A q	is a quality, or monadic character;		is necessary
A r	is a dyadic relation;	(g)	possible that necessary
A s	is a triadic relation;		possible
x⌒	is a graph or proposition;		

x⌒Y is a quality, or monadic character, of Y; or Y possesses the character X

x⌒^Y_Z stands in the relation X to Z;

Convention No. VIII. ¶ 1.⁹ A cut with many little interruptions aggregating about half its length shall cause its enclosure to be a graph, expressing that the entire graph on its area is logically contingent (non-necessary).

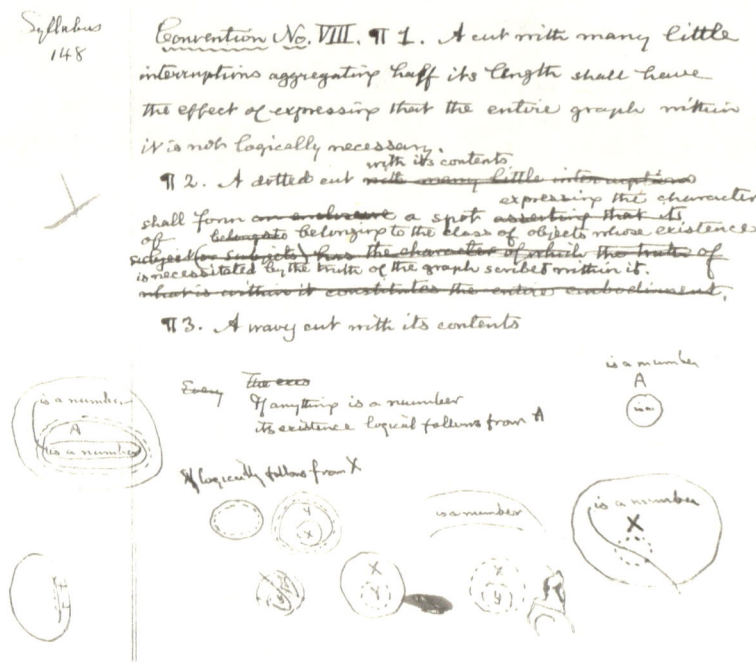

[A holograph page (Harvard Peirce Papers, R 478, ms p. 148, Alt.).]

---

9 [Alt.1] **Convention No. VIII.** ¶ 1. A cut with many little interruptions aggregating half of its length shall have the effect of expressing that the entire graph within it is not logically necessary.

¶ 2. A dotted cut with its contents shall form a spot expressing the character of belonging to the class of objects whose existence is necessitated by the truth of the graph scribed within it. A dotted cut with many little interruptions shall form an enclosure asserting that its subject (or subjects) has the character of which the truth of what is within it constitutes the entire embodiment.

¶ 3. A wavy cut with its contents [text breaks off here, followed by drafts of graphs for "If anything is a number its existence logically follows from A" and "Y logically follows from X", among others. See the holograph Figure R 478, ms p. 148, Alt.]

[Alt.2] ¶ 1. A cut with many little interruptions aggregating half its length shall cause its enclosure to express that the entire graph on its area is not logically necessary.

¶ 2. A dotted cut containing a graph some part of which is enclosed by an interior dotted part, with heavily dotted lines extending from places on this part to hooks on the outer cut, shall express that character which the truth of the graph within the outer cut essentially imparts to

Convention No. IX. ¶ 1. By a *rim* shall be understood an oval line making it, with its contents, the expression either of a rheme or a proper name of an *ens rationis*. Such a rim may be drawn as a line of peculiar texture, or a gummed label with a colored border may be attached to the sheet. A dotted rim containing a graph some part of which is itself enclosed by a similar inner dotted oval and with heavy dotted lines proceeding from marked points of this graph to hooks on the rim, shall be a spot expressing that the individuals denoted by lines of identity attached to the hooks (or the single such individual) have the character constituted by the truth of the graph, to be possessed by the individuals denoted by those points of it to which the heavy dotted lines are attached, in so far as they are connected with the partial graph within the inner oval.

¶ 2. A rim represented by ~~an oval~~ a wavy line containing a graph of which some marked points are connected by wavy lines with hooks on the rim shall be a spot expressing that the individuals denoted by lines of identity abutting on these hooks form a collection of sets, of which collection each set has its members ~~related~~ characterized in the manner in which those individuals must be which are denoted by the points of attachment of the interior graph, when that graph is true.

¶ 3. A rim ~~with~~ shown as a saw line denotes an individual collection of individual single objects or sets of objects, the members of the collection being all those in existence which are such individuals as the truth of the graph within makes those to be that are denoted by points of attachment of that graph to saw lines passing to hooks of the rim.

Rules of Transformation of Existential Graphs[10]

A *Transformation* is any act occupying a lapse of time considered only in respect to its triadic relation, first, to the entire graph on the sheet of assertion just before the act and, secondly, to the entire graph of the sheet of assertion just after the act.

---

what is denoted by the points of that graph connected to the hooks in reference to the part in the inner cut.

¶ 3. A wavy cut containing a graph of which points are connected by heavy wavy lines to points on the cut shall be a hook expressing the character of being any collection, wholly composed of such individuals as are denoted by those parts of the interior graph that are attached to the cut.

¶ 4. A saw cut [P.H.] shall denote the individual [end]

10 [Peirce replaced this section, which begins at ms page 150 of R 478 in its original pagination, with pages Syllabus B1–Syllabus B5 of R 508 consisting of "Rules of Transformation" and the first two sections of "Pure Mathematical Definition of Existential Graphs, regardless of their Interpretation" on "I. Alpha Part" and "II. Beta Part". These were renumbered as pages 150–155 in the

A *Rule* of Transformation is a general principle rendering certain Transformations *permissible* under expressed conditions. No transformation is *permissible* unless a Rule renders it so.

As a matter of interpretation it may be explained that the rules are so constructed that the permissible transformations are all those, and all those only, by which it is logically impossible to pass from a true graph to a false one. But this explanation is no part of the rules, which simply permit, but do not say why.

Archegetic Rules of Transformation[11]

The *archegetic* rules of transformation are the rules of any code which is such that none of its rules follows as a consequence from the rest, while all other permissibilities are consequences of its rules. No doubt, various codes of archegetic rules might be drawn up. Only one will be here given. The archegetic rules should not make any reference to the Conventions, except to borrow technical terms from them, and from the definitions of these terms all reference to the interpretation of the ~~symbols~~ graphs should be eliminated. Thus, the Code of Archegetic Rules will constitute a Pure Mathematical Definition of Existential Graphs in a sense so generalized that they will not be restricted to any particular meaning, or to being Representamens at all, but will be regarded simply as subjects of permissions of transformation. But it will be necessary to recognize the distinction between a general description of a subject of permission which description is perfectly determinate in every respect that can affect the transformability of anything, except in respect to its occurrence and connections, and an individual object of such description, which may be termed a *Replica* of it. For convenience, all the individual objects will be spoken of as existing on a surface.

---

final copy-text that was sent to the printer and were included in the printed *Syllabus*. The third section, "Gamma Part of Existential Graphs", paginated as Syllabus B6 but not renumbered, was not printed. This third section is followed by five sheets of studies entitled "Gamma Graphs 1–5" preserved in R 509 and eleven substantially and compositionally closely related worksheets located in R 510. The material from R 508–R 510 is provided in the present selection as a continuous segment following the material below that was omitted from the printed *Syllabus* until the beginning of the section "Pure Mathematical Definition of Existential Graphs".]

11 [Alt.1] Archegetic Rules of Transformation. The *archegetic* rules of transformation [are] the rules of a code of rules none of which is deducible from the others, but from which all permissibilities can be deduced. They do not refer to the Conventions, except to borrow certain technical terms to which they attach generalized significations. They constitute a Pure Mathematical Definition of Existential Graphs in a sense so generalized that the graphs are not necessarily Representamens, but are simply objects to which certain permissions of transformation attach. An individual object is said to be a *Replica* of a general description of object, that is perfectly determinate in every respect relevant to the rules except as regards to its occurrences.

These Rules suppose a single total diagram to be present and capable of being transformed. This is the *Entire Graph of the Sheet*. Any general description of diagram perfectly determinate in all respects to which these rules apply, which might some time be the Entire Graph of the Sheet is termed a *Graph*; but nothing is a graph which geometrically encloses anything not part of itself. A *partial graph of the sheet* is a graph forming an unenclosed part of the Entire Graph of the Sheet, and connected with the other parts in certain ways defined in the system, called *the forms of connection* of the system. Graphs are of three kinds, according to the nature of the forms of connection of their parts; namely, *Alpha Graphs*, *Beta Graphs*, and *Gamma Graphs*. Alpha Graphs are graphs whose parts have no other forms of connection than that of standing side by side detached from one another; but they may have *Cuts* which, with their *Places*, *Areas*, and *Enclosures*, are defined in a purely geometrical way as in the Conventions. Of these, the Enclosures alone are Graphs. Every Area has its Entire Graph, like the sheet, be it only a blank. A partial graph which has no parts connected by Forms of Connection of the System is a *Spot-graph*; and any Replica of it is a *Spot*. No cut passes through a spot. *Beta Graphs* differ from Alpha Graphs [end, fragment abandoned]

[Alt.2] Archegetic Rules of Transformation. The archegetic rules form a code from which all permissions to transform are deducible. They do not refer in any way to the Conventions, except to borrow terms ~~expressive of parts~~ descriptive of graphs and relations of ~~such parts~~ graphs. They constitute a pure mathematical definition of Existential Graphs, which so generalizes the conception of the system that the graphs are no longer restricted to being representamens but are any objects in which some condition or general circumstance renders certain transformations in some sense allowable.

Rule I, called *the Rule of Erasure and Insertion*. Any heavy line having a part evenly enclosed may there be broken; and any evenly enclosed detached part of a graph may be wholly erased with all it encloses.

Within an odd number of cuts *already existing* any graph may be inserted; and any parts of heavy lines on the same oddly enclosed area may be joined by a heavy line.

Rule II, called *The Rule of Iteration and Deiteration*. Any partial graphs (including any part of a heavy line) may be copied on the same area or within any additional cuts *already existing*, provided that if the ~~iterated~~ original replica of the iterated graph be connected to heavy lines, each of those very lines be extended by branches so as to connect with the corresponding part of the copy.

If any partial graph is already scribed in two replicas one of which is enclosed within all the cuts that enclose the other (if not in more besides) and if the corresponding parts of the two replicas are joined to identically the same ligatures, then that one which is enclosed in all the cuts that enclose the other may be erased.

Rule III. The removal of pairs of cuts is not prevented by the passage of ligatures from inside the inner cut to outside the outer one.

A detached line of identity is an immaterial form, like the double cut, and may always be inserted unenclosed.

Modifications of the Rules to make them applicable to Gamma Graphs. The Gamma part of the subject is not yet so matured that we can pronounce with certainty that any list of rules covers all permissions. Far less can an archegetic code be drawn up. ~~It is only possible to noti~~ We have

These Rules suppose that on any single occasion of their application there is a single total subject of permissions of Transformation, which subject is termed the *Entire Graph of the Sheet*. Any general description of a subject of permissions to transform, that is perfectly definite in all respects relative to these Rules, except as to its actual occurrence and actual connections, and which might at some time be the Entire Graph of the Sheet, but does not geometrically enclose anything not a part of itself (unless by the aid of certain heavy lines), is termed a *Graph*. A *Partial Graph of the Sheet* is a graph forming an unenclosed part of the Entire Graph of the Sheet, and connected with the other parts only in certain defined ways called the *forms of connection* of the[12] system. Graphs are of three kinds, according to the Forms of Connection of their parts; namely, *Alpha Graphs*, *Beta Graphs*, and *Gamma Graphs*. Alpha Graphs are graphs having no other form of connection than *Dinection*, that is, standing side by side detached from one another; but they may have *Cuts*, which, with their *Places*, *Areas*, and *Enclosures*, are defined in a purely geometrical way, as in the Conventions. Of these, the Enclosures alone are Graphs; and no Graph is partly inside and partly outside any cut, but is wholly in one Area or on the sheet. Every Area has its Entire Graph, like the Sheet, be it only a blank. A graph-replica which has no parts connected by Forms of Connection is a *Spot*. Beta Graphs differ from Alpha Graphs, in that some of their Spots may have certain places on their peripheries called *Hooks*, and every hook is invariably occupied by the extremity of a single heavy line, called a *ligature*, which heavy line may have three-way furcations, and a part, all, or none of the extremities of a *ligature* may occupy a Hook. Ligatures can cross cuts. Any part of a ligature on one area or on the sheet is called a *line of identity* and is subject to the rules, as a Graph. Beta Graphs have also a peculiar kind of spots called *Singulars*. Gamma Graphs differ from Beta Graphs in that they almost always have a peculiar kind of ligatures (or equivalent Selectives, which are Singulars that have the effects of ligatures). They also have a peculiar kind of cut, and several peculiar *Envelopes* of Spots, all of which are Forms of Connection. An archegetic code cannot yet be given for Gamma Graphs.

---

no reason to be confident that the symbols have taken their definite form. We can only give *some* rules.

Rule I applies to the broken cut. This rule may be extended, so as to give the proposition that unenclosed a full cut is transformable into a broken one, which within either a full or a broken enclosure a broken cut is transformable into a full one. Any graph can be inserted within a broken as within a full enclosure. In short, as far as Rule I is concerned the two sorts of cuts are alike. [End of fragment]

12 [The following was crossed out until "Some Modifications of the Rules for Gamma Graphs" (ms pp. 153–157).]

The Archegetic Code for Alpha Graphs

Rule I, called the *Rule of Erasure and Insertion*. Any evenly enclosed Graph,— Partial or Entire,—may be erased; and in any oddly enclosed area, *already existing*, any Graph may be inserted.

Rule II, called the *Rule of Iteration and Deiteration*. Any replica of a Graph anywhere ~~existing may be copied in the same any oddly/evenly~~ evenly enclosed may be[13] copied on the same Area; and every Replica of a Graph that is in an oddly enclosed Area ~~containing~~ carrying, in addition, a Cut, may be copied in the Area of that Cut. Further, if two Replicas of the same Graph lie in the same oddly enclosed Area, either of them may be erased; and if an evenly enclosed Area carries, in addition to a Replica of a Graph, a Cut in whose Area is another Replica of the same Graph, the latter may be erased.

Rule III, called *the Rule of Immaterial and Pseudographic Forms*. An unenclosed vacant cut may have any graph added to it; and the enclosure of an oddly enclosed cut on whose area is a vacant cut may be erased.

Further, two cuts the one containing only the other, and the latter containing nothing, can be added unenclosed to the Entire Graph of the sheet; and two cuts, one enclosing nothing but the enclosure of the ~~latter~~ other, can be removed, leaving what was on the area of the inner cut unenclosed by either of those cuts.

Additional Archegetic Rules for Beta Graphs

Rule I. Any evenly enclosed line of identity may be broken (though no hook can be left without any attached line of identity, and the point where a ligature emerges from a cut is to be considered as a hook of the enclosure of the cut), and two lines of identity on the same oddly enclosed area can be joined by a line of identity running from one to the other.

Rule II. This rule applies to Beta Graphs, provided that the copy of an iterated graph have all its hooks attached to the very same ligatures as the corresponding hooks of the original replica, these ligatures being extended inward for the purpose (but never out beyond their original areas). No ligatures must be severed or

---

13 [Alt.] [[...] enclosed] area that is within every cut that the original replica was within; and if there are any two Replicas of the same Graph of which one [while oddly enclosed] is within every cut that the other is within, the latter may be erased.

The rule is ~~better~~ simpler without the words in brackets, which are only inserted to avoit duplicating permissions already given in Rule I. [On the verso on this abandoned page appears Peirce's one-time proposal for the dual of the broken cuts, in which the broken cut is notated by small outward curved breves surrounding a graph. Its signification is that the surrounded graph is *impossible*, in contrast to the signification of the standard broken cut which is that of *contingency*. See the last selection of "Fragments" for an image of that page.]

joined to others, in the process. The rule also applies to portions of lines of identity, as graphs. In particular, it allows ~~loose ends of~~ ligatures to be extended inwards through cuts, or, so extending, to be retracted outwards. Hooks of cut-enclosures that have no connections within, cease to be hooks, and are to be regarded as outside the enclosures.

Rule III. The removal of a double cut is not prevented by the circumstance that ligatures traverse the annular space between the inner and the outer cut.

A detached line of identity is an immaterial form, like the double cut, and may always be inserted unenclosed. A cut on whose area is nothing but a line of identity, and whose enclosure has no hook, is a form of the pseudograph.

Some Modifications of the Rules for Gamma Graphs

The Gamma part of the system is in an imperfect state. It is impossible, as yet, to draw up a regular Archegetic Code, or to state the rules so that they can be used regardless of the significations of the symbols. It is also probable that undiscovered rules exist, and that additional symbols will be needed; while some of those now given may, hereafter, be dispensed with. For the broken cut, perfect rules may be given.

The Rule of Erasure and Insertion applies to the broken cut in this form: Evenly enclosed, a full cut can be transformed into a broken cut; while oddly enclosed a broken cut can be transformed into a full one. It makes no difference whether the enclosure here spoken of is by a full or a broken cut. In regard to Graphs the Rule of Erasure and Insertion applies to enclosures by broken cuts precisely as to those by full cuts.

The Rule of Iteration and Deiteration does not apply to the broken cut.

The Rule of Immaterials and the Pseudograph practically does not apply to broken cuts. For although two broken cuts one within the other, both otherwise vacant, or a broken and a full cut so circumstanced, may be written unenclosed, yet, owing to the failure of Iteration and Deiteration, this leads to nothing.

For these ligatures and selectives that are attached to q, r, s, and to the left hand side of ⩘, ⋀, ⩙, ⩚, which may be called *Potentials*, there is a remarkable rule that has no parallel in the Beta Graphs. It has not been fully formulated; but so far as formulated, is as follows:

1   A broken cut ~~surrounding~~ enclosing no other ~~line of identity than these~~ ligature than Potentials is equivalent to a full cut. (For these are logical possibilities; and a logically possible logical possibility has all the being it is capable of.)
2   Every evenly enclosed graph which contains in its innermost enclosure a new selective or a ligature of a Potential, and no ligature of an Existent Individual,

is either capable of being permissibly transformed into the pseudo-graph or may be ~~written~~ scribed unenclosed. (For ~~that which is presented as~~ a proposition ~~asserting~~ affirming a logical possibility is either logically impossible or has all the truth that it professes to have.) In these clauses, as elsewhere, it is to be understood that a ligature is not enclosed by a cut unless it is wholly so enclosed.

(The following numbered rules of Potentials have not been precisely worked out, although such formulation appears to be easy. But it is now twenty-four years ago and more since the writer, perceiving that he had come upon an extensive field of virgin soil, was obliged to adopt certain rules of Economy of Research, which require him to leave others the solution of problems for the solution of which he possesses no special facilities, unless the solutions are needed for his own purposes.)

3   If a Graph contains existential junctures more enclosed than its Potentials, and if, regarding only the latter, if it were not for the former, it would violate the above rule, then, if the Graph be true this must be due to a limitation or limitations of existence, which must give rise to the truth of a corresponding graph in which the innermost potentials are evenly enclosed. This will ~~easily~~ be discovered and proved, usually without difficulty, if we bear in mind that the potentials are logical possibilities.

4   In aid of this, it is necessary to take account of the number of times in which existential ligatures pass through full ovals containing nothing else.

If there is no such case, a pertinent conclusion will be reached by erasing every Potential and every $q, r, s, ⚭, ⋀, ⋀, ⋀$, of the graph, whose Potentials are oddly enclosed. This is permissible since whatever is true of all characters, is true of existence, whatever is true of all dyadic relations, is true of coexistence, and whatever is true of all triadic relations is true of tricoexistence. This done a similar ~~substitution~~ erasure of the Potentials, and their spots that are evenly enclosed, though not necessary, will often show the necessity of the proposition expressed by the Graph.

The cases in which there is but a single cut completely traversed by a ligature and containing nothing else are the most[14] important cases. The above process will commonly be useless in such a case; but it will always be permissible to scribe the graph of the figure here given; and this will lead one sufficiently familiar with the system not to be bewildered by many varying recurrences of the same form to important consequences. Much study will be required to learn how to manage this.

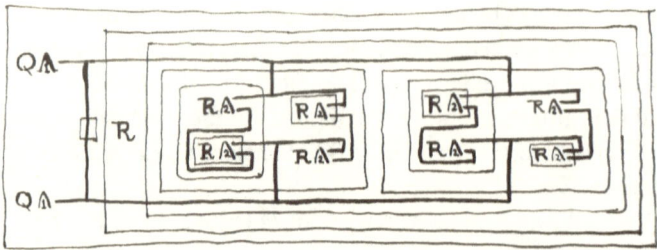

The cases in which there are more than one cut traversed only by a ligature afford no particular difficulty to one who has learned by practice to manage cases in which there is one such cut.

Remark on the Gamma Rims

The writer knows no way of distinctly formulating the whole transformational value of the three rims; nor does he know any partial expressions that are not quite obvious. The late Dr. Ernst Schröder, who for many years was the leader in exact logic, greatly admired two logical algebras of the present writer, which were less analytical, though in some respects more convenient, expressions of Beta graphs, alongwith the $q, r, s,$ and the ⋏ s. To this system Professor Schröder contributed a sign in so modest a way as to suggest a doubt as to whether he fully appreciated its fundamental importance. Namely, while the writer had the symbols Σ_i and Π_i, where the i below the line denotes a ligature and Σ shows that it is evenly enclosed, or Π that it is oddly enclosed, Schröder *also* wrote Σ_u and Π_u, where the u was a Potential referring to the whole universe of logical possibility, and obtained important results by the use of this particularly German mode of notation. The writer was at no time so enamoured of his own algebras as Schröder was, but thought both, and especially Schröder's pet, to be faulty from every point of view.

---

14 **[Alt.]** [...] important cases. The above process will commonly be useless in such a case; but it will always be permissible to scribe unenclosed this graph, which will almost always lead to an important conclusion by means of the Beta Rules

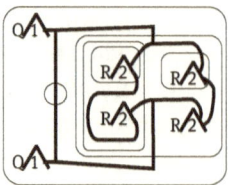

[end; fragment abandoned]

Thus arose a correspondence between the writer, attacking his own ideas, and Schröder defending them. Once, the writer asked Schröder how he would express either that something was true of the collection of all men or that something was one of the possible collections of men; to which Schröder replied "by your own algebra". When the posthumous papers of Schröder come to be published by Professor _ [Jacob Lüroth] (to whose competent hands this duty has been entrusted), we may hope to learn to what this enigmatical reply refers. Meantime, the writer remains confident that it is impossible to express such ideas, or to attain any distinct apprehension of them, without resort to very different symbols from these of the Beta Graphs even with ~~Schröder's~~ the Potentials and their accessories. The Gamma part of the system of Graphs can never be perfected until we have precisely analyzed all the conceptions of logic in terms of the three Categories, together with such other exact ~~ideas~~ conceptions as it may be found necessary to add to those of the Categories. But this is a labor for generations of analysts, not for one.

Rules of Transformation demonstrable from the Archegetic Rules

I. If any Graph, A, would, if scribed on the Sheet of Assertion, be permissively transformable into another Graph, B, then any evenly enclosed Enclosure, consisting of a Cut containing only B on its Area is permissively transformable into an Enclosure consisting of a Cut carrying only A on its area.

II. If a Graph A would, if scribed, unenclosed, be permissively transformable into an Enclosure consisting of a Cut with a Graph, B, alone on its area, then the Graph B, when evenly enclosed, is transformable into an Enclosure consisting of a Cut carrying on its Area only A.

III. If an Enclosure consisting of a Cut carrying on its Area only the Graph A would, if scribed unenclosed, be transformable into a Graph, B, then an Enclosure consisting of a Cut with B alone on its Area will, when evenly enclosed, be transformable into A.

IV. If an Enclosure consisting of a Cut carrying A alone on its Area would, if scribed unenclosed, be transformable into an Enclosure consisting of a Cut carrying B alone on its Area, then A, when evenly enclosed will be transformable into B.

V. Any Graph, however enclosed, may permissively have a Double Cut made around it; and any Graph within a Double Cut (that is a pair of Cuts of which one contains on its Area the Enclosure of the other and nothing else) may permissively be scribed in the same Area without the Double Cut.

VI. If a Graph, A, when unenclosed, would be permissively transformable into a Graph, B, then A will be permissively transformable into B whenever it may be evenly enclosed, and B into A whenever oddly enclosed.

VII. If the insertion of any graph, A, in any area, would make any evenly enclosed partial (or entire) graph permissively transformable into the pseudo-graph, then on that same area may be inserted an Enclosure consisting of a Cut containing A alone on its Area.

VIII. Any enclosure the Area of which carries at once a Graph, A, and also an Enclosure consisting of a Cut whose Area carries nothing but A may be erased.

IX. In any Area it is permitted to insert an enclosure containing at once any graph, A, and also an enclosure consisting of a Cut carrying on its Area nothing but A.

X. If any one graph, A, could, if scribed unenclosed, be transformed into another, B, then it is permitted in any area to insert an Enclosure consisting of a Cut carrying A on its area together with an Enclosure consisting of a cut carrying only B on its Area.

XI. Any Graph may be iterated with the same ligatures within any number of additional cuts; and if any Graph occurs in two Replicas with the same ligatures one of which is within all the Cuts that the other is within, the former Replica may be erased. But Iteration and Deiteration are commonly only useful within an even number of additional Cuts.

XII. If a Cut contains only Enclosures, it makes no difference whether any Graph is scribed just outside it or in the Areas of all the Enclosures.

XIII. A ligature is equivalent to a Selective at all the places where its extremities and outermost parts are.

XIV. Two Graphs not connected in their innermost common enclosure and not so connected without their ligature entering any other cut are virtually not connected at all, not even through another Graph.[15]

XV. A branch of a Ligature extending into the Area of a Cut without their being connected with any Hook is of no effect.

XVI. If two Selectives, Proper Names or other Individual Symbols are joined by a Ligature passing from without to within a Cut, it makes no difference whether both, only one, or neither are within the Cut.

---

15 [While Peirce was revisiting the minimum set of basic rules, Rule XIV appears, nearly verbatim, as a note dated June 9, 1903, inscribed on the *Logic Notebook* verso page [119v] with reference to Theorem XXVI of that notebook entry originally written on June 18, 1898.]

Existential Graphs. Rules of Transformation.[16]
Pure Mathematical Definition of Existential Graphs, regardless of their Interpretation

I. Alpha Part

1. The *System of Existential Graphs* is a certain class of diagrams upon which it is permitted to operate certain transformations.
2. There is required a certain surface upon which it is practicable to scribe the diagrams and from which they can be erased in whole or in part.
3. The whole of this surface except certain parts which may be severed from it by 'cuts' is termed the *sheet of assertion*.
4. A *graph* is a legisign (i.e., a sign which is of the nature of a general type) which is one of a certain class of signs used in this system. A *graph-replica* is any individual instance of a graph. The sheet of assertion itself is a graph-replica; and so is any part of it, being called the *blank*. Other graph-replicas can be scribed on the sheet of assertion, and when this is done the graphs of which those graph-replicas are instances is said to be "scribed on the sheet of assertion"; and when a graph-replica is erased, the graph is said to be erased. Two graphs scribed on the sheet of assertion constitute one graph of which they are said to be *partial graphs*. All that is at any time scribed on the sheet of assertion is called the *entire scribed graph*.
5. A *cut* is a self-returning finely drawn line. A cut is not a graph-replica. A cut drawn upon the sheet of assertion severs the surface it encloses, called the *area* of the cut, from the sheet of assertion; so that the area of a cut is no part of the sheet of assertion. A cut drawn upon the sheet of assertion together with its area and whatever is scribed upon that area constitutes a graph-replica scribed upon the sheet of assertion, and is called the *enclosure* of the cut. Whatever graph might, if permitted, be scribed upon the sheet of assertion might (if permitted) be scribed upon the area of any cut. Two graphs scribed at once on such area constitute a graph, as they would on the sheet of assertion. A cut can (if permitted) be drawn upon the area of any cut, and will sever the surface which it encloses from the area of the cut, while the enclosure of such inner cut will be a graph-replica scribed on the area of the outer cut. The sheet of assertion is also an area. Any blank part of any area

---

16 [The text in the printed *Syllabus* resumes here (p. 20), from "Rules of Transformation. Pure Mathematical Definition of Existential Graphs, regardless of their Interpretation", until "Gamma Part of Existential Graphs".]

is a graph-replica. Two cuts one of which has the enclosure of the other on its area and has nothing else there constitute a *double cut*.
6. No graph or cut can be placed partly on one area and partly on another.
7. No transformation of any graph-replica is permitted unless it is justified by the following code of Permissions.

Code of Permissions

Permission No. 1. *In each special problem such graphs may be scribed on the sheet of assertion as the conditions of the special problem may warrant.*

Permission No. 2. *Any graph on the sheet of assertion may be erased, except an enclosure with its area entirely blank.*

Permission No. 3. *Whatever graph it is permitted to scribe on the sheet of assertion, it is permitted to scribe on any unoccupied part of the sheet of assertion, regardless of what is already on the sheet of assertion.*

Permission No. 4. *Any graph which is scribed on the inner area of a double cut on the sheet of assertion may be scribed on the sheet of assertion.*

Permission No. 5. *A double cut may be drawn on the sheet of assertion; and any graph that is scribed on the sheet of assertion may be scribed on the inner area of any double cut on the sheet of assertion.*

Permission No. 6. *The reverse of any transformation that would be permissible on the sheet of assertion is permissible on the area of any cut that is upon the sheet of assertion.*

Permission No. 7. *Whenever we are permitted to scribe any graph we like upon the sheet of assertion, we are authorized to declare that the conditions of the special problem are absurd.*

II. Beta Part

8. The beta part adds to the alpha part certain signs to which new permissions are attached, while retaining all the alpha signs with the permissions attaching to them.
9. *The line of identity* is a Graph any replica of which, also called *a* line of identity, is a heavy line with two ends and without other topical singularity (such as a point of branching or a node), not in contact with any other sign except at its extremities. Otherwise, its shape and length are matters of indifference. All lines of identity are replicas of the same graph.
10. A *spot* is a graph any replica of which occupies a simple bounded portion of a surface, which portion has qualities distinguishing it from the replica of any other spot; and upon the boundary of the surface occupied by the spot

are certain points, called the *hooks* of the spot, to each of which, if permitted, one extremity of one line of identity can be attached. Two lines of identity cannot be attached to the same hook; nor can both ends of the same line.

11. Any indefinitely small dot may be a spot-replica, called a *spot of tri-identity*,[17] and ~~several~~ three lines of identity may be attached to such a spot. Two lines of identity, one outside a cut and the other on the area of the same cut, may have each an extremity at the same point on the cut. The totality of all the lines of identity that join one another is termed a *ligature*. A ligature is not generally a graph, since it may be part in one area and part in another. It is said to lie within any cut which it is wholly within.

12. The following are the additional permissions attaching to the beta part.

Code of Permissions,—*Continued*

Permission No. 8. *All the above permissions apply to all spots and to the line of identity, as Graphs; and Permission No. 2 is to be understood as permitting the erasure of any portion of a line of identity on the sheet of assertion, so as to break it into two. Permission No. 3 is to be understood as permitting the extension of a line of identity on the sheet of assertion to any unoccupied part of the sheet of assertion. Permission No. 3 must not be understood [as implying][18] that because it is permitted to scribe a graph without certain ligatures, therefore it is permissible to scribe it with them, or the reverse.*

Permission No. 9. *It is permitted to scribe an unattached line of identity on the sheet of assertion, and to join such unattached lines in any number by spots of teridentity.[19] This is to be understood as permitting a line of identity, whether within or without a cut, to be extended to the cut, although such extremity is to be understood to be on both sides of the cut. But this does not permit a line of identity within a cut that is on the sheet of assertion to be retracted from the cut, in case it extends to the cut.*

Permission No. 10. *If two spots are within a cut (whether on its area or not), and are not joined by any ligature[20] within that cut, then a ligature joining them outside the cut is of no effect and may be made or broken. But this does not apply if the spots are joined by other hooks within the cut.*

---

17 [Copy-text indeed spells this "triidentity", which Peirce in his offprints of the printed *Syllabus* consistently corrected to the more customary term "teridentity".]
18 [Peirce's correction to the copies located in R 478 and in R 1600, Nos. 1 and 2.]
19 [Corrected from "tri-identity" by Peirce in the copies from R 1600 (Nos. 1 and 2) and Peirce (n.d.,b).]
20 ["by any ligature" crossed out and replaced by "in any way" by Peirce in a copy from R 1600.]

Permission No. 11. *Permissions Nos. 4 and 5 do not cease to apply because of ligatures passing from without the outer of two cuts to within the inner one, so long as there is nothing else in the annular area.*

Gamma Part of Existential Graphs

The Gamma part of existential graphs being still under investigation cannot now be stated in its final form; and the following statement may not entirely agree with that given above. The special signs required in gamma graphs seem to be divisible into two classes; namely, *Potentials*, or signs of possibilities, with their adjuncts, and signs of graphs and graph-elements.

A *Potential* is any one of the spots $-p$, $-q$, $-r$, $-s$, ⊸0̸, ⊸1̸, ⊸2̸, ⊸3̸. At the left hand of Potentials a selective is used, instead of a ligature. A *Selective* is an improvised proper-name, like the letters A, B, C, employed by lawyers as substitutes for relative pronouns. (A noun substantive might be defined as a word instead of a pronoun. At any rate, the ancient definition of a pronoun, as "a word used instead of a noun", a definition rightly discarded in the thirteenth century as inexact, but revived at the revival of learning is preposterous. The pronoun '*that*' more directly denotes its object than does a noun describing that object.) But the Selectives placed at the left of potentials are proper nouns of a strange kind, since they do not denote ordinary individuals but qualitative possibilities which, in themselves, have no individuality. Along with Potentials, a broken cut is employed.

Gamma Graphs 1

There are ~~eight~~ eleven spots signifying parts of graphs, namely:

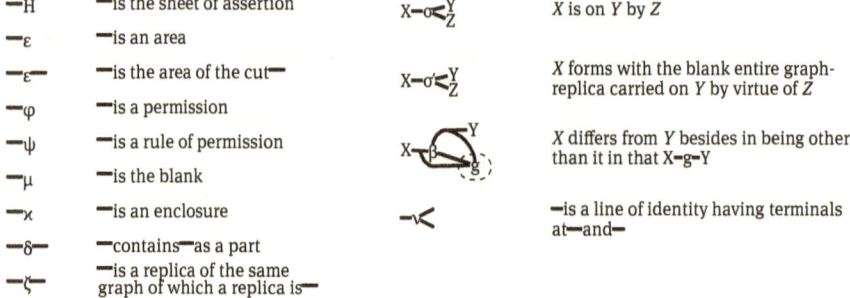

—H	—is the sheet of assertion	X—σ⊂^Y_Z	X is on Y by Z
—ε	—is an area		
—ε—	—is the area of the cut—	X—σ'⊂^Y_Z	X forms with the blank entire graph-replica carried on Y by virtue of Z
—φ	—is a permission		
—ψ	—is a rule of permission	X—β (Y, g)	X differs from Y besides in being other than it in that X-g-Y
—μ	—is the blank		
—χ	—is an enclosure	—⋋	—is a line of identity having terminals at— and—
—δ—	—contains— as a part		
—ζ—	—is a replica of the same graph of which a replica is—		

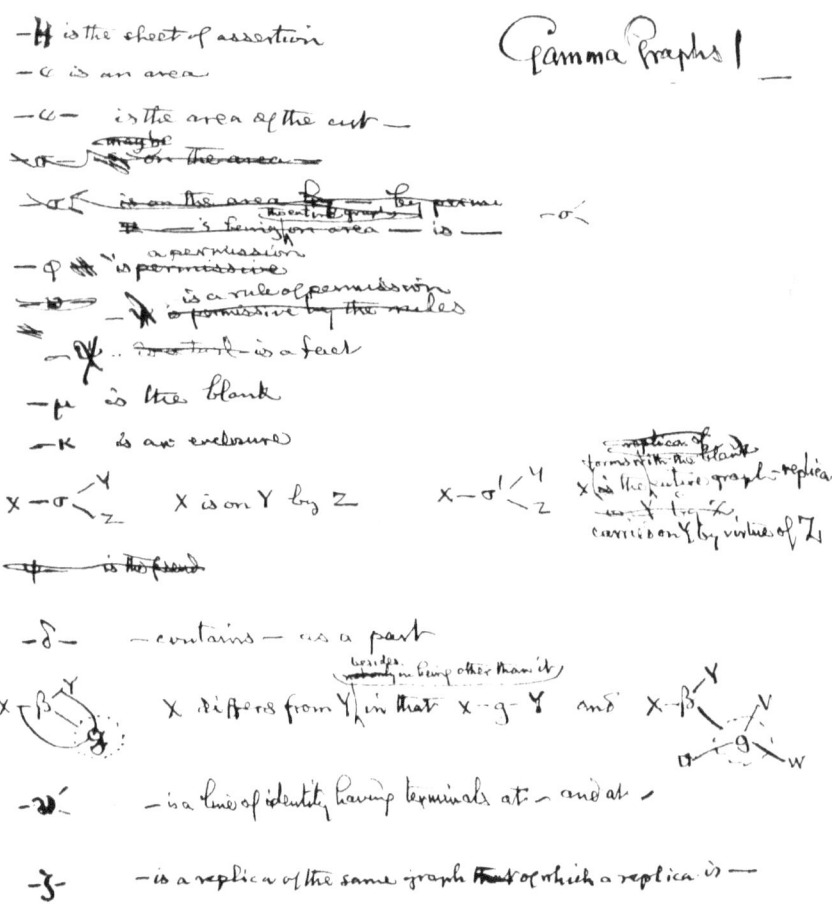

[A holograph page "Gamma Graphs 1" (Harvard Peirce Papers, R 509).]

Gamma Graphs 2

If any graph is permitted to be on the sheet of assertion, it is the blank or an enclosure of a cut on whose area nothing is but the blank or its not being on the sheet of assertion is permitted.

1. The sheet of assertion does not by virtue of any fact carry any entire graph unless it contains a blank.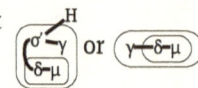

1 ½. The sheet of assertion carries a graph-replica.

2. The sheet of assertion if, by virtue of any fact, it carries an entire graph containing an enclosure whose area carries an entire graph which does not contain anything but blanks, then whatever permission permits whatever graph to be carried on the sheet contains that enclosure.

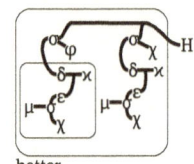
better

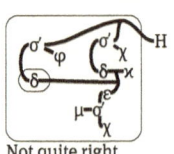
Not quite right

41 A Syllabus of certain Topics of Logic (R 478)

Gamma Graphs 2

If any graph is permitted to be on the sheet of assertion, it is the blank or an enclosure of of a cut on whose area nothing is but the blank or its not being on the sheet of assertion is permitted.

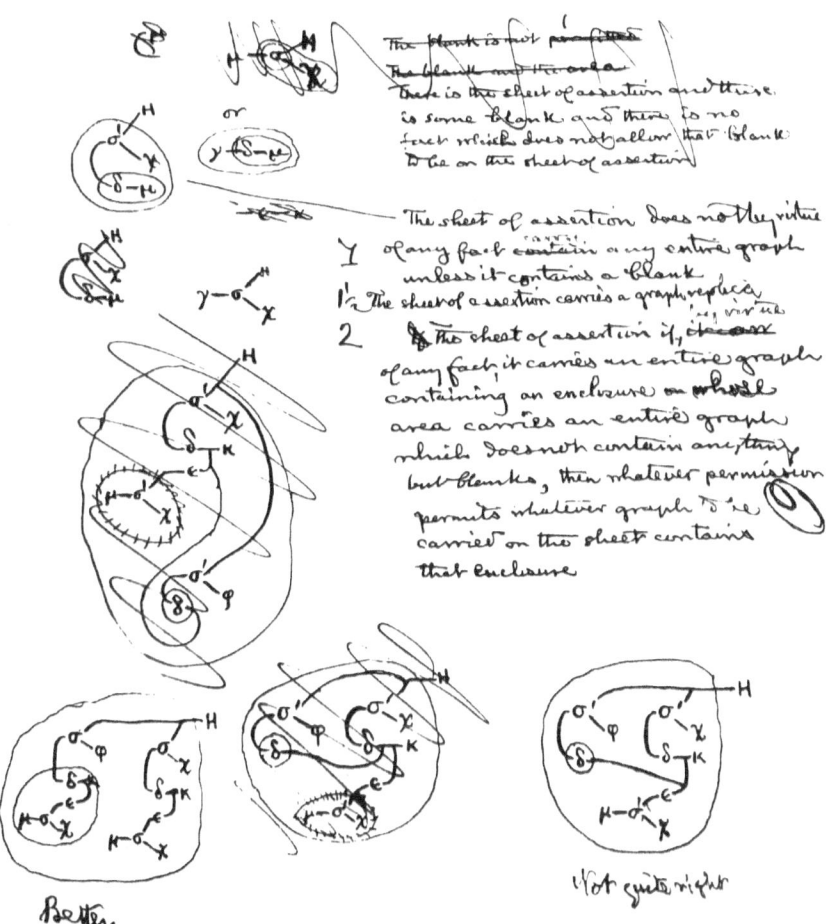

The blank is not permitted
The blank not the ...
There is the sheet of assertion and there is some blank and there is no fact which does not allow that blank to be on the sheet of assertion

1. The sheet of assertion does not by virtue of any fact contain any entire graph unless it contains a blank.
1½. The sheet of assertion carries a graph replica, by virtue,
2. The sheet of assertion if, of any fact it carries an entire graph containing an enclosure on whose area carries an entire graph which does not contain anything but blanks, then whatever permission permits whatever graph to be carried on the sheet contains that enclosure.

Better   Not quite right

[A holograph page "Gamma Graphs 2" (Harvard Peirce Papers, R 509).]

Gamma Graphs 3

On the sheet of assertion if the entire graph is permitted to contain any graph not a blank nor a cut ~~that does not as a fact contain as its containing~~ whose area carries as its entire graph

    Use "sheet" for sheet of assertion
    Use "carry" for "carry as the entire graph, a replica"
    Use "contain" for "contains as a part of the area"

3. The sheet if is it permitted to carry a graph$_1$ containing a graph$_2$ not a blank and not a cut whose area carries a blank is permitted to carry any graph-replica not differing from that graph-replica$_1$ in any other respect than that it does not carry that graph-replica$_2$.

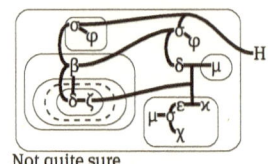
Not quite sure

4. If the sheet of assertion is permitted to carry a graph-replica and is permitted to carry ~~another~~ a second graph-replica and there is a third graph-replica that it is not permitted to carry than the third contains some part such that if anything is contained in it it is not a coreplica of any thing contained on the second and is not a coreplica of anything contained in the third.

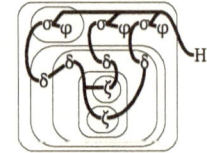

Gamma Graphs 3

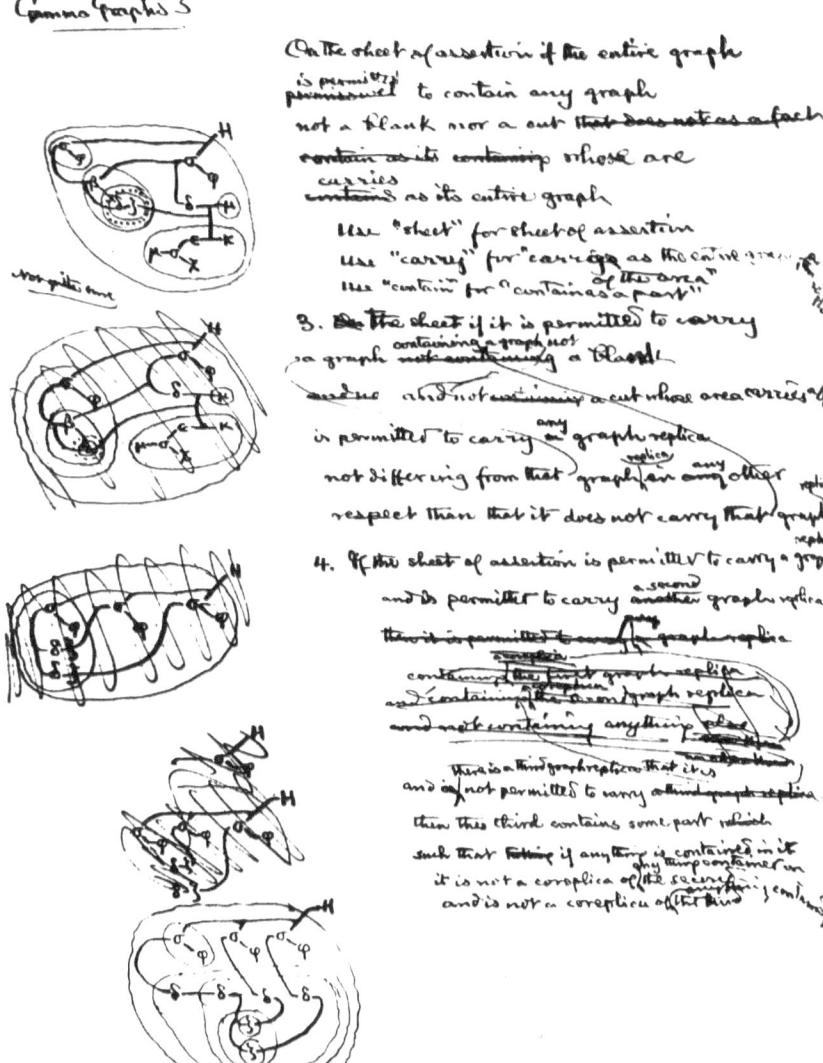

On the sheet of assertion it the entire graph is permitted to contain any graph not a blank nor a cut whose area carries as its entire graph

Use "sheet" for sheet of assertion
Use "carry" for "carriage as the entire area"
Use "contain" for "contains a part"

3. The sheet if it is permitted to carry a graph containing a graph not a blank and not containing a cut whose area carries is permitted to carry any graph replica not differing from that graph in any other respect than that it does not carry that graph

4. If the sheet of assertion is permitted to carry a graph and is permitted to carry a second graph replica there is a third graph replica that is and is not permitted to carry then this third contains some part which such that if anything is contained in it it is not a coreplica of the second and is not a coreplica of the third

[A holograph page "Gamma Graphs 3" (Harvard Peirce Papers, R 509).]

Gamma Graphs 4

5. Any line of identity joining any two points A and B, C being any third point, is a coreplica of any graph-replica containing a line joining A and C and containing a line joining B and C and not containing anything else but a blank.

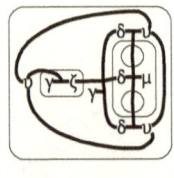

6. It is always permissible to draw a cut on the sheet of assertion with *some* graph in it.

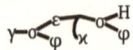

7. If it is permissible that the sheet of assertion should carry a cut whose area carries nothing but a cut, then it is permissible that the sheet of assertion should carry the graph carried on the area of the last cut.

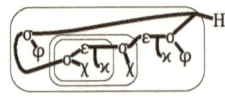

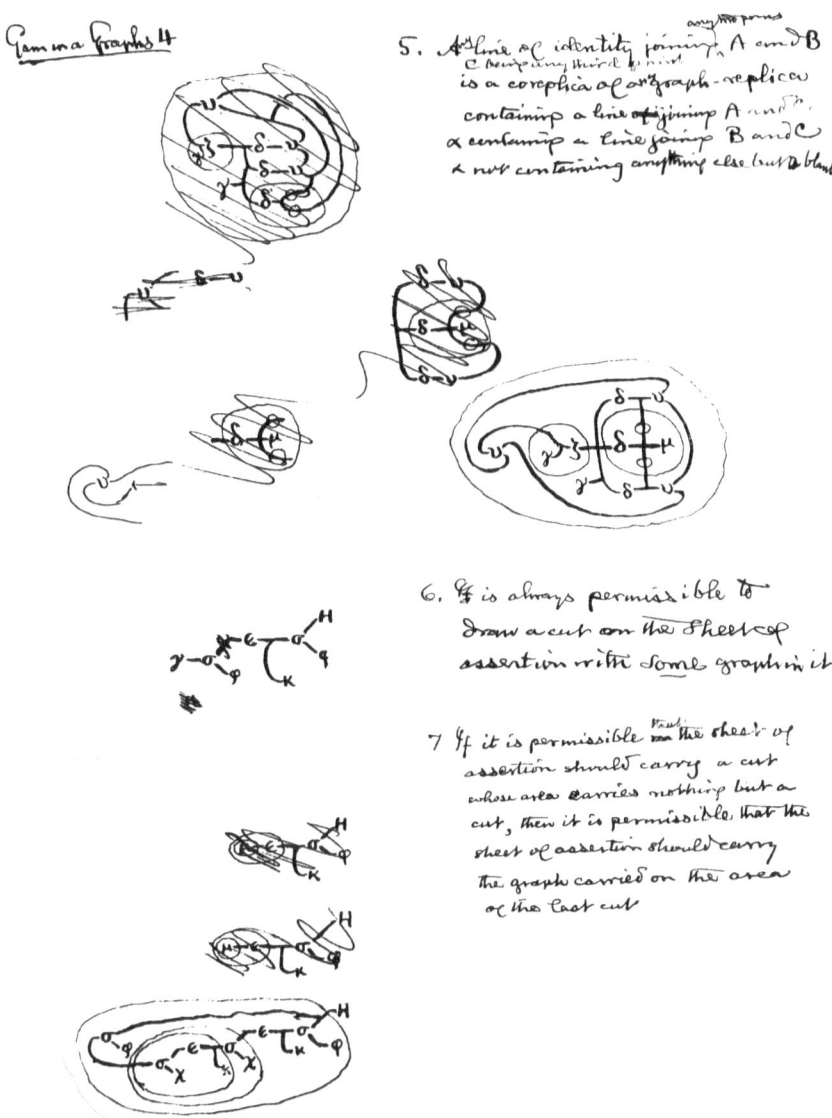

[A holograph page "Gamma Graphs 4" (Harvard Peirce Papers, R 509).]

Gamma Graphs 5

8. *Principle of Contraposition.* If it would become permissible if a graph-replica A were carried on the sheet of assertion to scribe a graph-replica, B, on the sheet of assertion then if a cut were on the sheet of assertion whose area carried a coreplica of B it would be permissible that the sheet should carry a cut whose area should carry a coreplica of A.

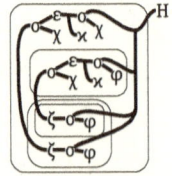

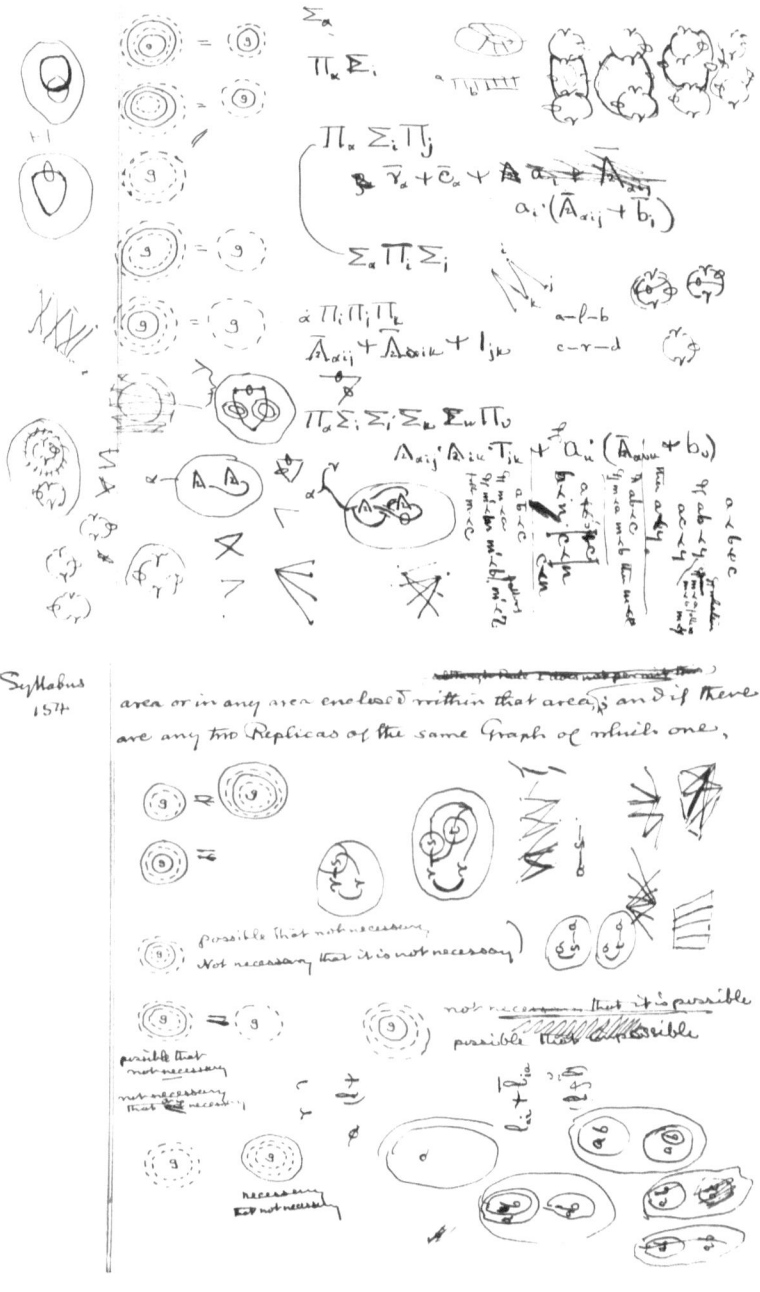

[Two holograph images (Harvard Peirce Papers, R 478(s)): a reversed verso of an abandoned ms draft page 137 (above) and an abandoned ms draft page 154 (below).]

Appendix ["'Pragmatism' as Our Method" and other comments on William James's "Syllabus of Philosophy 3"]

Pragmatism. It is a singular instance of that over-modesty and unyielding self-underestimate on my part of which I am so justly proud as my principal claim to distinction that I should have omitted *pragmatism*, my own offspring, with which the world resounds. See Baldwin's *Dictionary* [1902] where is my original definition of 1878 and an exegesis, not very deep, of William James. Pragmatism is a method in philosophy. *Philosophy* is that branch of positive science (i.e., an investigating theoretical science which inquires what is the fact, in contradistinction to pure mathematics which merely seeks to know what follows from certain hypotheses) which makes no observations but contents itself with so much of experience as pours in upon every man during every hour of his waking life. The study of philosophy consists, therefore, in reflexion, and *pragmatism* is that method of reflexion which is guided by constantly holding in view its purpose and the purpose of the ideas it analyzes, whether these ends be of the nature and uses of action or of thought.

[...][21] of every man in almost every hour. This truth is *necessary*, in the sense that only with great difficulty can a man in some particulars come to conceive it as other than it is. By far the most important part of man's experience he thus finds himself already possessed of; and his only business in philosophy is to reflect upon it.

Philosophy as so defined has three parts, as follows:[22]

(1) **Phenomenology**, or the Doctrine of the Categories, which states what are the peculiar kinds of elements in all experience. According to me, they are, *first*, the element of Quality, given first in immediate consciousness, such as *blue, pity*, etc., *second*, the element of Relation, or Reaction, which enters into every *event*, especially every exertion and is essentially two-sided, the effort and the resistance, and is antigeneral; *third*, the element of Representation, finding its fullest development in Continuity.

(2) **The Normative Science**, which are essentially dualistic in distinguishing good from bad, and are all but mathematical in the abstractness and there are *Esthetics*, the science of the Immediately Good; *Ethics*, the Science of the Good in Action, being thus doubly dualistic; Logic, the Science of the Good in Representation, thus leaning strongly toward the third part of philosophy.[23]

---

21 [The first page of the present sequence is lost; what follows is from the manuscript pages 2–23. The opening paragraph is a proxy for the lost page taken from Peirce's text of the *Minute Logic* written in early 1902 (CP 5.13fn1).]

22 [From Section 1 of the *Syllabus*, "An Outline Classification of the Sciences":] Philosophy is divided into (a) *Phenomenology*; (b) *Normative Science*; (c) *Metaphysics*.

Phenomenology ascertains and studies the kinds of elements universally present in the phenomenon; meaning by the *phenomenon*, whatever is present at any time to the mind in any way. Normative science distinguishes what ought to be from what ought not to be, and makes many other divisions and arrangements subservient to its primary dualistic distinction. Metaphysics seeks to give an account of the universe of mind and matter. Normative science rests largely on phenomenology and on mathematics; metaphysics on phenomenology and on normative science.

(3) **Metaphysics**, which endeavors to make a scheme or representation of what is.[24]

– An investigation in the object-world as well as into the subject world.

I don't much like these phrases. Philosophy must begin with familiar conceptions and philosophical terms can only be used after severe criticism. The world of reality and the world of imagination are phrases representing a distinction that every man has been accustomed to draw long before he comes to philosophy. Whatever their precise analysis may be, they refer to an incontestible distinction; for to contest it is to use it. But as for "object-world",—which would seem to be the only world there is,—and still worse "subject-world", which would seem to [be] no world at all, I cannot admit that they can pass without severe criticism, nor that such criticism can be satisfactory until philosophy has gone for upon its road.

– "Pragmatism" as our method.

I am sure you don't mean this as an *ipse dixit* or pure hypothesis. The merits of pragmatism have got to be proved to begin with. No doubt, they must be confirmed later; but before this method is used at all, I doubt not you intend to show why it ought to be used. Since you do not say what reason you propose to give, I will just intimate what my reason would be. Philosophical inquiry consists, by the definition given above, of reflection upon the knowledge that all men, so to say, already possess; and in point of fact the beginner in the study of philosophy is already possessed of knowledge far greater in weight than all that science can ever teach him. This is Common Sense; and one of the most solid principles of common sense is that when we begin any serious undertaking we ought to do so deliberately. Now this deliberation consists in making out as well as we can what the upshot of our efforts is likely to be. I propose to show the Pragmatism is nothing but deliberation so conceived. Suppose at a council of war held on the eve of a battle, one of the officers should propose to draw up the troops in the form of a bicyclic curve (a curve like the outline of a wryneck squash of any kind) and on being asked why, should say "Because these curves are so lovely". He would strikingly resemble the non pragmatist philosopher. That speech would not have convinced Napoleon Bonaparte, because his mind was eminently a pragmatistic mind; that is to say, he always thoroughly studied what his purpose was, to begin with, and then made the minutest movements of his army, every phrase of his utterances, to be determined exclusively by that. In the operations of reflection which make the warp and woof of philosophical inquiry, the method of Pragmatism is to consider what thought is *for*, and to take no step in reflection that is not required by that *purpose*. No more definite statement of the distinctive character of Pragmatistic Philosophy is possible until we can examine into Thought and see what it does. That is to say that Pragmatism first of all requires us to begin philosophical reflection with the study of Phenomenology. To accomplish our purpose we must first examine what it is that we are dealing with, what a Phenomenon in general is composed of. Now a Phenomenon, that is to say, anything that

---

23 [Marginal note:] But whether there is a science of Esthetics separate from Ethics is questiona[ble]

24 [Alt.] This ~~classification~~ scheme of classification differs from the great majority of those I have ~~considered~~ examined in that the forms classified are of an altogether different nature. Some of those quite certainly, and other presumably, relate to "sciences" in the sense of ἐπιστέμε or *scientia*; and a great many others ~~mean by~~ science [end, fragment abandoned]

can emerge in knowledge or in fancy, has in the first place its own peculiar smell, apart from any reflexion or comparisons. But in the second place, the coming of this phenomenon is an event. It strikes me, and I am conscious that it *insists* on recognition. That consciousness of insistence betrays the fact that I have in conservatism *resisted* it. For force without reaction cannot be. Perhaps I even will it to be otherwise; and if so it will be the Phenomenon that will resist. This element is what we chiefly have in mind when we talk of *experience*, which is so much of a cognitive character as insists on sticking. The only remaining element of the Phenomenon is Thought. If we will to alter the phenomenon, we have to make some representation to ourselves of what we propose to do. This is thought. All representation is this third element. We must now compare the categories. The first category is simply the phenomenon as it is present in itself regardless of anything else. It therefore is absolutely simple and without parts; for parts are different from one another, and no one is more identical with the whole than is another; so that one is the whole; therefore to say that the present phenomenon has parts is to take into consideration something other than itself. No doubt that the presentation as a fact has parts; but this is considering it *as a fact*; which is just what it is not; for a fact is a dualistic abstraction. As it is in itself the total phenomenon in its presentness is absolutely simple and absolutely unrelated either as like or as unlike any other. It is simply a peculiar smell, *sui generis*. There is therefore no reason why it should not be entirely present at an instant of time, if there were no such thing as change. This is not quite so of the second category which is essentially two-sided. But if time were nothing but a succession of discrete instants, this category would be possible in the sequence of one instant upon another. But it is not so with the Third Category. A representation represents an object to an interpretant, which is a representation of the same object determined by the first representation. The whole being of a representation lies in being represented; and a representation must be at least a part of a complete representation. This complete representation without which there can be no representation must comprise the entire fact, including object and interpretant. It must therefore represent itself to itself; and it must represent every relation of object and interpretant, since without being represented such a fact of representation would have no being. Since then its interpretant is itself a representation, it must have its own interpretant and there must be a series which cannot be completed by successive accretions of units. Yet the entire series must be represented and therefore its limit. Moreover, all the relations of these interpretants which are of denumeral multitude must be re-presented and these are of the first abnumerable multitude. On the same principle every abnumerable multitude must be represented; and this transcends all multitude. Consequently, a representation can only have its being in a continuum. (If it be objected that a continuum cannot be "realized", probably what is meant is what is certainly true, namely that it cannot be experienced as a "fact", that is, under the second category. But the same may be said of everything that is most real in life and in the world.) Consequently a Thought, being of the nature of a Representation, cannot be "present" to consciousness. A thought is something that has to be enacted, and until it is enacted, its meaning has not been given, even to itself. I know the "Elegy in a Country Churchyard". But what is that? I can only tell by repeating it; I cannot have the whole thing in mind at once. (The doctrine of the Time-span is only relatively true; and the phenomenon is only one of these miniatures of fundamental laws which so often present themselves in nature. It is really quite irrelevant to what I am here saying.) Still, it is quite true that I do know the poem now this minute, and my knowing consists in no more nor less than this, that I can say it if I have time. It is so with every thought whatever from the most simple, up to the thought act of creation which lasts as long as the universe develops. This third Category is Hegel's *Begriff*. In fact the Hegelian Philosophy is nothing but a development of the doctrine that there is no other category than this one. It is my belief that if Hegel could have read *Substance and Shadow* [1863, by Henry James Sr. (1811–1882)] he would have seen that it is a deeper book than it has ever had the credit of being, and that this very category requires the independence of the others. But to return: it would certainly be most contrary to common sense (and not merely absurd) to represent that there can be no such thing as a representation. And if there *can be* there is; for the possibility is a representation. But if there is a representation there is a whole representation. Now logical analysis shows that a whole representation must essentially have three functions. The first and lowest is that it is present to itself, and vicariously to every moment of itself. It therefore causes the first Category. It will be commendable to use reserve in admitting the logical deduction here merely sketched. The best computers always seek a check upon a complicated piece of necessary reasoning, be it but the summation of a column of figures; and where a complete check is not forthcoming they are glad to get a partial one. Now a partial check on the logical deduction is afforded by common sense. For nobody would so much as be able to form a clear idea of what was meant by a representation which should never appeal to a mind, so that that mind could be conscious of knowing it somewhat as I know that I know the 'Elegy written in a Country Churchyard' [Thomas Grey, 1751]. It is true that most persons will draw back from admitting that in all its states, the representation is present to itself. "What, attribute consciousness to a book!" Well, but come; why not? "Well, we are ignorant of what the physical conditions of consciousness may be; but apparently such metabole as takes place in the brain is one of them". But permit me to call your attention to the circumstance that the phrase "physical conditions of consciousness" is hopelessly devoid of meaning. The only physical conditions are masses, positions, velocities, and accelerations, and these are absolutely unlike consciousness. "That is true; but we know that nitrous oxide introduced into the pulmonary circulation will produce, or if you like, be followed by complete unconsciousness; and therefore it is permissible to use the phrase 'physical conditions of consciousness'; and they are evidently all-important". I admit that such facts are important enough; but of what kind is that importance? It is obviously impossible to prove that the exhibition of nitrous oxide is followed by a condition of unconsciousness. It is only to be proved that it is followed by a loss of the government of the body by the consciousness; and to go further is to beg the very question before us. It locks the book up in the closet: more we cannot say. Just as a good night's sleep may bring it out and pull up the window-shades, and let the light of heaven fall upon the page. It is certainly, when you come to consider it, purely a question of connection and disconnection *in fact*,—that is, in the second category,—and has nothing to do with the pure immediate feeling of the first category. However, let the matter be as you will. One person will go one lap with me, and another two or three; but everyone will, if he gives sober reflexion to the matter, go quite far enough for my purpose of establishing the propriety of the method of philosophizing called Pragmatism. The second function of the Representation,—the *Begriff*,—a much higher one, though still a condescension,—is that it stands in Reaction with the world of reactions, the real world, the "material" world. It does not however react in the same manner in which a physical mass reacts upon another, in gravitation, in electrical induction, etc. Its causality is of an altogether different kind; and the non-recognition of this other kind of causation,—now going the length of downright denial, now simple ignoring, now admitting with an emotional "merely" attached to it,—has been and still is productive of more philosophical error and nonsense than any or than every other source of error and nonsense. If there is any goddess of nonsense, this must be her haunt. Goodness gracious, does M. du Perron mean to tell me that if I feel a draught on the nape of my neck I can't go and shut the window? Then, if I can do this, of my own notions, what is the sense of his theory of divine assistance? The truth is he thinks it impossible for mind to act upon matter because it takes it for granted that there is but one form of causation and that that one is the action of physical forces. His Excellency the Privy-Counsellor Leibniz has a similar theory of Preëstablished Harmony. Let me not be understood to begrudge the Seigneur du Perron all the Divine Assistance he likes, nor to the good Gottfried Wilhelm his Preëstablished Harmony. Only, I can open and shut my window when I like regardless of such arrangements. The notion that every fact of the physical universe is caused by physical force is one that will not bear examination. One factor of the confusion of thought is that people talk of the causes of *events*. It is in that way that J. S. Mill is led to his stupid notion that the cause of any event is the sum total of everything that concerns the thing moved. A pragmatist would instantly correct that by asking to what *use* the proposition that A causes B is put. It will then be seen that it is not *events* that are caused but *facts*, which are fluid extracts of events carrying away so much of them as a proposition will hold. 'What was the cause of the eruption of Mount Saint Relée?' That means, 'What is the *fact* from which according to the principles of physics, necessarily resulted the *fact* that the mountain suddenly burst?' Bear in mind that it is *facts* that are caused, and not (primarily at any rate) raw events, and it is obvious enough that the most striking facts of the universe have other causes than physical forces. Thus, it is a fact that prisms in the sunlight are apt to make spots of high colored light. None but the most giddy head will attribute this to the forces of refraction; for those same forces will operate just as much to recombine the spectral colors. The true cause is the ordinary neutralization of colors by being compounded in the same rays. For thence it follows that dispersion must ordinarily enhance the chromatic effect, and only the most singular chance can cause decomposed rays to be reunited. Another striking fact is that things grow all one way and none in the reverse sequence of states. It is easy to see that no conservative force can be the cause of that. Very well then. Physical force give plenty of room for the action of other causes, since it is only one little group of facts that it meddles with at all, the accelerations of particles. Mind does not act on matter in that way at all. I am using *mind* now as synonym of Representation; and mind that this mind is not the mind that the psychologists mind if they mind any mind. I think they mainly talk about consciousness, in the sense of the first category, and hypothetical arrangements in the brain. The way in which Mind acts upon matter is by imposing upon it conformity to certain peculiar Laws, called Purposes; and the manner of the reaction is that the Purposes themselves become modified and developed in being thus carried out. Logical analysis shows that it is essential to the nature of representation that it should so develop itself by imposing purposes upon matter. This is the great logical operation of Deduction; where the Action (as in the operation of Volition) is more prominent and prevailing in these reasonings we call direct, but the Reaction (as in Sense-perception) in those cases in which the facts surprise us by rising in revolt, and we have an Indirect Reasoning or *Reductio ad absurdum*. The third and noblest function of the Representation is Growth. "ἄνευ [γὰρ] τοῦ γίγνεσθαι γενέσθαι ἀδύνατον" says Socrates in the *Theætetus* (155c), "a thing cannot happen without going through a process of coming to pass". But this is not the deepest philosophy: the process of growth is the *summum bonum*. Only, it must be remembered that the growth of the Idea includes Reproduction; nay that it is unsupposable and meaningless except in a Creation. For thought *is* an operation and a creative operation. The fault of *Substance and Shadow* is that it represents the desire of God to confer independence upon that which is most opposite to Himself to be a special peculiarity of God. But God has no whimsies nor pet weaknesses: it is on the contrary the essential nature of Purpose that it cannot be directed toward itself but develops itself in Creating. The Representation is directed toward its object. In the course of bringing that object into rationalization, making a statue out of a stone, the thought accomplishes itself. I am just scribbling as fast as pen will run. But let all this be more artfully put and I think almost any person without a violent prepossession will go along with what I say sufficiently to admit that a thought is a purpose and that in order to perform the reflexion necessary to the straightening out the threads of thought and laying them orderly and parallel will consist mainly or at least first of all in defining to ourselves what the purpose is a purpose to bring about and what use, theoretical or practical, it is designed to subserve; and that is Pragmatism.

– Berkeley's Idealism as an example of it.

Yes, of all possible examples this is the fittest; and for three reasons. First, because Berkeley is so illuminatively more pragmatistic than any of the philosophers who had preceded him, or than any who for a century or more followed him, that Pragmatism ought not bo be mentioned with approval without a reference to this very great philosopher. Secondly, because Berkeley is an extreme nominalist and Nominalism is itself of pragmatistic origin and its falsity is owing to its not fully planting itself upon pragmatistic ground. Thirdly, because the faults of Berkeley's system, which are prominent and obvious enough, arise simply from his deficient grasp of the pragmatistic principle. Berkeley's theory of vision was a great thing in itself. It springs entirely from the innate pragmatism of the British mind. It is also a very great thing as illustrating the pragmatistic method of reflexion. Let us also mention, in this connexion, among the great examples of Pragmatic thought, Kant's refutation of Berkeley's idealism. Berkeley is forever saying that he fully shares the belief of all ordinary people in regard to the existence of the material world. There is nothing upon which he insists more. But he thinks the philosophers have a different opinion. Yet how is it possible that they should have any other opinion? According to him, their theory would be the most extraordinarily original of all human theories. Who, then, originated it and when? There never was any such theory. The philosophers simply aim to reproduce the instinctive belief in the independent existence of matter which Berkeley himself is so extremely concerned to explain that he fully shares. Why use one mode of exegesis for the vulgar and and another for philosophers, the extreme vulgarity of whose thought is the most striking feature of their writings? The truth is that Berkeley wavers. He is pragmatist enough to see that the vulgar opinion is quite right and yet he does not seem to be satisfied with a pragmatism which does not convict anybody at all of error. Berkeley was a theologian and his philosophical doctrine partook of the character of a theological creed. Now no single creed of christendom,—as I can say by a painstaking study of Dr. Schaff's [1875] three volumes, —was ever put forward of which the principal purpose was not to proclaim somebody to be damned. Not one single creed contains anything about love, although that is generally recognized, as the central principle of christianity. But because nobody denied it, there was no motive to put it into the creed. In like manner, Berkeley would not have felt that he had made any contribution to philosophy at all, if he did not refute somebody; and in order to refute somebody, he gives his idealism a second meaning quite inconsistent with his admission of the vulgar tenet.

42 Fragments

[Copy-text consists of selected pages from R S-28, R S-1, R 510, R 478, R 1333, R 496, R S-46 and R 1070.] This last chapter is a collation of assorted images, illustrations and holograph pages from various sketchbooks and manuscript leaves from 1903. Peirce filled a significant number of sheets with studies and sketches of graphs, some rather experimental. Most of them do not appear elsewhere, and many are scattered across the Peirce Papers: relevant notebooks, worksheets, manuscript drafts and cut-out pages can be identified in a number of Robin folders and supplementary call numbers that are often unrelated, while some appear on fragmentary sheets misplaced in the archives. With the possible exception of a single folio from R 1070 and the pages from R S-46, the images included in the selection can be ascertained to have been produced during Peirce's preparation for his Lowell Lectures, even though they lack clear indications with which pre-drafts and lecture notes they are associated. Even so, they evince both the breadth and scope of the evolving theory of EGs, as well as the progress Peirce made on its development during his *annus mirabilis*.

Excerpts from R S-28, notebook pages 54, 64–78

[Page 54]

[A proposal of alternative notations for the spots of potentials appearing on the notebook page 55 of R S-28, opposite to "Convention No. 10" (the wavy line, Lowell Lecture II(a), R S-28). These marks suggest that Peirce contemplated, perhaps sometime in September, several alternatives to the 'envelope notation' of his logic of potentials (see pp. 64–71 of the same notebook). On this page we find Π and σ-shaped spots, as well as geometric shapes—such as a triangle for the zero-place relation of "___ is a graph"; a box for "___ is a quality", a diamond for "___ stands in a dyadic relation ___ to ___ ", etc., that stand for the spots of the second-order logic of potentials. Peirce's papers commonly feature doodles of face profiles that accompany his studies in logic.

The following studies on pp. 64–78 of R S-28 relate to the pre-drafts of Lecture V on the logic of mathematics and multitudes. Spots and lines are typically inscribed in red ink in the original.]

[Pages 64–65]

There is a relation in which no X stands to

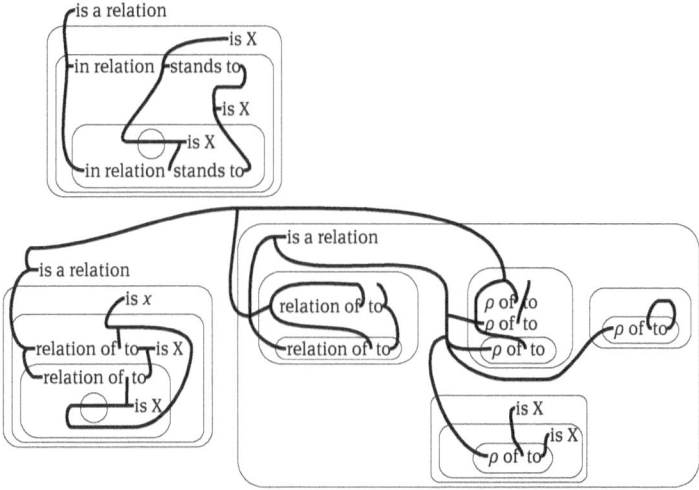

There is a relation ρ such that any X and whatever thing Z may be either Z is not in that relation to that X' or is not an X or is identical with X.

Moreover this relation ρ is such that no matter what ρ' may be, either there is something A and something C
- such that A is ρ to C
- or A is ρ to something that if ρ' to C
- or A is C and yet A is not ρ' to C
- or else there is an X, say P, such that whatever Q may be whether Q is not X or P is ρ' to Q.

[Page 67]

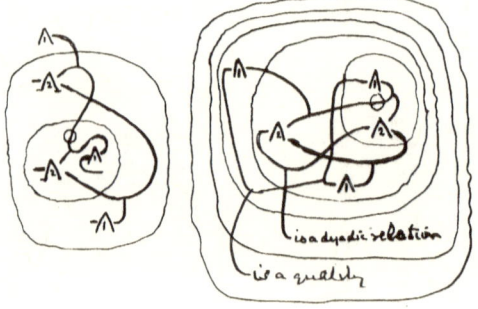

[Page 69]

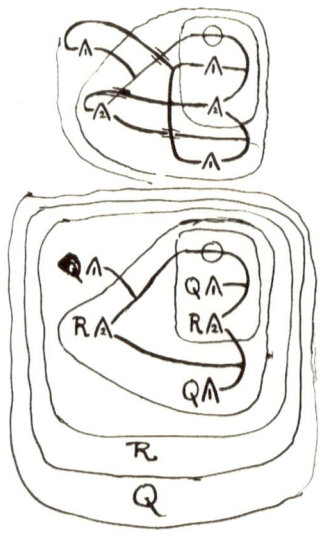

[Page 71]

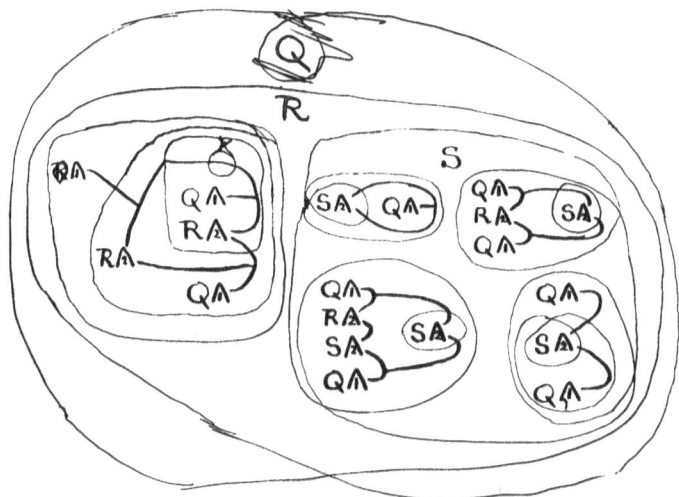

Whatever quality Q may be, there is a relation, R, such that (left-hand side) if anything possesses the quality Q it stands in the relation R to some thing which possesses that quality to which nothing else possessing the quality Q stands in the relation R; and further (right-hand side) whatever relation S may be that either (above left) something possessing the quality Q is not in the relation, S, to itself or (above right) something possessing the quality Q stands in the relation R to something possessing the quality Q without being in the relation S to that thing, or (below on left) something possessing the quality Q is in the relation R to something in the relation S to something possessing the quality Q without the first being in the relation S to the last or finally (below on right) some possessing the quality Q is in the relation S to everything possessing the quality Q.

[Page 73]

By a *number* is meant a *finite multitude* in contradistinction to a *numeral*

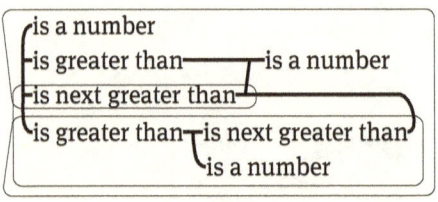

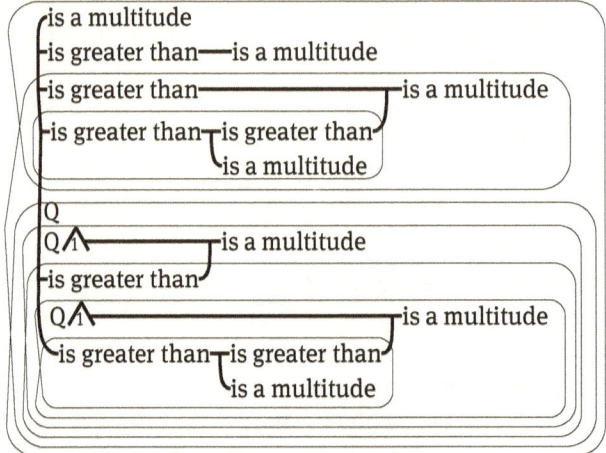

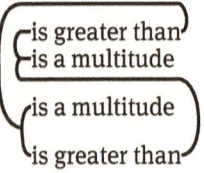

[Page 78]

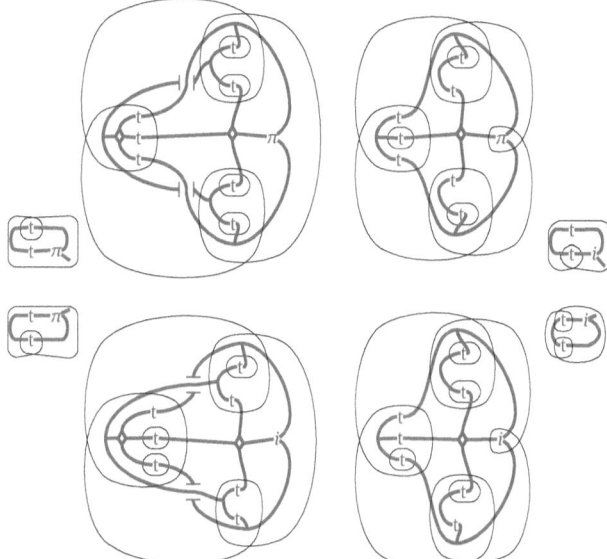

Excerpts from R S-1, notebook pages 70–81

[Possibly the first sketch of the fourth planned lecture on modal graphical logic (R 467). The broken-cut operators sketched here on the notebook page 70 mean "is possible" and although identical in looks, are not equivalent in meaning to the modal broken-cut notations that signify contingencies ("possibly, not") in Lecture IV (R 467) and elsewhere. This possibility interpretation of the broken cut predates the contingency interpretation that appears on p. 72 of the notebook.]

[Page 70]

The fact that c—⊢—w shows that c—⊢—w cannot be transformed into some apparent graph[1] and there is some real graph into which it cannot be transformed by the rules.

And from this it follows that there [is] some quality (c—⊢—w) and some quality (c—⊢—w) and some relation (c—⊢—w).

g ≺ (g) = g is possible

(g) ≺ (g) = non g is possible

(g) = non g is not possible ≺ g

(g) = g is not possible ≺ (g)

If this means logical possibility [end]

[Page 71]

The assertion of a graph is equivalent to saying that the graph itself may be written That is a blank may (as a fact) be transformed into that graph

produces the permission to transform a blank into it.

fact permits the transformation of a blank into it.

Let A be the actual universe

Contingent fact   A━permits━the graph
Possibility   ━permits━the graph

Necessity   ⎰permits⎱
                  ⎱the graph⎰

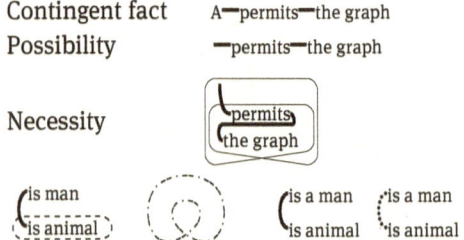

---

1 [See R 464(s) on the definition of "apparent graph".]

71

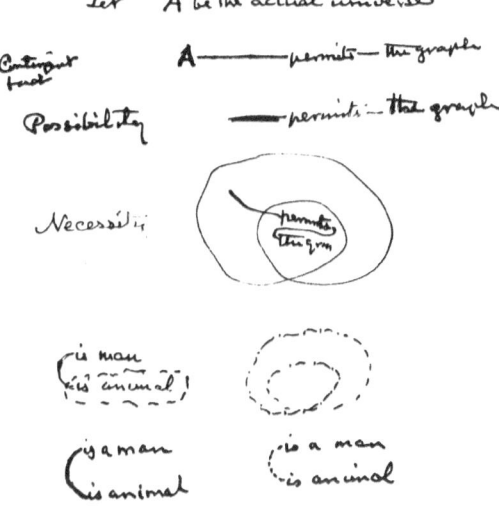

A holograph page 71 from R S-1 (Harvard Peirce Papers).

[Appearing as novelties on this page are the dotted line of identity and the dashed-dotted boundary of the scroll. These proposals are related to the development of the theory of graphs of graphs, section "Facts involving permissions" (Lowell Lecture IV, R 468).]

[Page 72][2]

Assume (̇g̣) means that *g* is not necessary

((g))   *g* is necessary

((̇g̣))   *g* is possible

(((̇g̣)))   *g* is impossible

(̇g̣) ≺ (g) ≺ (̇g̣)
(g) ≺ (̇g̣)
g ≺ (̇g̣)

Can fill broken cut inside full cut
Can break cut outside full cut
Unenclosed can remove (̇ ̣) can insert (○)
Inside broken cut
can insert (̇ ̣) can remove (○) can fill broken
Outside [broken cut]
can insert (○)

(̇g̣) = ((̇g̣)) ≠ (((̇g̣)))

(̇g̣) The rules don't know *g* is true   they may not know it not true (̇g̣)
                                                 or they may know it not true ((̇g̣)) ≺ *g*

((̇g̣))   don't know *g* is false   may not know it is true (̇g̣)
                                          or may know it is not true ((̇g̣))

If I don't know that I know it ~~not~~ true ((̇g̣)) I don't know it is true (̇g̣) ?
                        I may not know that I don't know it true ((̇g̣))
                        I may know that I don't know it true (̇ ̣). Surer ((̇ ̣))

---

[2] [See "Introduction" for explanations.]

72

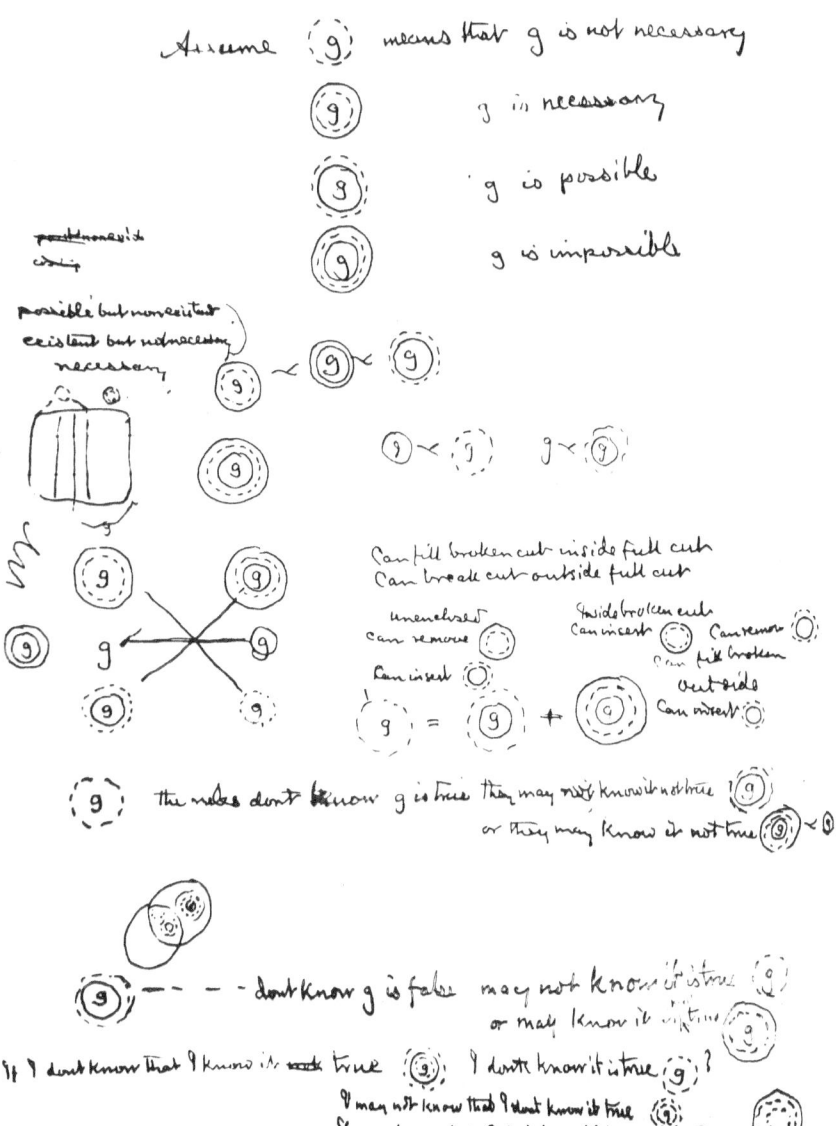

A holograph page 72 from R S-1 (Harvard Peirce Papers).

[Page 73][3]

If I don't know it false that I know g ⦅g⦆

        I may not know that it is true that [I] know g ⦅g⦆

        or I may know that it is true I know (⦅g⦆)

If the rules do not enable me to know that they enable me to know g ⦅g⦆

        then they do not enable me to know g ⦅g⦆ ?

Conclusion of the Matter

⦅g⦆	means that beta rules	do not prove that	g is true
(g)			g is false
(g)		prove that	g is true
(⦅g⦆)			g is false

The Rules of Transformation are

~~Outside a~~ Within an even number of cuts (whether interrupted or not) an interrupted cut can be made uninterrupted

~~Inside a~~ Within an odd number of cuts (interrupted or not) an uninterrupted cut can be interrupted.

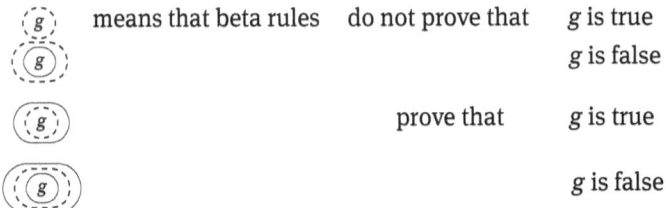

---

3 [See "Introduction" for explanations.]

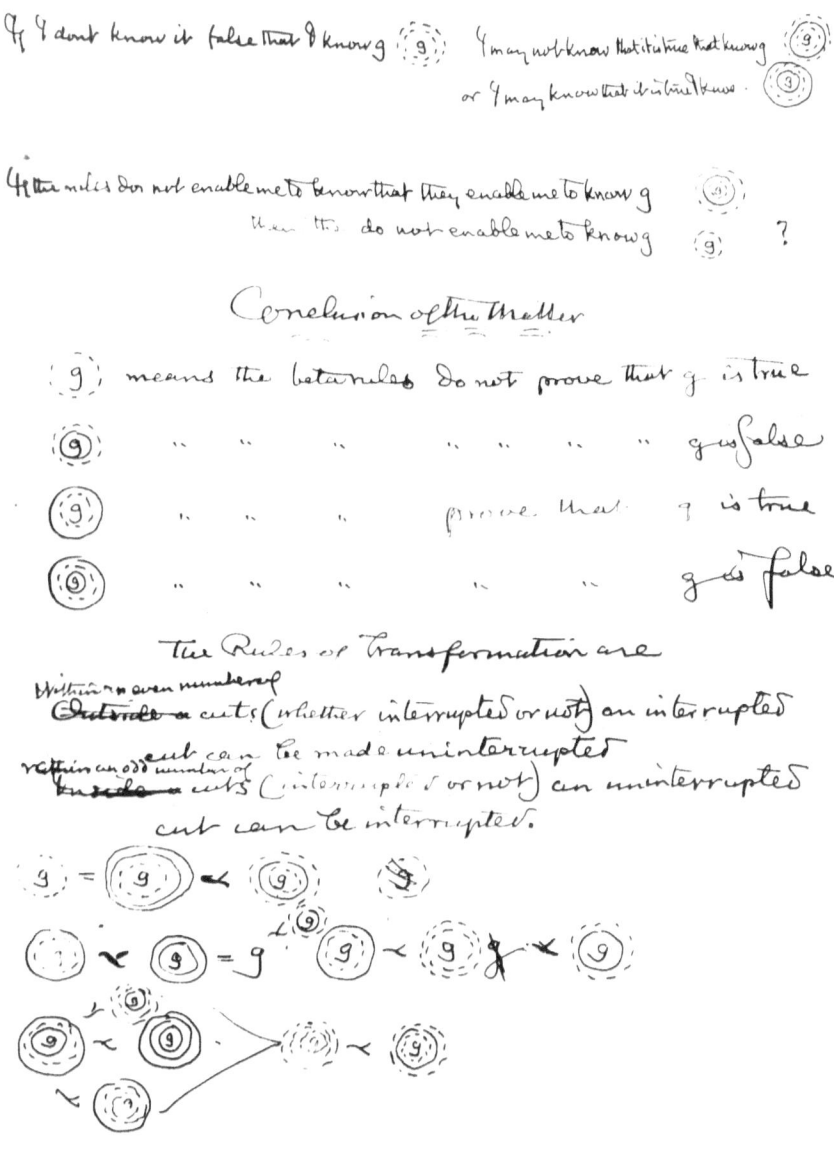

A holograph page 73 from R S-1 (Harvard Peirce Papers).

[Related to Lowell Lecture IV (R 467).]

74

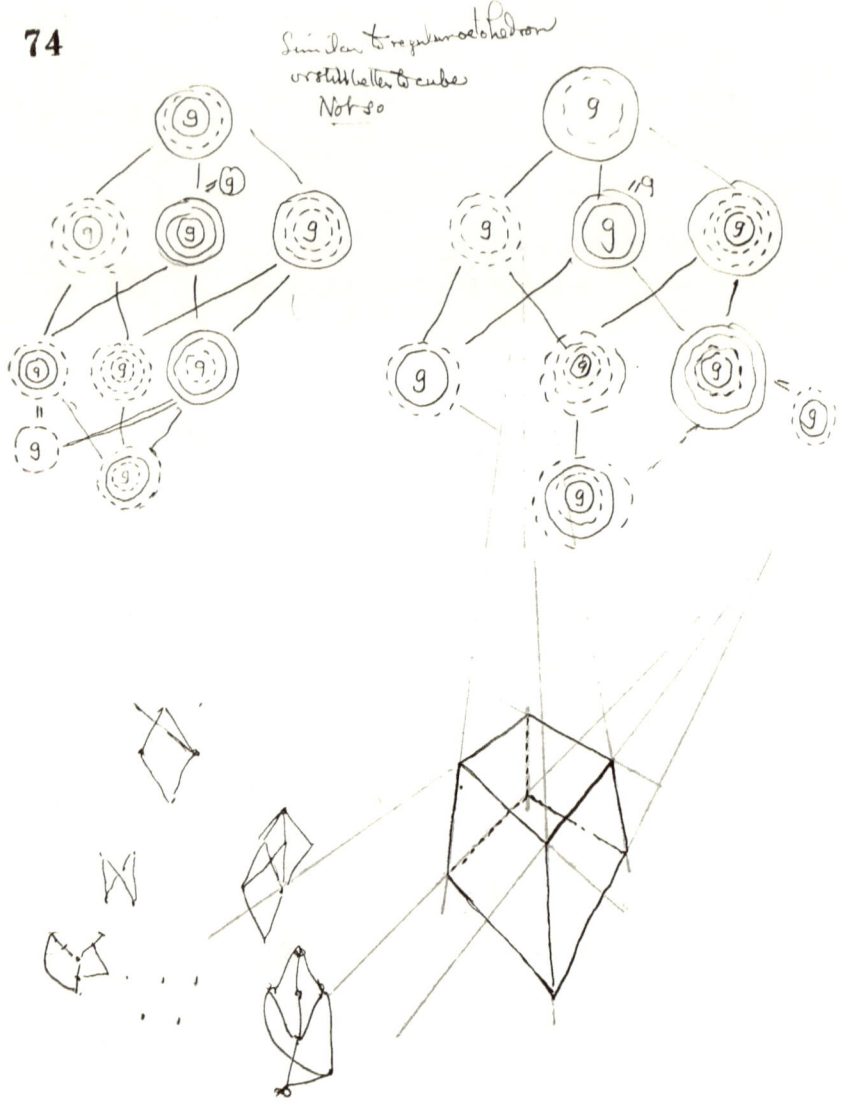

A holograph page 74 from R S-1 (Harvard Peirce Papers).

[See "Introduction" for explanations. The five long parallel double lines in the two figures above and the next page are equality signs.]

[Page 74]

Similar to regular octahedron, or still better to cube
Not so

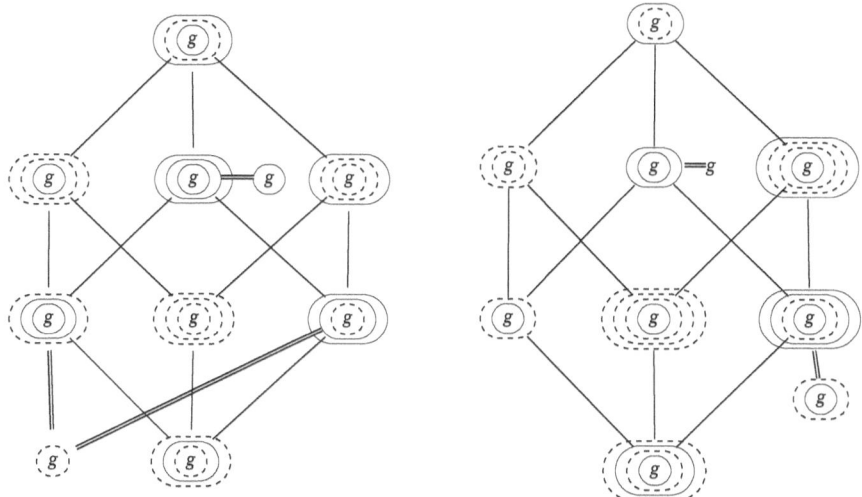

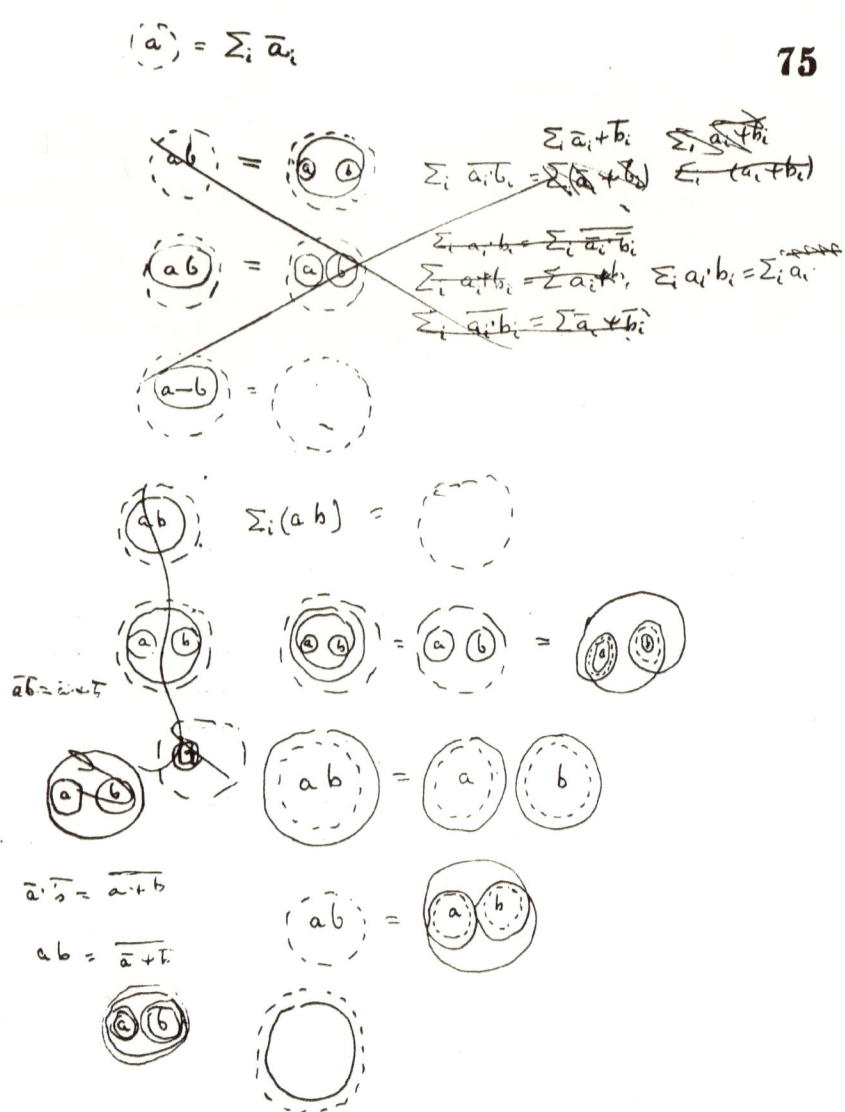

A holograph page 75 from R S-1 (Harvard Peirce Papers).

[See "Introduction" for explanations.]

76

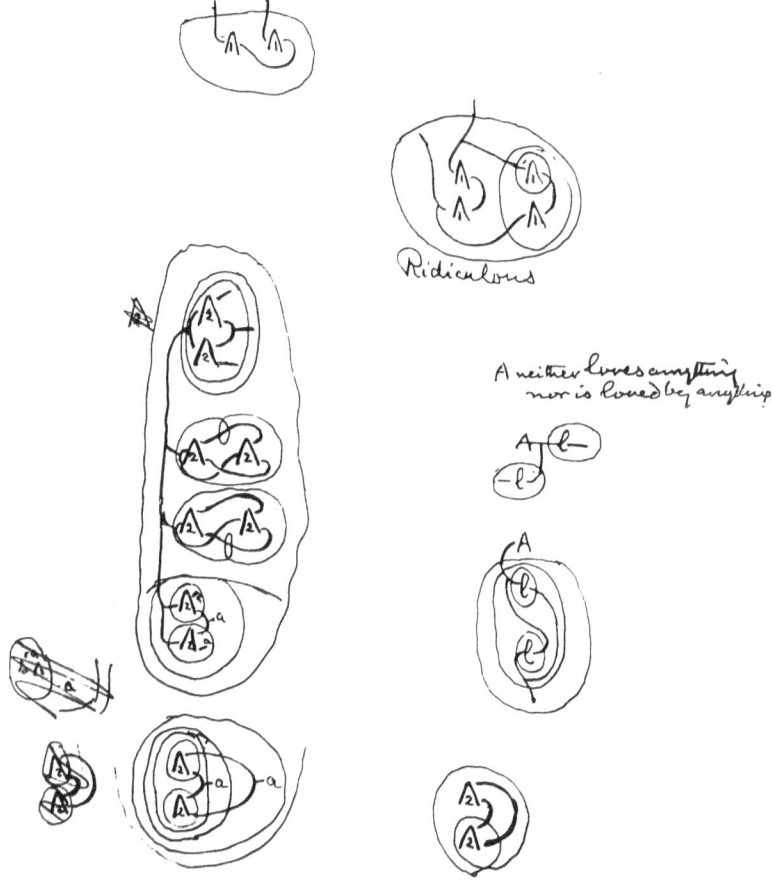

A holograph page 76 from R S-1 (Harvard Peirce Papers).

[Related to Lowell Lecture V(d), R 469–R 471.]

77

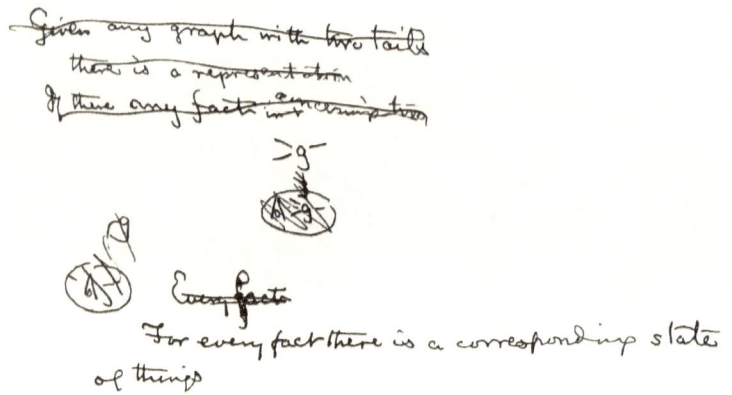

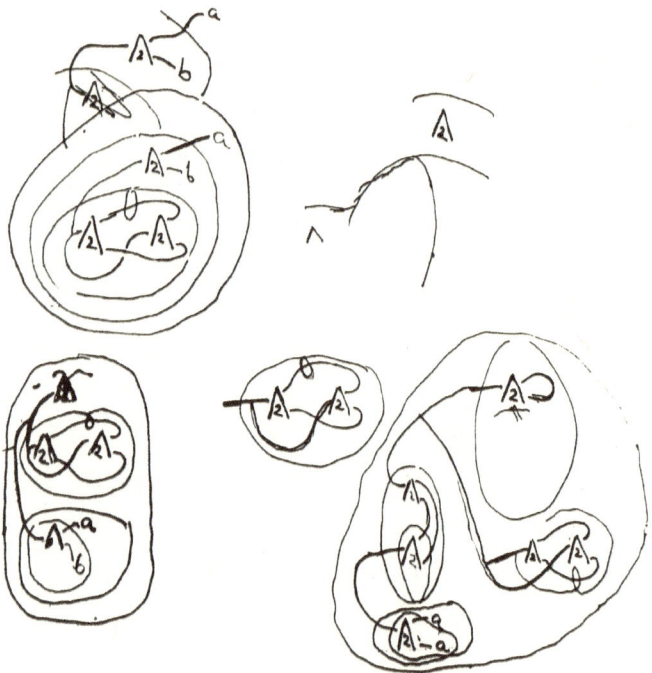

A holograph page 77 from R S-1 (Harvard Peirce Papers).

[More applications of potentials in Peirce's graphical logic of potentials, related to Lowell Lecture V(d), R 469–R 471. Indeed propositions of the form "For every A there is a B" are of second-order, and quantification over "representations" and "states of things" (cf. R S-46) suggests a further modal element involved in the logic of potentials.]

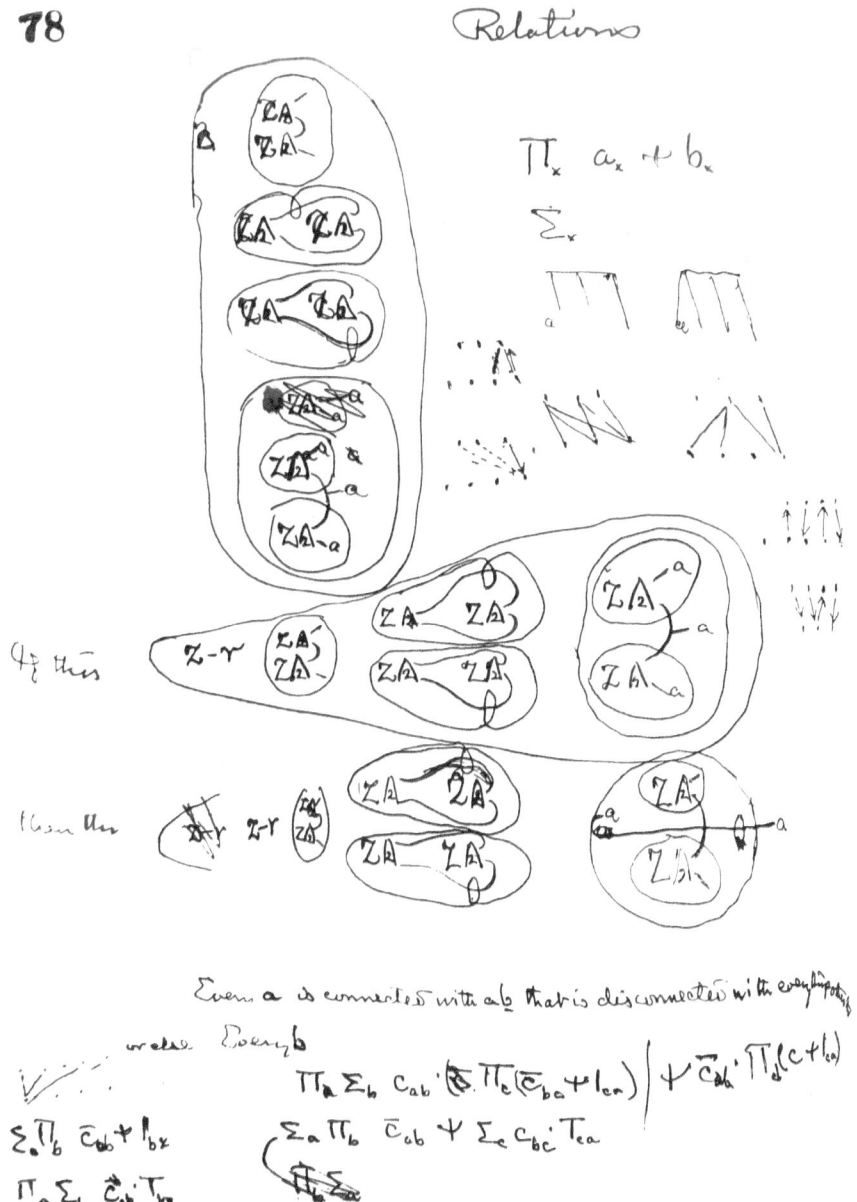

A holograph page 78 from R S-1 (Harvard Peirce Papers).

[Related to Lowell Lecture V(d), R 469–R 471, and NDDR (R 539).]

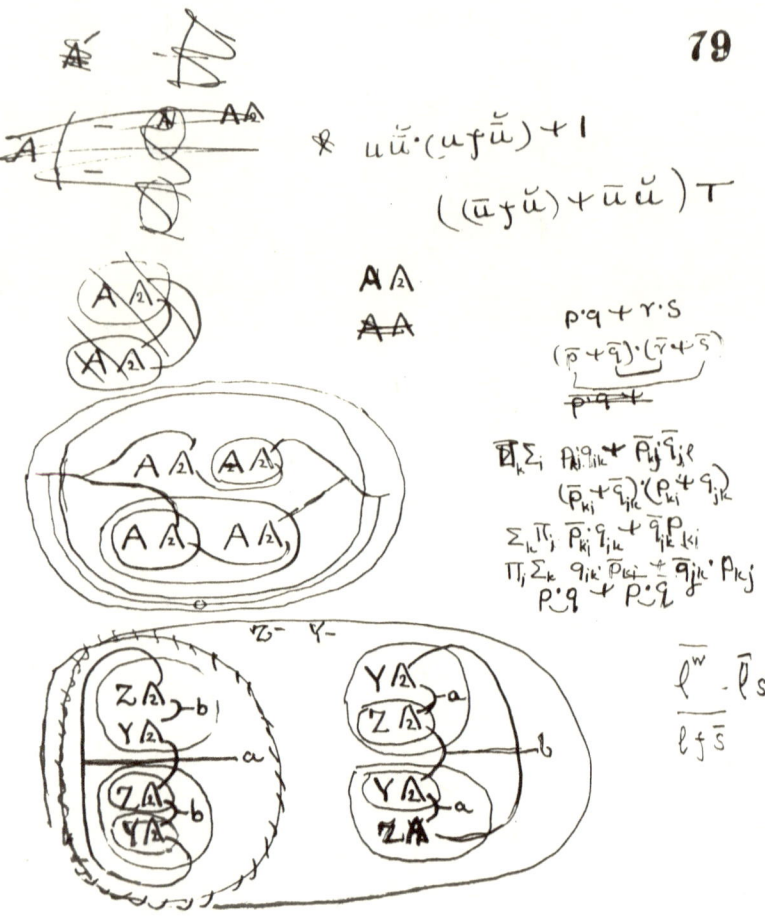

A holograph page 79 from R S-1 (Harvard Peirce Papers).

[Related to Lowell Lecture V(d), R 469–R 471, and NDDR (R 539).]

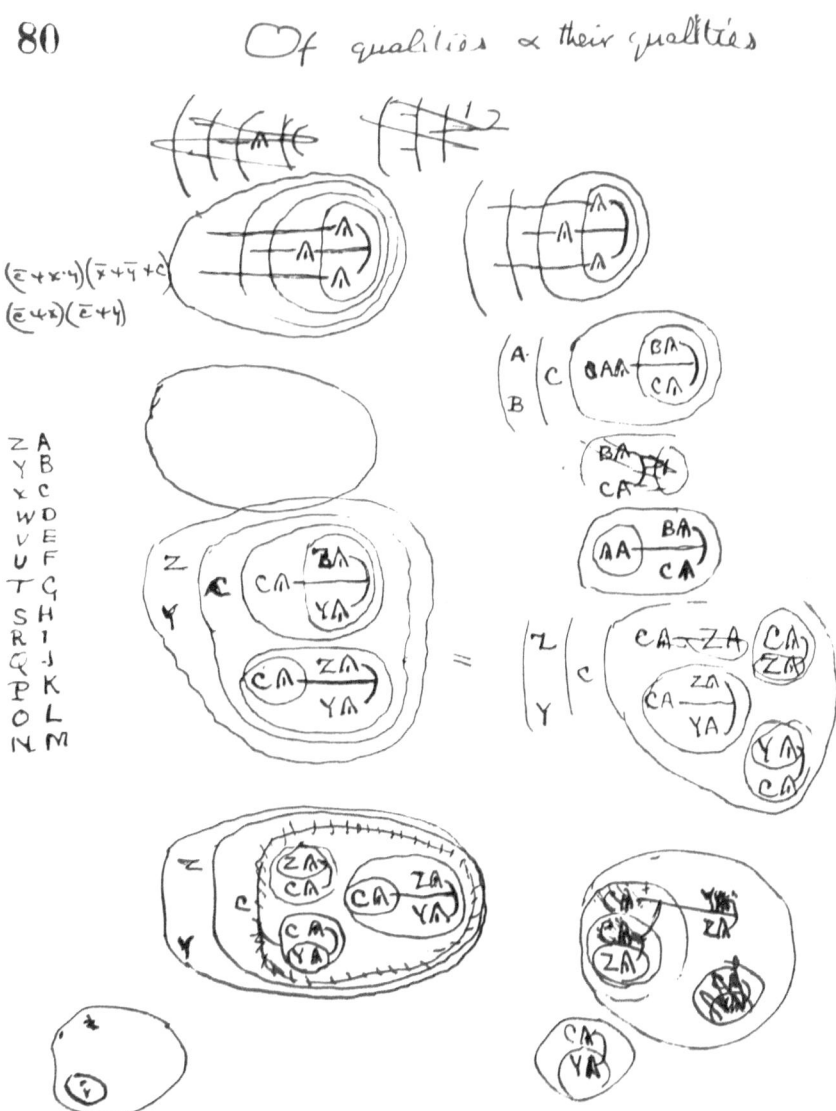

A holograph page 80 from R S-1 (Harvard Peirce Papers).

[Related to Lowell Lecture V(d), R 469–R 471.]

406 — 42 Fragments

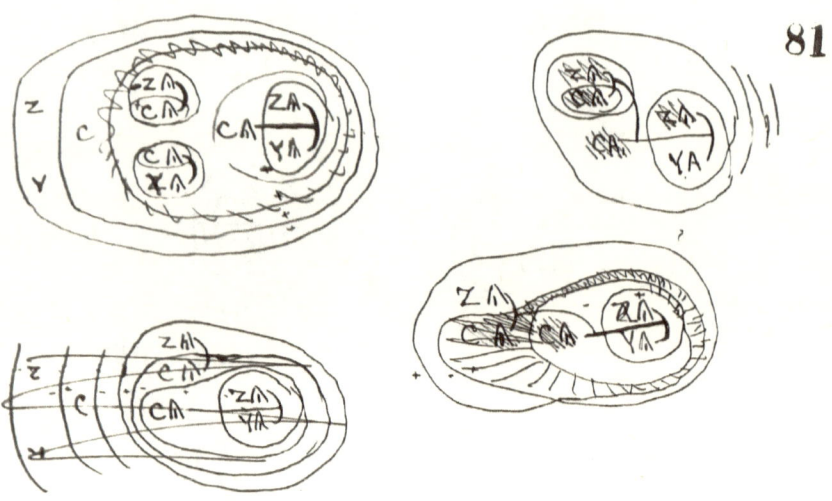

A holograph page 81 from R S-1 (Harvard Peirce Papers).

[Related to Lowell Lecture V(d), R 469–R 471.]

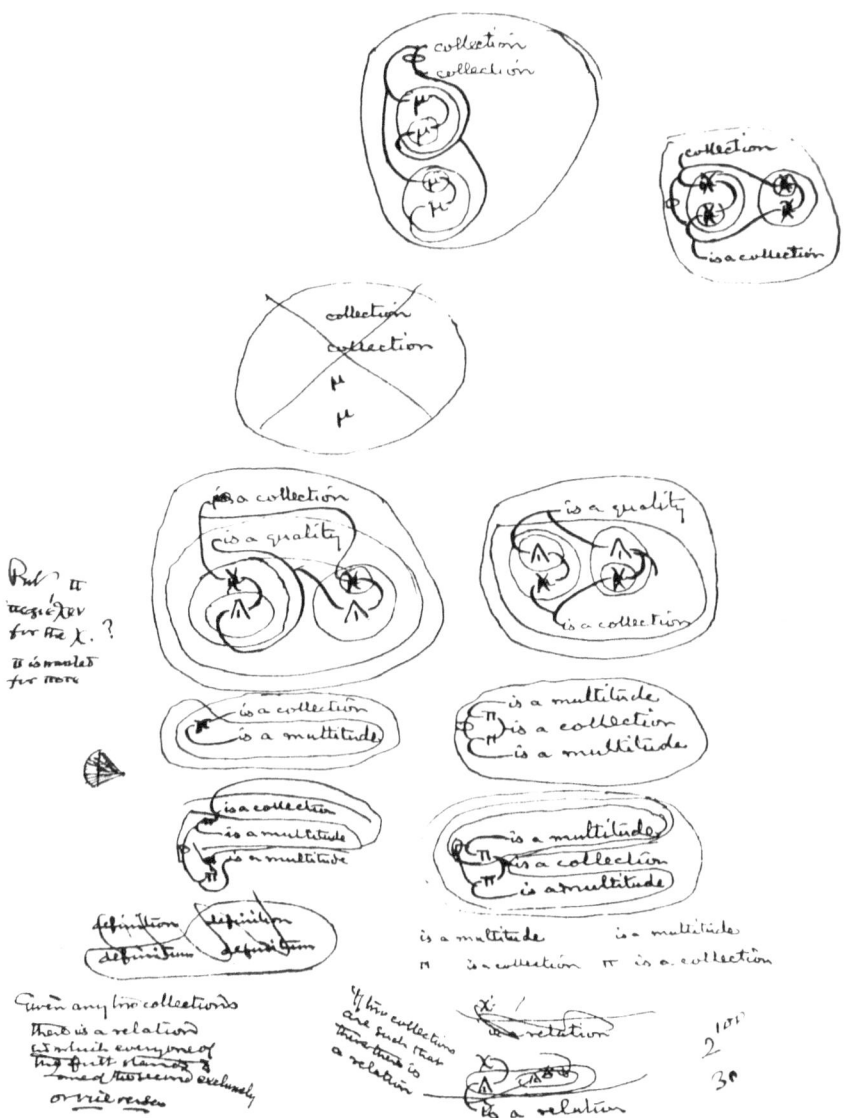

A holograph page (Harvard Peirce Papers, R 510).

[A worksheet on a study of collections with potentials. Related to Lowell Lecture V(d), R 469–R 471.]

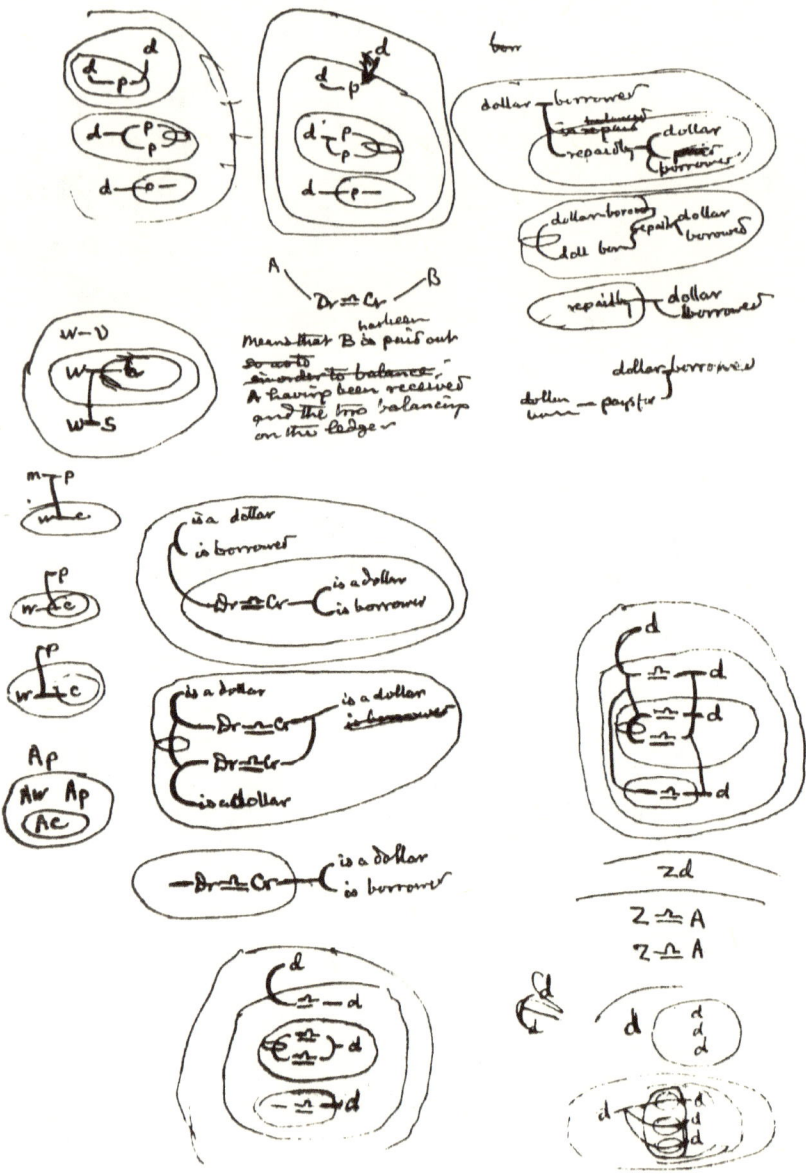

A holograph page (Harvard Peirce Papers, R 510).

[A worksheet proposing a 'ledger-spot' notation, to mean quantities that are "balancing on the ledger". (Some background inscriptions by lead pencil that appear on the original page have been removed for clarity.)]

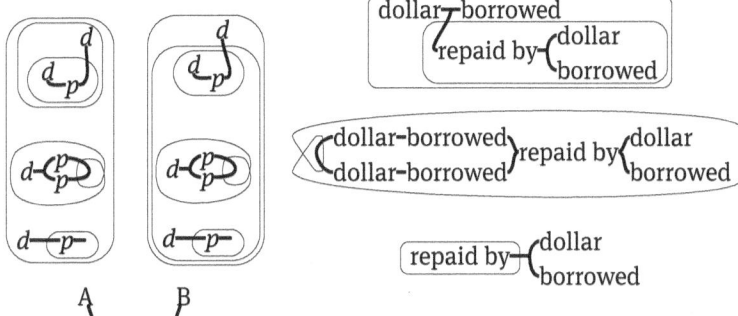

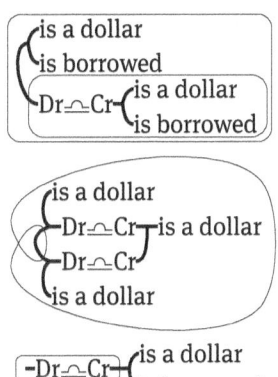

A   B
  Dr⌢Cr

Means that B ~~is~~ has been paid out ~~so as to in order to balance~~   A having been received and the two balancing on the ledger

is a dollar
is borrowed
-Dr⌢Cr- is a dollar
         is borrowed

is a dollar
-Dr⌢Cr- is a dollar
-Dr⌢Cr-
is a dollar

-Dr⌢Cr- is a dollar
         is borrowed

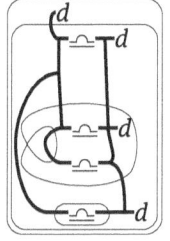

A holograph page (Harvard Peirce Papers, R 510).

[A worksheet illustrating examples of Peirce's alternative 'line-feed' notation for graphs. An adjacent page explains the procedure as follows:]

> [i] A selective, or capital letter, is to be substituted for ~~every~~ each least enclosed juncture, a juncture not being within a cut unless it is wholly within it, and this is to be repeated until all the junctures are abolished. [ii] Junctures evenly enclosed are to be replaced [by] early letters of the alphabet A to L, [iii] junctures oddly enclosed by late letters Z to M.
>
> The entire graph is to be transcribed, [iv] more enclosed spots being scribed lower down ~~than less~~ in the same columns and [v] spots enclosed in cuts within the same cut to be in parallel columns, the columns being split by braces.
>
> In place of ~~the cuts~~ each evenly enclosed cut is to be placed a single large parenthesis mark to the left and [vii] in place of each oddly enclosed cut is to be placed a single large square bracket to the left. [viii] Oddly enclosed spots are to be put a little further to the right than evenly enclosed spots in the same column.

[What Peirce is proposing here is a kind of graph rewriting algorithm, which by following the eight steps (numbers (i)–(viii) added here for clarity) would transform existential graphs into a quasi-linear notation, which has eliminated junctures and replacing them with selectives. Thus the notation uses only standard typesetting, such as line skips, indentations and large multi-line parentheses, brackets and braces. A couple of loose worksheets located in R 278 are also connected to this proposal which apparently was not pursued any further, however (see Bellucci, Liu & Pietarinen 2020 for details).]

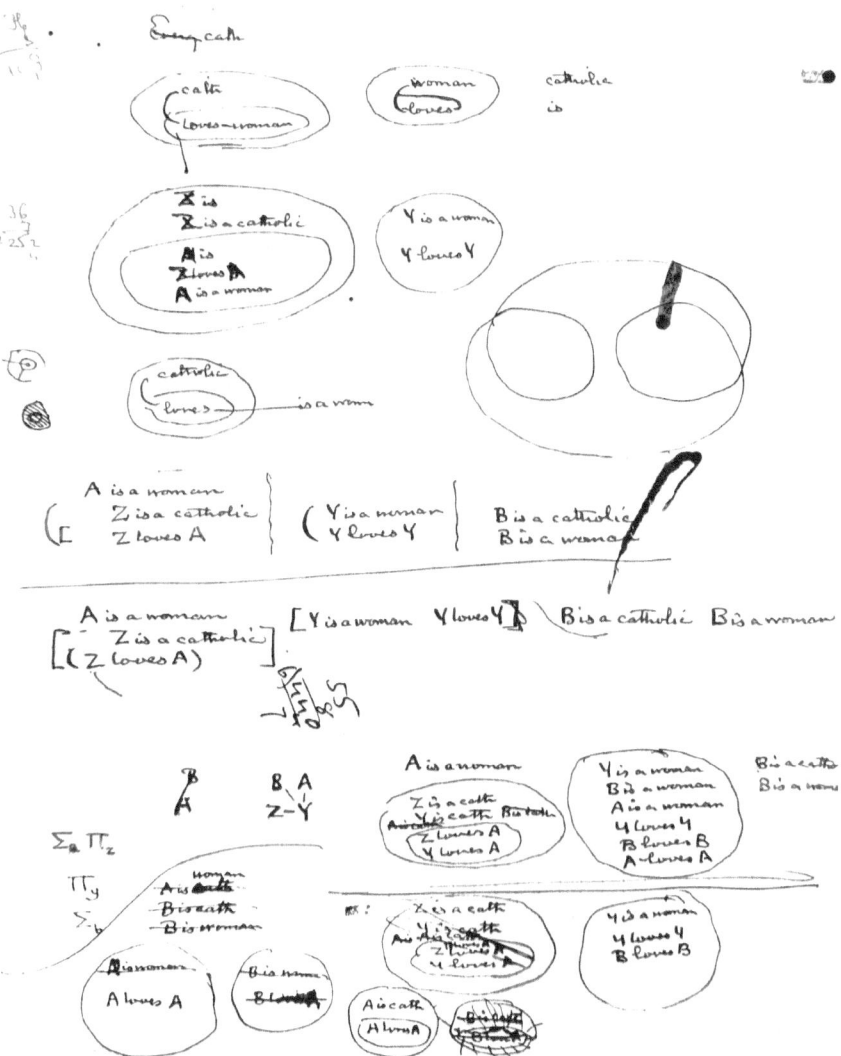

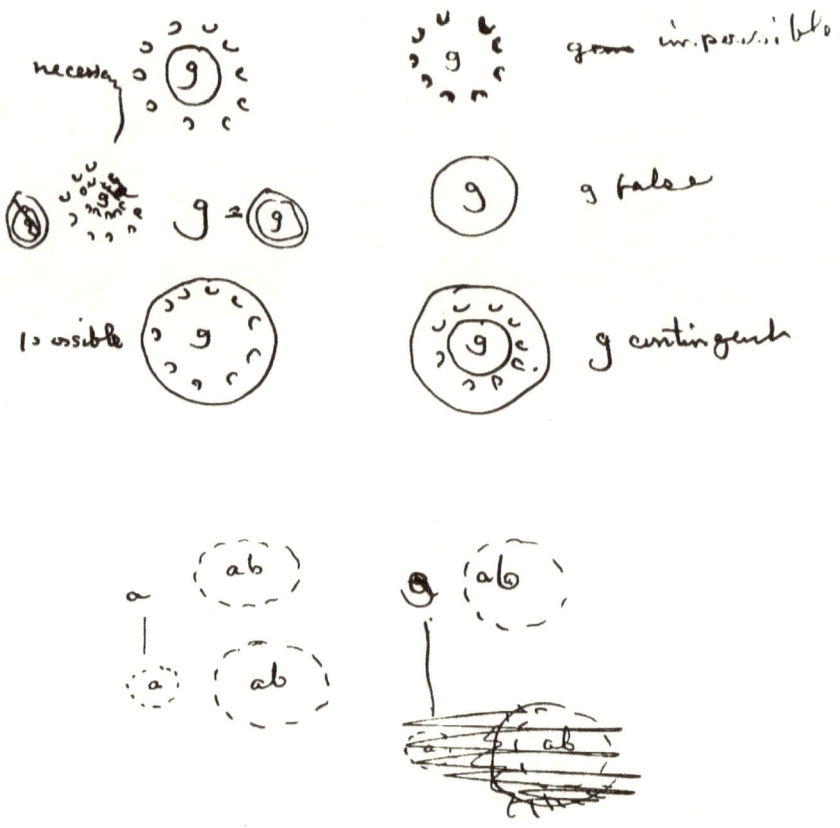

A holograph page (Harvard Peirce Papers, R 478).

[An image of the page on the verso on an abandoned manuscript page 154 of the draft *Syllabus* text. It shows a unique proposal to define a modality that is dual to the broken cuts, here notated by a ring of small outward-curved breves surrounding a graph. Its signification is that the surrounded graph is *impossible*, in contrast to the signification of the standard broken cut which is that of *contingency* of a graph *g*, namely that it is not impossible that not *g*. Contingency is defined by continuous cuts appearing both immediately outside and inside of the dual-broken cut, as depicted in the third graph on the right hand column. Peirce did not adopt the breve-cut notation that takes impossibility as the basic modality anywhere else in his studies, instead settling on broken-cuts and contingency.]

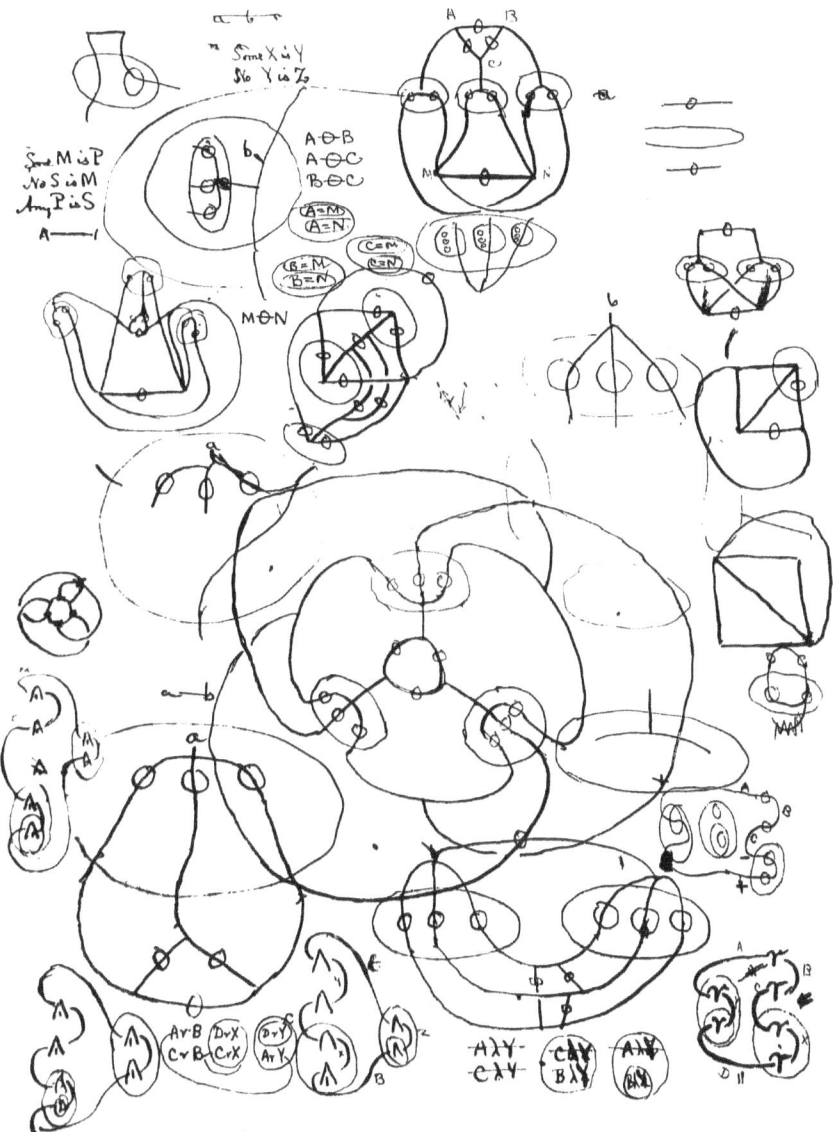

A holograph page (Harvard Peirce Papers, R 1333).

[A verso page filled with studies on graphs. The recto of this loose sheet is part of the draft of Peirce's review on English scientists, published in *The Nation*, October 1, 1903. The graphs are related to the topics taken up in the pre-drafts of his fifth Lowell Lecture (V(a,b,c)).]

Excerpts from R 496

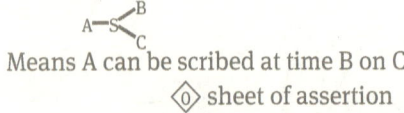

Means A can be scribed at time B on C

 sheet of assertion

1. Whatever could be scribed on the sheet at any time when this or that is scribed can be scribed (whatever is or is not scribed) at all times

2. If anything A can be scribed on the sheet of assertion at any time

Then at all times a cut can be made containing a cut containing A

At the time B a cut A can be scribed containing D

If at no time a graph A can be scribed on the sheet of assertion, then at any time, a cut can be made containing A

That is taking any graph whatever A and any circumstances C whatever, either that graph may be scribed on the sheet of assertion under these circumstances, or a cut containing it can be so scribed under the same circumstances.

If a cut can be scribed on the sheet of assertion

If under any circumstances a graph A were being scribed on the sheet of assertion a graph B could be scribed then under the same circumstances if B were contained in a cut.

If on the sheet (certain graph being scribed and certain graph not scribed) ~~can be scribed a cut~~ [end]

Take any detached graph you please and any state of the sheet you please then either this graph cannot be ~~written~~ veraciously scribed or else in any state of the sheet it can be scribed

Better begin by taking S to mean scribable on the sheet of assertion in a given state of the sheet ⟨S̄/S̱⟩

Now let $A\text{-}c{<}^B_C$ mean that in a state B of the sheet C may be scribed in a cut

{ A
  on the sheet
  permissibly

That should be in place in the state of sheet is permissible
That should be in place in the state of sheet is—known to be permissible

We must draw the distinctions	and still better
may be scribed	known to be insertable
may be unscribed	known to be omissible
must not be scribed	known not to be insertable
must not be unscribed	known not [to] be omissible
	not known to be insertible
	not known to be omissible
	not known not to be insertible
	not known not to be omissible
of a graph—it is known that ⟨	A—is a graph of which it is known ⟨

means that the presence of A in area C in state of sheet B has the character D

A—a—B
A is attached to B

The presence of A attached to B in the state C on the sheet ~~attached~~ in area D has character E

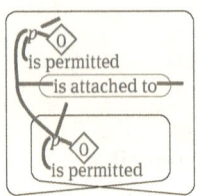

 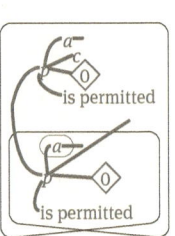

Geometrical conditions

A—c—B A is *present connected* B
A—d—B A is present dinected[4] to B

In every state of the sheet there is some graph neither connected nor dinected with any

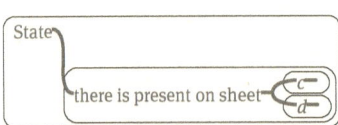 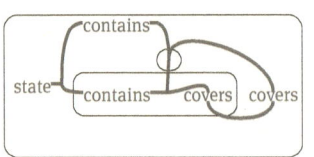

In every state of the sheet [end, fragment abandoned]

---

4 [Peirce wrote "denicted". See R 492, *Logical Tracts No. 2*, for the definition of "dinected". Cf. R 458 to which R 496 is related and probably composed about the same time, before October, as an early study intended for the lecture on multitudes.]

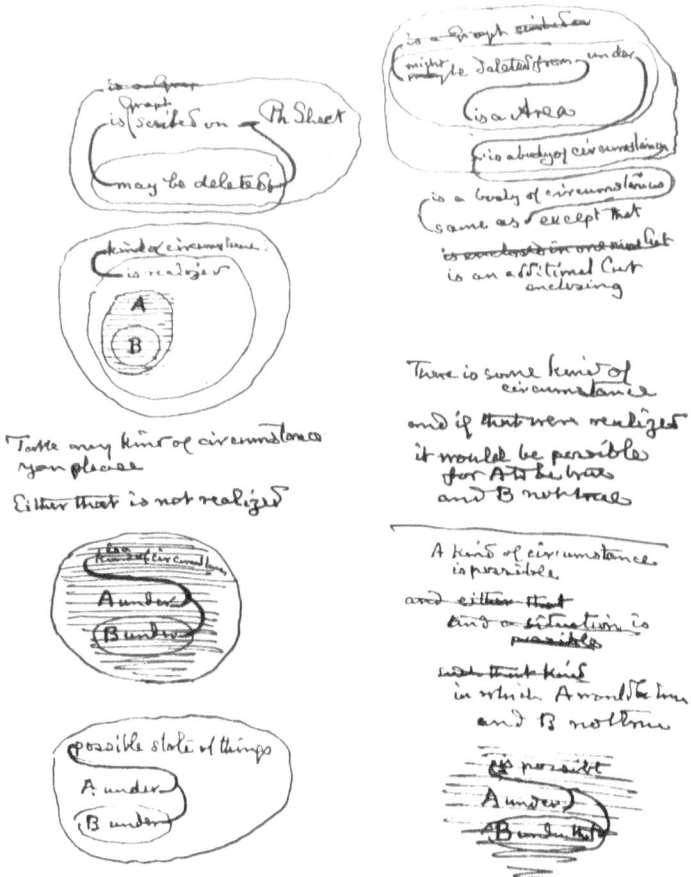

A holograph page (Harvard Peirce Papers, R S-46).

[A unique study that proposes modal graphs of graphs (e.g., "is scribed on Ph[emic] Sheet"; "is a kind of circumstance", "is realized"), with quantification over predicate terms that denote possible worlds ("states of things") and with graphical representations of facts involving permissions, appearing undated on the first page of a Harvard cooperative notebook R S-46. Probably later than 1903, given that (i) the term "phemic sheet" and Peirce's proposed further extension of dicisigns to phemes are later undertakings, appearing e.g. in the drafts of the 1906 article "Prolegomena to an Apology for Pragmaticism" composed in late 1905 and early 1906 (R 292a,b; LoF 3), and that (ii) the notebook text that follows these graphs continues several pages on "provisional table of the Division of Signs", the closely related studies of which date from 1906. These higher-order Beta graphs are thus created prior to Peirce's formulation of his later, semeiotic argument for pragmaticism, and may have been invented for that purpose.]

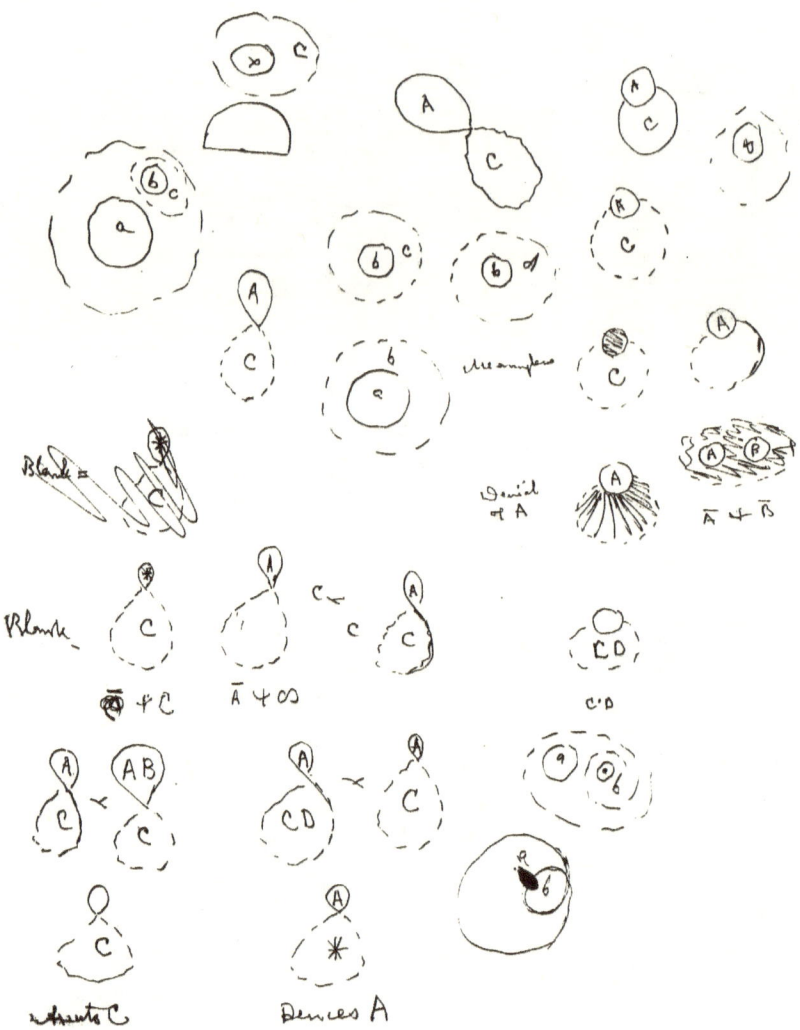

A holograph page (Harvard Peirce Papers, R 1070).

[An undated proposal representing variants of logical graphs that have a rather special look. This one-page study is inscribed on the back page of a leaflet, "Inventory of Instruments", which Peirce had retained from the Coastal and Geodetic Survey perhaps since late 1880s. Three pages of that leaflet have been preserved in R 1070; perhaps Peirce kept them as scrap paper which he was constantly in shortage of. The graphs are likely to have been scribed much later, however, and possibly date from the post-1903 era. Non-standard notations are created especially for the blot, thus effecting contradictions ("meaningless") and denials of an assertion, as well as for the scroll, in which the inloops are pulled out from the outloop to form these 8-shapes distinguished from the latter by dashed boundaries. Rules for inserting on the antecedent and erasing from the consequent appear near the bottom left of the page.]

Bibliography of Peirce's References

This bibliography encompasses those books, volumes and editions that Peirce referred or is most likely to have referred to in the relevant parts of the texts included in the volumes of the *Logic of the Future*. His self-references are included in the bibliography at the end of the introductory chapters of each volume.

At various times in his life, Peirce owned extensive and valuable collections of books, journals and reference works that was likely to consist of several thousand items. Details of the editions that Peirce owned or had in his possession when producing the relevant studies are included after the item information, and if known, with their present provenance (JHU = Johns Hopkins University, Special Collections).

The list below comprises approximatively some 1/30 of the books that Peirce might have acquired during his lifetime. Sadly the bulk of his collection, including countless books rife with marginalia, is no longer recoverable as most of the items that once belonged to his library have been lost, damaged, discarded, destroyed, stolen, given away or sold to collectors over the years.

Abelard, Peter (Abelardus Petrus). *Ouvrages Inédits d'Abelard Pour Servir À l'Histoire De La Philosophie Scolastique En France*. Edited by Victor Cousin. Paris: Imprimerie Royale, 1836. (Peirce's Library) [Only mentioned by name, no specific book detailed. This edition was owned by Peirce.]

Agrippa, Cornelius (Heinrich Cornelius Agrippa von Nettesheim). *De incertitudine et vanitate scientiarum et artium*. Parisiis: Apud Ionnem Petrum, 1531.

Alstedius (Alsted), Johann Heinrich. *Sientiarum omnium encyclopaediae*. Lyon: Hvgetan and Ravavd, 1649. (Peirce's Library, two copies of the same item, JHU) [Peirce's reference is to Alstedius's *Logic*, 1614, as referred to by W. R. Hamilton (LoF 2).]

Apuleius, Lucius. *Opuscula quæsunt de philosophia*. Edition A. Goldbacher, 1876.

Aquinas, Thomas. *Summa totius logicae Aristotelis*. Edidit Hieronymus Monopolitanus. 1496. [Of Thomas Aquinas's works, Peirce owned at least three incunabula, with Peirce's marginal notes: *Quaestiones de anima* (Venice: F. Renner, 1472), *Opuscula* (Venice, 1508), and *Quaestiones de quodlibet* (Nüremberg: Johann Sensenschmidt & Andreas Frisner, 1474). *Opuscula* is identified as "From the Library of Ludovico Manini [1726–1802], Doge of Venice". Provenance JHU.]

Aquinas, Thomas. *Opuscula sancti Thome: quibus alias impressis nuper hec addidimus videlicet Summam totius logice. Tractatum celeberrimum De usuris nusquam alias impressum*. Venice: cura & ingenio Giacomo Penzio mandato & expensis Peter Liechtenstein, 1508. (Peirce's Library, JHU) [Peirce's reference is: "Aquinas ... or the writer of the treatise on logic attributed to him" (LoF 3), probably referring to the *Summa logicae*. It is this particular edition that was in Peirce's possession.]

Aristotle. *Aristoteles Graece*. Two volumes. Edited by Theodor Waitz. Leipzig: Georg Reimer, 1831. (Peirce's Library, JHU) [Peirce mentions a few books in Aristotle's œuvre by name: *Metaphysics, Prior Analytics, Posterior Analytics, Perihermeneias* (ed. F. Michelis) and *Sophistical Elenchi*.]

Aristotle. *Aristotelis Organon graece*. Edited by Theodor Waitz. Lipsiae: Sumtibus Hahnil, 1844–1846. (Peirce's Library, JHU)

Arnauld, Antoine & Pierre, Nicole. *The Port Royal logic*. [*l'Art de Penser*] Translated by T. S. Baynes. 5th edition. Edinburgh: James Gordon, 1861. (Peirce's Library) [Lowell Lectures reading list. Peirce refers to the 5th edition of 1861 (R 454; LoF 2). This translation contains Leibniz's *Mediationes de Cognitione, Veritate et Ideis* (1684). Peirce's Library contained the 1851 edition, Edinburgh: Sutherland and Knox.]

Bachmann, Carl Friedrich. *System der Logik: Ein Handbuch zum Selbststudium*. Leipzig: F. U. Brockhaus, 1828. (Peirce's Library, JHU)

Bayes, Thomas. "An essay towards solving a problem in the doctrine of chances". *Philosophical Transactions of the Royal Society* 53(1763): 370–418.

Berkeley, George. *A Treatise Concerning the Principles of Human Knowledge*. Dublin: Jeremy Pepyat, 1710.

Berkeley, George. *The Works of George Berkeley, D.D. Late Bishop of Cloyne in Ireland—To which is added An Account of His Life, and several of his Letters to Thomas Prior, Esq., Dean Gervais, and Mr Pope*. In Two Volumes. Dublin: John Exshaw, 1784. (Peirce's Library, JHU)

Bertrand, Joseph Louis François. *Calcul des probabilités*. Paris: Gauthier-Villars et fils, 1889. [Lowell Lecture's reading list, Lecture VI.]

Boethius. *Anitii Manlii Severini Boethi: opera omnia*. Two Volumes. Basileæ: ex officina Henricpetrina [1570], 1546. (Peirce's Library, JHU. Peirce owned or attempted to acquire also the Migne edition of Boethius's *Opera*.)

Boltzmann, Ludwig. "Über die Grundprincipien und Grundgleiehuugen der Mechanik". In *Clark University 1889–1899: Decennial Celebration*, Edited by W. E. Story et alii, (261–309). Worcester, Mass., 1899.

Bolzano, Bernard. *Wissenschaftslehre: Versuch einer ausführlichen und größtentheils neuen Darstellung der Logik mit steter Rücksicht auf deren bisherige Bearbeiter*. Sultzbach: J. E. v. Seidel, 1837.

Bolzano, Bernard. *Paradoxien des Unendlichen*. Leipzig: C. H. Reclam sen., 1851.

Boole, George. *The Mathematical Analysis of Logic: Being an Essay Towards a Calculus of Deductive Reasoning*. Cambridge: MacMillan, Barclay, and MacMillan, 1847.
Boole, George. *An Investigation of the Laws of Thought, On which are founded the mathematical theories of logic and probabilities*. London: Walton & Maberly, 1854. [Lowell Lecture's reading list, Lecture VI.]
Bosanquet, Bernard. *Knowledge and Reality. A Criticism of F. H. Bradley's "Principles of Logic"*. London: Swan Sonnenschein & Co., 1892. [Lowell Lecture's reading list, Lecture I.]
Bossuet, Jacques-Bénigne. "Logique". Oeuvres inédites de Bossuet, évêque de Meaux dédiées à S. A. R. Monseigneur le Duc de Bordeaux. Paris, 1828.
Boutell, Charles. *The Handbook to English Heraldry*. London: Cassell, Petter, & Galpin, 1867.
Bradley, Francis Herbert. *The Principles of Logic*. London: Kegan Paul, Trench & co., 1883. [Lowell Lecture's reading list, Lecture I.]
Bradley, F. H. *Appearance and Reality: A Metaphysical Essay*. London: Swan Sonnenschein & Co, 1899. (Peirce's Library, Harvard University Robbins Library)
Byrne, James. *General Principles of the Structure of Language*. Two volumes. London: Trübner & Co, 1885.
Cantor, Georg. "Beiträge zur Begründung der transfiniten Mengenlehre". *Mathematische Annalen* 49(1897): 207–246. [Lowell Lecture's reading list, Lecture V.]
Cantor, Georg. *Zur Lehre vom Transfiniten: gesammelte Abhandlungen aus der Zeitschrift für Philosophie und Philosophische Kritik*. Halle: Pfeffer, 1890.
Cantor, Georg. "Une contribution à la théorie des ensembles". *Acta Mathematica* 2(1883): 311–328. [Peirce's reference is: "Acta Mathematica Vol. II, p. 321" (LoF 3).]
Cantor, Georg. "De la puissance des ensembles parfaits de points". *Acta Mathematica* 4(1884): 381–392.
Cantor, Moritz. *Vorlesungen über Geschichte der Mathematik*. Volume 2. Leipzig: B. G. Teubner, 1900.
Carus, Paul. *Ursache, Grund und Zweck: Eine philosophische Untersuchung zur Klärung der Begriffe*. Dresden: R. von Grumbkow, 1883.
Castrén, Matthias. *Grammatik der samojedischen Sprachen*. St. Petersburg: Buchdruckerei der Kaiserlichen Akademie der Wissenschaften, 1854. [Mentioned by name ("...Castrén, a grammarian of those [Samoyeed] languages...", LoF 1).]
Cayley, Arthur. "Fifth Memoir on Quantics". *Philosophical Transactions of the Royal Society of London* 148(1858): 429–460.

Cayley, Arthur. "Metrics". In: Salmon, George. *A Treatise on the Higher Plane Curves: Intended as a Sequel to A treatise on Conic Sections*, (108–128). Dublin: Hodges, Foster & Figgis, 1879.

Clarke, Frank Wigglesworth. *Data of Geochemistry*. Bulletin No: 330. Series E, Chemistry and Physics, 54. Washington: Government Printing Office, 1908.

Clifford, William K. *Lectures and Essays*. London: Macmillan, 1879. (Peirce's Library)

Darwin, Francis, Sir. *The Life and Letters of Charles Darwin: Including an Autobiographical Chapter*. Three volumes. London: John Murray, 1887.

Davidson, Thomas. *Aristotle and Ancient Educational Ideals*. New York: C. Scribner, 1892.

Dedekind, Richard. *Stetigkeit und irrationale Zahlen*. Braunschweig: F. Vieweg und sohn, 1872.

Dedekind, Richard. *Was sind und was sollen die Zahlen?* Braunschweig: Vieweg, 1887.

Dedekind, Richard. *Essays on the Theory of Numbers, 1. Continuity and irrational numbers. 2. The Nature and Meaning of Numbers*. Translated by Wooster Woodruff Beman. Chicago: Open Court, 1901. (Peirce's Library) [A copy of this book was sent to Peirce on July 13, 1903, by Fred. Sigrist, printer and compositor from Open Court who corresponded with Peirce on Carus's alleged plagiarism and misconduct issues in 1903 (FS to CSP, July 13, 1903, R L 77). Its present provenance is unknown. Included in the Lowell Lecture reading list, Lecture V, with reference to "Authorized translation by W. W. Beman. Chicago, 1901".]

De Morgan, Augustus. "On the Structure of the Syllogism". *Transactions of the Cambridge Philosophical Society* 8(1846): 379–408.

De Morgan, Augustus. *Formal Logic, or The Calculus of Inference, Necessary and Probable*. London: Taylor & Walton, 1847. (Peirce's Library) [The book has Peirce's abundant marginalia and its provenance has in the past been at the Harvard University's Library System. The item is no longer to be located in Harvard's collections.]

De Morgan, Augustus. "On the syllogism no: II. On the symbols of logic, the theory of the syllogism, and in particular the copula". *Transactions of the Cambridge Philosophical Society* 9(1850): 79–127.

De Morgan, Augustus. "On the syllogism no: III and on logic in general". *Transactions of the Cambridge Philosophical Society* 10(1858): 173–230.

De Morgan, Augustus. "On the syllogism no: III and on the logic of relations". *Transactions of the Cambridge Philosophical Society* 10(1860): 331–358.

De Morgan, Augustus. *A Syllabus of a Proposed System of Logic*. London: Walton & Maberly, 1860.

Descartes, René. *Geometria*. Second Edition. Amstelædami: apud Ludovicum & Danielem Elzevirios, 1659. (Peirce's Library, Harvard Robbins Library)

Diogenes Laertius. *Diogenis Laertii de vitis, dogmatibus et apophthegmatibus clarorum philosophorum libri X, Graece et Latine*. Volumes 1 and 2. Amstelædami: Apud Henricum Wetstenium, 1692. (Peirce's Library, JHU)

Drummond, William. *Academical Questions*. London: W. Bulmer and Co., 1805. [Peirce refers to Diodorus Cronus, "as related by Cicero toward the end of the Lucullus' book of his Academical Questions" (LoF 3).]

Erdmann, Benno. *Logik. I. Band: Logische Elementarlehre. Zweite, völlig umgearbeitete Auflage*. Halle a. S.: Max Niemeyer, 1907.

Erdmann, Johann Eduard. *Outlines of Logic and Metaphysics*. Translated by B. C. Burt. London: Sonnenschein, 1896. [Lowell Lecture's reading list, Lecture I.]

Euclid. *Euclidis Opera Omnia*. Edited by J. L. Heiberg & H. Menge. 8 Volumes. Lipsiae: B. G. Teubneri, 1883–1916. [Peirce's reference is: "Heiberg admits 27 corollaries as genuine in the Elements" (LoF 1).]

Euler, Leonhard. *Lettres à une princesse d'Allemagne sur divers sujets de physique & de philosophie*. Saint-Pétersbourg: Imprimerie de l'Académie Impériale des Sciences, 1768–1772.

Flint, Robert. *Philosophy as Scientia Scientiarum and A History of Classifications of the Sciences*. New York: Charles Scribner's Sons, 1904. [Peirce's Library]

Girard, Albert. *Invention nouvelle en l'algèbre*. Amsterdam: W. J. Blaeuw, 1629.

Glanvill, Joseph. *Saducismus triumphatus: or, Full and plain evidence concerning witches and apparitions. In two parts. The first treating of their possibility. The second of their real existence*. London: Printed for J. Collins & S. Lownds, 1681.

Goethe, Johann Wolfgang von. "Den Originalen", 1812. In *Berliner Ausgabe. Poetische Werke (Band 1–16)*. Band 1, Berlin, 1960.

Grassmann, Robert. *Der Formenlehre oder Mathematik*. Five Volumes. Volume three, *Die Bindelehre oder Combinationslehre*. Stettin, 1872. (Peirce's Library, JHU)

Hamilton, William Rowan. "Recent Publications on Logical Science". *Edinburgh Review* 58(1833): 194–238.

Hamilton, William Rowan. *Lectures on Metaphysics and Logic. Volumes III and IV. Logic I and II*. London: William Blackwood, 1860.

Helmholtz, Hermann von. "On the Conservation of Forces". *Popular Lectures on Scientific Subjects*, (317–362). Translated by Edmund Atkinson. New York: D. Appleton & Co., 1885.

Hibben, John Grier. *Hegel's Logic. An Essay in Interpretation*. New York: Charles Scribner's Sons, 1902. (Peirce's Library) [Lowell Lecture's reading list, Lecture III.]

Hume, David. *A Treatise of Humane Nature*. London: Printed for John Noon, 1738.

Hume, David. *An Enquiry Concerning Human Understanding*. In Volume 2 of *Essays and Treatises on several Subjects*. London: Printed for T. Cadell, 1788.

Isidorus Hispalensis (Isidorus of Sevilla). *Isidori Hispalensis episcopi Etymologiarum sive Originum*. In J.-P. Migne, *Sancti Isidori Hispalensis Episcopi: Opera Omnia*. Paris, 1830. [No information on the year or publisher of the edition that Peirce would have consulted in found in his text. References are to "Isodorus Hispalensis about A.D. 600 refers to [obelus] as an old sign" (LoF 1), "A.D. 600 by Isidorus Hispalensis (*Etymologiarum* lib.I.cap.xxi.3) as [obelus] being an old sign" (LoF 1) and to "his great work usually called his *Origines* (lib.XIII, cap.xi.tertus 2)" (LoF 1).]

James, Henry. *Substance and Shadow. On Morality and Religion in their Relation to Life: An Essay upon the Physics of Creation*. Boston: Ticknor and Fields, 1863. (Peirce's Library)

James, William. *Pragmatism, A New Name for Some Old Ways of Thinking*. Popular Lectures on Philosophy. New York: Longmans, Green, and Co, 1907. (Peirce's Library) [Peirce received a copy of this book from James on June 13, 1907.]

James, William. "Experience of Activity". In: *Essays in Radical Empiricism*. Edited by Ralph Barton Perry, (155–190). New York: Longman Green & Co, 1912. [Mentioned in a letter to Josiah Royce in June 30, 1913, but may refer to an earlier edition from 1909 (LoF 3).]

Jevons, William Stanley. *Pure Logic or the Logic of Quality apart from Quantity: with Remarks on Boole's System and on the Relation of Logic and Mathematics*. London: Edward Stanford, 1864. (Peirce's Library, JHU)

Jevons, William Stanley. *The Principles of Science: a Treatise on Logic and Scientific Method*. London: Macmillan & Co., 1877. [Peirce makes multiple references e.g. to Jevon's •|•, but no specific book or source is mentioned (LoF 1). The Lowell Lecture's reading list, Lecture VIII, has a reference to "2d edition. London, 1877". Peirce owned also Jevons's *Studies in Deductive Logic*, London, 1880, and *Substitution of Similars*, London, 1889; the provenance of all four volumes is JHU.]

Jordan, Camille. *Traité des substitutions et des équations algébriques*. Paris: Gauthier-Villars, 1870.

Kant, Immanuel. *Kritik der reinen Vernunft*. Part 2 of *Sämmtliche Werke*. Edited by K. Rosenkranz & F. W. Schubert. Leipzig: L. Voss, 1838. (Peirce's Library, JHU)

Kant, Immanuel. *Disputatio de mundi sensibilis atque intelligibilis forma et principiis*. Part 1 of *Sämmtliche Werke*. Edited by K. Rosenkranz & F. W. Schubert. Leipzig: L. Voss, 1838. (Peirce's Library, JHU)

Kant, Immanuel. *Critique of Pure Reason*. Translated from the German of Immanuel Kant by J. M. D. Meiklejohn. London, Henry G. Bohn, 1855. (Peirce's Library, Houghton) [Heavily annotated, virtually every page up to p. 160, including extensive corrections which bear mostly on the terminology of the translation, together with extensive marginal notes on the content. A separate leaf on Bacon is glued on p. 278. Very few annotations from the beginning the second division and virtually no annotations from p. 365 onwards (Div. II, Chap. III, Sect. IV).]

Kempe, Alfred Bray. "A Memoir on the Theory of Mathematical Form". *Philosophical Transactions of the Royal Society* 177(1887): 1–70. [Lowell Lecture's reading list, Lecture II. Peirce's abundant marginalia appears on nearly every of the first 40 pages of his offprint of Kempe's article located in R 1599.]

Kepler, Johannes. *Astronomia Nova* αιτιολογητος *seu physica coelestis, tradita commentariis de motibus stellae Martis ex observationibus G. V. Tychonis Brahe*. Heidelberg: Vogelin, 1609. [Peirce refers to this as "De Motu stellas Marties", not *Astronomia Nova*, but this is the most likely source, as it contains *De Motibus Stellae Martis* (LoF 3).]

Ladd-Franklin, Christine. "On the Algebra of Logic". In: Charles S. Peirce (ed.), *Studies in Logic, by Members of the Johns Hopkins University*. Boston: Little, Brown & Company, 17–71, 1883.

Lambert, Johann Heinrich. *Anlage zur Architektonik, oder Theorie des Einfachen und Ersten in der philosophischen und mathematischen Erkenntnis*. Riga: Hartknoch, 1771.

Lambert, Johann Heinrich. *Neues Organon oder Gedanken über die Erforschung und Bezeichnung des Wahren und dessen Unterscheidung vom Irrthum und Schein*. Two Volumes. Leipzig: Johann Wendler, 1764. (Peirce's Library, JHU) [No marginalia or annotations by Peirce.]

Lange, Friedrich Albert. *Logische Studien: Ein Beitrag zur Neubegründung der formalen Logik und der Erkenntnistheorie*. Iserlohn: J. Baedeker, 1877.

Lange, Johann Christian (Langii, Iohannis Christiani). *Nucleus Logicae Weisianae*. Auctore Christiano Weisio (Weise, Christian). Gissae-Hassorum: Henningi Mülleri, 1712. [The Heidelberg Edition, Universitätsbibliotek Heidelberg.]

Laplace, Pierre-Simon. *Théorie analytique des probabilités*. Paris: Ve. Courcier, 1812.

Laurent, Hermann. *Traité du calcul des probabilités*. Paris: Gauthier-Villars, 1873. [Lowell Lecture's reading list, Lecture VI.]

Legendre, Adrien-Marie. *Éléments de géométrie*. Paris: F. Didot, 1794.

Leibniz, Gottfried (Godefridus Guilielmus Leibnitius). *Meditationes de Cognitione, Veritate et Ideis*. Acta Eruditorum Lipsiensum, 1684. [Peirce's own copy at Houghton Library is Leibniz's *The Monadology and Other Philosophical Writ-*

ings, translated with introduction and notes by Robert Latta, London: Oxford at the Clarendon Press, 1898, with Peirce's marginalia. His Arnault & Nicole 1861 includes translation of the *Meditationes*.]

Leibniz, Gottfried. *Nouveaux Essais sur l'entendement humain* (New Essays on Human Understanding). In *Oeuvres philosophiques latines & francoises de feu*, Amsterdam et Leipzig: Chez Jean Schreuder, 1765.

Le Jeune Dirichlet, Gustav. "Beweis des Satzes, dass jede unbegrenzte arithmetische Progression, deren erstes Glied und Differenz ganze Zahlen ohne gemeinschaftlichen Factor sind, unendlich viele Primzahlen enthält". *Abhandlungen der Königlichen Preußischen Akademie der Wissenschaften zu Berlin*, 48(1837): 45–71.

Listing, Johann Benedict. "Vorstudien zur Topologie". *Göttingen Studien* 2(1847): 811–875.

Listing, Johann Benedict. *Vorstudien zur Topologie*. Göttingen: Vandenhoeck und Ruprecht, 1848. [Peirce's reference is: "J. B. Listing, who was a colleague of Gauss in Göttingen. He published two papers on *Topologische Studien*. One of these in an octavo publication called as well as I remember *Göttingen Studien*, or something like that, the other later on in the quarto Vandenhoeck und Ruprecht" (LoF 1).]

Listing, Johann Benedict. "der Census räumlicher Complexe, oder Verallgemeinerung des Euler'schen Satzes von den Polyädern". *Abhandlungen der Königlichen Gesellschaft der Wissenschaften zu Göttingen* 10(1862): 97–182.

Locke, John. *An Essay concerning Humane Understanding*. London: Awnsham and John Churchill, 1694. (Peirce's Library, JHU) [Second edition.]

Lutosławski, Wincenty. *The Origin and Growth of Plato's Logic; with an account of Plato's style and of the chronology of his writings*. London, New York and Bombay: Longmans, Green, and Co., 1897. (Peirce's Library, Houghton).

Mach, Ernst. *Popular Scientific Lectures*. Translated by T. J. McCormack. Second edition. Chicago, 1897. [Lowell Lecture's reading list, Lecture VIII.]

MacColl, Hugh. "The calculus of equivalent statements". *Proceedings of the London Mathematical Society*, 9(1877): 9–22. [Peirce's citation is "McColl, (1877)" (LoF 1). Three out of the series of eight papers were published in 1877.]

Mansell, Henry Longueville. *Prolegomena Logica: an Inquiry into the Psychological Character of Logical Processes*. London: Whittaker and Co., 1851.

Maxwell, James Clerk. *A Treatise on Electricity and Magnetism*. Two Volumes. Oxford: Clarendon Press, 1873.

Mill, John Stuart. *A System of Logic, Ratiocinative and Inductive*. New York, 1846. [Peirce mentions "the first edition of his *System of Logic, Ratiocinative and Inductive*, published in March, 1843" (LoF 3), and that "Mill's went through 9 editions (though with the advantage of containing no special novelty)"

(LoF 3). Peirce's copy at Houghton is a heavily annotated *A System of Logic, Ratiocinative and Inductive: being a connected view of the principles of evidence and the methods of scientific investigation*. Longmans, Green, and co., 1886 edition (London), "People's edition". [Lowell Lecture's reading list, Lecture VI, with reference to "New York, 1846" edition.]

Mitchell, Oscar Howard. "On a New Algebra of Logic". In *Studies in Logic by Members of the Johns Hopkins University*. Charles S. Peirce, editor. Boston: Little Brown & Company, 1883, 72–106. (Peirce's Library, Houghton)

Müller, Max. *Three Introductory Lectures on the Science of Thought*. Chicago: Open Court, 1887. [Peirce's reference is "two little books by Max Müller published by the Open Court Co. at a quarter each" (LoF 1).]

Müller, Max. *Three Lectures on the Science of Language*. Chicago: Open Court, 1889. [Peirce's reference is "two little books by Max Müller published by the Open Court Co. at a quarter each" (LoF 1).]

Murphy, Joseph John. *Habit and Intelligence Vol. II*. London: Macmillan & Co., 1869. (Peirce's Library)

Newton, Isaac. *Philosophiæ naturalis principia mathematica*. London: Jussu Societatis Regiae ac typis Josephi Streater, 1687. Glasgow: G. Brookman; London: T. T. and J. Tegg, 1833.

Ockham, William. *Tractatus Logicae*. Paris: Johann Higman, 1488. [Peirce borrowed this incunabulum of his, now at JHU, to a Harvard graduate student, with a contract; the item's provenance is now at Houghton Library. He refers to it as "The distinction [between *objectively general* and *subjectively general*], so far as I know, was first drawn, though not very accurately, by William Ockham, as is stated in his book variously called *Summa logices*, *Tractatus logicae* and *Logica aurea*, Pars 1ma, cap. xiiii, and in the two following chapters is made the basis of his variety of nominalism, which denies the reality of subjective generality" ("The First Part of an Apology for Pragmaticism", R 296; LoF 3). Peirce owned three other works of Ockham from the late 15th century.]

Pearson, Karl. *The Grammar of Science*. 2nd edition. London: Adam & Charles Black, 1900. (Peirce's Library) [Lowell Lecture's reading list, Lecture VI.]

Peirce, Benjamin. *An Elementary Treatise on Plane and Solid Geometry*. Boston: James Munroe, 1837. [Charles Peirce refers from memory to his father's "textbook of Elementary Geometry, 1832" (LoF 3).]

Peirce, Benjamin. *A System of Analytic Mechanics*. Boston: Little, Brown & Company, 1855. (Peirce's Library) [Peirce probably refers to this item from memory as "1852" (LoF 3).]

Peirce, Benjamin. *Linear Associative Algebra*. A Memoir read before the National Academy of Sciences in Washington, 1870. By Benjamin Peirce. With Notes and Addenda, by C. S. Peirce, Son of the Author. New York: Van Nostrand, 1882. (Peirce's Library)

Petrus Hispanus (Hispani, Petri/John XXI). *Summulae logicales (ff. 1 r. -84 v.) followed by a Propositio exponibilis (in a different hand) elucidating obscure points in the foregoing treatise.* de Ricci, Census, 753, no. 1. 15th Century. (Peirce's Library, JHU)

Petrus Hispanus (Hispani, Petri/John XXI). *Compendiarius parvuorum logicalium.* Vienna: Vietor, 1512. (Peirce's Library, JHU)

Philodemus. *On Signs and Semiotic Inferences* (Περὶ Σημείων καὶ Σημειώσεων/ Περὶ Φαινομένων καὶ Σημειώσεων). T. Gomperz. *Herkulanische Studien, i Philodem über Induktionslüsse.* Leipzig: Teubner, 1865. (Peirce's Library)

Plato. *Platonis Opera.* Edited by John Burnet. Oxford Classical Texts, Oxford University Press, 1903. (Peirce's Library)

Prantl, Karl von. *Geschichte der Logik im Abendlande.* Three volumes. Leipzig: S. Hirzel, 1855.

Priscianus Caesariensis. *Priscianus Caesariensis Grammatici Opera, ad vetustissimorum codicum, nunc primum collatorum, fidem recensuit, emaculavit, lectionum varietatem notavit et indices locupletissimos adiecit Augustus Krehl.* Two volumes. Edited by Krehl, August Ludwig Gottlieb. Lipsiae: Weidmann, 1819–1820.

Recorde, Robert. *The Whetstone of Witte.* London: Jhon Kyngstone, 1557.

Renouvier, Charles Bernard. *Essais de critique générale.* Four volumes. Paris: Bureau de la Critique Philosophique, 1854–1864. [Peirce's citation is "Essai de philosophie critique" (LoF 3).]

Risteen, Allan Douglas. *Molecules and the Molecular Theory of Matter.* Boston and London: Ginn & Co., 1895. Reprinted 1896.

Royce, Josiah. *The World and the Individual.* New York: Macmillan, 1900.

Russell, Bertrand. *The Principles of Mathematics.* Vol. 1. Cambridge: Cambridge University Press, 1903. (Peirce's Library, Houghton) [Peirce's copy is lightly annotated, and includes two EGs in the margin (p. 18): "Carroll is not right. $\overline{q\ \overline{r}}$ $\overline{p\,q\,r}$ for if q is absurd $q \prec r$ and $q \prec \bar{r}$ may both be true". Lowell Lecture's reading list, Lecture V, with reference to "London, 1903" edition.]

Salmon, George. *A Treatise on the Higher Plane Curves.* Dublin: Hodges, Foster & Figgis, 1879.

Sayce, Archibald Henry. "Grammar". *Encyclopaedia Britannica.* 11th edition, 1911.

Schaff, Philip. *History of the Christian Church.* Translated by Edward D. Yeomans. New York: Scribner, Armstrong & Co., 1874. ["Now no single creed of christendom,—as I can say by a painstaking study of Dr. Schaff's three volumes,—was ever put forward of which the principal purpose was not to proclaim somebody to be damned" (LoF 2). Schaff published eight volumes under the same title in 1858–1890.]

Schönflies, Arthur. "Die Entwickelung der Lehre von den Punktmannigfaltigkeiten". *Jahresbericht der deutschen Mathematiker-Vereinigung* 8, part 2(1900): 1–250.

Schröder, Ernst. *Der Operationskreis des Logikkalküls*. Leipzig: B. G. Teubner, 1877.

Schröder, Ernst. *Vorlesungen über die Algebra der Logik*. Three volumes. Leipzig: B. G. Teubner, 1890–1895. [Lowell Lecture's reading list, Lecture II.]

Schubert, Hermann. *Kalkül der abzählenden Geometrie*. Leipzig: B. G. Teubner, 1879.

Sigwart, Cristoph von. *Logic*. Second edition, enlarged and revised. Translated by Helen Dendy. London: Swan Sonnenschein & Co., 1895. [Lowell Lecture's reading list, Lecture I.]

Smith, James & Smith, Horace. *Rejected Addresses: or, The new theatrum poetarum*. London: John Murray, 1879.

Southey, Robert. *The Doctor*. New York: Harper & Brothers, 1836.

Stout, George Frederick. *Analytic Psychology*. London: Swan Sonnenschein & Co., 1896.

Trendelenburg, Friedrich Adolph. *Elementa Logices Aristotelicae*. Berolini, 1836. [Lowell Lecture's reading list. Peirce owned its 1862 edition, Berlin: Gustavi Bethae, JHU.]

Trendelenburg, Friedrich Adolph. *Logische Untersuchungen*. Berlin: S. Hirzel, 1840. [Lowell Lecture's reading list, Lecture I.]

Tucker, Abraham. *The Light of Nature Pursued*. (Together with some account of the life of the author by John Mildmay). Cambridge: Hilliard and Brown, 1831.

Überweg, Friedrich. *System der Logik und Geschichte der logischen Lehren*. Bonn: Bei Adolph Marcus, 1865. (Peirce's Library, JHU)

Ueberweg, Friedrich. *System of Logic, and History of Logical Doctrines*. Translated by T. M. Lindsay. London: Longmans, Green, & Co., 1871. [Lowell Lectures reading list, Lecture I.]

Überweg, Friedrich *Grundriss der Geschichte der Philosophie*. 9te Auflage. Herausgere M. Heinze. Four volumes.

Valla, Laurentius (Valla, Lorenzo; Laurentius, Vallensis). *Dialecticae Disputationes contra Aristotelicos*. Venice, 1499. Original publication c.1439. Printed in the *Laurentii Vallae Opera*, Basel, 1540, reprinted with a second volume, Turin: Bottega d'Erasmo, 1962, and as *Dialectical Disputations*. Latin text and English translation the *Repastinatio* by B. P. Copenhaver and L. Nauta. The I Tatti Renaissance Library, Cambridge: Harvard University Press, 2012. [Peirce's reference occurs in his library book list of R 1574: "Laurentius Valla, Dialecticae Disp (1499) or Opera *containing this*". The list contains several items that Peirce was canvassing from libraries in Boston or in Cambridge, Mass., in 1903.]

Vaugelas, Claude Favre de. *Remarques sur la langue française,* Paris: Vve J. Camusat et P. Le Petit, 1647. (Peirce's Library)

Venn, John. *The Logic of Chance. An Essay on the Foundations and Province of the Theory of Probability, with Especial Reference to Its Application to Moral and Social Science.* London: Macmillan & Co., 1876. (Peirce's Library) [Lowell Lecture's reading list, Lecture VI, with reference to "3d edition. London, 1888".]

Venn, John. *Symbolic Logic.* First edition. London: Macmillan & Co., 1881.

Venn, John. *The Principles of Empirical or Inductive Logic.* London and New York: Macmillan & Co., 1889. [Lowell Lecture's reading list, Lecture VIII.]

de Villadi, Alexander (Alexander of Villedieu). *Doctrinale puerorum XXII*, 1374. [Peirce's reference is to p. 354 of his copy of Thurot, Charles. *Notices et extraits de divers manuscrits latins pour servir á l'histoire des doctrines grammaticales au moyen age.* Notices et extraits des manuscrits de la Bibliothéque nationale 22.2, Paris: Imprimerie Impériale, 1868.] (Peirce's Library, JHU)

Vives, Juan Luis. "De Censura Veri et falsi". In: *De disciplinis Libri XX.* Antwerp: Michael Hillenius Hoochstratanus, 1531. (Peirce's Library)

Wadding, Luke (ed.). *Scotus, Duns. Ioannis Duns Scoti Opera Omnia.* Twelve Volumes. London: Laurent Durand, 1639. (Peirce's Library, JHU) [Peirce owned Volumes 1–4 of Duns Scotus's *Opera Omnia,* together with at least thirteen other 15th, 16th and early 17th century works by Scotus (JHU). Thomas of Erfurt's *Tractatus de modis significandi sive Grammatica Speculativa* is included in Volume 1 of the Wadding edition.]

Watts, Isaac. *Logick, Or, the Right Use of Reason in the Inquiry After Truth. With a variety of rules to guard against error, in the affairs of religion and human life, as well as in the sciences.* London: Printed for J. Buckland, T. Caslon etc., 1772. (Peirce's Library, JHU)

Welby, Victoria. *What is Meaning? Studies in the Development of Significance.* London: Macmillan and Co., 1903. (Peirce's Library)

Whately, Richard. *Elements of Logic.* 4th edition. London: B. Fellowes, 1831. (Peirce's Library) [Lowell Lecture's reading list (New York, 1875).]

Whewell, William. *History of Scientific Ideas. Being the first part of the Philosophy of inductive sciences.* London, 1858. [Lowell Lecture's reading list, Lecture VIII.]

Whewell, William. *History of Scientific Ideas. Being the second part of the Philosophy of inductive sciences.* London, 1858. [Lowell Lecture's reading list, Lecture VIII.]

Whitehead, Alfred North. "The logic of relations, logical substitution groups, and cardinal numbers". *American Journal of Mathematics* 25(1903): 157–178. [Lowell Lecture's reading list, Lecture II.]

Wilkins, John. *An Essay towards a Real Character, And a Philosophical Language.* London: Printed for Sa. Gellibrand, and for John Martin Printer to the Royal Society, 1668. (Peirce's Library, JHU) [Inscribed, on the frontleaf (not in Peirce's hand): "This design was pursued with great application, but has failed in the success, it was expected, would attend it. Nevertheless, the Book us very valuable, as containing a general reduction of things to their proper heads, and exhibiting at once an entire analytical system of the Universe. Some divisions perhaps are not exactly agreeable to the Philosophy now in vogue, or that which will come after, But. Who expects a perfect work to see, Expect what never was, not is, nor e'er will by, [undersigned] $\mathcal{M}$."]

Wilson, John Cook. *On the Traversing of Geometrical Figures.* Oxford: Clarendon Press, 1905. (Peirce's Library)

Wolff, Christian. *Vernünfftige Gedancken Von den Kräfften des menschlichen Verstandes Und ihrem Richtigen Gebrauche In Erkäntniß der Wahrheit.* Halle im Magdeburgischen Renger Halle, Saale Halle, 1713. [Peirce's citation is "*Vernünftige Gedanken von den Kräften des menschlichen Verstanden*, 1710" (LoF 1). Peirce owned at least thirteen volumes of Wolff's works, provenance JHU.]

Woods, Frederick Adams. *Mental and Moral Heredity in Royalty.* New York: Henry Holt & Co, 1906. (Peirce's Library)

Wundt, Wilhelm Max. *Logik, eine Untersuchung der Prinzipien der Erkenntnis und der Methoden Wissenschaftlicher Forschung.* 2nd edition. Stuttgart: Ferdinand Enke, 1893–1895. [Lowell Lecture's reading list, Lecture I.]

Catalogue of Peirce's Writings

This list references Peirce's writings—manuscripts, letters, papers and pieces—that have been included in Volumes 2/1 (Selections 29–31) and 2/2 (Selections 32–42) of *Logic of the Future*. The writings are in an approximate chronological order. Peirce did not date most of the notebooks and drafts; the third lecture and its drafts are a notable exception and are written during the first part of October. The prefaces of the syllabus manuscript R 478 have a (possibly post-dated) designation of November 1, R 468 has a date of December 4, and R S-28 is dated to the first part of September. All the rest of the material included in the present volume is undated; uncertainties remain as to the exact timing of their composition or relative ordering. It is not known, for example, whether Peirce worked on the lectures in sequence or whether he may have produced some of his pre-lecture drafts in parallel and was led to rearrange and revise them sometime later.

Alternatives, variants and pages from collateral sources are included and are also listed as separate items only if they bear a separate original title, label, designation or indication of their approximate contents and purpose. Label inscriptions appearing on the notebook covers and first pages are included. Some notebooks are without labels and some cover information was added by the editors of the *Collected Papers of Charles S. Peirce*. The details as well as references to sources from the published papers of Charles S. Peirce are included in the introductory essays and surveys of individual selections.

R 454 What Makes a Reasoning Sound?
   Lowell Lecture I [Early Draft]
   – Spring–Summer 1903.   *Selection 32.*
   "Lectures on Logic, to be delivered at the Lowell Institute. Winter of 1903–1904"

R 491 *The Logical Tracts No. 1.* On Existential Graphs
   – Early Summer (June) 1903.   *Selection 29.*

R 492 *The Logical Tracts No. 2.* On Existential Graphs, Euler's Diagrams, and Logical Algebra
   – Summer–Autumn (July–September) 1903.   *Selection 30.*

R 479 *The Logical Tracts No. 2.* Part II. On Logical Graphs [Euler's Diagrams]
   – Summer–Autumn 1903.   *Selection 31.*

R S-28 The Conventions.
   Lowell Lecture II(a)
   – September 1–15, 1903.   *Selection 33.*

R S-28 [Fragments.]
  – September, 1903. *Selection 42.*
R S-27 Graphs, Little Account.
  Lowell Lecture II(a)
  – September 1903. *Selection 33.*
R 450 A System of Diagrams for Studying Logical Relations. Exposition of it begun. (Existential Graphs—Alpha & Beta).
  Lowell Lecture II(a)
  – September 1903. *Selection 33.*
R S-29 Existential Graphs: The Initial Conventions.
  Lowell Lecture II(b)
  – September 1903. *Selection 34.*
R 455 A System of Diagrams for Studying Logical Relations. Exposition of it begun. (Existential Graphs—Alpha & Beta).
  Lowell Lecture II(b) (Includes R 455(s), R 456 and pages from R S-29, R S-32, R S-33, R S-34)
  – Late September–early October 1903. *Selection 34.*
  "Lowell Lectures by C. S. Peirce"
R 1333 [Fragments.]
  – Before October 1903. *Selection 42.*
R 496 [Fragments.]
  Lowell Lecture V(c).
  – Before October 1903. *Selection 42.*
R 458, R 458(s) The Doctrine of Multitude, Infinity and Continuity. (Multitude.)
  Lowell Lecture V(c).
  – Before October 1903. *Selection 38.*
  "May be useful for 3rd or 4th. Lecture 3. First Draught"
R 459 The Doctrine of Multitude, Infinity and Continuity. (Multitude.)
  Lowell Lecture V(a) (Includes pages from R 459(s), R 466)
  – Before October 1903. *Selection 38.*
  "Lowell Lectures. by C. S. Peirce. 1903. Lecture 3. Won't do"
R 466 The Doctrine of Multitude, Infinity and Continuity. (Multitude.)
  Lowell Lecture V(a)
  – Before October 1903. *Selection 38.*
  "? Useful for Third or Fourth ?"
R 457 The Three Universal Categories and their Utility. (General Explanations. Phenomenology and Speculative Grammar.)
  Lowell Lecture III(b)
  – October 2, 1903. *Selection 36.*
  "1st Draught of 3rd Lecture"

R 462 The Three Universal Categories and their Utility. (General Explanations. Phenomenology and Speculative Grammar.)
Lowell Lecture III(a) (Includes pages from R S-31)
– October 5, 1903.   *Selection 35.*
"The Main holt of Lecture 3. C. S. P's Lowell Lectures of 1903. 2nd Draught of 3rd Lecture. Begun 1903 Oct 5, 10:30am"

R 464 The Three Universal Categories and their Utility. (General Explanations. Phenomenology and Speculative Grammar.)
Lowell Lecture III(b) (Includes pages from R 464(s), R 465, R S-34)
– October 8, 1903 (R 464, R 464(s)); October 12 (R 465).   *Selection 36.*
"Lowell Lectures of 1903. Lecture III. Second Draught"

R 464(s) "Part I of the 3rd Draught of the Third Lecture"
Lowell Lecture III(b)
– October 8, 1903.   *Selection 36.*

R 465 "Second Part of the Third Draught of Lecture III"
Lowell Lecture III(b)
– October 12, 1903.   *Selection 36.*
"To be used. Lecture III. Vol. 2. C. S. P's Lowell Lectures of 1903. 2nd Part of 3rd Draught of Lecture III"

R 478 *A Syllabus of certain Topics of Logic.* (Includes pages from R 478(s), R 508, R 509)
– October 1903 (R 478, R 478(s) written before October 30).   *Selection 41.*

R 508 Existential Graphs. Rules of Transformation. Pure Mathematical Definition of Existential Graphs, regardless of their Interpretation (Syllabus B)
– Late October–early November 1903.   *Selection 41.*

R 509 Gamma Graphs.
– Late October–early November 1903.   *Selection 41.*

R 510 [Fragments]
– November 1903 (Includes pages from R 278)   *Selection 42.*

R 2, R 3, R 511, R 512 On the Simplest Branch of Mathematics, Dyadics.
– November 1903.   *Selection 40.*

R S-1 Notes on the Theory of Multitude.
Lowell Lecture IV (Notebook pages 61–85 are on existential graphs)
– From July to early December, 1903.   *Selection 42.*

R 460 Lowell Lecture IV
– November 30–December 3, 1903.   *Selection 37.*
"Lect. III a b d"

R 467 Exposition of the System of Diagrams Completed. (Existential Graphs: Gamma Part.)
Lowell Lecture IV (Includes pages from R 468, R S-31)

    – Late November–early December, 1903. *Selection 37.*
    "C. S. Peirce's Lowell Lectures 1903. Lecture 4. Vol. 1. Lowell Lectures for 1903"
R 468 Introduction to Lecture V.
    Lowell Lecture IV
    – December 4, 1903. *Selection 37.*
    "C. S. P's Lowell Lectures of 1903. Introduction to Lecture 5. 1903 Dec 4"
R 469 The Doctrine of Multitude, Infinity and Continuity. (Multitude.)
    Lowell Lecture V(d) (Including R 470)
    – December 3–7, 1903. *Selection 39.*
    "1903. Lowell Lectures. Lecture 5. Vol. I"
R 470 The Doctrine of Multitude, Infinity and Continuity. (Multitude.)
    Lowell Lecture V(d) (including R 471)
    – December 3–7, 1903. *Selection 39.*
    "1903. Lowell Lectures. Lecture 5. Vol. 2"
R 1070 [Fragments.]
    – post 1903. *Selection 42.*
R S-46 [Fragments.]
    – late 1905. *Selection 42.*

Name Index

Abbot, Francis Ellingwood 253
Agrippa, Cornelius 253
Aristotle 222, 253, 254 ; On diagrams 152
Arnauld, Antoine 57

Bacon, Robert 252
Baldwin, James Mark 2, 110
Beman, Wooster Woodruff 58, 87, 280
Berkeley, George 75, 253, 385
Boethius 282
Bolzano, Bernard 247, 297, 323, 331
Boole, George 1, 58, 252, 257

Cantor, Georg 58, 87, 280, 284, 321–323, 331
Carroll, Lewis 428
Carus, Paul 80
Cattell, James McKeen 16, 60, 89, 112, 113
Caucer, Geoffrey 252
Cicero 423

Dante Alighieri 252
De Morgan, Augustus 1, 252, 257 ; Universe of discourse 153
Dedekind, Richard 58, 87, 91, 280, 282, 285, 291, 292
Descartes, Rene 253
Dewey, John 110, 111

Euclid 69, 151, 180, 193 ; *Elements* 180, 193, 239 ; XVI proposition 69

Fermat, Pierre de 328
Franklin, Christine see Ladd-Franklin, Christine
Franklin, Fabian 110
Frege, Gottlob XIII, 2, 80
Froissart, Jean 252

Gardner, Martin 15

Halley, Edmund XV
Hartley, David 253
Hegel, G.W.F. 37, 57, 76, 219, 253, 266, 382
Helmholtz, Hermann von 244

Herbert, Francis 57, 63, 137
Hume, David 226, 253
Huntington, Edward V. 110

James, Alice Howe Gibbens 50
James, Henry Sr. 383
James, William VIII, 2, 3, 12, 16, 36, 42, 44, 47, 49–52, 59, 60, 74, 77, 97, 110, 117, 148
Jastrow, Joseph 110
Jevons, William Stanley 257

Kant, Immanuel 253, 323 ; On regulative and constitutive principles 225, 226 ; Refutation of Berkeley's idealism 385
Kempe, Alfred Bray 6, 57, 67, 98, 150

Ladd-Franklin, Christine 80, 110
Legendre, Adrien-Marie 180
Leibniz, Gottfried 253, 383
Locke, John 227, 253
Lounsbury, W. C. 38, 79, 90
Lowell, Lawrence A. 31
Lüroth, Jacob 365

Mansell, Henry Longueville 252
Marco Polo 252
Mill, John Stuart 58, 253, 384
Mitchell, Oscar Howard 23, 80, 258
Moore, Eliakim Hastings 91, 112, 113
Münsterberg, Hugo 104

Newcomb, Simon 53, 110, 113–115
Newton, Isaac XV
Nicole, Pierre 57

Ogden, Charles Kay 110–112

Peano, Giuseppe 61
Pearson, Karl 58
Peirce, Benjamin 115; Definition of mathematics 281, 291, 312
Peirce, James Mills 31, 53, 110
Peirce, Juliette 15, 109, 233
Putnam, George Haven 89

Ramsey, Frank Plumpton 110, 111
Reid, Thomas 253
Rémusat, Charles de 253
Richardson, Ernest Cushing 110
Risteen, Allan Douglas 25, 115, 300
Robert of Lincoln 252
Robin, Richard S. XV, 22
Royce, Josiah 50, 60, 268, 331 ; *The World and the Individual* 243
Russell, Bertrand 58, 87, 109–111, 280 ; *Principia Mathematica* 285 ; *The Principles of Mathematics* 48, 109
Russell, Francis C. 43, 110

Schaff, Philip 385
Schelling, F.W.J. von 253
Schiller, Ferdinand Canning Scott 16, 17, 75, 109, 117
Schröder, Ernst 57, 67, 80, 102, 150, 258, 285, 364 ; *Logik* 258

Scotus, Duns 252, 253
Sedgwick, William T. 38, 48, 49, 53, 55, 97, 98, 108, 111
Sigwart, Cristoph von 57, 63, 137
Socrates 65, 384
Spencer, Herbert 51, 61, 313

Tarski, Alfred 24
Thomas Aquinas 80, 252

Venn, John 58

Welby, Victoria 109–111, 116
Whately, Richard 57
Whewell, William 252
Whitehead, Alfred North 57, 67, 150 ; *Principia Mathematica* 285
Woodbridge, Frederick James Eugene 113

Keyword Index

Abduction XIII, XVI, 1, 31, 33, 41–43, 47, 50, 58, 60, 69, 81, 100, 106–108, 116, 149, 348
Abstraction 25, 80–84, 86, 88, 102, 116, 160, 171, 172, 203, 204, 226, 242, 257, 266, 310, 314, 339, 382 ; and Gamma graphs 254
Absurdity see Blot
Action 243, 384 ; as prediction 231
Adaptible pair 72, 73, 177, 224, 240
Algebra 239; Boole's algebra of logic 257
Antisep 173
Archegetic code see Transformations
Argument 37, 46, 75, 82, 161, 265
Arithmetic 295
Atom; and Collections 290
Axiom; Euclid's axioms 239

Belief see also Religion; as base for future conduct 244
Blot 62, 68–70, 170, 185–187, 189, 192, 195, 196, 206, see also Existential Graphs, Pseudograph
Brain; and consciousness 383, 384

Calculus; Differential Calculus 328
Cardinal numbers 284, 285, 337, 342 ; and applied mathematics 296
Chemistry 245, 246
Cognition 242, 299 ; of relation 229
Collections 25, 54, 66, 90, 91, 102, 205, 247, 248, 284, 288, 290, 291, 294–298, 300, 313, 314, 322, 324, 328, 330–333, 357, 365, 419
Common experience 153, 159, 163
Common sense; and pragmatism 381, 383
Consciousness 382, 384 ; and reasoning 151 ; Dyadic consciousness 243 ; field of 169 ; physical conditions of 383
Conservation of energy 245, 246, 384
Contingency 356; Alpha-contingency 209 ; Beta-contingency 208 ; Contingent graph 199, 209

Continuity XVI, 13, 32, 33, 40, 52, 58, 77, 79, 87, 88, 91, 92, 256, 259, 260, 280, 291, 310, 311, 330, 333, 337, 380, 433 ; and dimensionality 259 ; and gamma graphs 251
Continuum 259, 382
Critical logic 1, 77, 237
Cut see also Existential Graphs

Decidability 45, 71, 72, 76, 177
Deduction XIII, 1, 13, 23, 24, 31–33, 41, 43, 47, 67, 69, 70, 81, 83, 151, 161, 177, 211, 338, 383, 384, see also Reasoning, necessary ; Necessary 151 ; Probable and Necessary 161
Diagram 152, 229, 337 ; and mathematics 283 ; diagrammatic thought 283 ; geometrical 232
Diagrammatic syntax 10, 20, 24, 45, 68, 82, 177
Dialogue; Dialogical thinking 151, 153
Dimensionality; of the Phemic Sheet 169
Dinected graphs 360, 416
Disposition 152, 232
Doubt 244, 264

Economy of Research 42, 363
Electricity 178
Endoporeutic principle 24
Ens Rationis 225, 230, 254 ; and character 248 ; and collection 290 ; and graphs 314, 316, 317, 357 ; and quality 290
Entitative Graphs 66, 85, 94, 168, 258
Epicureanism 252
Epistemic Logic 26
esse in futuro 73, 221
Ethics 293; and logic 1 ; of terminology 53, 59, 68, 98, 266, 314, 348
Evolution 246, 253
Existential Graphs 143, see also Endoporeutic principle, Grapheus, Graphist, Hook, Line of Identity, Nex, Replica, Rhema, Selective, Sheet, Spot ; Alpha graphs 233, 239, 241, 261, 312, 342, 351 ; Alpha, Beta

and Gamma graphs 189, 257, 258, 338, 359, 360 ; Alpha-contingency 209, 210 ; Alpha-impossibility 221, 224 ; Alpha-permissibility 220 ; Alpha-possibility 207, 237, 242 ; Beta graphs 239, 242, 312 ; Beta-contingency 208 ; Beta-impossibility 208, 224 ; Beta-necessity 207 ; Beta-possibility 207, 220, 238, 242, 249 ; Delta graphs 25, 26 ; Evenly enclosed 142, 145, 196, 200, 224, 240, 289, 293, 352, 363, 364, 410 ; Exposition of the simplest possible form of mathematics 284 ; Gamma expressions of alpha graphs 269 ; Gamma graphs 370 ; Gamma rims 364 ; Gamma-impossibility 207 ; Gamma-possibility 207, 249 ; Oddly enclosed 142, 145, 224, 235, 240, 293, 352, 363, 364, 410 ; Pseudograph 62, 68–70, 74, 101, 143, 159, 160, 174, 196, 197, 351, 353, 361–363, 366 ; Scroll 156, 166, 184, 185, 189, 190, 194, 234, 287, 296, 297, 352 ; Sheet of Assertion 414, 415 ; Tincture 26, 27, 66, 85 ; Unenclosed 146, 234, 352, 360

Experience 69, 138, 169, 171, 172, 182, 189, 197, 225, 226, 229–231, 242, 243, 245, 253, 255, 283, 293, 297, 300, 380, 382

Experimentation 178; and 'hardness' 225, 299 ; and graphs 185, 193 ; versus definition 323

Feeling; Qualities of feeling 243
Firstness 230, 243, 246, 251, 254, 255, 314–316, 324

Gath 314–319, 323–325, 327, 330
Geometry; and graphs 359, 360 ; projective 283
Graph 182; Total and Partial 165 ; versus Calculus 220, 238
Graph-instance 19, 20, 22–24, 68, 90, 310, see also Replica
Graph-replica 18, 93, 164, 171, 184, 185, 189, 191, 193, 241, 271, 273, 338–340, 342–345, 360, 367, 368, 374, 376
Grapheus 22, 154, 171

Graphist 22, 26, 27, 154, 163–166
Graphist and Interpreter 153, 159, 164, 169–173, 182, 198, 351
Growth 230; as *summum bonum* 384

Habit 232; and self-control 246 ; of graphist and interpreter 169
Hook 81, 157, 167, 175, 199, 224, 240, 241, 345, 353, 354, 356, 360, 369

Idealism; Berkeleyan idealism 385
Indefinite individual 140
Indesignate individual 175
Index 229, 232, 263
Induction 283
Inference XIII, 17, 146, 161, 162, 187, 200, 206, 211, 282, 288, 294 ; and observation 193
Infinitesimal 160
Infinity 251, 311 ; Infinite collections 247 ; Infinite process 172 ; Infinite thought 169
Interpretant 170, 245, 263, 273, 311, 382
Interpreter 22, 173, 174, see also Graphist and Interpreter ; and Sign 230
Intuition 266

Languages; and children 231, 246 ; and logic 151, 181, 257
Law 81, 140, 172, 226, 245 ; and Gamma graphs 254 ; and habit 246 ; as mental 230 ; Laws of Dynamics 246 ; Laws of nature 227 ; of space 267
Leading Principle of Logic 69
Lexis 71, 199, 224, 240, 241
Ligature 19, 175, 201, 220, 224, 238, 239, 354 ; and selective 258, 268 ; Furcation 360
Line of Identity 19, 140, 145, 199, 240, 249, 258, 360, 368 ; and Illative transformations 200
Logic; and science 283
Logical breadth & depth 263
Logical equivalence 26
Logical Graphs see Entitative Graphs, see Existential Graphs, see Graph
Logical machines 138, 238
Logistic 282, 301

Map 260; projections 260
Mathematics; and logic 282 ; Applied 281 ; as a branch of logic 282, 291, 292 ; as science that draws necessary conclusions 291 ; as the science of quantity 282 ; Definition of 281, 292, 294 ; Logic of 249, 294 ; Mathematical definition of EGs 358, 359, 367 ; Mathematical hypotheses 281 ; Mathematical theories 240 ; Pure 281, 283, 287, 294, 312, 337 ; Reasoning in 151, 160, 161, 203, 282, 283, 292 ; Simplest possible 284, 293, 342
Meaning 225, 243, 244, 265 ; and mind 243 ; and triadic relation 245 ; as Quality and Reaction 244 ; Exact 181 ; of a proposition 259
Methodeutic XVI, 2, 41, 238
Mind 151, 153, 154, 159, 161, 172, 230, 288 ; Natural tendencies of human mind 148
Modal Logic 26, 44, 79, 88, 101, 116, 256, 265
Modality XVI; subjective possibility 27
Multi-modal Logics 26, 27
Multitude 32, 34, 40, 50, 58, 66, 73, 78, 87, 91–93, 205, 219, 220, 228, 247, 251, 256, 260, 271, 280, 284, 285, 287–289, 291, 294, 296, 297, 300, 310, 311, 313, 314, 320–325, 327–330, 333, 337, 339, 342, 382, 390

Necessity 263, 319
Nominalism 252–254, 385, 427

Obelus 424
Omniscience 227
Ordinal numbers 284, 285, 287, 296 ; and Pure Mathematics 285, 296

Peirce's Puzzle 27
Peirce's Rule 70
Perception 243; Direct 161, 172 ; Perceptual judgment 172
Phaneron 1, 35
Phenomenology 1, 242, 288, 293, 381
Phenomenon 242, 288, 382 ; Tripartite division of 246
Pons asinorum see Euclid

Possibilities 165, 183, 225, 228, 251, 263 ; and Collections 300 ; and Gamma graphs 370 ; and Qualities 227, 288, 298 ; Logical 227, 260, 261, 269, 362, 363 ; Mere 227 ; Qualitative 370 ; Range of 165 ; Substantive 249, 288, 289 ; Unrealized 243
Potentials 25, 267, 268, 362–365, 370 ; and Gamma graphs 370
Pragmaticism VIII, XIII, XIV, 2, 3, 50, 82, 117, 427
Pragmatism XIII, 16, 17, 49, 50, 74, 75, 91, 104, 116, 117, 226, 380, 381, 383, 385
Predication 193–195, 222
Principle of contradiction 221, 224
Principle of contraposition 195, 196, 378
Principle of excluded middle 81, 224
Probability; Boolean 257
Proper names XIII, 157, 160, 167, 174, 175, 197, 198, 354, 357, 366, see also Selective
Provability 91, 95, 262
Psychology 384; and logic 230, 288
Psychophysical 288
Purpose 384

Quality 173, 243, 248, 260, 289, 298–300
Quantifiers XIII, 2, 39, 71, 76, 77, 177, 233, 237
Quantity 205, 282, 283, 300, 301
Quasi-proposition 46

Reaction; and existence 267, 291 ; and force 382 ; and representation 383 ; and surprise 384 ; Consciousness of reaction 243 ; with a non-ego 230
Real; and *ens rationis* 248 ; Realism 253 ; Reality of laws 231
Reasoning; and graphs 238, 269 ; as self-controlled thought 148 ; Dissection of 152, 162, 180, 195, 226, 292 ; Indirect 384 ; Methodical 238 ; Necessary 138, 154, 180, 181, 257, 287, 292, 383 ; Scientific 138 ; Study of 181
Reduction Thesis 77
Relation 225, 248, 249, 298 ; and proposition 248 ; of similarity 228 ; Re-relation 228, 248

Religion (theology) 385
Replica 152, 154, 155, 162, 351, 353, 358, 359;
    Graph-replica 166, 170, 182, 312, 351,
    352, 367; Prime-replica 174
Representamen 46, 100, 247, 358, 359
Residuation see Peirce's Rule
Resistance and Effort 229, 242, 254
Retroduction XVI, 1, 41
Rheme 25, 157, 167, 175, 250

Sam 315, 316, 322, 327
Scepticism 253; and Pragmatism 226;
    mendacious and wholesome 244
Science 282
Scriptibility 6, 190, 276, 303, 308, 415
Secondness 230, 243, 246, 247, 251, 254,
    267, 276, 314
Selective 160, 174, 198, 354, 355; and Existential Graphs 258, 263, 264, 360, 366;
    and Potentials 268, 362, 370
Self-control 231, see also Reasoning, as
    self-controlled thought
Set 228, 229, 248, 255, 318
Sheet 342; Blank 159, 351; Entire graph of
    359; of assent 18, 154, 155; of assertion
    18, 163, 164, 169, 181, 241, 259, 351,
    367; of consciousness 171; of
    unexcluded possibility 209
Sign; Dicisign 46, 255; Legisign 267, 312,
    367; Primisign 46; Suadisign 46;
    Sumisign 46; Triadicity of 232
Singularity, Topical 368
Singulars 172, 360
Speculative Grammar 1, 18, 32, 39, 44, 53, 57,
    72, 76, 77, 99, 100, 107–109, 116, 233,
    237, 242, 255, 256, 433
Speculative Rhetoric see Methodeutic
Spot 157, 182, 240, 245, 258, 353; of teridentity 369; Spot-graph 355; Spot-symbol
    355
Stereopticon 38, 78, 79, 181, 190
Stoicism 252
Syllogism; Barbara 147; of transposed quantity 327; versus existential graphs
    146

Symbol 232; and Graph 351

Teridentity 26, 48, 276, 346, 353; Point of
    273; Spot of 369
Thirdness 37, 60, 232, 244, 246, 247, 251,
    254, 255, 314
Thought see also Dialogue, Dialogical thinking; active factor in the world 246; and
    expression as one 246; and signs 152;
    enacting 382; reality of 231
Topical Geometry see Topology
Topology 93, 337, 342
Transformability 6
Transformation rules; Contraposition 195;
    Deiteration 176, 359, 362; Double cut
    238; Double enclosure 194; Erasure
    176, 190, 238, 359; Insertion 176, 193,
    238, 359; Iteration 176, 238, 359, 362;
    of the Point on a Cut 176; of Two Cuts
    176; Permissible 189; Scribability 190
Transformations of graphs 233, 357;
    Archegetic 358, 359, 365; Basic four
    rights 146; Code of permissions 368;
    Compounding 190; Five fundamental
    rules 284; Fundamental Illative 176;
    Fundamental rules 293; Hypotheses respecting permissions of 344; Nine
    Basic Rules 213; Permissible 189; Simplicative and complicative rules 238;
    Three Permissions 241
Triadic relations; and meaning 244; and
    thought 229; Degenerate 245; Genuine 245; Irreducibility of 230, 244,
    246; Tricoexistence 363
Truth; as a working power 246
Type 152, 162, 172, 252, 310; and graph 170,
    273, 312, 367

Uniformity; in nature 225; of nature 227
Universe 138, 140; empty 325; of alpha possibility 210; of discourse 153, 163, 182,
    241; of existence 260; of possibilities
    155, 165; of propositions 264; of supposition 184; of unexcluded possibility
    208; Real 283, 293; states of 237
Utterer XIII, 22, 83

Verb 212, 213
Vexed questions of logic 3, 40, 46, 225

Volition 384

www.ingramcontent.com/pod-product-compliance
Lightning Source LLC
Chambersburg PA
CBHW030515230426
43665CB00010B/621